The Legal and Ethical Environment of Business

AN INTEGRATED APPROACH

Aspen College Series

The Legal and Ethical Environment of Business

AN INTEGRATED APPROACH

Gerald R. Ferrera • Mystica M. Alexander
William P. Wiggins • Cheryl Kirschner
Jonathan J. Darrow

Wolters Kluwer
Law & Business

Published by Wolters Kluwer Law & Business in New York.

Wolters Kluwer Law & Business serves customers worldwide with CCH, Aspen Publishers, and Kluwer Law International products. (www.wolterskluwerlb.com)

To contact Customer Service, e-mail customer.service@wolterskluwer.com, call 1-800-234-1660, fax 1-800-901-9075, or mail correspondence to:

Wolters Kluwer Law & Business
Attn: Order Department
PO Box 990
Frederick, MD 21705

Printed in the United States of America.

1 2 3 4 5 6 7 8 9 0

ISBN 978-1-4548-1520-4

Library of Congress Cataloging-in-Publication Data

The legal and ethical environment of business : an integrated approach / Gerald R. Ferrera, Mystica M. Alexander, William P. Wiggins, Cheryl Kirschner, and Jonathan J. Darrow.
    pages cm
  Includes bibliographical references and index.
  ISBN 978-1-4548-1520-4 (alk. paper)
  1. Industrial laws and legislation—United States. 2. Trade regulation—United States.
3. Commercial law—United States. 4. Business ethics—United States. 5. Trade regulation—Moral and ethical aspects. I. Ferrera, Gerald R. author. II. Alexander, Mystica M., author. III. Wiggins, William P. author.

  KF1600.L43 2014
  346.73'065—dc23
                                2014000168

Certified Chain of Custody
At Least 20% Certified Forest Content
www.sfiprogram.org
SFI-01042

SFI label applies to the text stock

About Wolters Kluwer Law & Business

Wolters Kluwer Law & Business is a leading global provider of intelligent information and digital solutions for legal and business professionals in key specialty areas, and respected educational resources for professors and law students. Wolters Kluwer Law & Business connects legal and business professionals as well as those in the education market with timely, specialized authoritative content and information-enabled solutions to support success through productivity, accuracy and mobility.

Serving customers worldwide, Wolters Kluwer Law & Business products include those under the Aspen Publishers, CCH, Kluwer Law International, Loislaw, ftwilliam.com and MediRegs family of products.

CCH products have been a trusted resource since 1913, and are highly regarded resources for legal, securities, antitrust and trade regulation, government contracting, banking, pension, payroll, employment and labor, and healthcare reimbursement and compliance professionals.

Aspen Publishers products provide essential information to attorneys, business professionals and law students. Written by preeminent authorities, the product line offers analytical and practical information in a range of specialty practice areas from securities law and intellectual property to mergers and acquisitions and pension/benefits. Aspen's trusted legal education resources provide professors and students with high-quality, up-to-date and effective resources for successful instruction and study in all areas of the law.

Kluwer Law International products provide the global business community with reliable international legal information in English. Legal practitioners, corporate counsel and business executives around the world rely on Kluwer Law journals, looseleafs, books, and electronic products for comprehensive information in many areas of international legal practice.

Loislaw is a comprehensive online legal research product providing legal content to law firm practitioners of various specializations. Loislaw provides attorneys with the ability to quickly and efficiently find the necessary legal information they need, when and where they need it, by facilitating access to primary law as well as state-specific law, records, forms and treatises.

ftwilliam.com offers employee benefits professionals the highest quality plan documents (retirement, welfare and non-qualified) and government forms (5500/PBGC, 1099 and IRS) software at highly competitive prices.

MediRegs products provide integrated health care compliance content and software solutions for professionals in healthcare, higher education and life sciences, including professionals in accounting, law and consulting.

Wolters Kluwer Law & Business, a division of Wolters Kluwer, is headquartered in New York. Wolters Kluwer is a market-leading global information services company focused on professionals.

To my dear wife, Judith, and to our beloved granddaughter, Sophia Asha,
and her beloved dog, Logan.
— G.R.F.

To my grandparents, who were my first teachers; to my mom,
who is a constant source of support; and to my son, Michael,
who has brought such happiness into my life.
— M.M.A.

To my lovely wife, Joanne, and our four wonderful children, Erik, Jonathan,
Hannah, and Mark, for their endless love, encouragement, and support.
— W.P.W.

With much love, to my wonderful sons, Michael, Philip, and Adam;
to my dear, supportive husband, Roger; to my dependable mother;
and to the memory of my beloved father. Like so many things in life,
this would not have been possible without all of you.
— C.K.

To my parents, Marion and Roselyn, and my brother, Stephen,
for all their love and support.
— J.J.D.

SUMMARY OF CONTENTS

Part IV: The Business Sale

Part V: Business Liability

CONTENTS

Chapter 2: Ethics in the Business Environment   33

Chapter 5: Legal Aspects of the Global Business Environment   131

Chapter 8: Intellectual Property   225

Chapter 11: Antitrust   323

PART IV: THE BUSINESS SALE

Chapter 15: Contracts: Contract Formation   449

Chapter 17: Sales Law, Consumer Protection, and E-Commerce   515

Chapter 18: The Debtor-Creditor Relationship   559

PART V: BUSINESS LIABILITY

Chapter 21: Environmental Law and Sustainability   637

We are pleased to introduce this first edition of *The Legal and Ethical Environment of Business: An Integrated Approach*. The new approach taken in this textbook was developed in response to the realities of learning to do business in the contemporary global context. The book covers, comprehensively and crisply, all the topics traditionally found in the legal environment of business textbooks, presented in a readable, accessible writing style. But in addition, it integrates that law with two themes of paramount importance in today's business world: the pursuit of ethical business practice and the understanding of the international dimensions of business and law.

To prepare students for the new realities of the workplace, regulatory and legal environment curricula must include meaningful ethics coverage. Current industry norms, practices, and legislation call for the incorporation of ethics into decision making and for a new approach to business structures that satisfies legal requirements and adopts and implements best practices. Most major corporations in the United States, for example, have adopted a Compliance and Ethics Program that includes a corporate Code of Ethics and mandates training for executives and managers in understanding legal compliance, corporate ethical codes, due diligence, risk assessment, and the resolution of ethical dilemmas. Many large companies now have chief ethics and compliance officers, reporting directly to the board or to the chief executive officer, who are responsible for protecting and enhancing the company's reputation, oversight of legal compliance, complying with the company's Code of Ethics, and maintaining ethical standards within the company. Legislative initiatives over the past decade, responding to high-level and widely publicized ethical infractions and criminal wrongdoings, have resulted in the passage of far-reaching initiatives such as the Sarbanes-Oxley Act of 2002 and the U.S. Sentencing Guidelines. Corporate boards increasingly include ethics committees charged with reviewing and approving major corporate initiatives, such as whistleblower protection, and compliance with the company's internal code of ethics.

This high-level focus on ethics, both internally and externally, demands increased, thoughtful ethics coverage to prepare students for the business world they will encounter. Traditionally, ethical coverage in many legal environments of business texts has been limited to a single chapter, perhaps coupled with brief case questions on ethics scattered elsewhere in the book. *The Legal and Ethical Environment of Business* takes a new approach. Here, a foundational chapter is devoted entirely to ethical theory and analysis, and ethics coverage is integrated throughout the book and featured in nearly every chapter. Ethical theory is interwoven with practical applications using several novel pedagogical tools we developed to promote focused, thoughtful inquiry and to highlight the interplay of ethics and law. We have found in our own teaching that these methods can help students learn to analyze judicial opinions more effectively and to achieve a deeper understanding of the legal environment of business:

- *An Ethical Insight.* Boxes throughout the text spotlight the thinking of selected ethicists and business executives, illustrating the basis of legal and business strategies in ethical theory, principle, or practice.
- *Manager's Compliance and Ethics Meeting.* Frequent simulations of managers' meetings address ethical issues, along with applicable law, to help readers explore fundamental ethical dilemmas, often through multiple perspectives.
- *In-Depth Ethical Case Analysis.* These extended case reviews identify the ethical issue in an appellate decision and review the case from an ethical perspective, applying classical ethical principles and theory to the judicial decision and case holding.

Although a thorough and deep understanding of the ethical and legal environment of business in the United States is fundamental to this text and course, this knowledge has today an ever-widening applicability. Economic interdependence, advances in technology and transportation, liberalization of international trade law, and greater political freedom in many countries around the globe are just a few of the factors contributing to the enormous increase in and reliance on international business transactions. This book pursues two distinct approaches to international business. First, it integrates international coverage by including, in addition to a chapter devoted to international business transactions, relevant international law components at the ends of most chapters. Second, and more importantly, the international coverage offered goes beyond the usual comparative law topics. Instead, most chapters include substantial coverage of a central topic in international business law, such as bribery and the Foreign Corrupt Practices Act, key provisions of the Convention of Contracts for the International Sales of Goods, and a comparison of the Uniform Commercial Code and the UN Convention on Contracts for the International Sale of Goods. Selected for their relevancy, practicality, and importance, knowledge of these international topics will help prepare students to embark on a career in the expanding world of business.

The accreditation requirements of business schools reinforce the need for thorough ethical coverage within the Legal Environment of Business context. In April 2013, the Association to Advance Collegiate Schools of Business adopted new accreditation standards, and this textbook was written in part to help academic institutions comply with those new standards. In particular, the book addresses Standard 9: "Curriculum content is appropriate to general expectations for the degree program type and learning goals." The standard further specifies:

- *General Skill Area. Ethical* understanding and reasoning (able to identify ethical issues and address the issues in a socially responsible manner)
- *General Business and Management Knowledge Area.* Economic, political, *regulatory, legal,* technological, and social contexts of organizations *in a global society* and *social responsibility*, including *sustainability*, and *ethical* behavior and approaches to management [Emphasis added.]

This textbook is also an ideal choice for schools holding or aspiring to achieve EQUIS accreditation from the European Foundation for Management Development. It provides the comprehensive coverage of international law expected of schools holding EQUIS accreditation.

Our objectives in writing this book were to provide comprehensive legal and ethical coverage of the business environment, to convey information clearly and concisely, to integrate ethical and international perspectives throughout the book, to develop an appreciation of the engaging nature of law and ethics, and to share with students the insights we have gained from our many cumulative years of study and experience in the field. We welcome instructors and students to this text and to the fascinating and challenging journey it represents: pursuit of a deep understanding of and appreciation for the productive integration of law, ethics, and global issues in the twenty-first-century legal and ethical environment of business.

Welcome to this textbook and congratulations on undertaking the study of the Legal and Ethical Environment of Business. We were motivated to write this book to help you understand and appreciate how law and, in a special way, ethics should be understood and used by executives, managers, and entrepreneurs in today's global business environment.

As you proceed through this book, you will be challenged from a professional perspective to see how ethical dilemmas and legal problems permeate the business environment. Chapter 2, "Ethics in the Business Environment" introduces classic ethical principles that will support you in your efforts to learn to think about business and legal issues from an ethical perspective. Our objective is to help you understand what it means to "do the right thing" as a manager prepared to contribute to the development and maintenance of an ethical corporate culture. Elements in our approach include case illustrations and court decisions that demonstrate the legal resolution of business disputes; insights in most chapters into the global business environment through explanations of relevant international business practices or agreements; and practical examples throughout illustrating the ethical dilemmas and legal problems that frequently arise in business situations.

Specific features show these ideas in practice. The *Ethical Insight* features, for example, provide brief but practical insights on ethics from business executives and philosophers. Building on these insights, the *In-Depth Ethical Case Analysis* feature shows court decisions from a legal and ethical perspective. The *Manager's Compliance and Ethics Meeting* feature offers practical illustrations of how managers discuss and resolve business and legal problems through the application of ethical principles. These concerns and methods are knit together as well in Chapter 8, "Corporate Social Responsibility," a concept increasingly embraced by companies worldwide.

We are honored to assist you in developing your understanding of the international, ethical, and legal dimensions of today's business environment.

ACKNOWLEDGMENTS

I gratefully acknowledge the mentoring of Chancellor Gregory H. Adamian of Bentley University when Dr. Adamian chaired the law department and later when he was president of Bentley. I also acknowledge the wisdom and support of the late Prof. Edwin W. Tucker and his many years of treasured friendship. I gratefully acknowledge my development in business ethics through the teaching of Dr. Michael Hoffman, the founder of the Bentley Center of Business Ethics, and especially the instruction in ethics by the late philosopher Prof. Frank Reeves, also associated with the Bentley Center of Business Ethics. I acknowledge the assistance of Prof. Tony Buono, director of the Alliance of Ethics and Social Responsibility at Bentley University, for his informative guidance on business ethics issues. Any misinterpretations of selected ethical theories applied to business problems are my own, especially those that go beyond their traditional use. My colleagues on the team of authors for this book and the publishing staff have made this venture a memorable joy.

A final loving acknowledgment to my wife, Judith, who for many years has patiently endured my constant response: "I'm almost finished."

— **Gerald R. Ferrera**

I acknowledge the support and guidance of my friend and mentor, Gerald Ferrera, who has made my work on this project possible. I also thank my pastor of 20 years, Father John Connelly, for his encouragement and support throughout this process. A special thanks to Fred Costantino who provided countless hours of technical help. Thanks to Grace Alexander, Michael Alexander-Yang, and John Hayward for their useful advice, and thanks also to Marianne DelPo Kulow and Cynthia Pasciuto for sharing their expertise. Last, I thank my coauthors who have made working on this project a joy.

— **Mystica M. Alexander**

I gratefully acknowledge the support and friendship of Dr. Michael Page, Provost and Vice President for Academic Affairs at Bentley University. Special thanks to my longtime friend and colleague, Jerry Ferrera, whose vision and leadership made this book possible, and to my other coauthors for their insight, dedication, and humor, all of which contributed immensely to the joy and pleasure of this intellectual journey.

— **William P. Wiggins**

I am deeply grateful to Dean Carolyn Hotchkiss and Professor Ross Petty, both of Babson College, for their sage advice and guidance over the past many years. My professional successes are due in some part to their guidance; my failures are due to my shortcomings. I am also grateful for Beverly Balconi's administrative support and cheerfulness and for Kathy Esper's encouragement, wisdom, and friendship. Last, my coauthors have been a dream to work with — my thanks for the opportunity to work on this project and, more importantly, to work with you.

— **Cheryl Kirschner**

I gratefully acknowledge Stephen M. Darrow and Katherine E. King for their substantial efforts in reviewing and making suggestions to the antitrust, intellectual property, and administrative law chapters, and thank Michael Adelman for his able research assistance. Thanks also to Deniz Tuncel and Ceylan Kara for providing research leads regarding certain international materials.

— **Jonathan J. Darrow**

The authors all also gratefully acknowledge David Herzig, associate publisher, for seeing the value of the new model of integrating ethics, global issues, and law and for sharing our vision.

The authors also gratefully acknowledge the professional work of Susan Boulanger, developmental editor, and her collaborative efforts in moving the project along. She has provided us with invaluable assistance and insight on this endeavor.

The authors thank art editor Naomi Kornhauser for guidance and assistance in the selection of photographs and for her professional attention to detail and her patience in selecting appropriate illustrations and securing copyright permissions.

The authors gratefully acknowledge permissions editor Trish O'Hara and her valuable, professional assistance in obtaining copyright permissions.

The authors gratefully acknowledge Steven Silverstein, senior account manager, Legal Education, for seeing the value of this textbook at the start of the project.

Last, the authors are deeply appreciative of the invaluable assistance and the many hours Fred Costantino devoted to the development of this text. We are in awe of his computer skills. His patience, attention to detail, and energy truly helped make this book possible.

Cover photo by Jon Feingersh/Blend.

U.S. Capitol Building Architect of the Capitol; **George Washington** Courtesy National Gallery of Art, Washington; **Supreme Court** Architect of the Capitol; **Senator Muskie** AP Photo/Henry Griffin; **U.S. Capitol Building** Architect of the Capitol; **White House** © cristinaciochina - Fotolia.com; **Corps of Army Engineers flag** Chris Granger/Times-Picayune/Landov; **Bulldozer** © Jakub Cejpek - Fotolia.com; **Gavel** © Africa Studio - Fotolia.com; **Water glass** © pasha66 - Fotolia.com; **Map of appellate (circuit) courts** Administrative Office of the U.S. Court; **Supreme Court justices** Steve Petteway, Collection of the Supreme Court of the United States; **Zappo's boxes with logo** © Ruaridh Stewart/ZUMA-PRESS.com; **Warren Buffet** JIM RUYMEN/UPI/Landov; **Amy Rees Anderson** Courtesy of Amy Rees Anderson; **Due diligence** VStock/Alamy; **Meg Whitman** AP Photo/Paul Sakuma; **Cartoon** Clay Bennett/© 1998 The Christian Science Monitor (www.CSMonitor.com). Reprinted with permission; **W. Michael Hoffman** Courtesy of W. Michael Hoffman; **Bentley University** ©Brian Smith; **Ronald Dworkin** AP Photo/New York University, Leo Sorel; **Aristotle** cenker atila/shutterstock; **Thomas Aquinas** Abegg Collection, Riggisberg, Switzerland/The Bridgeman Art Library; **United Nations headquarters** © James Steidl - Fotolia.com; **Immanuel Kant** Private Collection/The Bridgeman Art Library; **Jeremy Bentham** © UCL Art Museum, University College London/The Bridgeman Art Library; **John Stuart Mill** Library of Congress; **W. D. Ross** Kurt Hutton/Getty Images; **John Rawls** Gamma-Rapho via Getty Images; **Chinese pagoda** Songquan Deng/shutterstock; **Taj Mahal** Mazzzur/shutterstock; **Signing of Constitution** Architect of the Capitol; **Woman ordering a product online** Andrey Popov/shutterstock; **Cigarette advertisements** © SHANNON STAPLETON/Reuters/Corbis; **Ernesto Miranda** AP Photo/Matt York; **FDA scientist** JASON REED/Reuters/Landov; **CPSC agent inspecting toys** © Ann Johansson/Corbis; **Steven J. Heyman** Courtesy of Steven J. Heyman; **ILO World Day Against Child Labor** VERI SANOVRI/Xinhua/Landov; **WTO Building** Jonathan Darrow; **Signing treaty** AFP/Getty Images; **Cargo ship in port** tcly/shutterstock; **Ecuadorians protest Texaco** AP Photo/Eduardo Valenzuela; **United Nations General Assembly** Kyodo via AP Images; **Model T Ford** By permission of Ford Motor Company; **Ben & Jerry logo** By permission of Ben & Jerry's; **Newman's Own logo** By permission of Newman's Own; **Seventh Generation products** © David Young-Wolff/PhotoEdit; **Tom's of Maine products** GLEN ARGOV/Landov;

GERALD R. FERRERA is the Gregory H. Adamian Professor of Law Emeritus at Bentley University and was the first member of the law faculty to hold that endowed chair. In 2002 Professor Ferrera received the Academy of Legal Studies in Business Senior Faculty Award of Excellence. He chaired the Law Department at Bentley for 17 years. Over his teaching career of 45 years at Bentley University, he has been active in the legal environment of business curriculum development with an ethical component and has coauthored textbooks on business law, the legal environment of business, and cyberlaw. His scholarly articles on ethics and jurisprudence, authored or coauthored, were published in *The American Journal of Jurisprudence* and the *Richmond Journal of Law and the Public Interest*. He has also authored or coauthored published material in the New York University School of Law *Journal of Legislation and Public Policy*, the *Northwestern Journal of Technology and Intellectual Property, Texas Intellectual Property Law Journal*, the *American Business Law Journal, Marquette Law Review, Pepperdine Law Review, Journal of Legal Studies Education, Business Law Review*, and *Cleveland State Law Review*. He is currently a research fellow at the Center for Business Ethics, Bentley University, and a past president and current member of the executive committee of the North Atlantic Regional Business Law Association. He received the Ralph C. Hober publication award given by the Academy of Legal Studies in Business and the Bentley University Scholar of the Year Award. His teaching awards include the Bentley University Gregory H. Adamian Excellence in Teaching Award, numerous Bentley University Innovation in Teaching Awards, and the Master Teacher Award from the Academy of Legal Studies in Business. He holds a B.S. in Finance from Boston College, a J.D. from the New England School of Law/Boston, and an M.S. in Taxation from Bentley. He is a member of the State Bar of Massachusetts and federal bars.

MYSTICA M. ALEXANDER is Assistant Professor in the Law, Taxation, and Financial Planning Department at Bentley University. A graduate of Harvard Law School, Mystica practiced corporate and tax law for several years before moving into academia. She currently teaches business law and ethics as well as courses in the Masters of Science in Taxation Program. In addition to her role in the classroom, Mystica has been involved with curriculum development at the undergraduate and graduate level. She is a past Holmes Cardozo finalist for best conference paper at the Academy of Legal Studies in Business and the recipient of an Innovation in Teaching Award from Bentley University.

WILLIAM P. WIGGINS is Professor in the Law, Taxation, and Financial Planning Department at Bentley University. In addition to his faculty responsibilities, Professor Wiggins serves as chair of the Bentley University Institutional Review Board and coordinator of the Bentley Research Council. Over the years, Professor Wiggins has held a variety of administrative positions at the university and has chaired many of the university's major task forces. Most recently, he served as Associate Dean of Business for Academic Affairs, which included responsibilities for directing the university's AACSB and EQUIS accreditation processes.

Professor Wiggins is recipient of Bentley's highest teaching award: The Gregory H. Adamian Excellence in Teaching Award. He has developed and taught a wide variety of courses at the undergraduate and graduate levels, including a tax controversy practicum for graduate tax students for which he received a Bentley University Innovation in Teaching Award. Professor Wiggins has coauthored a leading textbook and a leading treatise on tax practice and procedure and has published articles in academic and professional journals and presented his work at international, national, and regional conferences. Professor Wiggins holds a bachelor's degree and a master's degree from Bentley University and a JD from Suffolk University Law School. He is a member of Beta Gamma Sigma, the honor society for business students and faculty.

CHERYL KIRSCHNER is Senior Lecturer in Law at Babson College. She received a BA from the University of Rochester in English and political science and a JD from Boston University School of Law. At Babson, she teaches undergraduate and graduate courses in business law and international business law. She was awarded the Babson College Dean's Award for Excellence in Undergraduate Teaching and is deeply involved in curriculum development and revision. She also serves as editor-in-chief for the Babson Case Publishing Center. The Academy of Legal Studies in Business awarded her the Best International Case in 2008 for her best-selling case, *Zidane's Last Red Card*. She coteaches Babson's offshore course in South Africa, where, in partnership with the University of Stellenbosch, students from both colleges teach entrepreneurship to underserved populations in the Cape Town area.

JONATHAN J. DARROW holds a BS in biological sciences from Cornell, a JD from Duke, and an MBA from Boston College, and completed the LLM and SJD programs (the PhD of the law discipline) at Harvard Law School. After admission to the bar, Dr. Darrow practiced law in the Silicon Valley offices of Cooley Godward and later worked on patent litigation matters at Wiley Rein & Fielding in Washington, DC. He has taught law at Boston College and Plymouth State University, provided research assistance to the World Trade Organization and the World Health Organization, spoken widely on legal topics throughout the United States and in Europe, given testimony before the Massachusetts Joint Committee on the Judiciary, and has published more than 20 articles and other works in numerous publications, including the *Stanford*

Technology Law Review, the NYU *Journal of Legislation and Public Policy*, and the *Harvard Journal of Law and Technology*. Dr. Darrow is a coauthor of the leading textbook *Cyberlaw: Text and Cases*. He currently teaches at Bentley University and researches issues of pharmaceutical law and policy at Brigham and Women's Hospital/Harvard Medical School.

The Legal and Ethical Environment of Business

AN INTEGRATED APPROACH

PART I

Legal and Ethical Overview

CHAPTER 1

The United States Legal System

Chapter Objectives

1. To understand the structure of the U.S. legal system and the significance of the balance of power
2. To know the various sources of law and to understand the relative authority of such sources
3. To understand the basics of the process by which a case moves through the court system, with emphasis on the concepts of jurisdiction, venue, and standing to sue
4. To understand the special jurisdictional challenges posed by online transactions
5. To recognize that the majority of cases are resolved, not through litigation, but through an alternative form of dispute resolution

Practical Example: Early Beginnings of the Legal System

They were steaming hot and humid days in the State House of Philadelphia in 1787. The small room, without air conditioning, was stuffy and uncomfortable, the curtains were closed, and the press was not allowed to hear the deliberations. In this room, 55 white males, 25 without any formal education, gathered together; the youngest was 26, and the oldest, a fellow named Ben Franklin, was 81. Most of the men were living out of suitcases in hotels far from their homes. A tall, dignified, quiet war hero presided over the assembly. George Washington was by then the most respected person in the nation. At the end of five months of deliberations that resulted in the U.S. Constitution, something was still lacking for a necessary ratification by the states. Between 1787 and 1788 the New York newspapers published essays under the name "Publius," written by James Madison, John Jay, and Alexander Hamilton. Those political essays are now known as *The Federalist Papers*. Our Bill of Rights, the first ten amendments of the U.S. Constitution, is a reflection of the values found in those essays. They essentially guarantee individual liberties and limit the role of the federal government.

Throughout this chapter you will see how the U.S. legal system tries to preserve the delicate balance between individual rights and the need for a federal government that attempts to provide for the common welfare of the nation. Keep in mind as you read and study the legal environment of business, including applicable federal and state laws and regulations, that many of the underlying principles of business laws and traditional ethical values are found in the U.S. Constitution and the Bill of Rights. Our contemporary hi-tech business environment could not possibly have been foreseen in any remote fashion by the 1787 assembly in Philadelphia that created the U.S. Constitution. It is the role of our legal system to guarantee and further develop those values as technology, a diverse group of employees, and marketing distribution systems continue to grow and adapt to the global marketplace.

Can you think of any current business laws that have their supporting values in the Bill of Rights? The U.S. court system has its foundation in the U.S. Constitution. Do you think our business laws and regulations are moving in the right direction or might they be too burdensome for American companies to compete in a global economy? In this chapter and throughout the book, we will discuss many similar questions to assist you in better understanding our contemporary legal environment of business.

Take a moment and think about what first comes to mind when you hear the phrase "the **law**?" Do you immediately associate the phrase with law enforcement and think of the local police officers and sheriffs who enforce the law? Do you think of the classic courtroom scenes portrayed in one too many television dramas? Perhaps you think of Judge Judy or Judge Joe Brown handing down their pronouncements from the "bench" in their television studios. Does the phrase immediately bring to mind the lawmakers in Congress charged with shaping the law for the United States? If your initial reaction is a more global one, perhaps you are wondering whether there is a set of enforceable international laws that transcend national boundaries.

What Is the Law?

So, what exactly is the law? There is no one-size-fits-all answer to that question because the law is a chameleon-like concept, with a precise definition varying to fit a particular situation. Consider, for example, the Yanomami tribal people, one of the largest groups of Amerindian people living in South America. Do these indigenous people who continue the hunting and farming practices put into place by their ancestors hundreds of years ago live by a system of law? Indeed, they do. In the context of the Yanomami, we can define the law as the practices or customs of a community considered by the members of that community to be binding. How the binding practices will be enforced is often left to the tribal elders.

Perhaps you are a member of a fraternity or sorority — Kappa Sigma, Tau Kappa Epsilon, Kappa Alpha Psi, or Chi Omega. What is the law within the context of that Greek organization? Most likely a "national" organization dictates the requirements for the individual chapters through a constitution and bylaws that form the laws for that fraternity or sorority. Such laws clearly set out penalties and consequences for violations.

Bringing our focus into the business context, consider a contract that you may have entered into with a cell phone provider such as AT&T or T-Mobile to secure cell phone service, or the membership agreement you may have signed with Planet Fitness, Gold's Gym, or Curves. That contract or agreement brings with it certain rights and responsibilities, not only those terms dictated in the contract itself, but also the broader dictates of rules that have been formally recognized by society as governing contracts.

At this point you are likely getting a clearer sense of what law is. It can be defined as "the regime that orders human activities and relations through systematic application of the force of a politically organized society . . ."[1] But this definition leaves us with even greater and more questions. Who prescribes these laws by which members of society are supposed to act? Who enforces these laws? If laws are not carefully drafted and leave room for interpretation, how will they be interpreted? If a law no longer serves the good of the community, should it be changed? If so, how can that change come about, and who has the authority to change it? What process is in place to ensure all people receive equal treatment under the prescribed set of rules?

The answers to these questions lie in an understanding of the sources of law and the legal system. This chapter will provide you with an overview of the U.S. sources of law and the legal system. Although this book is primarily focused on U.S. law and the U.S. legal system, it is important to recognize that we live in a global society. When we think of global transactions, our tendency is to first think of the dealings of widely recognized, multinational corporations such as Johnson & Johnson and Coca-Cola. Thanks to modern communications and technology, the global community has become

---

[1]Black's Law Dictionary (9th ed., 2009).

increasingly interconnected, and even the average individual is likely to engage in a global transaction, whether it is a student studying abroad for a semester or an eBay shopper in the United States who buys an item from a seller located in Hong Kong. Cross-border exchanges are becoming more commonplace, and for this reason, incorporated throughout this text is a look at the international law arena and its impact on a variety of business transactions. In addition, Chapter 5, "Legal Aspects of the Global Business Environment," provides an in-depth look at the global perspective.

The U.S. Legal System

Any attempt to understand how the legal system works must begin with an understanding of the federalist form of government.

Understanding the Federalist System

The United States is a **federalist system** of government meaning that a strong federal government operates alongside a parallel, sometimes complementary, sometimes competing state system of government. For example, you are no doubt aware that the U.S. Constitution, discussed in Chapter 3, "Constitutional Issues in Business," is at the center of the legal system. It is the foundation upon which all other laws are enacted and interpreted. Are you also aware that each state also has its own state constitution which serves as the guiding principle for that state? Elected U.S. senators and representatives enact federal laws, and corresponding state elected officials enact state laws.

The key to understanding the reasons behind this dual federal/state system lies in the very history of the United States. Recall that before the United States of America came into being, the founders were citizens under English rule living in colonies in America. These colonies united and fought against what they considered to be their common enemy — the English monarchy. When they were victorious in breaking free from English rule, they had to create a workable system of government balancing the concerns of those who were wary of a strong central, authority figure (after living under English rule) with the recognition that the individual colonies could only continue to survive and grow through concerted action. The federalist system — a compromise — brought together the two systems of government operating side by side, ideally with each side operating with a clear understanding of its rights and responsibilities.

Unfortunately, the boundary line between federal and state authority was not clear at the country's founding and to a certain extent remains unclear today, resulting in an endless tug-of-war between federal control and state authority. Even though there are some areas that are clearly within the purview of the state, such as the laws of marriage, adoption, and divorce, authority over some of the more controversial issues surrounding drugs, guns, and healthcare is less certain. At times, states have lobbied the federal government directly, seeking to have a greater voice in federal legislation affecting the states. At other times some states have found it necessary to file lawsuits against the federal government seeking to nullify federal laws believed to be an over-reach by the federal government. On occasion, states have taken even more extreme actions such as adopting measures in direct opposition to federal statutes. Exhibit 1.1 provides a brief snapshot of some recent areas of controversy between the federal and state governments. These examples illustrate that the federal and state governments exist together in a delicate balance of power.

Exhibit 1.1. Tensions Between the Federal and State Governments

Topic	Federal Law	State Reaction	Outcome
Driver's license	Real ID Act passed in May 2005 mandating certain documentation required for issuance of state driver's license	Between 2007 and 2008 25 states adopt resolutions opposing the Real ID Act; 15 of these states enact statutes vowing nonacquiescence	Federal government grants extension on compliance
Medical marijuana	Controlled Substances Act of 1970 prohibiting the use of marijuana for medicinal purposes	Since 1996, 20 states have adopted some form of authorization of manufacturing and use of marijuana for medical purposes	*Gonzalez v. Raich* (2005): the Supreme Court upholds the right of the federal government to regulate marijuana
Guns	1993 Brady Handgun Violence Protection Act requiring background checks on all handgun purchases	Since 2009, 21 states have adopted Firearms Freedom Acts (FFAs) to declare that firearms made and retained in a state are beyond the control of Congress	*Montana Shooting Sports Assn. v. Montana* (2013): the Ninth Circuit Court of Appeals ruled that federal rules take precedent over Montana's FFA; an appeal to the Supreme Court is expected
Healthcare	Patient Protection and Affordable Care Act of 2010 mandating health insurance coverage except for certain exempt categories of individuals	Fifteen states adopt statutes or constitutional amendments challenging individual mandates; Florida leads the way and is joined by 26 states that believe the Health Care Act exceeds the federal government's constitutional authority	*National Federation of Independent Business v. Sebelius* (2012): the Supreme Court upholds the individual mandate as a valid exercise of the taxing power

Sources of Law

Constitutional law, treaties, statutory law, administrative law, and case law are the primary sources of U.S. law.

The U.S. Constitution

Our starting point in understanding the U.S. legal system is the U.S. Constitution: "the supreme law of the land." Adopted in 1787 by delegates from 12 of the original 13 states, the U.S. Constitution remains one of the oldest federal constitutions in existence. The framers of the Constitution were faced with quite a challenge — they had to create a strong and effective national government but at the same time ensure that this national government did not infringe on the rights of the states or the rights of the individual. In setting up the parameters of the national government, the framers created three equal branches of government, each to serve as a check on the other and to prevent any one branch from becoming too powerful. There were some who pushed for a statement of individual rights in the text of the Constitution, but instead of including these rights in the Constitution itself, they were incorporated in the first ten amendments to the Constitution in the Bill of Rights. The rights granted under the Constitution will be explored more fully in Chapter 3.

Treaties

Treaties are agreements entered into between two or more nations. Those between two nations are referred to as bilateral, and those between three or more nations are multilateral. Treaties may address a variety of issues including trade relations, taxation, immigration, and human rights. In the United States, treaties are negotiated through the Department of State and must be ratified or endorsed by the U.S. Senate in order to have the force of law. Chapter 5 will provide additional information on the role of treaties.

Statutory Law

Statutory laws are those laws adopted through the legislative process. U.S. statutory law is adopted and approved by Congress. To become statutory law, proposed legislation must be approved by a majority of the members of both houses of Congress: the Senate and the House of Representatives. There are 100 senators, two from each state. There are 435 representatives. The number of representatives for each state varies by the population of the state, with some states, such as Alaska and Montana, having only one representative and others, such as California, having as many as 53. Laws that are passed by Congress and signed by the president become part of the U.S. Code. The U.S. Code is divided into 51 Titles, or subject matter categories, governing a broad array of issues including food and drug safety (Title 21), taxation (Title 26), protection of intellectual property such as patents and copyright (Titles 17 and 35), labor (Title 29), and agriculture (Title 7). The official version of the U.S. Code is published by the Office of the Law Revision Counsel of the U.S. House of Representatives.

Administrative Law

Standing alone, statutory law often does not contain an adequate level of detail needed to implement a statutory mandate. The task of describing how the law is to be implemented and enforced is left to federal administrative agencies that carry out this function through issuance of administrative regulations that are published in the Code of Federal Regulations. For example, Congress has enacted revenue laws that require payments of personal income tax on incomes over a certain threshold amount. The Treasury Department is responsible for adopting tax regulations that explain the details of this income tax, and the Internal Revenue Service is responsible for the implementation and enforcement of these revenue laws. Administrative law and the unique role of administrative agencies in our legal system will be explored in detail in Chapter 4, "Administrative Law."

Case Law

The United States is a Common Law system that has its roots in the English Common Law system. This means that in addition to the Constitution and statutory law, the legal system also rests upon judicial decisions that interpret the law. Relying on the doctrine of *stare decisis* ("to stand on decided cases"), judges place great weight on following the precedent of previous court decisions. This means that cases decided today will be decided in accordance with past cases that involve the same legal issues. Given the pivotal role the judiciary plays in the U.S. legal system, we will revisit this topic in more detail later in the chapter.

Understanding the Branches of Government and the Balance of Power

The U.S. system of government operates through a balance of separate powers designed to prevent any one branch from being too powerful, as each one serves as a check on the other's authority. It is the role of the legislative branch to enact statutory laws. The executive branch, the office of the president, is responsible for enforcing the laws, which is done through federal administrative agencies. The president also has the limited authority to enact law through the use of executive orders. It is the role of the judicial branch, or the court system, to apply and interpret the laws in resolving disputes. The balance of power is illustrated in Exhibit 1.2 on page 10.

Exhibit 1.2. The Balance of Power

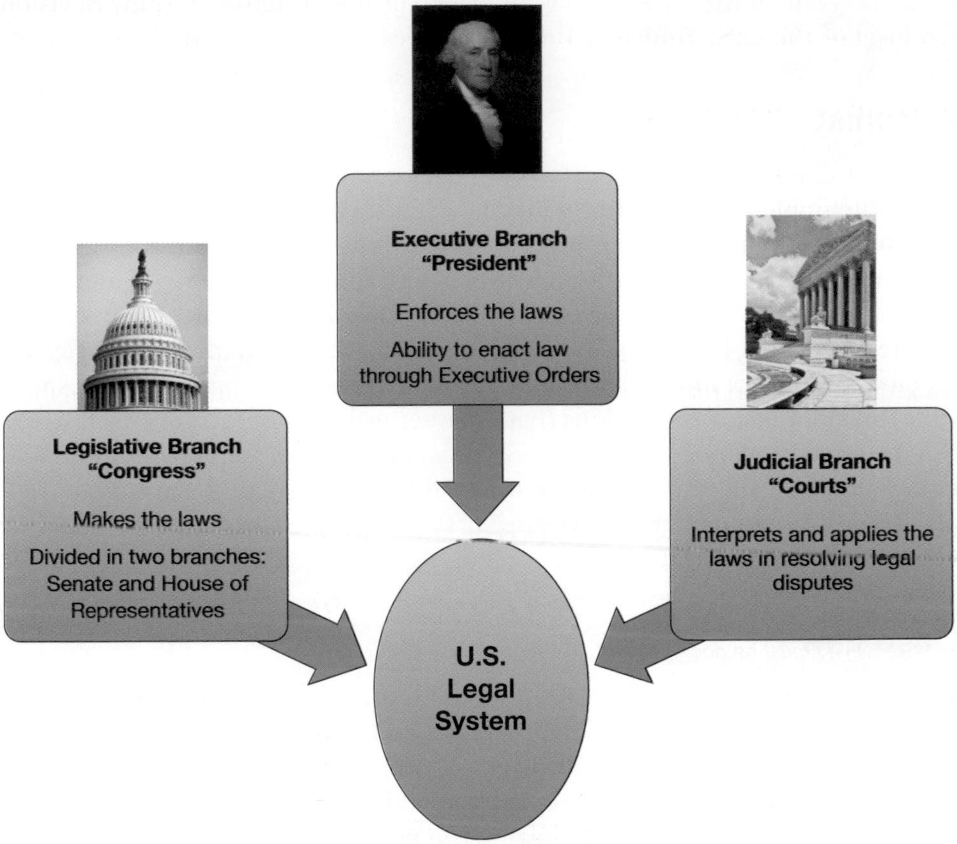

As already discussed, the U.S. federalist system consists not only of the central, federal government but also of the independent governments of the states. State governments also rely on this balance of power. State legislatures make the laws; the state executive branch, the governor, enforces the laws; and the state court system applies and interprets the laws in resolving disputes.

The Balance of Power in Action

Consider the following question: What is the connection between the construction of a shopping center in Michigan in 1988 and a glass of water in 1972? To answer this question, we must first journey through a legal labyrinth that will illustrate how the balance of power works.

An Example of the Balance of Power

Mr. Rapanos is a land developer who, in 1988, owned approximately 715 acres of land in Michigan. In 1988 he decided to build a shopping center on a portion of this land. The construction site included wetlands, and because of this Rapanos was cautioned by the Michigan Department of Natural Resources that these wetlands might be federally regulated property. Mr. Rapanos disagreed and proceeded to fill the wetlands with sand even though the Michigan Department of Natural Resources and the Environmental Protection Agency issued orders that he stop this action. Ultimately, the federal government stepped in and brought both civil and criminal charges against Mr. Rapanos for defying the orders and filling in the wetlands on his property. What would allow the federal government to dictate what a property owner can do with land that he owns? In the instant case, the answer to that question begins with a look at a contaminated glass of water.

It All Begins with Congress

In 1971 it came to the attention of the public that the average glass of drinking water contained an unsafe level of contaminants (see Exhibit 1.3). Sharing the

---

Exhibit 1.3. The Legal System at Work

In 1971 the U.S. Government realizes that over half the country's drinking water is being contaminated from sources such as underground storage tanks. Experts realize it is a matter of time before surface waters are also affected. *Something must be done.*

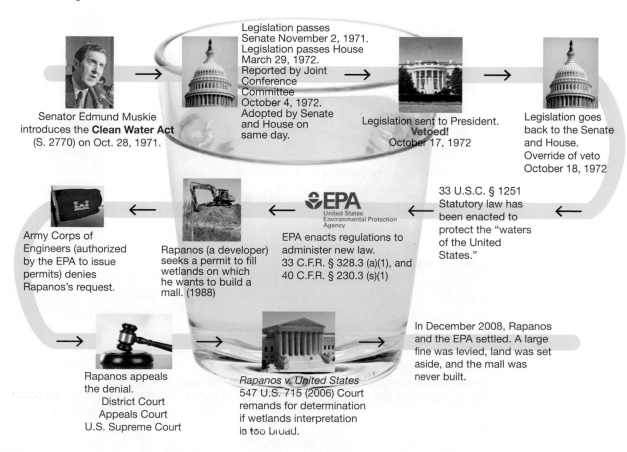

Senator Edmund Muskie introduces the **Clean Water Act** (S. 2770) on Oct. 28, 1971.

Legislation passes Senate November 2, 1971. Legislation passes House March 29, 1972. Reported by Joint Conference Committee October 4, 1972. Adopted by Senate and House on same day.

Legislation sent to President. **Vetoed!** October 17, 1972

Legislation goes back to the Senate and House. Override of veto October 18, 1972

33 U.S.C. § 1251 Statutory law has been enacted to protect the "waters of the United States."

EPA enacts regulations to administer new law. 33 C.F.R. § 328.3 (a)(1), and 40 C.F.R. § 230.3 (s)(1)

Rapanos (a developer) seeks a permit to fill wetlands on which he wants to build a mall. (1988)

Army Corps of Engineers (authorized by the EPA to issue permits) denies Rapanos's request.

Rapanos appeals the denial. District Court Appeals Court U.S. Supreme Court

Rapanos v. United States 547 U.S. 715 (2006) Court remands for determination if wetlands interpretation is too broad.

In December 2008, Rapanos and the EPA settled. A large fine was levied, land was set aside, and the mall was never built.

public sentiment that the government should take action to protect the nation's waters, Senator Edmund Muskie proposed the Clean Water Act on October 28, 1971. The legislation would bring all "navigable waters of the United States" under the jurisdiction of the federal government. In order for Senator Muskie's proposed legislation to become law, it first had to be approved by the House of Representatives and the Senate. The legislation gained Senate approval on November 2, 1971. On March 29, 1972, the House also voted in favor of the legislation. The versions of the legislation passed by the House and Senate varied slightly, and so a Congressional Joint Conference Committee stepped in to shape the legislation into a version that could be approved by both the House and Senate. This process was completed on October 4, 1972, and that same day both the House and the Senate approved the legislation.

Next Stop: The President

As part of the next step in the legislative process, the legislation was sent to President Nixon for his signature of approval. Instead, on October 17, 1972, President Nixon vetoed the proposal. A presidential veto can only be overcome by a two-thirds vote of both the Senate and the House of Representatives. The House and Senate did indeed override the presidential veto, and on October 18, 1972, the Clean Water Act was enacted and became Title 33 of the U.S. Code.

The Role of the EPA

The Environmental Protection Agency (EPA) is the executive agency responsible for enforcing the Clean Water Act. Among other things, the law requires that before filling or dredging or otherwise polluting any "navigable waters of the United States" a permit must be obtained from the Army Corps of Engineers, a federal agency. The Army Corps of Engineers was given the task of providing a working definition of the term "navigable waters."

It Is All in the Interpretation

The Clean Water Act is intended to govern and protect the "navigable waters" of the United States. At the center of the government's dispute with Mr. Rapanos's desire to build a shopping mall was whether the wetlands on the shopping mall location were brought within the control of the federal government by the Clean Water Act. The Army Corp of Engineers provided regulations that interpreted the phrase "navigable waters" very broadly to include not only traditionally navigable waters but also any "tributaries of such waters" and wetlands "adjacent to such waters or tributaries." Since the wetlands on Mr. Rapanos's property were near ditches or man-made drains that emptied into traditional navigable waters, the government believed his property was within their authority. Mr. Rapanos disagreed. The correct interpretation of the Clean Water Act was not clear, so it was left to the court system to decide the proper interpretation of the law.

The Court Steps In

In 1994 the U.S. Justice Department brought both civil and criminal proceedings against Mr. Rapanos in the federal District Court in Michigan for violations of the Clean Water Act. The civil litigation proceeded as follows. In February 2003, the District Court ruled that Mr. Rapanos had in fact discharged pollutants into federally protected wetlands in violation of the Clean Water Act. In April 2003, Mr. Rapanos appealed this decision to the next highest court, the 6th Circuit Court of Appeals. In July 2004, the Court of Appeals affirmed the decision of the District Court, meaning they agreed that Mr. Rapanos had violated the Clean Water Act. At this point Mr. Rapanos's only recourse in the matter was the Supreme Court, the nation's highest court, and so, in January 2005, he filed a petition to ask the Supreme Court to hear his case. The Court agreed. Oral arguments before the court occurred in February 2006, and the Supreme Court issued a decision shortly thereafter. Four of the nine justices on the court agreed with Mr. Rapanos that the Army Corp of Engineers' interpretation of the extent of the waters covered by the Clean Water Act was too expansive and should cover only those waters that have a natural, continuous flow to navigable waters. One justice wrote his own opinion that a natural flow should not be required but instead the Army Corp of Engineers should consider the nexus of the wetlands to the "navigable water" on a case-by-case basis, and the remaining four justices sided with the government. Because there was no solution agreed to by a majority of five justices, it was ultimately left to the lower courts to rule on the proper interpretation of the statute on a case-by-case basis. The Supreme Court sent the decision back down to the 6th Circuit for additional fact finding to determine whether the Army Corp of Engineers applied the statute too broadly. The 6th Circuit sent the case back down to the District Court for the fact finding. In 2007 the parties to the case decided to enter into settlement negotiations, and in December 2008 a settlement agreement was finally reached which resulted in the payment of fines and certain remedial actions required by Mr. Rapanos. His shopping center was never built.

The Court System

Notice the pivotal role of the court in resolving Mr. Rapanos's dispute. When parties to a legal dispute cannot resolve the situation between themselves, the parties often look to the courts for recourse. In fact, each year more than three hundred thousand disputes are filed in the federal court system, and more than 18 million civil cases are filed in the state courts. Approximately 90 percent of all decided cases are state court cases. Therefore, it is important to have an understanding of both the federal court and the state court systems.

The Federal Court System

To ensure the independence of the judicial branch, the majority[2] of federal judges are appointed by the president (subject to the approval of the Senate) for life terms and can only be removed by Congress for substantial cause such as bribery, treason, and other "high crimes and misdemeanors." In addition, the compensation of federal judges can never be reduced.

"The judicial power of the United States shall be vested in one Supreme Court, and in such inferior courts as the Congress may from time to time ordain and establish. The judges, both of the supreme and inferior Courts, shall hold their Offices during good Behaviour, and shall, at stated Times, receive for their Services, a Compensation, which shall not be diminished during their Continuance in Office."
U.S. Constitution — Article III

District Court

The U.S. District Court is the trial court of the federal system. It is often the court in which cases are initially heard. Judges determine how the law applies to a particular set of facts, but to ascertain the exact facts and circumstances of the dispute, judges may rely on a jury, witnesses, expert witness testimony, and other admissible evidence submitted by the parties. There are 94 district courts. Within each district there is also a U.S. bankruptcy court that hears bankruptcy cases.

Court of Appeals

The district courts are divided into regional circuits. There is one court of appeals for each of these regional circuits. In addition, there is a U.S. Court of Appeals for the Federal Circuit.[3] Exhibit 1.4 provides a snapshot of the federal circuit courts. The appeals court hears cases on appeal from the District Court and the other specialized courts. The first, sixth, eighth, ninth, and tenth circuits each have a bankruptcy appellate judge panel. These three judge panels hear appeals of bankruptcy court cases.

The U.S. Supreme Court

The U.S. Supreme Court is the highest court in the federal system. The Supreme Court is composed of one Chief Justice and eight Associate Justices.[4] Article III, section 1 of the Constitution confers broad powers on the court to hear all cases, in law and equity, arising under the Constitution, the laws of the

---

[2]Justices of the Supreme Court, judges of the courts of appeals and the district courts, and judges of the court of international trade are nominated by the president. Bankruptcy judges and other magistrate judges are not selected by the president and Congress, but instead are appointed by the district court and the courts of appeals.
[3]Unlike the other regional courts of appeal, the jurisdiction of the U.S. Court of Appeals for the Federal Circuit is determined by subject matter rather than geography. It hears nationwide appeals from only certain courts and agencies, such as the U.S. Court of International Trade, the U.S. Court of Federal Claims, and the U.S. Patent and Trademark office.
[4]28 U.S.C. § 1.

Exhibit 1.4. Geographic Boundaries of the U.S. Courts of Appeals and U.S. District Courts

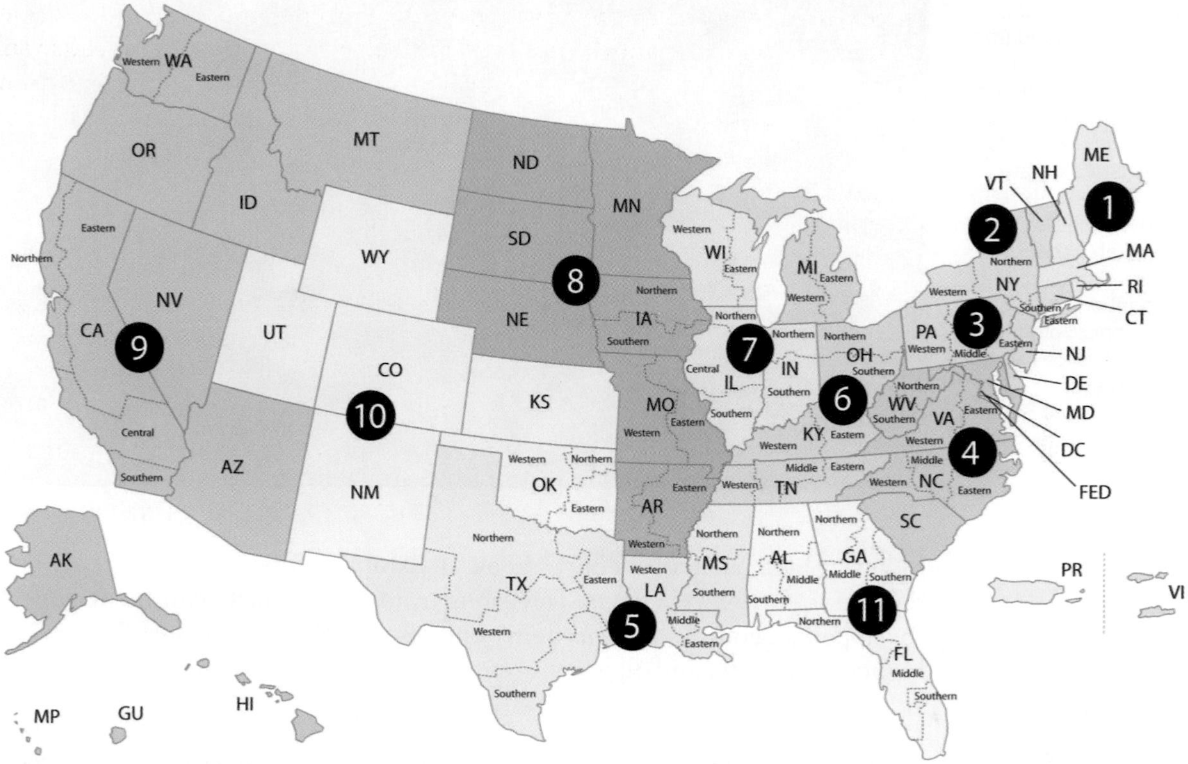

Source: www.uscourts.gov/uscourts/images/CircuitMap.pdf.

United States, and treaties.[5] The Supreme Court exercises discretion in choosing which cases to accept. To request the Supreme Court to hear a case, a petitioner must file a **petition for the writ of certiorari.** This is a formal request asking the court to agree to hear the case. At least four of the nine judges must agree to hear the case before a writ will be granted. (This is referred to as the rule of four.) Getting the attention of the Supreme Court is no easy task, since about 7,000 petitions are filed with the court each year, and the court can only hear and rule on about 150 of those cases.

Before moving on to a discussion of the state court system, a further explanation of the notion of *stare decisis* is relevant here. Recall that *stare decisis* means relying on past case precedent. But what past court decisions must be

---

[5]"The judicial Power shall extend to all Cases, in Law and Equity, arising under this Constitution, the Laws of the United States, and Treaties made, or which shall be made, under their Authority; to all Cases affecting Ambassadors, other public Ministers and Consuls; to all Cases of admiralty and maritime Jurisdiction; to Controversies to which the United States shall be a Party; to Controversies between two or more States; between a State and Citizens of another State; between Citizens of different States; between Citizens of the same State claiming Lands under Grants of different States, and between a State, or the Citizens thereof, and foreign States, Citizens or Subjects."

Supreme Court Justices, as of 2010, when the most recent justice appointed, Elena Kagan, took the judicial oath. Seated from left to right are: Associate Justice Clarence Thomas, Associate Justice Antonin Scalia, Chief Justice John G. Roberts, Associate Justice Anthony M. Kennedy, Associate Justice Ruth Bader Ginsburg. Standing from left to right are: Associate Justice Sonia Sotomayor, Associate Justice Stephen Breyer, Associate Justice Samuel Alito Jr., and Associate Justice Elena Kagan.

followed by a particular court? Look at Exhibit 1.5 below. Items 4, 5, and 6 represent entry-level courts. Decisions from these courts can be appealed to the appellate courts shown as items 2 and 3. The Supreme Court, item 1, is the highest authority, and all lower courts must follow Supreme Court precedent.

Exhibit 1.5. The U.S. Court System

1. U.S. Supreme Court	One Chief Justice Eight Associate Justices Hear less than 10% of cases appealed
2. U.S. Court of Appeals	Circuit Courts 11 Regional Circuits + Court of Appeals for the Federal Circuit
3. Bankruptcy Appellate Panel	Three-judge panel Hears appeal of Bankruptcy Court In place in 1st, 6th, 8th, 9th, and 10th circuits
4. District Courts	Trial courts 94 Federal district courts, including those in Puerto Rico, Guam, Virgin Islands, and Northern Marianna Islands
5. Bankruptcy Court	One in each of the districts
6. Other specialized courts (e.g., Court of International Trade, Court of Federal Claims, U.S. Tax Court)	Various specialized courts have jurisdiction over certain matters such as resolving international trade and customs issues, resolving monetary claims against the government, or resolving tax disputes

Consider the following example of how *stare decisis* works. Let us say that an appeal is being heard in the 8th Circuit Court of Appeals on a matter in which there is no Supreme Court precedent. To reach a decision, the appeals judge will look to existing precedent within the 8th circuit for guidance. If no such cases exist in the 8th circuit, the appeals judge might opt to look to what the other circuit court judges have ruled on similar issues, but she is not required to do so. Consider another example. Assume that a case is being heard by a judge in the district court in Louisiana. District court judges are bound by the precedent within their circuit and by Supreme Court decisions, but are not bound by the decisions from other jurisdictions. Louisiana is in the 5th circuit. A district court judge in Louisiana will consider Supreme Court decisions and decisions of the 5th Circuit Court of Appeals binding authority, while decisions issued by other district courts and circuit courts may be of interest and merely persuasive, but not determinative.

The State Court System

While each state has its own structure of court system, the most common state court structure includes two entry-level courts, an intermediate appellate court, and the highest state court. Unlike the federal judges, state court judges are either appointed by the governor or state legislature, or elected by the people. Generally, their term lasts for a set period of years.

Entry-Level Court

Most states have a trial court of general jurisdiction as well as a court of limited jurisdiction. The trial court of general jurisdiction is the main trial court of the state and hears both civil and criminal cases not heard by the courts of limited jurisdiction. As in the federal trial court, cases in this court are heard by one judge, usually in the presence of a jury. These courts go by various names but are often called superior courts, circuit courts, or district courts, depending on the state. The courts of limited jurisdiction only hear specific types of cases, and these cases are generally heard by one judge, without the assistance of a jury. Courts of limited jurisdiction include family court (dealing with family matters such as adoption, divorce, etc.), traffic court (dealing with violations of traffic laws), probate courts (handling matters relating to the distribution of assets upon death), and small claims court (dealing with cases involving a low dollar amount, generally under $5,000).

Intermediate Appellate Court

Most states also have intermediate appellate courts to which an appeal may be made from the trial court. Generally speaking, these appeals are considered a matter of right. These courts may be called by a variety of names, but the most common are courts of appeals and circuit courts of appeals. The appellate courts consist of a panel of either two or three judges. These judges generally will not review questions of fact, but rather hear appeals as to whether a procedural error was made or whether the law was applied incorrectly by the trial court.

Highest Court

All states have a highest court, which in most states is called the supreme court. In some states the highest court is referred to as the court of appeals, the supreme judicial court, or the supreme court of appeals. These courts use a panel of judges that vary in number. Some states have as few as three judges on the panel, and others have as many as nine. In states that have an intermediate appellate court, the highest court may exercise discretion on whether to hear a case. In states without an intermediate appellate court, appeal to the highest court is considered a matter of right.

Right of Appeal to the U.S. Supreme Court

Certain state cases are eligible for review by the U.S. Supreme Court. For example, if the highest state court has decided a federal question in a manner that conflicts with a decision of the high court of another state, a decision of a federal court of appeals, or a prior decision of the U.S. Supreme Court, the U.S. Supreme Court may agree to step in to resolve the issue.

Understanding Jurisdiction

Another key to understanding the workings of the court system is the concept of jurisdiction. Jurisdiction refers to the power or authority of the court to hear a case. The court must have jurisdiction over the subject matter of a particular case *and* must have jurisdiction over the parties to the dispute *or* the property at issue in the case. We examine jurisdiction because we must feel confident that everyone is in the right court. If the case is not in the right court, then any judgment that the court renders would be considered void and, therefore, unenforceable.

Subject Matter Jurisdiction

There are several types of cases over which the federal and state courts both have jurisdiction (concurrent jurisdiction), but the majority of cases must be addressed exclusively in federal or state court. For example, state courts have jurisdiction over family law matters such as divorce, adoption, and child custody; real estate cases; cases involving contracts; most criminal actions; and personal injury cases. Federal courts, on the other hand, have jurisdiction over cases that involve a federal question. Cases that involve a federal question are those that arise under the U.S. Constitution, the laws of the United States, and treaties. These cases include, for example, suits between states, cases involving ambassadors and high-ranking officials of foreign countries, bankruptcy, antitrust, securities and banking regulations, intellectual property, and federal crimes (such as treason, piracy, and counterfeiting). The other types of cases that can be heard by the federal courts are those cases in which there is diversity jurisdiction. Diversity jurisdiction exists when the parties to the case are residents of different states and the amount in controversy exceeds the amount specified by federal law that currently is $75,000.

Jurisdiction over Persons

In order for a court to hear a particular case, that court must have jurisdiction over the parties to the dispute. This jurisdiction over persons is called *in personam* **jurisdiction**. This is generally based on the presence of the person or a business in the geographic region of the court. Assume that Jordan and Jonathan, both residents of Massachusetts, have entered into a contract that Jonathan breaches. The state court of Massachusetts has jurisdiction over both individuals, as they are residents of the state. Let's change the facts a bit so that Jordan is a resident of Massachusetts but Jonathan is a resident of South Dakota. If Jordan wants to bring a suit against Jonathan in Massachusetts, she can do so only if the court in Massachusetts has jurisdiction over Jonathan. Because Jonathan is not a resident of Massachusetts, the court will have to consider what type of contact Jonathan has had with the state. In order to bring a nonresident defendant under the jurisdiction of the court, the court will always ascertain whether the person (or business) has sufficient minimum contacts within that state so that exercising jurisdiction over the person will "not offend traditional notions of fair play and substantial justice."[6] In *Burnham v. Superior Court* on page 20, the Supreme Court considered whether a brief visit to a state was sufficient to establish *in personam* jurisdiction.

Jurisdiction over Property

Jurisdiction over real or personal property is called *in rem* **jurisdiction**. It is the location of the property that determines which court has jurisdiction. Court judgment is enforced upon the property itself rather than on the person. Going back to our example involving Jordan and Jonathan, let us assume that their dispute is over a piece of real estate in Wyoming. Even though Jordan is a resident of Massachusetts and Jonathan is a resident of South Dakota, a case could be brought in Wyoming because the court in Wyoming has *in rem* jurisdiction.

The jurisdiction principles U.S. courts apply to foreign residents are similar to those applied to U.S. residents. The Supreme Court case *Republic of Argentina v. Welton* on page 21 provides guidance on this issue.

---

[6]*International Shoe Co. v. Washington*, 326 U.S. 310, 316 (1945)

Burnham v. Superior Court, 495 U.S. 604 (1990)

Facts: Prior to their separation, Mr. and Mrs. Burnham lived in New Jersey. Mrs. Burnham moved to California with the couple's children and filed for divorce. Mr. Burnham remained a New Jersey resident but on occasion visited California both for business and to visit his children. On one such visit to California, Mr. Burnham was served with divorce papers.

Mr. Burnham filed a motion in the Superior Court of California to quash this service on the basis that his limited contacts with the state of California were insufficient to give the courts of the state of California personal jurisdiction over him. Both the superior court and the appeals court denied Mr. Burnham's petition, ruling that his physical presence in the state was sufficient grounds for personal jurisdiction.

Issue: Did the court of the state of California have *in personam* jurisdiction over Mr. Burnham?

Holding: Yes. The Supreme Court upheld the right of the California court to exercise jurisdiction over Mr. Burnham. The Due Process Clause does not deny jurisdiction over a nonresident who is temporarily in a state in furtherance of activities unrelated to the suit.

From the Court's Opinion: *To determine whether the assertion of personal jurisdiction is consistent with due process, we have long relied on the principles traditionally followed by American courts in marking out the territorial limits of each State's authority. That criterion was first announced in Pennoyer v. Neff . . . in which we stated that due process "mean[s] a course of legal proceedings according to those rules and principles which have been established in our systems of jurisprudence for the protection and enforcement of private rights," . . . including the "well-established principles of public law*

respecting the jurisdiction of an independent State over persons and property." . . . In what has become the classic expression of the criterion, we said in International Shoe Co. v. Washington, 326 U.S. 310 (1945), that a state court's assertion of personal jurisdiction satisfies the Due Process Clause if it does not violate "traditional notions of fair play and substantial justice"

Among the most firmly established principles of personal jurisdiction in American tradition is that the courts of a State have jurisdiction over nonresidents who are physically present in the State. The view developed early that each State had the power to hale before its courts any individual who could be found within its borders, and that once having acquired jurisdiction over such a person by properly serving him with process, the State could retain jurisdiction to enter judgment against him, no matter how fleeting his visit . . . That view had antecedents in English common-law practice, which sometimes allowed "transitory" actions, arising out of events outside the country, to be maintained against seemingly nonresident defendants who were present in England.

Decisions in the courts of many States in the 19th and early 20th centuries held that personal service upon a physically present defendant sufficed to confer jurisdiction, without regard to whether the defendant was only briefly in the State or whether the cause of action was related to his activities there . . . The short of the matter is that jurisdiction based on physical presence alone constitutes due process because it is one of the continuing traditions of our legal system that define the due process standard of "traditional notions of fair play and substantial justice." That standard was developed by analogy to "physical presence," and it would be perverse to say it could now be turned against that touchstone of jurisdiction.

Republic of Argentina v. Welton, 504 U.S. 607 (1992)

Facts: The country of Argentina issued bonds called Bonods which were repayable in U.S. dollars through transfers on the market in various locations including New York City. When it was time to begin repayment on the bonds Argentina did not have the funds to do so and asked bondholders to reschedule the debt. Three of the bondholders, two Panama corporations and a Swiss bank, did not agree to this and insisted on repayment in New York which Argentina refused to pay. The bondholders then brought a breach of contract action against Argentina in the District Court in New York. Argentina filed a motion to dismiss on the grounds that the U.S. federal court lacked jurisdiction over the case.

Issue: Did the District Court have jurisdiction over this dispute between foreign parties?

Holding: Yes. The Supreme Court, affirming the judgment of the appeals court, found that the District Court had jurisdiction over the parties under the Foreign Services Immunities Act of 1976 that subjects foreign countries to suit in American courts if the acts taken by that country "in connection with a commercial activity" have a direct effect in the United States.

From the Court's Opinion: *We nonetheless have little difficulty concluding that Argentina's unilateral rescheduling of the maturity dates on the Bonods had a "direct effect" in the United States. [The foreign bondholders] had designated their accounts in New York as the place of payment, and Argentina made some interest payments into those accounts before announcing that it was rescheduling the payments. Because New York was thus the place of performance for Argentina's ultimate contractual obligations, the rescheduling of those obligations necessarily had a "direct effect" in the United States: Money that was supposed to have been delivered to a New York bank for deposit was not forthcoming. We reject Argentina's suggestion that the "direct effect" requirement cannot be satisfied where the plaintiffs are all foreign corporations with no other connections to the United States.*

Online Jurisdiction

The information age and the rapid growth of e-commerce has brought with it new challenges in the area of jurisdiction. In the days before online shopping, most of your purchases would likely be made via a trip to a local retailer. So, for example, if you wanted to purchase a music compact disc you would go to your local Sam Goody or Tower Records and purchase the CD. If a dispute arose with regard to that purchase, the geographic location of the seller was known and thus a court with *in personam* jurisdiction over the seller could readily be identified. E-commerce has changed this dynamic. Think for a moment about your most recent purchase from an online retailer. Although you are familiar with the retailer's Web site, do you know the retailer's "geographic location"? By its very nature, Internet communication lacks a clear physical location, and so the court has had to interpret traditional concepts of jurisdiction to e-commerce. One of the leading cases in this area is *The Zippo Manufacturing Co. v. Zippo Dot Com, Inc.*

Case Illustration

Since 1934, Zippo Manufacturing, a Pennsylvania corporation and maker of the well-known Zippo lighters, has registered and owned a variety of trademarks on the word "Zippo." The other party to the case, Zippo Dot Com, Inc., a California corporation, is an Internet news service that registered domain names such as zippo.com, zippo.net, and zipponews.com. Zippo Manufacturing brought a trademark infringement and dilution lawsuit against Zippo Dot Com in the federal district court in Pennsylvania. In response to the suit, Zippo Dot Com asked the court to dismiss the case due to a lack of jurisdiction because Zippo Dot Com did not have an office, employees, or other physical presence in Pennsylvania.

The court disagreed, finding that Zippo Dot Com had sufficient contacts with Pennsylvania to allow the court to exercise jurisdiction. In reaching its result, the court created what is referred to as a sliding scale of jurisdiction. At one end of the spectrum are those with an online presence that clearly constitutes doing business over the Internet, such as entering into contracts and conducting other transfers of information. In such instances jurisdiction is clear. At the other end of the sliding scale are those operating a purely passive Web site in which information is simply made available to users. Such sites do not establish jurisdiction. The more interesting and complex situations are those falling into the mid-range of the scale in which some interactivity on the Web site takes place. In those cases, a closer look at the level of commercial activity and exchange of information is necessary to determine whether jurisdiction over an out-of-state defendant is proper.

Zippo Manufacturing v. Zippo Dot Com, Inc., 952 F. Supp. 1119 (W.D. Pa. 1997).

Venue and Standing to Sue

Once it is determined that a court has jurisdiction over a particular case, further questions must be asked before the court will agree to hear the case. The first question is whether that court is the best location for a trial. Going back to our contract dispute between Jordan and Jonathan, let us assume that Jonathan, the South Dakota resident, traveled to Massachusetts on several occasions to negotiate the contract for the sale of the Wyoming land to Jordan. In that case it would appear that Jordan has several options. She can file her dispute in Massachusetts as it is likely that Jonathan's behavior gives him adequate minimum contact with Massachusetts; she can submit herself to the jurisdiction of the court in South Dakota which clearly has jurisdiction over Jonathan since he is a resident of that state; or she can file her claim in Wyoming, the location of the disputed property. The question of **venue** asks the court to consider which of these locations is the most appropriate physical location for a trial. The final question the court will consider is whether the party bringing the case has "**standing to sue**." This simply means considering whether the party has an actual tangible interest in the dispute. In the case of Jordan and Jonathan, the answer is clearly yes since she has been affected by his breach of their contract.

The Litigation Process

Whether a dispute is within the jurisdiction of a state or federal court, the legal process of a civil litigation generally involves several distinct phases: pleadings, discovery, trial, and possible appeals.

The Pleadings

A legal case commences when a plaintiff files a complaint with the court that describes the harm caused by the defendant, the legal grounds on which the lawsuit is based, and a description of the recovery and amount of damages requested. Recall that in order to hear a case, the court must have jurisdiction over the case. A plaintiff must also include in the complaint a statement explaining the court's jurisdiction over the case. The complaint must be served on the defendant in order to give the defendant notice of the lawsuit. This is referred to as **service of process**, and it puts the defendant on notice that she must file an answer to this complaint. There is no one set of rules on how the defendant must be served with the complaint: some states require service to be made in person, and others allow the complaint to simply be left at the defendant's address. The defendant must file an answer to the complaint within a certain period of time (generally 20–30 days, but rules vary). Missing this deadline absent compelling circumstances will result in an automatic default judgment for the plaintiff.

The defendant's answer to the complaint must respond to each of the items raised by the plaintiff in the complaint. The defendant may also use the answer as an opportunity to countersue the plaintiff. This means that not only does the defendant deny the allegations of the complaint, but she also offers her own claims against the plaintiff. If an answer does not raise any counterclaims, the plaintiff has the option of filing a reply to the defendant's answer. If the answer raises a counterclaim, the plaintiff must file an answer in reply.

Motions

A motion is a request made to the court. At this point in the process, the defendant may file a motion with the court asking the judge to take action on the case prior to trial. One such motion is the motion to dismiss in which the defendant asks the court to dismiss a case, generally because the facts do not support the liability of the defendant, there has been a procedural error (such as failure to serve the defendant correctly), or the court lacks jurisdiction over the case. You saw an example of this in the *Burnham* case at page 20. Recall that Mr. Burnham claimed that the court in California did not have personal jurisdiction over him and, therefore, asked the court to dismiss the case against him.

After receiving the defendant's answer to the complaint, it may be apparent that the parties are in agreement on the facts of the case. Because fact-finding is a function of trial, and that is no longer necessary, at this point in the process the judge can apply the law to the facts of the case and provide what is called a judgment on the pleadings (a ruling based on the facts as expressed in the pleadings). A request for this judgment can be made by either the plaintiff or the defendant.

Another motion you will see referenced in some cases in this text is the motion for summary judgment. This is a motion that either party can raise either before trail or even after the trial has already begun. The motion must convince the judge that there are no material facts in the case which are in dispute and as a result the party is entitled to judgment as a matter of law. In deciding on a motion for summary judgment, the court may consider not only the pleadings in the case but any additional supporting documentation such as witness testimony.

Discovery

The next phase of the litigation process is discovery, the process that allows the parties to obtain relevant information from each other and also from third parties about the facts and circumstances of the case. In the discovery process, information is gathered through a variety of methods including requests for documents, interrogatories (written questions), and oral depositions, in which witnesses are questioned under oath. The discovery process is usually the longest part of the litigation process, and it is an important one because it helps to clarify the case for both sides. Sometimes during or upon completion of discovery, a party might find that the gathered evidence so clearly represents a winning case that a motion for summary judgment is filed, asking the court to rule on the legal issues without a trial.

Trial

Once the discovery process is completed, a case is scheduled for trial. This part of the litigation process requires that each party submit a brief to the court detailing the legal arguments in defense of their position. Prior to trial the judge may hold a pretrial conference with the parties to discuss how the trial will proceed and to determine whether settlement before trial is possible. Trials may be conducted with or without a jury. Trials in which a jury is not used are called bench trials. During the trial, witnesses are called and questioned, and the opposing party is given an opportunity for cross examination. Once all the evidence has been presented to the court, each side makes a closing argument. Before the case is then turned over to a jury (in a jury trial), the parties also have the right to file a motion for judgment as a matter of law. This motion states that no reasonable jury could find for the opposing party in light of all the evidence. After closing arguments, the parties await the jury verdict (in a jury trial) or the judge's ruling (in a bench trial).

Once a decision has been rendered, the parties have several options. One is to file a motion for a new trial claiming either that there were errors made in how the trial was conducted or that the jury or judge clearly reached the wrong conclusion. These motions are not commonly granted. If it is believed that no reasonable jury could rule on behalf of the prevailing party, a motion for judgment n.o.v. (notwithstanding the verdict) can be made in state court. In federal court this motion will be a renewal of the motion for judgment as a matter of law that was filed before the case went to the jury. If the judge grants this request, the jury's verdict is set aside.

Appeal

Either party that is dissatisfied with the outcome of the case also has the right to appeal the case to a higher court seeking a reversal of the lower court decision. Appeals are generally limited to issues involving the procedural aspects of the trial itself. Appellate judges do not revisit the accuracy of the facts that have been determined by the lower court, and new evidence is not permitted.

Alternative Dispute Resolution

Litigating a case is time consuming, expensive, and opens the affairs of the individual/corporation to public view. For these reasons the parties may pursue alternatives to litigation. Television series such as *The Good Wife, Suits*, and *Boston Legal* all portray lawyers spending much of their time eloquently and vigorously defending their clients before a judge and jury. In reality, approximately 95 percent of all cases settle before trial, and so understanding the alternative approaches to dispute resolution is vital, especially for those engaged in myriads of business transactions.

Negotiation

The simplest, least costly method of resolving a dispute is for the parties to seek to settle their disputes between themselves through negotiation. This allows the parties to control the process. Lawyers may or may not be involved in the process as determined by the preference of the parties involved.

Mediation

For those situations in which the parties would like to settle their case but are unable to come to an agreement on their own, the parties may opt to try mediation. Nonbinding mediation is the most popular dispute resolution technique utilized today. In fact, some state and federal courts routinely require that parties engage in mediation before their case is allowed to proceed to trial. In mediation, a neutral third party, the mediator or facilitator, helps to keep the lines of communications open between the parties and helps them find common ground. A single mediator or a panel of mediators may be used. The mediator does not render a decision in the case.

Court-ordered mediation was imposed to resolve a claim against the National Football League (NFL) by former players suffering from neurological conditions believed to be caused by head injuries experienced during the game. The suit against the NFL was filed by more than 4,500 former players suffering from dementia, Alzheimer's, or depression. The former players sued the NFL for concealing the long-term dangers of concussions and for not providing players adequate recovery time from head injuries before putting them back on the field. Federal Judge Anita Brody required the parties to submit to mediation. Retired Judge Layn Phillips was appointed by Judge Brody to be on the mediation panel. Two additional mediators were chosen by the NFL and the players. As a result of the mediation, in August 2013, the NFL agreed to spend $765 million to settle the claims. However, in January 2014, Judge Brody refused to accept this proposed settlement, questioning the "fairness, reasonableness, and adequacy" of the $765 million. She has asked the parties to submit documentation that would convince her that this amount will adequately compensate the potential future claims of those covered under the settlement agreement.

Arbitration

Another commonly used dispute resolution alternative is arbitration. Like litigation, arbitration involves a neutral third party who will render a decision in a case. Arbitration permits a limited amount of discovery and applies simplified rules of evidence. As in litigation, the arbitrator will listen as both sides present their evidence and witnesses. The arbitration may be guided by a single arbitrator or a panel of arbitrators. An award issued through arbitration may be binding or nonbinding. In nonbinding arbitration, the parties retain the option to commence litigation after the completion of the arbitration process. Although an agreement to arbitrate a claim is often upheld by the court, exceptions can be made, as shown in the Case Illustration.

Case Illustration

Soon after Carol Warfield became the chief of anesthesiology at Beth Israel Deaconess Medical Center (BIDMC), she signed an employment agreement that included a provision that all claims would be submitted to mandatory arbitration. Dr. Warfield filed a suit against BIDMC in Massachusetts Superior Court claiming gender-based discrimination by her employer in violation of Massachusetts General Laws ch. 151B. Immediately, BIDMC filed a motion to dismiss, asking the court to compel Dr. Warfield to submit to mandatory arbitration as required by her employment agreement. The Supreme Judicial Court of Massachusetts ruled in favor of Dr. Warfield, explaining that while parties are free to agree to submit discrimination claims to arbitration, any contractual agreement to do so must be specifically and unambiguously worded. Because Dr. Warfield's employment agreement did not contain any explicit statement that discrimination claims would be subject to arbitration, the Massachusetts high court denied BIDMC's motion to dismiss.

Warfield v. Beth Israel Deaconess Medical Center, Inc., SJC-10375, 2009 WL 2195791 (Mass. 2009).

The Federal Arbitration Act[7] (FAA), initially enacted in 1925 and amended over time, provides guidelines for arbitration in contracts that involve interstate commerce. Because the FAA covers all contracts involving interstate commerce, its provisions apply in both federal and state cases. In fact, the U.S. Supreme Court has determined that the terms of the Federal Arbitration Act take precedence over state-law requirements when both apply to a case, as shown in a case involving a dispute over a franchisee's operation of a Subway sandwich shop in Montana.[8] The franchise agreement contained a provision that required the parties to submit all disputes to arbitration. Montana law required that any contract that is subject to arbitration must contain a notice of this fact on the first page of the contract. The first page of the Subway franchise agreement did not contain such a notice, and so one of the parties argued that arbitration requirement was therefore unenforceable. The Supreme Court disagreed and determined that the arbitration agreement was valid

---

[7]9 U.S.C. § 1, et. seq.
[8]*Doctor's Associates Inc. v. Casarotto*, 517 U.S. 681 (1996).

because the FAA requirements were met, and those requirements take precedence over any state-law requirements.

Practical Application of Arbitration in Business Transactions

Chances are you have recently engaged in a sales transaction in which you forfeited your rights to a "day in court" and instead agreed to submit any potential dispute to binding arbitration. Recall from the discussion of jurisdiction that a person/business will be under the jurisdiction of the court in any location in which the party has certain minimum contacts. Also recall that an interactive Web site is often adequate to establish this minimum contact. This leaves open the possibility that an online retailer could potentially be brought into court in every state in which they have customers. Businesses have anticipated this possibility and to limit their potential legal exposure may opt to include a provision in their sales agreements requiring that disputes be submitted to binding arbitration. Consider, for example, Zappos, the largest online shoe retailer. Zappos is based in Nevada and has annual gross sales in excess of a billion dollars. Customers making a purchase on the Zappos Web site must agree to the Zappos terms. These terms include a requirement that any disputes arising from an online transaction must be submitted to binding arbitration. The arbitration will be held in

Nevada and must be kept confidential. Zappos is not alone in requiring arbitration. Many sales agreements contain such terms, including the sales agreement of Amazon.com, one of the largest online retail sites, which includes the following language: "Any dispute or claim relating in any way to your use of any Amazon Service, or to any products or services sold or distributed by Amazon or through Amazon.com will be resolved by binding arbitration, rather than in court, except that you may assert claims in small claims court if your claims qualify." Similar terms can also be found in T-Mobile and AT&T cell phone service contracts.

You now have some familiarity with U.S. sources of law and workings of the legal system, but keep in mind that the U.S. common law system is just one system among many at work in the global marketplace. The following will give you an overview of the diversity of those systems internationally.

Global Perspective: Comparative Law and Legal Systems

Not surprisingly, legal systems around the world vary tremendously. Different regions and countries of the world developed, and continue to develop, legal systems based on factors like historical experience, social and economic conditions, and religious context. A particular event or a leader's decision made a dozen or a thousand years ago could have changed, fundamentally or slightly, the course of jurisprudential evolution in that part of the world. Despite these differences, comparative law scholars since the late nineteenth century have grouped legal systems into a few "legal families" based on common characteristics. Comparative law literature continues to be based on, and to examine, these classifications.

For example, many countries are thought of as pure common law or pure civil law systems. In reality, the number of pure systems is small and dwindling. Legal systems in almost every country are a mixture of elements from different influences, with laws and conventions transplanted or borrowed or imposed from other places. Latin American countries transformed the legal materials transplanted by their colonizers more than other regions because they have been independent for longer than other former colonies and because they have been dominated by the United States. In reference to continental European legal systems, one scholar commented, "All our national private laws in Europe today can be described as mixed legal systems. None of them has remained 'pure' in its development since the Middle Ages. They all constitute a mixture of many different elements: Roman Law, indigenous customary law, Canon law, mercantile custom, and Natural law theory, to name the most important ones in the history of the law of obligations."[9] Another scholar concluded, "I believe it is not at all unusual or surprising to discover five or six layers of exogenous elements in any single private law system one cares to examine."[10]

Factors Influencing Legal Systems

The major factors influencing legal systems of the world are as follows:

Conquest and Colonization. European colonization had a profound influence on the legal systems of countries on every continent. As the British, Dutch, French, Belgians, Germans, Italians, Scandinavians, and Portuguese fanned out to conquer and colonize all over the globe, they transplanted their laws, which mixed with systems already established by indigenous peoples.

Often, colonizing powers allowed some measure of local law to remain in force to mix with the law of the colonizing power. There are many reasons for this. Sometimes, the European law did not transplant easily to the colony. Sometimes, the imperial power wanted to cede some limited control in an effort to obtain and retain better overall control of the population.

Legal Education and Cultural Exchange. Interestingly, European law often continues to influence many entirely independent former colonies. Why, do you suppose? It can take time to migrate from one legal system to another. Some newly independent countries were poorly equipped to construct a wholly new legal system, so they imitated what was already familiar. Often, lawyers in the former colonies received their training in the colonizing country and used law texts, treatises, court decisions, and legal templates from there. In many cases, it is practical to

---

[9]Reinhard Zimmermann. *Roman Law, Contemporary Law, European Law: The Civilian Tradition Today* 159 (2001).
[10]Vernon Valentine Palmer, *Mixed Legal Systems . . . And the Myth of Pure Laws*, 67 Louisiana Law Review 1208 (Summer 2007).

model legislation after a former imperial power because the laws are written in a language legislators speak or are familiar with. For example, former French colonies in sub-Saharan Africa remain francophone and continue to emulate the French in legal matters, even long after their independence. Emulation is particularly common in certain areas of law, such as first-time adoption of securities law.

Legal Cooperation and Aid to Developing Countries. European and North American industrialized countries, as well as the United Nations, the European Union, the World Bank, and others, promote legal development in countries with emerging economies. Often, the pressure they exert for legal reform is influenced by the legal backgrounds of the leaders in those countries or organizations. In efforts to harmonize law globally, especially business law, securities law, and intellectual property, models are often based on the legal systems and laws of stronger, developed nations.

There are many examples of countries banding together and agreeing to harmonize their laws or coordinate their legislative efforts. For example, in the Helsinki Agreement of 1962, Norway, Sweden, Denmark, Finland, and Iceland agreed to coordinate legal development "with the aim of attaining the greatest possible uniformity in the field of private law."[11] A prime example of intentional legal convergence today is the European Union. Its members have adopted common standards pertaining to hundreds of different subjects, ranging from food labeling to bankruptcy. Efforts are even underway to harmonize contract law and criminal law.

Origins of Legal Families

Even though convergence, mixing, and evolution of countries' legal systems make it difficult to categorize, we can identify some enduring similarities by classifying systems according to primary origin. In general, there are three types of legal systems in the world, with many countries drawing on two or three of these categories: (1) common law, (2) civil law, and (3) religious or tribal law.

Systems Based on the Common Law Tradition. As explained previously in this chapter, common law countries adhere to the doctrine of judicial review. Common law originally developed in England and is followed by many former British Commonwealth countries, including the United States.

Systems Based on Civil Codes. Several continental European countries (and their current and former colonies) have civil code systems, such as France, Germany, and Spain, and they trace their legal frameworks back to Roman law. The Romans embarked on a system of written law to avoid the ambiguities and arbitrary applications that result from oral traditions previously followed by magistrates. Civil code systems feature statutes that are detailed, specific, and anticipate many different circumstances and situations, leaving less need for interpretation by

---

[11]Helsinki Treaty of 1962, Article 4.

judges. Because their laws are so detailed, civil code legal systems do not depend on court decisions to advance or develop the law.

Systems Based (in Whole or in Part) on Religious or Tribal Laws. The very nature of religious and tribal legal systems is different than civil or common law systems. The former is rooted in religious doctrine and founded upon faith in God, gods, deities, spirits, and/or prophets. Contrast that with, for example, the beginning of the preamble to the U.S. Constitution, "We the people," which implies that the source of governmental and legal authority rests with citizens. From this basic distinction, many other differences emerge. Religious and tribal laws are designed in part to dictate and facilitate moral behavior. As such, they cover a broader scope of matters, including relationships with other people, religious practice, and various aspects of daily life, such as eating habits. In contrast, common law and civil code systems tend to center on property rights, freedoms, and criminal activity. The methods of resolving disputes and the people empowered to resolve them are also different. Usually, a clergy member, tribe of elders, or other figurehead operates as judge in religious and tribal systems. Secular systems, especially democratic ones, rely on an independent judiciary composed of judges appointed based on their legal expertise.

Religious legal systems are more static, and secular-based systems tend to be more flexible. For example, Islamic law (also called Shari'a) is based on the Qur'an, the holy book of Islam, and the Sunnah, decisions and sayings of the prophet Muhammad (570–632 CE). Scholars and religious leaders in the centuries after Muhammad interpreted Islamic law. Around the year 900 CE, Sunni jurists agreed that the law was settled and all necessary legal precedent had been established, thus "closing the door" on further evolution. In contrast, Shi'i Muslims believed that human reasoning (ijtihad) is an important supplement to the Qur'an. In Saudi Arabia, where about 85 percent of the population is Sunni Muslims, judicial decisions are not published or publicly available; there is no reason for their distribution because Saudi Arabian law is not based on judicial precedent. Law in Saudi Arabia is relatively constant. In contrast, common law provides inherent flexibility for legal evolution.

The legal system in some countries, such as Saudi Arabia, is based purely on religion, whereas other countries have a dual system of religious (or tribal) and civil law. For example, in Israel, religious courts have jurisdiction to adjudicate disputes involving issues relating to marriage, divorce, children, and estates, while secular courts adjudicate other types of disputes. In most of India, family law is determined by one's religion.

In the last two centuries, there has been an expansion of the common law, diffusion of Islamic law, and reception to constitutional models. Intentional, planned harmonization of laws facilitates international trade. Cooperation and coordination help countries develop their legal systems. International conventions aimed at global or regional efforts to tackle bribery, crime, and environmental issues lead to unified or harmonized laws and regulation. All of these factors influence the world's legal systems to mix and globalize — a trend that is likely to continue.

Summary

An understanding of the workings of the U.S. legal system is essential for any student of business law. The law permeates every aspect of a business transaction. This chapter has acquainted you with various sources of law and the balance of power by which laws are made, enforced, and interpreted. Inevitably, legal disputes arise, and although the vast majority of those disputes are ultimately resolved through alternate dispute resolution methods, such as negotiation, mediation, or arbitration, a small percentage work their way through the court system. Given the global dimensions of today's marketplace, it is important to keep in mind that the U.S. legal system coexists with a variety of legal systems throughout the world. Multinational enterprises are responsible to adhere to the requirements of the legal system in which they operate.

Questions for Review

1. Federalist system

The state of Arizona in recent years has taken various legislative measures to effectively deal with the growing number of residents in the state who are in the United States illegally. One such measure passed by Arizona would require an individual to submit proof of citizenship as a condition of registering to vote. By requiring an individual to submit proof of citizenship, the state of Arizona imposed requirements beyond those of the federal government. Under federal voter registration laws, in order to prove eligibility to vote, an individual must only sign the voter registration form oath declaring, under penalties of perjury, that he is a U.S. citizen. The form can be submitted through the mail, and no documentation to prove citizenship is required. Will the court allow the Arizona legislation to stand? Explain your response. *Arizona et al. v. United States*, 132 S. Ct. 2492 (2012).

2. Jurisdiction

Shirley Jones, a well-known actress and California resident, brought a lawsuit in California court against the president of the *National Enquirer* newspaper and one of its reporters. The *National Enquirer* printed a story defaming Ms. Jones by alleging that she had a drinking problem that was so severe it affected her ability to act. The *National Enquirer* is a Florida-based corporation, and both its president and the reporter are Florida residents. The defendants filed a motion for the court to dismiss the case based on a lack of *in personam* jurisdiction. What factors should the court take into account to decide whether the California court has jurisdiction over the defendants? *Calder v. Jones*, 465 U.S. 783 (1984).

3. Jurisdiction and venue

Marla, a North Dakota resident, decides to take a road trip to Arkansas. While she is vacationing in Arkansas she is hit by a car driven by Jasper, a Georgia resident who also happens to be vacationing in Arkansas. Jasper refuses to pay for Marla's medical expenses, and she is forced to file a lawsuit against him. Which court(s) have jurisdiction over Jasper? Which court is the most appropriate venue for the case? Why? Explain your answer.

4. Motions

Explain the distinction between the various motions discussed in this chapter.

5. Writ of certiorari

What factors might the Supreme Court take into account in deciding whether to grant a writ of certiorari in a case?

6. Online activities and jurisdiction

Jeffrey Hansing, of Wyoming, wanted to sell his 1964 Ford Galaxie. He decided to put the car for sale on eBay. The winning bidder was Paul Boschetto who purchased the car for $34,106. Mr. Boschetto, a resident of California, arranged with the seller to have the car shipped to California. When the car arrived, Mr. Boschetto found that it did not match the eBay description of "awesome condition, not restored, rust-free chrome in excellent condition." Mr. Boschetto asked Mr. Hansing to rescind the transaction, but to no avail. Mr. Boschetto then brought suit against Hansing in the U.S. District Court in the Northern District of California. Mr. Hansing asked the court to dismiss the case based on lack of personal jurisdiction. What result?

Boschetto v. Hansing, 539 F.3d 1011 (9th Cir. 2008).

7. Alternative dispute resolution

What are the primary advantages of resolving a case through alternative dispute resolution methods rather than going to trial? In what situations might a trial be preferable?

8. International considerations

Imagine you are the legal adviser to a country that has just gained independence after years of colonization. What are the advantages and disadvantages of continuing to utilize the legal system imposed by the colonial power? Are there some areas of law (business, family, estates, etc.) where it would be preferable to use a newly developed law?

Further Reading

Kotz, Hein, *Civil Justice Systems in Europe and the United States*, 13 Duke Journal of Comparative and International Law, 3 (2003).

Larson, David E., *Technology Mediated Dispute Resolution (TMDR): A New Paradigm for ADR*, 21 Ohio State Journal on Dispute Resolution 629 (2006).

Reidenberg, Joel, *Technology and Internet Jurisdiction*, 153 University of Pennsylvania Law Review 1951 (2005).

Riskin, Leonard, & Nancy Welsh, *Is That All There Is? "The Problem" in Court-Ordered Mediation*, 15 George Mason Law Review (2008).

Stipanowich, Thomas, & J. Ryan Lamar, *Living with ADR: Evolving Perceptions and Use of Mediation, Arbitration, and Conflict Management in Fortune 1,000 Corporations*, Pepperdine University Legal Studies Research Paper No. 2013/16.

CHAPTER 2

Ethics in the Business Environment

Chapter Objectives

1. To understand the value of ethics in the legal environment of business
2. To know what is meant by developing and maintaining an ethical corporate culture
3. To understand the role of the U.S. Sentencing Commission in business ethics
4. To recognize how ethical principles apply in maintaining an ethical corporate culture
5. To understand how a code of ethics may differ in a foreign country

Practical Example: Cool Facts, Inc.*

Cool Facts, Inc., a successful social-networking Web site dealing mostly with recent college graduates, is seeking venture capital with a long-term goal of going public. Cool Facts is especially concerned with preserving the privacy of its users who register with the site and provide it with personal information including where they shop and their likes and dislikes about computer products. In a thoughtful strategy session, the company decided to publish on its Web site a privacy policy that states, "... *we respect your privacy and will not disclose any personal information to third parties*." Their reason for including that statement in the privacy policy was to encourage subscribers to use the site knowing the company would protect their privacy interests. Funds Associates, LLP, a venture-capital firm, has sent Cool Facts a "letter of intent" promising to invest $1 million providing they disclose the names of its users and any information they may have about their buying habits and preferences for computer products. Although Funds Associates has assured Cool Facts it will maintain their users' privacy, the personal information will be sold by Funds Associates to a marketing firm that claims it will not disclose the names of the users. The marketing firm expects to gain valuable insight into the buying habits and preferences of young college graduates and will sell this information to retailers. The managers of Cool Facts anticipate receiving substantial raises when the deal is finalized. Do you see any ethical issues in the proposed transaction?

---

*Cool Facts, Inc., is a fictitious company developed by the authors to demonstrate and illustrate key legal and ethical concepts, theories, practices, and strategies.

Venture capital firms often invest funds subject to a contract with the funded company for a controlling stock interest, a seat on the board of directors, top executive positions, and asset acquisitions to assure the success of the enterprise and their investment. In this case do you think the managers' ethical judgment will be obscured by anticipating substantial raises when the deal is finalized? Is disclosing the buying habits and names of Cool Facts subscribers to Funds Associates who will sell that information to a marketing firm, an invasion of the subscribers' privacy? Some of the managers, the ethics and compliance officer, and the company's board of directors have raised a few ethical questions. They are wondering if a business transaction can be "perfectly legal" and simultaneously unethical. If so, should management ignore its unethical implications and proceed with the business? Could there be a loss in the company's reputation by disclosing the confidential private information resulting in a long-term loss of profits? Some of the executives are arguing the proposed transaction is ethical because the users' privacy will be maintained: only their buying preferences will be disclosed and not their names. Others are taking the position the transaction would violate the spirit of privacy as expressed in the privacy policy, and that would ultimately lead to fewer subscribers.

This textbook will assist you in developing a repertoire of ethical principles that are applicable to similar ethical dilemmas. Understanding classical ethical principles, discussed throughout this textbook, will be useful in helping to resolve ethical disputes and negate exclusive reliance on your emotional and subjective feelings.

Practical Applications of Business Ethics

Business managers, confronted with an ethical dilemma, are often told to just "do the right thing." What does that mean? How does one arrive at that ultimate goal? This textbook is unique in using Features on Ethics in the vast majority of chapters as a way of reinforcing the application of ethics in the business environment. Through the use of these applications, we help you understand what it means to "do the right thing." More than 50 practical applications on how to ethically analyze a business problem and ultimately "do the ethical thing" appear throughout this textbook. Each Feature on Ethics gives you valuable ethical insight on a particular topic discussed in the chapters. It is important for you to understand the ethical principles explained in this chapter and that appear throughout this book in the Features on Ethics illustrated in Exhibit 2.1 below.

Business Ethics

A starting point in discussing how ethics relates to business requires an understanding of what is meant by business ethics. **Business ethics** is a branch of philosophy that applies to ethical decision making in the business environment. Understanding business ethics will be valuable in resolving ethical dilemmas similar to the Practical Example: Cool Facts, Inc. case on page 33. As you read this chapter, keep in mind there are many ways that reasonable people can view an ethical problem that may differ from yours. Presenting a thoughtful and persuasive business ethics argument is enhanced by an understanding of the ethical principles discussed in this chapter. Because there is often a rule of law involved in a business transaction, there is an emphasis throughout this textbook on the importance of integrating law and ethics to assist in crafting persuasive ethical arguments and in identifying potential or actual unethical business behavior. In the above social-networking

---

Exhibit 2.1. Features on Ethics

An Ethical Insight

Selected ethicists and business executives will be highlighted throughout the textbook in a feature called "An Ethical Insight" that illustrates how our laws and business strategies are often based on an ethical theory, principle, or practice useful in bringing about a just result. This feature has value in helping you understand a business proposal from an ethical perspective.

Manager's Compliance and Ethics Meeting

The manager's meeting is an effective process to satisfy a compulsory training program to inform employees of ethical issues and legal compliance as required by the 2004 Amendments to the U.S. Sentencing Guidelines. Ethical issues are discussed in this meeting along with the applicable laws to ensure legal compliance and help resolve any ethical dilemmas.

In-Depth Ethical Case Analysis

This feature identifies the ethical issues in an appellate decision and reviews the case from a legal and ethical perspective by applying classical ethical principles and theories to the facts of the case. Special emphasis is made throughout the text to illustrate and explain how a court's reasoning is often related to a classical ethical theory. This feature will assist you in understanding the law from an ethical perspective and will be helpful in discussing court decisions from a broader perspective.

scenario, an executive who understands the laws and can articulate ethical values to the decision makers will be an effective agent in implementing an ethical corporate culture. Because the business objective should be to maintain and sustain an ethical corporate culture, you should know the meaning of that concept.

Ethical Corporate Culture

An **ethical corporate culture** is an ongoing development of the company's values and moral attributes for the ultimate benefit of its stakeholders. The company's strategy to develop and maintain a sustainable ethical culture is implemented in its published **code of conduct** (e.g., see Exhibit 2.2 at the bottom of the page) that enumerates and explains the company's values, and a **compliance and ethics program** adopted by the board of directors with an aggressive **"due diligence"** and **"risk assessment"** policy, all discussed below, to ensure that

---

Exhibit 2.2. Google's Code of Conduct (Preamble)

Our informal corporate motto is "**Don't be evil**." We Googlers generally relate those words to the way we serve our users — as well we should. But being "**a different kind of company**" encompasses more than the products we make and the business we're building; it means making sure that our **core values** inform our conduct in all aspects of our lives as Google employees.

The Google Code of Conduct is the code by which we put those values into practice. This document is meant for public consumption, but its most important audience is within our own walls. This code isn't merely a set of rules for specific circumstances but an intentionally expansive statement of principles meant to inform all our actions; we expect all our employees, temporary workers, consultants, contractors, officers, and directors to study these principles and apply them to any and all circumstances which may arise.

The core message is simple: Being a Googler means **holding yourself to the highest possible standard of ethical business conduct**. This is a matter as much practical as ethical; we hire great people who work hard to build great products, but our most important asset by far is our reputation as a company that warrants our users' faith and trust. That trust is the foundation upon which our success and prosperity rests, and it must be re-earned every day, in every way, by every one of us.

So please do read this code, then read it again, and remember that as our company evolves, the Google Code of Conduct will evolve as well. Our core principles won't change, but the specifics might, so a year from now, please read it for a third time. And always bear in mind that each of us has a personal responsibility to incorporate, and to encourage other Googlers to incorporate, these principles into our work and our lives . . . [emphasis added].

applicable laws are understood and obeyed. Legal compliance and the company's ethical values are discussed and explained to the employees in periodic **training sessions**. The ultimate objective of an ethical corporate culture is a profitable and well-respected company that reasonably provides for the well-being of its stakeholders, namely, the stockholders, customers, employees, suppliers, community, and environment. See Chapter 6, "Corporate Social Responsibility," for a further discussion of stakeholders.

Ethical Corporate Culture and the Good Reputation of the Company

As Warren Buffet's quote on page 36 reminds us, a significant part of an ethical corporate culture is maintaining the good reputation of the company. A loss in business reputation is generally accompanied by a loss in profits over the long term as customers and investors lose trust in a company that is viewed to be unethical by the general public.

Creating and sustaining an ethical corporate culture should be at the forefront of business activity as expressed in the company's mission statement and code of ethics. Some cynics would claim an ethical corporate culture is a public relations ploy to placate an aggressive media convinced that corporate America is a greedy group of overpaid executives unconcerned with anything but making excessive salaries and profits at the consumers' and investors' expense. Corporate America is, however, quite capable of exercising good faith attempts to implement an ethical corporate culture. Statutes, regulations, and government agencies are now holding public corporations, boards of directors, and executives to high standards of legal compliance and ethics. Managers who understand business laws and the ethical principles that support their policy are in the best positions to explain the need of an ethical corporate culture to their subordinates. Being ethical is not merely a nice thing to do but is often legally required as discussed and explained in this chapter and throughout the textbook. In a court of law, legal and ethical violations can result in awarding the plaintiff substantial punitive damages, to make an example out of the defendant, and to convince the defendant/company to change its business practices that caused harm to the injured plaintiff.

Ethical Corporate Culture and "Doing the Right Thing"

Amy Rees Anderson, the current managing partner and founder of Rees Capital and prior CEO of MediConnect Global, Inc., gave advice on her blog on how to be a successful person by doing the right thing and letting the consequences follow. The integrity of a business executive is striving to consistently "do the right thing" based on a value system of rational and

An Ethical Insight: "Do What Is Right"

Amy Rees Anderson was the award-winning CEO of Medi-Connect Global, recently acquired by Verisk Analytics. She is currently the managing partner and founder of Rees Capital.

"Do what is right, let the consequence follow." That quote is a quote that has been on the wall of my office every single day since I came to MediConnect. That quote has come to mean a great deal to me in my life and the truth is that it is living by that quote that I attribute the successes that have happened in my life and it is living by that quote that you will find the greatest successes in your lives.*

_____

*Amy Rees Anderson, Do the Right Thing, http://www.amy reesanderson.com/blog/do-the-right-thing/.

ethical principles. One may ask: What is the right thing to do? This chapter acquaints you with classical ethical principles that will assist you in doing the right thing.

Due Diligence and Risk Assessment

An essential part of establishing an ethical corporate culture is management constantly engaging in "due diligence" and "risk assessment."

Due Diligence

Due diligence is an extensive method of legal review to ensure legal compliance. Recall in the last chapter, "The U.S. Legal System," we discussed the administration of justice and how it provides the process for resolving business disputes in our contemporary business environment. In this chapter we explain the need to constantly train business executives and managers to prevent illegal acts by the company's employees, managers, and boards of directors leading to possible criminal prosecution for committing "white collar" crimes, as discussed in Chapter 10, "Business Crimes."

Risk Assessment

Risk assessment reviews a wide range of potential business losses to the company including possible corporate liability for carelessly enabling its employees to perform civil wrongs or criminal acts. Once the applicable rules of law are identified and legal compliance is improved by periodic "due diligence" and continual "risk assessment" by management, the company must then take positive steps to reduce the risk of an employee violating the laws. This goal is achieved by adopting and implementing an effective compliance and ethics program, a code of ethics, and training programs that explain the law and the company's ethical values.

"Due diligence" requires applicable laws and regulations to be reviewed with the "highest standard of care" to ensure legal compliance.

Compliance and Ethics Programs, Codes of Ethics, and Training Sessions

The U.S. Sentencing Guidelines Manual defines an effective compliance and ethics program as one that *"exercises due diligence to prevent and detect criminal conduct and otherwise promotes an organizational culture*

Do you think ethics is important in business? If so, is it equally important in education, politics, sports, entertainment, and family relationships?

that encourages ethical conduct and a commitment to compliance with the law."[1] The Society of Corporate Compliance and Ethics has stated "*an effective compliance program — must be a living, ongoing process that is part of the fabric of the organization. A compliance program must be a commitment to an ethical way of conducting business and a system for helping individuals to do the right thing.*"[2] Both definitions strongly indicate that an organizational ethical culture is best illustrated as a system for helping rank-and-file employees as well as top-level management to do the right thing. Keep in mind that a compliance and ethics program is legally required for publicly traded companies.[3] When properly implemented, such programs and codes demonstrate that the company acted with the highest degree of care in attempting to prevent the occurrence of a crime. Compliance programs and codes of ethics can be used as evidence in a criminal trial to possibly reduce the prison sentence of a corporate executive and/or reduce the fine against the corporation. Compliance with business laws and regulations is just the beginning of creating an ethical culture. For example, at Wal-Mart's annual stockholders' meeting, in response to a question on an alleged bribery allegation and violation of the Foreign Corrupt Practices Act (FCPA) (see Chapter 5, "Legal Aspects of the Global Business Environment") by its Mexican subsidiary, Chairman Rob Walton told

---

[1]U.S. Sentencing Guidelines Manual, sec. B2.1 (Nov. 2006).
[2]See *The Complete Compliance and Ethics Manual* (Society of Corporate Compliance and Ethics 2004).
[3]For example, the *Sarbanes-Oxley Act* requires all publicly traded companies to have compliance procedures to ensure internal accounting controls are in order.

investors, "*Acting with integrity is not a negotiable part of this business. It is our business; we will not tolerate violations of the FCPA or ethical wrongdoing of any kind.*"[4] If legal violations are found, could due diligence and risk assessment have prevented their occurrence? The role of an ethics and compliance officer should help promote corporate ethical conduct.

Chief Ethics and Compliance Officer

The **chief ethics and compliance officer (CECO)** performs the "risk assessment" function of constantly reviewing any risks associated with a business venture including potential civil or criminal liability for wrongful company conduct along with ongoing "due diligence" to ensure legal compliance. The first step in maintaining an ethical corporate culture is to obey applicable laws and regulations. The CECO explains the ethical values to the corporation and its stakeholders. Beyond that there may be other ethical concerns, for example, the possibility of initiating a "green company" that is socially responsible. (See Chapter 6, "Corporate Social Responsibility.") Other responsibilities of the ethics officer include constantly updating the compliance and ethics program and the company's code of ethics to ensure their implementation and understanding by the company. This is accomplished by having periodic training programs with the company's employees. Ethics officers generally report directly to the CEO to assure top management is informed of any potential or actual legal and/or ethical violations.

> ### An Ethical Insight: Corporate Ethics Starts from the Top
>
>
>
> **Meg Whitman** is the President and CEO of Hewlett-Packard and former eBay CEO.
>   *Companies form culture very early on and they get imprinted very early on with a sense of right and wrong. **And it starts from the top**. It started with the CFO, the President, and CEO. And so, I think I had this innate sense that we needed to establish very early on what the code of behavior was going to be, what the code of ethics would be*[*] [emphasis added].
>
> ———————
> *See an interview with Ms. Whitman, http://www.youtube.com/DruckerInst (type Meg Whitman in the search channel).

Ethical Corporate Governance Starts from the Top

A **code of ethics** is a published document that clearly enumerates the legal compliance requirements of the company including its ethical values. The code should be explained to the employees along with the consequences of violating its provisions.

Ms. Whitman's reference to the formation of an ethical corporate culture and the code of ethics is significant in understanding the ethical role of top management and the board of directors. Rank-and-file employees will generally develop a strong attitude of ethical

———————
[4]Wal-Mart Chairman: Integrity "Is Our Business," http://www.theglobeandmail.com/report-on-business/international-business/us-business/wal-mart-chairman-integrity-is-our-business/article4224932/.

behavior only if it is recognized and rewarded by the corporation. If the CEO and corporate board seem disinterested in ethics, it will be impossible to have an ethical culture regardless of a rigorous code of ethics.

Publicly traded companies must publish codes of ethics and make them available to the general public.[5] The code of ethics represents company promises made to its stakeholders and could be used as evidence in court by injured plaintiffs seeking damages for violations of the code. The development of a code of ethics should be carefully reviewed by legal counsel and the ethics and compliance officer and ultimately formally adopted by the board of directors.

Center for Business Ethics, (CBE) Bentley University (http://www.bentley.edu/centers/center-for-business-ethics) . . . *promotes integrity and trust in business by encouraging the establishment of ethical cultures everywhere.* Reviewing the website of a business ethics center is a way of keeping current in business ethics discussions by top executives.

Ethical Culture and the Practical Problems of Business

Although ethical principles are useful in understanding the reasons for business law and resolving ethical dilemmas, there is a practical application of ethics to law and business decisions as commented on by Dr. Hoffman. This practical application of ethics to a business situation will be emphasized by examples and features in this textbook. Business ethics applies to business situations and should always be viewed as a useful method to resolve an ethical dilemma. Although the theory of ethics as discussed must be understood, the practical application of the ethical principles developed by the theory is most important.

The practical problems of business and ethics are introduced in each chapter by a feature entitled, "Practical Example," and are generally accompanied by laws and regulations explained in the chapter relevant to the specific topic being discussed. The application of ethical principles to the practical problems of business by the board of directors and its ethics committee is an essential practice to maintain a viable ethical corporate culture.

An Ethical Insight: Ethics and the Practical Problems of Business

W. Michael Hoffman, PhD, Executive Director, Center for Business Ethics, and Hieken Professor of Business and Professional Ethics, Bentley University, Massachusetts. Dr. Hoffman is a renowned ethics scholar and founder of the Center for Business Ethics at Bentley University in 1976.

One of the important things I've learned over the years is that business ethics is not so much about erudite theories and arcane debates among scholars as it is about responding to the practical problems of business.*

*See, W. Michael Hoffman, Center for Business Ethics, Bentley University, *Raytheon Lecture in Business Ethics*, April 2012, *Toward a Sustainable Future*, Muhtar Kent, Chairman and CEO of The Coca-Cola Company; introduction comments at 3.

---

[5]Sarbanes-Oxley, sec. 406, 15 U.S.C., sec. 7264, and listed companies on the NYSE and NASDAQ must have published codes of ethics, 17 C.F.R., sec. 228.406, 229.406.

Manager's Compliance and Ethics Meeting

Federal Sentencing Guidelines

The 2004 Federal Sentencing Guidelines require a company to have an effective training strategy and incentives to implement the Compliance and Ethics Program. Manager's Compliance and Ethics Meetings (illustrated throughout this textbook) could be used as training programs to satisfy this requirement. The manager should report the minutes of this meeting to the appropriate person who oversees the ethics program (e.g., the ethics and compliance officer and/or the corporate board ethics committee). Each company will have its own potential unique liability risks that should be evaluated and explained to employees. This strategy known as *risk assessment* is an essential part of a compliance program. In the event the company is sued for violating a federal law, the adoption of a Compliance and Ethics Program, Code of Ethics, and effective training programs for the employees are all relevant to demonstrate a "good faith" attempt to be in compliance with the laws and are admissible evidence to mitigate damages and fines. Periodic Manager's Compliance and Ethics meetings are evidence of *due diligence* to ensure that the employees are aware of the laws that may apply to their company. Chapters in this textbook will utilize a Manager's Compliance and Ethics Meeting feature and apply a topic discussed in the chapter to its agenda seeking an ethical result. The analysis will utilize ethical theories and principles discussed in this chapter.

The U.S. Sentencing Commission

The **U.S. Sentencing Commission** (USSC) was approved by Congress as an independent agency and made part of the judicial branch of the federal government in order "*to establish sentencing policies and practices for the federal courts, including guidelines to be consulted regarding the appropriate form and severity of punishment for offenders convicted of federal crime.*"[6]

The USSC has defined a Compliance and Ethics Program as one that "**promotes an organizational culture that encourages ethical conduct and a commitment to compliance with the law.**"[7] Corporate governance,

---

[6]An Overview of the United States Sentencing Commission, http://www.ussc.gov/About_the_Commission/Overview_of_the_USSC/USSC_Overview.pdf.
[7]U.S. Sentencing Guidelines Manual, sec. 8B2.1 (b) (1)-(7).

from the board level to lower management, should implement procedures and policies that promote an ethical corporate culture.

Training Programs and the 2004 Federal USSC Sentencing Guidelines

The 2004 Federal Sentencing Guidelines of the USSC require companies to implement ongoing training programs with high- and lower-level employees as well as company agents which provide information about compliance with the law and ethics.[8] An effective training program could be implemented by having periodic **Manager's Compliance and Ethics Meetings**. This feature will be illustrated throughout this textbook to show how adequate training sessions address *due diligence* along with adequate *risk assessment* to ensure an ethical business environment and a sustainable ethical corporate culture.

    The following section will discuss philosophers and their principles of ethics that can be applied to a business ethical dilemma. An understanding of ethical principles is especially useful in appreciating various ethical points of view that may differ from your own.

Ethical Principles[9]

Consider this conversation between an employee and her supervisor:

EMPLOYEE: *"It's just totally wrong!"*
SUPERVISOR: *"It may be to you but, under the circumstances, I think it's entirely appropriate!"*
EMPLOYEE: *"That's because you have no morals!"*
SUPERVISOR: *"You are living in the dark ages, everyone is doing this and besides, it's perfectly legal."*

When considering the ethics of a situation, what standards do you apply? Your instincts may be useful in knowing when something is morally wrong, but are there acceptable ethical principles that are traditionally used to analyze an ethical dilemma? Traditional and classical ethical theories, discussed below, have been used in business ethics to analyze business situations from an ethical perspective.

---

[8]U.S. Sentencing Guidelines Manual, sec. 8B2.1(b)(4) makes "compliance and **ethics training a requirement**, and specifically extends the **training requirement to the upper levels of an organization**, including the governing authority and high-level personnel, in addition to all the organization's employees and agents" [emphasis added]. Commentary, 2004 Federal Sentencing Guidelines.
[9]See, generally, Gerald R. Ferrera and Mystica M. Alexander, *Appellate Judges and Philosophical Theories: Judicial Philosophy or Mere Coincidence?* Richmond Journal of Law and the Public Interest, vol. 14, no. 4, Spring 2011.

Unethical Corporate Behavior in Violation of the "Public Trust"

Note the counsel from Prof. Dworkin that lawsuits have a *moral dimension* and unless properly decided, there is a grave risk of a public injustice. Unethical corporate behavior is in breach of the public trust that its customers and investors have allotted to it, and in that sense, by engaging in unethical conduct, a "public injustice" occurs.

There is often a *moral dimension* to business decisions as well as lawsuits. Applying ethical principles to a situation will be helpful in avoiding a *public injustice* resulting in a loss of business reputation and possibly costly litigation, including criminal punishment. Keep in mind that this textbook does not address the details of philosophical inquiry and the specific questions of ethical theory; we leave that to the experts in philosophy and their ethics courses. Our task is to acquaint you with a few prominent ethicists; there are others equally relevant, who have contributed to the understanding of jurisprudence (the philosophy of law) and business ethics. Understanding their principles and underlying theories will assist you in developing a depth of ethical analysis appropriate for crafting and explaining ethical business strategies.

Ethical theories are duty oriented (deontology) or ethically evaluated based on the *consequences of the act* (teleology). Both theories have value in ethical analysis although they approach a situation from different ethical perspectives.

An Ethical Insight: Prof. Ronald Dworkin: The "Moral Dimension" to a Lawsuit

Prof. Ronald Dworkin was a world-renowned philosopher and constitutional law scholar. He was Frank Henry Sommer Professor of Law and Philosophy at New York University and Emeritus Professor of Jurisprudence at University College London. He previously taught at Yale Law School and the University of Oxford.

*Lawsuits matter in another way that cannot be measured by money or liberty. There is inevitably a **moral dimension** to any action at law, and so a standing risk of a distinct forum of public injustice* [emphasis added].*

---

* Ronald Dworkin, *Law's Empire* 1 (Harvard University Press, 1986).

Ethical Theory: Deontology and Teleology

Traditionally there have been two ethical theories that characterize a philosophical position: **deontology** and **teleology**. In discussing a business ethics dilemma, first clearly understand the facts of the case and the applicable law. Legal compliance is a prerequisite to an ethical corporate culture. Then review the ethical theories (see Exhibit 2.3) that will assist you in perceiving the problem from a variety of ethical perspectives. It is especially helpful in critical thinking to see the problem from different ethical points of view that will be useful in understanding why others, acting in good faith, may not agree with your ethical reasoning.

Deontology

Deontology (duty ethics) derives from the Greek words for duty (*deon*) and science (*logos*). This theory is based on a duty to do what one ethically ought to under the circumstances regardless of the consequences. For example, cheating on a corporate expense account, which is common practice in some companies, would be ethically wrong as managers have an ethical (deontological) duty to be honest in reporting their business expenditures regardless of the consequences of not being caught.

Teleology

Teleology (consequential ethics) is a word derived from the Greek words *telos* or root meaning an "end or purpose." It is commonly referred to as *consequentialism* because it is primarily concerned with the consequence of behavior. Rather than emphasize the duty to act (deontology) a certain way which is generally based upon a rule of law and acceptable moral norms, teleology seeks out the consequence of the decision and how it affects the common good. For example, from a business perspective, a teleological analysis often considers the overall consequences of a decision on the stakeholders involved, generally including the customers, employees, stockholders, suppliers, creditors, community, and environment. (See Chapter 6 for a further discussion of stakeholders.)

The philosophers presented in Exhibit 2.3 have made contributions to our jurisprudence. It is useful to note their ethical principles and consider how they apply to the resolution of an ethical dilemma. Others could be added to this list, but for the sake of an introduction to ethical thinking, the following philosophers and their ethical theories are often discussed in ethics and jurisprudence and provide a useful start in discussing the principles of ethics.

Exhibit 2.3. Philosophers: Ethical Principles and Ethical Theory

Philosopher	Classical Ethical Principles	Ethical Theory
Aristotle (384–322 BC)	Virtue Ethics	Teleological
St. Thomas Aquinas (1226–1274)	Natural Law	Teleological
Immanuel Kant (1724–1804)	Categorical Imperatives	Deontological
Jeremy Bentham (1748–1832)	Utilitarianism	Teleological
John Stuart Mill (1806–1873)	Utilitarianism	Teleological
W.D. Ross (1877–1971)	Prima Facie Duties	Deontological
John Rawls (1928–2002)	A Theory of Justice	Deontological

The philosophers and their theories are discussed chronologically and not by their order of importance or significance to the study of ethics. It is necessary to consider their philosophy within its cultural context at a particular place and time in history. Although the philosophers did not develop their ethical theories for use in corporate governance or establishing an ethical corporate culture, and some of the philosophers lived and wrote their theories many years ago, they collectively have crafted a path of Western ethical culture that continues to be relevant to contemporary business problems. Throughout this textbook you will be exposed to their ethical principles and how they apply to current business situations.

Aristotle (384–322 BC)

Students in Athens who lived at the time of the ancient Greeks may have attended school at the **Academy at Athens**, considered to be the center of Greek culture. Today we would refer to Plato, who was Socrates' student, as the director of the Academy. Aristotle was 17 years old when he attended the Academy, and he was a student of Plato. **Aristotle** was born in Macedon, in what is now northern Greece. He spent most of his adult life in Athens, first as a member of Plato's Academy (367–347 BC) and later as director of his own school, the Lyceum (334–323 BC). Among his many works, Aristotle wrote two ethical treatises — the ***Nicomachean Ethics*** and the ***Eudemian Ethics*** — and a treatise on political justice entitled ***The Politic****.*

* Aristotle, http://plato.stanford.edu/entries/aristotle/.

Virtue Ethics and Executive Responsibility

Aristotle has had more influence than any other scholar on philosophy and ethics. His *virtue ethics* is not a concrete series of ethical principles but rather a virtuous disposition, induced by good habits, to develop appropriate attitudes about ethical behavior.

Virtue Ethics

Virtue ethics is a teleological theory (see Exhibit 2.3 on page 45) that, for business ethics purposes, relates to the character traits and virtues of a business executive. Aristotle considered justice more important than other virtues, such as temperance, prudence, and courage, because it concerns itself with the well-being of others. Executives who perform their business duties with virtuous character traits and practical reasoning skills, especially by applying the virtue of justice to their decisions, will be especially conscious of the relationship and needs of the company's stakeholders.

Aristotle and the Virtue of Justice

Michael J. Sandel, the Anne T. and Robert M. Bass Professor of Government at Harvard University, is one of today's leading political philosophers. In his best-selling book, *Justice, What's the Right Thing to Do?* he states, "Aristotle

Exhibit 2.4. Virtue Ethics and an Ethical Corporate Culture		
Virtue Ethics	**Application to Business Ethics**	**Ethical Corporate Culture**
Justice →	concerns the rights of others →	benefits the stakeholders

teaches that justice means giving people what they deserve."[10] This notion of justice as giving *"people what they deserve"* has broad applications and is useful as an ethical principle in business relation-ships. For example, consumers *deserve to know* if a product is harmful by the company displaying a conspicuous, adequate warning on their product. (See Chapter 20, "Product Liability and Warranties.") This legal requirement to warn customers of a potentially dangerous product is ethically supported by the virtue of justice as it seeks to protect consumers from any unknown dangers that may accompany the product's use. The virtuous business executive should have valued character traits and apply them to a business situation seeking the best ethical decision for its customers and other stakeholders.

> "Justice alone of the virtues is 'the good of others,' . . . because it does what is for the advantage of another."[11]
> Aristotle, *Nicomachean Ethics*

A highlight of virtue ethics applicable to establishing an ethical corporate culture is Aristotle's preference of justice over other virtues because it benefits others in the business environment, per Exhibit 2.4.

Virtue Ethics and Ethical Corporate Culture

As illustrated throughout this textbook, Aristotle's virtue ethics has value in resolving ethical problems and understanding laws and regulations that benefit others, especially as business executives make hard decisions, for instance, reducing the workforce to increase the company's cash flow to prevent it from going into bankruptcy. Although the laid-off employees could object to this process on other ethical grounds, the virtue of justice may support management's decision, as it will benefit the long-term best interests of the other stakeholders, including the stockholders and the nondismissed employees by keeping the company in business. The laid-off employees could ethically argue, using ethical principles of equality, that they should be offered reduced time or even a temporary absence (furlough) from work rather than permanent dismissal. Keep in mind, as illustrated by this example, that hard business decisions are always subject to difficult ethical resolutions, and reasonable, ethical people can and often do differ in their analyses.

---

[10]Michael J. Sandel, *Justice, What's the Right Thing to Do?* 187 (Farrar, Straus and Giroux, 2009).
[11]See *The Great Legal Philosophers, Selected Readings in Jurisprudence*, edited by Clarence Morris, University of Pennsylvania Press, *Nicomachean Ethics*, Book V, at 17, translated by H. Rackham, Loeb Classical Library. Reprinted by permission of the Harvard University Press.

St. Thomas Aquinas (1226–1274)

Students in Paris around the year 1260 would have heard of a very popular Dominican priest, Fr. Aquinas, who taught classes at the University of Paris to standing-room-only audiences. Aquinas is best known for his famous work entitled "**Summa Theologica**," which includes a section on ethics and the philosophy of law. He had great respect for Aristotle and often referred to him in the **Summa** not by his name but rather as "the Philosopher." Aquinas was a philosopher and theologian whose theory of natural law continues to be discussed as it relates to law and business ethics. For instance, natural law scholars in a leading book on law and ethics, entitled **Natural Law Theory, Contemporary Essays** (Oxford Press, 1991), explain justice and rights and how natural law applies to contemporary legal reasoning.*

* See *Natural Law Theory, Contemporary Essays* (Robert P. George ed., Clarendon Press, Oxford, 1991).

The virtue of justice and its concern for others is a valuable starting point in ethical analysis.

Natural Law and Ethics

St. Thomas Aquinas and his theory of natural law further developed Aristotle's philosophy. Aristotle had an enormous influence on Aquinas, and his leading treatise, the *Summa Theologica*, often makes frequent reference to Aristotle simply as "*the Philosopher.*"

Natural law is a teleological ethical theory that holds, regardless of cultural differences, that all people have an innate ability and duty to make rational decisions that should be used in resolving ethical disputes. Contemporary defenders of natural law, within a jurisprudential context, view it as an assertion that law is a part of ethics. Aquinas was a Catholic Dominican priest, and his definition of natural law, as quoted on page 49, was based on his orientation of man sharing in divine providence and participating in Eternal Reason. Natural law may also be viewed, in a nonreligious sense, as an intuition based on rational inquiry, that just laws should be supported by moral principles. However, as Prof. Lloyd L. Weinreb, the Dane Professor of Law at Harvard Law School, cautioned, "The *practical danger of natural law is that it may discourage reliance on the rule of law.*"[12] Unless a law is clearly unjust, it should be obeyed until it is amended or overruled by the U.S. Supreme Court.

Natural Law and Common Law

The ethical principle that reason is the basis of law may sound rather simplistic, but the notion that law must be founded on principles of reason and above all appeal to our rational instincts is significant, because reason guides human behavior and is imbedded in our contemporary jurisprudence. For example, common law notions of "*good faith,*" the "*reasonable person,*" a "*reasonable expectation of privacy,*" and "*beyond a reasonable doubt*" all have natural law origins. They are not defined because they assume all people have the ability to act reasonably, including jurors and arbitrators. In keeping with Aquinas's deference to reason and natural law, business executives should always rely on

---

[12]Lloyd L. Weinreb, *Natural Law and Justice* 263 (Harvard University Press, 1936).

reasonable judgments when resolving ethical dilemmas and defining ethical behavior in the company's code of ethics. It is important to keep in mind that although reasonable people can differ, for an ethical argument to be persuasive, it must be logical and reasonable. The Uniform Commercial Code (see Chapter 17, "Sales Law, Consumer Protection, and E-Commerce") that establishes the laws of sales for personal property often refers to "*commercial reasonableness*" that is a natural law standard.

What is *commercially reasonable* is based on *trade practice* suggesting that society accepts that standard because it is rational and reasonable.

Natural Law Is Self-Evident

Aquinas regarded the principles of natural law as self-evident to people acting in good

> "Among all others, the rational creature is subject to divine providence in the most excellent way, insofar as it partakes of a share of providence, being provident both for itself and for others. Thus it has a share of the Eternal Reason, whereby it has a natural inclination to its proper act and end. This participation of the eternal law in the rational creature is called natural law."[13] Aquinas, *Summa Theologica*

conscience and "*good faith*." That notion of natural law is found in the preambles to the Declaration of Independence stating, "*We hold these Truths to be Self-Evident*" and the United Nations Declaration of Human Rights that states, "*Whereas recognition of the inherent dignity and of the equal and inalienable rights of all members of the human family is the foundation of freedom, justice and peace in the world.*"

Natural Law and Reasonable Differences

Because natural law allows for a rich diversity in moral life, regardless of religious views, a natural law argument could be made that is reasonable to one person and quite unreasonable to another, both of whom are acting in good faith. In our legal system, in a negligence case, the jury by their collective judgment that often reflects the morality of the community determines whether the defendant was acting reasonably. By following the judge's instructions, the jury *reasonably* applies the facts to the law in the case and is thereby utilizing natural law principles. Because natural law is based on reasonable arguments, in order to avoid lapsing into "moral relativism" that hold that truths of moral judgments are never absolute, one should carefully review the facts of the case and, if possible, give scientific reasons why one argument is stronger than another. In a court of law, this is often accomplished by *expert testimony* allowing the expert witness to give an opinion of liability based on the facts of the case. Contradictory expert testimony is resolved by the jury who, based on their reasonable judgment, decide to believe one expert rather than another.

The reference to "inherent dignity" of "all members of the human family" found in the UN Declaration of Human Rights is a natural law concept that holds, regardless of cultural heritage, there is an "inherent dignity" found in all human beings. Do you agree?

---

[13]Thomas Aquinas, *Summa Theologica*, Treatise on Law Q. 91.

Exhibit 2.5. Natural Law and an Ethical Corporate Culture		
Natural Law	**Application to Business Ethics**	**Ethical Corporate Culture**
law should be based on rules of reason →	law is a part of ethics →	natural law integrates law and ethics

Natural Law and Ethical Corporate Culture

Rational and accurate representations of the facts are always an important part of resolving ethical dilemmas. Natural law's contribution to an ethical corporate culture is the theory that law is a part of ethics and together they contribute to forming an ethical corporate culture as illustrated in Exhibit 2.5 above.

Immanuel Kant (1724–1804)

Students who attended the University of Konigsberg would want to enroll in Prof. Kant's courses on ethics. Kant was a demanding professor who insisted that students think for themselves, and his students always enrolled in his classes early because they filled to capacity. Immanuel Kant is considered by some authorities as the most influential and greatest philosopher of the eighteenth century. Prof. Kant was a curious person who, with all of his intelligence, spoke only his native German language and never traveled far from where he taught at the University of Konigsberg in Eastern Germany. He was, nevertheless, considered by many to be the most prominent philosopher of his generation, and his works on reasoning and ethics are found in three major treatises: *Critique of Pure Reason, Critique of Practical Reason*, and *Critique of Judgment*, and a treatise on morals, the *Fundamental Principles of the Metaphysics of Morals.**

---

*Immanuel Kant, http://plato.stanford.edu/entries/kant/#CatImp/.

Categorical Imperatives and Ethics

Ethical theory can be duty oriented (deontological) as discussed in Kant's *categorical imperatives*. Kant would insist that ethical conduct is the dutiful thing to do regardless of the consequences.

Kant had a lot to say about morals and ethics, and his ethical theories are relevant to contemporary business ethics. In the discipline of ethical philosophy, Kant is best known for his "categorical imperatives," as explained next.

Notice in the following quotes from Kant's categorical imperatives that our conduct should be worthy of universal imitation, and we have a moral duty not to manipulate others in order to accomplish a goal.

Kant's "Categorical Imperatives"

I. *Act only on that maxim whereby thou canst at the same time will that it* [your action] *should become a universal law.*[14]

In other words, an ethical executive would ask the question: *What if everyone in the company did what I am about to do? For*

---

[14]Immanuel Kant, *Fundamental Principles of the Metaphysics of Morals*, sec. II, 1787.

Exhibit 2.6. Kant's Categorical Imperatives and Ethical Corporate Culture

Categorical Imperatives	Application to Business Ethics	Ethical Corporate Culture
universalize conduct $\rightarrow$	acts worthy of imitation $\rightarrow$	self-imposed honesty to do the right thing
conduct as an end, not as a means $\rightarrow$	not to manipulate $\rightarrow$	benefits company and customer morale

instance, what if a manager is considering cheating only a small amount on his or her expense account, after all, everyone in the company is doing it. Kant would respond that it is the principle of universality that should guide one's conduct, regardless of the consequences of getting away with the unethical act of cheating. If everyone cheated even a small amount on their expense accounts, the obligation of holding employees accountable to submitting to management where corporate funds were expended would become meaningless.

II. *Act so that you always use humanity, in your own person as well as in the person of every other, never merely as a means, but at the same time as an end in themselves.*[15]

Moral or ethical acts always treat individuals with great respect as ends in themselves, and they should not be manipulated as a means to accomplish an ulterior motive. For example, Kant would argue a mortgage loan officer should respect and protect loan applicants' privacy and not manipulate them to disclose personal information without their consent, even if that practice would benefit the bank in making loans to the best, qualified applicants.

An executive's traits of integrity and transparency have their foundation in Kant's ethical principles as illustrated in Exhibit 2.6 at the top of the page. A manager's transparency and full disclosure to subordinates are essential parts of developing an ethical business environment.

Kant's "Categorical Imperatives" and Ethical Corporate Culture

There are no exceptions to Kant's categorical imperatives and he would find even a small act of dishonesty to be unethical. For example, a corporate board member who is privy to trade secrets and uses them for his own financial benefit is violating Kant's categorical imperative of universalizing conduct. The major contribution of Kant's categorical imperatives in creating an ethical corporate culture is found in his insistence upon honesty regardless of the consequences. Kant's categorical imperatives would hold executive behavior to a high standard of morality that some would argue is not feasible in today's business environment. For instance, they would argue not to manipulate in

---

[15]*Id.*

advertising and to always act in such a manner that your conduct could become universalized is impossible in a highly competitive free-enterprise global legal environment. Do you agree? Applying Kant's categorical imperatives to a company's compliance and ethics policy and its codes of ethics would be an extraordinarily strict standard with zero tolerance for an infraction. Kant was not one to compromise and would expect a carefully drafted code of ethics to be rigorously obeyed. Giving inexpensive gifts to foreign officials to expedite a business transaction may be legally permissible under the Foreign Corrupt Practices Act (see Chapter 10 for a discussion of the FCPA) but would violate Kant's categorical imperatives. Kant would find the use of even an inexpensive gift as a means to finalize a business transaction an insult to a person's integrity. A standard business practice of misrepresenting a product's durability could be considered a "white lie" but would violate Kant's duty to always tell the truth. Insisting that we always "do the right thing" regardless of the consequences is Kant's worthwhile contribution to maintaining an ethical corporate culture.

Utilitarianism and Ethics

Utilitarianism defined and developed by Jeremy Bentham and John Stuart Mill ethically justifies laws and business practices that seek the best interests and happiness of the majority in society as distinguished from Kant's categorical imperatives that create moral duties regardless of the consequences. Utilitarianism is concerned with the happiness and well-being of the parties affected by the decision. In utilitarianism, the *consequences* of a business decision are more important than the executive's moral duty to behave a certain way as in Kant's categorical imperatives.

Utilitarianism is a teleological ethical theory that is summarized as seeking the "*greater good for the greater number*." It is a useful theory in considering a management strategy that concerns the well-being of the stakeholders. Utilitarianism generally follows one of two theories.

■ *Rule utilitarianism* calculates the greater good for the greater number before confronted with the ethical dilemma. Executives who insist on "due diligence" to ensure legal compliance are generally following the principle of rule utilitarianism that will benefit the common good. For example, a rule-consequentialist would follow legal guidelines on

Jeremy Bentham (1748–1832)

Some lawyers become law professors because they would rather teach and research the laws than engage in the practice of law. Jeremy Bentham, the father of utilitarianism, was one of them. Bentham's main utilitarian concern, his "*principle of utility*," was whether the act produces pleasure or happiness and prevents pain and suffering. The notion of "*the greater good for the greater number*" often justifies a majority rule mentality that ignores the right of the minority for the greater good and happiness of the majority. Although utilitarianism is controversial, it is commonly used to ethically justify our laws where not all but "the greater number" will benefit from their use. The ethical theory of utilitarianism was further refined by John Stuart Mill.

what constitutes sexual harassment in the workplace as the greater number of workers would benefit in a harassment free working environment. Its concern is the long-range benefit to society. The UN Global Compact's 10 principles, seeking the greater good for the environment, women and children's rights and challenging corrupt practices, are an example of rule utilitarianism. (See Chapter 6, "Corporate Social Responsibility" for a discussion of the U.N. Global Compact.)

■ *Act utilitarianism* is a teleological theory that requires the acting agent to calculate the greater good for the greater number at the time of its execution. There is no pre-act calculation on the greater good for the greater number. Act-utilitarianism runs the risk of not having carefully examined beforehand the various alternatives and the meaning of the greater good for the greater number. For example a salesperson not well versed on the laws of the Foreign Corrupt Practices Act may illegally make a bribe to a foreign official believing the final contract will benefit his company as well as its stakeholders by generating greater revenues.

Both rule and act utilitarianism seek the happiness and well-being of others and not the doer or agent performing the act.

Utilitarianism as a Pragmatic Philosophy

Utilitarianism is a pragmatic philosophy, and it is often a useful principle that ethically justifies hard business decisions where a number of people will suffer in order to protect the greater good. For example, massive layoffs may be necessary in order to allow the company to continue in business. Although a large number of discharged employees would suffer pain, utilitarianism would ethically justify this procedure, because by discharging some employees the company is allowed to reestablish a positive cash flow allowing the remaining (greater number) of employees to keep their jobs. The business decision to have massive layoffs leads to a greater good as some employees keep their jobs rather than a decision not to dismiss employees which would eventually lead to bankruptcy and an entire unemployed workforce. Hard and unpopular business decisions often protect the greater good, as in this example, by allowing the company to regain its profitability.

John Stuart Mill (1806–1873)

John Stuart Mill was the son of James Mill, a philosopher committed to furthering the utilitarianism of his friend, Jeremy Bentham (discussed previously). Mill was a genius who was home schooled by his father. He could read Greek at age 3, Latin at age 8, and at age 14 he could read the Greek and Latin classics. He was greatly influenced by Bentham and expanded his theory of utilitarianism.

John Stuart Mill is one of the most influential philosophical scholars of ethics. He was strongly influenced by Bentham and expanded his theories of utilitarianism.

Utilitarianism and the Greater Good to the Company's Stakeholders

Mill's notion of a legal right is based on a *legal system* that protects that right because of its *general utility*, meaning that right is useful to the possessor and society because it brings about a greater good. As you will learn in Chapter 18, "The Debtor-Creditor Relationship," bankruptcy under Chapter 11 allows a financially insolvent company to continue in business providing it meets the court-approved schedule of payments to creditors. The Chapter 11 bankruptcy procedure is based on utilitarianism because it is useful to the insolvent company, the creditors, and the greater happiness and good of society. This point is illustrated by the many commercial airlines and other companies that continue in business operating in a Chapter 11 bankruptcy status. As illustrated in Exhibit 2.7 at the bottom of this page, managers will generally be successful if their policies and strategies attempt to produce legitimate pleasure and well-being in the employees and customers who will bring about greater company morale and happiness.

> *"The utilitarian morality does recognize in human beings the power of sacrificing their own greatest good for the good of others. . . . In the golden rule of Jesus of Nazareth, we read the complete spirit of the ethics of utility. To do as you would be done by, and to love your neighbor as yourself, constitute the ideas of utilitarian morality . . . laws and social arrangements should place the happiness or the interest of every individual, as nearly as possible in harmony with the interest of the whole."* [16] Mill, *Utilitarianism*, Ch. II, What Utilitarianism Is.

Utilitarianism and Ethical Corporate Culture

Bentham would examine the ethics of a corporate strategy based on its consequences to the entire corporate culture. Notice how this differs from the strict "duty ethics" [deontology] of Kant's *categorical imperatives* that are not concerned with the consequences of the act but rather with the ethical act itself. Utilitarianism employs a practical and useful approach to maintaining an ethical corporate culture. Bentham would view the corporate culture as a continuing process that constantly evolves to accommodate the changing needs of the company. For example, a company strategy that demands higher sales production each quarter may be controversial as working a hardship on the employees but ethically justified as necessary in a competitive business environment.

Exhibit 2.7. Utilitarianism and an Ethical Corporate Culture

Utilitarianism	Application to Business Ethics	Ethical Corporate Culture
"greater good for the greater number" →	practical use to benefit the majority of stakeholders →	hard business decisions can be justified if they benefit the majority

---

[16] John Stuart Mill, *Utilitarianism*, ed. George Sher (Hackett, 1979) 16–17.

Utilitarianism would find this to be ethical as the long-term consequences would be the profitability and survival of the company that would justify the extra work effort by the sales force.

Mill would probably be opposed to the extensive corporate regulations in today's business environment. However, if the evidence showed the company policy was causing harm to society, one could argue he would recognize the need for government regulations to benefit the common good. The utilitarian principle of *"the greater good for the greater number"* is useful in explaining to employees a company policy that seems to work a hardship on a few but in the long term the company's strategy will work for their benefit.

"Prima Facie" Duties and Ethics

A radically different ethical theory than utilitarianism is that of W.D. Ross's *prima facie* duties that are deontological theories that seemingly relate to common sense but are frequently overlooked in ethical discussions. Ross finds *"special obligations"* to behave a certain way because we have inherent duties or obligations to perform regardless of the consequences.

Notice the importance Ross places on doing the right thing regardless of the consequences based on the *"prima facie"* duties to act (see Exhibit 2.9 on page 57). His theory is consistent with Amy Rees Anderson's guiding deontological principle of *"Do what is right and let the consequences follow."* For example, an executive having access to inside information on a corporate development that will increase the value of its stock creates a prime facie duty of fidelity not to disclose it until the information goes public. This *prima facie* duty of fidelity ethically supports the law on insider trading, making it a serious crime to use confidential information when buying or selling stocks.

> *"Our acts, at any rate our acts of special obligation, are not right because they will produce certain results — which is the view common to all forms of utilitarianism."*[17] Ross's *prima facie* duties are deontological and not concerned with the consequences of their execution. For example, keeping a serious promise may work a hardship on a business, but in the absence of grave extenuating circumstances, there is a moral duty to do so. W.D. Ross, *The Right and the Good.*

Ross and the Value of "Promise Keeping"

Ross states that in exceptional cases, *"the consequences of fulfilling a promise . . . would be so disastrous to others that we judge it right not to do so."*[18] From a legal perspective, his fiduciary duty is useful in developing legal arguments based on contractual obligations. Of special interest is his insistence that *"[t]he moral order . . . is just as much part of the fundamental nature of the universe . . . as is the spatial or numerical structure expressed in the*

---

[17]*Id.* at 46.
[18]*Id.* at 18.

W.D. Ross (1877–1971)

W.D. Ross was the provost of Oriel College, Oxford, and professor of moral philosophy. He was a "moral intuitionist" who established prima facie duties that are generally binding irrespective of their consequences based on a moral obligation to perform. His book, "***The Right and the Good***," published in 1930, is considered one of the most important works of moral philosophy.*

Ross states that, "*To make a promise is not merely to adopt an ingenious devise for promoting the well-being; it is to put oneself in a new relationship to one person in particular, a relationship which creates a specifically new prima facie duty* [of fidelity] *to him, not reducible to the duty of promoting the general well-being of society.*"** Consider the application of this statement to the law of contracts, discussed in Chapter 15, "Contracts: Contract Formation," where we explain how serious promises create contractual duties that will be enforced in court and the breaching party will pay damages for their wrongful violation. The adoptions of Ross's "prima facie" duties (see Exhibit 2.8 on page 57) into a compliance and ethics program and a code of ethics are useful in implementing an ethical corporate culture.

---

* William David Ross, http://plato.stanford.edu/entries/william-david-ross.
** W.D. Ross, *The Right and the Good* 38 (Oxford at the Clarendon Press, 1955).

axioms of geometry or arithmetic."[19] This proposal, based on natural law, compels Ross to apply his ethical theory when conflicting duties create ethical dilemmas that can often be resolved when one of his prima facie duties has preference over another.

"Prima Facie" Duties and Moral Obligations

Ross's duties are useful in strategizing a business plan, especially the duty to prevent harm. Traces of Ross's prima facie duties can be found in court decisions where judges use language that reflects moral obligations that integrate law and ethics into their opinions (Exhibit 2.8). See the feature "In-Depth Ethical Case Analysis" found throughout this textbook that illustrates that concept.

"Prima Facie" Duties and Ethical Corporate Culture

Prima facie duties are especially useful in drafting a code of ethics because they represent expressed and implied promises inherent in employment relationships and business transactions. They are duties that are useful in resolving ethical dilemmas (see Exhibit 2.9) that can be explained to employees during training sessions as in the Manager's Compliance and Ethics Meetings as illustrated throughout this textbook. For example, the illegality of insider trading is supported by the "prima facie" duties of fidelity, nonmalfeasance, and the duty to prevent harm. Business managers acquainted with prima facie duties are better equipped to explain the integration of law and ethics to their subordinates.

---

[19]*Id.* at 29–30.

Exhibit 2.8. W.D. Ross's Prima Facie Duties and Their Application to the Legal Environment of Business*

1. **Duty of Fidelity:** The duty of fidelity relates to "promise keeping" that may be contractual, expressed, or implied, depending on the circumstances. From a legal perspective, expressed contractual duties are in the contract's "terms and conditions." An example of an implied contractual duty is found in the relationship the board of directors has with the stockholders to govern the company on their behalf. All contractual promises impose upon the parties' duties of fidelity to perform them in accordance with the agreement.

2. **Duty of Reparation:** The duty of reparation is an obligation to compensate for injuries done to others. For example, contract and tort damages are based on the defendant's duty to compensate the aggrieved plaintiff for a loss resulting from the wrongful acts or omissions of the defendant.

3. **Duty of Gratitude:** The duty of gratitude is based on an obligation when a benefit is received, individual or social, without cost, for example, the tax advantages the state and federal government grants to nonprofit corporations. The nonprofit corporate entity, in return for the tax advantage provided by the government, has a duty to perform a social service to the public.

4. **Duty of Nonmalfeasance:** The duty of nonmalfeasance is an ethical obligation not to cause harm to another. Our common law of negligence is based on the duty of nonmalfeasance. When a duty to perform carefully has been negligently violated, resulting in injury to the plaintiff, the court will award damages to compensate for the sustained loss.

5. **Duty to Prevent Harm:** Statutes that prohibit discrimination, such as Title VII of the Civil Rights Act, are based on duties owed to prevent harming minority employees.

6. **Duty of Beneficence:** Ross is concerned with a duty of beneficence that enhances the well-being of others. Statutory laws often follow that precept in an attempt to remedy a social malady. Consider, for example, the Americans with Disability Act that requires an employer to offer "reasonable accommodations" to a disabled employee.

7. **Duty of Self-Improvement:** Laws often obligate a person to self-improve, for example, probation for good behavior and required compulsory driver's education in a driving under the influence case.

8. **Duty of Justice:** Of special interest is comparing Ross's duty of justice with Rawls's **equal liberty principle**. Ross, along with Rawls, finds a social duty to distribute societal benefits fairly. Our federal tax code has provisions that generally follow this duty. The theory of the **Patient Protection and Affordable Care Act** is an example of a duty to distribute healthcare to all as a precept of social justice.

* W.D. Ross, *The Right and the Good* 22 (Oxford at the Clarendon Press, 1955).

Exhibit 2.9. Ross's Prima Facie Duties and an Ethical Corporate Culture

Prima Facie Duties		Application to Business Ethics		Ethical Corporate Culture
moral obligations to perform duties	→	helps resolve ethical dilemmas	→	ethical duties to benefit the business environment

John Rawls (1921–2002)

John Rawls was the James Bryant Conant University Professor at Harvard University. His leading classic books, *A Theory of Justice* and *Justice as Fairness, A Restatement*, develop a political liberal perspective of what he believes are the most basic rights of all in society. Students studying law and ethics in business should be exposed to them as helpful and useful methods to view our legal environment of business in a manner most sensitive to the "least advantaged." Keep in mind that Rawls was directing his theories of justice as fairness to government policy and political liberalism rather than corporate governance, but since corporate size and influence in society is enormous (e.g., abusive corporate practices of financial institutions as one of the causes of the last recession), it is useful to apply them to the legal environment of business. Although Rawls would limit his conception of justice to enhancing political values, his principles of justice are useful in broadening a business discussion of equality and fairness in the corporate culture.

"Theory of Justice" and Ethics

Ethical principles, based on the consequence of the act, as illustrated in utilitarianism, are disputed in John Rawls's theories of liberty and equality. Rawls stated in his book, *A Theory of Justice*, "*What I have attempted to do is to generalize and carry to a higher order of abstraction the traditional theory of the social contract as represented by Locke, Rousseau, and Kant. . . . The theory that results is highly Kantian* [deontological] *in nature.*"[20]

Rawls's book *A Theory of Justice* explains how social justice can be acquired by a group viewing a proposal from an *original position* functioning behind a *veil of ignorance* and applying the *equal liberty principle* and the *difference principle*. As stated in *Justice as Fairness, A Restatement*: "*Justice as fairness thus develops a theory of justice from the idea of a social contract.*"[21]

Rawls developed two principles of justice that he believed would be applied by people deciding behind the veil of ignorance (i.e., a group of people who are unaware of their social status in society and come together to form a social contract and make judgments based on the **equal liberty principle** and the **difference principle**.)

Rawls argued that people acting in this hypothetical "*original position*" would apply the following two principles of justice.

The First Principle: Equal Liberty Principle

Each person has the same indefeasible claim to a fully adequate scheme of equal liberties, which scheme is compatible with the same scheme of liberties for all.[22] Notice how this differs from utilitarianism because it protects minority interests rather than "the greater good for the greater number." Rawls stated, "*My aim is to work out a theory of justice that represents an alternative to utilitarian*

---

[20]John Rawls, *A Theory of Justice* viii (The Belknap Press of Harvard University Press, 1971; rev. ed., 1999; citations are from the 1971 ed.).

[21]John Rawls, *Justice As Fairness, A Restatement* xi (Erin Kelly ed., Belknap Press of Harvard University Press, 2001).

[22]*Supra* at 41.

thought."[23] The Bill of Rights in the U.S. Constitution that seeks to provide equal liberty for all is a reflection of one of the *equal basic liberties* defined by Rawls as *"the rights and liberties covered by the rule of law."*[24]

The Second Principle: Difference Principle

Social and economic inequalities are to satisfy two conditions: first, they are to be attached to offices and positions open to all under conditions of fair equality of opportunity; and second, they are to be to the greatest benefit of the least advantaged members of society.[25]

Rawls used the "original position" as a hypothetical situation where *"no one knows his place in society, his class position or social status; nor does he know his fortune in the distribution of natural assets and abilities, his intelligence, and strength, and the like."** The application of this concept may be useful for executives who want to maintain an ethical corporate culture that increasingly progresses toward a socially just workplace.

*See John Rawls, *A Theory of Justice* 137 (Belknap Press of Harvard University Press, 1971).

Some would argue that the difference principle is not applicable to the business environment; however, the concept is useful in searching for a corporate ethical culture to be as all-inclusive as possible. Companies may be influenced by this principle to assist the least advantaged. Currently many companies are using charitable foundations to assist those in need.

Rawls's Principles of Justice and Ethical Corporate Culture

Rawls's principles hypothesize how members in the original position, operating behind a veil of ignorance and applying the *equal liberty principle* and the *difference principle*, seek a just result in their decisions. Aristotle's "virtue ethics" that prioritized justice over the other virtues because it is concerned with the benefit of others, is reflected in Rawls's *Theory of Justice* where he stated, *"Justice is the first virtue of social institutions . . . laws and institutions no matter how efficient and well-arranged must be reformed or abolished if they are unjust."*[26] An example of how the equal liberty principle is relevant to the legal environment of business is found in Raytheon's Code of Conduct that states, *"Treat People with Respect and Dignity: Raytheon leaders at all levels have a special obligation to encourage an open work environment and **ethical culture**, where employees are treated respectfully and may raise issues or concerns without fear of retaliation"* [emphasis added]. Notice that the employees are given *"an equal basic liberty"* compatible with management to raise controversial issues without fear of being fired. An essential part of developing an ethical corporate culture is recognizing equal rights in the workplace. (For a further discussion of rights in the workplace, see Chapter 13, "Employment Law," and Chapter 14, "Discrimination in the Workplace"). Rawls's principles of justice are useful in

---

[23]*Supra* note 21,
[24]*Id.* at 41.
[25]*Id.* at 42.
[26]*Supra* note 21, at 3.

	Exhibit 2.10. Rawls's Theory of Justice and an Ethical Corporate Culture

Theory of Justice	Application to Business Ethics	Ethical Corporate Culture
"equal liberty principle" →	basic liberty for all →	same basic rights for all employees
"difference principle" →	benefit the "least advantaged" →	possible use of a charitable foundation

assisting management in strategizing a just working environment. For instance, does the business assist the "*least advantaged*" in the company? Are customers, as part of a corporate scheme of basic liberties, adequately warned of dangerous latent defects in their products? A Rawlsian ethical corporate culture (see Exhibit 2.10) considers the values of the equal liberty principle and the difference principle, especially how the latter may apply to the least advantaged in society by a company often utilizing a charitable foundation.

A business executive should constantly be reminded of ethical theories and principles as objective moral standards that are useful in reviewing a corporate strategy. Exhibit 2.11 illustrates that proccess.

Exhibit 2.11. Executive Summary of Ethical Theories

ARISTOTLE. *Virtue Ethics*: Aristotle taught that we become just by acquiring the habit of doing just acts. The virtue of justice is paramount to the other virtues of temperance, courage, and prudence because it provides fairness to others. This notion is especially useful in stakeholder analysis that seeks fairness to all affected by the business strategy.

AQUINAS. *Natural Law*: Aquinas believed people of good conscious acting in "good faith" have an innate ability to act reasonably and ethically regardless of their cultural heritage. Natural law has value as it requires an open mind willing to listen to other reasonable points of view and is useful in executives' understanding a reasonable ethical principle that differs from their own.

KANT. *Categorical Imperatives*: Kant proposed our conduct should be something all could imitate (a universal law) without harm, and it must respect human dignity as an end in itself. The duty to act ethically, based on Kant's principles, regardless of the consequences, distinguishes the categorical imperatives from utilitarianism. The categorical imperatives hold business executives to the highest degree of honest ethical behavior.

BENTHAM and MILL. *Utilitarianism*: The principle of utilitarianism states that actions are ethical if they promote *happiness* or *pleasure*, and wrong if they tend to produce *unhappiness* or *pain*. *Rule utilitarianism* finds the action to be ethical if it conforms to a rule that contributes to *the greater good in society*. *Act utilitarianism* judges the ethics of an individual's act based on its *consequences* to society, rather than strict adherence to the rule. Utilitarianism is helpful in seeking to provide for the well-being of stakeholders.

ROSS. *"Prima Facie" Duties*: Ross provides a series of "prima facie" duties based on relationships that should be performed as moral obligations. They are useful in analyzing business ethics and legal relationships, especially in contract and tort law.

RAWLS. Rawls's **"equal liberty principle"** and **"difference principle"** have special value in seeking to provide a socially just working environment.

Global Perspectives and Business Ethics

We have been explaining the integration of law and principles of ethics in the United States and how they apply to an ethical corporate culture. Because most major companies have a global presence, throughout this textbook the chapters will discuss some relevant aspects of international law.

Apple's Global International Code of Conduct

A typical example of a company doing extensive foreign business is Apple, whose sales from business in China were $23.8 billion in 2012.[28] Apple's Code of Conduct, **"Business Conduct: The Way We Do Business Worldwide,"**[29] applies to all of the company's employees, its executives, and the board of directors.

Foreign Culture's Ethical Values

It is important to keep in mind as you read about global perspectives throughout this textbook that various cultures often perceive ethical values from their unique historical heritage. It is important that an American company doing business in a foreign country does not impose its code of ethics in that environment without carefully reviewing and changing its provisions, if morally acceptable, to accommodate that ethical culture. It is generally necessary to adopt a code of ethics and have training sessions on ethics which are sensitive to the foreign cultural environment. Throughout this textbook the majority of chapters have reference to international transactions in a section entitled "Global Perspectives."

China

The People's Republic of China has its own unique court system and overview of business ethics. A U.S. company doing business in China should understand that the imposition of a foreign Western system of ethics in China is not an acceptable way to proceed.

Codes of Ethics in The People's Republic of China
Stephen Rothlin, a renowned, international scholar and general secretary of the Center for International Business Ethics at Beijing University, commented on the result of using an American code of ethics in China without consulting with Chinese executives in its development.

---

[28]Apple's iPhone 5 officially goes on sale in China, http://news.cnet.com/8301-13579_3-57559157-37/apples-iphone-5-officially-goes-on-sale-in-china/.
[29]Apple, Business Conduct: The Way We Do Business Worldwide, http://media.corporate-ir.net/media_files/irol/10/107357/BC_Policy_0209.pdf.

"If you translate your existing code [of ethics] from English and distribute it, the Chinese will say, Yes, thank you,' and then throw it away." Stephan Rothlin, S.J., general secretary of the Center for International Business Ethics, Beijing University. (Business Ethics in China, http://www.scu.edu/ethics/publications/ethicalperspectives/business-china.html.)

Because codes of ethics used in a foreign country are promises made to the public by the corporation, they should be carefully drafted and reviewed by legal counsel from both countries and the compliance and ethics officer before their publication.

India

Code of Ethics in India

India is a global commercial player and has a unique business culture that should be understood and respected by American companies doing business in India. Prime Minister Manmohan Singh, addressing the inauguration of India Corporate Week in 2010, noted: "Ethics encompass a wide sphere of actions, economic, social and human, involving the consumer, labor, society at large and the government. Mahatma Gandhi repeatedly used to emphasize the importance of not only good ends but also of the use of fair means to attain them. It is the large companies that have to set the pace in this regard. The rest of the corporate sector will quickly follow as this becomes a national norm." Sing recalled Mahatma Gandhi's counsel of the use of fair means to obtain an objective. This advice would apply to the use of a fair (ethical) means to accomplish a company's mission and perform its strategic plain. Gandhi's ethical guidance is comparable to Kant's categorical imperative to "*Act so that you always use humanity, in your own person as well as in the person of another, never merely as a means, but at the same time as an end.*" Both Gandhi and Kant would insist on the ethical assurance that the means to accomplish a company objective must be fair and just.

An Indian company that has "set the pace" is Tata Industries, one of India's largest international companies. Tata has a Code of Conduct that is an example for other Indian companies and American companies doing business in India to follow (Exhibit 2.12). Its requirements are similar to what is found in many American companies' Codes of Conduct.

Exhibit 2.12. Tata's Code of Ethics

"Every employee of a Tata company, including full-time directors and the chief executive, shall exhibit culturally appropriate deportment in the countries they operate in, and deal on behalf of the company with professionalism, honesty and integrity, while conforming to high moral and ethical standards. Such conduct shall be fair and transparent and be perceived to be so by third parties.

Every employee of a Tata company shall preserve the human rights of every individual and the community, and shall strive to honor commitments.

Every employee shall be responsible for the implementation of and compliance with the Code in his/her environment. Failure to adhere to the Code could attract severe consequences, including termination of employment."

http://www.tata.com/aboutus/articles/inside.aspx?artid=NyGNnLHkaAc

Summary

The U.S. Sentencing Commission and the 2001 amendments to the U.S. Sentencing Guidelines have established corporate obligations to "*promote an **organizational culture** that encourages **ethical conduct***" [emphasis added]. For publicly owned companies the Sarbanes-Oxley Act requires corporations to engage in "*honest and ethical conduct*."[29] Ethics and compliance officers, a relatively new corporate position, monitor "***due diligence***" and "***risk assessment***" to ensure the law is being followed and potential and actual business transactions are legal and ethical. The managerial strategy to create an ethical corporate culture is accomplished by adopting and publishing a code of ethics reflecting company values and a compliance and ethics program with appropriate training sessions that explain their provisions to the employees. An effective ethics program consists of the following:

■ Due diligence: Because business ethics starts with legal compliance, corporate counsel and high-level management must ensure that the company is in compliance with the laws and regulations that govern the business.
■ Risk assessment: Management should review the company's potential business risks from a broad perspective, including the avoidance of possible criminal and civil violations.

■ Code of ethics: Management should publish, online and offline, a code of ethics that reflects the company's unique value system.
■ Corporate training: Periodic corporate training (e.g., manager's compliance and ethics meetings) will ensure that employees are aware of the company's ethical values and legal compliance program.

Because laws and regulations continually change, maintaining a sustainable ethical corporate culture must be an ongoing process.

Collectively these corporate governance initiatives contribute to a sustainable ethical corporate culture that ought to be the goal of corporate America. Remember that legal compliance and avoiding criminal and civil liability are only the beginnings of an ethical corporate culture. As you will see throughout this textbook, it is often necessary to go beyond the baseline of legal requirements to ensure the company is engaging in ethical activities. Keep in mind that ethical analysis will not always provide a "correct answer" but will promote a vigorous discussion on various ethical "points of view" that will be useful in "doing the right thing" that may avoid expensive and time-consuming lawsuits resulting in a public relations disaster, possible criminal liability, and ultimately a loss in customers' and investors' trust.

Questions for Review

1. Ethics and negligence

In 2005, plaintiff, a motorcycle driver, was injured when his motorcycle collided with a vehicle driven by Mathias, a pizza delivery driver. At the time of the accident, Mathias was employed by and was delivering pizzas for Zzeeks Pizza & Wings, Inc. (Zzeeks), doing business as one of approximately 4,500 franchises of Domino's Pizza, LLC (Domino's). Plaintiff filed this negligence action against Mathias, Zzeeks, and Domino's Pizza. Were the defendants, Zzeeks Pizza and Domino's

---

[29]17 C.F.R. sec. 229.406(b).

Pizza, ethically responsible for the plaintiff's injury? Give your ethical reasons using ethical principles. *Viado v. Domino's 217 P. 3d 199 (2009).*

2. Ethics and whistle blowing

The plaintiff worked in a maintenance department for the defendant, a railway company, as a forklift operator. As the only female worker in that department, her supervisor repeatedly told her a woman should not be working in the maintenance department. She was reassigned to a "track laborer" position. In her new job, her supervisor complained that she had been insubordinate and she was suspended without pay during her suspension. She sued, alleging her suspension without pay amounted to retaliation. What are the ethical issues in this case? How would you decide the case from an ethical perspective? *Burlington Northern and Santa Fe Railway Co. v. White, Supreme Court of the United States,* 548 U.S. 53 (2006).

3. Ethics and board of directors' responsibility

The defendant is a highly respected corporation with no record of civil or criminal acts by its employees. Hanna, the CEO, suggested to the board of directors that the company should have an ethics and compliance program including a published code of ethics and a new position for a compliance and ethics officer who will conduct periodic training sessions in legal compliance and corporate ethical values. Hanna is concerned with a flow of information concerning legal compliance and ethical issues directly to the board of directors. Edward, the chairman of the board of directors, is opposed to Hanna's suggestion. He and the majority of the board members are basing their objection on the company's perfect record of legal compliance and want to leave "well-enough alone." What is your advice to the CEO and the board of directors?

See *In re Caremark International Inc. Derivative Litigation* 698 A.2d. 959, (1996) for an explanation of directors' potential liability.

4. Ethics and product liability

Conway, Inc., has developed and is selling artificial hips. Its chief engineer has discovered that upon extensive use it may leach metal from the artificial hip into the patient's bloodstream. This is not conclusive evidence and the FDA has approved its use. She asks you if there is a legal or moral obligation to report and publish her findings. Answer only the ethical question utilizing the ethical theories discussed above.

5. Ethics and insider trading

Harold, a board member of a Fortune 500 corporation, has just discovered at a board meeting that the company will acquire a competitor. Harold is assured the company stock will increase once this becomes public knowledge. Peter, another board member, has told Harold this is the time to buy stock in the company. He has assured Harold this goes on all the time. Harold asks your ethical advice.

6. Rawls's "Theory of Justice" and an ethical corporate culture

Rawls was not writing his "Theory of Justice" and "Justice as Fairness" for executives working in corporations but rather for governmental institutions forming public policy. Explain how the equal liberty principle and the difference principle are useful in developing an ethical corporate culture.

7. Corporate ethics and the U.S. Sentencing Commission and SOX

What is the role of the U.S. Sentencing Commission in encouraging corporate ethical conduct? What is the role of the Sarbanes-Oxley Act (SOX) in developing an ethical corporate culture for publicly owned corporations?

8. Global ethics

Jennifer is a salesperson for a major chemical company doing business in China. In order to close a multimillion dollar contract, she has been asked by a Chinese government official for a payment of $50,000. Jennifer has been told by her company to pay the requested fee and close the deal. Jennifer will make a bonus over $100,000 if the deal is closed but is nervous about the payment. She asks your ethical advice.

Further Reading

Ferrera, Gerald R., and Mystica M. Alexander, *Appellate Judges and Philosophical Theories: Judicial Philosophy or Mere Coincidence?* 14(4) Richmond Journal of Law and the Public Interest (Spring 2011).

Hoffman, W. Michael, Frederick, Robert E., Swartz, Mark S., Eds, *Business Ethics: Readings and Cases in Corporate Morality* (Wiley Blackwell 2014).

Morris, Clarence, Ed., *The Great Legal Philosophers, Selected Readings in Jurisprudence*, Trustees of the University of Pennsylvania (1959).

Salbu, Steven R., *Law and Ethics* 38(2), American Business Law Journal 209–214 (Jan. 2001).

Sandel, Michael J., *Justice, What's the Right Thing to Do?* (Farrar, Straus and Giroux 2009).

Zalta, Edward N., Ed., *Stanford Encyclopedia of Philosophy*, http://plato.stanford.edu/.

CHAPTER 3

Constitutional Issues in Business

Chapter Objectives

1. To understand the purpose and functionality of the system of checks and balances of the U.S. Constitution
2. To know how the commerce clause applies to the legal environment of business
3. To know how commercial speech applies to business advertising
4. To know what constitutional safeguards exist for business executives accused of committing a business crime
5. To understand how equal protection of the law applies to businesses

Practical Example: Inappropriate, Inc.*

Inappropriate, Inc., an interstate business, is financially prospering from its sales of leisure clothing and backpacks with crude and vulgar language printed on the fabric. Inappropriate is based in Massachusetts and has three retail locations and a warehouse in that state. The majority of its sales are made online through its website to customers in all 50 states and around the world. College students are its primary consumers. Massachusetts imposes no restrictions on the manufacture and sale of these products. But the speech printed on the items is offensive to many people, and some states have passed laws prohibiting the sale of these products in the state by both retail stores and through Inappropriate's online websites. Inappropriate, Inc., has no physical presence in any state except in Massachusetts. Many other states want to impose a state sales tax for products purchased online and want Inappropriate, Inc., to collect the tax from its online customers and remit it to the states.

Some of the employees of Inappropriate, Inc., were storing controlled drug substances, including powdered opium, in its warehouse and selling the illegal drugs from the Massachusetts stores. Two of the employees engaged in this practice were vice presidents and majority stockholders of Inappropriate, Inc. The police were suspicious that customers were buying illegal drugs in the stores and broke into the warehouse and the stores without a warrant. The vice president and owners were arrested along with a 16-year-old customer, a minor under state law. In the police car on the way to the police station, the offenders were given Miranda warnings after they spoke to the police in the stores and admitted buying and selling the drugs, and the minor admitted purchasing them in the Massachusetts store. The arrested minor was indigent but refused the court-appointed lawyer because she did not like the attitude of the lawyer. The judge refused to appoint another lawyer.

Inappropriate is facing a variety of legal challenges. Can a state ban the sale of their products just because some people find them offensive? Can states with which the company has very minimal contact require Inappropriate to collect sales tax on behalf of the state? Were police within their rights to break into the company warehouse and search the premises without a warrant? The answers to such questions are grounded in constitutional law.

---

*Inappropriate, Inc., is a fictitious company developed by the authors to demonstrate and illustrate key legal and ethical concepts, theories, practices, and strategies.

The Making of the U.S. Constitution

What does it mean to *constitute* something? To *constitute* means to form, compose, or set up something, usually joining together elements. A country's Constitution does just that—it sets up the legal foundation upon which the government and indeed the entire country rest. It describes the structure and powers of the government and its components. It establishes and protects freedoms for its citizens, such as the freedom of speech, freedom of the press, freedom of religion, and so forth. Most people's impression of the U.S. Constitution[1] is based on the structure of the government and the individual personal liberties and rights granted in this extraordinary document. Yet

---

[1]Many countries have constitutions—Brazil (1988), Russian Federation (1993), India (1950), P.R. China (1982), Mexico (1917), Indonesia (1945), and Turkey (1982), to name a few. However, for purposes of this chapter, *Constitution* refers to the U.S. Constitution.

"A republic, if you can keep it." Benjamin Franklin's response to "what have we got, a republic or a monarchy?" after signing the Constitution.

many provisions in the Constitution relate to business and economics. Explicitly or implicitly, the Constitution contains provisions relating to employment law, advertising, business litigation, intellectual property, taxation, the extent of the government's power to regulate business, and many other aspects of business.

The authors of the U.S. Constitution (often called *framers*) began this famous document with a description of their objectives: "We the people of the United States, in order to form a more perfect union, establish justice, insure domestic tranquility, provide for the common defense, promote the general welfare, and secure the blessings of liberty to ourselves and our posterity, do ordain and establish this Constitution for the United States of America."

The political context in which the framers lived and the historical realities they inherited meant they worked within certain constraints and were faced with particular challenges. In reaction to these challenges, they set other goals. They strived to unify an assortment of states that were distinct, separately governed, and different in fundamental ways: in size, population, economic bases, terrain, climate, and even currencies. They hoped, on the one hand, to unify these states and, on the other, to allow for sufficient local governance. They guarded against the power of the larger states swallowing the interests of the smaller states. They sought to prevent the overbearing authoritarianism to which they had been subjected under British rule. They determined to establish a viable country that could grow with economic stability and prosperity.

In a remarkably short document, the framers strove to accomplish these goals by delineating the powers and power limitations of the government and describing and protecting the liberties of its citizens. Despite its brevity, this document has remained in effect, with few changes, since 1787. But although the Constitution itself has changed little, the world today would be unrecognizable to the framers. Advancements in technology, architecture, transportation, engineering, and agriculture have modernized every aspect of our lives. Historical experiences, wars, conflict, social movements, industrial revolution, immigration, commercial development, and so on, have also transformed how we live. The Constitution was written with flexibility, foresight, and a deep understanding of the enduring issues relating to power and to freedom. But much of the Constitution's ability to flex with the times is thanks to numerous court decisions, especially by the U.S. Supreme Court, over the past two centuries which have helped adapt the Constitution to contemporary disputes and situations.

The Supreme Court's adaptation and interpretation of the Constitution over the decades has met with controversy. Strict constructionists construe the text of the Constitution exactly as it is written, without expansion or even small variation. Others argue for a more flexible interpretation to accommodate the needs and realities of modern society. Competing views on how to best interpret the language of the Constitution have led, over the years, to spirited academic debate, public discourse, and even violence.[2]

The first three articles of the Constitution design a functioning system of government. Recall from Chapter 1, "The U.S. Legal System," the framers approached formation of the government by separating powers into three branches. Each branch has a distinct function. The legislative branch makes law, the executive branch enforces law, and the judicial branch interprets law. Each branch operates as a check on the other two. The combination of dispersing government power across three branches and a system of checks on power and balances against other branches addressed the framers' concerns about concentration of too much power in the hands of too few people.

Article I establishes the legislative branch. It creates a Congressional body comprised of two houses—the Senate and the House of Representatives—and specifies the procedure for enacting legislation. Article II establishes the executive branch and details the qualifications for candidacy for the presidency of the United States and the rules for presidential elections. Article III establishes the judicial branch, including the U.S. Supreme Court and other federal courts. Exhibit 3.1 on page 71 depicts the balance of power established by the Constitution.

---

[2]One notable instance of violence resulting from interpretation of the Constitution is the protests in Little Rock, Arkansas, after the *Brown v. Board of Education of Topeka, Shawnee County, Kansas* 347 U.S. 483, 74 S. Ct. 686 (1954) required that public schools desegregate.

Exhibit 3.1. Checks and Balances

	Legislative (Article I)	Executive (Article II)	Judicial (Article III)
Legislative check	—	Treaties and U.S. Supreme Court appointments must be ratified or approved. Also, Congress can impeach a president.	Can enact statutes that override court decisions (as long as such statutes are not unconstitutional)
Executive check	Has veto power over Congressional bills; however, Congress can override the veto with a 2/3 majority vote.	—	Can appoint federal judges
Judicial check	Can strike down laws it decides are unconstitutional through a process known as judicial review (although not specified in the Constitution)	Can declare unconstitutional acts of the executive branch	—

Federal Powers, State Powers, the Supremacy Clause, and Preemption

Perhaps the greatest challenge the framers faced was balancing central authority by the federal government with dispersed local power by the state governments. The framers realized conflict and disagreement between states and the federal government were inevitable. The Supremacy Clause (Article VII, section 2) establishes a rule for resolving such conflicts: "This Constitution, and the Laws of the United States which shall be made in Pursuance thereof; and all Treaties made, or which shall be made, under the Authority of the United States, shall be the supreme Law of the Land; and the Judges in every State shall be bound thereby, any Thing in the Constitution or Laws of any State to the Contrary notwithstanding." Under the **Supremacy Clause**, if a state or local law conflicts with a federal statute, regulation, or treaty, the federal law takes precedence. This is the case as long as the federal law is pursuant to the powers granted to the federal government in the

Constitution. For example, the federal government and the states regulate the securities markets. If there is conflict between the two, federal law takes priority.

In some cases, federal law *preempts* (that is, replaces) state law. Sometimes Congress passes a statute that expressly states that it preempts state law. Other times, courts examine Congressional intent and decide that a particular federal statute or regulation preempts states legislation. For example, if Congress has legislated heavily on a particular topic, courts will infer that Congress intended to preempt state regulation on that topic. In other cases, courts have invoked the preemption doctrine if national security warrants it. In other situations, federal statutes authorize states to legislate if they choose, subject to whatever guidelines Congress provides.

The Commerce Clause

Understanding the commerce clause is useful in appreciating the legitimate power of a state to enact legislation that may affect interstate commerce and when that state legislation may be unconstitutional if it "substantially affects trade and commerce among the states."

Congress has limited powers under the Federal Constitution of the United States. Among the enumerated powers granted to Congress is the **commerce clause** that states in part "*To regulate Commerce . . . among the several States. . . .* " This power allows Congress to regulate, among other things, commerce among the 50 states and prohibits the states from enacting laws that would interfere with **interstate commerce**.

Federal Regulation of Business and an "Interdependent National Economy"

The U.S. Supreme Court characterized the commerce clause as the basis of our new era of federal regulations of business (see Chapter 4, "Administrative Law") when it stated,

> *The Commerce Clause emerged as the Framers' response to the central problem giving rise to the Constitution itself: the absence of any federal commerce power under the Articles of Confederation. For the first century of our history, the primary use of the Clause was to preclude the kind of discriminatory state legislation that had once been permissible. Then, in response to rapid industrial development and an increasingly interdependent national economy, Congress "ushered in a new era of federal regulation under the commerce power," beginning with the enactment of the Interstate Commerce Act in 1887 and the Sherman Antitrust Act in 1890.* (Gonzales v. Raich, 545 U.S. 1 2005).

Congress continues to regulate business (through legislation such as the Dodd-Frank Act and the Sarbanes-Oxley Act. See Chapter 9, "Sale of Securities and Investor Protection"). Internet technology and online business activity have contributed to an exponentially growing "*interdependent national economy*" fueled by the ability to order online practically any product that is delivered to your doorstep within days from any state in the country.

State Activities That "Might Have a Substantial and Harmful Effect upon Interstate Commerce"

When we consider the configuration of the U.S. economic landscape in the twenty-first century, it becomes increasingly evident that Congress will continue to regulate interstate commerce when it deems a state law to have a "*substantial and harmful effect upon . . . commerce.*" In *Heart of Atlanta Motel v. United States*, 379 U.S. 21 (1964), the owners of a small locally owned Atlanta motel refused to rent rooms to African Americans in violation of the federal Civil Rights Act of 1964. The motel owners alleged the Act was unconstitutional and did not apply to their privately owned local motel. Evidence disclosed the small, local motel rented to 75 percent of guests from states outside of Georgia, the owners advertised on national billboards, and the motel was accessible to motorists from interstate highways. The court ruled "*the power of Congress to promote interstate commerce also includes the power to regulate local incidents thereof, including local activities in both the States of origin and destination, which might have a substantial and harmful effect upon that commerce.*"

Dormant Commerce Clause

In instances where Congress has not regulated interstate commerce, it still maintains the power to do so under the dormant commerce clause. In *Wilson v. Blackbird Creek Marsh Co.*, 27 U.S. 245 (1829) Chief Justice Marshall described this legal principle as Congress having the "*power to regulate commerce in its dormant state.*" For example, although there is no federal statute expressly prohibiting a state censoring free speech on clothing sold in interstate commerce, the Supreme Court in *New Energy Co. of Indiana v. Limbach*, 486 U.S. 237-74 (1988) stated the **dormant commerce clause** "*prohibits economic protectionism — that is, regulatory measures designed to benefit in-state economic interests by burdening out-of-state competitors.*"[3]

State Sales Tax

State sales tax is a tax on the consumer collected by the merchant and submitted to the state on a periodic basis. Before a state may impose a sales tax collection obligation on the merchant, the merchant must have a physical presence in that state. Online sellers who have no physical presence in a state (e.g., Amazon) need not collect a sales tax from the buyer. Retailers

---

[3]See *Santa Fe Natural Tobacco, Inc. v. Spitzer* (S.D. N.Y. 2000).

Quill Corporation v. North Dakota, 503 U.S. 298 (1992)

Facts: "Quill is a Delaware corporation with offices and warehouses in Illinois, California, and Georgia. None of its employees work or reside in North Dakota, and its ownership of tangible property in that State is either insignificant or nonexistent. Quill sells office equipment and supplies; it solicits business through catalogs and flyers, advertisements in national periodicals, and telephone calls. Its annual national sales exceed $200 million, of which almost $1 million are made to about 3,000 customers in North Dakota. It is the sixth largest vendor of office supplies in the State. It delivers all of its merchandise to its North Dakota customers by mail or common carrier from out-of-state locations. As a corollary to its sales tax, North Dakota imposes a use tax upon property purchased for storage, use, or consumption within the State."

Issue: Is a mail-order company doing business in a state with no physical presence subject to the state's sales tax or use tax?

Holding: No. The Due Process Clause "requires some definite link, some minimum connection, between a state and the person, property or transaction it seeks to tax." A mail-order transaction does not have a sufficient physical connection between the state and the transaction to subject it to collecting a sales tax from its customers.

From the Court's Opinion (Justice Stevens):
As in a number of other cases involving the application of state taxing statutes to out-of-state sellers, our holding in Bellas Hess relied on both the Due Process Clause and the Commerce Clause. Although the "two claims are closely related," Bellas Hess, 386 U.S., at 756, the Clauses pose distinct limits on the taxing powers of the States. Accordingly, while a State may, consistent with the Due Process Clause, have the authority to tax a particular taxpayer, imposition of the tax may nonetheless violate the Commerce Clause. See, e.g., Tyler Pipe Industries, Inc. v. Washington State Dept. of Revenue, 483 U.S. 232 (1987). The two constitutional requirements differ fundamentally, in several ways . . . the Due Process Clause and the Commerce Clause reflect different constitutional concerns. Moreover, while Congress has plenary power to regulate commerce among the States and thus may authorize state actions that burden interstate commerce, see International Shoe Co. v. Washington, 326 U.S. 310, 315 (1945), it does not similarly have the power to authorize violations of the Due Process Clause.

The Due Process Clause "requires some definite link, some minimum connection, between a state and the person, property or transaction it seeks to tax," Miller Brothers Co. v. Maryland, 347 U.S. 340, 344-345 (1954), and that the "income attributed to the State for tax purposes must be rationally related to 'values connected with the taxing State,'" Moorman Mfg. Co. v. Bair, 437 U.S. 267, 273 (1978) (citation omitted). Here, we are concerned primarily with the first of these requirements.

Prior to Bellas Hess, we had held that that requirement was satisfied in a variety of circumstances involving use taxes. For example, the presence of sales personnel in the State or the maintenance of local retail stores in the State justified the exercise of that power because the seller's local activities were "plainly accorded the protection and services of the taxing State." Bellas Hess, 386 U.S., at 757. The furthest extension of that power was recognized in Scripto, Inc. v. Carson, 362 U.S. 207 (1960), in which the Court upheld a use tax despite the fact that all of the seller's in-state solicitation was performed by independent contractors. These cases all involved some sort of physical presence within the State, and in Bellas Hess the Court suggested that such presence was not only sufficient for jurisdiction under the Due Process Clause, but also necessary.

We expressly declined to obliterate the "sharp distinction . . . between mail-order sellers with retail outlets, solicitors, or property within a State, and those who do no more than communicate with customers in the State by mail or common carrier as a part of a general interstate business." 386 U.S., at 758. Although Congress can and should address itself to this area of law, *we should not adhere to a decision, however right it was at the time that by reason of later cases and economic reality can no longer be rationally justified.**

---

*Notice in the Quill case, the court stated that "Congress . . . should address itself to this area of the law." That suggestion was finally materialized in 2013 with the Senate passage of the Marketplace Fairness Act. The Act would require online out-of-state retailers, with no physical presence in the state of sale, to collect a sales tax from customers. As of this writing, the House of Representatives has not yet voted on the bill.

Assuming this online retailer has no physical presence in the state of sale, is it fair to require it to collect a sales tax from this consumer?

with a store in the same state have to collect the sales tax for the same item purchased in its store, and they argue that this is an unfair burden on their business. In the Inappropriate case, there were no retail stores or other physical presence in the states attempting to impose a sales tax, and to this date that would violate the due process and commerce clause of the U.S. Constitution.

Although the case on page 75 involves mail-order sales and not online sales, the reasoning follows the prohibition of imposing a sales tax on an out-of-state retailer with no physical presence in the state.

The Constitutional Protection of Liberty

As discussed in Chapter 1, at the time the Constitution was adopted, there were some who pushed for the document to include a statement of individual rights. Such rights were not included in the Constitution itself, but instead were incorporated as amendments to the Constitution. The first ten of these amendments, known as the Bill of Rights, were adopted in 1791. Other amendments have followed. Exhibit 3.2 on page 76 highlights the protection of individual liberties guaranteed by these amendments.

A discussion of each of these amendments is beyond the scope of this text. Rather, attention will be given to those amendments that have a significant impact on business transactions.

First Amendment Protection of Speech

The First Amendment of the U.S. Constitution provides that *"Congress shall make no law respecting an establishment of religion, or prohibiting the free exercise thereof; or abridging the freedom of speech, or of the press; or the right of the people peaceably to assemble, and to petition the Government for a redress of grievances."* Because we focus on Constitutional issues as they affect business issues, we explore freedom of speech as it potentially affects commercial transactions. In the introductory example at the start of the chapter, Inappropriate is in the business of selling clothing and backpacks with crude and vulgar language. Let us assume that the language on the clothing and backpacks is offensive to some, and offensive to such an extent that some states have passed statutes banning crude and vulgar speech on clothing and backpacks. Is this permissible? Can manufacturers be prohibited from making

Exhibit 3.2. Constitutional Protections

Amendment	Protection Guaranteed
First Amendment	Freedom of speech, press, religion, and the right to assemble peaceably or petition government (1791)
Second Amendment	Right to bear arms (1791)
Third Amendment	No obligation to house soldiers during peacetime (1791)
Fourth Amendment	Freedom from unlawful search and seizure (1791)
Fifth Amendment	Right to grand jury; right against self-incrimination; prohibition against double jeopardy; no punishment without being found guilty at trial; no government taking of property without just compensation (1791)
Sixth Amendment	Right to a fair and speedy trial in criminal cases; right to know charges and hear witnesses; right to a court-appointed attorney if unable to afford legal services (1791)
Seventh Amendment	Right to a jury trial in civil suits involving more than $20 (1791)
Eighth Amendment	Restriction on cruel and unusual punishment and on excessive fines or excessive bail (1791)
Ninth Amendment	Ensures retention of other rights not enumerated in the Bill of Rights (1791)
Tenth Amendment	Powers not given to federal government are reserved to the states and to the people (1791)
Eleventh Amendment	Guidelines for lawsuits against states (1795)
Thirteenth Amendment	Abolition of slavery (1865)
Fourteenth Amendment	Grants citizenship to black Americans (1868)
Nineteenth Amendment	Suffrage for women (1920)

such products? Can retailers be prevented from selling such products? Can consumers be prohibited from wearing such clothing or carrying such backpacks? To understand the answers to these questions, we look to the protections provided by the First Amendment, keeping in mind that "freedom of speech" does not protect all speech but rather will permit certain limitations on this freedom as necessary for the public welfare.

Different Types of Speech

What qualifies as "speech?" As a starting point, keep in mind that the term *speech* includes both oral and written forms of communications as well as expressive conduct known as symbolic speech (for example, wearing an armband as a symbol of protest, wearing a t-shirt with a message, burning an American flag). While each of these types of speech has received constitutional protection against government limitations, the extent of that protection depends on the context and content of the speech. Over time, the courts have created different categories of speech with different levels of protection. For example, political speech (c.g., protest against government actions) is considered "pure" speech given the highest level of protection, while other types of speech, such as slanderous speech, are considered unprotected speech.

Regulating Speech

Any governmental regulation of speech, by a federal, state, or local government, will be tested for constitutional validity under one of three standards of review (or scrutiny) that have been articulated by the Supreme Court: strict scrutiny, intermediate scrutiny, or rational review. Exhibit 3.3 below summarizes the characteristics of each type of scrutiny.

Exhibit 3.3. Judicial Scrutiny

Scrutiny	Characteristics	Situations in Which Applied
Strict scrutiny	Restriction on speech must "promote a compelling interest" and must be the "least restrictive means to further the articulated interest."	Pure speech; government seeks to directly limit *content* of speech
Intermediate scrutiny	Restriction should be narrowly tailored to serve a substantial interest but does not have to be the least restrictive means available.	Non-content-based restrictions; restrictions on time, place, and manner of speech; restrictions on commercial speech
Rational basis	The court is highly deferential to government interest in restricting the speech.	Incidentally burden speech; burden communications that are not considered protected speech such as obscenity, fighting words, or speech advocating an illegal activity such as drug use

As noted in Exhibit 3.3, the First Amendment is most protective in those instances in which a government seeks to limit the content of speech, meaning the ability of the person to express his or her opinion or ideas, or convey information. The First Amendment protects a person's right to express himself or herself, even if the message is unpopular. The same standard is applied to symbolic speech as to oral or written speech. If the government seeks to repress the *message* of the expression, the actions will be subject to the highest level of scrutiny by the court.

First Amendment protection does not mean that reasonable restrictions as to the time, place, and manner of the speech cannot be imposed. For example, a company has a right to disseminate advertisements of its product or services and solicit customers, but laws limiting solicitation to certain times have been upheld. The U.S. Supreme Court has also upheld a municipal law that limited the size, placement, and number of "for sale" signs that could be posted on real estate within a municipality based on the fact that the law furthered the government's interest in maintaining the appearance of the residential neighborhood while at the same time not diminishing the ability of prospective buyers to be made aware that the real estate was for sale. Time, place, and manner restrictions that are content neutral are held to a lesser level of scrutiny by courts, because the government in such a situation is not seeking to suppress a *message* but rather, only the time, place, or manner in which the message can be expressed. To uphold such restrictions, the court must be convinced that the restrictions are narrowly tailored and that adequate alternative means of communication are available.

Some types of messages are not protected by the First Amendment. For example, in Chapter 19, "Business Torts," you will learn about the tort of commercial disparagement that includes publishing a falsehood that affects a company's products or services. The First Amendment does not protect an act of defamation. Likewise, words or actions that incite a crowd to violence or encourage illegal activity may be suppressed by the government as long as the government can show that it had some rational basis for doing so, such as preserving public safety.

Understanding the Limits of Commercial Speech

Commercial speech has a commercial transaction as its goal — the sale of a product or service. The Supreme Court has helped to clarify the limits on commercial speech by supplying a four-part test to determine whether regulation of commercial speech is constitutional. These steps included (1) whether the commercial speech is protected by the First Amendment (concerns a lawful activity and is not misleading); (2) whether the asserted governmental interest in restricting it is substantial; (3) whether the restriction directly advances the governmental interest asserted; and (4) whether the restriction is not more restrictive than needed to meet the government interest.[4] If a more narrowly tailored option is available for regulating speech which will satisfy the government's asserted interest, then the government regulation will be struck down by the court. The cases below and on page 80 illustrate the types of challenges that have been brought against state regulation of commercial activity.

Knowing that excessive smoking causes cancer, are the warnings adequate?

Obscene Speech

As noted earlier in the chapter, certain types of speech are considered unprotected speech and are subject to greater government regulation. Included in this category are defamation, fighting words, incites to rioting, and obscenity. According to the court in *Chaplinsky v. New Hampshire*,[5] the reason such speech is often considered unprotected is because "it contains no ideas or viewpoint and doesn't advance any socially worthwhile goals."[6] The U.S. Supreme Court has upheld state legislative bans on obscene speech if such bans protect "the social interest in order and morality."[7]

To determine whether something is obscene, the Supreme Court applies the Miller test that considers (1) whether the "average person applying contemporary community standards" would find that the work, taken as a whole, appeals to the prurient interest; (2) whether the work depicts or describes in a patently offensive way, sexual conduct, specifically defined by applicable state law; and (3) whether the work, taken as a whole, lacks serious literary, artistic, political, or scientific value. To be considered obscene, the work must meet all three of these tests. When applying these tests, keep in mind that in evaluating the first prong, a jury has to decide how an average member of that community would perceive the work. For example, a community in Spokane, Washington, might adopt a different standard than a community in Portland, Oregon. The third prong of the test, however, applies a much broader reasonable person standard,

Case Illustration

In *Greater New Orleans Broadcasting, Inc. v. United States*,* the U.S. Supreme Court declared illegal a federal statute that prohibited a broadcaster from advertising for casinos in broadcasts that might be heard in states in which gambling was illegal. The broadcasters in the case successfully argued that the restrictions on their advertisement of a lawful activity went beyond the means necessary to achieve the stated government interests of reducing the social costs of gambling and assisting the states that limit gambling or prohibit casino gambling. The court based its result on the fact that the statutory restrictions did not limit advertisements by tribal casinos and also did not limit advertisements of general "Vegas-style excitement," without mention of a particular casino name; therefore, the restrictions on the broadcaster's First Amendment rights went beyond those needed to serve a government purpose.

---

*527 U.S. 173 (1999).

---

[4]Cohen, Henry, *Freedom of Speech and Press: Exceptions to the First Amendment*, Congressional Research Service, October 16, 2009.
[5]315 U.S. 568 (1942).
[6]Hayward, John, *Selected Cases in the Student T-Shirt Wars*, 45 Business Law Review 31 (2012).
[7]*Roth v. United States*, 354 U.S. 476, 483 (1957).

Case Illustration

Lorillard Tobacco Co. v. Reilly,[†] involved a government restriction on advertising. In that case, the U.S. Supreme Court considered the constitutionality of a regulation imposed by the Massachusetts Attorney General that prohibited advertising for smokeless tobacco and cigars within 1,000 feet of schools or playgrounds if the advertisement was "placed lower than five feet from the floor of any retail establishment." The Court agreed with the tobacco manufacturers that this restriction was unconstitutional, finding that the Attorney General had not provided sufficient justification for the restriction because (1) not all school-age children are less than five feet tall, and (2) even if the child was shorter than five feet, the child could simply look up and see the advertisement.

[†]533 U.S. 525 (2001).

not tied to the sentiment of a particular community but instead to a more national, general standard.

Returning to our initial example involving the sale of Inappropriate's products, let us consider the actions of those states that have banned the sale of the products to state residents. To decide whether such an action is constitutional, we would first have to apply the Miller test to the products to determine if such products are obscene. If they meet all three prongs of the Miller test, the products are considered obscene. Then the Court will uphold the state's authority to regulate the use and sales as long as the state can make a basic showing that such a restriction serves the public interest and well-being. If the products do not rise to the level of obscenity but are vulgar and offensive to some, it is unlikely that state legislative bans against such products will withstand judicial scrutiny.

Limits on Distasteful Ideas?

Assuming the message on Inappropriate's shirts is vulgar and distasteful to some, but not obscene, no restrictions can be placed on the ability of the seller to sell or the consumer to buy and use such products. Although a consumer has a right to purchase and wear such items, this does not mean that no restrictions can be imposed on the ability to wear that t-shirt. Two cases help illustrate this point. In *Barr v. LaFon*,[8] a school board prohibited students from wearing clothing that depicted the confederate flag. That ban was upheld by the 6th Circuit Court of Appeals. In that case there was already racially motivated tension among the student body at the Knoxville, Tennessee, school, and the court found it likely that allowing students to wear such clothing would cause substantial disruption to both schoolwork and school discipline. A different decision was reached by the 7th Circuit Court of Appeals in *Zamecnik v. Indian Prairie School District*[9] that involved t-shirts that some students wanted to wear to school on the school's observance of the national Day of Silence during which some students remain silent to call attention to the harassment faced by those who are lesbian, gay, bisexual, and transgender. Some students wanted to wear a t-shirt that read "My Day of Silence, Straight Alliance" on the front and on the back read "Be Happy, Not Gay." The

[8]538 F.3d 554 (6th Cir 2008).
[9]636 F. 3d 874 (7th Cir. 2011).

administrators of the school opposed the phrase "not gay" and sought to ban the t-shirts based on the school's policy of prohibition of derogatory comments that refer to race, ethnicity, religion, gender, sexual orientation, or disability. The Court of Appeals did not find compelling evidence that the t-shirt rose to the level of being derogatory, nor was it convinced that allowing students to wear the shirt would be a disruption to the educational process or incite others to violence. The court held that "people in our society do not have a legal right to prevent criticism of their beliefs or even their way of life."[10] Taken together the *Barr* and *Zamecnik* cases give you some sense of the type of intermediate level of scrutiny the courts impose in evaluating time, place, and manner restrictions on protected speech.

Constitutional Safeguards for the Criminally Accused

This section of the chapter covers important constitutional safeguards for those individuals and entities charged by government officials with criminal offenses. Specifically, the Fourth, Fifth, and Sixth Amendments are reviewed and illustrated. Examples focus on criminal cases brought against individuals as well as business entities. As discussed in Chapter 10, "Business Crimes," the constitutional protections provided by the Bill of Rights help define the limits imposed on law enforcement officials and prosecutors in their pursuit of criminal defendants. At this time, you may want to review Exhibit 10.3, which depicts the various steps involved in the criminal investigative and prosecutorial processes.

The Fourth Amendment

The Fourth Amendment to the U.S. Constitution provides the following:

> The right of the people to be secure in their persons, houses, papers, and effects, against unreasonable searches and seizures, shall not be violated, and no Warrants shall issue, but upon probable cause, supported by Oath or affirmation, and particularly describing the place to be searched, and the persons or things to be seized.

The Fourth Amendment defines and limits the actions of government officials when conducting criminal investigations and prosecuting defendants. If the government exceeds these limits, evidence obtained during an investigation may be excluded from presentation by the prosecution at trial. Although the

---

[10]Hayward, *supra*, n.6.

word "privacy" does not appear in the Fourth Amendment, the concept of privacy permeates the Fourth Amendment.

A Fourth Amendment violation by government officials prevents the prosecution from being able to use the seized evidence at trial. The exclusion of evidence is referred to as the exclusionary rule. The **exclusionary rule** was established by the U.S. Supreme Court nearly 100 years ago in the case of *Weeks v. United States*, in which the Court stated the following:

> The effect of the Fourth Amendment is to put the courts of the United States and Federal officials, in the exercise of their power and authority, under limitations and restraints as to the exercise of such power and authority, and to forever secure the people, their persons, houses, papers and effects against all unreasonable searches and seizures under the guise of law. This protection reaches all alike, whether accused of crime or not, and the duty of giving to it force and effect is obligatory upon all entrusted under our Federal system with the enforcement of the laws. The tendency of those who execute the criminal laws of the country to obtain conviction by means of unlawful seizures and enforced confessions, the latter often obtained after subjecting accused persons to unwarranted practices destructive of rights secured by the Federal Constitution, should find no sanction in the judgments of the courts which are charged at all times with the support of the Constitution and to which people of all conditions have a right to appeal for the maintenance of such fundamental rights.[11]

The exclusionary rule provides constitutional safeguards for the defendant, and it also serves other societal purposes as expressed by U.S. Supreme Court Justice Brandeis in his dissenting opinion in the case of *Olmstead v. United States*:

> In a government of laws, the existence of the government will be imperiled if it fails to observe the law scrupulously. Our Government is the potent, the omnipresent teacher. For good or for ill, it teaches the whole people by its example. Crime is contagious. If the Government becomes a lawbreaker, it breeds contempt for law; it invites every man to become a law unto himself; it invites anarchy. To declare that in the administration of the criminal law the end justifies the means — to declare that the Government may commit crimes in order to secure the conviction of a private criminal — would bring terrible retribution. Against that pernicious doctrine this Court should resolutely set its face.[12]

As a corollary to the exclusionary rule, the fruit of the poisonous tree doctrine provides that evidence obtained in violation of the Fourth Amendment, including ancillary evidence that may have been tainted or "poisoned" by an unconstitutional search, must be excluded at trial. For example, if law enforcement officials conduct an unconstitutional search and as part of the search obtain a

---

[11]*Weeks v. United States*, 232 U.S. 383 (1914).
[12]*Olmstead v. United States*, 277 U.S. 438 (1928) (dissenting opinion).

constitutionally valid confession from the defendant, both the unconstitutionally obtained evidence and the otherwise valid confession must be excluded at trial. The theory underlying the *fruit of the poisonous tree* doctrine is simple; it precludes law enforcement officials from benefitted from their own illegal activities.

Initially, the Fourth Amendment, like other Amendments included in the Bill of Rights, applied only to federal cases and federal courts. However, over 60 years ago in the case of *Wolf v. Colorado*, the U.S. Supreme Court held that the constitutional safeguards provided by the Fourth Amendment apply equally to state cases and state courts through the due process clause of the Fourteenth Amendment.[13] The Fourteenth Amendment provides that the citizens of each of the states shall have the right to due process and equal protection of the laws of the United States.

It is clear that the Fourth Amendment applies to individuals, but does it apply also to business entities? Federal and state governmental officials are sometimes allowed to conduct what are called "administrative inspections" as part of the government's role in regulating commercial activities. As an example, consider the federal legislation regarding the U.S. Food and Drug Administration (FDA) in Exhibit 3.4 on page 84.

Legislation like that presented in Exhibit 3.4 serves to protect consumers, and it also provides governmental officials with expanded authority to enter a business premises without the need to secure a warrant or have probable cause that a crime has been (or is about to be) committed. So, does the Fourth Amendment apply to business entities?

Consider the following case: In *See v. City of Seattle*,[14] a business owner was convicted in state court for refusing to allow a fire inspector to conduct a warrantless search of the business's locked commercial warehouse. The owner's refusal violated provisions of the state's fire code. In response, the business owner argued that the warrantless search of his warehouse would have violated his Fourth Amendment rights. The U.S. Supreme Court reversed the conviction, holding that the state's prosecution of the defendant based on his refusal to allow a warrantless search of his locked commercial warehouse violated his Fourth Amendment rights. The Court ruled that this type of administrative search of a commercial warehouse not otherwise open to the public required the fire inspector to obtain a search warrant. In its holding, the Court found little distinction between the government conducting a search of a residence or a business. Therefore, the Court ruled that a warrant must generally be obtained before conducting a search of a business premises if the owner does not consent to the search.

The issue litigated in *See v. City of Seattle* raises the question of the need to obtain a search warrant before conducting an inspection of a business establishment in a *noncriminal* case. The holding in the *See* case has undergone

---

[13]*Wolf v. Colorado*, 338 U.S. 25 (1949).
[14]*See v. City of Seattle*, 387 U.S. 541 (1967).

Exhibit 3.4. New Inspection and Compliance Mandates Under the FDA
Food Safety Modernization Act*

About 48 million people (1 in 6 Americans) get sick, 128,000 are hospitalized, and 3,000 die each year
from foodborne diseases, according to recent data from the Centers for Disease Control and Prevention.
This is a significant public health burden that is largely preventable.

The FDA Food Safety Modernization Act (FSMA), signed into law by President Obama on Jan. 4,
2013, enables the FDA to better protect public health by strengthening the food safety system. It
recognizes that preventive control standards improve food safety only to the extent that producers
and processors comply with them. Therefore, it will be necessary for the FDA to provide oversight,
ensure compliance with requirements, and respond effectively when problems emerge.

* * *

FSMA provides the FDA with important new tools for inspection and compliance:

- Mandated inspection frequency: The FSMA establishes a mandated inspection frequency, based on
  risk, for food facilities and requires the frequency of inspection to increase immediately. All high-risk
  domestic facilities must be inspected within five years of enactment and no less than every three
  years thereafter. Within one year of enactment, the law directs the FDA to inspect at least 600
  foreign facilities and double those inspections every year for the next five years.
- Records access: the FDA will have access to records, including industry food safety plans, and the
  records firms will be required to keep documenting implementation of their plans.
- Testing by accredited laboratories: The FSMA requires certain food testing to be carried out by
  accredited laboratories and directs the FDA to establish a program for laboratory accreditation to
  ensure that U.S. food testing laboratories meet high-quality standards.

*Food and Drug Administration, Inspection and Compliance, http://www.fda.gov/Food/GuidanceRegulation/FSMA/
ucm257978.htm (May 29, 2013).

---

review, analysis, and modification by the U.S. Supreme Court in the years
following the case, but the basic tension between valid commercial inspections
of a business premises versus unconstitutional searches remains vibrant in
today's legal environment of business. When does the government need to
obtain a search warrant before entering a business premises in a noncriminal
case? No bright line rule exists, but the current trend is to expand the powers of
the federal and state governments to conduct warrantless inspections of
commercial enterprises, particularly when issues of public health and safety
are involved.

As an application of the rules involving the search of a business, consider
the case of Inappropriate, Inc., which was introduced at the beginning of the
chapter. The facts of the case reveal that some of Inappropriate's employees
were storing controlled drug substances in the company's warehouse and selling the drugs from its stores. The police became suspicious that customers
were buying illegal drugs in the stores and broke into the warehouse and
the stores without a search warrant. Based on the warrantless search, the
police found illegal drugs and arrested several employees and a customer.
The offenders admitted buying and selling the drugs before they were read
their Miranda warnings (discussed next under the Fifth Amendment). The
Miranda warnings were read to the offenders only after they were in the police
car and on their way to the police station.

Consider the following questions about Inappropriate, Inc., and the offenders as you reflect on the discussion of the Fourth Amendment:

- Will the Exclusionary Rule prevent the government from using the drugs seized during the warrantless search as evidence in its case against the offenders?
- Will the fruit of the poisonous tree doctrine preclude the use of the confessions obtained by the police from the offenders?
- Will the government be able to argue that it made an allowable warrantless "administrative inspection" of the company's warehouse and stores?

Finally, it is important to remember that the Fourth Amendment protects persons against unreasonable searches and seizures. In deciding what are "unreasonable" searches and seizures, the U.S. Supreme Court has identified a number of situations where persons do not have a constitutionally protected right to privacy. For example, the Court held that a person does not have a right to privacy in "open fields or wooded areas" that are part of a person's property, even though the person has a right to privacy in his or her home.[15] Also, a person does not have a right to privacy in matters involving "personal characteristics" such as handwriting samples or fingerprint samples.[16] Accordingly, law enforcement officials may request that a person provide a handwriting sample or fingerprint sample without the need for a search warrant.

The Fifth Amendment

The constitutional safeguards provided by the Fifth Amendment focus on law enforcement procedures that occur during an arrest and subsequent court trial. An easy way to compare the Fourth Amendment to the Fifth Amendment is to think of the Fourth Amendment as dealing with law enforcement activities leading up to an arrest. For example, the Fourth Amendment focuses on "searches and seizes" that provide law enforcement officials with the evidence they need to make an arrest and prepare for trial. The Fifth Amendment provides persons with constitutional protections during and after an arrest.

The Fifth Amendment to the U.S. Constitution provides the following:

> No person shall be held to answer for a capital, or otherwise infamous crime, unless on a presentment or indictment of a Grand Jury, except in cases arising in the land or naval forces, or in the Militia, when in actual service in time of War or public danger; nor shall any person be subject for the same offence to be twice put in jeopardy of life or limb; nor shall be compelled in any criminal case to be a witness against himself, nor be deprived of life, liberty, or property, without due

---

[15]*Hester v. United States*, 265 U.S. 57 (1924).
[16]*United States v. Dionisio*, 410 U.S. 1 (1973).

process of law; nor shall private property be taken for public use, without just compensation.

The Fifth Amendment provides five distinct constitutional protections against potential law enforcement and prosecutorial abuses:

- Before a person can be charged with a capital crime, the government must secure a presentment or indictment from a grand jury. (This provision prevents the government from making capricious or arbitrary charges against individuals.)
- If a defendant is found not guilty in a criminal case, the government is precluded from charging the defendant with the same crime again (prohibition against double jeopardy).
- The government may not force a defendant to testify (be a witness against himself) in a legal proceeding initiated by the government (prohibition against self-incrimination).
- The government may not deprive a person of life, liberty, or property without due process of law (requirement of a fair trial).
- The government may not seize a person's private property without offering a fair price in exchange (prohibition against the government appropriating private property without providing fair consideration).

As with the Fourth Amendment, the U.S. Supreme Court ruled that the Fifth Amendment applies to the various states through application of the Fourteenth Amendment's "due process and equal protection" guarantees.

While the **double jeopardy** clause precludes the government from prosecuting a defendant for the same offense after the defendant has been acquitted or convicted, it does not shield a defendant from being involved in a civil (private) lawsuit based on the same set of facts as those presented at the criminal trial. Consider, for example, the criminal and civil trials of O.J. Simpson. In the criminal trial, O.J. Simpson was not required to testify against himself under the Fifth Amendment's prohibition against self-incrimination. After a trial of nearly ten months, the jury acquitted Simpson of the murders of his former spouse and an acquaintance. However, the families of the murder victims filed a civil lawsuit against Simpson for the wrongful deaths of the victims. Because the Fifth Amendment applies only to government actions, Simpson was required to testify during the civil trial. The jury found Simpson responsible for the deaths of Nicole Brown Simpson and Ronald Goldman and awarded the families $33.5 million in damages.

The **privilege against self-incrimination** applies to individuals, but a question often arises about whether the privilege extends to business entities. Unless a business takes the form of a sole proprietorship, the privilege does not extend to business entities such as corporations, limited liability companies, or limited liability partnerships. In the case of a sole proprietorship, the U.S. Supreme Court has held that the privilege against self-incrimination does not apply to business records that the government knows exist. Because business records are produced voluntarily during the ordinary course of business, they exist without any coercion from the government to produce them. Thus, when the government requests business records known to exist, the Fifth Amendment may not be used to shield them. If the government does not know of the existence of particular business records, the government may not compel the production of unknown documents.[17]

The U.S. Supreme Court added a major component to the right against self-incrimination in the case of *Miranda v. Arizona*.[18] In *Miranda*, the Court mandated that all custodial defendants must be informed of their basic constitutional rights under the Fifth and Sixth Amendments. These rights are commonly referred to as "**Miranda warnings**," which require government officials to inform individuals of the following rights once they have been told they are the target of a criminal investigation, or have been charged with a crime, or are in police custody:

- You have the right to remain silent.
- Anything you say can and will be used against you in a court of law.
- You have the right to an attorney.
- If you cannot afford an attorney, one will be appointed for you.

Chapter 10, which covers business crimes, provides an in-depth examination of the right against self-incrimination.

Returning to the case of Inappropriate, Inc., we know that the offenders confessed to the police their involvement in the buying and selling of drugs before they were read their Miranda warnings. Based on the above discussion, do you believe the government will be able to use the confessions as evidence against the offenders, or will the Fifth Amendment's prohibition against self-incrimination combined with the Supreme Court's requirement of Miranda warnings bar the use of the confessions as evidence at trial?

The Sixth Amendment

The Sixth Amendment to the U.S. Constitution provides that

> In all criminal prosecutions, the accused shall enjoy the right to a speedy and public trial, by an impartial jury of the State and district wherein the crime shall have been committed, which district shall have been previously ascertained by law, and to be informed of the nature and cause of the accusation; to be confronted with the witnesses against him; to have compulsory process for obtaining witnesses in his favor, and to have the Assistance of Counsel for his defense.

---

[17]*U.S. v. Doe*, 465 U.S. 605 (1984); *U.S. v. Hubbell*, 530 U.S. 27 (2000).
[18]*Miranda v. Arizona*, 384 U.S. 436 (1966).

The Sixth Amendment provides seven distinct constitutional safeguards for criminal defendants:

- The right to a speedy trial
- The right to a public trial
- The right to an impartial jury
- The right to be informed of pending charges
- The right to confront and to cross-examine adverse witnesses
- The right to compel favorable witnesses to testify
- The right to legal counsel

In reviewing these constitutional protections, the U.S. Supreme Court in the case of *United States v. Gaudin* offered the following observations about the Sixth Amendment:

> The [Sixth Amendment] guarantees that in all criminal prosecutions, the accused shall enjoy the right to a speedy and public trial, by an impartial jury. We have held that these provisions require criminal convictions to rest upon a jury determination that the defendant is guilty of every element of the crime with which he is charged, beyond a reasonable doubt. The right to have a jury make the ultimate determination of guilt has an impressive pedigree. Blackstone [a great judge and scholar] described "trial by jury" as requiring that "the truth of every accusation, whether preferred in the shape of indictment, information, or appeal, should afterwards be confirmed by the unanimous suffrage of twelve of [the defendant's] equals and neighbors. Justice Story wrote that the "trial by jury" guaranteed by the Constitution was "generally understood to mean . . . a trial by a jury of twelve men, impartially selected, who must unanimously concur in the guilt of the accused before a legal conviction can be had." This right was designed to guard against a spirit of oppression and tyranny on the part of rulers, and was from very early times insisted on by our ancestors in the parent country [Great Briton], as the great bulwark of their civil and political liberties.[19]

As noted by the U.S. Supreme Court in the above case, "the accused shall enjoy the right to a speedy and public trial, by an impartial jury." How does the requirement of a "speedy trial" protect criminal defendants? By requiring the government to conduct a speedy trial, defendants are not forced to endure months or years in prison without having the opportunity to present their defense to an impartial jury of their peers. Another reason for requiring a speedy trial is to ensure that witnesses for the defense are available to testify. If a trial takes too long, defense witnesses could move, die, or not otherwise be available to testify. Their testimony could also become stale, for their memories of events may fade with the passage of time. Additionally, supporting documentary evidence may be lost or destroyed with the passage of time.

The right to a "public trial" includes two components. The first component relates to the defendant. The Sixth Amendment right is a "personal" right; it

---

[19]*United States v. Gaudin*, 515 U.S. 506 (1995) (footnote references omitted).

does not extend to others. This personal right affords defendants the opportunity to be supported by family and friends in the courtroom. The second component of a "public trial" relates to the First Amendment, which essentially allows media coverage of a trail. However, courts may impose restrictions on the type and extent of media coverage. For example, some courts, including the U.S. Supreme Court, do not allow television coverage of their proceedings.

The Sixth Amendment protects criminal defendants by requiring the government to inform defendants of the charges against them. This constitutional safeguard gives the defendant time to prepare for trial. Furthermore, the government is restricted to litigating these charges only; no new charges may be raised by the government once the trial begins. During the trial, the defendant has the right to confront and cross-examine the witnesses against him. This safeguard ensures that the defendant has a right to be present during all aspects of the trial, especially when the prosecution is presenting evidence against the defendant. In turn, after the defendant has heard the testimony of the government's witnesses, the defendant has the opportunity to impeach the testimony of the witnesses through the cross-examination process.

A cornerstone of the Sixth Amendment relates to a criminal defendant's right to have a lawyer present during an interrogation and at trial. Although the right to counsel does not formally begin until the government has brought charges against a defendant, the right to counsel may be invoked during a custodial interrogation, as guaranteed by the Miranda warnings.

Returning to the defendants in the Inappropriate, Inc., case, we are told that a minor customer was arrested. Because this customer was indigent, the court offered her a court-appointed lawyer based on the Sixth Amendment's right to be represented by legal counsel. The defendant refused the court-appointed lawyer because she did not like the attitude of the lawyer. The court refused to appoint a second attorney. Based on this situation, do you believe the government has satisfied the Sixth Amendment requirement to provide a court-appointed attorney if the defendant cannot afford one? Another way of asking the question is do you believe the defendant has a constitutional right to "select" an attorney, or is the defendant required to accept the attorney appointed by the court?

Equal Protection of the Laws

The Equal Protection Clause of the Fourteenth Amendment states that no state shall "deny to any person within its jurisdiction the equal protection of the laws." This means that individuals in the same situation must be treated in a similar manner under the law. When a law is enacted which treats similar individuals differently, the court will determine whether this is constitutional by using the three tests illustrated earlier in the chapter in Exhibit 3.3 on page 77. If a law distinguishes between persons based on race or nationality, the law will be subject to strict scrutiny, and the government must be able to show a compelling interest in order to prevail. If a distinction between persons is based on gender, intermediate scrutiny applies, and the government must be able to convince the court that there is a substantial relationship between the discriminatory treatment under the law and an important government interest. Those laws that govern economic interests, for example, those impacting business, are subject to a rational basis review, and the government need only show that the distinction furthers some legitimate government objective. For example, let us suppose that one of the states that sought to ban Inappropriate's products in the introductory example had passed a law that made it illegal for Inappropriate to sell its products online via the company website to state residents, but at the same time did not take any action against in-state retailers that also carry t-shirts that some considered to be vulgar as part of their inventory in the state. It is unlikely the state could justify unequal treatment of substantially similar businesses.

Summary

The U.S. Constitution has application to business transactions, and it also provides constitutional safeguards to executives and others accused of committing "white-collar" crime. Under the commerce clause, Congress has the power to regulate local activities in a state which might have a substantial and harmful effect upon interstate commerce. Because many businesses are now online, there is a movement to impose a burden on them to collect a sales tax from the consumer and remit it to the state. Generally there must be some physical presence in the state to do so, such as a warehouse or a retail store; however, the Marketplace Fairness Act, if enacted into law, will require the collection of a sales tax, regardless of it not having a store or warehouse in the state. Commercial speech (advertising) can be regulated by the state or federal government in limited circumstances. The government must provide sufficient justification for restricting commercial speech. Executives accused of committing a crime are entitled to constitutional safeguards to protect their presumption of innocence. They are found in the Fourth (search and seizure), Fifth (right to remain silent), and Sixth (right to a fair trial) Amendments to the U.S. Constitution. The Equal Protection Clause protects employees from workplace discrimination and companies from economic discrimination. Management should always consult with legal counsel to ensure that constitutional issues are reviewed when they apply to a business transaction. An executive accused of committing a business crime should immediately retain counsel to protect his interest and presumption of innocence.

Questions for Review

1. Constitutional interpretation

What are some of the limitations of strict constructionism? What are the advantages and drawbacks to this way of interpreting the Constitution?

2. The Commerce clause and regulating guns in school zones

In 1990 Congress passed the Gun-Free School Zone Act that made it unlawful to possess a firearm in a school zone. A high-school senior carried a concealed and loaded handgun into his high school and was arrested and charged with firearm possession on school premises in violation of the Act. The student brought a motion to dismiss the indictment arguing that Congress had no power or authority under the commerce clause to regulate guns in school zones because possession of a firearm on school premises had nothing to do with economic activity. The motion to dismiss the indictment was denied by the District Court. The Federal Court of Appeals reversed the decision and allowed the motion. The case was appealed to the U.S. Supreme Court. Did the Gun-Free School Zone Act exceed Congress' authority under the commerce clause? What categories of commerce may Congress regulate under the commerce clause? *United States v. Lopez*, 514 U.S. 549 (1995).

3. The First Amendment and restrictions on advertising

A state legislature is concerned about the increasing number of drivers who have been driving under the influence of alcohol and decides that one way to address this public safety concern and discourage alcohol consumption in the state is to prohibit any advertisements for alcohol that include pricing information. The price advertising ban is put into place despite opposition from liquor retailers. One liquor retailer, LiquorLicense, creatively tries to get around this restriction by placing an ad in the paper that includes pictures of vodka and rum but does not include any price information for those items, rather the ad just says "Wow." Also in the advertisements are pictures of various kinds of chips and pretzels, each with corresponding low sale prices for those items included in the ad. The state liquor authority fines LiquorLicense $400 for the ad on the grounds that the tone of the ad suggests that the store's prices for the liquor are low. In response, LiquorLicense files a complaint in the U.S. District Court alleging, among

other things, that the advertising restriction violates the First Amendment. You are the judge in the case. What factors will you take into account in determining whether the advertising restriction violates the First Amendment? How will you rule? *44 Liquor Mart, Inc., v. Rhode Island*, 517 U.S. 484 (1986).

4. The Fourth Amendment and prisoners' rights

The Fourth Amendment prohibits searches without a reasonable suspicion to justify them. When an individual is arrested, law enforcement officers routinely fingerprint and photograph prisoners for identification purposes. Suppose a police department proposes adding a new procedure to its prisoner intake routine for prisoners arrested in connection with a serious crime—taking a DNA sample via a cheek swab. Such samples could then be submitted into a national crimes database for a potential match to unsolved crimes. Is obtaining the DNA sample without a search warrant a violation of the prisoner's Fourth Amendment rights? *Maryland v. King*, 133 S. Ct. 1958 (2013).

5. The Fifth Amendment and computer passwords

An increasing number of electronic files are secured by encryption measures for added levels of protection. Such measures may make it difficult for law enforcement officials to access computer hard drives and files on the drives that have lawfully been seized from individuals accused of a crime. Would compelling such individual to turn over passwords or encryption codes to law enforcement officials be a violation of the person's Fifth Amendment right against self-incrimination?

6. The Sixth Amendment and plea bargaining

Defendants in a criminal proceeding have a right to the assistance of counsel. Petty

Crime Pat was charged with driving with a revoked driver's license four times. Under the law the fourth offense was considered a felony that had a potential maximum jail sentence of three years. The district attorney offered Pat's attorney two alternative plea bargains: (1) a 90-day prison sentence or (2) a lowering of the charge to a misdemeanor along with a one year sentence. Pat's attorney did not mention the plea bargains to Pat, and the offers expired. Pat later pleaded guilty, and the judge sentenced him to three years in prison. Was the attorney's conduct a violation of Pat's Sixth Amendment rights?

7. The Fourth Amendment and the right to privacy

Do you think that the Fourth Amendment adequately protects the privacy rights of individuals in light of concerns such as the extensive collection of data by the National Security Agency of the United States?

8. The First Amendment and limitations of commercial speech

When are limitations of commercial speech constitutional? When may a state limit commercial advertising, if ever?

Further Reading

Dorf, Michael C., *Constitutional Law Stories* (2d ed. Foundation Press 2010).

Garrison, Michael J., *Should All Cigarette Advertising Be Banned? A First Amendment and Public Policy Issue*, 25(2) American Business Law Journal 169–205 (June 1987).

Kanovitz, Jacqueline R., *Constitutional Law* (13th ed. Anderson Press 2012).

Langvardt, Arlen W., *The Incremental Strengthening of First Amendment Protection for Commercial Speech: Lessons from Greater New Orleans Broadcasting*, 37(4) American Business Law Journal, 587–652 (June 2000).

Reed, O. Lee, *Is Commercial Speech Really Less Valuable than Political Speech? On Replacing Values and Categories in First Amendment Jurisprudence*, 34(1) American Business Law Journal 1–38 (Sept. 1996).

Tribe, Lawrence H., *Constitutional Choices* (Harvard University Press 1986).

CHAPTER 4

Administrative Law

Chapter Objectives

1. To understand the nature of administrative agencies
2. To understand how administrative agencies are created
3. To examine the powers that administrative agencies exercise over businesses
4. To explore the limits on agency power
5. To understand how international bodies affect U.S. businesses

Practical Example: Google, Inc.

Google, Inc.* is a company whose technology-centered services have a striking reach into daily life. Consumers "Google" the answers to questions, communicate via Gmail, and find their way around town using Google Maps. Just as Google products are all around consumers, administrative agencies form the regulatory environment that is all around Google. In 2011, the Federal Trade Commission (FTC) sanctioned Google for using deceptive tactics when it launched its now-defunct Buzz social network. The following year, the Federal Communications Commission (FCC) fined Google $25,000 for obstructing an investigation related to Google's Street View project. According to reports, Street View involved not only the photographing of buildings along public roads, but the surreptitious

---

*Google, Inc., is a global technology company best known for its Internet search engine.

collection of private e-mail, passwords, and other records as the camera-toting Google vehicles drove by. Google must be careful to operate within the rules of the FTC, FCC, and other agencies as it continues to roll out new products. One of these new products is Google Glass, a computer that is worn like eyeglasses and that allows its wearers to access the Internet, take videos, and see virtual information superimposed on the real world. As you read the chapter, consider what issues may be raised by Google Glass that could attract the attention of administrative agencies. Also consider how Google might respond to any of their concerns.

Overview of Administrative Law

In Chapter 1 you learned that the Constitution establishes three branches of government with distinct roles: the legislative branch (Congress), which makes the laws; the executive branch (headed by the president), which enforces the laws; and the judicial branch (federal courts), which interprets the laws. This separation of powers and the system of checks and balances established by the Constitution are intended to ensure a stable system of government where no one branch becomes too powerful.

In this chapter, you will explore a "fourth branch" of government — virtually unmentioned in the Constitution — that exercises all three functions. This "fourth branch" is made up of administrative agencies that pass regulations that have the force of law, investigate and prosecute violations of those regulations, and sit in judgment when businesses or individuals are accused of violating those regulations. You will discover how and why these agencies are created. You will also learn about the significant checks on administrative agency power exercised by the legislative, executive, and judicial branches of government.

The "Fourth Branch" of Government

Administrative agencies are pervasive in modern society, influencing nearly every aspect of business operations. If an entrepreneur wishes to raise funds for a new company by offering to sell stock to the general public, the regulations of the Securities and Exchange Commission (SEC) must be considered. Businesses seeking to hire or promote employees must be cognizant of the laws administered by the Equal Employment Opportunity Commission (EEOC). If a business wishes to merge with or acquire a competitor, it must satisfy the Federal Trade Commission (FTC) or Department of Justice (DOJ) that the merger will not raise antitrust concerns. Exhibit 4.1 illustrates some of the ways that administrative agencies impact the business environment.

Exhibit 4.1. Administrative Agencies and the Business Environment — Examples

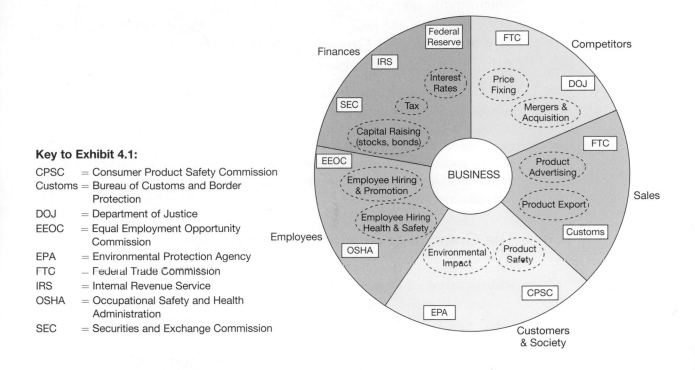

Key to Exhibit 4.1:

CPSC	= Consumer Product Safety Commission
Customs	= Bureau of Customs and Border Protection
DOJ	= Department of Justice
EEOC	= Equal Employment Opportunity Commission
EPA	= Environmental Protection Agency
FTC	= Federal Trade Commission
IRS	= Internal Revenue Service
OSHA	= Occupational Safety and Health Administration
SEC	= Securities and Exchange Commission

What Is an Administrative Agency?

An administrative agency is a unit of the government other than a court or legislature.[1] The definition of "agency" is therefore broad and flexible, even bringing within its reach units of the government that are "subject to review by another agency." Under this definition, the Food and Drug Administration (FDA) is an "agency," even though it is part of the U.S. Department of Health and Human Services (HHS), which also meets the definition of an "agency." Thus, just as Russian dolls fit one inside the other and have similar physical characteristics, agencies housed within larger administrative agencies share similar legal characteristics for purposes of administrative law.

Naming Administrative Agencies

Although the names of some agencies include the term "agency" in their title, such as the Environmental Protection Agency (EPA), other agencies may use terms such as "commission," "office," "service," "bureau," or "authority." For

---

[1] 5 U.S.C. § 551(1).

example, the Federal Communications Commission (FCC), the U.S. Patent and Trademark Office (PTO), and the Internal Revenue Service (IRS) are all administrative agencies.

The Number and Growth over Time of Administrative Agencies

In 1952, Supreme Court Justice Robert H. Jackson stated that "the rise of administrative [agencies] probably has been the most significant legal trend of the last century."[2] More than a half century later, administrative agencies continue to exert their substantial influence on the business environment. The federal government's official website, USA.gov, offers an alphabetized list of approximately 480 federal agencies. In addition, many more agencies exist at the state and local levels.

The Creation of Administrative Agencies

When Congress perceives a governmental or regulatory need, it may choose to address that need by the creation of an administrative agency. The legislation enacted by Congress that creates the administrative agency is known as an **enabling act**.

Case Illustration

In 2007 the United States began to experience the most severe financial crisis since the Great Depression. In response, Congress passed the Dodd–Frank Wall Street Reform and Consumer Protection Act of 2010, which created the Consumer Financial Protection Bureau (CFPB). The CFPB monitors financial markets, guards against unfair or deceptive financial practices, and receives consumer complaints. Although consumer financial protection was not new, the act creating the CFPB consolidated most authority for such protection in one new agency.

Pub. L. No. 111-203, 124 Stat. 1376 (2010).

Why Create Agencies?

Given the deliberate separation of governmental powers by the Constitution into the legislative, executive, and judicial branches, one might wonder why Congress would create a vast infrastructure of administrative agencies that combine all three functions. The two justifications that are most commonly cited to explain this are (1) agency specialization and (2) legislative gap-filling.

Agency Specialization

Congress is made up primarily of generalist legislators, while the judiciary is staffed primarily by generalist judges. In contrast, an administrative agency can hire specialists who are highly educated and experienced in a particular field. For example, in a recent year the FDA employed more than 11,000 people in areas such as drug evaluation, toxicology, and veterinary medicine, including more than 300 pharmacists and more than 100 veterinarians.

---

[2]*FTC v. Ruberoid Co.*, 343 U.S. 470, 487 (1952) (Jackson, J., dissenting).

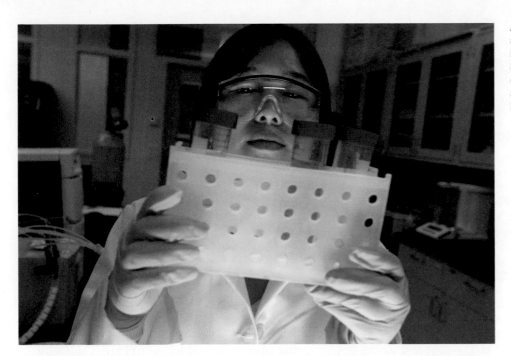

A scientist at the Food and Drug Administration inspects test tubes. Specialization and expertise enable agencies to regulate in highly technical areas.

Legislative Gap-Filling

Administrative agencies can also "fill in the gaps" of legislation enacted by Congress. For example, the Endangered Species Act prohibits businesses or others from selling or transporting endangered species, but the task of determining which species are "endangered" has been delegated to the Fish and Wildlife Service, an agency within the Department of the Interior. Similarly, federal law provides that imports shall be taxed by category according to the Harmonized Tariff Schedule of the United States, but delegates to Customs the responsibility of determining in which category a given item belongs.

Other Explanations for the Rise of Administrative Agencies

The ability of administrative agencies to aggregate specialists within a single regulatory entity and fill in the details of national legislation has become all the more important in light of a changing commercial environment. The U.S. population has increased by a factor of more than 75 since the founding of the nation, from less than 4 million in 1790 to over 316 million today. As the population has grown, the volume and complexity of commerce has increased dramatically as well. Concerns over particular social issues have led to the establishment of agencies to oversee issues such as fair business practices (FTC, created 1914), securities law (SEC, 1934), environmental protection (EPA, 1970), and workplace safety (OSHA, 1972). New areas of technology have created the need for new regulations in fields such as radio and telephone communication (FCC, 1934), aeronautical transportation (Federal Aviation Administration, 1958), and nuclear energy (Nuclear Regulatory Commission, 1975).

State and Local Agencies

All of the examples of administrative agencies provided so far have been federal agencies, including the SEC, EEOC, FTC, DOJ, FDA, EPA, FCC, PTO, and IRS. States and localities also create administrative agencies that have substantial relevance to businesses. In some cases, these agencies have a federal counterpart. For example, the Ohio Environmental Protection Agency is that state's counterpart to the federal EPA, and businesses must comply with the regulations of both.

Case Illustration

Thomas Jefferson was not only the author of the Declaration of Independence and the third President of the United States, he was also the nation's first patent examiner. In 1790, Congress enacted the first federal patent statute, which authorized the Secretary of State (along with the Secretary of War and the Attorney General) to grant patents on any invention that was deemed "sufficiently useful and important."* During Jefferson's tenure as Secretary of State from 1790 to 1793, only 57 patents were granted. It was soon realized, however, that the increasing volume and complexity of patent applications necessitated the delegation of the examination process to federal employees. Today, the U.S. Patent and Trademark Office is an administrative agency that employs about 9,500 people and issues more than a quarter of a million patents per year.

---

*Patent Act of 1790, 1 Stat. 109-112, § 1.

State Agencies

State administrative agencies regulate a wide array of business activities. For example, entrepreneurs seeking to obtain limited liability by incorporating or by operating as an LLC (see Chapter 7, Business Organizations) must file appropriate documents with the unit of the state responsible for licensing and regulating corporations. Most businesses must purchase workers' compensation insurance, which pays medical and disability benefits to employees for work-related injuries and diseases, and comply with the requirements of the state workers' compensation office. Businesses may also have to register with and pay unemployment insurance taxes to the state workers' unemployment division. Other state agencies regulate commercial driver licensing, banking, insurance, and real estate licensing.

Local Agencies

Administrative agencies also exist at the local level. For example, Chicago's Department of Business Affairs and Consumer Protection protects consumers from fraud by resolving complaints and taking action against offending businesses located in Chicago. The same agency also administers a system of business licensing, including liquor licensing, body piercing licensing, day care licensing, manufacturing licensing, and restaurant licensing.

State and local administrative agencies can vary from jurisdiction to jurisdiction. The remainder of this chapter focuses on federal administrative agencies.

Independent Versus Executive Agencies

Agencies may also be classified as either executive or independent. The president possesses varying levels of influence and control over agency action

Exhibit 4.2. Examples of Executive Agencies	
Agency	**Housed Within**
OSHA*	Department of Labor
IRS	Department of the Treasury
FDA	Department of Health and Human Services

* OSHA = Occupational Safety and Health Administration.

depending on the provisions of the enabling act drafted by Congress. If Congress decides that an agency can be most effective if it is subject to greater control by the president, it can create an *executive agency*. Executive agencies are generally considered to be "housed" within one of the executive departments and are usually headed by a single officer who can be removed by the president with or without cause. Examples of executive agencies are provided in Exhibit 4.2.

Where greater independence from executive influence (and therefore from political or partisan influence) is considered to be more important, Congress may create an *independent agency*. Independent agencies are usually headed by several individuals from both political parties who serve staggered terms and who can only be removed by the president for poor performance or wrongdoing. Independent agencies are therefore sometimes collectively referred to as the "headless fourth branch" of government. Examples of independent agencies include the

- SEC
- FTC
- Small Business Administration (SBA)

There is no bright line that distinguishes "independent" from "executive" agencies, and courts will classify an agency as one or another based upon a number of factors related to the degree of the agency's independence from the executive branch.[3] The distinction could be important, for example, if a court were called upon to determine the extent of the president's power to remove an agency head. Although the degree of agency independence may have important political and constitutional ramifications, businesses may notice little difference between the two types of agencies.

---

[3]See *Free Enterprise Fund v. Pub. Co. Accounting Oversight Bd.*, 130 S.Ct. 3138, 3215 (2010) (listing "six criteria that may suggest independence").

Administrative Agencies: Legislative, Executive, and Judicial Powers

As mentioned in the chapter introduction, the U.S. Constitution generally divides the federal government into three branches, each with different functions: the legislative branch makes the laws; the executive branch enforces the laws; and the judicial branch interprets the laws. Even though this simplistic conception of the separation of powers doctrine is generally accurate, many exceptions exist: The president (the head of the executive branch) can make law by issuing executive orders; the judiciary can promulgate procedural rules that have the force of law; and the Senate (legislative branch) is empowered by the Constitution to try all impeachments, thus performing a court-like function. If the separation of powers is incomplete when one considers these traditional actors in the legislative, executive, and judicial branches, administrative agencies blend the three governmental functions to an even greater extent.

Legislative Powers

Unless otherwise specified in the enabling act, administrative agencies generally have the power to **promulgate** (enact) regulations that have the force of law. These regulations, like agency action in general, must be consistent with all relevant statutes and cannot overrule or contravene Congressional enactments or the U.S. Constitution.

Agency Regulations

Regulations (also called "regs" or "rules") are similar to statutes except that they are promulgated by administrative agencies rather than by Congress. The term *regulations* most commonly refers to provisions that affect the substantive rights of businesses or others. For example, the FCC has promulgated regulations that prohibit telemarketing businesses from using automated dialers to call cell phone numbers. This type of regulation is also known as a *legislative rule*. Agencies may also promulgate *interpretive rules* that do not create new rights or obligations but instead clarify existing statutes or agency regulations. These interpretive rules are sometimes called "nonlegislative rules" but are more commonly referred to as "guidance documents" or simply **guidance**. For example, the EEOC has issued enforcement guidance on the issue of when employers will be vicariously liable for the unlawful racial or sexual harassment of employees by supervisors. Agencies may also promulgate *procedural rules*, which relate either to internal agency operations or procedural technicalities. For example, the Secretary of Health and Human Services (HHS) has promulgated procedural rules that relate to the consequences of missing Medicare reimbursement filing deadlines. A summary of the types of rules issued by agencies is presented in Exhibit 4.3.

Exhibit 4.3. Types of Administrative Agency Rules

	Type of Rule	Description
Substantive	Legislative rules	Analogous to federal statutes
	Interpretive rules ("guidance")	General statements of policy, or clarifications of the meaning of a regulation
Procedural	Procedural rules	Rules that relate to internal agency operations (e.g., employee promotion) or rules that relate to procedural technicalities (e.g., required filings must use 12-point font)

Where Can a Business Find Regulations?

Just as Congressional statutes are *codified* (compiled and ordered by topic) into a set of printed volumes known as the **United States Code** (USC), administrative rules are codified into a set of printed volumes known as the **Code of Federal Regulations** (CFR). For example, if a business wishes to locate applicable statutes and regulations relating to trademarks, it could consult Title 15 of the USC ("Commerce and Trade") and Title 37 of the CFR ("Patents, Trademarks, and Copyrights"). Both the USC and the CFR are freely available online (www.gpoaccess.gov).

Executive Powers

Not only do agencies make laws, but they also enforce these laws in a number of ways, such as by gathering information, issuing licenses, and entering into settlement agreements known as "consent decrees."

Agency Information Gathering

Administrative agencies may require businesses to periodically submit information to the agency in an information submissions process known as *periodic reporting*. For example, the SEC requires, at a minimum, the quarterly (every three months) filing of financial statements by covered entities. These statements help the SEC to verify whether company financial information that is legally required to be made available to the public has been properly disclosed. Similarly, IRS regulations require the quarterly prepayment by corporations of estimated income taxes in many cases as well as the familiar annual filing of income tax returns. Reporting may often be completed electronically. The SEC, for example, maintains the Electronic Data Gathering, Analysis, and Retrieval (EDGAR) system that allows businesses to submit most required forms and reports electronically.

Periodic reporting is only one of several means of agency information gathering. In some cases, members of the public may voluntarily provide

Federal agents inspect toys arriving from China. Why might imported toys need to be inspected?

information to agencies, as when a consumer files a complaint with the FTC alleging that a company has engaged in fraudulent or abusive business practices. Agencies may also inspect premises to verify safety, environmental, or other standards. For example, the Kansas Department of Agriculture, a state agency, tests about 26,000 gas pumps every 18 months to ensure that they accurately measure and display the number of gallons pumped. Also within the arsenal of administrative agency information collection tools is the *administrative subpoena* that, like a court-issued subpoena, is a document requiring an individual to appear and provide information. A *subpoena duces tecum* is a type of subpoena that requires an individual to appear and bring documents or other records.

When businesses fail to comply with agency information disclosure requirements, they may be subject to sanction. However, even if an agency approves a given disclosure, this does not necessarily mean that a business is immune from all liability related to it.

Although the Court in *Wyeth v. Levine* (see Case Illustration) concluded that a drug company could be liable for inadequate labeling notwithstanding the involvement of the FDA, in some cases the degree of agency

Case Illustration

Since 1955, Wyeth Pharmaceuticals (now a part of Pfizer) has manufactured a drug known as Phenergan® (promethazine) for the treatment of nausea. On April 7, 2000, a physician assistant administered a dose of Phenergan to Diana Levine, injecting the drug into her arm via the "IV-push" method. Following the injection, Levine, a professional guitarist and pianist, developed gangrene that necessitated the amputation of her hand and forearm. Although the FDA-approved product labeling warned that "extreme care" must be taken to properly administer the drug and that amputation could be the result of faulty administration, Levine argued that the warnings should have been even stronger and that Wyeth should be liable. Notwithstanding the FDA-compliant disclosure, the Supreme Court held that Wyeth could be liable for negligent labeling and affirmed a jury verdict of $7.4 million.

_____

Wyeth v. Levine, 555 U.S. 555 (2009).

regulation may be so significant as to absolve a business of legal responsibility for the regulated disclosures. This was the case in *Pliva v. Mensing*, in which the Court concluded that a generic drug manufacturer (in contrast to a brand name drug manufacturer like Wyeth) could *not* be liable for inadequate labeling.

In-Depth Ethical Case Analysis

Pliva, Inc. v. Mensing, 131 S.Ct. 2567 (2011)

Facts

Metoclopramide is a drug used to treat digestive disorders such as heartburn, nausea, and vomiting, which sometimes occur in connection with diabetes or chemotherapy treatment. It was first approved by the FDA in 1980 under the brand name Reglan and since 1985 has also been produced by generic manufacturers. Following its original approval, evidence accumulated that long-term use (more than 12 weeks) could cause a severe neurological disorder known as tardive dyskinesia in up to 29 percent of patients, and in response the warning label was strengthened repeatedly in 1985, 2004, and 2009. Gladys Mensing was prescribed Reglan in 2001, and after taking the drug as prescribed for about four years she developed tardive dyskinesia.

Critically, Mensing used generic metoclopramide rather than branded Reglan. Mensing sued the generic manufacturers, alleging that they failed to provide adequate warning labels and that the risk of tardive dyskinesia was far greater than indicated on the label. In response, the manufacturers argued that they were required by federal statutes and FDA regulations to use the same labeling as that used for the branded Reglan product, and that therefore they could not have strengthened the label warning without violating federal law. The federal appeals court found in favor of the plaintiff, holding that FDA regulations did not prevent the manufacturers from proposing changes to the warning label and that in any event the generic manufacturers could have

suggested that the FDA send out warning letters to healthcare professionals. The Supreme Court reversed, noting that although the generic companies could have worked with the FDA to change the warning label, they could not have altered the label "independently" (i.e., without FDA assistance).

Justice Thomas delivered the opinion of the Court joined in part by Justice Kennedy. Justice Sotomayor filed a dissenting opinion joined by Justices Ginsburg, Breyer, and Kagan.

Issue

Are generic drug manufacturers subject to state tort suits for failure to include adequate warnings on drug labels?

Holding

No.

From the Court's Opinion

State tort law places a duty directly on all drug manufacturers to adequately and safely label their products . . . . [T]his duty required the [generic] Manufacturers to use a different, stronger label than the label they actually used. . . . Federal law, however, demanded that generic drug labels be the same at all times as the corresponding brand-name drug labels. See, e.g., 21 CFR § 314.150(b)(10). Thus, it was impossible for the Manufacturers to comply with both their state-law duty to change the label and their federal law duty to keep the label the same. . . . Although requesting FDA assistance would have satisfied the Manufacturers' federal duty [to work with the FDA to strengthen the warning], it would not have satisfied their state tort-law duty to provide adequate labeling. State law demanded a safer label; it did not instruct the Manufacturers to communicate with the FDA about the possibility of a safer label.

Wyeth [v. Levine] is not to the contrary. In that case, as here, the plaintiff contended that a drug manufacturer had breached a state tort-law duty to provide an adequate warning label. The Court held that the lawsuit was not pre-empted [i.e., the manufacturer could be liable under state law] because it was possible for Wyeth, a brand-name drug manufacturer, to comply with both state and federal law. Specifically, the [relevant] regulation, 21 CFR § 314.70(c)(6)(iii), permitted a brand-name drug manufacturer like Wyeth 'to unilaterally strengthen its warning' without prior FDA approval . . . . But here . . . federal law directly conflicts with state law [because the generic manufacturer could not have changed the labeling without the FDA's special permission and assistance].

We recognize that from the perspective of Mensing . . . finding pre-emption here but not in Wyeth [v. Levine] makes little sense. Had Mensing . . . taken Reglan, the brand-name drug prescribed by their doctors [rather than generic metoclopramide], Wyeth [v. Levine] would control and [Mensing could maintain her suit]. [However, it] is beyond dispute that the federal statutes and regulations that apply to brand-name drug manufacturers are meaningfully different than those that apply to generic drug manufacturers. Indeed, it is the special, and different, regulation of generic drugs that allowed the generic drug market to expand, bringing more drugs more quickly and cheaply to the public.

From the Dissenting Opinion (Sotomayer, J., joined by Ginsburg, Breyer, and Kagan, JJ.)

Today's decision introduces a critical distinction between brand-name and generic drugs.

Consumers of brand-name drugs can sue manufacturers for inadequate warnings; consumers of generic drugs cannot. These divergent liability rules threaten to reduce consumer demand for generics, at least among consumers who can afford brand-name drugs. They may pose "an ethical dilemma" for prescribing physicians. Brief for American Medical Association et al. as Amici Curiae 29. And they may well cause the States to rethink their longstanding efforts to promote generic use through generic substitution laws. See Brief for National Conference of State Legislators as Amicus Curiae 15 (state generic substitution laws "have proceeded on the premise that . . . generic drugs are not, from citizens' perspective, materially different from brand ones, except for the lower price"). These consequences are directly at odds with the Hatch-Waxman Amendments' goal of increasing consumption of generic drugs.

Ethical Issue

Generic drug manufacturers profit from the sale of their drugs to the public. However, FDA regulations substantially limit the ability of generic manufacturers to use a label different from that of the brand-name company. Do generic manufacturers have an ethical obligation to work with the FDA to update product labeling in light of new risk information? Suppose their efforts with the FDA are unsuccessful but that potential health risks remain. Do they then have an obligation to exit the market? What are the potential consequences of imposing multi-million-dollar liability on generic drug companies, which may operate with thin profit margins?

Ethical Theory Analysis

The first concern in using any drug is generally: "Is it safe?" If there are side effects, is the drug worth the risk? Adequate warning labels disclosing the drug's risks are an ethical obligation of the manufacturer that assists the consumer in making a decision based upon "informed consent." Guided by physicians, the majority of consumers select generic drugs over brand-name drugs because generics are less expensive. Even with knowledge of an inadequate warning, a manufacturer of generic drugs is required by federal law and the FDA not to strengthen the warning label beyond that adopted by the brand-name manufacturer. This means that users of generic drugs (or any drugs) are potentially at risk of not having full information regarding side effects.

Ethical Arguments that Would Support the Dissenting Opinion

W.D. Ross — Prima Facie Duties
The deontological prima facie duty of nonmalfeasance is a duty not to harm others. This case illustrates the harm experienced by a consumer, Gladys Mensing, who may not have been adequately warned of the risk.

Immanuel Kant — Categorical Imperative
Kant's ethical principle "Always act in such a manner that your actions could become a universal law" calls into question the majority decision, because that decision is now the "law of the land" (a "universal law") that broadly limits the ability of future patients who are injured by generic drugs to obtain compensation.

John Rawls — "The Original Position"
In the "original position," those acting behind a "veil of ignorance" (i.e., not knowing whether they will be in the role of vulnerable patient or generic manufacturer) would in any case want adequate warnings on all drugs. In addition, treating consumers of generic drugs differently from consumers of brand-name drugs may violate Rawls's *Equal Liberty Principle* that "Each person has the same indefeasible claim to a fully adequate scheme of equal liberties . . . with the same scheme of liberties for all." Providing a legal remedy for consumers of generic drugs is compatible with providing the "same scheme of liberties" (i.e. rights) for consumers of brand-name drugs.

Ethical Arguments that Would Support the Majority Opinion

John Austin — Legal Positivism
John Austin, the founder of legal positivism, stated that "[t]he existence of law is one thing; its merit and demerit another." The decision to exempt generic drug companies from liability could be defended as the result of a purposeful legislative enactment that, according to the majority, "allowed the generic drug market to expand, bringing more drugs more quickly and cheaply to the public." Those who wish to ensure a right to sue may do so by purchasing the branded product. The warnings are the same for either product.

John Stuart Mill — Utilitarianism
The utilitarian principle of "the greater good for the greater number" could support the absence of liability: Because the majority of consumers (71 percent) using the drug will not contract tardive dyskinesia, and the imposition of liability might induce some generic manufacturers to either exit the market or raise prices to the point where some cannot afford them, the "greater good" might be served by a rule that ensures low-cost generic drugs will continue to be affordable and widely available.

Conclusion

The basic ethical principle of "do no harm" suggests that the generic drug manufacturer should have at least tried to persuade the FDA to send warning letters to physicians. In addition, given that the contraction rate of tardive dyskinesia — a severe disease — is as much as 29 percent for long-term users of metoclopramide, a manufacturer might ethically decide to cease marketing the drug.

Manager's Compliance and Ethics Meeting

Executives' Ethical Responsibility

The chief executive officer of a generic drug company has been informed of the *Mensing* decision and has asked the company's marketing manager to meet with her subordinates to discuss the possibility of ceasing production of metoclopramide. The manager is to report to the CEO on any ethical findings. The manager and her group have identified a number of stakeholders including consumers, stockholders, and suppliers. The group has decided, in view of the 29 percent of consumers at risk, that consumer interests should be given primacy over other stakeholders. A group member has suggested an immediate conference with the FDA to persuade it to allow the generic manufacturer to display a warning that exceeds that of the brand-name drug. This might be beyond the power of the FDA, however, as it must act consistently with the statute. Given the company's modest size and limited budget, the group does not believe the company could be successful in persuading the Senate and House to change the underlying legislation. Even if successful, a change in the rules could subject the generic drug company to greater liability exposure, adversely affecting stockholders. Because a large number of consumers are at risk without an adequate warning, the group has decided the company should stop manufacturing the drug. They are convinced this is the correct ethical decision, and over the long run it will be good for profits as the company's reputation among consumers will be enhanced. Do you agree?

Licensing

Local, state, and federal administrative agencies exert substantial influence over businesses through their ability to grant and revoke business licenses. For example, in order to protect the public from dishonest or unsafe contractors during the construction of a new home or business, many states maintain a system of contractor licensing. At the federal level, those seeking to operate a television or radio station or wireless telephone service must comply with FCC licensing provisions.

Consent Decrees

Just as the large majority of formal legal disputes are settled out of court prior to trial, many potential administrative violations are settled by voluntary agreement between the regulated entity and the agency. Settlement may often be negotiated even before a formal complaint is filed by the agency. More formal settlement agreements will take the form of a *consent decree*, which may be subject to court approval.

Consent decrees are treated as contracts between the agency and the regulated business and can be enforced in court without regard to the underlying agency regulations at issue.

Alternative Dispute Resolution

Administrative agencies may also settle disputes via alternative dispute resolution (ADR). Under the 1990 Administrative Dispute Resolution Act,[4] Congress explicitly authorized agency use of binding arbitration and other types of ADR, so long as the regulated party consents and certain other conditions are met.

Product Recalls

Certain agencies can exert influence on businesses by negotiating the recall of products that are or may be unsafe.

Although recalls are frequently described as "voluntary," administrative agencies often play a significant role in negotiating the recall, with the negotiation sometimes taking place in the shadow of mandatory recall authority. In addition to the CPSC-negotiated recall of bicycle trailers (see Case Illustration), examples include FDA recalls of food, drugs, and medical devices, and National Highway Transportation Safety Administration (NHTSA) recalls of vehicles. Since the NHTSA's predecessor was empowered to require recalls in 1966, more than 390 million vehicles, 46 million tires, and 42 million child safety seats have been recalled.

Case Illustration

In 2010 State Street Bank entered into a consent decree with the Massachusetts Securities Division (the state counterpart to the SEC) following allegations that State Street had misled investors into thinking that one of its bond funds was highly diversified by sector. In fact, the fund was heavily invested in bonds backed by risky subprime mortgages. Under the terms of the consent decree, State Street agreed to (1) permanently cease and desist from further violations, (2) pay a $10 million civil penalty to the state of Massachusetts, and (3) hire a consultant to help ensure against future securities law violations. (In a related enforcement action brought by the SEC, State Street agreed to pay an additional $50 million federal civil penalty and contribute $250 million to compensate injured investors.)

In re State Street Bank & Trust Co., Docket No. E-2007-0084 (Mass. Securities Division, issued Feb. 4, 2010).

An Ethical Insight: Steven J. Heyman

"For Aristotle . . . freedom is subject to regulation for the public good . . . . In particular, the law seeks to inculcate the virtue of particular justice, the disposition to respect the good of the community and that of one's fellow citizens."

Steven J. Heyman, *Aristotle on Political Justice*, 77 Iowa Law Review. 861 (1992). The Case Illustration on page 108 would support Aristotle's ethical notion that "the good of the community" requires a recall of defective products.

---

[4]Pub. L. No. § 101–552, 104 Stat 2736 (1990) (codified at 5 U.S.C. §§ 571-84).

Fines and Warning Letters

Agencies have increasingly been given the power to impose fines and other penalties on the businesses they regulate. In many cases, penalties are imposed via the court system. For example, the SEC has the authority to bring suit in federal district court in order to seek civil fines for insider trading, which can be as much as three times the profit gained (or loss avoided) by the use of insider information.[5] In other cases, however, the agency itself may be able to impose fines. The administrator of the EPA, for example, is authorized to impose civil fines of up to $200,000 on automobile manufacturers for selling cars that fail to meet environmental standards.

Agencies may also issue *warning letters*. For example, the FTC sent warnings to the marketers of Four Loko, a fruit-flavored malt beverage, alleging that the marketers falsely claimed that a 23.5-ounce can of Four Loko contained the alcohol equivalent to two beers, when in fact it contained the alcohol equivalent of four to five beers. In response to the warning letters, the marketers of Four Loko agreed to re-label and repackage their product. Similarly, the FDA issued a warning letter to Genentech based on a print advertisement for the osteoporosis drug Boniva (ibandronate), which was alleged to have "misleadingly overstate[d] the efficacy of Boniva." Genentech was ordered to immediately cease dissemination of the offending advertisements.

Case Illustration

Bicycle trailers have become increasingly popular in recent years, allowing kids to pedal along behind while attached to their parent's bicycle. One of these trailers is the "iGo," a single-wheel trailer sold by Weehoo, Inc., that attaches to the seat post of the bicycle in front. In 2011 it became apparent that a portion of the seat post hitch could crack and cause the trailer to detach. In cooperation with the Consumer Product Safety Commission (CPSC), Weehoo agreed to recall about 2,700 iGo trailers.

See Press Release, *Weehoo Recalls Bike Trailers Due to Fall and Crash Hazards*, Consumer Prod. Safety Comm'n, http://www.cpsc.gov/cpscpub/prerel/prhtml11/11323.html (Sept. 13, 2011).

Judicial Powers

If a dispute cannot be resolved informally, the agency may issue a formal complaint against the accused party, known in administrative law as the *respondent*. As with civil litigation in the court system, a *complaint* is the document that initiates the adjudicative process and informs the respondent of the charges being asserted. An **administrative law judge** (ALJ) presides over the hearing and has the power to administer oaths, issue subpoenas, take depositions, receive testimonial or documentary evidence, and hold conferences to facilitate settlement or resolution via ADR. Eventually, in the absence of settlement, the ALJ concludes the proceedings by issuing an *initial order* (decision). The initial order becomes a *final order* if neither party appeals

---

[5]15 U.S.C. § 78u-1.

the decision. There are approximately 1,584 ALJs working in federal administrative agencies.

Appeal Within the Agency

Either party may appeal an ALJ's initial order to a higher body within the agency, often composed of the commissioners or board members who head the agency. For example, the National Labor Relations Board (NLRB) is an independent federal agency governed by a board of five individuals who are appointed by the president. In addition to overseeing the actions of the agency, the board members act as an appellate body, hearing appeals from decisions of the agency's approximately 40 administrative law judges. Further appeal can be taken in federal court (see the section entitled "Exhaustion of Administrative Remedies" on page 119).

Cease-and-Desist Orders

Some agencies have the power to issue *cease-and-desist orders*, which are similar to injunctions in that they command a party to refrain from some action. (See Case Illustration.)

Attorney Fee Shifting

Administrative agencies do not always prevail in disputes. Where small businesses are the subject of agency enforcement actions that are found by an ALJ to not be "substantially justified," those businesses may be entitled, under the Equal Access to Justice Act (EAJA), to compensation for attorney fees and other costs incurred in defending the action. The EAJA defines a small business as one having a net worth of no more than $7 million and no more than 500 employees.

Agency Hearings Versus Court Trials

Although administrative hearings are similar to court proceedings in many ways, there are important differences. See Exhibit 4.4 on page 110. Administrative hearings do not involve a jury. Because there is no jury, the rules of evidence may be relaxed, meaning that evidence that might be excluded in a court trial is more likely to be admitted in an agency hearing. The rationale is that an ALJ, who is a professional administrator of the law, is less likely to be swayed by inflammatory, unreliable, or irrelevant evidence than is a jury of ordinary citizens. Thus, for example, an ALJ is more likely to admit hearsay evidence (and appropriately discount its probative value) than is a trial court judge.

Case Illustration

The North Carolina Board of Dental Examiners (Dental Board) is a state agency that regulates the practice of dentistry in North Carolina. As teeth whitening services and products became more popular during the early 2000s, a number of nondentists sought to compete for this market niche. The Dental Board, however, concluded that the provision of teeth whitening services by these nondentists constituted the unlawful practice of dentistry and sent cease-and-desist letters ordering them to stop. The story, however, did not end there. In 2010 the FTC, a federal agency, issued a complaint against the state Dental Board alleging that the Dental Board's cease-and-desist letters constituted exclusionary tactics that unreasonably restrained competition in the teeth whitening market, in violation of federal antitrust law. The following year, an FTC administrative law judge issued an order requiring the Dental Board to cease-and-desist from threatening nondentist providers.

North Carolina State Board of Dental Examiners v. FTC, 717 F.3d 359 (4th Cir. 2013).

Exhibit 4.4. Court Trial Versus Administrative Agency Hearing	
Court	**Agency**
Judge	ALJ
Jury (sometimes)	No jury
Rules of evidence protect jury from unreliable or irrelevant evidence	Rules of evidence are relaxed

Limits to Agency Power

At the same time that agencies exercise substantial legislative, executive, and judicial powers — perhaps *because* they exercise these combined powers — there are significant checks on agency action by all three government branches, as well as limits imposed by the U.S. Constitution. As the supreme law of the land, the U.S. Constitution guarantees rights that administrative agencies must respect, including the Fourth Amendment right to be free from unreasonable search and seizure. Congress defines the scope of powers of each agency in the enabling act and has also enacted legislation applicable across agencies designed to increase transparency while minimizing the impact of agency action on small businesses, the environment, and the public at large. The executive and judicial branches of government also exert significant control over agency action through their respective oversight powers. Each of these limits on agency power is explored below.

Constitutional Limits

Agency actions are limited in a number of ways by the U.S. Constitution, including the First Amendment (speech), Fourth Amendment (search and seizure), Fifth Amendment (self-incrimination; due process), and Sixth and Seventh Amendments (jury trial).

However, each of these rights has been construed quite narrowly by the Supreme Court in the administrative context, leaving agencies with substantial freedom to operate. For example, corporations (as distinct from their employees) do not enjoy the Fifth Amendment privilege against self-incrimination and so cannot refuse to disclose relevant documents. The constitutional rights to a trial by jury contained in both the Sixth and Seventh Amendments have been held to be consistent, in general, with the power of ALJs to preside over administrative hearings without a jury, at least as long as the agency's decision is subject to review by a court.

Notwithstanding the protections of the Fourth Amendment, the Supreme Court has upheld the ability of the EPA to fly airplanes at low altitudes (1,200 feet) in order to take precision photographs of business premises for the

FCC v. Fox Television Stations, 132 S.Ct. 2307 (2012)

Facts: During the 2002 Billboard Music Awards, broadcast by Fox Television, the singer Cher exclaimed during a supposedly unscripted acceptance speech: "I've also had my critics for the last 40 years saying that I was on my way out every year. Right. So f * * * 'em." Following similar incidents during televised awards in 2003, the Federal Communications Commission (FCC or Commission) issued an order that found "fleeting expletives" indecent pursuant to a federal statute (18 U.S.C. § 1464). That statute provides: "Whoever utters any obscene, indecent, or profane language by means of radio communication shall be fined . . . or imprisoned not more than two years, or both." Although the FCC had applied this provision to both radio and television broadcasters in the past, it had previously distinguished between "sexual or excretory references [that] have been made once or [that] have been passing or fleeting in nature" (i.e., "fleeting expletives") and the "repetitive occurrence of [] indecent words." Fox and other parties challenged the "180-degree turn" in policy and the FCC order that had characterized the broadcast as "indecent," even though no fines had been imposed.

Issue: May the FCC issue an order condemning the 2002 Fox broadcast based on a "fleeting expletives" policy that was significantly changed following the broadcast?

Holding: No. Regulated businesses and individuals must have prior notice of what the law is so that they may adjust their conduct accordingly.

From the Court's Opinion: *A fundamental principle in our legal system is that laws which regulate persons or entities must give fair notice of conduct that is forbidden or required. This requirement of clarity in regulation is essential to the protections provided by the Due Process Clause of the Fifth Amendment. It requires the invalidation of laws that are impermissibly vague. . . . When speech is involved, [prior notice] is necessary to ensure that ambiguity does not chill protected speech. . . . In addition . . . reputational injury provides further reason for granting relief to Fox. As [one of the defendants] points out, findings of wrongdoing can result in harm to a broadcaster's "reputation with viewers and advertisers . . . ." The Commission failed to give Fox . . . fair notice prior to the broadcasts in question that fleeting expletives . . . could be found actionably indecent. Therefore, the Commission's standards as applied to these broadcasts were vague, and the Commission's orders must be set aside.*

purpose of regulatory enforcement.[6] In highly regulated industries such as firearms, liquor, and mining, even surprise inspections by agency personnel have been held constitutional. In some cases a warrant must be obtained prior to a surprise inspection, unless the regulated party consents to the inspection. For example, many of the 111 million businesses regulated by OSHA frequently consent to unannounced workplace safety inspections, knowing that OSHA could obtain a warrant for such inspections in any event.

---

[6]*Dow Chemical Co. v. United States*, 476 U.S. 1819 (1986).

FCC v. Fox Television Stations on page 111 addresses the ability of the FCC to levy fines on television broadcasters for the fleeting use of expletives, in light of the Fifth Amendment's guarantee of due process.

An Ethical Insight: W.D. Ross and Indecent Speech

Although indecent speech receives some protection under the First Amendment, the FCC's statutory authority to regulate indecency is supported by W.D. Ross's duty of nonmalfeasance — in this case the duty to prevent, in the words of the Supreme Court, the "harmful effect of broadcast profanity on children."

Legislative Limits

Because most administrative agencies are created by Congress, they are subject to its control through both agency-specific legislation as well as generally applicable legislation. In addition, the Constitution specifies that the president may appoint agency heads only "with the Advice and Consent of the Senate."[7]

Agency-Specific Legislation: Enabling Acts and Amendments

Congress initially defines the scope and powers of an agency, subject to constitutional limits, when it drafts an enabling act. The powers established by the enabling act can be, and frequently are, later modified by Congress via legislative amendments. For example, in 2009 Congress enacted the Family Smoking Prevention and Tobacco Control Act in order to expand the power of the FDA to regulate cigarettes, which had previously been held by the Supreme Court to be beyond the reach of the FDA.[8]

In addition to defining agency powers directly, Congress can indirectly expand or contract the scope of an agency's operations to a great extent through the annual appropriations bill, both by setting an agency's overall budget or by special provision. An example of a special provision is the Weldon Amendment to the Consolidated Appropriations Act of 2004, which provided that "[n]one of the funds appropriated or otherwise made available under this Act may be used to issue patents on claims directed to or encompassing a human organism," thus limiting the power of the USPTO to grant certain patents that some considered objectionable.

Case Illustration

Horses may be most commonly thought of in the context of horse racing or horseback riding, but they may also be slaughtered and consumed as food. Seeking to limit the use of horses for human consumption, Congress in a rider to the 2007 appropriations bill prohibited the U.S. Department of Agriculture (USDA) from using federal funds to inspect horse slaughterhouses. Although the absence of USDA inspections means that horses cannot be slaughtered for food in the United States, other countries continue to allow the practice. In 2012, more than 166,000 U.S. horses were shipped to Canada and Mexico to be slaughtered for food, while during the same year Europeans consumed 119,000 tons of horse meat (about 18 percent of which came from U.S. horses).

See Elizabeth Weise, *Oklahoma Lawmakers Vote to Allow Horse Slaughter*, USA Today (Mar. 21, 2013).

---

[7]U.S. Const., art. 2, § 2.
[8]*FDA v. Brown & Williamson Tobacco Corp.*, 529 U.S. 120 (2000).

Congress may also eliminate agencies completely in light of changed societal circumstances. For example, the Interstate Commerce Commission (ICC) Termination Act of 1995 abolished the ICC more than a century after its founding. Its abolition followed deregulation of the trucking, railroad, and bus industries during the 1980s, which left the ICC with fewer functions to fulfill.

General Legislation: The Administrative Procedure Act of 1946 (APA)

In addition to imposing limits via enabling acts and their amendments, which apply to individual agencies, Congress in 1946 enacted the *Administrative Procedure Act* (APA) to impose procedural limits that are generally applicable across agencies. The passage of the APA occurred in the wake of the dramatic expansion of administrative agencies during the Great Depression and resulting concern over increasing agency power. In the absence of specific requirements provided in an enabling act, the APA creates a set of default procedural rules that agencies must follow. Thus, one must generally look to two sources of law when evaluating agency action: (1) the particular enabling act at issue and (2) the APA. State legislative enactments analogous to the APA create similar procedural requirements at the state level.

Types of Rulemaking

The APA requires that most agency regulations be promulgated only after the public is given notice of the proposed rules and an opportunity to comment on them. This procedure is therefore known as *notice-and-comment rulemaking*. Despite the structured approach of notice-and-comment rulemaking, it is sometimes known as "informal rulemaking." The APA also provides for *formal rulemaking*, which allows interested parties to present oral testimony in a trial-type environment, but this type of rulemaking is rarely used. In some cases, Congress provides for special rulemaking requirements in the enabling act of a particular agency that are more rigorous than notice-and-comment rulemaking but may not require all the formalities of formal rulemaking. When rules are promulgated via these intermediate procedural requirements, which may vary from agency to agency, the process is sensibly known as *hybrid rulemaking*. Guidance documents and procedural rules, because of their less substantial impact on the public, generally are not subject to any particular type of procedural rulemaking requirements. See Exhibit 4.5 on page 114.

Notice-and-Comment Rulemaking

Under notice-and-comment rulemaking, agencies must first provide *notice* to the general public by publication of the date, time, place, and subject matter of the proposed rulemaking proceedings in the *Federal Register*, a daily publication of the federal government (federalregister.gov). Usually, the actual text of the proposed rule will be reproduced in full in the Federal Register. This notification therefore enables interested parties to critically examine the rule and offer feedback to the agency, usually in the form of written *comments*. Businesses, law firms, nonprofit organizations, individuals, and others may offer

Exhibit 4.5. APA Safeguards Against Abuse of Administrative Rulemaking

	Type of Rulemaking	Used	Safeguards
Substantive	Informal rulemaking ("notice-and-comment rulemaking")	Frequently	Notice-and-comment
	Hybrid rulemaking	Sometimes	Notice-and-comment *plus* additional requirements specified in the enabling act
Procedural	Formal rulemaking	Rarely	Trial-type procedure
	Interpretive rulemaking ("guidance" documents or policy statements)	Frequently	Possible voluntary use of notice-and-comment procedure by agency
	Procedural rulemaking	Frequently	Limited judicial review

feedback regarding the likely impact of the proposed regulations, contributing to the public accountability of agency operations. These comments may cause the agency to reformulate its proposed rule, in which case the agency must provide notice of the revised rule and offer an additional comment period. If, following the initial comment period, only minor changes or no changes are made, the agency may publish the final rule not less than 30 days before its effective date.

The APA sets forth only default rules, and some enabling acts require a longer period for comment. In 2011 President Obama signed Executive Order 13,563 which stated that the comment period "should generally be at least 60 days." The Order also requires agencies to accept comments via the Internet. Established in 2003, the website www.regulations.gov enables the public to submit comments on the proposed regulations of nearly 300 federal agencies.

Negotiated Rulemaking

Under the Negotiated Rulemaking Act of 1990, agencies are encouraged to identify businesses or other interested parties who might be affected by a proposed rule, even prior to its initial publication in the Federal Register. Representatives of these parties may be convened by the agency into a negotiated rulemaking committee, usually comprised of no more than 25 people, for the purpose of formulating a proposed rule that would then be published for wider public comment. Negotiated rulemaking is optional unless mandated by an enabling act.

Transparency

In order to ensure public accountability, Congress requires that much of what agencies do be made *transparent* (openly viewable by the public). Transparency is accomplished by the daily publication of new government regulations in the Federal Register, the ability of the public to request specific information from government agencies under the Freedom of Information Act, and the public announcement of most agency meetings.

The Federal Register

Enacted in 1935, the Federal Register Act created the Federal Register, a daily publication of the Government Printing Office in which executive orders and other government documents that have "general applicability and legal effect" must be published. Regulations that are first published in the Federal Register will be compiled in the appropriate Title of the Code of Federal Regulations (CFR) once they become law. Both the Federal Register and the CFR are available online (www.gpoaccess.gov).

The Freedom of Information Act (FOIA)

Administrative agencies collect, produce, and maintain a vast amount of valuable information in the form of written documents. The *Freedom of Information Act* (FOIA, pronounced "FOY-uh") provides that any person has a right to obtain access to this information. Businesses may therefore be able to obtain information about their business environment or even about their competitors by examining documents maintained by agencies such as the SEC, FTC, or FDA. Information that is not freely available on the agency's website can usually be requested electronically, either via a Web form or e-mail. Although FOIA only applies to federal government agencies, state analogues to FOIA often provide access to state agency documents. In 2013, however, the Supreme Court held that a state may limit information requests under that state's freedom of information law to the state's own residents.[9]

As might be suspected, the general rule under FOIA in favor of public availability of documents is not without limit. In order to promote fair competition, respect personal privacy, and maintain national security, FOIA exempts from public disclosure certain categories of information, including

- Trade secrets
- Confidential commercial or financial information
- Personnel files and medical files
- Documents that could compromise national security

In some cases, documents may be made available to the public only after sensitive information has been *redacted* (deleted or blacked out) as shown in Exhibit 4.6 on page 116. FOIA also allows agencies to charge

---

[9]*McBurney v. Young*, 133 S.Ct. 1709 (2013).

Exhibit 4.6. Publicly Available SEC Document with Information Redacted

---

UNITED STATES
SECURITIES AND EXCHANGE COMMISSION
WASHINGTON, D.C. 20549

OFFICE OF
INSPECTOR GENERAL

MEMORANDUM

TO: Mary Schapiro
              Chairman, Securities Exchange Commission

FROM: H. David Kotz
              Inspector General

DATE: April 22, 2010

SUBJECT: Report of Investigation, Case No. OIG-526
              Investigation of the SEC's Response to Concerns Regarding Robert Allen
              Stanford's Alleged Ponzi Scheme

Subsequent to the issuance of the above-referenced Report of Investigation ("ROI") on March 31, 2010 and subsequent to approval by the Commission for release of the ROI to Congress and the public, the Office of the Inspector General ("OIG") learned from the Texas State Securities Board ("TSSB") further information about an aspect of the OIG investigation relating to the TSSB.

Specifically, the OIG stated in Section IV of the ROI that the SEC had received a letter dated October 28, 2002, from [Complainant 1] _____ ("the [Complainant 1] letter"), a citizen of Mexico who raised concerns about Robert Allen Stanford and his companies ("Stanford"), and its CDs in which her mother had invested. *See* ROI at 53. The OIG reported that it found evidence that the SEC staff had decided to forward the [Complainant 1] letter to the TSSB on December 10, 2002, without responding to [Complainant 1] or investigating her concerns. ROI at 56.

The OIG also reported, based on interviews of Denise Crawford, TSSB Commissioner, and [TSSB Empl 1] [PII] _____, that the TSSB

Government-held documents are often redacted before being made available to the public. Why is redaction necessary?

the public reasonable search and copying fees, but in practice there is usually no charge for the first two hours of search time or for the first 100 pages of duplication. In 2012, more than 650,000 FOIA requests were received with about 93 percent of those being granted in whole or in part.

Government in the Sunshine Act

The Government in the Sunshine Act of 1976 requires agencies headed by two or more individuals (i.e., most independent regulatory agencies) to open most meetings to public observation. The time, place, and subject matter of each meeting must be publicly announced at least one week in advance, generally by publication in the Federal Register. Meetings may be closed for a number of reasons, most of which overlap with the exemptions under FOIA. Some states have analogous "open meeting" laws.

General Legislation: Additional Checks

Congress has sought to reduce the adverse impact of agency regulation by enacting legislation that applies generally across agencies. These acts of Congress attempt to address the impact of agency action on the environment, personal privacy, and small business, as well as other societal issues. Perhaps most important among them is the 1996 *Congressional Review Act*, under which "major rules" proposed by an agency are subjected to a legislative preapproval process. The Congressional Review Act and several other principal enactments are presented in Exhibit 4.7 on page 118.

> **An Ethical Insight: John Rawls and The Government in the Sunshine Act**
>
> Rawls's *Democratic Equality Principle* states: "Social and economic inequalities are to be arranged so that they are both (a) to the greatest benefit of the least advantaged and (b) attached to offices and positions open to all under conditions of fair equality of opportunity." The Government in the Sunshine Act, discussed on this page, which opens government agency meetings to the public, allows minority groups to observe the rulemaking process and should assist in developing Rawls's *Democratic Equality Principle* as the public and the free press become aware of agency rules and discussions.

Executive Limits

The executive branch also exerts considerable influence on administrative agencies. The president has the constitutional powers to both veto agency-related legislation passed by Congress (which veto may then be overridden by a two-thirds vote in each house of Congress) as well as appoint agency heads with the advice and consent of the Senate. The president may also remove agency heads, though for independent (as opposed to executive) agencies he may generally do so only "for cause" — that is, for inefficiency, neglect of duty, or malfeasance in office. The president may also issue executive orders, which may mandate particular action or prescribe general policies that agencies should follow. For example, President Obama's Executive Order 13,563, as noted on page 114, requires agencies to accept comments via the Internet and states that the comment period under notice-and-comment rulemaking "should generally be at least 60 days."

The executive branch also influences agency action by less direct means. Although agencies generally possess enforcement powers, they may not themselves bring enforcement actions in court unless otherwise provided in an enabling act. Instead they must refer the matter to the Department of Justice (DOJ) which will take the lead in conducting litigation. Because the DOJ is one of the fifteen executive departments, the president can influence whether and

Exhibit 4.7. Selected General Legislation that Regulates Agency Action

Legislation	Year	Limit or Check
The National Environmental Policy Act (NEPA)	1969	Requires agencies to give advance consideration to the environmental consequences of major federal actions and prepare "environmental impact statements" that describe these consequences as well as alternatives to the proposed action.
Privacy Act	1974	Agencies may maintain information about individuals only to the extent "relevant and necessary to accomplish the purpose of the agency."
Paperwork Reduction Act	1980	Requires agencies to obtain clearance from the Office of Management and Budget (OMB) prior to collecting information from the public, for the purpose of minimizing the paperwork burden of agency regulation on individuals, businesses, and others.
Regulatory Flexibility Act	1980	Requires agencies to consider the impact of new regulations on small businesses.
Congressional Review Act	1996	Requires agencies to submit proposed rules to Congress before they can take effect. Major rules do not take effect until at least 60 days after Congress receives the rule. "Major rules" are defined as those the OMB determines are likely to (1) have an effect on the economy of at least $100 million; (2) cause major increases in costs or prices; or (3) cause significant adverse effects on employment, productivity, innovation, or the ability of U.S.-based enterprises to compete. If Congress enacts a joint resolution of disapproval that is then signed by the president, the rule will not take effect, creating a type of "veto" power over agency rules.

how particular enforcement or defense proceedings are undertaken. Finally, the Office of Management and Budget (OMB), which reports directly to the president, reviews proposed regulations prior to their enactment in order to ensure consistency with presidential priorities.

Judicial Limits

If businesses or individuals are adversely affected by agency rulemaking or enforcement actions, they can seek redress in the courts.

In general, federal courts will review federal agency actions for compliance with the Constitution as well as with the procedural requirements of the APA or enabling act. Similarly, actions by state agencies are generally reviewable in state courts. Judicial review of agency actions is not without limit, however. Courts may dismiss suits brought by businesses or individuals if certain threshold requirements are not met. Even where a court accepts a case for review on the merits, it will generally give some level of deference to the agency's underlying findings of fact and conclusions of law. These threshold requirements for judicial review, as well as the concept of deference, are discussed below.

Ripeness, Mootness, and Standing

Plaintiffs in any lawsuit, whether or not an administrative agency is involved, must meet certain constitutional hurdles if they wish to obtain judicial review. The agency action must be far enough along that it is *ripe* for review, but not so far along that it is rendered *moot*. Under Article III of the Constitution, federal courts may decide only "cases" or "controversies," a provision that has been interpreted by the courts to require that plaintiffs have standing to sue. *Standing*, in turn, requires that a plaintiff has

1. Suffered an "*injury* in fact"
2. That is *caused* by the action of the defendant
3. And that "will be *redressed* by a favorable decision" of the court

Case Illustration

In 2009, the EPA issued a decision allowing California to impose higher automobile emission standards than required under the federal Clean Air Act. The National Association of Automobile Dealers (NADA) challenged the law, expressing concern that the EPA's decision would result in higher manufacturing costs that would depress dealer profit margins. The D.C. Circuit, however, held that NADA lacked standing. According to the court, any injuries that its member-*dealers* would sustain were indirect (occurring only via the effects of the emission standards on automobile *manufacturers*), and would be sustained, if at all, only in the future.

_____

Chamber of Commerce v. EPA, 642 F.3d 192 (D.C. Cir. 2011).

Most of the time, plaintiffs will meet these requirements. After all, if a plaintiff was not "injured," why would the plaintiff bring suit? However, in some cases the injury may be too speculative or may be caused only indirectly via the independent action of some third party, and the plaintiff will then lack standing to sue.

Exhaustion of Administrative Remedies

Those seeking judicial review of agency action must generally **exhaust administrative remedies** prior to filing suit in court. That is, the plaintiff must usually first pursue internal agency appeals prior to asking a court to intervene, or the court may dismiss the case.

Agency Discretion

Finally, where an agency decision has been "committed to agency discretion,"[10] the courts will not intervene. For example, because agency resources are limited, decisions about which violations to prosecute are generally considered to be committed to agency discretion and thus are not reviewable in court. (See the Case Illustration on page 120.)

Deference to Agency Action

When courts engage in judicial review of agency actions, they will accord various levels of **deference** (weight and respect) to the determinations and decisions made by the agency. For example, agency determinations of fact receive the greatest amount of deference because the agency, unlike the reviewing court, may be composed of highly trained experts who may have received or

_____

[10]*See* 5 U.S.C. § 701(a)(2).

Exhibit 4.8. The Continuum of Judicial Deference to Agency Action

Type of Agency Action	Level of Deference to Agency	Standard of Judicial Review
Discretionary actions or determinations	Very high	Courts will uphold the agency action unless it is "*arbitrary or capricious*"
Findings of fact	Very high	Courts will defer to agency findings of <u>fact</u> so long as they are supported by "*substantial evidence*," even if the court would have decided differently
Issues of law (legislative rulemaking and adjudication)	Moderately high	Court will defer to agency interpretation of <u>law</u> if (1) statute is ambiguous and (2) agency interpretation is *reasonable* ("*Chevron* deference")
Constitutional issues	Very low	Courts will engage in *de novo* review (i.e., courts will not defer to agency determinations)

Case Illustration

During the late 1970s, a number of states enacted statutes adopting lethal injection as a means of human execution, with the first such execution occurring in Texas in 1982. Even before Texas made use of its new law, however, death row inmates asked the FDA to intervene. They claimed that the drugs used for execution by lethal injection were "unapproved and unsafe for human execution," and thus violated the Food Drug and Cosmetic Act (FDCA). The FDA, however, declined to intervene. When the inmates challenged the FDA's decision to not investigate and enforce the relevant provisions of the FDCA, the Supreme Court sided with the agency, stating that "agency refusals to initiate investigative or enforcement proceedings [are not reviewable] unless Congress has indicated otherwise."

Heckler v. Chaney, 470 U.S. 821, 838 (1985).

observed the evidence first-hand. Such findings will only be rejected if they are "*arbitrary and capricious*" or unsupported by "*substantial evidence*." In practice this means that agency determinations of fact are unlikely to be overturned by a reviewing court. See Exhibit 4.8.

Courts will give somewhat less deference to agency determinations of law, because the reviewing judges *are* experts in law. Nevertheless, judicial deference to agency determinations of law is still significant. Following the 1984 landmark case of *Chevron v. Natural Resources Defense Council*,[11] agency determinations of law are subject to *Chevron deference*, under which a court conducts a two-part inquiry to determine whether an agency has properly applied a statute:

1. First, the court must determine whether the statute is ambiguous. If the statute directly addresses the precise question at issue, then the statute is unambiguous and must be followed.
2. However, if the statute is ambiguous, the court must then determine whether the agency's interpretation of the ambiguous statute is reasonable. So long as the agency's interpretation is not arbitrary or manifestly contrary

---

[11]*Chevron USA, Inc. v. Natural Resources Defense Council, Inc.*, 467 U.S. 837 (1984).

Exhibit 4.9. Legislative, Executive, Judicial, and Constitutional
                Checks on Agency Power

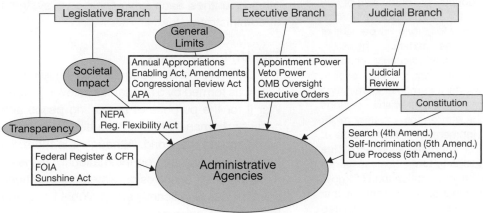

to the statute, a court will defer to the agency's view even if the court might
believe another interpretation is more reasonable.

When disputes relate to international trade, courts add a third step to their
review. That is, under the *Charming Betsy Doctrine*,[12] even an otherwise-
reasonable interpretation of an ambiguous statute by an administrative
agency can be overturned if it is inconsistent with U.S. obligations under
international law.

Not all agency decisions receive substantial deference, however. For
example, a court will engage in **de novo** review of agency determinations of
constitutional matters, meaning that it will not give any deference to the
agency's judgment and instead will decide the matter anew.

Exhibit 4.9 summarizes the legislative, executive, judicial, and
constitutional checks on the actions of administrative agencies.

Global Perspective

In the United States, the term "administrative law" generally refers to the study of U.S. administrative agencies and
especially to the limits placed on those agencies by the
legislative, executive, and judicial branches. See Exhibit
4.9. However, there are two international dimensions
that might be included as part of the study of administra-
tive law. First, certain international organizations coordinate or influence the
regulation of business at the global level, and as such are a type of "international

---

[12]*Murray v. Schooner Charming Betsy*, 6 U.S. (2 Cranch) 64 (1804).

Case Illustration

Makers of smart phones, electric car batteries, and other high-technology products rely on a class of raw materials known as the "rare earths," as well as on tungsten and molybdenum. More than 90 percent of the world's supply of these materials, however, comes from China, which has allegedly imposed fees, quotas, and other restrictions on their export. Companies could respond to this market dominance by innovation, seeking to develop alternative designs that are less reliant on the rare earths. Or, they might try to promote the development of mines outside of China that could provide alternate sources of the required materials. In addition to these business strategy solutions, companies might petition the U.S. government to make use of international organizations that administer global trade rules. In 2012, the United States, Japan, the European Union, and Canada did just that, jointly engaging China in dispute resolution proceedings before the World Trade Organization, which ruled against China in late 2013. An appeal within the WTO's Dispute Settlement Body is likely.

Source: Chuin-Wei Yap, *Beijing Says WTO Rules Against China in Rare Earth Dispute*, Wall St. J., Oct. 30, 2013.

Case Illustration

In the 1990s, Argentina sought to boost its economy by attracting foreign business investment. To allay fears that it might be too difficult for foreign firms to protect their rights in Argentine courts, Argentina entered into treaties that guaranteed recourse to ICSID should disputes arise. Following a dramatic inflow of foreign investment, the Argentine economy entered a severe recession in 2001, and businesses turned to ICSID to rectify losses caused by trade restrictions imposed by Argentina in response to the crisis. Although Argentina prevailed in many of these disputes, foreign businesses prevailed in others and were awarded compensation totaling $400 million.

Source: See *Come and Get Me*, Economist, Feb. 18, 2012.

agency." Second, there are a number of U.S. administrative agencies that regulate or affect trade to or from the United States. In addition, other countries each have their own systems of administrative law.

The United Nations

The United Nations, headquartered in New York City, was formed by 51 countries following World War II for the purpose of promoting peace and security, human rights, and better living standards around the world. Although it is therefore not primarily focused on international business, a number of its agencies or related organizations nevertheless significantly affect global trade and the business environment.

UN Agencies Affecting Business

The *International Center for Settlement of Investment Disputes* (*ICSID*, pronounced "IK-sid"), headquartered in Washington, DC, is a specialized UN agency that provides facilities for the arbitration of international investment disputes between national governments and businesses or individuals from other countries. Businesses that have made investments abroad, such as the building of manufacturing facilities, may be able to settle disputes via ICSID arbitration rather than attempt to bring suit in the courts of the foreign country. However, while the United States, China, and 146 other countries are members of ICSID, a number of countries are not, including Brazil, Russia, India, and Mexico.

Based in Geneva, Switzerland, the *International Labour Organization* (*ILO*) is a specialized agency of the UN that facilitates the setting of labor standards for its 185 member states (including the United States), including issues of workplace discrimination, organized labor, and occupational safety and health. For example, in 1996 the ILO adopted a "code of practice" on the Protection of Workers' Personal Data that recommends, among other things, that employers "reduce as far as possible the

Children demonstrate against unfair labor practices on World Day Against Child Labour in Jakarta, Indonesia, June 12, 2013. Should child labor ever be permitted?

kind and amount of personal data collected" from workers. Although ILO codes of practice are nonbinding, they may establish baseline norms and influence national legislation. In addition, the ILO has adopted over 180 conventions and protocols, which are binding on countries that ratify them. Mexico, for example, has ratified 78 ILO conventions including the Workman's Compensation Convention of 1925, which requires that compensation be paid to workers injured in the course of employment.

The *World Intellectual Property Organization* (*WIPO*), another UN specialized agency based in Geneva, administers 24 treaties governing intellectual property and provides a forum for the settlement of Internet domain name disputes (see Chapter 8, "Intellectual Property").

The *UN Commission on International Trade Law* (*UNCITRAL*) is a Vienna-based UN body that seeks to harmonize international trade law through the formulation of conventions and model laws. The most famous of these is the UN Convention on Contracts for the International Sale of Goods (CISG), which provides default rules that will govern international contracts for the sale of goods unless the parties affirmatively choose to apply some other law.

The United Nations is organized into a number of principal organs, including the General Assembly, Security Council, Economic and Social Council, and Secretariat. A number of related organizations either report to or are affiliated with the principal organs, including the WTO, ILO, WIPO, and UNCITRAL. Exhibit 4.10 provides a schematic view of the relationships of the principal UN organs and a few of its related organizations, programs, and agencies.

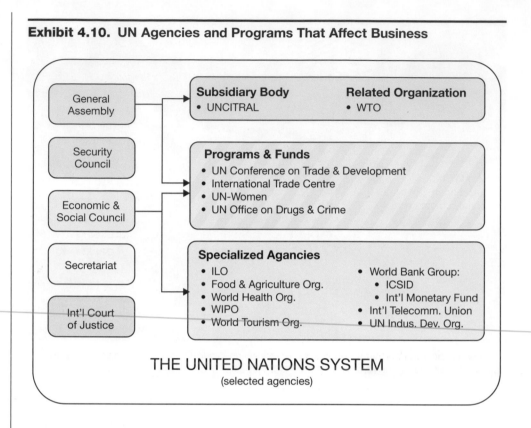

Exhibit 4.10. UN Agencies and Programs That Affect Business

THE UNITED NATIONS SYSTEM
(selected agencies)

World Trade Organization (WTO)

Perhaps the organization that has most substantially affected global trade is the *World Trade Organization* (*WTO*), a UN-affiliated organization whose 629-person *secretariat* (administrative office) is located in Geneva, Switzerland. The WTO's primary role is to liberalize trade by serving as a forum where countries can negotiate the reduction of tariffs and other barriers to trade, thereby facilitating exports. The importance of the WTO stems not only from its role in negotiating the reduction of trade barriers, but also from its *Dispute Settlement Body* (*DSB*), which helps to ensure that countries honor their treaty obligations. Only governments of the 159 countries that are members of the WTO may file disputes in the WTO's DSB, and these suits may be brought only against other WTO member countries. The DSB thus contrasts with ICSID arbitration, where businesses or individuals may directly bring disputes with foreign governments. Nevertheless, businesses or trade organizations who believe their interests are being harmed by another country's violation of its trade obligations may petition their own government to bring a dispute before the WTO's DSB.

Intergovernmental Organizations Outside the UN that Affect Business

Numerous organizations outside the United Nations system also significantly affect the business environment. The *World Customs Organization* (*WCO*) facilitates international trade by harmonizing customs standards. In the United States, the

The World Trade Organization in Geneva, Switzerland, hosts an open house each year. Why is transparency important to international organizations?

classification of imported products for tariff purposes is based on the WCO's 1983 Harmonized System Convention, to which 139 countries have acceded. The *International Organization for Standardization (ISO)* has developed over 19,000 voluntary industrial standards that affect virtually every aspect of business and technology. The most famous ISO standards are the ISO 9001 quality management standards and the ISO 14000 environmental standards. Although these standards are "voluntary," businesses may find that they are more competitive if they obtain an ISO compliance certification because some customers may demand such certification. ISO also promulgates standards addressing matters as diverse as the machine-readability of passports, the format of magnetic strips for credit cards, screw thread dimensions, paper sizes, shoe sizes, and musical pitch, among many others.

U.S. Agencies that Affect International Business

A number of administrative agencies within the United States impact imports and exports. Following the attacks of September 11, 2001, the U.S. Customs Services was reorganized into the *U.S. Customs and Border Protection (CBP* or *Customs)*. Simultaneously, it was moved from the Department of the Treasury to the newly created Department of Homeland Security, reflecting the shift in emphasis from tariff collection to safeguarding U.S. borders against terrorists and their weapons. Nevertheless, CBP not only continues to collect tariffs but also enforces quotas and embargoes, classifies imported products to determine the appropriate tariff rate, and imposes monetary penalties on importers who provide false information to CBP.

The *International Trade Administration (ITA)* is an agency of the Department of Commerce that facilitates exports by U.S. businesses. The ITA helps businesses understand export licensing needs, packaging laws, and tariff rates, provides sector-specific industry reports, and offers information and individualized export assistance by phone at 1-800-USA-TRADE. In addition, the ITA works to prevent foreign companies from *dumping* goods in the United States (i.e., selling them at less than fair value) and thereby making it difficult for U.S. businesses to compete at home.

Not to be confused with the ITA, the *U.S. International Trade Commission* (USITC) is an independent, quasi-judicial agency that is not housed within the executive branch. A business may file suit in the USITC to prevent the mportation of products that violate that business's intellectual property rights. If the complaining business is successful, the USITC can issue an *exclusion order*

Businesses that believe foreign competitors are dumping goods in the United States may visit the ITA website (trade.gov) to learn how to file a petition to initiate government action. A joint investigation by the ITA and USITC (see below) could ultimately lead to the imposition of import tariffs that offset the unnaturally low prices of the foreign goods, and thereby bring relief to U.S. businesses. In general, if at least 25 percent of an industry supports a petition, an anti-dumping investigation will be initiated. 19 U.S.C. § 1673a.

directing Customs to block the infringing items at the port of entry. A second principal function of the USITC is to work with the ITA in conducting antidumping investigations.

Many other U.S. agencies impact global trade. The Office of the U.S. Trade Representative (USTR) is part of the Executive Office of the President and is the agency that directly negotiates international trade treaties on behalf of the United States. The Overseas Private Investment Corporation (OPIC) offers loans and political risk insurance for businesses that wish to expand into emerging markets. And the Department of Labor provides "trade adjustment assistance," including monetary payments, to both workers and businesses that have been harmed by increased imports or the outsourcing of production to other countries.

Administrative Law in China

An extensive network of administrative bodies regulate business across the expansive Chinese market. The State Administration for Industry and Commerce (SAIC) administers China's antitrust law, licenses corporations to do business in China, registers trademarks, and promotes consumer protection. The General Administration of Quality Supervision, Inspection and Quarantine (AQSIQ) has responsibility for recalling defective products, preventing the counterfeiting of products, inspecting goods entering or exiting the country, ensuring the safety of certain worksite equipment, regulating food safety, and collaborating with the WTO on product standards issues.

Since 2003, businesses seeking to export certain products to the Chinese market must first obtain the China Compulsory Certification mark (CCC), a type of "stamp of approval" that helps ensure minimum standards of safety, quality, or performance have been met. To obtain the mark, product samples must be sent to accredited testing laboratories in China and businesses must pay for Chinese regulators to visit manufacturing facilities located in the United States, a process that can take 90 days or longer and cost several thousand dollars. Although not all products require the CCC mark, it is needed for items as varied as toy dolls, rearview mirrors, and X-ray diagnostic equipment.

China's centralized government and political ideology do not fully embrace the concept of separation of powers. As a result, administrative bodies in China are subject to more limited judicial review and tend to be less independent from the legislature than their counterparts in the United States. In addition, the regulatory system has been criticized as corrupt, ineffective, and in some cases subject to the influence of local pressures. Nevertheless, a number of reforms have taken place. China's Administrative Procedure Law, adopted in 1989, provides for limited judicial review of agency action. Although notice-and-comment rulemaking is not the norm, China has experimented with this type of rulemaking in the recent past, with mixed results. The Administrative Licensing Law of 2004 reduces the number of activities for which a government license is required and aims to reduce the burden on businesses seeking to obtain such licenses.

Administrative Law in Turkey

Turkey's legal framework has been criticized as involving lengthy, nontransparent procedures, unpredictable outcomes, and poor implementation of regulations. This lack of legal robustness is one of many reasons that Turkey's bid for membership in the European Union (EU), begun in 1987, has not yet been achieved.

Despite the slow progress in negotiations with the EU, Turkey has made great efforts to develop its regulatory infrastructure. Six "independent regulatory authorities" (IRAs) regulate different aspects of the economy. Among these is a Capital Markets Board, analogous to the U.S. Securities and Exchange Commission, which regulates the Turkish securities markets,

Although Turkey is not a member of the EU, it nevertheless requires many imports to bear the EU's "CE" mark ("conformité européenne"), analogous to China's CCC mark. The CE mark indicates compliance with the EU's health, safety, and environmental standards and does not necessarily indicate that goods were made in the EU.

The CE mark is a symbol that indicates compliance with European standards. Are there any drawbacks to obtaining a CE mark?

including the regulation of corporations that have more than 250 shareholders or whose shares are traded on the national stock exchange. In 1997, a Competition Agency was established to guard against antitrust violations. Other IRAs regulate telecommunications, energy, banking, and alcohol and tobacco.

Turkey has no equivalent to the U.S. Administrative Procedure Act. Instead, each IRA is governed primarily by its enabling act. Within an IRA, decisions are made by a governing board, the members of which are appointed by the Turkish cabinet, known as the Council of Ministers. Board members may be investigated for misconduct with permission of the appropriate Minister, and decisions of the IRAs are subject to judicial review by a specialized court (the "Onüçüncü Daire," or Thirteenth Department). In addition, a 2002 law obligates all IRAs to report annually to the Council of Ministers, although the specific content of these reports is not specified in the law. Finally, the Right to Obtain Information Law of 2003 serves an analogous function to that of the U.S. Freedom of Information Act, allowing individuals or businesses to obtain access to information in the possession of an agency, while providing exceptions to protect trade secrets, national security, and privacy.

Summary

Thousands of administrative agencies exist on the local, state, and national levels and exert considerable influence on nearly every aspect of the business environment, from incorporation and capital-raising to employee hiring and merger

activity. At the federal level, these agencies are created by Congress to carry out specialized functions such as environmental protection or securities regulation. Administrative agencies combine legislative, executive, and judicial powers — powers normally kept separate in the American system of governance under the separation of powers doctrine. Legislative functions of agencies include the promulgation of regulations and the issuance of guidance documents that help businesses understand how various statutes and regulations should be interpreted. Executive functions include investigation of possible violations, licensing of business activity, and negotiation of settlement agreements. Judicial functions include resolution of disputes via hearings that are presided over by Administrative Law Judges as well as the issuance of cease-and-desist orders.

Although agencies wield substantial powers, there are also significant checks on their actions. Like other government actors, agencies are subject to constitutional protections against unreasonable search and seizure and must comply with the Constitution's due process requirements. Each branch of government also exercises control over administrative agencies. Congress defines the scope of an agency's power and has enacted generally applicable legislation known as the Administrative Procedure Act that requires agencies to follow certain procedures during rulemaking or adjudication proceedings. Additional legislation facilitates transparency of agency action to promote public accountability and mandates the consideration by agencies of various constituencies, such as small businesses. Within the executive branch, the president appoints agency heads with the advice and consent of the Senate, and the Office of Management and Budget reviews proposed regulations prior to their enactment. Finally, most agency actions are subject to judicial review.

Questions for Review

1. Freedom of information act

Larry Bryant researches information concerning unidentified flying objects ("UFOs") as the Director of the Washington, DC, Office of Citizens Against UFO Secrecy, and also writes for the monthly periodical *UFO Magazine*. In 2008, Bryant sent the Central Intelligence Agency ("CIA") a request for information under FOIA requesting "CIA-generated records [pertaining to] . . . cases of airborne UFO encounters reportedly occurring since Nov. 17, 1986." Assuming the CIA has such records, on what basis might it object to their release? *Bryant v. CIA*, 818 F. Supp. 2d 153 (D.D.C. 2011). (The CIA in fact offered to release 2,779 pages to Bryant, noting that it had received "numerous previous request[s]" of a similar nature and that the information had already been provided to the public.)

2. President's removal power

After a series of celebrated accounting debacles, Congress enacted the Sarbanes-Oxley Act of 2002, which introduced tighter regulation of the accounting industry under a new Public Company Accounting Oversight Board ("Board"). The Board is composed of five members who are appointed by the SEC to serve staggered, five-year terms. The SEC can remove board members only for good cause. In turn, the president can remove the SEC commissioners only for good cause. In *Humphrey's Executor v. United States*, 295 U.S. 602 (1935), the Supreme Court held that Congress has the power to create independent agencies headed by officers that are appointed by the president, but whom the president may remove only for good cause. Do you think that Congress should have the power to create an agency such as the Board whose members are protected by a "double-layer" of for-cause removal? Or does such a structure insulate board members from executive accountability and thereby subvert the president's ability to ensure that the laws are faithfully executed? *Free Enter. Fund v. Pub. Co. Accounting Oversight Bd.*, 130 S.Ct. 3138 (2010).

3. Ethical considerations

A company manufacturing artificial hip devices approved by the FDA has been informed that a number of patients (about 35 percent) using their artificial hips are experiencing a high level of lead in their blood due to a leaching process caused by the hip articulating on the metal of the artificial hip as the patient walks. The manufacturer has decided this is a risk that accompanies a hip transplant and continues to manufacture and sell the device. The manufacturer has informed physicians that this has occurred and has encouraged them to explain the risk to their patients as part of the "informed consent" process. The manufacturer feels this is an ethical decision because the FDA has approved the company's artificial hips and the majority of patients do not experience the blood disorder. Do you agree? State your reasons based on the ethical theories discussed in this textbook.

4. Nature of administrative regulations

Enbrel (etanercept) is a prescription medication that is FDA approved for the treatment of psoriasis (among other indications), a condition characterized by raised, thick, red, and scaly patches of skin. Amgen, the maker of Enbrel, sought to promote its treatment for psoriasis using a television advertisement entitled "Freedom" that described the drug as a "BREAKTHROUGH" that would provide relief "MONTH after MONTH." The advertisement depicted 12 "patients" with no visible signs of psoriasis, including one scene in which a young woman with unblemished skin runs in a care-free manner along the beach. Another scene showed apparently healthy people jumping with joy, all with no visible signs of psoriasis. The advertisement stated in small print that "Your results may vary" and that "not everyone will respond." According to the FDA, there was no evidence that Enbrel could clear skin completely. As a general matter, must businesses comply with the regulations of administrative agencies, or do they merely issue advisory guidance that businesses should follow as good practice? In this particular case, do you think the FDA could require the drug company to modify its advertisement? To what sources of law might we look to answer this question? *Warning Letter from Thomas W. Abrams (FDA) to Kevin W. Sharer (Amgen)*, Feb. 18, 2005.

5. Agency discretion

The rise of portable electronic devices such as laptops and smart phones is made possible in part by the availability of lithium ion battery technology. Unfortunately, in some cases these batteries have caught fire and caused serious injury, and in several cases the Consumer Product Safety Commission (CPSC) has facilitated recalls of dangerous batteries. But can consumers *compel* the CPSC to recall a dangerous battery? Suppose that a consumer has been injured by a faulty battery, provides information about the problem to the CPSC, and asks it to take action. If the CPSC declines, can the injured person ask a court to order the CPSC to take action? What would be the likely outcome? *Messier v. U.S. Consumer Product Safety Commission*, 741 F. Supp. 2d 572 (D. Vt. 2010).

6. Meaning of transparency

What does "transparency" mean in the context of administrative agency law? In what ways have administrative agency rules and operations been made more transparent?

7. Limits to agency power

Which branches of government serve to check agency power? Provide at least one example of a power exercised by each branch.

8. Global concerns

A large solar panel device company based in the United States has noticed a sharp decline in its domestic sales. Upon investigation, it is discovered that customers have been switching to solar panels imported from Asia, which are being sold at an impossibly low price. Furthermore, the solar panels appear to be nearly identical to the U.S. company's own solar panels, which are protected by multiple patents. In what U.S. administrative agency might the company bring a complaint in order to prevent further importation by its competitor? What is the legal basis of such a claim? What remedy could that agency offer? What other agency would enforce the remedy? Are there any other legal or business options that the company might consider?

Further Reading

American Bar Association, Administrative and Regulatory Law News, www.americanbar.org/groups/administrative_law/publications/administrativeandregulatorylawnews.html (quarterly newsletters available for download).

GPO Access: A Service of the U.S. Government Printing Office, www.gpoaccess.gov (online access to the USC, CFR, and Federal Register).

O'Brien, Christine Neylon, *The First Facebook Firing Case Under Section 7 of the National Labor Relations Act: Exploring the Limits of Labor Law Protection for Concerted Communication on Social Media*, 45 Suffolk U. L. Rev. 29 (2011).

Orozco, David, *Administrative Patent Levers*, 117 Penn St. L. Rev. 1 (2012).

Regulations.gov: Your Voice in Government Decision-Making, www.regulations.gov (allows the public to comment on proposed regulations).

CHAPTER 5

Legal Aspects of the Global Business Environment

Chapter Objectives

1. To understand the concepts of sovereignty, sovereign immunity, and comity
2. To know where international law comes from and to distinguish between public and private international law
3. To be able to strategize how to prevent international business disputes and to understand how private international disputes are resolved
4. To understand the basic concepts involved in international trade law and the origins and function of the World Trade Organization (WTO)
5. To understand the purposes and structure of the United Nations (UN) and be familiar with the agencies that report to it

Practical Example: Exploring a Start-Up Business

Serina just graduated from college as a business major and could finally live her dream: to start her own business. She started thinking about how the Internet could enable her to sell products anywhere. Eventually, she decided to base a business around this idea: she would buy up small hardware items like screwdrivers and pliers from hardware stores and distributors in the United States that were going out of business or that would sell below the usual price due to large surpluses. Because the U.S. market for these products is saturated, she would then investigate in which country she could sell the items. She would export the hardware to those countries, aiming for a cost below both U.S. and overseas market price but higher than the price she paid for the goods. Her goal would be to undercut the competition regularly but always make a profit.

To obtain initial inventory, she needed capital, so she met with a venture capitalist about the possibility of obtaining financing. When the venture capitalist heard Serina's plan, he exclaimed, "Not only won't I back you — I'll have no part of this business, ever. I don't want to get caught up in a potential violation of international trade regulations." What was the venture capitalist referring to? What rules affect import or export businesses? What risks would Serina face that she would not face if she were launching a domestic business, and how could she help minimize the risks of doing business internationally?

International trade has been conducted in most parts of the globe for centuries. People bartered, sold, and traded when traveling or sailing to distant lands. Leaders throughout history spearheaded efforts to seek out, secure, and use long-distance trading opportunities such as the Silk Route and to devote resources and priorities to the development of navigational and maritime strength. European powers formed colonies overseas to capitalize on economic opportunities. More recently, advances in transportation, communication, and technology have led to an explosion of international business. Goods, services, money, and people cross international boundaries at rates and in numbers never imagined a few decades ago. Companies nowadays not only buy and sell goods overseas, they also send employees overseas, set up factories abroad, license technology to foreign companies, and invest abroad. Increased globalization of business corresponds to an increased interdependency and interconnectedness. More and more, to be competitive, businesses must understand and work in the context of an international landscape.

Sovereignty, Sovereign Immunity, and Comity

Before considering rules and bodies of law that apply to international business transactions, first consider concepts relating to internationalism. What is nationhood? Can countries sue each other in court, and if so, for what? Because each country's laws are so different, is one country's law recognized in another country?

Sovereignty

What does it mean that a country is **sovereign**? What are the common features or characteristics of sovereign states[1]? Sovereignty involves

- International recognition
- Control over a specified geographic region
- A government that commands control over the population
- Identifiable symbols like flags and a national anthem
- Some uniform law
- Common currency
- Postal system
- A defined population

A sovereign state is self-governing and independent. While countries have fixed geographical borders, people are mobile—so what happens if you are a U.S. citizen and travel to Namibia? Which state's law governs your actions? You must abide by the laws of Namibia, just as any Namibian traveling to the United States must abide by U.S. law.

Sovereign Immunity

Based on the concept of respecting a foreign nation's sovereignty, the doctrine of sovereign immunity means that courts in one country should refrain from hearing lawsuits against foreign governments. In the United States, this doctrine and its exceptions are codified in the **Foreign Sovereign Immunities Act (FSIA)**. This federal statute allows a foreign government's public-sector acts to fall outside the scope of a U.S. court's jurisdiction. Essentially, the act states that a sovereign government's public-sector act should not be subject to review and scrutiny by U.S. courts. Keep in mind the FSIA applies only when a foreign country (not a foreign citizen) is named as defendant in a U.S. lawsuit.

Originally, the FSIA excluded all sovereign acts from a U.S. court's jurisdiction, but over time, this absolute immunity gave way to some exceptions. Currently, under the FSIA, there are a few exceptions under which U.S. courts *will* have jurisdiction over a sovereign government's actions. (Keep in mind that this law applies only to actions against governments, not private parties like companies). The most common of these exceptions are as follows:

1. The country **waived** its immunity. Why would a country voluntarily choose to be sued? Suppose the Danish government wanted to purchase a large quantity of timber from a U.S. logging company to construct a public housing development. In the contract for this transaction, Denmark could waive immunity, so that if a dispute arose in connection with the

---

[1]In international law, the term "country" and the term "state" are often used synonymously.

contract, the Danish government could be sued. The timber supplier would likely not enter into the contract if there would be no recourse in court for nonpayment of the goods. To ensure access to a remedy in the event of a breach of contract, the U.S. timber company would insist on a contractual waiver of immunity.

2. The country is engaged in **commercial activity** (as opposed to governmental activity).[2] This is the most commonly litigated FSIA exception. To determine whether a foreign government's activities are considered commercial, "the issue is whether the particular actions that the foreign state performs (whatever the motive behind them) are the type of actions by which a private party engages in 'trade and traffic or commerce.' . . . [For example] a foreign government's issuance of regulations limiting foreign currency exchange is a sovereign activity, because such authoritative control of commerce cannot be exercised by a private party; whereas a contract to buy army boots or even bullets is a 'commercial' activity, because private companies can similarly use sales contracts to acquire goods."[3] Governments could engage in commercial activity by buying goods or services, leasing property, or borrowing or lending money.

3. The country violated property rights in violation of international law. If the lawsuit involves a claim that the foreign government seized property in violation of international law, then there is no sovereign immunity. Note that seizure of private property is lawful if the owner is fairly compensated (**expropriation**) but is unlawful if the owner is not fairly compensated (**confiscation**).

Comity

Does the fact that foreign nations are generally exempt from jurisdiction by U.S. courts mean that U.S. laws and decisions are never recognized by foreign governments? Or that the laws and decisions of foreign governments are never recognized by the United States? Not exactly. The U.S. Constitution requires that each state give "full faith and credit" (that is, give effect) to the valid public act of every other U.S. state unless doing so would violate public policy. A similar type of concept, called comity, applies internationally. Comity is not actually a law; it is a voluntary principle that many countries, including the United States, recognize. It is grounded in the acknowledgement and respect countries have for each other's sovereignty. The doctrine of **comity** holds that, in some circumstances, nations will recognize and defer to the legislative, executive, or judicial acts (including court decisions) of other countries.

---

[2]This exception applies to actions that are based on commercial activity occurring in the United States or to actions performed in the United States in connection with commercial activity elsewhere or to actions and commercial activity elsewhere that cause a direct effect within the United States.
[3]*Republic of Argentina v. Weltover, Inc.*, 504 US 607 (1992).

In the case of judicial proceedings, comity can apply during an international dispute or after the dispute has been decided. For example, often, two or more countries could exercise jurisdiction over the parties to an international dispute. Comity requires that a U.S. court abstain from exercising jurisdiction over the dispute if a foreign court is in a better position to adjudicate the dispute or if applying foreign law is more appropriate than applying U.S. law. The reverse is also true: comity requires that a foreign court abstain from jurisdiction over the dispute if the U.S. court is in a better position to adjudicate the dispute or if applying U.S. law is more appropriate than applying foreign law. Once a foreign judicial decision is rendered, U.S. courts will recognize the foreign decision as long as

1. The foreign court had jurisdiction;
2. The foreign procedings have been "orderly, fair and not detrimental to the nation's interests";[4] and
3. Recognizing the decision will not violate U.S. laws or U.S. public policy.

U.S. court decisions are generally recognized by other countries under similar conditions.

Sources of International Law and Public and Private International Law

Why Abide by International Law?

If sovereignty means that a nation's authority to govern, legislate, hear cases, etc., extends only within its territorial borders, how can the concept of international law exist? And why would a sovereign country choose to abide by rules that it did not exclusively author? There are many reasons countries choose to relinquish some of their sovereign control. For example, 18 of the member countries of the European Union currently use the euro as legal currency. In doing so, they choose to be bound to a central international monetary system in the belief that the cost of giving up some control over domestic monetary policy is worth the benefits of a stronger,

Case Illustration

The United States brought a lawsuit requesting forfeiture of a $38.5 million jet purchased by Teodoro Nguema Obiang Mangue ("Nguema") because the government believed the jet had been purchased with funds derived from extortion, misappropriation, theft, and embezzlement. Nguema was Equatorial Guinea's Minister of Forestry and Agriculture and the son of Equatorial Guinea's president. The United States brought the lawsuit to enforce U.S. anti-money-laundering laws and prevent the United States from being a haven for the proceeds of illegal activity abroad. A motion to dismiss was filed on the basis of international comity, based on the argument that adjudicating the case might require the U.S. court "to pass judgment over Equatorial Guinea's application of its own laws." The court held that the doctrine of international comity does not bar the lawsuit because (1) there is no other proceeding in Equatorial Guinea for the United States to pursue the claim; (2) courts do not need to decline jurisdiction any time a case involves foreign affairs (as Nguema had claimed); and (3) dismissal of the case is not appropriate when doing so "would be contrary to the policies or prejudicial to the interests of the United States." *United States v. One Gulfstream G-V Jet Aircraft*, 2013 WL 1701831 (2013).

---

[4] *Basic v. Fitzroy Engineering, Ltd.*, 949 F. Supp. 1333 (ND Ill. 1996) aff'd 132 F.3d 36 (7th Cir 1997).

multinational currency. In other instances, countries form military alliances or agree to abide by international environmental standards because the perceived common benefit outweighs the costs of abiding by treaty terms. Countries gain economic benefit by agreeing with other countries to reduce tariffs on international trade. The African Economic Community, for example, aims to create economic and monetary union by creating free trade areas and a central bank. In these examples, countries affirmatively agree to abide by an international set of rules and in doing so, relinquish a small amount of sovereign control.

Legal Validity of International Law

Is international law recognized as binding law in U.S. courts? In a famous case decided in 1900 called *The Paquette Habana*, the U.S. Supreme Court stated that "[i]nternational law is part of our law, and must be ascertained and administered by the courts . . . as often as questions of right depending upon it are duly presented for their determination."[5] The United States is not alone in its recognition of the importance of international law. A well-respected international scholar estimated, "[i]t is probably the case that almost all nations observe almost all principles of international law and almost all of their obligations almost all of the time."[6] This famous observation underscores the power of international law while acknowledging the lack of total, uniform acceptance of international law.

Public and Private International Law

Public international law refers to law that applies to the relationships between or among sovereign nations. **Private international law** refers to law that applies to the resolution of disputes between private individuals and business entities, typically when parties are engaging in international commercial transactions. Private international law refers to the body of laws that apply to moving people, goods, money, and services across state borders for business reasons.

Sources of International Law

Because there is no single governing body with authority to enact law binding on citizens of all countries, how is public international law made? According to the International Court of Justice, established by the United Nations to hear

[5]*The Paquette Habana*, 175 US 677 (1900).
[6]Henkin, Louis, *How Nations Behave* 47 (2d ed. 1979).

disputes between nations, international law is determined, in order of importance, by

1. International treaties and conventions
2. Customary international law
3. General principles of law
4. Judicial decisions and scholarly teachings by international law experts

International treaties and conventions and customary international law are discussed below.

Treaties and Conventions

What is a treaty? The Vienna Convention on the Law of Treaties defines a **treaty** as "an international agreement concluded between States in written form and governed by international law, whether embodied in a single instrument or in two or more related instruments."[7] A treaty is an agreement between sovereign nations to cooperate in some way, signed by authorized representatives and ratified (if so required) by the signatory countries. Treaties between two countries are called **bilateral** treaties; treaties between three or more countries are called **multilateral** treaties. Normally, a treaty does not take effect until it is **ratified**. In the United States, the executive branch negotiates and signs treaties. The U.S. Senate must then provide advice and consent by approving a resolution to ratify it by two-thirds vote. It then is signed by the president, at which point it becomes binding on the United States.

Treaties can serve several purposes. Historically, treaties were used to end wars and prevent continued conflict. Records of peace treaties between warring nations date back hundreds, and even thousands of years.[8] In modern times, treaties have been used for many other purposes, involving both public and private international law. For example, in addition to cessation of military hostilities, modern treaty provisions can relate to taxation, trade, intellectual property rights, extradition, environmental policy, navigation, monetary policies, human rights, or a host of other issues. Although treaties can address a wide variety of matters, for business law purposes, treaties that involve trade are of particular importance. Many modern treaties aim to harmonize rules between and among countries, often with enormous value for economies and businesses. When rules relating to trade, intellectual property, or monetary policies are standardized across international borders, goods and services can be imported and exported more cheaply and foreign investment is more attractive.

---

[7]*Vienna Convention on the Law of Treaties* (1969) Article 2(1)(a).
[8]For example, the Treaty of Kadesh, enacted in 1247 BCE in Ancient Egypt, is one of the earliest recorded treaties. Written on a clay tablet, it declared a truce in hostilities between Hittite and Egyptian forces and is now preserved at the Istanbul Archeology Museums in Istanbul, Turkey.

A **convention** is a type of treaty. It is a vehicle by which representatives of many countries meet to discuss international or global issues of mutual concern. When successful, through the deliberation process, countries achieve consensus on policies designed to address those concerns. It is a collaborative process. Often, conventions are facilitated by an international organization, such as the United Nations or the World Trade Organization, both of which are discussed below.

Customary International Law

Not all international law is based on agreements between and among countries. The evolution of widely recognized legal principles forms the basis of **customary international law**. Over time, established practice eventually is acknowledged as recognized legal authority. Customary international law refers to legal principles to which many countries voluntarily assent. For example, centuries ago, Europeans relied on *lex mercatoria* (Latin for "merchant law"), a set of legal principles based on the customs and practices used on trade routes. Recognizing these principles increased predictability when conducting international business. (See Chapter 17, "Sales Law, Consumer Protection, and E-Commerce.")

Relationship Between Domestic and International Law

In addition to the sources of international law noted above, domestic law can play an important role, especially in private international law. First, individual countries adopt laws that affect the way their citizens do business

Through treaties, countries agree on a range of issues, from ending wars to facilitating trade to cooperating on environmental protection.

internationally. For example, you will learn that the Foreign Corrupt Practices Act, discussed in Chapter 10, "Business Crimes," prohibits U.S. businesses from bribing or offering bribes to non-U.S.-government officials for the purpose of influencing business. Second, countries adopt laws that affect the way foreign companies do business in their countries. For example, many countries restrict foreign investors by imposing different rules for foreign and domestic investment; restricting the amount of foreign-owned equity; prohibiting foreigners from investing in certain industries; and capping the amount of profit a foreigner can take out of the country. Last, parties to a contract will often choose to forge a connection between their international transaction and domestic law by selecting which country's law will govern their transaction. You will learn in Chapter 16, "Contracts: Performance, Public Policy, and Global Contracts," that in the United States, courts will generally uphold choice of law provisions. In an international contract, if parties agreed to the application of the law of a particular country, courts will apply that law as long as there is a reasonable relation between the transaction and the law of the selected jurisdiction.

Preventing and Resolving International Disputes

International business disputes can be more problematic than domestic ones. First, there is greater risk associated with international transactions. In general, each additional layer of complexity in an international agreement could lead to potential problems. Second, when international business disputes arise, they can be more difficult to resolve than domestic business disputes. How can international business-related disputes be managed?

Although not always possible, preventing international disputes is ideal. Sensible and informed parties can significantly reduce the likelihood of a dispute through awareness of the risks international transactions pose and the ways to prevent problems before they arise. Broadly, international risks can be categorized as follows.

Communication and Cultural Misunderstandings

Parties to an international agreement are more likely to have problems cooperating and communicating due to language differences, cultural misunderstandings, and differences in historical, ethical, and religious contexts. There are some practical ways to overcome some of these difficulties. For example, buyers can request product samples and visit the seller's factory. Buyers can engage the services of trading companies or import/export houses to make introductions to potential sellers and facilitate communication and negotiations (a common practice in Japan, for example). Parties can and should choose a language as the official language for the contract to help minimize disputes over contract interpretation. Trade references can help parties evaluate the reputation of a foreign company. And of course, devoting time to developing personal rapport is invaluable for building mutual trust that can ultimately reduce the risks stemming from communication and cultural differences.

Transportation and Delivery Problems

There is greater risk in the transportation and delivery of goods because of the longer distance involved. Goods are more likely to be received late or not received at all. The longer the goods must travel, the greater the likelihood of extreme weather; pilferage; theft; accidents during loading, transportation, or unloading; spoilage; civil unrest; and labor strikes. To minimize these risks, insurance is imperative. The party bearing the risks during transportation may want to insist on a *force majeure* clause. As discussed in more detail in Chapter 16, a *force majeure* clause excuses a party from performance if performance is prevented due to any one of a list of extraordinary events. Some countries, including the United States, provide government-sponsored services, such as financing, guarantees, and political risk insurance in order to encourage exports and advance the country's foreign policy.[9] Freight forwarders (companies that organize shipment from the manufacturer to the place designated by the buyer) can help navigate transportation and logistical issues, thereby minimizing the chance of disputes relating to transportation and delivery.

Financial Risks

There is greater financial risk in international business contracts than in domestic ones because transportation expenses are higher, currencies fluctuate, and creditworthiness of foreign buyers is more difficult to evaluate. Just the longer time lapse between shipment and delivery can create problems. Because buyers often wait longer for the goods, if the goods arrive and do not conform to the contract, it is often too late to rectify problems. While waiting for goods, a buyer could find goods more cheaply from another source or could become insolvent. Again, there are practical ways to minimize these financial risks. Parties can choose a currency for payment and can hedge fluctuations in exchange rates by buying currency futures. Buyers can obtain a letter of credit from a bank or other financial institution that guarantees payment to the seller under certain conditions. When possible, investigation of a buyer's credit report is helpful, as are trade references. If risk of expropriation in the foreign country is a concern, it is possible to keep more control and more assets in the United States by choosing carefully how to structure expansion. For example, having overseas sales agents who supply a company with leads risks less foreign capital than purchasing an ongoing business overseas and running it from the home base.

---

[9]In the United States, the Overseas Private Investment Corporation is responsible for this program. See OPIC, http://www.opic.gov/.

Approximately 90 percent of the world's goods are transported by sea.

Source: Witness, "International Shipping: Globalization in Crisis," http://www.visionproject.org/images/img_magazine/pdfs/international_shipping.pdf.

Resolving International Business Disputes

Not only are business disputes more likely to arise in the international context, but they are more difficult to resolve than domestic disputes. There is no single body empowered to regulate, legislate, or adjudicate for everyone in the world. Different countries have different laws, government regulations, court systems, and civil administrations. Pursuing a claim in a foreign court is often more expensive. Parties may be unfamiliar with a foreign legal system and may have difficulty finding local legal counsel. Again, if disputes do arise, parties can facilitate speedier and cheaper resolution of disputes by planning in advance. For example, it is common for parties to international business contracts to contractually agree to a **forum selection clause** (designating which court would hear any dispute arising from the transaction). Forum selection clauses are upheld by U.S. courts unless a party can "clearly show that enforcement would be unreasonable and unjust, or that the clause was invalid for such reasons as fraud or overreaching."[10] It is also common for parties to include a choice of law provision (designating which body of law would apply to any dispute arising from the transaction). Such provisions are generally upheld as long as there is a reasonable relation between the transaction and the law of the selected jurisdiction.

---

[10]*M/S Bremen v. Zapata Off-Shore Co.*, 407 U.S. 1 (1972).

Negotiation

Normally, parties will first attempt to negotiate and settle, as with any legal claim. As always, it is important that any settlement of claims be reduced to writing.

Mediation

Mediation is a voluntary, nonbinding, private process in which a neutral third party facilitates a negotiated settlement between the parties. Although mediation is not a common method of resolving international business disputes, it does have some advantages:

- It can resolve a dispute quickly and relatively inexpensively.
- Mediators focus on parties' real commercial needs and not just their legal rights.
- Parties have the opportunity to participate directly in the mediation process and have some control over both the process and the outcome.
- Parties are more likely to be comfortable with the settlement and to comply with it if they have taken part in helping shape it.
- The mediation process can help to diffuse conflict and hostility.
- The mediation process can improve relations between parties, which is especially important if they have an ongoing commercial relationship.

Arbitration

Arbitration proceedings are held by tribunals. In an arbitration proceeding, a neutral third party hears the dispute and issues a binding award. (Arbitration decisions are called *awards*, not judgments or decisions.) Usually, parties to a transaction include a provision in their contract agreeing to arbitration in the event of a dispute. Such clauses, which are common in major international contracts, typically specify which law will govern the arbitration, which arbitration tribunal and how many arbiters will hear the dispute, what language will be used during the arbitration, and who will pay for arbitration costs. Unlike litigation, where jurisdictional principles require a connection to the forum, arbitration is usually heard in a country in which neither party resides. Arbitration awards are legally binding and internationally enforceable, subject to the tests listed below.

There are three major arbitration tribunals in the world: the International Chamber of Commerce International Court of Arbitration (ICC) in Paris; the London Court of Arbitration (LCIA) in London; and the American Arbitration Association (AAA) in New York. Each has different procedural rules, but the overall process is similar[11] for commencement of arbitration, exchange of

---

[11]The American Arbitration Association applies its own rules only in the absence of any designated rules.

arbitration pleadings, appointment and removal of arbitrators, and so forth. One major difference is that under ICC arbitration rules, the parties must submit to the arbiter and to the opposing party a summary of claims, along with a list of issues to be determined and applicable procedural rules, called **terms of reference**. Although this can be time consuming, the process of articulating claims and issues can help facilitate settlement and reduce time and costs overall. Neither the LCIA nor the AAA rules require terms of reference.

Arbitration has many advantages for resolving international commercial disputes and is a popular way to resolve large private international disputes. It tends to be cheaper and faster than litigation. Whereas court proceedings in many countries are public, arbitration proceedings are confidential. Parties have more control over the process as compared with litigation. Parties choose the arbiter (often selected for particular expertise) and the location of the proceedings (often a location not home to either party). Generally, the arbitration process is more streamlined and easier for parties to understand than litigating in a foreign court.

Arbitration has disadvantages, too. It is less suited to multiparty litigation because arbitration tribunals do not have the power to bring into the lawsuit any party who has not voluntarily agreed to arbitration. Partly because, as noted above, the process is generally faster than litigation, there is limited pretrial discovery. U.S. lawyers accustomed to learning their opponent's case in advance of trial do not have this opportunity. Arbitration cases do not serve as precedent the way court decisions in common law countries do. Many in the legal community are concerned that the development of law, which relies so heavily on previously decided opinions, is stinted when too many cases are decided by private tribunals. Last, parties to arbitration lack the ability to appeal the decision, even if that decision is inconsistent with well-established legal principles.

Can a party who has agreed to an arbitration clause be compelled by a court to submit to arbitration? If one party refuses to comply with the terms of an arbitration award, is there a remedy in court? The **UN Convention on the Recognition and Enforcement of Foreign Arbitral Awards** (often called the **New York Convention**) governs arbitration of private international disputes and has been ratified by 149 countries, including the United States. Like many UN conventions, it is designed to standardize how signatory countries approach this area of law. The convention encourages use of arbitration clauses in commercial agreements. It also addresses two legal issues that arise in international arbitration:

1. **Can a contractual arbitration clause be enforced in a domestic court?** Yes. U.S. courts apply the New York Convention and will uphold written arbitration clauses of a valid contract which arise in the commercial setting.
2. **Can the arbitration award be enforced in a domestic court?** Yes. U.S. courts will set aside arbitration awards only in rare circumstances, such as (1) lack of contractual capacity or other reason to set aside the contract that contains the arbitration clause; (2) the defendant was not given notice of the proceeding or the opportunity to be heard; (3) the arbitration award

Case Illustration

Texaco entered into a long-term contract to help drill oil wells, install pipelines, and manage the oil refinery and distribution process in Ecuador in 1964 and continued operating there until 1992. Shortly thereafter, residents of the Amazonian rain forest filed a lawsuit, claiming environmental damage caused by Texaco's oil exploration and extraction. Texaco had left behind almost no assets in Ecuador, presumably to prevent seizure in the event of an adverse judgment.

Initially, the Ecuadorian plaintiffs sued Texaco in the United States. Texaco requested that the case be moved to Ecuador, arguing that Ecuador has a reliable legal system and was a preferable location because all the evidence and alleged damage were there. The plaintiffs opposed this request, but the U.S. judge held that the trial should be conducted in Ecuador.

In 2001, Texaco merged with Chevron, and Chevron continued to defend the lawsuit. Chevron claimed that Texaco met all local and international regulations and that a $40 million cleanup effort in the 1990s resolved any environmental liability. The case proceeded, and in 2009, in expectation of losing the case, Chevron told its shareholders it did not expect to pay any judgment against it and told the *Wall Street Journal*, "We are not paying and we're going to fight this for years if not decades into the future."

In February 2011, Ecuadorian Judge Zambrano ordered Chevron to pay $8.6 billion, "believed to be the largest-ever judgment in an environmental case" and stated that if Chevron did not apologize in the next 15 days, the amount would double. Surprisingly, Chevron stock rose 1.3 percent — apparently shareholders were expecting the judgment to be higher. Chevron refused to pay the fine or apologize and said the proceedings in Ecuador did "not provide impartial tribunals or procedures compatible with the requirements of due process." About a year later, Judge Zambrano was dismissed from the bench for inappropriately granting a narcotics defendant bail in an unrelated case. Eventually, the judgment increased to $18 billion because Chevron did not apologize.

Early in 2013, Chevron filed a statement in U.S. District Court by a former Ecuadorian judge, Alberto Guerra, stating that Judge Zambrano authorized him to approach Chevron to ask for a bribe in exchange for ruling in Chevron's favor. Chevron's lawyers refused, and eventually, a deal was struck with the plaintiffs instead. Zambrano would receive $500,000 (which he promised to share with Guerra) in exchange for moving the case along quickly and generally ruling in plaintiff's favor. According to Guerra, in the end, Zambrano allowed plaintiffs' lawyers to ghostwrite the entire 188-page decision in the plaintiff's favor in exchange for the promise of receiving $500,000 from the proceeds of the case.

In exchange for his cooperation in bringing forward evidence of the alleged bribe, Chevron agreed to pay Guerra $38,000 for the value of the physical evidence he gave them. Chevron also committed to protect his security, which meant helping him and four family members leave Ecuador and move to the United States and paid him $10,000 a month for living expenses, $2,000 a month for housing, and covered his health insurance and legal fees.

As of this writing, the case is ongoing.

relates to issues beyond the scope of the arbitration clause; (4) the arbitration process did not conform to the particulars of the parties' contractual agreement; or (5) enforcing the award would violate the public policy of the country where enforcement is sought.[12]

---

[12]United Nations Convention on the Recognition and Enforcement of Foreign Arbitral Awards, Article 5.

Texaco's activity in
Ecuador from 1964 to
1992 has led to complex
litigation, protests, and
scandals.

International Litigation

If parties have failed to prevent a dispute from arising and if other means of
dispute resolution have either failed or are not available, parties may be forced
to litigate in a domestic court. As noted above, international business contracts
often contain forum selection and choice of law clauses.

International Trade Law and the World Trade
Organization (WTO)

Free trade has many benefits. It reduces economic waste and inefficiency,
decreases the cost of living, increases wealth, promotes peace, stimulates economic growth, and encourages good government. Yet countries for centuries
have engaged in a variety of economic protectionist policies.

Tariff and Nontariff Barriers to Trade

There are two types of barriers to international trade:

1. *Tariffs.* A tariff is a tax levied on imported goods. Governments levy tariffs
   (1) to create a price advantage to domestically produced goods as compared
   to imported goods and (2) to generate revenue for governments. Tariffs can
   be calculated in several ways: as a percentage of the value of the imported

goods, on the basis of the number or weight of the imported goods, by the unit, or some combination of these.

2. *Nontariff barriers.* A nontariff barrier is any type of restriction on imports other than tariffs. The most transparent nontariff barriers are *quotas*, which are government-imposed restrictions on the number or value of goods that can be imported, and **embargoes**, which are government bans on trade with a particular country. Nontariff barriers also can include technical regulations.

World Trade Organization Origins

Located in Geneva, Switzerland, the World Trade Organization (WTO) describes itself as "the only global international organization dealing with the rules of trade between nations"[13] working to open trade, provide a forum for settling trade disputes, and operate a system of trade rules.[14] In its own words, "[e]ssentially, the WTO is a place where member governments try to sort out the trade problems they face with each other."[15] Now 159 member countries strong, the WTO began as the General Agreement on Tariffs and Trade (GATT) in 1948 with only 23 members. In reaction to the recent war, conflicts, and economic difficulties, countries realized the value in opening and strengthening international trade through tariff reduction and removal of trade barriers. This foundation was continued with the creation of the World Trade Organization in 1994 during the Uruguay Round.[16] The WTO took over GATT's trade agreements, treaty obligations, and overall objectives.

One important function of the WTO is hearing trade disputes between member countries. A three-member panel of judges hears disputes filed by member countries and prepares a report with its findings of fact, conclusions of law, decision, and remedy. The report is sent to the WTO Dispute Settlement Body for review. A party can appeal to the WTO Appellate Body.

World Trade Organization Principles

The WTO aims to liberalize trade by invoking these principles:

- *Most favored nation (MFN) also called Normal Trade Relations (NTR).* Each member must give equal trade privileges and benefits to all member nations in relation to the same imports. If a country improves benefits for one trading partner, it must improve benefits in the same way for other WTO members. This is sometimes referred to as the principle of

---

[13]World Trade Organization, What Is the WTO? http://www.wto.org/english/thewto_e/whatis_e/ whatis_e.htm.
[14]World Trade Organizaiton, Who We Are, http://www.wto.org/english/thewto_e/whatis_e/ who_we_are_e.htm.
[15]World Trade Organization, Who We Are, http://www.wto.org/english/thewto_e/whatis_e/ who_we_are_e.htm.
[16]A *round* is a conference.

nondiscrimination. All member countries must be treated the same for trading purposes.

- *National treatment.* Each member must apply the same standards to imports that are applied to domestic goods. Domestic products cannot be favored over imported products.
- *Elimination of trade barriers.* Nontariff barriers, such as boycotts and quotas, are prohibited. Although tariffs are permitted, they are disfavored, and the WTO strives to reduce or eliminate tariffs.

Dumping

The WTO prohibits dumping. Dumping occurs when products of one country are introduced into the commerce of another country at less than the normal value of the product.[17] The **normal value** of the product is the price charged for that product in the exporter's home market. The normal value might be less than the cost of production but is not necessarily so. The comparison must always be at the same level of trade — that is, wholesale compared to wholesale; retail compared to retail. Adjustments can be made for the costs of shipping, packing, customs brokerage fees, insurance, etc., to make an accurate comparison.

Why would a seller want to dump goods? Given the costs of shipping and the risks of doing business internationally, when would a seller have the incentive to sell goods in a foreign market for less than could be charged in the home market? Suppose a company has surplus inventory. Selling the surplus at reduced prices in the domestic market could be unattractive because it would drive domestic prices down. However, to recoup some costs, the surplus could be "dumped" cheaply in another country while still protecting prices in the domestic market. Wouldn't the receiving country be pleased that inexpensive goods are being sold in its country? Doesn't it benefit their consumers? Dumped goods are not just priced low. They are priced artificially low. Selling at artificially low prices is unfair competition for the domestic market for those goods.

Recall Serina's business plan at the beginning of this chapter. Why was the venture capitalist concerned that her plan might violate international trade law? If Serina sold tools overseas at less than their U.S. cost, then Serina would be dumping the goods. Note that if she sold the goods overseas for a price above the normal cost of the goods in the United States, she would not be dumping the goods.

If dumping causes or threatens to cause material injury to an established industry, the injured country can impose antidumping duties. In the United States, the International Trade Commission of the Department of Commerce determines whether material injury was caused. In assessing this, the ITC considers "all relevant economic factors, including the domestic industry's output, sales, market share, employment, and profits."[18] Antidumping duties are tariffs equal to the difference between the export and domestic prices.

---

[17]General Agreement on Tariffs and Trade, Article 6(1).
[18]*An Introduction to US Trade Remedies,* http://ia.ita.doc.gov/intro/index.html.

Subsidies

Dumping is based on anticompetitive behavior that is usually undertaken by private companies. Governments also engage in anticompetitive behavior, for example, through imposition of subsidies. The WTO's Agreement on Subsidies and Countervailing Measures defines a **subsidy** as (1) a financial contribution; (2) by a government or any public body within the territory of a member country; (3) which confers a benefit.[19] Subsidies can involve loans, loan guarantees, grants, tax credits, or price supports, for example. Tax credits for fuel-efficient cars and government payments to supplement farmers' incomes when prices are low are subsidies. Government loans to companies for less than market interest rates and grants to companies to support research for business purposes are also subsidies. Like dumping, government subsidies artificially reduce prices and distort the natural competitive landscape.

Not all subsidies are illegal. First, only certain types of **specific subsidies** are illegal. A **specific subsidy** is a subsidy available only to a particular enterprise or industry. For example, a tax credit given to all companies that use primarily solar-powered energy or that engage in research and development are not targeted to any specific enterprise or industry. These are not specific subsidies and therefore would not be illegal.

Next, the WTO categorizes specific subsidies into **prohibited subsidies**, which are automatically illegal, and **actionable subsidies**, which are illegal if the subsidy has an adverse effect on the complaining country. Export subsidies are one kind of prohibited subsidies. For example, a subsidy conditional on the exporting of goods or conditional on recipients meeting certain export targets are export subsidies and, therefore, are prohibited. Import substitution subsidies are also prohibited subsidies. These are subsidies granted for using or buying domestic goods instead of imported goods. Both export subsidies and import substitution subsidies are illegal because they distort international trade and are therefore presumed to be harmful.

Actionable subsidies are permissible unless a complaining country shows an adverse effect on its interests. Examples of adverse effects include (1) hurting a domestic industry in the importing country; (2) hurting rival exporters from another country when the two compete in third markets; and (3) hurting exporters trying to compete in the subsidizing country's domestic market.

If a country has engaged in illegal subsidies, how can this be rectified? Countries complaining of subsidies can request the appointment of a WTO panel to begin a Dispute Settlement Procedure and, if appropriate,

---

[19]Agreement on Subsidies and Countervailing Measures, section 1.1.

countervailing duties will be imposed. **Countervailing duties** are duties designed to offset the effects of subsidies. They are calculated to eliminate the market distortion caused by the artificial effects of subsidies. Alternatively, a subsidized exporter can agree to raise its export prices instead of being charged a countervailing duty.

The United Nations

Several international organizations exist to facilitate dialogue between countries; improve trade relations; expand markets; reduce barriers to trade; minimize violence and hostilities; resolve disputes; improve social, environmental, and living conditions; and strengthen international relations in other ways. Much of this work is done by or under the umbrella of the United Nations.

An Ethical Insight: Rawls and a Just World Order

Rawls stated, *"A just world order is perhaps best seen as a society of people, each maintaining well-ordered and decent political (domestic) regime, not necessarily democratic but fully respecting basic human rights."*[*] In international business transactions, it is useful to consider Rawls's definition of a just world order that must maintain basic human rights. This is an ongoing challenge as U.S. companies have a significant presence in China and other countries that are trading partners but where basic human rights are often challenged.

---

* Rawls, John, *Justice as Fairness, A Restatement* 13 (Erin Kelly ed., Belknap Press of Harvard University Press 2001).

Written in 1945, the preamble to the UN's charter states that the organization was formed "to save succeeding generations from the scourge of war."

Exhibit 5.1. Purposes of the United Nations

The UN's stated purposes are as follows:

1. To maintain international peace and security, and to that end: to take effective collective measures for the prevention and removal of threats to peace, and for the suppression of acts of aggression or other breaches of the peace, and to bring about by peaceful means, and in conformity with the principles of justice and international law, adjustment or settlement of international disputes or situations which might lead to a breach of the peace
2. To develop friendly relations among nations based on respect for the principle of equal rights and self-determination of peoples, and to take other appropriate measures to strengthen universal peace
3. To achieve international co-operation in solving international problems of an economic, social, cultural, or humanitarian character, and in promoting and encouraging respect for human rights and for fundamental freedoms for all without distinction as to race, sex, language, or religion; and
4. To be a center for harmonizing the actions of nations in the attainment of these common ends[*]

More specifically, these purposes translate into work on a broad range of issues "from sustainable development, environment and refugees protection, disaster relief, counter terrorism, disarmament and non-proliferation, to promoting democracy, human rights, gender equality and the advancement of women, governance, economic and social development and international health, clearing landmines, expanding food production, and more."[†]

[*] United Nations Charter, Chapter 1, Article 1, http://www.un.org/en/documents/charter/preamble.shtml.
[†] *UN at a Glance*, http://www.un.org/en/aboutun/index.shtml.

UN Formation and Purpose

Formed on June 26, 1945, a few weeks before the conclusion of World War II, the United Nations was established with 51 original country members.[20] With immediate impressions of World War II in mind, the charter's authors wrote in the first sentence of the preamble of their determination "to save succeeding generations from the scourge of war" and to that end, the charter authorizes "collective measures for the prevention and removal of threats to peace, and for the suppression of acts of aggression or other breaches of the peace."[21] To be considered for admission as a member, a country must pledge to abide by the UN charter, excerpted in Exhibit 5.1.

Structure and Power Allocation Within the United Nations

The United Nations is composed of five active bodies: the General Assembly, Security Council, Secretariat, International Court of Justice, and Economic and Social Council.[22]

---

[20] The United Nations currently has 193 member countries.
[21] United Nations Charter, Chapter 1, Article 1.
[22] A sixth body, the Trusteeship Council, was originally charged with administration of trust territories, most of which were mandated by the League of Nations or taken from countries defeated in World War II. All territories are currently independent, and although the Trusteeship Council has not been dissolved, its mission has been completed.

General Assembly

All member nations participate in the **General Assembly**, which functions as the UN's main deliberative and legislative body. Each member nation has one vote. The General Assembly considers and votes on recommendations relating to any of the UN's wide scope and varied purposes enumerated above. Recommendations, however, have limited force because enforcement is generally through persuasion, diplomatic pressure, or economic sanctions. Several committees, funds, programs, research organizations, and advisory boards report to the General Assembly. The General Assembly votes on the budget of the United Nations; votes to admit new members and suspend current ones; elects members to the Security Council and to the Economic and Social Council; and elects judges to the International Court of Justice.

Security Council

The **Security Council** has 15 members in total, five of whom are permanent: China, France, Russian Federation, United Kingdom, and United States. The initial selection of the five permanent members was based on the role they played during World War II. The permanent members have veto power over any action proposed in the council. The privilege of serving on the Security Council, with its corresponding veto power, has been a source of controversy.[23] The remaining ten Security Council members are elected by the General Assembly to two-year terms. The Security Council has "primary responsibility for the maintenance of international peace and security,"[24] As such, it may "investigate any dispute, or any situation which might lead to international friction or give rise to a dispute"[25] and may "recommend appropriate procedures or methods of adjustment."[26] This includes, for example, authorizing military action or recommending severing diplomatic and/or economic relations with countries.

Secretariat

The Secretariat is the administrative arm of the UN. It supports the overall activities of the UN by providing day-to-day administrative services, collecting and maintaining data, conducting studies, preparing annual reports, and more. The Secretary-General is the chief administrator of the UN and head of the Secretariat. Staff of the Secretariat take a pledge of international loyalty that prohibits them from seeking or receiving instructions from any individual nation.[27] The Secretariat maintains a daily journal and a radio station[28] featuring current activities of the UN.

---

[23]Contrary to popular belief, the vast majority of UN resolutions pass the Security Council by unanimous vote. In 2012, 53 resolutions were considered by the UN Security Council, of which 50 passed unanimously. *Highlights of Security Council Practice 2012*, United Nations Department of Political Affairs, http://www.un.org/en/sc/inc/pages/pdf/highlights/2012.pdf.

[24]United Nations charter, Article 24, section 1.

[25]United Nations charter, Article 34.

[26]United Nations charter, Article 36, section 1.

[27]United nations charter, Article 100.

[28]The United Nations radio link is located at http://www.unmultimedia.org/radio/english/.

International Court of Justice

Also known as the **World Court**, the **International Court of Justice (ICJ)** is the judicial branch of the United Nations. It has heard few cases in its history. Located in The Hague, Netherlands, it is composed of fifteen judges, each of whom serves a nine-year term. No two judges can be from the same country. Judges are elected by the Security Council and General Assembly. Interestingly, a judge cannot be disqualified from hearing a case on the grounds that he or she is a national of one of the disputing countries; in fact, each country involved in a proceeding before the ICJ is entitled to insist that a judge of its nationality participate on the court for the duration of the proceeding.

The ICJ exercises jurisdiction in two situations:

1. The ICJ resolves legal disputes submitted by member states. Only countries, not private parties, can submit claims or be sued in the International Court of Justice; hence, business-related cases are uncommon.[29] Many of the disputes involve interpretation of treaties and conventions. Countries voluntarily submit themselves to the jurisdiction of the ICJ. Member countries have handled voluntary jurisdiction in a variety of ways, for example,

   - By declaring compulsory jurisdiction and therefore submitting to the ICJ's jurisdiction in any case filed against it
   - By submitting to the ICJ's jurisdiction on a case-by-case basis
   - By ratifying treaties that require that any dispute concerning the treaty be resolved by the ICJ
   - By submitting to jurisdiction only conditionally

   For many years, the United States had submitted to compulsory jurisdiction, but it withdrew from compulsory jurisdiction in 1986. Since then, the United States accepts the ICJ's jurisdiction on a case-by-case basis.

2. The ICJ also renders advisory opinions on legal questions submitted by the UN General Assembly, the Security Council, or UN agencies.

The UN Charter authorizes the Security Council to make recommendations regarding the enforcement of the ICJ's decision,[30] subject to the veto power of a permanent member of the Security Council. Diplomacy and public opinion can play a part in enforcing ICJ decisions as well.

Economic and Social Council

Fifty-four member countries are elected to the **Economic and Social Council**, which prepares studies and arranges conferences relating to

---

[29]Occasionally, a state will take up the cause of a private individual or business and pursue a claim through the ICJ.

[30]United Nations charter, Article 94, section 2.

economic, social, cultural, educational, health or human rights issues and problems and makes related recommendations, including draft conventions, to the General Assembly or to a specialized UN agency.

UN Agencies

Some of the most valuable work in the United Nations is undertaken by its subsidiary agencies. All subsidiary agencies of the United Nations report to the General Assembly. UN agencies whose work is most relevant to business include the following.

United Nations Commission on International Trade Law (UNCITRAL)

UNCITRAL helps modernize and harmonize international trade law and standardize commercial practices and agreements, which has enormous value to international business. To do this, it coordinates the activities of institutions involved in international trade, encourages continued and expanded commitment to current treaties and conventions, and facilitates discussion of new international trade agreements. UNCITRAL's most important achievement was the facilitation of the Convention on Contracts for the International Sale of Goods.

World Intellectual Property Organization (WIPO)

Almost all members of the United Nations are members of WIPO. Headquartered in Geneva, Switzerland, WIPO's overall mission is "to promote innovation and creativity for the economic, social and cultural development of all countries, through a balanced and effective international intellectual property system."[31] Its expansive responsibilities include

- Administering systems that make it easier to obtain intellectual property protection internationally
- Arbitrating disputes relating to patents, trademarks, and copyrights, including disputes over Internet domain names
- Administering dozens of intellectual property treaties and conventions
- Building collaborative networks and technical platforms to share knowledge, transfer technology, and simplify intellectual property transactions, especially among developing countries
- Facilitating conferences for the discussion of intellectual property issues
- Publishing and distributing educational materials on intellectual property rights

---

[31]WIPO, What Is WIPO, http://www.wipo.int/about-wipo/en/.

Summary

While doing business internationally exponentially increases business opportunities, it also carries significantly more risk than conducting business domestically. Understanding basic international law principles and the international litigation process can help businesspeople minimize these risks and facilitate smoother international transactions. Being familiar with the sources of international law, such as key provisions of the WTO and WIPO, enables international business-people to avoid illegal activity. It also helps enhance the value of a business through adequate international protection of intellectual property and enhanced business strategy development.

Questions for Review

1. Effect of ICJ decision

Jose Medellin participated in the rape and murder of two teenage girls in Houston, Texas. He was arrested and read his Miranda rights, and he confessed. At the time, he was not informed that he could consult with Mexican diplomats. He was sentenced to death. Mexico successfully sued the United States in the International Court of Justice, claiming that the United States violated the rights of 51 Mexican citizens, including Medellin, by not providing them with assistance by Mexican diplomats, as required under the Vienna Convention. In response, President Bush ordered states to comply with the Vienna Convention and to review the convictions of defendants who had not been told of their right to receive diplomatic assistance. Medellin then challenged his conviction because he had not been told of his rights under the Vienna Convention. Must the U.S. Supreme Court treat the ICJ decision as binding precedent? Would a decision of the U.S. Supreme Court serve as binding precedent in the International Court of Justice? *Medellin v. Texas*, 552 U.S. 491 (2008).

2. Sovereignty

How and why would a country give up any of its sovereign powers?

3. Ethics in global business

Early in 2013, Chevron filed a statement in U.S. District Court by a former Ecuadorian judge, Alberto Guerra, stating that Judge Zambrano authorized him to approach Chevron to ask for a bribe in exchange for ruling in Chevron's favor. Chevron's lawyers refused, and eventually, a deal was struck with the plaintiffs instead. Zambrano would receive $500,000 (which he promised to share with Guerra) in exchange for moving the case along quickly and generally ruling in the plaintiff's favor. According to Guerra, in the end, Zambrano allowed plaintiffs' lawyers to ghostwrite the entire 188-page decision in the plaintiff's favor in exchange for the promise of receiving $500,000 from the proceeds of the case.

In exchange for his cooperation in bringing forward evidence of the alleged bribe, Chevron agreed to pay Guerra $38,000 for the value of the physical evidence he gave them. Chevron also committed to protect his security, which meant helping him and four family members leave Ecuador and move to the United States, and paid him $10,000 a month for living expenses, $2,000 a month for housing, and covered his health insurance and legal fees. Discuss the ethical issues.

4. Foreign Sovereign Immunities Act

In 1981, Argentina established a foreign exchange insurance program under which it assumed the risk of currency depreciation in international transactions. Argentina was then unable to cover the contracts, so it issued bonds that guaranteed repayment in U.S. dollars. When the bonds came due, Argentina was unable to repay the bonds and unilaterally decided to extend the time for payment and offered bondholders substitute means of repayment. Plaintiffs brought a breach of contract action in U.S. federal district court. Argentina claimed that the district court did not have jurisdiction under the Foreign Sovereign Immunities Act. Is Argentina correct in this assertion? *Republic of Argentina v. Weltover*, 504 U.S. 607 (1992).

5. Public versus private international law

Could a contract be difficult to categorize as either public or private international law? What would such a contract look like?

6. International Court of Justice

How helpful is it that jurisdiction of the International Court of Justice is voluntary only? Does this completely undermine the value of the court? What are the advantages and disadvantages of voluntary versus compulsory jurisdiction?

7. International Court of Justice

What is the purpose of allowing a country to ensure that a judge of its nationality sits on the ICJ?

8. WTO claims

In the Philippines, nearly all domestic distilled spirits (such as gins, brandies, rums, vodkas, whiskeys, and tequila-type spirits) are made from cane sugar. The majority of imported spirits are made from cereals or grapes. For many years, the Philippines imposed an excise tax on distilled spirits that consisted of a low flat tax on spirits made from certain raw materials, such as cane sugar, and a much higher tax on spirits made from other raw materials, such as cereals and grapes. In 2009, the European Union filed a complaint at the World Trade Organization. What arguments do you think the EU made, and do you think the suit was successful? Panel Reports, *Philippines — Taxes on Distilled Spirits*, WT/DS396/R/WT/DS403/R, adopted 20 January 2012, as modified by Appellate Body Reports WT/DS396/AB/R/WT/DS403/AB/R.

Further Reading

Christy, Jr., David S. *The Impact of the World Trade Organization: Its Many Successes and the Primary Challenges It Faces.* Aspatore (Dec. 2012) 2012 WL 5899380.

Lackert, Clark W., and Zhao, Zhongcheng. *Defending Intellectual Property Rights Cases in China: Leading Lawyers on Protecting Clients' Rights in China's Evolving IP Environment.* Aspatore (July 2013) 2013 WL 4192392.

Lester, Simon, *The Problem of Subsidies as a Means of Protectionism: Lessons from the WTO EC — Aircraft Case,* 12 Melbourne Journal of International Law 345–372 (Nov. 2011).

Noyes, John E., Dickenson, Laura D., and Janis, Mark W., eds., *International Law Stories* (Foundation Press 2007).

Roberts, Lawrence D., *Beyond Notions of Diplomacy and Legalism: Building a Just Mechanism for WTO Dispute Resolution,* 40 American Business Law Journal 511–562 (Spring 2003).

The U.S. Senate's Role in Treaties, http://www.senate.gov/artandhistory/history/common/briefing/Treaties.htm.

What Is the WTO? World Trade Organization, http://www.wto.org/english/thewto_e/whatis_e/whatis_e.htm.

CHAPTER 6

Corporate Social Responsibility

Chapter Objectives

1. To understand the nature of the corporation and its relationship to society at large
2. To distinguish between the various objectives and responsibilities of a business enterprise
3. To understand the competing, yet complementary purposes of profit maximization and social responsibility
4. To understand corporate stakeholder theory
5. To understand the role of corporate social responsibility in the global economy

Practical Example: Stanley's Innovations Inc.*

While an undergraduate business student, Stanley decided that he wanted to be an entrepreneur. His goal was to provide a product or service that would grab the public's attention. He spent countless hours observing human behavior and making notes of the types of products or services that could be useful for consumers. By the time he finished his undergraduate education, Stanley had a business idea for a new and improved toothbrush that he was sure would be a bestseller if his idea could break into the marketplace. He worked tirelessly (on average 18 hours a day) to perfect his product and develop a business plan that would attract investors. Eventually Stanley was able to secure $1 million in investment from approximately 10 shareholders who owned 40 percent of his new venture, Stanley's Innovations, Inc. Though Stanley was fresh out of college, Stanley exuded confidence and assured the investors that his business plan was solid and that they would receive a return on their investment. Innovations, Inc., manufactured a preliminary batch of 50,000 toothbrushes locally in a small Iowa town. Because the going labor rate for manufacturing was minimum wage, production costs were kept down. Stanley was able to convince a few local Iowa retailers to carry his product. After a few years he was able to convince a national chain store to carry his novel toothbrush brand of merchandise and sales began to pick up considerably. Stanley was still working 18 hours a day, but the corporation was starting to make a profit and his hard work began to pay off. The company shareholders could begin to get a return on their investment.

Before paying a dividend to his shareholders, Stanley decided to think a bit more about what else could be done with the corporate profits. The corporation could make a donation to a new local library in need of donors because, after all, an extensive library collection for town residents served the community interest. The corporation could opt to pay workers more than the mandatory minimum wage, allowing the workers to have greater discretionary income, and because more discretionary income means more money spent, that would benefit not only the workers but also the economy. The corporation could opt to buy the raw materials used to manufacture the toothbrush from a more expensive, environmentally conscious seller offering plastic and bristles that exceeded federal safety standards for such products. Stanley found all of these options compelling and thought about the best course of action.

Must the shareholders' interest come first and dividends paid before increasing wages and considering using corporate profits to assist in community social development? What *should* the corporation do?[†]

Is the corporation an entity that exists solely to make a profit and increase the wealth of its owners, or does the corporation have a social responsibility to other stakeholders, such as its consumers, suppliers, and even the environment?

This chapter will explore the answers to these questions.

---

* Stanley's Innovation Inc., is a fictitious company.

† In the next chapter you will learn about a variety of forms of businesses in which a business can operate. It should be recognized that it is not just businesses in the corporate form that have adopted socially responsible business practices. Many of the practices described in this chapter under the umbrella of corporate social responsibility are applicable to other types of businesses enterprises such as partnerships and Limited Liability Companies, but that discussion is beyond the scope of this chapter.

Understanding the Nature of a Corporation

To begin to understand how to determine what course of action Stanley's Innovations, Inc., should take, we first have to understand the nature and purposes of a corporation.

What Is a Corporation?

A complete answer to this question will be provided in Chapter 7, "Business Organizations." For purposes of this chapter, you should understand the basic fact that a corporation is a legal entity that has an identity distinct from that of its owners. As an entity, it can own assets, enter into contracts, and sue or be sued. In the United States, as in most of the world, a corporation is considered a legal person.

History of Corporations

Although there is evidence of a type of corporate form of business existing as far back as 800 BCE, at which time the *sreni* was used in Ancient India to conduct a variety of business, municipal, and political activities,[1] most researchers trace the development of modern corporations back to the guilds of Medieval Europe. Gradually, the central elements of a corporation began to develop: the presence of owners, the objective to carry on a business and divide the gains, limited personal liability of the owners for the actions of the corporation, continuity of life so that the corporation continues in existence even upon the death or withdrawal of one or more of its owners, centralized management for decision making, and free transferability by the owners of their share of the corporation.

As the notion of a corporation began to develop in the United States (and in much of the Western world), the idea of being able to conduct business in a corporate form was not an automatic right. Instead, the ability to do so was something that was granted either by the ruling royalty or by the state. For example, European monarchs issued corporate charters to public stock companies that were engaged in activities that would benefit the monarchy, often through increased trade opportunities. One example of this is the charter given to the British East India Company chartered in 1600 by Queen Elizabeth to trade with East and Southeast Asia, and later with the Americas. These early corporations had individual stockholders, but the sense was that the company did not exist to serve the stockholder but rather to achieve its broader objectives. In the early history of the United States, a limited number of corporate charters were granted often only by special legislative act. Over time this was expanded so that special legislative acts were no longer required for incorporation, and self-incorporation was made possible, although the scope of corporate purposes was initially limited to public benefit functions such as charitable, religious, or other municipal services. The scope and property holdings of these corporations were strictly regulated by the state government.[2]

North Carolina was the first state to pass a private incorporation statute in 1795. The incorporation was only available to canal builders and conditioned on the canals being passed to state ownership upon completion. Up until the early nineteenth century, American corporations were given charters with the intention that the corporation would serve the public interest. The shareholders had control over the corporation, but the early corporate charters often dictated that shareholder interests were second to those of the corporation's public interest goal.[3]

Eventually, however, states loosened the self-incorporation requirements, and corporations began to be formed to carry out private business enterprises.

---

[1]Khanna, Vikramaditya, *The Economic History of the Corporate Form in Ancient India* (2005), http://papers.ssrn.com/sol3/papers.cfm?abstract_id=796464.
[2]Hood, John, *Do Corporations Have Social Responsibilities?* 48 The Freeman Ideas on Liberty 11 (1998).
[3]Wallman, Steven, *Understanding the Purpose of a Corporation, an Introduction*, 807 Journal of Corporation Law (Summer, 1999).

In fact, by the start of the 1900s, the notion that a corporation existed for the purpose of making money for its shareholders was taking hold.[4]

Maximization of Shareholder Profit

As early as the start of the twentieth century, a common school of thought was that corporations existed to generate profits for the shareholder. An often cited advocate of this position was Milton Friedman, winner of the 1976 Nobel Prize in Economics, who generated quite a stir with his 1970 article in the *New York Times Magazine* in which he stated that, "There is one and only one social responsibility of business — to use its resources and engage in activities designed to increase profits so long as it stays within the rules of the game, which is to say, engages in open and free competition without deception or fraud."[5] Friedman's position is based, in part, on the notion that corporate executives making business decisions are working as employees of the owners of the corporation, the shareholders. As such, the executive's responsibility is to conduct business in accordance with their desires and to act in their best interest. To explain his point, Milton Friedman used the example of a corporate executive who believes the corporation has a social responsibility to contribute to the social objective of preventing inflation. To achieve this objective, the executive decides to forego price increases on company products even though price increases would be in the best interests of the corporation. In effect, says Friedman, the executive would be making a judgment about how to best spend the corporate shareholder's money.[6]

You are no doubt familiar with Henry Ford, the man who revolutionized transportation with the development of the Model T automobile. Henry Ford, like the hypothetical executive described by Mr. Friedman, also made an independent, socially conscious decision on how best to spend corporate shareholder money. The *Dodge v. Ford* case summarized on page 161 describes the court's unfavorable view of Mr. Ford's generosity with corporate funds.

In stark contrast to their early predecessor corporations that were strictly limited in size and scope, by the start of the 1900s "modern" corporations were beginning to amass significant wealth, and along with that wealth a corresponding amount of social and political influence. As the size and influence of corporations began to shift, so did opinions on the duty of a corporation.

A look at the origins of this shift in opinion would not be complete without mention of a debate on the issue between two prominent law professors in the 1930s. In 1931 the *Harvard Law Review* published an article by Columbia Law

---

[4]Hood, supra note 2.

[5]Friedman, Milton, *The Social Responsibility of Business Is to Increase Profits*, New York Times Magazine (Sept. 13, 1970).

[6]The purpose of this chapter is to explore the concept of corporate social responsibility and so its focus is on the strides that have been taken in that arena. However, it is important to keep in mind that the Friedman school of thought that the purpose of the corporation is to produce profit for its shareholders, continues to be a mainstream sentiment and a respected school of thought.

Dodge v. Ford, 170 N.W. 668 (Mich. 1919)

Facts: The Ford Motor Company that was founded by Henry Ford and a handful of other investors in 1903 achieved significant financial success by selling mass-produced cars at prices that an increasing number of consumers could afford. The firm did so well that by 1911 the average annual dividend paid to shareholders was $1.2 million. In 1913, 1914, and 1915, special dividends (extra dividends) between $10 and $11 million were also paid to the shareholders. In 1916, Henry Ford, as majority shareholder, decided that the company would no longer pay a special dividend but would instead use part of that money to double the salaries of the employees and lower the price of the cars. Mr. Ford gave the following reason for his actions, "My ambition is to employ still more men; to spread the benefits of this industrial system to the greatest possible number, to help them build up their lives and their homes." Two of the Ford Corporation shareholders, the Dodge Brothers, who collectively owned 10 percent of the company, objected to this plan and filed a lawsuit against the company seeking, in part, to compel the corporation to pay a special dividend to the shareholders.

Issue: Was the corporation required to pay a dividend to its shareholders?

Holding: The trial court concluded that while generally the decision whether to declare a dividend was within the discretion of the directors, such a decision could be subject to judicial review if it appears that the directors unreasonably withheld corporate surplus from the shareholders. The trial court required the corporation to pay a dividend to the shareholders. This decision was affirmed by the Michigan Court of Appeals.

Even though the Court of Appeals agreed that it would be permissible for a for-profit corporation to engage in incidental humanitarian expenditures, such as using corporate funds to build a hospital that benefits employees, the court was also clear that there should be no confusion as to the distinction between the duties a corporation owes to the public and the duties owed to the shareholders — the business corporation is organized primarily for the profit of the stockholders.

From the Court's Opinion: *[I]t is not within the lawful powers of a board of directors to shape and conduct the affairs of a corporation for the merely incidental benefit of shareholders and for the primary purpose of benefiting others, and no one will contend that if the avowed purpose of the defendant directors was to sacrifice the interests of shareholders it would not be the duty of the courts to interfere.*

There should be no confusion (of which there is evidence) of the duties which Mr. Ford conceives that he and the stockholders owe to the general public and the duties which in law he and his co-directors owe to protesting, minority stockholders. A business corporation is organized and carried on primarily for the profit of the stockholders. The powers of the directors are to be employed for that end. The discretion of directors is to be exercised in the choice of means to attain that end and does not extend to a change in the end itself, to the reduction of profits or to the non-distribution of profits among stockholders in order to devote them to other purposes.

But it is clear that the agents of a corporation, and even the majority, cannot arbitrarily withhold profits earned by the company, or apply them to any use which is not authorized by the company's charter.

The Michigan Court of Appeals in 1919 required Henry Ford to declare a dividend to shareholders.

Professor Adolf Berle, entitled "Corporate Powers as Powers in Trust." In this article, Berle argued that "all powers granted to a corporation or the management of a corporation are exercisable only for the benefit of the shareholders."[7] Berle viewed the corporation simply as a means of promoting shareholder interests. In 1932, the *Harvard Law Review* published a response to Berles's argument written by Harvard Law Professor E. Merrick Dodd. In his article, "For Whom are Corporate Managers Trustees?" Dodd proposed that "there is in fact a growing feeling not only that business has responsibilities to the community but that our corporate managers who control business should voluntarily and without waiting for legal compulsion manage it in such a way as to fulfill those responsibilities."[8] Dodd believed that corporations were not only impacted by corporate laws regulating the actions of a business but also by "the attitude of public and business opinion as to the societal obligations of business."[9] The case of *A.P. Smith Manufacturing Co. v. Barlow*[10] is an early case exemplifying this shift in opinion.

---

[7]Berle, Adolf, *Corporate Powers as Powers in Trust*, 44 Harvard Law Review 1049 (1931).
[8]Dodd, E. Merrick, *For Whom Are Corporate Managers Trustees?* 45 Harvard Law Review 1145 (1932).
[9]*Id.*
[10]97 A.2d 186 (1953).

Case Illustration

The A.P. Smith Manufacturing Company, a manufacturer of fire hydrants and valves, was founded in 1896. Over the years the corporation made a series of small contributions to a variety of charities. In 1951, the company Board of Directors voted to make a $1,500 donation to Princeton University. Although the ability to make charitable contributions was not authorized by the corporation's article of incorporation, the corporate president justified the contribution as part of the company's obligation to support the public good and promote the company's interest by helping to ensure there was an educated workplace available from which the company could find future employees.

The defendants in this case were the corporate shareholders who challenged the donation as an impermissible use of corporate funds.

The Superior Court of New Jersey upheld the contribution, acknowledging that a long-range view of what is best for the corporation is warranted. The judge stated, *"I am strongly persuaded by the evidence that the only hope for the survival of the privately supported American college and university lies in the willingness of corporate wealth to furnish in moderation some support to institutions which are so essential to public welfare and therefore, of necessity, to corporate welfare. What promotes the general good inescapably advances the corporate weal."*

Evidence of a shift of opinion is further shown by the following language of the court: *"[j]ust as the conditions prevailing when corporations were originally created required that they serve public as well as private interests, modern conditions require that corporations acknowledge and discharge social as well as private responsibilities as members of the communities within which they operate." A.P. Smith Manufacturing Co. v. Barlow,* 97 A.2d 186 (1953).

A year after the court's decision in *Barlow,* Adolf Berle published a book entitled *The 20th Century Capitalist Revolution* in which he acknowledged that at that time the law and public opinion seemed to side with Dodd. In the book Berle wrote, "the argument has been settled (at least for the time being) squarely in favor of Professor Dodd's contention."[11] While still not in agreement with Dodd's view, Berle was aware of the public sentiment.

Other early signs also pointed to a shift in the understanding of the role of the corporation. Beginning in the 1920s, a few states had added provisions to their corporate law to explicitly allow corporations to make financial, charitable contributions, but these early statutes often placed significant restrictions on the amount of the contribution. By 1950 the American Bar Association had added a philanthropic giving provision to the Model Business Corporation Act that did not limit the scope of corporate donations.[12] Inroads were clearly being made to the notion of a corporation having a social responsibility, a

---

[11]Rutkow, Lainie, Should Corporations Serve Shareholders or Society? The Origins of the Debate, Corporations and Health Watch (2011), corporationsandhealth.org.

[12]Balotti, Franklin, and Hank, James, *Giving at the Office: A Reappraisal of Charitable Contributions by Corporations,* The Business Lawyer (May 1, 1999).

responsibility beyond the duty owed to its shareholders. After all, proponents reasoned, if philanthropy/charitable giving was considered a legitimate corporate purpose, were there not perhaps other social goals that would also transcend returns to shareholders?[13]

Further evidence of a shift in the scope of the responsibilities of a corporation can be seen in the corporate **constituency statutes** that began to be adopted in various states starting with Pennsylvania in 1983. The purpose of a corporate constituency statute is to give corporate managers the option of considering more than just the interests of the shareholders when making business decisions. Today, more than half the states have such statutes, and while some statutes apply to only a limited number of corporate decisions (e.g., when a company is seeking to buy out or take control of another corporation.), other statutes extend these to the whole range of corporate decisions. All state statutes include employees and customers as constituents that can be considered, but some states statutes also include other parties such as suppliers, creditors, local communities, and both the state and the national economies as constituents.[14]

Corporate Stakeholder Theory

When R. Edward Freeman released his book, *Strategic Management: A Stakeholder Approach*, in 1984, he gave birth to the popular use of the phrase **"stakeholder theory."** The actual use of the term "stakeholders" has its origin in an internal memorandum written at the Stanford Research Institute in the 1960s which used the term *stakeholders* to mean, "those groups without whose support the organization would cease to exist."[15] The memo echoed Dodd's sentiments issued decades before that business has an obligation to take into account the interests of various groups.

Mr. Freeman initiated organized thinking about the concept of stakeholders, and he is, therefore, considered by many to be the father of contemporary stakeholder thinking.[16] According to Mr. Freeman, a stakeholder refers to any individual or group that "can affect or is affected by the achievement of an organization's objectives."[17] Stakeholder theory requires that the corporation consider the effect of its action not only on its shareholders, but on its customers, employees, vendors, suppliers, the community, and the environment.

---

[13]Hood supra note 2.
[14]McDonnell, Brett, *Corporate Constituency Statutes and Employee Governance*, 30 William Mitchell Law Review 1227 (2004).
[15]Hillenbrand, Jens, *Stakeholder Management in Small and Medium Sized Enterprises: The Case of Belgian Microbreweries*, GRIN (Verlag 2010).
[16]Id.
[17]Freeman, R. Edward, *Strategic Management: A Stakeholder Approach* (Pitman 1984).

Now that you have a bit better understanding of the nature of a corporation and the differences of opinion with regard to the influence of stakeholder theory for conducting business, let us take a closer look at some of the concerted efforts that have taken place in the last 30 years or so which challenge and seek to change the traditional shareholder-focused approach to business.

The Social Enterprise Movement

Along with the stakeholder theory of corporate management that gained prominence in the 1980s, the notion of using private corporate enterprise to help remedy social ills can also be traced back to this time with the birth of the social enterprise movement. The idea was based, in part, on the belief that acting alone, the government could not solve social problems, but what was needed was help from private enterprise. During this time, organizations began to be formed with the goal of encouraging and investing in companies working for social change/improvement. For example, the Alpha Center for Public and Private Initiatives was created in 1985 with the goal of encouraging entrepreneurs to get involved in solving social problems. Due to the popularity of its product, its incredible success, and its commitment to improving society, Ben and Jerry's is often seen as the face of the Social Enterprise Movement. Other notable social enterprises include Newman's Own, Seventh Generation, and Tom's of Maine. A glimpse of the missions and actions of these social entrepreneurs is provided in the Snapshots on this page and page 166.

Conscious Capitalism: Capitalism Needs a Conscience

The financial scandals of the twenty-first century, unethical and illegal actions at corporations such as Enron and WorldCom motivated by greed and a desire for short-term gains, and the ever-widening gap between the compensation of executives and average

Snapshot of Ben & Jerry's

Annual Sales: $132 million
Founded: In 1978 by Ben Cohen and Jerry Greenfield after the two took a $5 correspondence course in ice cream making and invested $12,000 in equipment and renovations of an old gas station in Vermont.
CSR Claim to Fame: Introduced the "Improvement of the Environment" as a second bottom line for businesses. Because of this it is sometimes considered to be the first socially responsible business.
Stated Social Mission: To operate the company in a way that actively recognizes the central role that business plays in society by initiating innovative ways to improve the quality of life locally, nationally, and internationally.

Snapshot of Newman's Own, Inc.

Annual Sales: $5.8 million
Founded: In 1982 by actor Paul Newman, who initially filled wine bottles with his homemade salad dressing as gifts for his neighbors. Newman was committed to philanthropy, and all profits from the corporation are given to charity.
CSR Claim to Fame: All after-tax profits contributed to the Newman's Own Foundation and donated to charities both in the United States and abroad. Since 1982, over $370 million has been donated.

Snapshot of Seventh Generation, Inc.

Annual Sales: $150 million
Founded: In 1988 by Jeffrey Hollender in Burlington, Vermont.
CSR Claim to Fame: Since its founding, the company was designed to consider effects of its actions on the next seven generations. Seventh generation designs products with sustainability in mind. New benchmarks have been established for ethical and sustainable corporate behavior. In 2011 the company was named *Leader for Change* by the United Nations and the Foundation for Social Change.
Quote from Company President: "We still aspire to be the company our founders envisioned 25 years ago; one that leads the world to more holistically organic ways of operating. We remain intent on being the strongest and clearest voice for consumer health and environmental issues."

wage earners, have caused some to deride the capitalist system as a propagator of the country's economic woes, the exploitation of workers, and a whole range of other abuses. In response to this, the **Conscious Capitalism** movement offers an alternate perspective. In their 2013 book, *Conscious Capitalism: Liberating the Heroic Spirit of Capitalism*, author John Mackey, founder of Whole Foods, and Raj Sisodia, marketing professor, explore the benefits of the free-enterprise capitalist system. "In the long arc of history, no human creation has had a greater impact on more people more rapidly than free enterprise capitalism. It is unquestionably the greatest system for social cooperation that has ever existed."[18] While advocating the vast good promoted by capitalism, the conscious capitalism movement acknowledges that corporations have a greater interconnectedness to society than ever before; therefore, they have a corresponding obligation to be more conscious in their decision making. We will use the experience of Whole Foods to explore the tenets of conscious capitalism.

When John Mackey founded SaferWay, Inc. (a health conscious supermarket that would eventually become Whole Foods, Inc.) in 1978 at one location in Austin, Texas, he did so with the mission of promoting healthier food alternatives. In less than 30 years he turned a company that had begun with $45,000 in capital and initial annual sales of $250,000 into a company with annual sales of $5.6 billion, net profits of $200 million, and a market capitalization of $8 billion. Although Mackey's vision for his corporation has evolved over time, one constant has been Mackey's desire to serve the interest of all the stakeholders of the corporation. For Whole Foods this means engaging in activities that promote the company's core values, which are: (1) selling the highest-quality natural products available; (2) supporting

Snapshot of Tom's of Maine

Annual Sales: $30.7 million
Founded: In 1970 by Tom and Kate Chappell with an initial investment of $5,000 and a desire to manufacture personal care products that would not harm people or the environment.
CSR Claim to Fame: The company offered the first natural toothpaste in 1975 and the first natural deodorant in 1976. The company's Statement of Beliefs emphasizes respect for individuals and the environment, and the importance of developing good relationships with a variety of stakeholders.

---

[18]Mackey, John, and Sisodia, Raj, *Conscious Capitalism: Liberating the Heroic Spirit of Business* 11 (Harvard Business School 2013).

employee (team member) happiness; (3) satisfying customers; (4) creating profits and growth; and (5) caring about communities and the environment.[19]

The conscious corporation sees the various stakeholders of a business as interdependent and takes a holistic approach to creating a win-win situation for the various constituencies, including employees, suppliers, customers, the community, the environment, and investors. The Whole Food's model of stakeholder theory considers the effects of these relationships. By focusing on their core values and the interest of various stakeholders, Whole Foods has created a successful business model in which interactions with one stakeholder impact the other stakeholders. For example, the happiness of the Whole Food's employees (referred to as team members), helps to translate into satisfied customers who are likely to return. This, in turn, is good for the investors, making them more likely to continue to desire to engage in activities that contribute to team member happiness such as providing opportunities to engage in activities that benefit the local community. You should recognize that while the goal of Whole Foods and other conscious companies is to create win-win situations for all stakeholders, it is not always possible to simultaneously keep all stakeholders equally satisfied. It is the job of the conscious manager to continuously monitor how well a business is striking a balance between stakeholder interests and continuously adjust the business model as the situation demands.

The conscious capitalist believes that the corporation should not put profit motivation first, but rather should focus on fulfilling the corporate mission or purpose, and in turn, profits will follow. This favorable financial performance results from overall lower marketing costs, lower than industry average employee turnover (due to employee satisfaction), and lower administrative costs (e.g., keeping healthcare costs lower by investing in employee wellness programs).[20]

> ### An Ethical Insight: Lucien J. Dhooge
>
> "Although ethics, guidelines, codes of conduct, and more detailed policies are no panacea for unethical behavior, they may provide significant benefits for corporations. Such guidelines, codes, and policies may increase shareholder confidence, thereby motivating individuals and institutions to invest or increase their stake. Of particular significance is the role of such guidelines, codes, and policies in motivating socially responsible investors to act."
>
> *Source:* Dhooge, Lucien, J. *Creating a Course in Global Business Ethics: A Modest Proposal*, 212 Journal of Legal Studies in Business, 28:2 (2011). Dhooge is the Sue and John Staton Professor of Law at the College of Management of Georgia Institute of Technology.

Corporations: Being a Good Corporate Citizen

In Chapter 2, "Ethics in the Business Environment," you learned about the essential role of ethics in business decision making. Following the law is

---

[19]*Id.*
[20]Mackey, note 16.

generally considered the minimum standard of behavior. When faced with a decision and considering the various alternatives, a business executive must first ask "is the action legal?" If not, no further consideration should be given to that option. If the option is legal, the next question to consider is, "Is it ethical?" When faced with a variety of alternatives that are both legal and ethical, the business manager must then decide which course is best. And so, we turn back to Stanley's dilemma at the start of the chapter. You will recall that after many years of effort, Stanley's business is finally making a profit. Rather than simply paying these profits to the shareholders as dividends, Stanley is considering what other options might be available. Such options include a donation to the town library, an increase in employee compensation, or an increase in the cost of raw material by purchasing products that exceed safety standards from an environmentally conscious seller.

Let us think about the first questions we raised in this chapter:

Is the corporation required to take a specific course of action?
Must the shareholders' interest come first and dividends be paid?

Based on what you have read in this chapter you know that the answer to these questions is no. A specific course of action is not required, and Stanley is not under an obligation to pay a dividend. He might decide to pay a dividend, and this would of course be a legal and ethical course of action. One aid to Stanley as he guides corporate decision making is the corporation's mission statement. Does Stanley's Innovations, Inc., have a mission statement that indicates that not only will the corporation seek to derive a profit for investors, but in doing so it will act in a socially responsible manner? Keep in mind that even if Innovations, Inc., does not yet have a corporate mission statement that reflects a commitment to integrating socially responsible choices, the company is not precluded from doing so. Part of the strategic planning for a company requires continuous review of its mission statement and a responsiveness to changes in the society in which it operates.

The next question posed at the start of the chapter was

Is it permissible for the corporation to instead opt to increases wages, make a charitable contribution, or increase production costs?

Yes, as long as Stanley acts in accordance with his fiduciary duty to the company, his choice of action is permissible. Fiduciary duty is discussed more fully in Chapter 7, and Chapter 12, "Agency Law." Essentially, fiduciary duty is an obligation to act in the best interests of the company.

The final question posed at the start of the chapter was

What should the corporation do?

There is no uniform response to this question. This is a business decision, impacted by the wide range of variables that have been discussed in this chapter.

A short-term view might point Stanley in the direction of paying a dividend to the shareholders as the best way of ensuring they get the best return on their investment. This might make the company even more attractive to additional investors. A more long-range view may indicate that more value can be created by making the donation to the library and increasing the company's goodwill in the community. Perhaps it is best to spend more on the product by doing business with an environmentally conscious company, similar to Tom's of Maine, highlighted as a Snapshot on page 166. A sustainable product might be more attractive to consumers in the marketplace.

The Manager's Meeting asks you to think about the Always Safe Warehouse Storage Company's decision to make an environmentally sound investment in infrastructure. Many companies are considering ways to reduce their "carbon footprint" and are "going green" with solar panels and other natural alternative energy sources.

Manager's Compliance and Ethics Meeting

Reducing Carbon Footprints and Adequate Disclosure

At a cost of $2,000,000 the Always Safe Warehouse Storage Company can install solar panels in all of its 25 New England locations. The potential financial benefits include federal and state tax credits and rebates, and substantial savings on its electricity.

Until the panels are installed and a few years' history of their effectiveness is determined, no accurate findings can be made on the ultimate savings on electricity. The company's board of directors thinks this would also be a human relations bonus that could be used in its "going green" advertising campaigns and would, in the long run, increase its profitability. Some members of the board remain skeptical and want further investigation. The board has hired two reputable natural energy consulting firms to investigate the effectiveness of solar energy and the potential savings on electricity.

Their findings were contradictory with one firm providing positive results and the other extremely skeptical results primarily due to the lack of ongoing sunlight in New England during the winter months. The board of directors must make a decision on whether to move ahead with the solar panel project.

The chief compliance and ethics officer is arguing that because there are unknowns with regard to the cost effectiveness of the project, moving ahead with the solar panels could be an ethical violation of the board's fiduciary duty owed to the stockholders, as there is a risk the project may be ineffective. The board members want to start construction.

At this manager's meeting you are asked for ethical arguments that would either support or negate the board's position. Keep in mind both expert reports are equally credible. Applying ethical principles, offer the board your advice.

	IBM Corporation	
Action	**Motivation**	**Outcome**
IBM management, after the tsunami in Asia, quickly agreed to send both technology and expertise to the region to assess how to best meet the needs of the community.	Long-time IBM employee Sunil Raghavan proposed that IBM do something to help in relief and recovery efforts. He approached his manager with a request that IBM capabilities be used in the region.	IBM created system registries that would (1) track those missing or deceased; (2) collect records of nongovernmental organizations (NGOs), governments, and others offering relief goods and services; (3) locate individuals living in relief camps; and (4) record health and management incidents.

Exhibit 6.1. A SuperCorp Snapshot

Doing Well by Doing Good

Engaging in socially responsible behavior does not necessarily negatively impact corporate profits. In fact, there is evidence that socially conscious behavior may actually enhance shareholder value.

The SuperCorps

Rossabeth Moss Kanter, a professor at Harvard Business School, in her 2009 best-selling book entitled *SuperCorp: How Vanguard Companies Create Innovation, Profits, Growth, and Social Good*, describes a business model for companies that undertake initiatives to remedy social problems without a direct profit motive. (See snapshot in Exhibit 6.1.) As an example of such efforts, Ms. Kanter cites the work of IBM in response to the tsunami in Asia in December 2004. In an act of good corporate citizenship, IBM played an important role in relief and recovery efforts.

The Firms of Endearment

In preparation for their book, *Firms of Endearment*,[21] Professors Sisodia, Wolfe, and Sheth researched hundreds of companies, looking for those that were most admired by a variety of stakeholders who came into contact with them. The term "firms of endearment" is used for those companies that were identified as adopting a "stakeholder relationship management" business model. This model is one in which the management continually strives to

---

[21]Rajendra Sisodia, David Wolfe, and Jagdish Sheth, *Firms of Endearment: How World-Class Companies Profit from Passion and Purpose* (Wharton 2007).

In April, 2013 more than 70,000 Comcast volunteers participated in Comcast Cares Day, the nation's largest single-day corporate volunteer effort.

develop good relationships with not just the stockholders, but with all stakeholders including, employees, suppliers, and communities, with the belief that this will then translate into positive relationships with customers. Looking at the financial data for these firms of endearment, the authors discovered that over a ten-year period, these companies outperformed the Standard and Poor's and Dow Jones averages.

Exhibit 6.2 on page 172 provides a look at some of the socially responsible actions taken by some of the companies on the firms of endearment list.

The Evolution of the Hybrid Entity

In Chapter 7 you will learn that the corporation is a commonly utilized form of for-profit business. As has been explained in this chapter, there has been a long-standing difference of opinion on whether the corporate focus must be on shareholders or whether a broader stakeholder approach is permissible and perhaps, even, preferable.

State Constituency Statutes

Recall that state corporate constituency statutes allow a corporation to take a variety of stakeholders into account when making business decisions. Keep in mind that even though these statutes allow the stakeholders to be taken into account, they do not *require* such consideration. So, in that sense, they are not specifically promoting socially responsible behavior but rather simply

Starbucks has been recognized for its commitment to corporate social responsibility.

Exhibit 6.2. Highlights of Actions by Selected Firms of Endearment

Company	Actions
Starbucks	Maintains Farmers Support Centers to work with farmers to help improve both the quality and productivity of their crops.
	Sponsors a Global Month of Service to mobilize employees and customers to perform acts of community service.
	In 2012, 93 percent of Starbuck's coffee was ethically sourced.
UPS	In 2012 the UPS Foundation awarded $5.5 million in grants to nonprofit organizations that promote community safety through humanitarian relief efforts and safety initiatives.
	Developed Logistic Action Teams to help humanitarian relief efforts enhance their capabilities before and during disasters.
New Balance	Established a responsible leadership program to focus on a safe and healthy work environment, improving environmental sustainability, and providing support to local communities in which the company operates.
	Since 2004, the New Balance Foundation has contributed more than $50 million to a variety of causes.

providing corporate decision makers with the greatest possible latitude. These statutes along with the business judgment rule, which will be discussed in Chapter 7, help to insulate corporate officers and directors from personal liability to shareholders for their business decisions. Recall that W.D. Ross's prima facie "duty of beneficence" has been defined as a moral duty to enhance the well-being of others. Constituency statutes that allow directors to craft business strategy that includes the well-being of the stakeholders follow Ross's moral "duty of beneficence" and contribute to maintaining an ethical corporate culture. This strategy should enhance a corporation's market value as investors perceive it as a profitable socially responsible company.

B-Lab

B-Lab was formed in 2006 by three friends, Andrew Kassoy, Jay Coen Gilbert, and Bart Houlahan, with the goal of helping entrepreneurs to use business to address both social and environmental concerns. **B-Lab** proposed the idea of certifying corporations as B Corporations if the corporation creates a general public benefit as measured by an independent third-party standard and also meets other performance benchmarks set by B-Lab to ensure that the company is meeting specific social and environmental performance standards. The companies must also submit to periodic audits.[22] In 2013, there were over 742 Certified B Corporations doing business in over 60 industries, in 26 countries.[23] These include companies such as the King Arthur Flour Company, which focuses on four core areas: environment, employees, products, and community. The company provides employees 40 hours of paid time off to volunteer and organizes companywide community service outings. Keep in mind that a B Corporation is essentially a company that has been certified as socially responsible, and it does not represent a new type of entity. However, one of the stated goals has been to encourage states to adopt a new form of corporation that would have a stated goal of stakeholder over shareholder; therefore, B Lab was actively involved in the adoption of Benefit Corporation legislation in the states.

Benefit Corporations

Beginning in 2010, state legislatures began to take the notion of corporate social responsibility a bit further, recognizing a new form of doing business which would *require* the corporate directors to take a broad range of stakeholders into account in corporate decision making, including, but not limited to, the community, employees, and consumers. This corporate form of business, called the Benefit Corporation, is called a hybrid entity because it not only has a profit motive but must also have the dual consideration of making a

[22]benefitcorp.net
[23]B Corporation, 2012 Annual Report (2012).

positive impact on society. Maryland was the first state to pass Benefit Corporation legislation in April 2010, and since that time almost half of the states have followed suit and continue to do so.

Purpose of a Benefit Corporation

The purpose of a Benefit Corporation is to have a "material, positive impact on society and the environment." Benefit Corporations may also opt to fulfill stated, additional, more specific purposes such as improving health, protecting the environment, etc. Language is included in the Benefit Corporation's organizing document which requires the directors to consider the interests of a variety of stakeholders. For example, South Carolina's Benefit Corporation statute requires that corporate directors consider the interests of stakeholders when making business decisions, including (1) the shareholders, (2) employees of the benefit corporation and the employees of its subsidiaries and suppliers, (3) customers, (4) community and societal factors, (5) local and global government, and (6) the short- and long-term interests of the benefit corporation.[24]

Model Benefit Corporation Legislation

Exhibit 6.3 highlights the general aspects of Benefit Corporation statutes. As you read through these provisions, keep in mind that states may choose to adopt legislation that deviates from the provisions contained in the model legislation.

Exhibit 6.3. Highlights of Model Legislation
Corporate Purposes
Create a general public benefit as measured by a third-party standard
Right to name a specific benefit
Creation of public benefit in best interest of the corporation
Accountability
Director's duty — make decisions in the best interest of the corporation
Director's duty — consider effects on stakeholders
Independent Benefit Director to attest board acted in accordance with duties
Transparency
Annual benefit report published in accordance with third-party standards
Annual Report delivered to shareholders and Secretary of State and published on the company's website.
Right of Action
Only shareholders and directors have a right of action
Right of action for violation of duty (purpose or standard of conduct)

Source: Benefit Corporation: Model Legislation: http://benefitcorp.net/storage/documents/Model_Benefit_Corporation_Legislation.doc

---

[24]S.C. Code of Laws § 33-38-400.

The hybrid corporate entity provides social-minded entrepreneurs with the unquestioned latitude to put social mission and consideration of stakeholders ahead of the financial bottom line for shareholders.

Global Perspective: International Guidelines

Although many governments around the world encourage corporate social responsibility, the notion of corporate awareness and a sense of obligation to the community in which it operates is not legally mandated. Strides taken by corporations to be good corporate citizens in the marketplace and in the world are taken voluntarily by corporations. That said, there have been steps taken by international organizations and governing bodies to provide guidance and support. Multinational companies seeking international guidance on Corporate Social Responsibility can look to the various internationally recognized principles and guidelines, including the following:

- OECD Guidelines for Multinational Enterprises
- The UN Global Compact
- The ISO 26000 Guidance Standard on Social Responsibility
- The ILO Tri-partite Declaration of Principles Concerning Multinational Enterprises and Social Policy

OECD Guidelines for Multinational Enterprises

The Organisation for Economic Co-operation and Development (OECD) promotes policies that encourage economic and social well-being worldwide. The OECD guidelines "are the most comprehensive set of government-backed recommendations on responsible business conduct in existence today."[25] First adopted in 1976, the guidelines are continually updated to keep up with changes in the global economy. The most recent changes were implemented in May 2011. The stated goals of the guidelines are to promote corporate contributions to social, economic, and environmental progress. The guidelines have been adopted by 42 governments committed to their implementation, including the United States, China, Israel, Canada, and Turkey, to name a few. Although a complete review of the guidelines is beyond the scope of this text, Exhibit 6.4 on page 176 illustrates some of the policies promoted by the guidelines.

The UN Global Compact

The UN Global Compact is a policy for businesses that are committed to aligning their operations with universally accepted principles in the areas of labor, environment, human rights, and anticorruption. "The Global Compact asks companies to

---

[25]OECD Guidelines for Multinational Enterprises, http://mneguidelines.oecd.org/.

embrace universal principles and to partner with the United Nations. It has grown to become a critical platform for the UN to engage effectively with enlightened global business."[26] Eight thousand companies in 140 countries have already committed to the UN Global Compact, which means committing to a principles-based management and operations approach. Exhibit 6.5 represents the ten principles of the UN Global Compact.

ISO 26000:2010 Guidance Standards on Social Responsibility

The International Organization for Standardization (ISO) has members from 163 national standards bodies from countries worldwide. The ISO is the world's largest developer of international standards. The ISO has members from 163 countries and over 600 international and regional organizations. ISO Guidance Standards were first announced in 2010 after five years of negotiations between many different stakeholders globally. This included representatives from government, NGOs, industry, consumer groups, and labor organizations. The ISO is considered to represent an international consensus that clarifies what social responsibility is, helps

---

Exhibit 6.4. Highlights of the OECD Model Guidelines

OECD Guidelines encourage enterprises to:

1. Contribute to sustainable, environmental, and social progress with a view to achieving sustainable development.

2. Respect the human rights of those affected by corporate activities.

3. Encourage local development through close cooperation with the local community.

4. Encourage human capital formation by creating employment opportunities.

5. Refrain from seeking or accepting exemptions from statutory or regulatory rules governing human rights, environment, health, safety, labor, tax, incentives, or other issues.

6. Develop and apply good corporate governance practices.

7. Refrain from taking disciplinary or discriminatory action against employees who blow the whistle on illegal corporate practices.

8. Seek to avoid adverse impacts from its activities.

9. Encourage business partners, including suppliers and contractors, to apply the principles of responsible business conduct.

10. Engage with stakeholders to allow their views to be taken into account when planning projects that significantly impact local communities.

11. Abstain from improper involvement in local politics.

12. Support promotion of Internet freedom.

13. Encourage social dialogue on responsible supply chain management.

Source: OECD Guidelines for Multinational Enterprises revised May 2011. www.oecd.org/daf/inv/mne/48004323.pdf.

---

[26] Comment by UN Secretary-General Ban Ki-Moon, http://www.unglobalcompact.org/.

Exhibit 6.5. Ten Principles of the UN Global Compact

1. Business should support and respect the protection of internationally proclaimed human rights.

2. Business should make sure they are not complicit in human rights abuses.

3. Businesses should uphold the freedom of association and the effective recognition of the right to collective bargaining.

4. Businesses should uphold the elimination of all forms of compulsory labor.

5. Businesses should uphold the effective abolition of child labor.

6. Businesses should uphold the elimination of discrimination in respect of employment and occupation.

7. Businesses should support a precautionary approach to environmental challenges.

8. Businesses should undertake initiatives to promote greater environmental responsibility.

9. Businesses should encourage the development and diffusion of environmentally friendly technologies.

10. Businesses should work against corruption in all its forms, including extortion and bribery.

---

businesses translate principles into action, and is used to share best practices relating to social responsibility. The core subjects addressed by the ISO are listed in Exhibit 6.6.

In September 2013, representatives from 128 countries met in St. Petersburg, Russia, to discuss ways to make the standard development simpler and better able to meet the demand of today's world. It is likely that modifications to the ISO Guidelines will be announced in the near future as a result of this collaboration.

The ILO Tripartite Declaration of Principles Concerning Multinational Enterprises and Social Policy

The International Labour Organization (ILO) was founded in 1919. It became a specialized agency of the United Nations in 1946. Its mission is to promote social justice and human and labor rights internationally. Its Declaration of Principles Concerning Multinational Enterprises and Social Policy was adopted in 2006 to offer

---

Exhibit 6.6. Core Subjects Addressed in ISO 26000:2010 Guidelines

1. Human Rights

2. Labor Practices

3. The Environment

4. Fair Operating Practices

5. Consumer Issues

6. Community Involvement and Development

7. Organizational Governance

Source: ISO 26000:2010 Guidelines, www.iso.org/iso/home/standards/iso26000.htm.

Exhibit 6.7. ILO Principles	
Principle	**Some of the Actions Encouraged**
Employment	Promotion of full, productive, and freely chosen employment. Corporations should keep their manpower plans in harmony with national social development policies. Policies should promote equality of opportunity and be designed to correct any historical patterns of discrimination.
Training	Corporations should support programs to encourage skill formation and development and support vocational guidance. Relevant training should be available to all employees.
Conditions of work and life	Employers should provide the best possible wages, benefits, and working conditions within the framework of government policies. Corporations should cooperate with international organizations working on the adoption of international safety and health standards.
Industrial relations	Workers should have the freedom to organize and bargain collectively.

guidelines in the areas of employment, training, conditions of work and life, and industrial relations. It recognizes the vital role multinational enterprises play in the process of social and economic globalization. Exhibit 6.7 illustrates some of the key principles advocated by the ILO.

The above has given you a sense of global framework that encourages and supports greater actions by corporations of all sizes to practice good corporate citizenship. A closer look at activities in the European Union will give you an idea of how CSR principles are being implemented.

Global Perspective: The European Union

The European Union Commission released a new policy on Corporate Social Responsibility in October 2011 which defines corporate social responsibility as "the responsibility of enterprises for their impacts on society." In order to meet this responsibility, business are expected to "have in place a process to integrate social, environmental, ethical, human rights, and consumer concerns into their business operations and core strategy in close collaboration with their stakeholders, with the aim of: (1) maximizing the creation of shared value for their owners/shareholders and for their other stakeholders and society at large and (2) identifying, preventing, and mitigating their possible adverse impacts." The Commission views these corporation actions as those that are "over and above" the company's legal obligations.

Exhibit 6.8. Europe's 2020 Initiatives

Initiative	Relationship to CSR
Integrated Industrial Policy for the Globalisation Era	Policy communication from the European Commission that proposes a new approach to industry in the EU, one that, among other things, helps enable the transition to efficient use of resources and a low-carbon economy.
European Platform Against Poverty and Social Exclusion	Launched in 2012, this initiative has proposed that 20 percent of the European Social Fund be earmarked for fighting poverty and social exclusion. The initiative also calls for enhancing coordination among EU countries and a more effective working relationship with civil society.
Agenda for New Skills and Jobs	Designed to help the EU reach a 75 percent employment target by 2020.
Youth on the Move	Policy initiatives on education and employment for young people, with a focus on training and other measures designed to aid in the transition from education to work.
Single Market Act	As part of this initiative, businesses interested in not only profit, but also social, ethical, or environmental development will be encouraged.
Innovation Union	This will enhance the ability of businesses to address societal challenges.

The Commission recognizes that it is through social responsibility that businesses will be able to build trust with their stakeholders. This, in turn, will foster a business environment of innovation and growth. Exhibit 6.8 summarizes those initiatives that are part of Europe's 2020 initiatives that reference CSR.

Although strides are being made in the advancement of corporate social responsibility, only about 15 of the EU member states have national policies that promote CSR, and many European companies have not yet integrated social concerns into their core strategy.

Summary

Shareholder and stakeholder interests are not necessarily in conflict when it comes to corporate decision making. While there is one long-standing school of thought that the sole purpose of a corporation is to generate profit for its investors, there is another school of thought that takes a broader view of a corporation's duty to all stakeholders impacted by its actions. Financial performance of socially conscious firms suggests that corporations committed to corporate social responsibility do not necessarily do so at the expense of the shareholder. In fact, being a good corporate citizen may indeed enhance shareholder value. Corporate social responsibility has become a global concept as corporations in the global marketplace increasingly play a role in bringing about social change and improvement.

Questions for Review

1. Corporate purpose

This chapter refers to an article by Professor Dodd in which he asks, "For whom are corporate managers trustees?" How would you respond to this question and why?

2. Constituency statutes

Explain the purpose of state constituency statutes and how they might aid a corporation's efforts to engage in socially conscious behavior.

3. Ethical considerations

Pharmaceutical Company manufactures one of the most widely used diabetes medicines in the United States and Asia. Recently, the Food and Drug Administration has been receiving an increasing number of complaints from consumers about the extensive amount of long-term side effects they have started to experience as a result of the drug. After reevaluating the drug, the FDA determined that this drug is no longer to be considered safe and has banned its sale in the United States. Because the authority of the FDA extends only to sales in the United States, Pharmaceutical Company remains able to continue to sell the drug in Asia. Applying ethical principles, decide whether the company should continue to do so. How, if at all, would your answer be impacted by the fact that Pharmaceutical Company has been the only Pharmaceutical Company willing to sell a diabetes drug at a discounted price in Asia to enable low income individuals to afford medication to help manage their disease?

4. Stakeholder theory

A friend has asked you for help. She is an entrepreneur and would like to start a company to pursue her dream of manufacturing and selling a new and improved lawn mower. She has heard of the term "stakeholder theory" and would like you to explain some practical steps she can take to apply stakeholder theory in her new company.

5. Firms of endearment

What might account for the fact that, on average, the investor return provided by the firms of endearment exceeded that of the Standard and Poor's and Dow Jones averages?

6. Researching CSR

Choose one of the companies you regularly patronize (e.g., the Gap, Oakley, etc.). Using information contained on the company website along with news sources, assess the extent to which the company engages in socially responsible behavior. If a company is very active in this regard, you may choose to focus on its activities in one area (e.g., environmental issues).

7. Benefit corporations

Critics of the new hybrid benefit corporation have suggested that there is no need for benefit corporation laws because corporations are already permitted to operate with a corporate social responsibility purpose. Do you agree with this sentiment? Explain why or why not.

8. International perspective

The UN Global Compact is a voluntary initiative. Explain why a company or business enterprise that already has a code of conduct in place might also decide to pledge participation in the Global Compact.

Further Reading

Bantekas, Ilias, *Corporate Social Responsibility in International Law*, 22 Boston University International Law Journal 309 (2009).

Carroll, Archie B., Lipartito, Kenneth J. Post, James E., Werhane, Patricia H., and Goodpaster, Kenneth E., eds., *Corporate Responsibility: the American Experience* (Cambridge University Press 2012).

Freeman, R. Edward, *Strategic Management: A Stakeholder Approach* (Pitman 1984).

Kanter, Rossabeth Moss, *SuperCorp: How Vanguard Companies Create Innovation, Profits, Growth, and Social Good* (Crown Business, 2009).

Mackey, John, and Sisodia, Raj, *Conscious Capitalism: Liberating the Heroic Spirit of Business* (Harvard Business School 2013).

Wallman, Steven, *Understanding the Purpose of a Corporation, an Introduction*, Journal of Corporation Law 807 (1999).

PART II

The Business

CHAPTER 7

Business Organizations

Chapter Objectives

1. To know the primary types of legal structures used by business organizations
2. To understand the advantages and disadvantages of each type of legal structure
3. To understand the business, legal, and tax reasons for selecting one legal structure over another
4. To know the circumstances under which creditors may pierce the veil of a corporation or a limited liability company
5. To understand the nature and purpose of the business judgment rule, the rights of minority shareholders in a closely held corporation, and the rights of shareholders to initiate derivative lawsuits

Practical Example: Green Earth Foods Company*

Amy founded Green Earth Foods Company, Inc. (Green Earth) in 1970, shortly after the first Earth Day in April 1970. Amy's philosophy about life and business has influenced the policies and management practices of Green Earth since the inception of the company. Over the past 40 years, the company has grown from two employees to 150. Its product line of organic foods has expanded from three products to more than 50. Green Earth purchases and sells certified organic foods to restaurants. Located in western Massachusetts, the company's customer list has grown from three local restaurants to approximately 200 dispersed throughout the six New England states.

The company's mission statement asserts that it preserves the earth's natural resources, promotes a healthy lifestyle, and treats all individuals with dignity and respect. Green Earth prides itself on providing customers with the healthiest foods that the planet has to offer. The company's promotional literature states that its food products contain no artificial ingredients or chemicals and are grown using processes that sustain the environment.

Green Earth boasts of using methods to package its food products in ways that elevate the safety and protection of the environment. For example, all products are packaged with 100 percent recycled materials using a custom-molded technique that minimizes the use of wrapping and covering materials. The management of Green Earth believes in encouraging all of its customers to develop environmentally friendly buying behaviors. Management recognizes and appreciates that this approach is good for the environment and good for business. With an increasing awareness among informed consumers that packaging accounts for approximately one-third of all nonindustrial waste in the United States, management hopes to attract new customers by promoting and advertising its healthy food options and the environmentally friendly way it packages all food products.

Green Earth is a closely held corporation. Amy, the founder and chief executive officer (CEO), owns 51 percent of Green Earth's outstanding common stock. Jeffrey, the chief financial officer (CFO), has a 24 percent stake in the company. Jeffrey has been employed by Green Earth since 1973; Allison, Green Earth's chief operating officer (COO), holds 15 percent of Green Earth's outstanding stock. She joined the company in 1993. Mark, the chief marketing officer (CMO), owns the remaining 10 percent of the stock. Mark has been an employee of Green Earth since 2005. These four individuals represent the management team of Green Earth Foods Company. Their individual salaries for the most recent year are presented in Figure 1.

Figure 1: Salaries of Green Earth's Management Team

Employee Name	Position	Salary
Amy	CEO	$450,000
Jeffrey	CFO	$275,000
Allison	COO	$225,000
Mark	CMO	$160,000

Over the past six months, Amy and the board of directors of Green Earth have expressed interest in exploring the possibility of selling some of the real estate owned by Green Earth. The company owns 37 acres of land in western Massachusetts. Roughly seven acres of the 37 have been developed by Green Earth and converted into a small commercial park for its three buildings: an office building, a processing plant, and a warehouse. The remaining 30 acres are composed of undeveloped fields and woodland. Amy and the board believe that some portion of the undeveloped land could be sold and used for additional commercial development.

With the consent of the board, Amy approached several commercial developers. After concluding detailed discussions with each developer, Amy decided to open preliminary negotiations with Big Mountain Commercial Developers, Inc. After several rounds of negotiations, a plan was developed whereby Amy would purchase 15 acres of land from Green Earth in her own name. She would then sell the land to Big Mountain. Because of her concern about a possible conflict of interest, Amy asked the chair of the board to sign the contract on behalf of Green Earth for the sale of 15 acres of land to her. In turn, Amy signed a contract in her personal capacity for the sale of the same land to Big Mountain. Amy paid Green Earth an amount significantly above the price Green Earth paid for the land 20 years earlier. The sale generated a profit of $140,000 for Green Earth. Amy sold the land to Big Mountain for a price equal to its current fair market value, which generated a $70,000 profit for Amy.

The minority shareholders of Green Earth (Jeffrey, Allison, and Mark) became aware of the real estate transactions after reading about them in the local newspaper. Because Amy resold the land previously owned by Green Earth for a personal profit of $70,000, the minority shareholders questioned the logic of selling the land first to Amy. In response, the chair of the board told the minority shareholders that the land was originally owned by Amy in her personal capacity and that she sold the land to Green Earth at a discounted price 20 years ago. Therefore, as majority shareholder, Amy informed the board that she would not agree to sell the land to Big Mountain unless she first recaptured her loss on the original sale of the land to Green Mountain. The board reasoned that it would be in the best interest of Green Mountain to sell the land to Amy and earn a profit of $140,000 for Green Mountain as opposed to no sale (or profit) at all. Unconvinced by the board's response, the minority shareholders are considering a legal action to recover their share of the $70,000 profit earned by Amy. The minority shareholders question the ethics and the business judgment of Amy and the board.

---

*Green Earth Foods Company is a fictitious company developed by the authors to demonstrate and illustrate key legal and ethical concepts, theories, practices, and strategies.

The preceding example illustrates the types of questions that may arise when selecting a legal structure for a business and the issues that often surface after a particular structure has been chosen. For example, the minority shareholders (Jeffrey, Alison, and Mark) believe that Amy and the board may have mistreated them in the way they handled the planning and selling of the 15-acre tract of land owned by Green Earth. They believe Amy and the board may have violated their rights as minority shareholders and may have engaged in unethical behavior. As you read the materials presented in the chapter, return to the Green Earth Foods Company illustration to examine these and other issues raised by the facts.

Different types of legal entities exist under state law to accommodate the needs of business owners. As we examine these entities, keep in mind that one type of entity is not necessarily better or worse than another. Deciding which type of legal structure to adopt depends on the purpose and goals of an individual or group of individuals who want to start a business. This chapter explores the characteristics of the main types of business organizations available to entrepreneurs and established enterprises.

Sole Proprietorship

If a person is thinking about starting a business, what is the simplest and least expensive way of getting started? The answer is easy—a sole proprietorship. What is a sole proprietorship? To help answer this question, think of the word *proprietor*. A proprietor is someone who has legal title to property, such as a business. We commonly use the phrase **sole proprietorship** to define a business structure where one person owns "property" in the form of a business enterprise. Think of a sole proprietorship as a "single-person" business entity.

In a sole proprietorship, one person is responsible for the affairs of the business. This person is the owner, the manager, and the person who enjoys the profits and losses of the business. Because the person and the business are "one and the same" in a sole proprietorship, the business does not have a legal identity separate from the person (the owner). This point was reinforced by the Texas Supreme Court in a case involving an accident and a sole proprietor by the name of Thompson:

> At the time of the accident, Thompson [a party to the lawsuit] was the owner and operator of a sole proprietorship known as Blue Streak Welding Service. There were no other persons involved in this venture, and it had no employees. Blue Streak Welding Service was, in law and in fact, *one and the same* as Thompson because a sole proprietorship has a legal existence only in the identity of the sole proprietor.[1] [Emphasis added.]

Although simple, the consequence of a single-person entity is that the owner is personally liable for the debts of the business. This exposure of personal assets to the creditors of the business represents one of the most significant disadvantages to organizing a business as a sole proprietorship.

On the other hand, a sole proprietorship has its advantages. For example, because a sole proprietorship does not have a separate legal existence, it is not required to file a tax return. Rather, the owner reports the profits and losses of the proprietorship on her personal tax return. Property used by the proprietorship remains in the name of the owner. Thus, the expense of transferring legal title from one entity to another is avoided. The owner may use his or her personal bank account for both personal affairs and the business affairs of the proprietorship. Consequently, the owner need not worry about comingling personal funds and business funds. As we will see later in the chapter, the comingling of personal and business funds is a major issue for businesses organized as a corporation or limited liability company.

A sole proprietorship is allowed to use a business or trade name different from the name of the owner. For example, assume that Sarah Smith owns and operates a consulting firm, which is organized as a sole proprietorship. Sarah could refer to her consulting business as *Sarah Smith Consulting*. Alternatively, if Sarah wished to call her consulting business a different name, such as *Brownstone Consulting*, state law allows her to use the alternative name as long as it is not being used by another entity operating within the same state.

Operating a business as a sole proprietorship does not require the preparation of a written document or any other kind of organizational formalities. Consequently, the sole proprietorship form of business organization serves as a

---

[1]*Ideal Lease Service, Inc. v. Amoco Production Co., Inc.*, 662 S.W.2d 951 (1983).

kind of de facto organizational structure when a business owner has not under-taken the steps necessary to form an alternative type of entity such as a cor-poration. For instance, in the Green Earth Foods Company example, if Amy had not formed a corporation (or some other form of legal structure), Green Earth Foods would, by default, take the form of a sole proprietorship with Amy as the sole owner of the business.

General Partnership

A **general partnership** provides the simplest organizational structure for start-ing a business when two or more individuals decide to associate for the purpose of owning and operating a business. Like a sole proprietorship, a general part-nership is not legally separate from its owners (partners). Consequently, part-ners are personally liable for the debts of the partnership. Unlimited personal liability represents one of the major disadvantages of organizing a business in the form of a general partnership.

Similar to what we learned about sole proprietorships, the personal affairs of the partners need not be separate from the business affairs of the partner-ship. For example, property used by the partnership can remain in the individual names of the partners. Personal bank accounts may be used to con-summate partnership transactions. The comingling of personal funds and part-nership funds is permissible, although such practices may not be wise from a management and control perspective. In many respects, a general partnership and a sole proprietorship share common attributes. The key difference, of course, is that one person owns and operates a sole proprietorship, and two or more persons own and operate a general partnership.

A general partnership allows two or more individuals to join forces in pursuit of a common business objective.

Forming a general partnership does not require the preparation of a written document. A general partnership can exist when two or more people decide to "join forces" in pursuit of a common set of goals. An oral arrangement suffices to establish a general partnership. Like a sole proprietorship, a general partnership is the de facto legal entity when two or more people decide to start a business and take no other affirmative steps to establish an alternative entity. For example, an alternative legal entity could take the form of a limited partnership, a limited liability company, or a corporation. However, establishing these entities requires the owners to prepare and file relevant legal forms with state agencies.

A partnership is classified as a "pass-through" entity. As a **pass-through entity**, a partnership is a nontaxable entity. This means its profits and losses are reported on the partners' individual tax returns (IRS Form 1040). Essentially, the taxable income of the partnership is treated as the income of the partners. Although they do not pay taxes, partnerships are required to file a tax return, which is essentially an information return. A partnership tax return discloses the revenue earned by the partnership and reports the various deductible expenses. However, the partnership tax return does not calculate a tax liability, as the tax liability is passed through to the partners and disclosed on an IRS tax form known as a "K-1." The partners attach Form K-1 to their individual tax return and pay the relevant tax liability.

While a partnership may be simple to form, it is generally more expensive to operate than a sole proprietorship. Because partnerships are required to prepare and file a separate tax return, even though partnerships are not subject to taxation, an accountant is usually hired to prepare the tax return. Partnership taxation laws and regulations are complex. To enable the accountant to prepare an accurate and complete partnership tax return, the books and records of the partnership must be properly maintained and supported by a system of internal controls. Satisfying these legal requirements adds to the administrative cost of operating a partnership. Another cost of forming and operating a general partnership relates to the managerial need for a written partnership agreement. Even though a written agreement is not required by law, good management practices dictate that a written agreement be prepared with the assistance of an attorney. The agreement then serves as the roadmap for directing the affairs and operations of the partnership. The Case Illustration demonstrates the importance of preparing a comprehensive written **partnership agreement**.

Because partnership agreements are not prescribed by law, they vary in form, structure, and content. However, a partnership agreement typically addresses how profits and losses will be shared among the partners, how management decisions will be made by the partners, and how the value of an existing partner's interest will be determined. Partnership agreements provide a set of guidelines for running the business on a day-to-day basis. Exhibit 7.1 on page 192 summarizes the major components of a typical partnership agreement.

Case Illustration

The question in this case was whether a partnership had been formed based on the following facts and circumstances. Fenwick owned a beauty shop. He employed Chesire to work as a cashier and reception clerk at a salary of $15 per week. Later on, Chesire requested an increase in her salary. Fenwick agreed to pay Chesire an increase, but only if the income of the business warranted it. Fenwick and Chesire then entered into a written agreement, the terms of which follow:

- The parties agree to form a partnership.
- The business shall be the operation of the beauty shop.
- The name of the business shall be United Beauty Shoppe.
- No capital investment shall be made by Chesire.
- The control and management of the business shall be vested in Fenwick.
- Chesire is to act as cashier and reception clerk at a salary of $15 per week and a bonus at the end of the year of 20 percent of the net profits, if the business warrants it.
- As between the partners, Fenwick alone is to be liable for debts of the partnership.
- Both parties shall devote all their time to the business.
- The books are to be open for inspection by each party.
- The salary of Fenwick is to be $50 per week and at the end of the year he is to receive 80 percent of the profits.
- The partnership shall continue until either party gives ten days' notice of termination.

The court noted that several elements come into play when determining the existence or nonexistence of a partnership. The first element is the intention of the parties. The court found that the agreement itself provided evidence of the intention of the parties to form a partnership; however, the court stated that this evidence alone was not conclusive. The second element

of partnership is the right to share in profits. Here, the court found that this right clearly existed based on the terms of the agreement. The third element is the obligation to share in losses, which the court found to be absent as the agreement provided that Chesire is not to share in the losses.

The fourth element is the ownership and control of the partnership property and business. Based on the agreement, the court determined that Fenwick alone contributed all the capital and that Chesire had no right to share in the capital of the business upon dissolution. Furthermore, Fenwick reserved to himself control of the business. The fifth element relates to community of power in administration. Here, the court found that Fenwick retained exclusive control of the management of the business; Chesire had no power to control the business. The sixth element is the language of the agreement itself. The court noted that although the parties call themselves partners and the business a partnership, the language used in the agreement excludes Chesire from most of the ordinary rights of a partner.

The seventh element is evidence of how the parties conduct themselves when dealing with third parties. The court observed that the business filed a partnership tax return and Fenwick and Chesire held themselves out as partners when dealing with the defendant. However, to no other third parties did they hold themselves out as partners. Based on this evidence, the court determined the conduct of the parties did not support a finding that they were partners. The eighth element is the rights of the parties on dissolution of the partnership. Here, the court found that Chesire had no rights to partnership property after leaving the business. Her salary simply ended, and Fenwick would carry on with normal operations of the business.

Based on all the facts and circumstances, giving due effect to the written agreement, the court determined that a partnership between Fenwick and Chesire had not been established. Furthermore, the court found that the agreement between Fenwick and Chesire was nothing more than a method of compensating Chesire for the work she had been performing as an employee. Chesire had no authority or control in operating the business, she was not subject to losses, and she was not effectively held out as a partner. Chesire received nothing from the agreement beyond a new arrangement for determining her wages. *Fenwick v. Unemployment Compensation Commission*, 44 A.2d 172 (1945).

Exhibit 7.1. Components of a Partnership Agreement

Component	Description
Ownership interest	The law presumes that partners have an equal ownership stake in the partnership. If, however, the partners wish to have an unequal ownership arrangement, a partnership agreement can describe the various interests. For example, if X invests $100,000 in the partnership, Y invests $200,000, and Z invests $300,000, the partnership agreement could specify that X has a 1/6 ownership interest, Y has a 2/6 ownership interest, and Z has a 3/6 ownership interest.
Sharing of profits and losses	Without a partnership agreement, the law presumes that partners share profits and losses equally. However, a partnership agreement could provide that partner A, who works 40 hours a week in the partnership, will receive two thirds of the profits and losses while B, who works 20 hours a week in the partnership, will receive one third of profits and losses.
Managerial decision making	Without a partnership agreement, the law presumes that the partners share equally in the decision-making process. Thus, each partner has an equal vote. However, a partnership agreement could provide for a different decision-making arrangement. For example, if partner X has invested twice as much capital in the partnership compared to partner Y, the partnership agreement could provide for X to have two "votes" and Y one "vote."
Partnership valuation	If a partner decides to leave the partnership, that person will expect to receive an appropriate amount of money for his or her ownership interest. When this occurs, the remaining partners typically buy the ownership interest of the departing partner. What price will the remaining partners be willing to pay for the departing partner's interest? If the partnership agreement does not prescribe a fixed price or a method for calculating the price, a major dispute may arise, causing disruption of partnership operations and the incurrence of significant legal fees. These problems can be avoided by including in the partnership agreement a clear methodology for determining the purchase price of the departing partner's ownership interest.
Partnership dissolution	If partners agree to terminate the partnership, a dissolution of the partnership will occur, and the assets of the partnership will be divided equally among the partners unless the partnership agreement calls for a different allocation.

Limited Partnership

Because limited partnerships share many of the same features as general partnerships, this section of the chapter focuses on some of the differences between the two types of partnerships. Like other artificial entities, state law authorizes the formation of limited partnerships and provides legal guidance for their operations. Limited partnerships provide a legal structure that has characteristics of both a corporation and a general partnership. Two classes of partners comprise a limited partnership: general partners and limited partners.

Like a general partnership, the **general partners** of a limited partnership have unlimited liability and responsibility for managing the business. On the other hand, **limited partners** have limited liability and no responsibility for managing the partnership. The financial exposure for limited partners is restricted to their capital investment in the partnership. If limited partners participate in the management of the partnership, they risk being reclassified as general partners. This situation should be avoided, as general partners have unlimited liability.

Unlike a general partnership, statutory provisions in most states require the preparation of a written partnership agreement to support the creation of a limited partnership. Limited partnerships do not enjoy the same level of popularity as corporations and limited liability companies. The lack of popularity is due in part to the cost of complying with state and federal laws. For example, at the state level, starting and maintaining a limited partnership can be as costly, if not more costly, than starting and maintaining a corporation.

Limited Liability Partnership (LLP)

A **limited liability partnership** operates like a general partnership except state statutes provide that non-negligent partners are not liable for the negligent conduct of another partner. Equally, a partner is not liable for the negligent conduct of an employee of the firm, unless the employee is under the direct supervision of a partner. Thus, the personal assets of non-negligent partners are insulated from the party injured by a negligent partner. All 50 states have enacted some form of limited liability partnership statutes. The most common users of LLPs are accounting firms and law firms.

Limited Liability Company (LLC)

State statutes authorize the formation of **limited liability companies** to operate as unincorporated entities with legal identities separate and distinct from their members. In 1977 Wyoming became the first state to recognize LLCs as a legal structure for operating a business; now all 50 states have statutes authorizing LLCs.

Characteristics of an LLC

Limited liability companies possess characteristics of both partnerships and corporations. Like a partnership, an LLC is a pass-though entity for tax purposes. Many businesspeople find this feature particularly appealing because of the avoidance of double taxation. On the other hand, members of LLCs enjoy limited liability as do the shareholders of a corporation. Where owners of a corporation are called shareholders, the owners of an LLC are referred to as members. In most states, **members** may include individuals, corporations, and other limited liability companies. Like a corporation, most state statutes do not place a limit on the number of members comprising an LLC, and all 50 states allow for a single-person LLC (i.e., only one member).

The Supreme Court of Delaware made the following observation about limited liability companies:

> The limited liability company ("LLC") is a relatively new entity that has emerged in recent years as an attractive vehicle to facilitate business relationships and transactions. . . . [It] is seemingly a simple concept—to permit persons or entities ("members") to join together in an environment of private ordering to form and operate the enterprise under an LLC agreement with tax benefits akin to a partnership and limited liability akin to the corporate form.[2]

Formation of an LLC

Forming a limited liability company is relatively easy and inexpensive. The LLC's promoters, the individuals who want to start an LLC, prepare what is commonly referred to as **articles of organization**. Some states refer to this document as a **certificate of organization**. To form an LLC, one or more of the promoters must prepare and file an LLC's articles of organization with the appropriate state agency, often the office of the secretary of state. Most states provide a template for completing the articles of organization. Exhibit 7.2 presents the basic information typically included in the articles of organization.

State statutes provide that an LLC comes into legal existence at the time of the filing of the articles of organization with the appropriate state agency. Once formed, an LLC continues as a separate legal entity until an authorized member or members officially terminate the LLC by canceling its articles of organization. Unlike a corporation, which has an unlimited life, an LLC generally has a limited life.

---

[2]*Elf Atochem North America, Inc. v. Jaffari*, 727 A.2d 286 (1999).

Exhibit 7.2. Articles of Organization (*components and features*)

1. Name of the LLC. The name must include the words *limited liability company*, *limited company*, or the abbreviation *L.L.C.*, *L.C.*, or some other abbreviation as required by state law.

2. Official mailing address of the LLC. This address need not be the LLC's principal place of business.

3. An official office in the state within which the LLC was organized for the maintenance of official records and the location of the resident agent for service of process on the limited liability company. This address need not be the LLC's principal place of business.

4. Name and address of the LLC's resident agent.

5. Name and address of the LLC's manager.

6. Names and addresses of other individuals authorized to execute documents on behalf of the LLC, which is typically a listing of the members of the LLC.

7. Description of the LLC's business.

8. Other matters of interest, as determined by the LLC's promoters.

Members usually make a contribution to an LLC, in the form of an investment, to get the company up and running. Contributions typically take the form of cash, noncash property (such as equipment), or a promissory note. However, a person may be admitted to a limited liability company as a member and may receive an interest in the limited liability company without making a contribution.

Management of an LLC

Management practices differ depending on the size of an LLC. Smaller LLCs rely on a practice commonly referred to as **member management**. In a member management arrangement, individual members (owners) participate equally in the management of the company. As the LLC's business grows, member management usually becomes impractical. To solve this problem, many LLCs form a **management team**. Active members (those members involved in the company's day-to-day operations) comprise the management team, while the remaining members assume a more passive role as holders of an ownership interest. As an alternative model, some LLCs will designate one member to serve as the **manager** of the LLC. The manager's duties and responsibilities are usually included in the operating agreement.

State laws vary, but an LLC must generally maintain the following types of records as part of its management policies and procedures:

- A current membership list: full name and last known address of each member;
- A copy of the LLC's articles of organization;
- A copy of the LLC's operating agreement, assuming that a separate operating agreement has been prepared;

- Copies of the LLC's federal, state, and local income tax returns and other official reports for the three most recent years; and
- Copies of the LLC's financial statements for the three most recent years.

Statutory provisions generally require that the above records be available for inspection at the request of any member of the LLC. Additionally, statutes require that LLCs prepare and file an annual report with the appropriate state agency, such as the office of the secretary of state.

Operating Agreement

Even though most state statutes do not mandate the preparation and maintenance of an operating agreement, the common practice among business owners is to prepare one. An **operating agreement** is typically a written document regarding the management of the company and the conduct of its business. It includes guidelines about the LLC's operational policies, practices, and procedures. An operating agreement also provides guidance for how members will share profits and losses, the percentage of ownership of each member, and the rights, privileges, duties, and responsibilities of each member. Compared to a corporation, an LLC offers fewer restrictions on the sharing of projects. In general, members share profits based on a formula determined by the LLC's members as opposed to a distribution based on the percentage of ownership, which is often the case with a corporation.

A comprehensive operating agreement helps to preserve the relationship among the members of the LLC by providing clarity and instructions about the running of the business. It also provides information about how new members may join the LLC and how existing members may leave. For example, some operating agreements provide instructions about determining the value of a member's share of the LLC when leaving the business. Unless restricted by the operating agreement, state statutes generally allow members to lend money to or borrow money from an LLC. Members may serve as a guarantor for a loan and provide collateral in support of the LLC's obligations. Members may also transact business with the LLC in ways similar to how third parties conduct business with the LLC. The Case Illustration demonstrates the importance of developing a comprehensive operating agreement.

Taxation of an LLC

Like a partnership, a limited liability company is a pass-through entity, a tax structure designed to avoid double taxation. An LLC is a nontax entity. Its profits and losses are reported on its members' individual tax returns. The members are responsible for paying taxes on the LLC's profits. In practical terms, an LLC, like a partnership, serves as an agent for the Internal Revenue Service (IRS) in collecting and reporting tax data about the company's revenue and expenses. The LLC files an annual tax return to report relevant tax data to the IRS. The LLC reports each member's share of the profits or losses annually on an IRS Form K-1. The members use the information included on Form K-1

Case Illustration

The plaintiff, Elf Atochem North America, Inc. ("Elf"), manufactured and distributed solvent-based maskants to the aerospace and aviation industries throughout the world. The defendant, Jaffari, had developed an innovative, environmentally friendly alternative to the solvent-based maskants that dominated the market. Because of concerns generated by the Environmental Protection Agency (EPA)'s reclassification of solvent-based maskants as a hazardous contaminant, Elf considered developing or distributing a maskant less harmful to the environment. Shortly thereafter, Elf approached Jaffari and proposed investing in his product and assisting in its marketing. After some discussions, Elf and Jaffari agreed to participate in a joint venture, which they organized as a limited liability company called Malek LLC (Malek). After forming Malek, Elf and Jaffari, in their capacities as members of Malek, entered into a series of agreements, including a single-spaced 38-page operating agreement. One of the provisions of the operating agreement called for an arbitration clause covering all disputes. Among other aspects of the arbitration clause, the parties agreed that all litigation would take place in the state of California.

After some time, litigation ensued between Elf and Jaffari. Elf alleged that among other claims, Jaffari breached his fiduciary duty to Elf and Malek. Elf initiated his litigation in a Delaware trial court, which dismissed his claim based on a lack of jurisdiction to hear the case. The court found that the operating agreement governed the question of jurisdiction, and that only a court of law or arbitrator in California was empowered to decide Elf's claims. Elf appealed the decision of the trial court. The Delaware Supreme Court heard the appeal.

The Delaware Limited Liability Company Act was adopted in October 1992. The Delaware Supreme Court noted that the LLC is an attractive form of business entity because it combines corporate-type limited liability with partnership-type flexibility and tax advantages. The court referred to the Delaware LLC Act as a "flexible statute" because it grants substantial freedom to members of an LLC to decide by contract (operating agreement) how they wished to be managed and governed. The court went on to characterize an LLC as the "best of both worlds." The Delaware LLC Act provides members with broad discretion in drafting an operating agreement. The Court noted that the LLC Act gives the maximum effect to the principle of freedom of contract and to the enforceability of LLC agreements. The plaintiff, Elf, claimed that the Delaware LLC Act gives jurisdiction to a Delaware court to hear claims for breach of fiduciary duty, even though the LLC's members contracted through the operating agreement to arbitrate all such claims in California.

In ruling against the plaintiff, Elf, the Delaware Supreme Court found that the members, in their operating agreement, designated California as the chosen jurisdiction for hearing disputes between themselves. In light of this decision between the members, the Court stated that it could find no reason to alter this contractual provision within the operating agreement. Therefore, the Court held for the defendant, Jaffari. The court concluded by stating that the dispute must be heard by an arbitrator or court in California as called for in the operating agreement. *Elf Atochem North America, Inc. v. Jaffari*, 727 A.2d 286 (1999).

to report their respective share of the LLC's profits and losses on their individual tax returns.

Under special tax laws designed for pass-through entities, a limited liability company is allowed to choose how it will be treated for tax purposes. The Internal Revenue Service has special rules allowing an LLC to be treated for tax purposes as either a corporation or a partnership. For example, the IRS classifies a limited liability company with at least two members as a partnership for tax purposes. However, members may elect by filing IRS Form 8832 to be classified and taxed as a corporation, in which case they would file an annual corporate income tax return. An LLC with only one member is treated like a sole proprietorship for income tax purposes with its income reported on the individual member's tax return. However, a single-member LLC may instead elect to be treated like a corporation for income tax purposes by making an election on Form 8832.

Termination of an LLC

While not in the forefront of the thoughts of most individuals when forming an LLC, considering how an LLC may be terminated in the future is an important decision. Unlike a corporation, which has an indefinite life, the law of most states dictates that an LLC terminates automatically by operation of law when one member leaves. If the members want to prevent this automatic dissolution, the operating agreement must specify the means by which the LLC will continue. Thus, the default option is dissolution, a situation most members wish to avoid.

The most common way to avoid automatic dissolution is to include in the operating agreement a process referred to as a "buyout" agreement. The buyout agreement addresses future situations involving the possible departure of a member. For example, a member may wish to retire or simply leave the company to start another business or go to work for a different company. The buyout agreement provides that the LLC will continue after the departure of a member. It also includes ways of valuing the worth of a member's ownership interest. A buyout agreement typically includes instructions about how to finance the purchase of the departing member's ownership interest. For example, assume the value of a departing member's ownership interest is $2 million. The buyout agreement may specify that the LLC will purchase the member's interest on an installment basis over four years at an interest rate of 4 percent.

Corporations

Statutes enacted by state legislatures authorize the creation of corporations. A **corporation** is an organization (often a business) that has a legal existence separate and distinct from its owners. The owners (shareholders) share in the profits and losses of the corporation. In many corporations, owners also work for the company. Historically, the corporate form of organization has been used by business owners and investors to facilitate commerce and encourage entrepreneurial ventures. By centralizing the management function of an enterprise, corporations attract

"A corporation is an artificial being, invisible, intangible, and existing only in contemplation of law. . . . [I]t possesses only those properties which the charter of its creation confers upon it." *The Trustees of Dartmouth College v. Woodward*, 17 U.S. 518 (1819).

capital investment from passive investors who seek a return on their investment without engaging in the day-to-day activities of the business. Passive investors do not control or manage business operations, but enjoy the profits, if any, generated by the corporation. This type of passive investment provides the basic structure for large, publicly traded corporations.

Characteristics

The law recognizes corporations as having legal characteristics similar to a person. For example, a corporation may own property in its own name, and it may enter into contracts with other parties. Corporations may also be the subject of a lawsuit or a criminal investigation, or may initiate a lawsuit against another party. State and federal statutes recognize corporations as taxpayers. Thus, unlike a pass-through entity, corporations are required to file annual tax returns in their own names, separate and distinct from their shareholders. When thinking about a corporation, it is helpful to remember that a corporation possesses many of the same rights, duties, obligations, and privileges as individuals. And like the members of an LLC, corporate shareholders enjoy limited liability.

"Under the designation of person [in the Fourteenth Amendment of the United States Constitution] there is no doubt that a private corporation is included. Such corporations are merely associations of individuals united for a special purpose, and permitted to do business under a particular name, and have a succession of members without dissolution." *Pembina Consolidated Silver Mining and Milling Company v. Pennsylvania*, 125 U.S. 181 (1888).

The corporate form of organization serves as one of the major ways of structuring a business enterprise. When one or more individuals contemplate starting a business, decisions about how to form and structure the business are vital to the long-term success and sustainability of the business. When a new corporation is formed, we often refer to it as a closely held corporation. In **closely held corporations**, the investors (owners) often serve as corporate officers and help manage the business. Conversely, in **publicly traded corporations**, the management team operates separately and distinctly from the shareholders.

The corporate form of organization encourages the creation of new enterprises by minimizing the risk of starting and running a business. Protecting personal assets from the reach of business creditors represents one of the primary reasons for organizing a business as a corporation. By separating the management of a business from the owners, two important features of corporate law emerge. First, a legal shield (**corporate veil**) insulates owners from corporate creditors. As a general rule, this protection safeguards the personal assets of the owners. Second, managers of the business have duties and responsibilities that differ from those of the owners. In a corporate setting, officers and other workers are employees of the corporation. They serve as agents

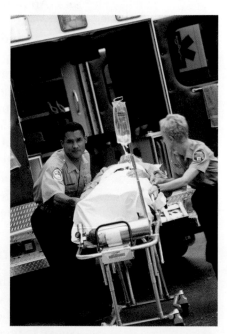

Some corporations are formed to serve the community at large, such as a not-for-profit hospital.

of the corporation and provide services designed to advance the mission, strategies, and goals of the corporation. On the other hand, the owners (shareholders) of the corporation are not usually involved in the day-to-day management of the business, unless it is a closely held corporation. Shareholders typically play a passive role in the running of the business as compared to a business organized as a sole proprietorship or general partnership.

Starting a Corporation

A corporation may be started for a variety of reasons and by people possessing a variety of backgrounds; the term **promoter** is commonly used to describe the person or persons who start a business. In addition to promoters, starting a corporation requires a business purpose, a business plan, a source of capital and financing, a physical place to house the corporation, a source of customers and vendors, and generally a cadre of experienced and skilled managers and workers. An attorney will usually be involved in the early stages of a corporation's existence, helping to draft the corporation's articles of incorporation, its bylaws, and other important documents. The attorney will also file all the necessary paperwork with the appropriate state agencies, such as the office of the secretary of state, and with the Internal Revenue Service.

A corporation's **articles of incorporation** serve as a type of constitution for a corporation. They establish the basic terms of the corporation's structure and operations and define its purpose. A corporation's **bylaws** provide guidance to officers and directors regarding a corporation's internal affairs and operations and its external relations. Bylaws set forth a corporation's most important policy statements and serve as the "terms of reference" for directors, officers, and managers when developing strategic plans and making significant business decisions.

An Ethical Insight: Jeremy Bentham and "Private Ethics"

Jeremy Bentham, an English jurist, philosopher, and social reformer, wrote in his Introduction to the Principles of Morals and Legislation (1790), *"acts really pernicious, which . . . may come . . . under the censure of private ethics . . . may no[t] be fit objects of the legislature to control."* Not every unethical act is illegal. Conflicts with legal but questionable company practices and so-called private ethics could lead to compromising your integrity. Understanding the principles of ethics discussed throughout this textbook will assist you in clarifying your private ethics and in crafting ethical arguments useful in challenging questionable company practices and in contributing to formulating an ethical corporate culture.

Where to Incorporate

Typically, the owners of a closely held corporation will incorporate their business in the state in which they live and work. For example, if the owners live in Texas and believe that most of their activities will occur in Texas, then it makes sense to incorporate their business in Texas. On the other hand, the promoters of a publicly held corporation may decide to go forum shopping. Because a publicly held corporation by its very nature involves large numbers of shareholders, employees, customers, supplies, and other stakeholders, one particular state may not dominate over another. Therefore, the promoters will usually search for a state that is friendly to business. The state of Delaware is viewed by many businesses as the most "friendly" state to incorporate a business. Statistically, more publicly held corporations are incorporated in Delaware than any other state. Delaware is known for having state laws, administrative agencies, and courts experienced in and accustomed to dealing with publicly held corporations.

Shareholders

All corporations (small or large, closely held or publicly held) must have the following three structural components: shareholders, directors, and officers. The **shareholders** of a corporation are the owners of the corporation. They invest in the corporation, providing it with the initial capital to get the business started. Shareholders provide subsequent capital as needed to help support and sustain the business during its years of operations. In addition to being a corporation's owners, shareholders possess certain powers regarding the corporation, including the power of electing members to serve on the corporation's board of directors.

Directors

In concert with corporate officers, **directors** set the strategic vision for the corporation. They make high-level decisions about the direction of the corporation, including whether to expand or reduce product lines, whether to make major asset investments, whether to establish a business presence in different regions of the United States or in foreign countries, and whether to undertake major financing obligations. Directors hire corporate officers such as the chief executive officer, the chief financial officer, the chief operating officer, and similar high-level positions. Directors also set the officers' levels of compensation. Directors, often with corporate officers, establish corporate policies and strategic goals. Directors also determine when to declare dividends and decide the amount of any dividend distribution. Directors operate as a unit, commonly referred to as the **board of directors**. Most corporate boards are comprised of committees, such as the audit committee, the nominating committee, and the compensation committee.

Officers

Corporate officers take direction from the board of directors and run the corporation on a day-to-day basis. Officers have the authority to commit the corporation to perform services, sell goods, and assume financial obligations, all within their stated levels of authority as set forth in the corporation's bylaws. Officers allocate the resources of the corporation through a comprehensive budgeting process and system of internal controls. Officers hire managers who report to them, often delegating duties to managers to implement the goals and objectives established by the officers.

Stock

Ownership of a corporation is represented by shares of stock. For example, if a corporation has issued 100 shares of stock, each share represents 1 percent of the total ownership of the corporation. Thus, if one person owns 40 shares, that person owns 40 percent of the corporation. Corporations may issue more than one class of stock. For example, a corporation may issue **common stock** (owners have voting rights, but are usually subordinate to preferred stockholders regarding dividends and corporate assets) and **preferred stock** (owners have a "preferred" claim to dividends and assets, but typically have no voting rights).

In closely held corporations, shareholders may agree to restrict the ownership of stock through a separate shareholder agreement. In a publicly held corporation, the value of a corporation's stock is determined through an open market as the shares are traded on one of the public exchanges such as the New York Stock Exchange. Therefore, the value of a publicly held corporation varies throughout the day as the stock is traded. Conversely, in a closely held corporation, the value of the corporation's stock is generally not known unless an expert is hired to conduct an appraisal, or an arm's-length sale to a third-party occurs.

Dividends

Dividends represent a distribution of the corporation's earnings to the shareholders. It is a way for the owners of a corporation to receive assets from the corporation, usually in the form of cash, as a return on their investment in the corporation. The amount of dividends received by shareholders depends on the number of shares owned. For example, assume a corporation issues a $10 cash dividend, and 1,000 shares of its stock are outstanding. If a shareholder owns 400 shares, that shareholder will receive a cash dividend of $4,000. As mentioned earlier, the board of directors has the responsibility to determine when to declare and pay dividends. The board also determines the amount of a dividend.

Taxation

Federal income tax laws and regulations impose taxes on corporations differently depending on whether an election has been made to have the corporation taxed as an S corporation. If a corporation has made an S corporation election, it becomes a flow-through entity for tax purposes with taxation occurring only at the shareholder level. If an election has not been made, then the corporation will be taxed as a C corporation. Like an individual taxpayer, a C corporation is taxed on its taxable income. Thus, when dividends from a corporation are distributed to its shareholders, a possibility exists for double taxation: 1) the corporation pays an income tax on its net income (taxable income) and 2) when some or all of that income is distributed to taxpayers in the form of a dividend, the shareholders also pay an income tax.

Consider the Green Earth Foods Company example introduced at the beginning of the chapter. The shareholders' salaries of $450,000 (Amy), $275,000 (Jeffrey); $225,000 (Allison), and $160,000 (Mark) would be taxed on their personal income tax returns. However, any profits made by Green Earth Foods would be taxed separately on the company's corporate tax return, assuming the company did not make an S corporation election to be taxed as a flow-through entity.

Dissolution

Although a corporation by state law usually has an indefinite life, the directors may decide nonetheless to terminate the legal existence of a corporation through the process of dissolution. In some ways, the process of dissolving a corporation is relatively simple and straightforward. Dissolution requires the board of directors to prepare and adopt a **resolution of dissolution**. The shareholders must then approve the resolution. Corporate offices and the directors prepare a plan of dissolution, which includes what is commonly referred to as a **winding-up period**. During this period, the corporation provides employees with notice of the expected duration of their employment with the corporation. Creditors are paid to the extent the corporation has liquidity. All necessary state and federal filings occur including the preparation and filing of "final" tax returns. Then, to the extent that assets remain in the corporation, a final **liquidating dividend** is made to the shareholders. Corporations may also dissolve through bankruptcy proceedings, as discussed in Chapter 18, "The Debtor-Creditor Relationship."

External Influences on Corporate Management Practices

The Dodd-Frank Wall Street Reform and Consumer Protection Act affects the corporate governance of all public companies regarding the disclosure to stockholders of executive compensation. Note how the following manager's meeting illustrates the need for ethical as well as financial justification for substantial increases in executive compensation when the company seeks to maintain an ethical corporate culture.

Manager's Compliance and Ethics Meeting

Executive Compensation — How Much Is Enough? Shareholders "Say-On-Pay"

Software Solutions, Inc.,* a publicly traded company listed on the New York Stock Exchange, has a substantial net worth, high earnings, and a history of dividend distributions. Software Solutions has a published code of ethics that states "we always act in the stockholders' best interests." At a board of directors' meeting, the board members voted unanimously to raise the CEO's salary 50 percent to $4,000,000 annually. The CEO is considered by the board to be an outstanding CEO, and they assert her past performance justifies the substantial increase in her salary. The Dodd-Frank Wall Street Reform and Consumer Protection Act (Dodd-Frank) requires shareholder advisory voting ("say-on-pay") on executive compensation. In their advisory vote, the shareholders voted against the raise primarily because the average pay for an outstanding CEO in the industry is $1 million. Although this is merely an advisory stockholders' vote, it must be taken seriously by the board's compensation committee. Nonetheless, the compensation committee decided to ignore the shareholders' advisory vote because they viewed the increase in salary to be appropriate due to the CEO's exceptional performance during the past five years.

The committee informed the stockholders of the CEO's outstanding company performance and of their conviction that the company's long-term success is going to be directly related to the CEO being awarded this incentive-based high compensation. The annual stockholders' meeting is planned for next month, and the compensation committee and the ethics officer are preparing appropriate responses to anticipated questions by the stockholders regarding the CEO's proposed salary. Software Solution's ethics officer argues that in view of the company's code of ethics, compliance with the Dodd-Frank Act for substantial increases in executive compensation should not be based exclusively on financial justification but should also include ethical reasons to justify their decision.

What are the ethical principles that would support the compensation committee's decision? Are there ethical arguments that would find a 50 percent increase in salary on its face unethical, especially when the total salary is now $4,000,000 and the average compensation in the industry for an outstanding CEO is $1,000,000? What would be the most convincing ethical arguments to justify the increase in compensation? Apply ethical principles to your analysis.

Utilitarianism. One approach to consider the ethics of this case is to apply the utilitarian principle of "*the greatest happiness (good) for the greater number of people*," an expression first used by Francis Hutcheon that further explained the utilitarian theories of **John Stuart Mill** and **Jeremy Bentham**. The ethical notion of stakeholder analysis from the perspective of publicly-traded corporations is appropriate because of their societal role in creating wealth and jobs. Corporate decisions utilizing stakeholder analysis have an effect on stockholders, customers, creditors, suppliers, and the environment.

Substantial executive compensation, as a fixed expense, has potential negative financial consequences that may affect, among other things, the financial well-being of the company. There will be positive effects of the increase in the CEO's compensation based on the director's compensation committees' comment that the company's long-term success will be directly related to the CEO continuing her outstanding performance. Additional potential negative effects could be that money available for dividend distribution and company expansion may no longer be available with this large compensation package.

Rule utilitarianism reviews the pros and cons of a situation and decides on the "greatest happiness (good) for the greater number." An argument could be made that a vast number of stockholders may suffer if the history of dividend distributions would be curtailed as a result of this substantial raise. If that is the case, one could argue the raise would be unethical under a "rule utilitarianism" theory of ethics.

Kant's Categorical Imperatives. Kant would find an absolute moral obligation to reduce the CEO's compensation since the shareholders should be treated as an end in themselves (meaning the recipients of potential dividends) and not merely as a means for deriving capital investment. Unlike the above utilitarian argument that is concerned with the consequences of a decision, Kant's categorical imperative to "*Act so that your conduct is not merely a means to an end but rather an end in itself*"[†] is a moral duty regardless of its consequence (deontology).

Conclusion. Whether or not the compensation committee acted ethically in ignoring the stockholders' advisory vote will to a great extent depend upon the company's assurance that the financial well-being of the company, including potential dividend distributions, will be enhanced. There may be some merit to that argument based on the company's history of dividend distributions under the leadership of the present CEO.

---

[*]A fictitious case and company name.
[†]*Fundamental Principles of the Metaphysics of Morals*, Immanuel Kant, section II (1785).

Business Judgment Rule, Minority Shareholder Rights, and Shareholder Derivative Actions

Three major legal theories affect the decisions and actions of the directors, officers, and shareholders of a corporation. The theories are (1) the business judgment rule, (2) minority shareholder rights, and (3) shareholder derivative actions. Each theory will now be explained and illustrated.

Business Judgment Rule

The **business judgment rule** protects directors and officers of a corporation against the risk of personal liability for making business decisions that others might find imprudent, unwise, and inappropriate. When a corporation incurs losses as a result of managerial decisions, people adversely affected by the decisions may be inclined to challenge them. Such challenges could lead to unnecessary and expensive litigation. Therefore, the business judgment rule provides immunity for business judgments and decisions that corporate directors and officers make as long as they acted on an informed basis, in good faith, and within the scope of their authority. The business judgment rule imposes on directors a duty of care and a duty of loyalty to the corporation and the shareholders. Further, the business judgment rule expects directors and officers to act on the belief that their decisions and actions are in the best interests of the corporation and the shareholders. Common reasons for shareholders to believe that directors have not acted in the best interests of the corporation include assertions of self-dealing, abuse of discretion, or an absence of good faith.

Running a business requires directors and officers of the corporation to make business decisions and implement business plans on a regular basis. Some business decisions are complex with uncertain outcomes. For example, directors and officers must decide whether to start a new product line or terminate an existing line, or how to price a product or a service. At times, they may also have to decide whether to acquire a business or sell a business, whether to expand the geographical reach of the business to global markets, and whether to hire employees or lay off employees as business cycles fluctuate. These are not easy decisions. They are complex decisions and involve many factors. Yet, they are business decisions that must be made.

An obvious question for those making these kinds of decisions is whether they will be challenged by others, including shareholders. Given the significance of their judgments, directors and officers require some level of assurance that their decisions will not be the subject of frequent litigation. Without this protection, a sense of paralysis would permeate the boardrooms and corporate offices of nearly every corporation in the United States. In very practical terms, there needs to be some standard by which managerial decisions can be made without fear of a "challenge" and costly litigation. The standard used in the United States to judge the decisions of corporate directors and officers is called the *business judgment rule*. Additionally, directors and officers often seek further insulation from personal liability through the use of **directors and officers liability insurance**, which provides financial protection from the consequences of litigation involving wrongful acts on the part of directors and officers.

Another source of insulation for directors and officers from personal liability comes in the form of statutory relief. The majority of states in the United States have enacted **constituency statutes**. These statutes, sometimes referred to as stakeholder statutes, allow directors and officers of a corporation to make non-shareholder-oriented decisions about a company's resources. For example, a company interested in contributing to the least advantaged in its community (Rawls, *The Difference Principle*) could establish a charitable foundation using company resources. (See Chapter 6, "Corporate Social Responsibility" for a discussion of constituency statutes.)

Minority Shareholder Rights

In *Donahue v. Rodd Electrotype Company of New England, Inc.*, the court established the rights of minority shareholders and expanded the duties of majority shareholders for closely held corporations. In its seminal decision, the Massachusetts Supreme Judicial Court concluded that the features of a closely held corporation resemble those of a partnership. Thus, like the partners in a partnership, the shareholders of a closely held corporation rely on the trust, confidence, and loyalty of their fellow shareholders to help ensure the long-term sustainability of the business. Consider, for example, the rights of the minority shareholders in the Practical Example (Green Earth Foods Company) introduced at the beginning of the chapter. As minority shareholders, do Jeffrey, Allison, and Mark have the right to demand a portion of the profit ($70,000) earned by Amy (the majority shareholder) in the sale of property owned by Green Earth Foods Company?

As illustrated by the following *In-Depth Ethical Case Analysis*, the Donahue decision raises legal and ethical questions about the relationship between a corporation and its shareholders as well as the relationship among the shareholders themselves. For example, what are the *legal* duties and expectations of shareholders in a closely held corporation? Do shareholders' legal duties and expectations differ from their *ethical* duties and expectations? As demonstrated by the following case analysis, a fine line may exist between legal duties and ethical duties.

In-Depth Ethical Case Analysis

Donahue v. Rodd Electrotype Company of New England, Inc.,
328 N.E. 2d 505 (1954)

Facts

Mrs. Donahue (the plaintiff), a minority shareholder in Rodd Electrotype Company of New England, Inc. (Rodd Electrotype), sued the board of directors of Rodd Electrotype along with Harry Rodd, a former director, officer, and controlling stockholder of Rodd Electrotype (the defendants). The plaintiff sought to rescind Rodd Electrotype's purchase of Harry Rodd's shares in Rodd Electrotype and compel Harry Rodd to repay the purchase price of the shares. In the alternative, the plaintiff sought to have Rodd Electrotype purchase her shares under the same conditions as it purchased Harry Rodd's shares. The plaintiff alleged that the defendants caused Rodd Electrotype to purchase Harry Rodd's shares in violation of their fiduciary duty to her in her capacity as a minority stockholder.

In 1935, Harry Rodd began his employment with Rodd Electrotype. A year later, the plaintiff's husband, Joseph Donahue (now deceased), began his employment with the company. In 1955, the board of directors of Rodd Electrotype made available to Harry Rodd and Joseph Donahue shares of the common stock of the company. Harry Rodd acquired 200 shares, and Joseph Donahue acquired 50 shares. After Joseph Donahue's death, the plaintiff, Mrs. Donahue, inherited her husband's 50 shares.

In 1970, Harry Rodd was 77 years old and not in the best of health. His children (Charles and Frederick) convinced their father to retire from the company. Harry Rodd reluctantly agreed, but insisted that some financial arrangement be made with respect to his shares of stock in Rodd Electrotype. In their capacity as members of Rodd Electrotype's board of directors, Charles and Frederick negotiated the company's purchase of their father's shares. When Mrs. Donahue learned of the purchase arrangement, she demanded that Rodd Electrotype also purchase her shares. However, the board of directors voted not to purchase Mrs. Donahue's shares.

Holding

The trial judge dismissed the plaintiff's suit, determining that the purchase of the stock of a majority shareholder in a closely held corporation had been carried out in good faith and with inherent fairness. The Massachusetts Appeals Court affirmed the decision of the trial court judge. The plaintiff then appealed her case to the Massachusetts Supreme Judicial Court, which reversed the decision of the trial court and held for the plaintiff.

Issue

Do the majority shareholders of a closely held corporation owe a strict duty of utmost good faith and loyalty to the minority shareholders of the corporation?

From the Court's Opinion

A closely held corporation bears striking resemblance to a partnership. Commentators and courts have noted that the closely-held corporation is often little more than an "incorporated" partnership. Ripin v. United States Woven Label Co. 205 N.Y. 442, 447 (1912). Just as in a partnership, the relationship among the stockholders must be one of trust, confidence, and absolute loyalty if the enterprise is to succeed. All participants rely on the fidelity and abilities of those stockholders who hold office. Disloyalty and self-seeking conduct on the part of any stockholder will engender bickering, corporate stalemates, and, perhaps, efforts to achieve dissolution.

* * *

In her argument, Mrs. Donahue, the plaintiff, characterized the corporate purchase of Harry Rodd's shares as an unlawful distribution of corporate assets to controlling stockholders. She alleged that the distribution constituted a breach of the fiduciary duty owed by the Rodds as controlling (majority) stockholders to her, a minority stockholder in the company. Mrs. Donahue asserted that the Rodds failed to accord her an equal opportunity to sell her shares to the corporation. The defendants replied that the stock purchase fell within the powers of the corporation and met the requirements of good faith and inherent fairness. Furthermore, the defendants stated that Mrs. Donahue has no right to an equal opportunity to have the corporation purchase her shares.

* * *

We agree with the plaintiff and reverse the decree of the Superior Court. However, we limit the applicability of our holding to "closely-held corporations." Rodd Electrotype is a closely-held corporation and Charles and Frederick Rodd control the corporation as majority shareholders. On its face, the purchase of Harry Rodd's shares by the corporation without extending the same opportunity to Mrs. Donahue is a breach of the duty, which the controlling stockholders owe to the minority stockholder, Mrs. Donahue. Mrs. Donahue is entitled to have her shares purchased by Rodd Electrotype under the same conditions as the corporation purchased Harry Rodd's shares, a majority shareholder.

Ethical Questions

1. According to the Donahue case, shareholders in a closely held corporation owe a strict *legal* duty of utmost good faith and loyalty to one another. Is this legal duty, imposed by the Massachusetts Supreme Judicial Court on the shareholders in a closely held corporation, strictly a legal duty or are there ethical principles embedded within it?

2. Mrs. Donahue was a passive shareholder; she did not work at Rodd Electrotype nor did she contribute actively to its success. Accordingly, is it reasonable for Mrs. Donahue to expect equal and fair treatment consistent with those shareholders who run the business? Do the majority shareholders in a closely held corporation have an ethical duty to treat minority shareholders in the same manner as they treat themselves?

Ethical Theory Analysis

A starting point for understanding the **ethical relationships** in the Donahue case is to keep in mind the general structure of the closely held corporation. After the sole proprietorship, the closely held corporation is the most commonly used business organization. It is especially common in a family business or one among friends where there are very few shareholders.

Perhaps for that very reason disputes exist among the majority and minority shareholders, the officers, and the board of directors. This intimate business relationship between the shareholders and management creates ethical duties of trust, loyalty, and confidence that are collectively referred to as **fiduciary duties**. A **fiduciary** is a person or group of people who legally act on behalf of others. A fiduciary's judgment may not be self-serving but ought to be made looking out for the best interests of those represented by the fiduciary. A corporate board is subject to this fiduciary obligation as it manages a company on behalf of the stockholders. As discussed previously, board members are accountable to the stockholders for their business decisions.

What are the **ethical principles**, if any, embedded in the legal duty of utmost good faith and loyalty the shareholders of a closely held corporation owe to each other?

1. W.D. Ross's *prima facie duty of fidelity*. The legal relationship between the stockholders of a closely held corporation is not contractual. It is rather a relationship that the law recognizes because the majority shareholders have the controlling votes on the election of the directors who manage the company at its highest level and make major policy decisions. One could argue the majority shareholders and the board of directors collectively manage the closely held corporation since members of the board and the executive officers are usually majority shareholders. For that reason, Ross's duty of fidelity would find an ethical obligation based on the stockholders' relationship to honor the ownership interests between the minority and majority shareholders by acting with the "utmost good faith and loyalty" toward each other.

2. Kant's *Categorical Imperative* to "Act so that your conduct is not merely a means to an end but rather an end in itself." Majority

shareholders who act in a manner that is self-serving to the detriment of the minority shareholders do so as a means to the end of protecting their own interests. Mr. Rodd's two sons who were majority shareholders and on the board of directors voted to have the company purchase their father's shares of stock without offering the same opportunity to the minority shareholder, Mrs. Donahue. That decision not only breached the board's legal fiduciary duty of loyalty to keep the minority stockholder (Mrs. Donahue) informed of its intent to purchase Mr. Rodd's stock before it occurred, but also violated Kant's ethical duty of not using others as a means to a self-serving end. Both Ross and Kant provide ethical principles that support the court's decision of good faith and loyalty the shareholders of a closely held corporation owe to each other.

What are the **ethical principles**, if any, supporting the "equal and fair treatment" of a "passive shareholder" in a closely held corporation?

Rule utilitarianism. Ethics is concerned with moral rules, and rule utilitarianism calculates in advance behavior that would lead to the greatest happiness for the greater number. In this case the common stock of the majority shareholders constitutes the "greater number." The *consequence* of a legal rule of granting "equal and fair treatment" between a passive minority shareholder and an active majority shareholder would *not* provide happiness to the "greater number "of majority stockholders. This argument would be less effective if Mrs. Donahue's minority interest was closer to 49 percent or if she participated in some significant fashion in the management of the company.

Ethical Conclusion

Note that the boards of directors and shareholders all have ethical as well as legal duties owed to each other. Although there are ethical principles that support the court's decision, relying exclusively on the law of closely held corporations and ethics to assist the interests of minority shareholders is an unnecessary risk. Was Mrs. Donahue, a "passive shareholder" who inherited her deceased husband's minority stockholder's interest of only 50 shares, ethically entitled to the same "equal and fair treatment" for the company to purchase her stock, presumably at the same price, as Mr. Rodd who served in the company for 35 years?

The best way to provide for the contingency of selling inherited stock in a closely held corporation is to establish a stockholder's agreement (a formal contract between the stockholders and the company) that is funded with life insurance that pays the stockholders' beneficiary, in this case Mrs. Donahue, a predetermined amount upon the stockholder's (her husband's) death, and in return she would transfer her inherited shares over to the company. Typically, the life insurance tax-deductible premiums are paid for by the closely held company. An appropriate "risk assessment" process should identify the possibility of inheriting stock as in this case, along with other potential problems relevant to stock held in a closely held corporation. The board of directors and shareholders should discuss potential risks with their attorney, accountant, and life insurance advisor and establish an appropriate business plan to provide for this type of contingency.

Donahue v. Rodd Electrotype Company of New England, Inc., 328 N.E.2d 505 (1975).

Shareholder Derivative Action

A **shareholder derivative action** is a legal claim brought by the shareholders of a corporation against the corporation's directors and officers. The essence of the claim is that the directors and officers failed to discharge their duties to the benefit of the corporation and its shareholders. Typically, a derivative action alleges fraud, mismanagement, or self-dealing on the part of the corporation's officers and the directors. As discussed earlier in the chapter, the separation of ownership from management distinguishes a corporation from other forms of organizing a business. By its very nature, the separation means that shareholders may have little influence over the management decisions of the corporation. This arrangement works most of the time, but there are situations in which shareholders may disagree with the decisions of the board and the corporate officers. When this occurs, shareholders have minimal rights or abilities to influence management decisions. For example, if the directors decide to declare and pay a dividend of $10 per share, but the shareholders believe it should be $12 per share, the shareholders' only vehicle to influence the board's decision is to initiate a shareholder derivative action.

To be successful in a derivative suit, shareholders generally must prove that the directors and officers committed fraud, engaged in self-dealing, or otherwise breached a fiduciary duty owed to the corporation and its shareholders. Generally, courts are reluctant to interfere with management's decision-making processes. Courts are inclined to defer to the judgment of those employed to manage the corporation. In other words, courts resist the temptation to second-guess the business judgments of management. Accordingly, in a derivative shareholder action, shareholders must satisfy a number of legal requirements. For example, many states require that shareholders provide a cash security in the form of a bond to pay for the legal expenses of the corporation should the derivative action fail. Not surprisingly, this hurdle alone often inhibits the initiation of a derivative shareholder suit. The *Kamin v. American Express Company* case illustrates the requirements of a shareholder derivative suit.

Piercing the Corporate Veil

As discussed earlier in the chapter, one of the primary reasons to organize a business as a corporation or as a limited liability company (LLC)[3] is to protect the personal assets of the principals.[4] As a general rule of corporate law, which has been a part of the U.S. legal system for over two centuries, the principals of a corporation are not personally liable for a corporation's debts and obligations.

---

[3]The term *corporation* is used to describe both corporations and limited liability companies (LLCs).
[4]The term *principal* is used in this section of the chapter broadly to describe the parties authorized to act on behalf of a corporation as well as parties having a vested interest in a corporation, such as corporate officers, directors, and shareholders.

Kamin v. American Express Company, 383 N.Y.S. 2d 807 (1976)

Facts: In this stockholders' derivative action, the individual defendants, who are the directors of the American Express Company, moved for an order dismissing the plaintiff's complaint for failure to state a cause of action. The complaint was brought derivatively by two minority stockholders of the American Express Company. The complaint asked the court to declare that a certain "in- kind" dividend is a waste of corporate assets, and to instruct the defendants not to proceed with the distribution.

In 1972 American Express acquired for investment 1,954,418 shares of common stock of Donaldson, Lufken and Jenrette, Inc. (hereafter DLJ), a publicly traded corporation, at a cost of $29,900,000. Three years later, the market value of those shares was approximately $4,000,000. The board of directors of American Express declared an in-kind dividend of the DLJ stock to the stockholders of American Express. The plaintiffs contend that if American Express were to sell the DLJ shares on the market, it would sustain a capital loss of $25,000,000, which could be offset against taxable capital gains on other investments. Such a sale, they allege, would result in tax savings to American Express of approximately $8,000,000, which would not be available if the DLJ shares were distributed to the American Express shareholders as an in-kind dividend. The plaintiffs demanded that the directors rescind the previously declared dividend in DLJ shares and take steps to preserve the capital loss that would result from selling the shares. The directors rejected the plaintiffs' demand.

Issue: Does the *business judgment rule* protect directors and corporate officers from challenges by shareholders when questions of fraud and self dealing are absent from the decisions made by the directors and officers.

Holding: Defendants (American Express Company) filed a motion for summary judgment arising from a plaintiff stockholders' (Kamin, et al.) derivative action challenging the decision of the board of directors of American Express Company to distribute an in-kind dividend. The Court granted the defendant's motion for summary judgment and dismissal of the plaintiff's complaint stating that questions of policy and business management were better left to the discretion of the board of directors unless the plaintiffs could show acts, such as fraud and self-dealing, that justified judicial interference. Here, the plaintiff stockholders' suit was based only on their disagreement with the board of director's business decisions. The Appeals Court upheld the summary judgment noting that "in this case it clearly appears that the plaintiffs have failed as a matter of law to make out an actionable claim. Accordingly, the motion by the defendants (American Express Company) for summary judgment and dismissal of the complaint is granted."

From the Court's Opinion: *The allegations of the complaint go to the question of the exercise by the board of directors of their business judgment in deciding how to deal with the DLJ shares. The crucial allegation that must be scrutinized to determine the legal sufficiency of the complaint is paragraph 19 of the complaint, which alleges that all of the Directors engaged in or acquiesced in or negligently permitted the declaration and payment of the dividend in violation of the fiduciary duty owed by them to American Express Company to care for and preserve the company's assets in the same manner as a person of average prudence would care for his or her own property. Nonetheless, the dividend was paid on October 31, 1975. Accordingly, that portion of the complaint seeking a direction not to distribute the shares is deemed to be moot, and the court will deal only with the request for declaratory judgment* or for damages.*

Examination of the complaint reveals there is no claim of fraud or self-dealing, and no contention of bad faith or oppressive conduct. The law is quite clear as to what is necessary to ground a claim for actionable wrongdoing. "In actions by stockholders, which assail the acts of their directors or trustees, courts will not interfere unless the powers have been illegally or unconscientiously executed, or unless it be made to appear that the acts were fraudulent or collusive and destructive of the rights of the stockholders. Mere errors of judgment are not sufficient as grounds for equity interference; for the powers of those entrusted with corporate management are largely discretionary." (Leslie v Lorillard, 110 NY 519, 532; see, also, Winter v Anderson, 242 App Div 430, 432; Rous v Carlisle, 261 App Div 432, 434, affd 290 NY 869; 11 NY Jur, Corporations, § 378.)

More specifically, the question of whether or not a dividend is to be declared or a distribution of some kind should be made is exclusively a matter of business judgment for the board of directors. "Courts will not interfere with such discretion unless it is first made to appear that the directors have acted or are about to act in bad faith and for a dishonest purpose. It is for the directors to say, acting in good faith of course, when and to what extent dividends shall be declared. The statute confers upon the directors this power, and the minority stockholders are not in a position to question this right, so long as the directors are acting in good faith" (Liebman v Auto Strop Co., 241 NY 427, 433-434; accord: City Bank Farmers Trust Co. v Hewitt Realty Co., 257 NY 62; Venner v Southern Pacific Co., 279 F 832, cert den 258 U.S. 628).

Thus, a complaint must be dismissed if all that is presented is a decision to pay dividends rather than pursuing some other course of conduct. A complaint that alleges merely that some course of action other than that pursued by the board of directors would have been more advantageous gives rise to no cognizable cause of action. Courts have more than enough to do in adjudicating legal rights and devising remedies for wrongs. The directors' room rather than the courtroom is the appropriate forum for thrashing out purely business questions that will have an impact on profits, market prices, competitive situations, or tax advantages. As stated by Judge Cardozo:

"The substitution of someone else's business judgment for that of the directors is no business for any court to follow." (Holmes v Saint Joseph Lead Co., 84 Misc 278, 283, quoting from Gamble v Queens County Water Co., 123 NY 91, 99.)

It is not enough to allege, as plaintiffs do here, that the directors made an imprudent decision, which did not capitalize on the possibility of using a potential capital loss to offset capital gains. More than imprudence or mistaken judgment must be shown.

The only hint of self-dealing that is raised, not in the complaint but in the papers on the motion, is that four of the twenty directors were officers and employees of American Express and members of its executive incentive compensation plan. Hence, it is suggested, by virtue of the action taken earnings may have been overstated and their compensation affected thereby. Such a claim is highly speculative and standing alone can hardly be regarded as sufficient to support an inference of self-dealing. There is no claim or showing that the four company directors dominated and controlled the sixteen outside members of the board. Certainly, every action taken by the board has some impact on earnings and may therefore affect the compensation of those whose earnings are keyed to profits. That does not disqualify the inside directors, nor does it put every policy adopted by the board in question. All directors have an obligation, using sound business judgment, to maximize income for the benefit of all persons having a stake in the welfare of the corporate entity.

In this case it clearly appears that the plaintiffs have failed as a matter of law to make out an actionable claim. Accordingly, the motion by the defendants (American Express Company) for summary judgment and dismissal of the complaint is granted.

---

[*] Parties to a lawsuit may petition the court for a *declaratory judgment* after the lawsuit has been initiated but before damages have been awarded. In issuing a declaratory judgment, a judge defines and declares the legal rights of each of the parties involved in the lawsuit. Once issued, a declaratory judgment binds the parties to the conclusions drawn by the judge, and the parties are barred from seeking future judicial relief of the same legal issue unless they appeal the decision of the trial judge.

In other words, a corporation's principals are generally immune from personal liability for the decisions they make and the actions they undertake on behalf of a corporation. For example, assume that Corporation A contracts with Corporation B to purchase equipment valued at $500,000. If Corporation A fails to pay Corporation B for the equipment it purchased, the principals of Corporation A are not personally liable to Corporation B. Rather, Corporation A, the party in privity of contract with Corporation B, remains liable for the liability it incurred. The *corporate veil* protects the principals of Corporation A, which insulates them personally from legal actions taken by Corporation B to collect the $500,000.

What Is the Corporate Veil?

Conceptually, the **corporate veil** is a legal assumption that the actions and obligations of a corporation are separate and distinct from the corporation's principals. This legal fiction exists to protect the individuals who manage, direct, or own a corporation. The need for a legal fiction becomes obvious when we consider the nature of a corporation. As an artificial entity created under the auspices of state law, a corporation is empowered to act as a "single person" distinct and separate from its principals. The U.S. Supreme Court also views a corporation as a *person*: "Corporations are merely associations of individuals united for a special purpose, and permitted to do business under a particular name, and have a succession of members without dissolution."[5]

Therefore, in its capacity as a "person," a corporation possesses the rights, duties, privileges, and authorization to transact business in its own name separate from those who manage, direct, or own the corporation. Why should state law offer protection to principals in the form of a corporate veil? In some ways, the answer is simple. The corporate veil affords individuals (people like you) the opportunity to start a business and assume the risks associated with a start-up business without the fear of jeopardizing personal assets.

Piercing the Corporate Veil

However, the corporate veil is not an impenetrable shield. Creditors of a corporation may be able to "breach the shield" through an equitable action known as **piercing the corporate veil**.[6] Once the veil has been pierced, the personal assets of the principals fall within the reach of the corporation's creditors. Creditors may find it necessary to seek recovery by "piercing the corporate veil" when the assets of a corporation are insufficient to satisfy their rightful and legitimate demands. For example, assume that a creditor has been successful in pursuing a breach of contract claim against a corporation by

---

[5]*Pembina Consolidated Silver Mining and Milling Company v. Pennsylvania*, 125 U.S. 181 (1888).
[6]The legal doctrine of "piercing the corporate veil" is not itself a cause of action. Rather, it is "an equitable tool that authorizes courts, in rare situations, to ignore corporate formalities, where such disregard is necessary to provide a meaningful remedy for injuries and to avoid injustice." *Attorney Gen. v. M.C.K., Inc.*, 432 Mass. 546, 555, 736 N.E.2d 373 (2000), citing *My Bread Baking Co. v. Cumberland Farms, Inc.*, supra at 620.

Case Illustration

The plaintiff, Kraft Power Corporation (Kraft), sold power equipment to Power Wiring & Emergency Response, Inc. (Power Wiring), a corporation owned and controlled by John Marino (Marino). Marino was the sole shareholder, sole director, president, and treasurer of Power Wiring. Because Power Wiring failed to pay Kraft the outstanding balance due on the sale of equipment, Kraft brought a breach of contract action against Power Wiring. Kraft received a judgment in the amount of $259,417. However, Kraft was unable to collect the judgment because Power Wiring had no assets at the time the court issued the judgment. Marino died shortly thereafter, and his estate assumed responsibility for his affairs. Merrill, the defendant in this case, was appointed by the court to manage Marino's estate.

Because Power Wiring had no assets at the time of the judgment, Kraft sought to pierce the corporate veil of Power Wiring and collect the judgment of $259,417 from Marino's personal assets, now owned and managed by his estate. In its complaint, Kraft asserted that the corporate veil of Power Wiring & Emergency Response, Inc. should be pierced and the corporation disregarded because Marino was personally responsible for Power Wiring's contractual obligations. In support of its assertions, Kraft alleged that Marino exercised pervasive control over Power Wiring for his personal benefit. For example, Kraft argued that when Power Wiring entered into the contract with Kraft for the purchase of the power equipment, Marino had already stripped away the assets of Power Wiring, thus causing it to become insolvent. Marino resold the equipment to a third party and used the proceeds to pay personal expenses. Consequently, Kraft was unable to collect any of the $259,417 judgment.

In its opinion, the court noted as a general principle of corporate law that a principal of a corporation is not liable for the acts of the corporation. However, this general rule gives way when it is necessary to look beyond the corporate form to address fraud and wrongful behavior of the principal, or to remedy an injustice. The court stated that the equitable doctrine of piercing the corporate veil can be used to disregard the corporation's existence and impose liability on the individual principals of the corporation.

The court stated that it is appropriate to pierce the corporate veil when the corporate principal exercises (1) some form of pervasive control over the activities of the corporation, and (2) there is some fraudulent or injurious consequence as a result of the pervasive control. In determining whether these two tests have been met, the court stated that the facts and circumstances of each case must be evaluated, based on the following 12 factors:

- Common ownership (the corporation and its principals are effectively one unit)
- Pervasive control by the principal over of the operations of the corporation
- Commingling of corporate and principal funds
- Thin capitalization of the corporation
- Nonobservance of corporate formalities
- Absence of corporate records
- No payment of dividends
- Insolvency at the time of the litigated transaction
- Siphoning away of the corporation's funds by a dominant shareholder
- Nonfunctioning officers and directors
- Use of the corporation for personal transactions of the dominant shareholders
- Use of the corporation to promote fraud

The court concluded that Kraft's claims for breach of contract and unjust enrichment were valid. *Kraft Power Corporation v. Merrill*, 464 Mass. 145, 981 N.E.2d 671 (2013).

securing a $1 million judgment award. The initial excitement generated by this judicial success may be extinguished quickly if the defendant corporation is defunct and has no assets. If the defendant corporation has no assets, how will the creditor collect its $1 million judgment? To help answer this question, consider the Case Illustration of Kraft Power Corporation v. Merrill.

In this case, the Massachusetts Supreme Judicial Court enumerates 12 factors for consideration in determining whether to allow a creditor to pierce the corporate veil. While these 12 factors capture the essence for allowing creditors to pierce the corporate veil, most states use some combination of the factors when considering a demand by a creditor to pierce the corporate veil.

Global Perspective: Global Business Organizations

Expanding a U.S. business internationally can provide a company with enormous opportunity. Companies can gain a competitive advantage by helping satisfy consumer demand for buying foreign goods. Strategically utilized, foreign capital and human resources can strengthen a business. Sometimes, lower tariffs and more lenient regulation abroad can provide new opportunities. Expanding internationally involves risks too. Greater distances mean higher transportation and insurance costs, more risk something will go wrong, and more difficulties in resolving problems that do arise. How does a U.S. business decide whether to enter the international market? When, where, and in what form should expansion take place? Ultimately, these questions are interconnected and the development of sensible strategies for international expansion involves many factors and choices. Also, the analysis may change over time. Businesses evolve and decisions made today could require reconsideration in coming years.

Factors Influencing Decisions to Expand Internationally

An assessment of the business's current situation and goals is critical. The types of legal and business issues involved in deciding whether to do business internationally include the following:

- What product or service is the business planning to export or import?
- What is the desired level of control over overseas operations?
- How mature is the business and how much experience does it have working internationally?
- How much risk is the business willing and able to bear?
- How much capital is available to invest?
- How does international expansion fit with the company's long-term goals and strategy?

Factors Influencing Geographic Choices

If international expansion appears feasible and profitable, what factors influence the choice of where to expand? This decision rests largely on an analysis of the

Shareholders of multinational corporations, such as Daimler AG, meet with directors and executives at annual shareholder meetings.

economic, political, cultural, and even historic context of the relevant country. A business considering international expansion must investigate, for example, currency exchange rates and volatility; economic climate; political stability; shipping costs to, from, and within the foreign region; labor laws and the employment market; and potential language barriers.

Legal Structures for International Expansion

Suppose, for example, you are the general manager of Apple Menagerie, Inc. ("AM"), a facility that grows, processes, and cans apples and manufactures apple products in Massachusetts. AM has a U.S. patent for a unique method for processing apples. You believe that the company has capacity to grow and expand operations. After reviewing the situation, you think the U.S. market for apple products is saturated, but there is potential outside the United States. How can you tap into international markets? Broadly, there are three categories of choices for international expansion, each with different risks, costs, efficiencies, and potential liabilities. These options are listed in order of increasing presence in the foreign market, from minimum to maximum involvement.

Import/Export The simplest and usually lowest risk way to expand internationally is by importing foreign goods or services or by exporting domestic goods or services. Selling directly to a buyer who takes delivery in a foreign country is called *exporting*; purchasing and taking delivery in the United States from a seller in a foreign country is called *importing*. This can be accomplished through direct import/export sales, sales representatives and sales agents, distributorships, export trading offices, or branch offices.

- **Direct import/export sales.** Normally, in a direct import or export sale, parties sign a sales contract providing for terms and conditions of the sale — a relatively straightforward arrangement. Suppose you locate a buyer for apples in France and sign a sales contract. The apples would be subject to U.S. export regulations, European Union import regulations, and European Union tariffs. The buyer might use the apples, resell them within France, or re-export them to a different foreign country. In comparison to other avenues for expanding internationally, direct import or export sales involve less political, economic, and legal risk. AM must solicit its own sales leads, which could be challenging. Also, disagreements can arise, such as contract disputes, nondelivery, delivery of nonconforming goods, or nonpayment. Sometimes these disputes are exacerbated due to language barriers, difficulty in communicating quickly and clearly, and problems in pursuing legal claims.

- **Sales representatives and sales agents.** A relatively low-risk way to cultivate international sales is by appointing a person in the foreign country to help facilitate sales. Engaging the services of a professional located in France could be an attractive arrangement for penetrating the French market. He or she is in a good position to understand and react quickly to the local market trends and to cultivate customer relationships. There are two possible arrangements. A *sales representative* finds sales leads. Usually the home office provides the foreign sales representative with marketing materials. The sales representative earns a commission upon forwarding a lead that materializes into a completed sale. A *sales agent*, as the name implies, is an agent for the company and is authorized to enter binding contracts with foreign customers on behalf of the U.S. principal. Neither sales agents nor sales representatives take title to the goods.

  Some countries do not allow sales representatives or agents at all; a few countries consider them employees and still other countries require specific procedures for terminating sales representatives and agents. All these issues are governed by the laws of the country in which representatives or agents operate. Unless otherwise specified by contract, both sales agents and sales representatives can work for other companies in a similar capacity. This can be advantageous if, for example, the representative or agent has a robust customer base in the food and restaurant industry and is selling complementary food products. On the other hand, it can be a drawback because the agent's or the representative's effort and time may be divided among several different companies.

- **Distributorship.** If there is sufficient sales potential in the foreign market, AM might choose to use a distributor. A *distributor* is a person or company that buys goods (usually in bulk), pays for the goods, and takes title to the goods, with the intent of reselling them. As such, distributors bear the financial risks that the goods cannot be resold or cannot be profitably resold. They are not agents of the company whose products they purchase. They are responsible for providing post-sales support, customer service, whether to extend credit, and extending and honoring warranties.

To establish a distributorship, AM and a French individual or company would enter a contract with many of the same terms and conditions as a sales contract. Additionally, distributorship contracts address whether the distributorship is exclusive. Either (or both) parties can promise exclusivity. For example, AM could promise not to contract with any other distributors in the European Union. The French distributor could promise not to sell any competing products from other companies. Exclusivity can be beneficial to both parties. The distributor need not compete with others, and AM receives the benefit of the distributor's full loyalty and energies. However, exclusive distributorships could violate antitrust laws and must be carefully reviewed to avoid conflict with a foreign jurisdiction's antitrust or competition laws.

Using a French distributor could offer several advantages for AM. In essence, AM would be transferring the risks that the product will not sell. AM would also be transferring the responsibility of post-sale support, honoring warranties, customer service, and the like. AM would not need to devote time or money to studying the French market and maintaining business operations in a foreign location. It can be an efficient arrangement — like the sales representative or agent, a French distributor, with its business contacts, knowledge of French markets, and understanding of French conditions, is in the best position to solicit and transact business in France.

■ **Export trading company.** Some regions of the world, notably Asia, rely heavily on transacting international business through the use of export trading companies. An export trading company is an independent company that operates as intermediary between a buyer and seller from different countries. An export trading company would negotiate with AM, to find a customer in, say, China. The export trading company would then buy the apples, pay for them, take title to them, and arrange for their transportation to the ultimate customer.

■ **Branch office.** As its name implies, a *branch office* is an extension of a company's main office, not a separate entity. As such, the company is legally liable for the actions of branch office workers in accordance with agency law. If AM wants to control foreign operations exclusively and directly, it could use an international branch office to gain presence and operate in a foreign market. Branch offices that conduct business in a foreign jurisdiction must be registered in the jurisdiction, abide by relevant laws, and may be subject to local taxation.

Licensing and Franchising A domestic firm can also generate revenue by (A) licensing its intellectual property to an existing foreign company or by (B) franchising.

■ **Licensing.** An intellectual property *license* is the right to use, manufacture, and/or distribute the licensor's technology, art, information, invention, trademark, or other intellectual property, usually in exchange for royalty payments. This exchange is effectuated by contract, called a *licensing agreement*. All forms of intellectual property — patents, copyrights, trademarks, and trade secrets — can be licensed. A technology license, for example, permits a manufacturer to produce the licensed product. In an international context, licensing has many strategic uses. AM could first obtain patent protection in Brazil and then enter a licensing agreement with the Brazilian manufacturer. There are a few variations of this arrangement. For example,

- The Brazilian company could use the patented technique and sell the resulting products in the local Brazilian market. AM would receive royalties. Often, royalties in such arrangements are based on a percentage of sales. In this scenario, AM could generate a stream of income, with little capital or direct foreign investment.

- Suppose that AM wanted to sell the apple products processed at the Brazilian plant. Instead of buying or building a plant in Brazil, AM could license the Brazilian plant to use the patented technique. Then AM could sell the finished products, either in Brazil or by importing them into the United States. This would allow AM to leverage lower costs for labor, equipment, and other necessities. If the final products were sold in Brazil, there would be no Brazilian import restrictions or tariffs, and the costs of shipping to retailers would be lower than if the products were transported from the United States. But there are also potential problems. Licensees must be carefully selected — poor quality at the factory level could harm AM's reputation. If the license involves know-how or trade secrets instead of patents, the licensor risks that its trade secrets will be misappropriated deliberately or revealed through a licensee's carelessness.

- **Franchising.** A **franchise** is a specialized type of license. It is a trademark license, accompanied by specific procedures and business plans relating to conducting a particular business. SUBWAY, for example, enters into franchise agreements permitting franchisees to use SUBWAY'S name, logo, marketing materials, etc., and requiring franchisees to sell certain menu items, make its sandwiches a certain way, and adhere to many other specifications. In exchange, SUBWAY receives a specified share of the franchisee's gross or net sales. The franchisee gains automatic credibility, reputation, and name recognition; the franchisor receives income and spreads its reputation globally. U.S. fast food restaurants in particular have franchises all over the world. As with other types of licensing, supervision and monitoring are key. A franchise's reputation can be quickly ruined by a rogue or careless franchisee.

Foreign Direct Investment Foreign direct investment refers to a U.S. firm directly investing in and actively controlling at least a portion of an ongoing business in another country. This is best suited to U.S. firms that seek maximum penetration of foreign markets, have capital available, and are experienced enough to oversee a substantial level of foreign business involvement. The two most common types of foreign direct investments are joint ventures and subsidiaries.

■ **Joint ventures.** A U.S. company and a foreign entity[7] can form a *joint venture* whereby they contractually agree to work together on a business or business effort, sharing both profit and liabilities. Typically, each party contributes different, complementary strengths or resources to the venture. Synergy and economies of scale can help add value to the endeavor. For example, AM could form a joint venture with an established fruit processing company in the Bahamas to process, distribute, and sell canned fruit. AM could contribute use of its patent and trade secrets relating to processing fruit, and the Bahamian firm could contribute use of its plant, equipment, experienced workers, knowledge of the local market, and established business contacts. This involves less capital investment than if AM solely owned a plant in the Bahamas, but it also involves less control over operations. A joint venture could be beneficial to the Bahamian firm if it lacks sufficient technological capabilities to develop state-of-the-art fruit processing techniques by itself. In countries where markets are restricted to those with local ownership, joint ventures can be one way to meet the local ownership requirement.

■ **Subsidiaries.** A **subsidiary** is a corporation, the controlling majority of whose stock is owned by another corporation. A subsidiary is a separate, independently managed legal entity, with its own board of directors and officers. Because it is a separate entity, the parent is ordinarily not liable for the obligations, debts, or torts of the subsidiary, and vice versa (unless laws of the country in which the subsidiary is incorporated provide otherwise). It is separately capitalized and subject to the corporate laws of the country in which it is incorporated.

Establishing a foreign subsidiary can be a strategic way to establish and maintain a strong international business presence. For example, a foreign subsidiary could be established to operate production facilities while minimizing risk. AM could either buy an existing plant in, say, India or build a new one. The plant would be separately incorporated and AM would own a majority of its shares. As majority shareholder, AM would have control over the board of directors and management. Yet, because AM and the subsidiary are separately incorporated, AM is shielded from responsibility for the subsidiary's accidents, negligence, and other liabilities arising from the manufacturing process and other operations. Not surprisingly, establishing an international subsidiary can be complicated and expensive. Legal and tax issues in particular must be evaluated carefully before embarking on the task of setting up a subsidiary.

---

[7]Or a foreign government.

Summary

A variety of legal structures exist to assist in the formation and operation of a business entity. These include sole proprietorships, general partnerships, limited partnerships, limited liability partnerships (LLPs), limited liability companies (LLCs), and corporations. Business owners decide what type of legal structure to adopt depending on their needs and goals. Over the years, laws have developed to assist minority shareholders in closely held corporations as well as minority shareholders in publicly held corporations. Judicial doctrines, such as piercing the corporate veil and the business judgment rule, influence how owners and managers operate their businesses. As an increasing number of businesses, large and small, transact business outside the United States, international laws affecting business structures, operations, taxation, and ethical requirements have assumed a greater role in the running of a business.

Questions for Review

1. Sole proprietorship and limited liability companies

Jalila owns and manages a small business (E Connections) that sells electronic connectors and network components. The following industries purchase products from E Connections: mechanical and plant engineering, broadcast and entertainment, and industrial electronics and telecommunications. Jalila has operated E Connections as a sole proprietorship for the past five years. E Connections employs five individuals on a full-time basis and seven on a part-time basis. The part-time workers are classified as independent contractors. Jalila expects the company's annual revenues to grow at a rate of about 10 percent during the coming five years. She uses a local bank for her commercial banking needs, which includes a credit line of $50,000. Currently, Jalila handles bookkeeping requirements at E Connections. A certified public accountant (CPA) prepares her annual tax return. Recently, a business associate suggested to Jalila that she consider converting the legal structure of E Connections from a sole proprietorship to an LLC. Discuss the advantages and disadvantages of operating E Connections as a sole proprietorship versus an LLC.

2. Limited liability and piercing the corporate veil

Best Equipment, Inc., sells a variety of landscaping equipment. Karl, the owner and CEO of Best Equipment, started the business twenty years ago. During its first ten years of operations, Karl organized the business as a sole proprietorship. During this period, Karl referred to the proprietorship as Karl's Equipment. When Karl incorporated Best Equipment, Inc., he received 100 shares of common stock with a par value of $1,500 per share. In exchange for the common stock, Karl transferred legal title of the sole proprietorship's assets to Best Equipment, Inc.

Best Equipment, Inc., grew at a comfortable pace until 2009. Like many companies during this period, Best Equipment began to feel the effects of the recession that began in 2008. To help maintain a reasonable cash position, Best Equipment borrowed funds from two sources in 2009. It secured a $75,000 commercial loan from Main Street Bank and a $20,000 shareholder loan from Karl in his capacity as Best Equipment's sole shareholder. Both loans are supported by signed promissory notes.

Despite its best efforts, Best Equipment was unable to recover from the recession.

Karl decided to cease operations and close Best Equipment, Inc., in 2013. One week prior to the closing date, Karl, in his capacity as CEO, used Best Equipment's remaining cash to pay the outstanding balance of the shareholder loan. However, the outstanding balance of Main Street Bank's commercial loan remains unpaid.

Discussion Questions

a. Describe the concept of "limited liability." If Main Street Bank decides to sue Karl and Best Equipment, Inc., for the outstanding balance of its loan, what legal theories is it likely to advance? Explain.

b. Would Best Equipment, Inc., be classified as a closely held corporation or a publicly held corporation? Identify three differences between a closely held corporation and a publicly held corporation.

c. Discuss the ethical implications and the legal consequences of Karl's decision, as CEO of Best Equipment, Inc., to instruct the corporation to use all of its cash to pay the outstanding balance of the shareholder loan, but not the outstanding balance of Main Street Bank's commercial loan.

3. Ethics in business organizations

Tony is a sole proprietor who owns 40 cabs doing business in Chicago under the name of Tony's Cabs. The company's total net worth is over one million dollars and Tony has personal assets totaling $800,000. Tony's lawyer recently formed four corporations. Tony is the sole shareholder of each corporation. Under Tony's instruction, his lawyer transferred 10 cabs into each corporation. The cabs were owned originally by Tony and used in his previous business, Tony's Cabs. A week after the four corporations were formed, a passenger was riding in a cab owned by one of the corporations and sustained serious injuries when the cab driver negligently smashed into another vehicle. A police investigation determined that the cab driver was operating the cab under the influence of drugs and alcohol. The passenger plans to sue the corporation and its sole shareholder, Tony, for $10 million. Discuss the ethical implications of the decision to form four corporations and transfer the assets of "Tony's Cabs" into these newly formed corporations.

4. LLCs and piercing the corporate veil

Planes-for-Rent, Inc., (PFR) leases airplanes. Dayton, LLC, is one of PFR's customers. Dayton is a limited liability company with one member, Jacob, who is Dayton's sole owner. Dayton and PFR executed a five-year contract that calls for PFR to make available to Dayton a certain model plane four business days each month. The arrangement worked well for approximately two years. However, in the third year of the contract, Dayton began to experience financial problems. Because of these problems, the chief financial officer of Dayton contacted PFR's chief executive officer to inform her that Dayton is unable to pay its $248,000 outstanding debt to PFR.

PFR initiated a lawsuit against Dayton and its sole owner, Jacob, alleging breach of contract against Dayton and unjust enrichment against Jacob. During the discovery phase of the lawsuit, PFR discovered that Jacob and his family regularly used Dayton's planes for personal use. Furthermore, PRF discovered that Jacob regularly transferred funds between his personal checking account and Dayton's checking account, and often borrowed funds from Dayton without any evidence of repayment of the alleged loans. Consequently, PFR asserts that Jacob should be held personally liable for the $248,000 debt because his frequent withdrawing of funds from Dayton caused the company to have minimal assets. Do you believe PFR will be successful in pursuing its legal claims against Dayton and Jacob? Explain. *Netjets Aviation, Inc. v. Zimmerman*, 537 F.3d 168 (2nd Cir. 2008)

5. Limited liability company versus corporation

Describe the advantages and disadvantages of forming a limited liability company (LLC) versus a corporation.

6. Business judgment rule, conflict of interest, minority shareholder rights

Sand Corporation, a publicly held corporation, owns 90 percent of the outstanding voting stock of Beach Corporation. Lance Jones, the CEO of Beach Corporation, owns the remaining 10 percent of Beach's outstanding voting stock. Most of the members of Beach's board of directors were nominated by the chair of Sand Corporation's board of directors. For the past five years, Beach Corporation has been very profitable, resulting in a large cash reserve. On the other hand, Sand Corporation's business operations have taken a turn for the worse. Its cash position is very weak.

Lance believes that recent decisions by Beach's board of directors have not been in the best interest of Beach Corporation. For example, Beach's directors voted recently to declare a cash dividend, which when distributed will effectively exhaust Beach's cash reserves. Lance has determined that the dividend will force Beach to borrow funds from a local commercial bank at an unusually high interest rate.

Discussion Questions

Lance has asked you if there is any legal action that can be taken to force Beach's board of directors to reverse its decision to declare and pay a cash dividend. In your response to Lance, consider the following rules and doctrines:

a. The business judgment rule
b. The doctrine that majority shareholders owe a strict duty of utmost good faith and loyalty to the minority shareholders

7. Derivative shareholder action

Explain the purpose, use, and limitations of a derivative shareholder action.

8. International considerations

If you wanted to expand your business to include international customers and vendors, what factors would influence your decision? Use examples to support your answer.

Further Reading

Cramer, K. D., *Back from the Brink: Boyd's Private Papers Protection and the Sole Proprietor's Business Records*, 21 American Business Law Journal, 367–402 (1984).

Langvardt, A. W., *A Principled Approach to Compensatory Damages in Corporate Defamation Cases*, 27 American Business Law Journal, 491–534 (1990).

Leibman, J. H., and Kelly, A. S., *Accountants' Liability to Third Parties for Negligent Misrepresentation: The Search for a New Limiting Principle*, 30 American Business Law Journal, 347–439 (1992).

Metzger, M. B., and Dalton, D. R., *Seeing the Elephant: An Organizational Perspective on Corporate Moral Agency*, 33 American Business Law Journal, 489–576 (1996).

Ostas, D. T., *When Fraud Pays: Executive Self-Dealing and the Failure of Self-Restraint*, 44 American Business Law Journal, 571–601 (2007).

CHAPTER 8

Intellectual Property

Chapter Objectives

1. To be able to define the term intellectual property, and list its principal types
2. To understand the kinds of business assets that can be protected by intellectual property
3. To understand how businesses acquire intellectual property rights
4. To explore the ethical theories that may justify intellectual property
5. To explore how intellectual property protection has increased over time

Practical Example: Who Owns Your Online Data?

The average person has 20 to 25 online accounts, each with a potential treasure trove of digital assets: e-mail accounts may contain thousands of messages; Facebook[*] can store years of photos and posts; and Dropbox can hold countless digital files of all types in password-protectable accounts. Who controls these digital assets, and what happens to them when the account holder dies? The law in this emerging area is unsettled, in part because the usual rules of inheritance and control can sometimes come into conflict with a service provider's "click-through" terms-of-service agreement. As you read the chapter, consider which types of intellectual property may be implicated in the storage and transfer of online digital assets. *See* Jonathan J. Darrow and Gerald R. Ferrera, *Who Owns a Decedent's E-Mails? Inheritable Probate Assets or Property of the Network?* 10 NYU Journal of Legislation and Public Policy 281 (2007).

---

[*] Facebook, Inc., is a social networking website where users can communicate and share photos with one another.

Overview of Intellectual Property

Intellectual property and the innovative and creative activities it protects are central to the modern information economy. Entrepreneurs are more likely to obtain venture capital funding if they have strong patent portfolios. For the U.S. economy as a whole, the U.S. Chamber of Commerce estimates that intellectual property intensive industries employ up to 19 million American workers and constitute up to 33 percent of U.S. gross domestic product. At the international level, intellectual property contributes to a positive balance of trade (exports exceed imports) in such industries as motion pictures, music, software, and video games. More broadly, technological innovation is estimated to be responsible for 75 percent of cumulative economic growth in the United States since World War II. It should be clear, then, that protection of intellectual property is of great concern in the modern world. This chapter explores the major types of intellectual property and explains their importance to the business environment.

Types of Intellectual Property

Intellectual property (IP) can be divided into four principal categories: patents, copyrights, trademarks, and trade secrets. A *patent* provides the right to prevent others from using an invention, such as a new drug or a more efficient lightbulb. A *copyright* provides the right to prevent others from copying an original work of authorship, such as a book, film, or musical recording. A *trademark* provides the right to prevent others from using a confusingly similar symbol to identify competing products or services. Only McDonald's, for example, can use the golden arches to identify its fast-food restaurants. Virtually any secret and valuable business information, such as a product formula, customer list, or undisclosed software code, can be protected as a *trade secret*. The formula for Coca-Cola is perhaps the most famous trade secret.

Businesses can provide notice that a particular product or service is protected by IP by using certain symbols or abbreviations, which are presented in Exhibit 8.1. These symbols may be placed, for example, on product packaging, in advertisements, or on products themselves.

Intellectual Property Rights Are "Negative Rights"

Intellectual property rights (IPR) are often misunderstood to confer the affirmative right to use a patented invention, copyrighted work, trademark, or trade secret. In fact, IP owners generally have only the "negative right" to *exclude others* from making, using, or copying IP. This negative aspect of IPRs becomes important when two or more related IP rights overlap, which occurs quite frequently. For example, the owner of an invention kept as a trade secret (rather than patented) may suddenly be legally unable to continue practicing its own trade secret if another party independently arrives at the same

Exhibit 8.1. Intellectual Property Symbols	
Type of Intellectual Property	**Symbol(s) or Abbreviation**
Patent	Pat.
Copyright	©, Copr.
Trademark	®, TM, SM
Trade Secret	[None]

invention and obtains a patent on it. An example in the trademark context is provided by the Masco Corporation of Indiana, which owns a trademark on the word "Delta" for use on water faucets and other plumbing products. Although Masco can prevent others from using an identical or confusingly similar mark on water faucets and other plumbing products, it does not have the affirmative right to use its trademark on airplanes because another company, Delta Air Lines, holds the trademark rights (i.e., rights to exclude) to "Delta" with respect to passenger air transportation services.

In the case of patents and copyrights, negative rights become most evident when later patented inventions or copyrighted works build upon earlier inventions or works. In these cases, which occur frequently, the owner of the earlier patent or copyright may be able to exclude later inventors or creators from exploiting their own creations. An example from the copyright context is provided in the Case Illustration at the right.

What Is Property?

A defining characteristic of all property is the right to *exclude others*. For example, a land owner may exclude others from the land, and the law will enforce this right by imposing liability for trespass. Similarly, the owner of an automobile or wristwatch can exclude others from using or taking those items, and violators may be prosecuted for theft. From the perspective of a business, IP can be conceived of as a right to exclude competitors from "stealing" an invention, product design, website layout, trade secret or other information protected by IPRs.

Case Illustration

Perhaps no comic book hero is more famous than Superman. Initially conceived by Jerome Siegel and Joseph Shuster between 1933 and 1934, the cape-wearing superhero could hurdle skyscrapers and run faster than an express train, all while aiding the down-trodden and oppressed. In 1978 the blockbuster film *Superman*, based on the earlier comic book work, was released in theaters. Although the copyright in a film enables its owner to *prevent others* from unauthorized copying, several rounds of litigation initiated by Siegel and Shuster created some uncertainty regarding the extent of Warner Brothers' affirmative right to make and distribute its own film. This is because the owner of an underlying copyright (in this case the Superman comic book copyright) is normally authorized to prevent the creation of derivative works, such as a film that is based on a book. Fortunately for Warner Brothers, a 1973 court decision held that Siegel and Shuster had assigned "all their rights" to Detective Comics in a 1938 agreement, and the rights were later acquired by Warner Brothers. Despite the 1973 ruling and the passing of Siegel and Shuster in the 1990s, the Superman litigation — first begun in 1947 — has continued to the present, with the heirs of Siegel and Shuster continuing to assert claims to the Superman profits. Due to repeated legislative extensions of the copyright term, Superman will not enter the public domain until 2033 at the earliest. *Siegel v. Warner Bros. Entm't Inc.*, 542 F. Supp. 2d 1098 (C.D. Cal. 2008).

Intellectual Property: A Strange Sort of "Property"

Although the term *intellectual property* accurately implies similarity with other forms of property, including the right to exclude, it is unlike ordinary property in number of ways. First, some IP is *limited in duration*. Patents, for example, expire 20 years from the date the patent application was filed, after which time anyone can use the patented information without compensation or even notification to the former patent holder. Second, IP is *intangible*, although it is usually embodied in tangible objects. For example, even though you may have purchased this textbook, a tangible object, the copyright in the book is intangible and remains with Wolters Kluwer, the publisher. Only Wolters Kluwer could assert the copyright to prevent a third party from making unauthorized copies of the book. Third, IP is **nonrivalrous**, meaning that it can be simultaneously used by multiple parties without diminishing the amount available to others. For example, the secret formula for Coca-Cola can be used to produce Coca-Cola syrup in an unlimited number of manufacturing facilities around the globe. In contrast, most goods and services are **rivalrous**. For example, a bite of steak can be consumed in its entirety by only one person. Similarly, if one person occupies an airplane seat, another person cannot simultaneously occupy the same seat.

An Ethical Insight: John Locke and the Justification for Intellectual Property

Intellectual property can be justified under a number of philosophical theories. One of these is the Lockean labor theory, which stems from the writings of English philosopher John Locke. In his *Second Treatise of Government* (1690), Locke argued that although God "hath given the world to men in common," an individual could acquire rights over particular property, to the exclusion of others, by "mix[ing] his labor with it." As an example, Locke suggests that if a person labors to gather apples from trees in the wilderness, the apples become that person's property. Lockean labor theory could be extended to justify intellectual property: by laboring to create a painting or to develop an invention, the painter and inventor have acquired rights to the resulting fruits of their labor.

Trademarks

The **Lanham Act of 1946**, also known as the Federal Trademark Act, defines a **trademark** as "any word, name, symbol, or device . . . used by a person . . . to identify and distinguish his or her goods . . . from those manufactured or sold by others. . . ."[1] Informally, trademarks are often called "brands." **Service marks** such as State Farm (insurance), Six Flags (amusement parks), or Rice University (higher education) serve to distinguish one service provider from another. Organizations such as the Boy Scouts of America or the National Honor Society may obtain **collective marks** to protect their names. Finally, organizations that certify the products or services of others

---

[1] 15 U.S.C. § 1127.

may obtain **certification marks**. For example, the Orthodox Union has obtained a certification mark consisting of the letter *U* in a circle, and authorizes third parties to use this mark on food that has been certified by the Orthodox Union as kosher, while the Association to Advance Collegiate Schools of Business was granted a certification mark to designate "AACSB Accredited" business schools.

Trademarks, service marks, collective marks, and certification marks are collectively known as **marks** and receive essentially the same legal protection under the Lanham Act. Therefore, when the term *trademark* is used, it should be understood that the same principles also apply to the other types of marks.

The Purpose of Trademarks

Trademarks simultaneously serve two complementary purposes: First, trademarks protect the goodwill and reputation of a business by, for example, preventing counterfeit or lower-quality imitation products from bearing the same or confusingly similar trademarks (i.e., preventing the imitation product from being "**palmed off**" as the originator product). Second, trademarks protect the public by ensuring that consumers are not deceived or confused into purchasing products other than the ones they expect and want to buy.

Trademark Registration and Renewal

Businesses seeking to protect a trademark may apply to register the mark with the **U.S. Patent and Trademark Office** (USPTO), a federal administrative agency that is located just outside of Washington, DC. The basic filing fee is currently $280 if submitted electronically. If the registration is granted, the trademark owner can then use the symbol ® to inform the public that the mark is registered. (This symbol should not be confused with the © symbol, which is used to designate a copyright.)

Trademarks receive protection under the Lanham Act even if not registered with the USPTO. However, registration is advisable as it establishes nationwide rights in the mark even if the product is not yet sold nationwide, enables criminal prosecution for counterfeiting, and may allow a business to recover more money should a judgment be rendered against an infringer. Businesses sometimes choose to use the symbols TM (trademark) or SM (service mark) to let other businesses know they are claiming rights in an unregistered mark, such as a mark whose registration is pending. The initial term of protection is ten years, and trademarks may be renewed for unlimited additional ten-year periods upon the payment of a fee (currently $400). The current fee schedule is available at uspto.gov.

Unusual Trademarks

The simplest type of mark is a word mark, consisting of words in nonstylized all-capital letters (e.g., YAHOO!). Trademarks may also consist of words combined with symbols, and can include specific fonts, colors, or sizes (e.g., **YAHOO!**). In fact, almost anything that serves to distinctly identify the products or services of one company can be used as a trademark:

■ **Sounds**. The sound of the New York Stock Exchange closing bell has been registered as a trademark, as has the distinctive lion's roar on MGM movies and the five-note sequence played during Intel commercials (below).[2]

■ **Touch**. Tactile trademarks are also possible, such as the distinctive touch and feel of a medicine bottle with a plasticized surface or the leather texture wrapping around the middle surface of a bottle of wine.
■ **Scent**. Scent marks have been obtained or applied for in connection with the sale of toothbrushes (strawberry scent) and for a retail store environment that sells flip-flops and other beach-related products (coconut scent).
■ **Color**. In some cases, color can be trademarked independently of words or symbols. United Parcel Service, for example, has registered its distinct shade of chocolate brown for use on its delivery trucks and uniforms, and Owens Corning has obtained a trademark for its particular shade of pink with respect to insulation products.
■ **Shape**. Distinctive shapes, such as the shape of Apple's iPod and PepsiCo's soft drink bottle (left), have also been registered.

The "Likelihood of Confusion" Standard

Trademark infringement occurs when someone other than the mark owner uses an identical or confusingly similar mark in connection with similar products or services such that there is a **likelihood of confusion** as to the origin of the products or services. Both the product market and the geographic market are relevant when determining the existence of a likelihood of confusion. For example, "Lexus" as a mark for automobiles is not confusingly similar to "Lexis" as a mark for online legal research services despite their similar pronunciations and spellings because the two terms are used in unrelated product markets. Similarly, when the owner of the Taj Mahal restaurant in Washington, DC, brought suit against Donald Trump for opening a casino and resort under the name Trump Taj Mahal in New Jersey, the district court found no likelihood of

---

[2]Registration No. 3,659,390 (July 21, 2009) ("The mark consists of a five tone audio progression of the notes D Flat, D Flat, G Flat, D Flat, and A Flat.").

confusion in part because the businesses were located in different geographic markets.[3] In order to avoid applying for a trademark that is confusingly similar to an existing mark, businesses can utilize the free Trademark Electronic Search System (TESS), available at uspto.gov.

Trademark Dilution

Even where two businesses operate in entirely separate product or geographic markets and there is no likelihood of confusion, it is still possible that the use of a similar or identical mark will constitute **trademark dilution**. The Federal Trademark Dilution Act of 1995 prevents third parties from selling such hypothetical anomalies as DuPont shoes, Buick aspirin, and Kodak pianos, even though those companies do not sell competing shoes, aspirin, or pianos, respectively. While infringement under the likelihood of confusion standard applies to all trademarks, only owners of "famous" trademarks can bring a cause of action for dilution. In the Lexis-Lexus example provided above, the court found no dilution in part because the plaintiff's Lexis mark was not famous in the general population.[4]

The Distinctiveness Continuum

Court decisions have established four levels of distinctiveness into which marks or potential marks can be classified. From least distinctive to most distinctive, these are (1) generic, (2) descriptive, (3) suggestive, and (4) arbitrary or fanciful.[5] A **generic** word is simply the name of a type of product and cannot be appropriated by a company for use as a trademark. "Ivory," for example, is a generic term for products made from the tusks of elephants, and so cannot be registered as a trademark for such products. **Descriptive** terms describe a product or service and can be registered only if the term has acquired **secondary meaning** (i.e., if consumers recognize the term as denoting a particular company or source rather than being merely descriptive). For example, The Scooter Store merely describes a store that sells scooters, but became eligible for trademark protection as a result of heavy advertising.

In contrast to generic and descriptive terms, some words or symbols are automatically eligible for trademark protection because they are "inherently distinctive." These include **suggestive** marks, which suggest but do not describe a product or service. Roach Motel, for example, is suggestive as a trademark for insect traps. Arbitrary or fanciful marks are considered the strongest marks and will normally be the easiest to register. An **arbitrary** mark consists of a common word used in an unfamiliar way. For example,

---

[3]*Taj Mahal Enterprises v. Trump*, 745 F.Supp. 240 (D.N.J. 1990).
[4]*Mead Data Central, Inc. v. Toyota Motor Sales, U.S.A., Inc.*, 875 F.2d 1026 (2d Cir. 1989).
[5]*Abercrombie & Fitch Co. v. Hunting World, Inc.*, 537 F.2d 4 (2d Cir. 1976).

Exhibit 8.2. The Trademark Distinctiveness Continuum

	Category	Registrable?	Examples
Most Distinctive	Arbitrary/ Fanciful	Yes	Exxon, Kodak, Hulu, Ivory (soap)
	Suggestive	Yes	Roach Motel, Facebook, Coppertone (sun tan lotion)
	Descriptive	Only if secondary meaning	Holiday Inn, Raisin Bran (cereal), Chap Stick
Least Distinctive	Generic	No	aspirin, computer, pilates (exercise)

although "Ivory" is the generic name for products made from elephant tusks, it is arbitrary as applied to soap and therefore registrable as to soap. **Fanciful** marks consist of words coined for the purpose of creating a trademark and do not have a separate ordinary meaning. Exxon and Kodak are frequently cited as examples.

The four categories just described are not rigidly discrete, and courts are often called upon to appropriately classify a disputed mark. In fact, all marks or potential marks may be considered to lie along a continuum from least likely to be registrable to most likely (Exhibit 8.2).

Genericide

A great irony of trademark law is that a mark can become so successful and well known that it becomes the generic term for a product, and trademark rights will then be lost. Once-famous trademarks that have become generic include dry ice, thermos, escalator, yo-yo, cellophane, and zipper. Companies aware of the risk of **genericide** sometimes advertise in order to discourage the public from using a trademarked term as if it were generic (Exhibit 8.3).

Domain Names

A **domain name** is the address for a website, such as www.google.com. Businesses or others can acquire the ability to use domain names from entities called "domain name registrars," which are accredited by a nonprofit organization known as the Internet Corporation for Assigned Names and Numbers (ICANN). Because the process of registering a domain name with an ICANN-accredited registrar is entirely separate from the process of registering a trademark with the USPTO, conflicts frequently arise over the rights to a given domain name. These disputes can take the form of **cybersquatting**,

Exhibit 8.3. Advertisement by Kimberly-Clark to Prevent Genericide of the Kleenex Trademark

do not erase

You may not realize it, but by using the name **Kleenex**®
as a generic term for tissue, you risk erasing our coveted
brand name that we've worked so hard for all these
years. **Kleenex**® is a registered trademark and should
always be followed by a ® and the words 'Brand Tissue.'
Just pretend it's in permanent marker.

the bad-faith registration of an Internet domain name that contains the trademark of another, with the intent to free-ride off of the goodwill associated with that trademark. **Typosquatting**, a subcategory of cybersquatting, is the registration of domain names that contain intentional misspellings of others' distinctive trademarks in order to divert Internet traffic to the typosquatter's site (e.g., "Microsof.com").

Case Illustration

In the landmark case of *Panavision v. Toeppen*, an individual named Dennis Toeppen registered more than 100 domain names containing the well-known trademarks of others, including "panavision.com," "yankeesstadium.com," and "nieman-marcus.com." Toeppen offered to sell "panavision.com" to Panavision for $13,000, but the company declined. Instead, Panavision brought suit in the federal district court, where a judge determined that Toeppen had violated both state and federal trademark dilution laws, and ordered the domain name transferred to Panavision. *Panavision Int'l, L.P. v. Toeppen*, 945 F.Supp. 1296 (C.D. Cal. 1996).

Although courts have the power to award money damages for trademark violations, the new Internet context created uncertainty about the effectiveness of existing remedies. In the *Panavision* Case Illustration (left), for example, Toeppen was forced to transfer the domain name and enjoined from further violations but was not ordered to pay any damages. Recognizing the growing problem of cybersquatting and seeking to tip the balance in favor of trademark owners in this important new environment, Congress enacted the **Anticybersquatting Consumer Protection Act (ACPA)**[6] in 1999. The ACPA prohibits registering in bad faith a domain name that is identical or confusingly similar to the trademark of another and allows trademark owners to recover between $1,000 and $100,000 per wrongfully registered domain name, as the court considers just. Businesses may also arbitrate domain name disputes through the World Intellectual Property Organization (WIPO). Although WIPO domain name arbitration generally costs less than ACPA litigation and can resolve a dispute more quickly, arbitrators are only able to cancel or transfer domain names and cannot award damages or attorney fees.

An Explosion of New Generic Top-Level Domains?

Until recently, there were only 22 generic top-level domains (gTLDs), such as .com, .edu, .gov, and .org. In 2012, ICANN began allowing private businesses to apply to operate new gTLDs, which could consist of virtually any suffix, such as .salsa, .berlin, or .pepsi. Unlike the registration of a domain name, which is relatively inexpensive, an application to operate a new gTLD requires a fee of $185,000. Moreover, if the application is granted, the applicant must be able to actively manage the associated domain registry, including the allocation to third parties of domain names within its gTLD. Even though the potential benefits to commerce of the new gTLDs may be substantial, some fear that these new gTLDs may increase the potential for trademark infringement by

---

[6]Pub. L. No. 106-113, 113 Stat. 1501 (1999).

opening up many more gTLDs that could contain the trademark of another (e.g., mcdonalds.berlin).

Copyright

A **copyright** protects creative works of expression, such as books, web pages, music, works of art, and motion pictures, from unauthorized copying by others. Under the federal **Copyright Act of 1976**, copyright owners have the right to prevent unauthorized copying of original works that are "fixed in any tangible medium of expression."[7] This right includes the right to prevent **piracy**, the intentional copying of entire works without any lawful pretext, often on a large scale and for commercial gain, and also includes the right to prevent unintentional or inadvertent copying. In addition, copyright owners may prevent the public distribution, performance, or display of a work, such as the unauthorized uploading of a document or video to the Internet. Finally, copyright guarantees authors the exclusive rights to create **derivative works**, that is, works based upon a preexisting work (such as a translation, musical arrangement, or motion picture version).

Copyright Duration

Copyright duration is very long, providing protection during the whole of an author's life and for 70 years thereafter. Thus, a work created in 2015 by a 25-year-old author who lives to age 75 would not expire until the year 2135.

Employers and Copyright Duration

In the business context, many copyrightable works are created by employees in the course of their employment, such as software, architectural designs, advertising copy, or entire motion pictures. Where a work is prepared by an employee within the scope of employment, the work is a **work made for hire** and the copyright belongs to the employer rather than the employee. The copyright duration of works made for hire is 95 years from date of publication (but in no case longer than 120 years from the date of creation).

Case Illustration

By law, copyright only applies to works that are fixed in a "tangible medium of expression," such as a book, videotape, sculpture, or computer hard drive. It might be wondered, then, whether concert attendees may legally "bootleg" (record without permission) live performances that are not previously fixed. The answer is that they cannot legally do so. A 1994 law, enacted to bring U.S. law into compliance with its international TRIPS obligation, prohibits the recording of "sounds and images of a live musical performance" and provides that violators are subject to the same civil remedies as are infringers of copyright. If the bootlegging is done for "commercial advantage or private financial gain," criminal fines and imprisonment may also result. *See* 17 U.S.C. § 1101 and 18 U.S.C. § 2319A.

---

[7] 17 U.S.C. § 102(a).

Obtaining a Copyright

Copyrights are extraordinarily easy to obtain. In fact, under the Copyright Act of 1976 as amended by the Berne Convntion, a work is protected by copyright automatically upon creation, without any act required on the part of the author. However, it is advisable to register works of authorship with the U.S. Copyright Office, which can be done for a modest fee (currently $35 for a basic registration, or about one tenth the cost of a trademark registration). There are significant benefits to registration. Most importantly, a copyright owner cannot bring suit until a work is registered. Although it is possible to register and bring suit after unauthorized copying occurs, the failure of a business to register the copyright prior to the unauthorized copying will in most cases significantly limit the amount of damages available.

Case Illustration

Joel Tenenbaum began downloading songs without authorization at his family's home in Providence, RI, in 1999. After entering Goucher College in 2002, he continued to download songs from peer-to-peer networks such as Kazaa, Limewire, and Morpheus, eventually accumulating at least 1,153 songs in his "shared directory," which made those songs available for others to download. In 2007, two years after sending Tenenbaum a warning letter, Sony BMG filed suit in federal district court. Following trial, at which Sony BMG established the unauthorized downloading of 30 specific songs, a jury determined that an appropriate level of statutory damages, taking into account the defendant's willfulness, was $22,500 *per song*, or $675,000 total. Rejecting a lower court ruling that $22,500 per song was unconstitutionally excessive, the First Circuit upheld the $675,000 award on appeal. *Sony BMG Music Entertainment v. Tenenbaum*, 660 F.3d 487 (1st Cir. 2011).

Copyright Damages

If a work is unregistered at the time of infringement, the copyright owner is limited to collecting an amount equal to either the loss caused by the infringement or the infringer's profits deriving from the infringement, whichever is greater. However, such **actual damages** can be difficult and expensive to prove and may often be so uncertain as to preclude recovery altogether. Therefore, for works registered prior to infringement, copyright law provides for the collection of **statutory damages**[8] that range from $750 to $30,000 per infringed work with the exact amount determined at the discretion of the court or jury. This basic range of statutory damages per infringed work can be expanded to $200 (if the infringement is unintentional) to $150,000 (if the infringement is willful). Even at the reduced amount of $200 per work, statutory damages can add up quickly. For example, an 80 gigabyte iPod or other portable device can hold up to about 20,000 songs. If those songs were obtained illegally, the *minimum* damages would be $4 million while the maximum damages would be $3 billion!

---

[8]17 U.S.C. § 412.

Fair Use

The long duration and potentially astronomical damages associated with copyright are tempered by a number of limitations to the exclusive rights of copyright owners. The most important among these is **fair use**, a statutory right that expressly permits use of a copyrighted work without authorization under certain circumstances.[9] The fair use doctrine, however, is a flexible standard, and it is often difficult to determine in advance of a court judgment whether a particular use is a fair use. Section 107 of the copyright statute indicates that fair use is more likely to exist if copyrighted works are being used for "criticism, comment, news reporting, teaching (including multiple copies for classroom use), scholarship, or research. . . . " The mere inclusion in one of these categories, however, does not necessarily make a given use fair. Instead, courts will flexibly balance four nonexclusive factors:

Case Illustration

University students create copyrighted works each time they write an essay or term paper, create a diagram, or draft an e-mail message of more than minimal length. In light of the work-made-for-hire doctrine, it might be wondered whether the copyrights in these works belong to the student or to the university. In general, the answer is that the copyright in works created in the context of academic courses (e.g., course assignments) belong to the student, while those created in the context of student employment may well belong to the university. Many universities have developed written intellectual property policies that help to clarify the allocation of rights to copyrightable (or patentable) works that are created in the university environment. See generally *A.V. v. iParadigms*, 562 F.3d 630 (4th Cir. 2009).

1. The purpose and character of the use (e.g., did the copyist seek commercial profit?)
2. The nature of the copyrighted work (e.g., fictional works receive greater protection than factual works)
3. The amount of the copyrighted work that was copied
4. The effect on the market for the copyrighted work (e.g., will the copying decrease sales of the original?)

There is no rigid formula for balancing these factors, meaning that one factor weighing strongly in one direction could potentially offset three factors weighing mildly in the other direction.

   Although fair use provides some room for creative expression that borrows or builds from earlier works, rights under copyright law extend well beyond the prevention of flagrant piracy, as RDR Books discovered the hard way in the "Harry Potter Case" (next page).

The Public Domain

The **public domain** consists of information or works that are not covered by IP protection. After a copyright (or patent) expires, for example, the creation (or invention) becomes a part of the public domain and can be freely used

---

[9]17 U.S.C. § 107.

Warner Bros. Entertainment Inc. v. RDR Books, 575 F.Supp.2d 513 (S.D.N.Y. 2008) ("The Harry Potter Case")

Facts: J.K. Rowling is the author of the highly acclaimed *Harry Potter* book series, made into a number of major motion pictures by Warner Brothers. Seeking to capitalize on the overwhelming public demand for all things Harry Potter, a Michigan-based publishing company called RDR Books arranged to publish *The Lexicon*, a comprehensive encyclopedia of the seven Harry Potter books arranged in A-to-Z format. Rowling had already written two companion books to the Harry Potter series, one of which was an A-to-Z encyclopedia of *Harry Potter*'s imaginary beasts and beings, but it was more limited in scope than *The Lexicon*.

Issue: Is an unauthorized encyclopedia of a fictional work a fair use of that work?

Holding: No. A copyright holder of a fictional work has the right to prevent the publication of an unauthorized encyclopedia, at least where the author of the original work has already produced companion works and where the unauthorized work takes more material from the original work than is reasonably necessary to create a reference guide.

From the Court's Opinion: *To the extent that Defendant seeks to provide a useful reference guide to the* Harry Potter *novels that benefits the public, the use is fair, and its commercial nature [first factor] only weighs slightly against a finding of fair use. . . . [However,] highly imaginative and creative fictional works are close to the core of copyright protection [and] . . . [a]s a result, the second factor [nature of the copyrighted work] favors Plaintiffs. Weighing most heavily against Defendant . . . is the Lexicon's verbatim copying and close paraphrasing of language from the* Harry Potter *works. In many instances, the copied language is a colorful literary device or distinctive description, as in the Lexicon entries for "Clankers," "Marchbanks, Madam Griselda," "Brain room," and "Dementors." This type of language is of great quality and importance; these phrases are, as Rowling testified, the "plums in [her] cake." [Therefore, the extent of the copying] raises a significant question as to whether it was reasonably necessary for the purpose of creating a useful and complete reference guide. . . . The amount and substantiality of the portion copied from the companion books [third factor] weighs . . . against a finding of fair use. . . . [Finally, although] the Lexicon does not present any potential harm to the markets for the original* Harry Potter *works, [it] could harm sales of Rowling's two companion books. [Therefore,] the fourth factor tips in favor of Plaintiffs. . . . The fair-use factors, weighed together in light of the purposes of copyright law, fail to support the defense of fair use in this case. . . .*

[B]ecause the Lexicon appropriates too much of Rowling's creative work for its purposes as a reference guide, a permanent injunction must issue. . . . Since the Lexicon has not been published and thus Plaintiffs have suffered no harm beyond the fact of infringement, the Court awards Plaintiffs the minimum award under the statute for each work with respect to which Plaintiffs have established infringement. Plaintiffs are entitled to statutory damages of $750 for each of the seven Harry Potter *novels and each of the two companion books, for a total of $6,750.*

Note: Following *Warner Bros. v. RDR Books*, the parties reached a settlement agreement under which a modified version of *The Lexicon* was published by RDR Books in 2009.[*]

---

[*] *Hammer v. RDR Books*, No. 10 Civ. 1007(CM), 2011 WL 4388849 (S.D.N.Y. Sept. 20, 2011).

Author J.K. Rowling addresses the public outside a New York City courthouse. Do copyright holders have the right to prevent the creation of derivative works, such as an encyclopedia based on a work of fiction?

by anyone. Because of the long duration of copyright and the loss or destruction of copyrighted works over time, only a small fraction of extant books, movies, software, photographs, music, and other works are in the public domain.

Patents

A **patent** is a federally granted right to exclude others from making, using, selling, or importing an invention. Patentable inventions can include any process, machine, manufacture, or composition of matter that is (1) new, (2) useful, and (3) nonobvious.

Patent Duration and Exceptions

Although patents provide much stronger rights than copyrights and have fewer exceptions to the owner's exclusive rights, they are much more difficult and expensive to obtain and last only 20 years from the date the patent application is filed—about one fifth of the copyright term.

> **An Ethical Insight: Ross, Bentham, and Copyright Statutory Damages**
>
> Like tort and contract damages, statutory damages under copyright law are based on the duty to compensate for injuries (e.g., lost royalties) done to others, or what W.D. Ross calls the "duty of reparation." However, this duty cannot explain the 100-fold disparity in damages between the Harry Potter Case ($6,750) and the *Tenenbaum* music downloading case ($675,000). Isn't the large-scale commercial publication of an unauthorized book far more injurious than the harm created when a college student illegally downloads 30 songs? This apparent lack of proportionality can be explained, if not necessarily justified, by Jeremy Bentham's reasoning in his Theory of Legislation: "The more deficient in certainty a punishment is, the severer it should be." Under Bentham's rule, the punishment for illegal downloading, which is difficult to detect and therefore infrequently punished, must be far more severe than the punishment for an unauthorized publication, which is highly visible and nearly certain to result in litigation or at least royalty negotiations.

Who Can Obtain a Patent?

Only inventors are entitled to patents. This means that an entrepreneur who observes someone else's neglected invention and seeks to develop it into a marketable product will *not* be able to obtain a patent. It might be possible, however, for that other person to patent the invention and then **assign** (transfer) the resulting patent rights to the entrepreneur. Even the inventor can be barred from obtaining a patent if that inventor does not timely apply for a patent. Under § 102 of the patent law, businesses must file a patent application within one year of selling or otherwise disclosing an invention, or the invention falls into the public domain. This provision is referred to as the **one-year on-sale bar**. Some countries do not have this one-year "grace period," meaning that the sale or disclosure of an invention in the United States can lead to the loss of the ability to obtain a foreign patent unless the foreign patent application was previously filed.

What happens if two or more businesses or individuals independently invent the same invention at about the same time? For more than 200 years, the United States followed a first-to-invent system, under which a patent would be awarded to the party that could prove it was the first inventor, regardless of who filed a patent application first, which might require litigation in expensive and time-consuming "interference proceedings."

Case Illustration

The Google Book Project is an undertaking of Google, Inc., to digitally scan and make available for search on the Internet every book in any language that exists anywhere in the world. By 2013, Google reportedly allowed users to engage in full-text searches of more than 20 million of the 130 million books estimated by Google to exist. Copyright, however, proved to be a thorny issue. Only about 16 percent of the books scanned by Google are in the public domain. Another 9 percent are under copyright but still in print, allowing Google to contact the publishers to arrange for copyright authorization. The remaining 75 percent consists of works still under copyright but no longer being commercially sold and includes many **orphan works** — works for which it is difficult or impossible to identify the copyright holder. In 2005, two separate lawsuits were filed against Google with respect to the 75 percent of works that remain under copyright but are out of print. In 2013, a federal court ruled that Google's activities constituted fair use, but further litigation and appeal may be likely. *The Authors Guild, Inc. v. Google Inc.*, 1:05-cv-08136 (D.D.C. Nov. 14, 2013).

In 2011, the Leahy-Smith America Invents Act simplified the law by changing to a **first-to-file** system, thus bringing U.S. law into harmony with the law of other jurisdictions around the world.

Costs of Obtaining and Maintaining a Patent

Businesses usually hire attorneys to **prosecute** (apply for) a patent in the USPTO, the same office that processes trademark applications. It takes an average of about three years and may cost $10,000 to $50,000, including attorney fees, to obtain a patent. Moreover, **maintenance fees** must be paid to the USPTO at 3.5 years, 7.5 years, and 11.5 years after issuance of the patent or the invention will fall into the public domain. If all fees are paid, patents still last only 20 years from the date the patent application was filed. In contrast, trademark renewal fees are substantially lower, and there are no maintenance fees at all for copyrights or trade secrets.

Exceptions to the Patent Right

A business that is sued for patent infringement will find that there are few exceptions to the patent right. In contrast to copyright law, patent law contains no exception equivalent to the fair use doctrine. Even if a business independently develops an invention without knowledge that the invention has already been patented, the business can still be held liable for infringement.

One rarely used exception to the patent right relates to use by the government. In general, the power of government to take private property for public use upon the payment of just compensation is known as **eminent domain** and is recognized in the Fifth Amendment to the U.S. Constitution. In the context of IP, the federal government may exercise an eminent-domain-like power to use, or authorize others to use, a patented invention (or, for that matter, a copyrighted work).[10] This power is rarely invoked, however, even where substantial public interests are at stake, such as public health. The following case provides a recent example of the tension between public health and patent rights.

In-Depth Ethical Case Analysis

Association for Molecular Pathology v. Myriad Genetics, 133 S. Ct. 2107 (2013)

Facts

The average woman in the United States has around a 12 percent risk of developing breast cancer in her lifetime. In contrast, women with certain mutations in the *BRCA* gene face a cumulative risk of over 50 percent of developing breast cancer. By studying the genetic makeup of individual family members, a group of researchers correlated the occurrence of breast cancer with certain *BRCA* sequences, leading to the invention and patenting of a diagnostic tool, the rights to which were assigned to Myriad Genetics. Diagnostic testing can provide patients with information on cancer risk that can in turn aid in difficult decisions regarding preventive options, such as prophylactic (preventative) surgery or chemotherapy.* Although Myriad offered

testing to the public, it charged what some regarded as an unreasonably high price—around $3,200. Myriad was able to charge this price because the patents allow it to prevent others, until the patent terms expire, from offering a similar test.

Myriad's patents were challenged on the ground that naturally occurring substances are unpatentable because they are "products of nature." That is, if something is found in nature, it cannot be a human-made "invention" under § 101 of the patent law. By 2005, however, the USPTO had granted about 40,000 DNA-related patents, including Myriad's patents, covering about 20 percent of the genes in the human genome. These patents were granted on the theory that "isolated" genes are sufficiently different

---

[10]28 U.S.C. § 1498.

from naturally occurring genes to constitute "invention" for purposes of the patent law.

Issue

Is naturally occurring DNA patentable?

Holding

No. However, modified DNA, such as cDNA, may be patentable.

From the Court's Opinion

It is undisputed that Myriad did not create or alter any of the genetic information encoded in the BRCA1 and BRCA2 genes. . . . Instead, Myriad's principal contribution was uncovering the precise location and genetic sequence of the BRCA1 and BRCA2 genes within chromosomes 17 and 13 . . . [†] *Myriad seeks to import these extensive research efforts into the § 101 patent-eligibility inquiry. But extensive effort alone is insufficient to satisfy the demands of § 101.*

Nor are Myriad's claims saved by the fact that isolating DNA from the human genome severs chemical bonds and thereby creates a nonnaturally occurring molecule. Myriad's claims are simply not expressed in terms of chemical composition, nor do they rely in any way on the chemical changes that result from the isolation of a particular section of DNA. Instead, the claims understandably focus on the genetic information encoded in the BRCA1 and BRCA2 genes. . . .

Finally, Myriad argues that the PTO's past practice of awarding gene patents is entitled to deference. We disagree. . . . Congress has not endorsed the views of the PTO in subsequent legislation [as it did with respect to PTO endorsement of plants as patent-eligible in a previous case]. . . . Further undercutting the PTO's practice, the United States [Solicitor General] argued in the Federal Circuit and in this Court that isolated DNA was not patent eligible under § 101, and that the PTO's practice was not a sufficient reason to hold that isolated DNA is patent-eligible. These

concessions weigh against deferring to the PTO's determination. [‡]

[The Court did not entirely invalidate Myriad's patents, holding that a type of DNA known as "cDNA" remains potentially patentable because it is not identical to naturally-occurring DNA. However, the Court expressed no opinion as to whether cDNA might meet the requirements of novelty and nonobviousness.]

Ethical Issue

Is it ethical for the government to grant patents on genes in light of the high prices that patent owners can charge for access to important gene-related inventions?

Ethical Theory Analysis

Legal Realism

Can human genes, found in nature, be patentable? Legal realism is an ethical theory that is opposed to the strict application of "rules of law" to resolve novel legal disputes and thereby rejects legal fundamentalism. One of its proponents, Roscoe Pound, wanted law students to consider the social and economic implications of legal issues. Justice Oliver Wendell Holmes, Jr., the founder of legal realism, stated that "what really is before us [in difficult legal disputes] is a conflict between two social desires, each of which seeks to extend its dominion over the case. . . . "[§] The gene patenting dispute in Myriad might be viewed as a conflict between the social desire for faster innovation and the desire not to withhold existing technology from those who could benefit from it. A legal realist might find it unethical for a company to charge a prohibitively high price for a diagnostic medical test, because an extraordinary number of women with the BRCA gene, at increased risk of developing breast cancer, could not possibly afford to be tested at that price. At the same time, a legal realist would welcome innovations in science and argue the augmentation of nature that results in a transformed gene with a new character, nature, and function ethically meets the patentability standard of § 101 of the patent statute. The desirable social objective is the progression of science. Justice Oliver Wendell Holmes, Jr., stated: "The real justification of a rule of law, if there be one, is that it helps to bring about a social end which we desire." You can see from this analysis there are different ethical arguments with contrary conclusions based on the theory of legal realism. You should decide which one supports your ethical position: allowing the patent to encourage future research that could help cancer patients, or disallowing the patent to help women afford the existing diagnostic test.

Utilitarianism
A utilitarian approach would ask whether the invention would have been invented at all if not for the patent incentive. Many biotech companies rely on venture capital to develop and process a scientific discovery through the Food and Drug Administration for government approval. This is an enormous research and development cost to the company as well as a time-consuming process; without patent protection, interest in developing new drugs would likely wane. If the diagnostic test would not have been created at all without the patent incentive, then by definition it would be unavailable to anyone at any price, and so the better rule would be to continue to grant gene patents, even though this results in high prices for a limited period of time. However, if the invention would have been invented just as quickly without the patent incentive, then the better rule would be to eliminate patent protection for gene products. A utilitarian perspective is reflected in the court's statement that "patent protection strikes a delicate balance between creating incentives . . . and impeding the flow of information that might permit, indeed spur, invention." This is an example of rule-utilitarianism that relies on case precedent and tradition rather than subjective personal judgments. Recall that by 2005 the USPTO had granted about 40,000 DNA-related patents.

A utilitarian could ethically argue in favor of the court's decision based on scientific progress for the greater good of society.

Natural Law
Natural law theory posits that certain obligations or rights are universal to all human beings. One such obligation might be to avoid harm, or its corollary, to help another person when the need is great enough and no other means of help is available. Under a natural law approach, one might argue that withholding an available diagnostic test from those who have no other means of assessing their health situation violates universal norms. By granting the patent and thereby denying other biotech firms from competing with Myriad during the 20-year patent term, millions of "at risk" women will be denied preventative treatment. A natural law ethicist could argue that is an unethical position because law should serve the common good.

John Rawls, A Theory of Justice
Recall the Rawlsian "original position" where "no one knows his place in society" and where "principles of justice are chosen behind a veil of ignorance." In this case, the veil of ignorance might mean not knowing whether one will be a woman who is unable to pay for Myriad's test, or a woman who will not have access to some future test (perhaps for a different disease) if the Court's removal of patent protection reduces incentives and thereby delays the development of that other test. Thus viewed, Rawls's Equal Liberty Principle might counsel against striking down the patent on Myriad's test: Although striking down Myriad's patent might help women who want to be tested for *BRCA* now, this gain would come only at the expense of future women, thus wrongly trading off a gain in liberty to one group for a loss in liberty to another.

Conclusion
The ethical theories do not unambiguously resolve the issue of whether genes should be patentable, as reflected in the Court's mixed determination that "isolated" DNA is unpatentable

while cDNA might still be patentable. Within hours of the Court's decision, Myriad's share price fell by 5.6 percent; at the same time, a competitor of Myriad announced it would immediately begin offering a basic *BRCA* diagnostic test for $2,200. Because Myriad's patents were only partially invalidated, competing tests might still be challenged, but Myriad's patents in any event began to expire in 2014.

---

* Actress Angelina Jolie brought increased attention to such difficult decisions in 2013 when, at the age of 37, she elected to

undergo a prophylactic double mastectomy after learning that she carried a mutation in the *BRCA* gene.

† Footnote 6 in the Court's opinion says: "Myriad first identified groups of relatives with a history of breast cancer . . . ; because these individuals were related, scientists knew that it was more likely that their diseases were the result of genetic predisposition rather than other factors. Myriad compared sections of their chromosomes, looking for shared genetic abnormalities not found in the general population. It was that process which eventually enabled Myriad to determine where in the genetic sequence the BRCA1 and BRCA2 genes reside."

‡ Footnote 7 in the Court's opinion says: "Myriad also argues that we should uphold its patents so as not to disturb the reliance interests of patent holders like itself. Concerns about reliance interests arising from PTO determinations, insofar as they are relevant, are better directed to Congress."

§ Oliver Wendell Holmes, Jr., *Law in Science and Science in Law,* 12 Harv. L. Rev. 443, 460 (1899).

Design Patents and Plant Patents

The term *patent* is usually used to refer to the most common type of patent, the **utility patent**, and this book follows that convention. However, two less common types of patents also exist. **Plant patents**, which also last for 20 years, may be obtained for any distinct and new variety of plant that may be asexually reproduced. **Design patents**, which last only 14 years, may be obtained for any new, original, and ornamental design for an article of manufacture (Exhibit 8.4).

Exhibit 8.4. U.S. Patent Grants 2012, by Patent Type

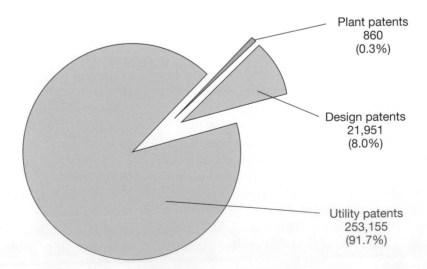

Plant patents
860
(0.3%)

Design patents
21,951
(8.0%)

Utility patents
253,155
(91.7%)

eBay Inc. v. MercExchange L.L.C., 547 U.S. 388 (2006)

Facts: The online marketplace eBay operates a popular Internet website that allows private sellers to list goods they wish to sell, either through an auction or at a fixed price. MercExchange owns a number of patents, including a business method patent for an electronic market designed to facilitate the sale of goods between private individuals by establishing a central authority to promote trust among participants. MercExchange sought to license its patent to eBay, as it had previously done with other companies, but the parties failed to reach agreement. MercExchange then filed a patent infringement suit during which the Federal Circuit noted the general rule that a permanent injunction will issue if a valid patent has been infringed.

Issue: As a general rule, are owners of valid patents that have been infringed automatically entitled to an injunction?

Holding: No. Patent holders may obtain injunctive relief only if a four-factor test is satisfied (see below).

From the Court's Opinion: *According to well-established principles of equity, a plaintiff seeking a permanent injunction must satisfy a four-factor*

test before a court may grant [an injunction]. A plaintiff must demonstrate: (1) that it has suffered an irreparable injury; (2) that remedies available at law, such as monetary damages, are inadequate to compensate for that injury; (3) that, considering the balance of hardships between the plaintiff and defendant, a remedy in equity is warranted; and (4) that the public interest would not be disserved by a permanent injunction.

From the Concurring Opinion (Kennedy, J.): *An industry has developed in which firms use patents not as a basis for producing and selling goods but, instead, primarily for obtaining licensing fees. For these firms, an injunction, and the potentially serious sanctions arising from its violation, can be employed as a bargaining tool to charge exorbitant fees to companies that seek to buy licenses to practice the patent. When the patented invention is but a small component of the product the companies seek to produce and the threat of an injunction is employed simply for undue leverage in negotiations, legal damages [i.e., money] may well be sufficient to compensate for the infringement and an injunction may not serve the public interest.*

Patent Trolls and Injunctions

A **patent troll** is an informal and pejorative term for a business that does not itself manufacture products but instead owns patents and asserts them against alleged infringers.[11] In the landmark decision of *eBay v. MercExchange* (2006), the Supreme Court weakened the bargaining position of patent owners by making it more difficult for patent owners, including patent trolls, to persuade a court to **enjoin** (prohibit) a defendant's infringing activities. In a

---

[11]*Taurus IP v. DaimlerChrysler Corp.*, 519 F.Supp.2d 905, 911 (W.D. Wis. 2007).

now-famous concurring opinion, Justice Kennedy explained how the threat of injunction could allow patent trolls or other patent owners to **hold-up** the production of a multicomponent product or system.

Trade Secrets

Any information that is valuable because it is not generally known to competitors can be protected as a **trade secret**. Famous examples of trade secrets include the formula for Coca-Cola, the secret chicken recipe of KFC, and the formula for the lubricant WD-40. Trade secrets are not limited to formulas or recipes, however. To the contrary, almost any information that is secret can receive protection, such as the release date of forthcoming software, technical specifications, and databases of customer contact information.

Case Illustration

With an estimated net worth of $13 billion, Mark Zuckerberg is the acclaimed founder and CEO of popular social networking site Facebook.com. However, according to a lawsuit filed in 2004, Zuckerberg achieved his success in part by stealing the idea from a rival network called ConnectU when Zuckerberg and ConnectU's founders were classmates at Harvard University. ConnectU alleged that although Zuckerberg had originally committed himself to working for ConnectU, he eventually used his position as an insider to misappropriate ConnectU's trade secrets to his own benefit, including computer source code and confidential business plans. The case was settled for $65 million in cash and shares of Facebook common stock, with these details of the settlement emerging only after they were inadvertently (and somewhat embarrassingly) disclosed by ConnectU's lawyers in 2009. The Facebook story inspired the major motion picture, *The Social Network* (2010).

State Law: The Uniform Trade Secrets Act

Unlike patents and copyrights, which are governed almost exclusively by federal law, trade secrets (and trademarks) are governed by both state and federal law. The **Uniform Trade Secrets Act** (UTSA) was promulgated as a model act in 1979 by the National Conference of Commissioners on Uniform State Laws and has been adopted by 46 states and the District of Columbia. Under the UTSA, businesses can obtain both money damages and injunctions to prevent competitors from using secret information that has been wrongfully misappropriated, such as by industrial espionage. Businesses may also be able to enjoin a former employee from departing to work for a competitor, if that employee would necessarily use or disclose trade secrets in the new position.

Federal Law: The Economic Espionage Act of 1996

In the 1990s Congress responded to a sharp rise in industrial espionage by criminalizing trade secret theft and imposing substantial penalties, particularly when the violation was committed to benefit a foreign business or government. Under the **Economic Espionage Act of 1996** (EEA), organizations that misappropriate trade secrets may be fined up to $10 million and individuals may be imprisoned for up to 15 years. The legislative history leading up to the EEA noted

Manager's Compliance and Ethics Meeting

Trade Secrets: Executives' Ethical Responsibility

There is a great likelihood that you, as a potential employee-manager, will be exposed to your employer's confidential information. Trade secrets present the opportunity for an employee to violate not only a legal obligation but an ethical duty to maintain confidential business information belonging to the employer. A well-drafted *compliance and ethics program* that includes a *code of ethics* must reference the importance of maintaining business-sensitive information. Ongoing training sessions should remind employees of their duty to protect trade secrets. Employees should also be reminded that their legal and ethical obligation to protect trade secrets continues beyond their current employment with the company.

At a manager's meeting discussing trade secrets, Jennifer, an executive employee, has notified the company she will leave next month for an executive position at a competing company. Jennifer has been informed that she cannot discuss her current company's strategy or plans with anyone after she leaves the company. Since she was involved in planning the strategy document, it is her belief that asking her to sign a nondisclosure agreement when she exits the company is unethical. Is it ethical to limit Jennifer's potential in her new job by prohibiting her from disclosing and discussing in any way the company's new strategy document? Yes.

W. D. Ross — Prima Facie Duties. In his treatise, "The Right and the Good," Ross stated that "[o]ur acts . . . are not right because they will produce certain results [in the above instance Jennifer disclosing the company's strategic plan to impress her new employer] — which is the view common to all forms of utilitarianism." Jennifer, as an employee privy to confidential information, has a prima facie *duty of fidelity* owed to the company based on an implied promise to maintain its confidentiality. Even without having signed a nondisclosure agreement, based on her relationship with the company as an executive acting on its behalf, she is ethically obligated to keep her implied promise to maintain the trade secret of the new strategy plan.

H.L.A. Hart — Natural Law. Hart wrote in "The Concept of Law" that "the doctrine of natural law is in fact nothing but an assertion that law is part of ethics." One could argue trade secret law has its foundation in natural law theory, which would claim it *is reasonable and ethical* to protect trade secrets that consist of information of economic value, present or potential, from not being generally known to other persons or competing companies who could obtain economic value from its disclosure.

Aristotle — Virtue Ethics. In his Fifth Book of the "Nichomachean Ethics," Aristotle stated the principle that *no one should be enriched at another's expense*. This concept supports the modern legal doctrine that prohibits "unjust enrichment," which might prevent Jennifer, even absent a nondisclosure agreement, from enriching herself at the expense of her employer by sharing the confidential information of the strategy plan with a competing company.

Conclusion. Jennifer should be referred to the company's *compliance and ethics program* and its *code of ethics*, which prohibit employees from disclosing trade secrets, and the underlying legal and ethical principles that support the doctrine of trade secrets. Her participation in developing the strategic plan was part of her employment duties, and the fruits of her efforts belong to the company in exchange for her salary. The manager should record minutes of the meeting and the discussion with Jennifer to memorialize her understanding of the strategy document as a trade secret. The minutes should be preserved for evidentiary purposes should a lawsuit against Jennifer be necessary to prevent or remedy wrongful disclosure.

Manager's Compliance and Ethics Meeting

Trade Secrets: Corporate Board Member Responsibilities

SEC Rule 10b5-1 prohibits the purchase or sale of a security on the basis of material nonpublic information.[*] Assume that the corporate board of a publicly owned company has just been informed that its scientists have filed a patent application on the design of a football helmet that will radically reduce the chance of brain injury. Once the patent issues, the stock of the company will significantly appreciate. Harry, a board member, has decided, based on this inside information, to purchase a substantial amount of the company's stock. Harry is also the vice president of sales. At a manager's meeting, Harry has been informed that the inside information related to the nonpublic patent application is a trade secret (a patent application is normally not made available to the public until 18 months after its filing date[†]). Since Harry has not signed a nondisclosure agreement, he thinks he can purchase the company's stock at its current market value. Rule 10b-5 prohibits trading on inside information if doing so would "breach . . . a duty of trust or confidence that is owed directly [or] indirectly . . . to the issuer of th[e] security or the shareholders of that issuer, or to any other person who is the source of the material nonpublic information." Is Harry acting ethically in purchasing the company's stock at its current value based in this inside information?

W. D. Ross — Prima Facie Duties. Ross proposed a *duty of fidelity* that may consist of an implied contract creating a duty to keep a promise. From an ethical perspective, Harry has an implied duty not to profit from inside information. Harry, as a board member, owes a *fiduciary duty* to the stockholders to act in their best interests.

Immanuel Kant — Categorical Imperative. One of Kant's categorical imperatives is: "I ought never to act except in such a way that I can also will that my maxim should become a universal law." Harry was acting unethically in purchasing the company stock, based on the inside information. Harry should ask: "What if insider trading became a universally accepted practice?"

Aristotle — Justice. Aristotle is concerned with virtues and stated in his book *Nicomachean Ethics* that "justice seems to be the good of someone else." Rule 10b-5, by prohibiting the purchase or sale of a security on the basis of material nonpublic information that gives the buyer or seller an unfair advantage over others, suggests that Harry would violate this ethical principle of justice that relates to the good of others, in this case the stockholders who would sell to him without knowledge of the inside information.

Conclusion. Even without having signed a nondisclosure agreement, Harry, as someone with inside information, is under a legal and ethical obligation not to trade on that information. The company's *ethics and compliance program* and *code of ethics* should reference and prohibit the practice of insider trading. Harry, and all employees, should be advised not to purchase any stock on the basis of material nonpublic information.

---

[*] 17 C.F.R. § 240.10b5-1.
[†] 35 U.S.C. § 122.

significant economic harm from the theft of information, including manufacturing process information ($110 million) and pricing data ($1 billion). Only the federal government can bring suit under the EEA.

The Rise and Rise of Intellectual Property

Intellectual property rights have expanded dramatically in both scope and duration since the first federal patent and copyright statutes were enacted in 1790.

Expanding U.S. Patent and Copyright Duration

Both the Patent Act of 1790 and the Copyright Act of 1790 provided for initial terms of protection of 14 years (renewable, in the case of copyright, for an additional 14 years). These relatively brief initial terms have been lengthened several times since then, reflecting a complex interplay of political interests that are beyond the scope of this text. The patent term was extended to 17 years in 1861 and then to 20 years (from date of filing) in 1995. The initial term of copyright protection was increased to 28 years in 1831, to 75 years in 1976, and finally to 95 years in 1998. The patent and copyright durations (first term only) since 1790 are summarized in Exhibit 8.5 on page 250.

IP Duration: Natural Rights or Utilitarian Rationale?

Critics of the ever-expanding length of copyright often argue that the current duration is far more than needed to incentivize the creation of new works. After all, they point out, few books, movies, and other copyrighted works are still earning their owners substantial revenues after 15 or 20 years . . . let alone 120 years. Those who

Case Illustration

Headquartered near Boston, American Superconductor (AMSC) supplies wind-turbine software and components that increase the efficiency of wind power generation. AMSC was taken by surprise when it discovered that Sinovel, a Chinese company and the world's second-largest wind turbine manufacturer, had somehow stolen AMSC's proprietary information and was producing pirate versions of its products. No longer needing AMSC's products, Sinovel canceled over $700 million worth of orders, causing AMSCs stock price to plummet by 90 percent. Eventually, it was discovered that a disgruntled AMSC employee, who had been demoted from the design team to the marketing department, had been enticed to sell software source code to Sinovel. In 2011, the employee was sentenced to a year in jail by an Austrian court. Sinovel, however, has no significant assets in the United States, and AMSC has therefore initiated legal action in Chinese courts where it is seeking $1.2 billion in damages. A ruling by a lower court in China dismissing the case has been appealed to China's supreme court. *See* Joan Lappin, *American Superconductor and Its Rogue Employee Both Duped by Sinovel*, Forbes, Sept. 17, 2011.

An Ethical Insight: Trade Secrets, John Stuart Mill — Utilitarianism

Mill stated that "laws and social arrangements should place . . . the interests of every individual, as nearly as possible in harmony with the interest of the whole. . . . " This ethical perspective supports SEC Rule 10b-5, which prohibits insider trading. If investors cannot be certain that other traders do not have secret information, they might hesitate to participate in the stock market. This would make it difficult both for firms to raise money and for honest sellers of investments to find willing buyers (and vice versa), thereby undermining the integrity of the stock market to the detriment of society as a whole.

Exhibit 8.5. Copyright and Patent Duration from 1790–Present (Initial Term Only[*])

Duration (years)

100
95
75
75
50
28
25
14
14
20
17

1800   1850   1900   1950   2000

- - - - - = Copyright

———— = Patent

[*] Patents were renewable for an additional seven-year term (for a total term of 21 years) between 1836 and 1861, while a 14-year copyright renewal term was established in 1790, extended to 28 years in 1909, and then eliminated (for new works) in 1976. Because under a renewal system most copyrights and patents are not renewed and therefore expire before their maximum term, the Exhibit presents only the initial terms of protection and omits renewal terms. Other complexities of patent and copyright duration are also omitted.

Mary Bono.

embrace a utilitarian justification of IP may well agree with these critics. However, an alternate justification for copyright is that creators have a natural right to the fruits their labor. In the congressional debates leading up to the Sonny Bono Copyright Term Extension Act of 1998, which extended copyright by 20 years to its current duration, Congresswoman Mary Bono (wife of the late singer and Congressman Sonny Bono, left) advocated the idea that copyright should last "forever less one day," a clear reflection of the natural rights approach. She has advocated for longer copyright based on a natural rights approach. Should authors have a permanent right to control the use of their works? Why might the drafters of the Constitution (see Article 8, § 8) have answered this question in the negative?

Case Illustration

In 1999, a Canadian company called Research in Motion (RIM) introduced the BlackBerry, a handheld device with a miniature keyboard that integrated telephone functionality with e-mail and, later, an Internet browser. The BlackBerry quickly rose from obscurity to become one of the most coveted devices in the world, adding 32,000 subscribers in the first quarter of 2002 alone. Even the U.S. Congress became a customer of RIM, investing $6 million to ensure effective communication among the nation's legislators following the attacks of September 11, 2001. Research in Motion, however, had stepped on a patent landmine. Unbeknownst to RIM, a company called NTP — a nonpracticing entity that some described as a patent troll — held a number of patents covering the BlackBerry technology. Although there was no evidence that RIM copied NTP's technology, patents allow their owners to prevent all others from making or selling an invention, even those who independently invent the same technology. In 2006, following several years of high-profile litigation, RIM paid NTP $612.5 million. Although that payment settled the matter as to RIM, an emboldened NTP then asserted the same patents in a spate of suits against Google, LG, HTC, Apple, Microsoft, Motorola, Yahoo, and others. These suits were settled in 2012 for an undisclosed sum.

Expanding Scope of Intellectual Property Protection

Intellectual property protection has expanded substantially not only in duration but also in scope. The Copyright Act of 1790 protected only maps, charts, and books. Over time a number of other types of works were brought under protection, including sheet music (1831), dramatic works (1856), photographs (1865), paintings and sculpture (1870), motion pictures (1912), musical recordings and choreography (1971), software (1978), and architecture (1990). Patentable subject matter has also expanded via statute or decision to include industrial designs (1842), plants (1930), microorganisms (1980),[12] software (1981),[13] nonhuman animals (1987), and business methods (1998).[14] Trademark law has also expanded to cover fictional characters (1921), sounds (1950), colors (1985), and scents (1990), as well as product packaging and product design. New forms of IP have even emerged, including rights related to domain names, **mask works** (integrated circuit layout designs), and clinical trial data generated during pharmaceutical or pesticide testing.

Implications of Expanded Intellectual Property for Business

Although there are a number of complex reasons for the dramatic expansion of IP duration and scope, the important implication for businesses is that IP must

---

[12]*Diamond v. Chakrabarty,* 447 U.S. 303 (1980).
[13]*Diamond v. Diehr,* 450 U.S. 175 (1981).
[14]*State Street Bank & Trust Co. v. Signature Financial Group, Inc.,* 149 F.3d 1368 (Fed. Cir. 1998).

be considered in any business plan or new product rollout. For example, an innovative electronic device with a creative, distinctive, and nonfunctional shape might be simultaneously protected by a design patent, by copyright law, and by trademark law, while its components may be covered by hundreds or thousands of utility patents. In addition to seeking protection for its own offerings, a business must also exercise caution so as not to step on an IP **landmine**. That is, the business must be careful not to inadvertently violate the IP rights of others.

Global Perspective: The Globalization of Intellectual Property

Although patents for inventions have been granted since at least the 1400s, a wave of national patent laws swept the globe beginning with the U.S. Patent Act of 1790 and followed by legislation in France (1791), Russia (1812), Brazil (1830), Mexico (1832), and India (1856), among others. This global expansion and institutionalization of national patent laws gave way in the 1850s to a vigorous antipatent movement that lasted through the 1870s, in which calls for the complete abolition of the patent system were based in part on the ideal of free trade in the underlying products.[15] The patent advocates emerged victorious, however, and in the 1880s two international IP treaties were adopted that remain in force today: the Paris Convention of 1883 and the Berne Convention of 1886.

The Paris and the Berne Conventions

Both the **Paris Convention** (1883) and the **Berne Convention** (1886) establish certain basic principles with respect to IP that member countries are bound to implement in national legislation. Most important among these is the concept of **national treatment**, an antidiscrimination principle that prohibits a member country from treating foreign nationals less favorably than its own nationals. Thus, for example, a country may not deny a trademark registration to an applicant simply because that applicant is a foreigner or does not have a manufacturing facility in the country where protection is sought. These treaties are

Case Illustration

John Wiley & Sons is a publisher of English-language academic textbooks that are sold both within the United States and abroad. Often the versions sold abroad are nearly identical to domestic versions but may cost less, reflecting a type of geographic price discrimination. Supap Kirtsaeng, a citizen of Thailand who came to the United States to study math at Cornell University, imported over 600 copies of the Thai versions of some of John Wiley & Sons' books into the United States and resold them, thereby making a profit. An exception to copyright law known as the **first-sale doctrine** states that once a copyrighted work is first sold with the permission of the copyright holder, it may then be freely resold. But does the first-sale doctrine apply when the first sale takes place abroad, at a substantially lower price? According to a 2013 Supreme Court decision, the answer is yes, meaning that Kirtsaeng's actions were lawful. *Kirtsaeng v. John Wiley & Sons, Inc.*, 133 S.Ct. 1351 (2013).

---

[15]Fritz Machlup and Edith Penrose, *The Patent Controversy in the Nineteenth Century*, 10 J. Econ. Hist. 1 (1950).

important for business because they make it easier to obtain IP protection in other countries. Almost all countries are members of both the Paris Convention, which applies to "industrial property" (patents and trademarks), and the Berne Convention, which applies to copyrights. The United States **acceded to** (joined) the Paris Convention in 1887 but did not accede to the Berne convention until 1988. One practical implication of U.S. accession to the Berne convention is that businesses and other authors no longer need to include notice of copyright (e.g., "© 2014 Wolters-Kluwer") to obtain copyright protection, although it remains advisable to do so.

World Intellectual Property Organization

The **World Intellectual Property Organization (WIPO)** is a specialized agency of the United Nations located in Geneva, Switzerland, that administers both the Paris and Berne Conventions, along with 22 other IP treaties. These conventions obligate member countries to provide WIPO with copies of all new laws relating to IP, which WIPO in turn makes freely available on its website.

WIPO serves a number of other important functions. It provides a forum for the ongoing development and global coordination of IP, including the negotiation of new treaties. It facilitates the accession of new countries to existing treaties. Although it is not yet possible to obtain a patent or trademark registration that is valid throughout the world, WIPO administers the Patent Cooperation Treaty (PCT) and the Madrid Protocol, which streamline the process of applying for foreign patents and trademarks, respectively. Finally, as noted above, WIPO provides arbitration services that businesses can use to resolve domain name disputes.

Geneva, Switzerland, is home to a number of international organizations, including the World Intellectual Property Organization (pictured), the World Trade Organization, the World Health Organization, the International Telecommunication Union, and the International Labor Organization. All of these, plus a major campus of the United Nations, are within walking distance of one another.

TRIPS

Notwithstanding the importance of WIPO and the 24 treaties that it administers, by far the most important IP treaty today is the **Agreement on Trade-Related Aspects of Intellectual Property Rights (TRIPS)**, which is administered by the World Trade Organization (WTO). TRIPS is important because (1) all members of the WTO must accede to TRIPS, meaning that it is broadly applicable around the world; (2) it provides certain minimum levels of IP protection, including a 20-year patent term; and perhaps most importantly, it (3) provides a meaningful enforcement mechanism via the WTO dispute resolution system, ensuring that countries abide by their international obligations. Since TRIPS entered into force in 1995, more than 23 TRIPS-related disputes have been brought before the WTO's dispute settlement body.

The adoption of TRIPS required many countries to change their IP laws. The United States, for example, was obligated to change its patent duration from 17 years, measured from the date the patent is issued, to 20 years, measured from the date the patent application is filed. A number of countries that did not provide patent protection for pharmaceutical products became obligated to do so, as TRIPS requires patents to be available "in all fields of technology." Least developed countries, however, need not comply with this particular provision of TRIPS until 2016. Finally, TRIPS **incorporates by reference** certain provisions of the Paris and Berne Conventions, making those provisions legally a part of TRIPS and thus enforceable via the WTO dispute resolution system.

Global Perspective: Intellectual Property Law in the European Union

All 28 countries of the European Union (EU) are members of the WTO, WIPO, and the Paris and Berne Conventions, and are therefore subject to the provisions of these organizations and treaties. For example, the Berne Convention requires the protection of copyrighted works for a minimum duration of the life of the author plus 50 years. The European Union has complied with this requirement via Directive 2006/116/EC, which requires all EU member states to protect copyrighted works for the life of the author plus 70 years, the same duration as in the United States. Note that IP treaties, such as the Berne Convention, generally provide only *minimum* required levels of protection, allowing countries to institute longer or higher levels of protection if they choose. This has led to some variations between countries. For example, Mexico, which is not a member of the EU, recently extended the protection of copyrights to the life of the author plus 100 years!

Although the IP laws of the various EU countries have been **harmonized** (made more similar and consistent) via EU directives such as the copyright directive just mentioned, most IP laws in the EU are national laws and may therefore be somewhat different from country to country. Nevertheless, a few Europe-wide IP initiatives facilitate the conduct of business in the EU. For example, the EU's Office for Harmonization in the Internal Market (OHIM) allows businesses to file a single trademark registration that provides protection within the EU's 28 member states. Similarly, the European Patent Convention (EPC), which is not an EU body, allows businesses to file a single patent application that can lead to patent protection in 40 European countries, including all 28 members of the EU. In 2013, an agreement on a Unified Patent Court was signed by 24 EU member states and, if ratified, would simplify patent litigation in most of the EU.

Although patents, copyrights, trademarks, and trade secrets constitute the principal types of IP, there are other types as well. **Geographical indications** are trademark-like rights given to producers located within a given geographic region, rather than to an individual business. Under TRIPS, WTO members must prohibit the use of geographical indications that would misleadingly indicate the geographical origin of the product. For example, only tea producers from the Darjeeling region of India may label their tea as "Darjeeling" tea, while only producers from Florida may label their oranges as "Florida" oranges. In certain cases, the IP rights of producers to use a given geographical indication have come into conflict with the public's understanding of that geographical indication as a common name for a particular product, as seen in the Case Illustration at right.

Global Perspective: Intellectual Property Law in India

India became a member of the WTO in 1995, obligating it to accede to TRIPS. In accordance with TRIPS, India provides for the registration of trademarks, which may be renewed indefinitely, the protection of copyrights, which endure for the life of the author plus 60 years, and the patenting of inventions, which last for 20 years. Despite these protections, the U.S. government has noted extensive pirating in India of copyrighted movies and music, difficulties in collecting royalties, and the wide availability of counterfeit medicines.

The most contentious IP issue in India relates to the patentability of pharmaceutical products. India is a global leader in the production and export of generic drugs, notably those related to HIV/AIDS. It obtained this leadership position due to a number of factors, one of which was a 1970 Indian law that dramatically reduced patent protection for all products and eliminated patent protection for pharmaceutical products, thereby allowing Indian companies to manufacture drugs invented in other countries without paying royalties. Under TRIPS, developing countries such as India were provided with a ten-year period to phase-in patent protection for pharmaceutical products,[16] an obligation India dutifully complied with in 2005.

Case Illustration

The European Union has taken the position that only sparkling wine from the Champagne region of France should be labeled as "Champagne." However, TRIPS provides exceptions for geographical indications that have become generic or which were used in good faith by a producer prior to 1994. Consistent with these exceptions, the European Union and United States in 2006 negotiated the Agreement on Trade in Wine, which generally prohibits American sparkling wine producers from using the term "Champagne" in their labeling, but includes a grandfather provision that allows such use for U.S. producers that were already using the term "Champagne" prior to 2006, provided that the brand name is also used. Thus, Korbel, a California company, may continue to label its Champagne as "Korbel California Champagne." The grandfather provision also applies to other alcoholic products, including Burgundy, Chianti, Port, and Sherry. *Agreement Between the United States of America and the European Community on Trade in Wine*, Art. 6(2), Mar. 10, 2006, www.ttb.gov/agreements/us-eu-wine-agreement.pdf.

---

[16]TRIPS Art. 65.

An Ethical Insight: John Rawls and Compulsory Licenses of Patented Products

Opponents of compulsory licenses sometimes argue that the beneficiaries of the licenses are free-riding on the efforts of others. This argument draws on the natural rights perspective that one should not reap where one has not sown. Proponents of compulsory licenses reply that patented information is nonrivalrous, and that therefore the grant of compulsory licenses benefits the poor without diminishing that which is available to others. This position might draw support from John Rawls's *Equal Liberty Principle*, under which "each person is to have an equal right to the most extensive basic liberty compatible with similar liberty for others."

Although India has strengthened its IP laws pursuant to its obligations under international treaties such as TRIPS, it has taken care to include a number of exceptions and limitations to IP rights. Among the most important of these exceptions is the right of the government to grant **compulsory licenses**, that is, permission to produce a patented product without obtaining authorization from the patent holder. Compulsory licenses are authorized under Article 31 of TRIPS and are thus compatible with international law. Although companies that manufacture under a compulsory license must pay royalties to the patent holder, these royalties are often very small. It remains controversial whether the TRIPS regime, including its exception for compulsory licenses, strikes an appropriate balance between incentivizing the development of new drugs and ensuring broad access to any new drugs that are developed.

Global Perspectives: Intellectual Property Law in Russia

Russia acceded to the World Trade Organization in 2012, following 19 years of accession negotiations. As a WTO member, Russia is now bound by TRIPS. Although Russia had already acceded

The Eurasian Patent Convention

Following the breakup of the Soviet Union in 1991, the Eurasian Patent Convention was adopted, which allows businesses to file a single patent application to obtain protection in Russia and eight other countries: Armenia, Azerbaijan, Belarus, Kazakhstan, Kyrgyzstan, Moldova, Tajikistan, and Turkmenistan. The Eurasian Patent Convention contains substantive patent law provisions similar to the law in the United States. For example, Eurasian patents may only be granted for inventions that are new (novel), industrially applicable (useful), and involve an inventive step (nonobvious). Also like U.S. patents, Eurasian patents last for 20 years from the date of filing. The Eurasian Patent Convention exists alongside national patent systems, and does not replace them. This means that businesses must work with their patent attorneys to decide whether to apply separately for one or more national patents, which might be sensible if protection is sought in only one or a small number of countries, or a Eurasian patent, which is applicable in the nine countries listed above but may be more expensive or time consuming to obtain.

to the Berne and Paris Conventions, its accession to the WTO allows some of the provisions of these agreements to be enforced via the WTO dispute resolution system. These developments are expected to lead to a strengthening of Russian IP laws and make it easier for U.S. businesses to obtain and enforce IP rights in Russia. Russia has long been criticized by the U.S. government for its failure to adequately enforce IP rights, particularly with respect to Internet piracy and counterfeit trademarked products. In addition, the United States has described Russia (along with China) as an "aggressive and capable collector of sensitive U.S. economic information and technologies," implying that the government is actively supporting the theft of U.S. trade secrets in potential violation of the Economic Espionage Act. Although some improvements are expected following WTO accession, change is likely to be gradual.

Summary

Intellectual property is of central and growing importance to the modern information economy. The negative rights conferred by IP law allow businesses to prevent others from free-riding on their efforts and reputation. Patents confer a temporary, 20-year right to exclude others from making, using, selling, or importing inventions that are novel, useful, and nonobvious. Copyrights protect creative works of expression such as books, films, music, or Web pages. If they are works made for hire, they will last for 95 years from the date of publication or 120 years from date of creation, whichever is shorter. Although copyrights last much longer than patents, they are subject to greater exceptions, including the right of others to make fair use of the work. Trademarks are distinct words, names, symbols, or devices that serve as source identifiers for products or services. They serve the dual purpose of (1) protecting the goodwill of a business and (2) protecting consumers from confusion in the marketplace. Valuable information that is secret, such as secret formulas or technical specifications, can be protected by state trade secret law. These trade secret laws are reinforced by federal legislation enacted in 1996 that creates significant criminal penalties for economic espionage, particularly when it benefits foreign businesses or governments. Intellectual property has expanded dramatically in both duration and scope since 1790, and businesses should therefore be proactive in securing protection for their own IP while also being careful to avoid violating the rights of others. While intellectual property laws in general can find support in ethical principles, in certain contexts (e.g., medicine) ethical principles may suggest that intellectual property protection should not be without limit.

Questions for Review

1. Obtaining rights/statutory damages

Martin Alexander created a pilot script for a new television sitcom entitled *Loony Ben*. Beginning in March 2006, Alexander submitted copies of the script to agents, producers, directors, production companies, and television networks. In September 2009, the sitcom *Modern Family* debuted on ABC and was, according to Alexander, remarkably similar to his own *Loony Ben*. Alexander sued for copyright infringement, alleging that both works included slapstick elements, focused on nontraditional families, and addressed issues of divorce, racial diversity, and sexuality, among other similarities. With what government office would Alexander have registered his work in order to preserve his rights? Assuming the work was registered, what is the range of damages to which Alexander might be entitled? *Alexander v. Murdoch*, 2011 WL 2802923 (S.D.N.Y. July 14, 2011).

2. Requirements for patentability

In 1997, Bernard Bilski and Rand Warsaw filed a patent application for a method of hedging risk in the field of commodities trading. In effect, the asserted invention was a method of protecting buyers from sudden spikes in the price of commodities, such as coal, by matching them with sellers who were averse to sudden dips in price or demand. After the patent application was rejected by the USPTO, the inventors appealed to the Federal Circuit, which affirmed the rejection. Finally, appeal was taken to the Supreme Court, which similarly affirmed the rejection of the patent application. The Court based its rejection on the ground that the purported invention was an "abstract idea." Under the Court's longstanding precedents, abstract ideas are unpatentable. What are the three principal requirements for patentability mentioned in this chapter? Which of these, do you think, might the Court have utilized as an alternate basis for rejecting Bilski and Warsaw's patent application? *Bilski v. Kappos*, 130 S.Ct. 3218 (2010).

3. Ethics and trade secret theft

Trade secret theft can be a serious crime. Employees leaving a company often consider taking their work product, possibly implicating trade secrets, with them to their new company. E-mails marked "confidential" or "top secret" to alert the employee of their confidentiality are commonly used to transmit trade secrets. Trade secrets are often posted on the company intranet and can be downloaded by an employee and copied to an external storage device. Upon leaving Intel, an employee-engineer was required to return a company computer, and it was discovered he had downloaded top-secret material and copied his Intel laptop's hard drive onto an external storage device. The engineer at Intel left the company with mission-critical documents describing Intel's latest generation of microprocessors valued at $1 billion. The employee-engineer claimed he took the information to help his wife who also worked at Intel. Assuming this is true, was this an ethical act? Base your analysis on ethical theories discussed in Chapter 2, "Ethics in the Business Environment".

4. Trademark landmines/negative rights

Pepperidge Farm's "Goldfish" snack competes with Nabisco's "Cheese Nips" in the cheese cracker snack market. In a 1998 joint promotion agreement with television network Nickelodeon, Nabisco planned to launch a new snack cracker product that combined three shapes of cheese crackers: (1) a "CatDog" shape (2) bones, and (3) fish, all of which were based on trademarked images from the popular Nickelodeon cartoon *CatDog*. The Second Circuit found Nabisco's planned product to wrongfully dilute Pepperidge Farm's Goldfish trademark. Which party could be said to have stepped on a trademark landmine? How does this case illustrate the concept of "negative rights"? *Nabisco v. PF Brands, Inc.*, 191 F.3d 208 (2d Cir. 1999).

5. Intellectual property duration

Create a table summarizing the duration of IP protection, including any required renewals. Be sure to consider patent, copyright, trademark, and trade secret protection.

6. Fair use/de minimis use

Acclaimed screenwriter and director Woody Allen directed *Midnight in Paris*, a 2011 film that is set in Paris, France. In the movie, one of the characters states, "The past is not dead. Actually, it's not even past. You know who said that? Faulkner, and he was right." In fact, William Faulkner, a well-known real-life author, wrote a fictional book that was published in

1950 called *Requiem for a Nun* in which one of the characters states: "The past is never dead. It's not even past." When the 2011 film was released, the holder of the copyright in Faulkner's book sued the film studio, alleging copyright infringement. What resulted? *Faulkner Literary Rights v. Sony Pictures Classics Inc.*, 2013 WL 3762270 (N.D. Miss. July 18, 2013).

7. Trademark continuum

The text notes that some trademarks can be characterized as "stronger" than others, based on the level of distinctiveness. What are the four categories of trademarks, within the trademark distinctiveness continuum, mentioned in the text? Think of examples of trademarks that you know and provide an example of a trademark or word that is likely to fall within each category.

8. Global considerations

Bayer, a global pharmaceutical company based in Germany, holds patents in a number of countries on sorafenib (Nexavar), a drug used to treat certain types of cancer. One of these is an Indian patent (Indian Patent No. 215758), which provides Bayer with certain rights to exclude others from making and using sorafenib within the territory of India. In 2012 India granted a compulsory license to Natco, an Indian generic drug manufacturer, authorizing it to manufacture and sell sorafenib within India, notwithstanding Bayer's Indian patent. Given that India is a member of the WTO, and must therefore comply with TRIPS, is India entitled to grant compulsory licenses? Search the WTO website for a full-text copy of the TRIPS agreement and examine Article 31. What limitations are there, if any, when a country wishes to grant a compulsory license? Must a recipient of a compulsory license, such as Natco, pay anything to the patent holder? *Natco Pharma Ltd v. Bayer Corp.*, The Patent Office Journal [India], Dec. 8, 2011, at 13,345.

Further Reading

Bessen, James, and Michael Meurer, Patent Failure: How Judges, Bureaucrats, and Lawyers Put Innovators at Risk (Princeton University Press, 2008).

Bird, Robert C., and Elizabeth Brown, *The Protection of Well-Known Foreign Marks in the United States: Potential Global Responses to Domestic Ambivalence*, 38 N.C. J. Int'l L. & Com. Reg. 1 (2012).

Boyle, James, The Public Domain: Enclosing the Commons of the Mind (Yale University Press, 2008).

Cahoy, Daniel R., *Breaking Patents*, 32 Mich. J. Int'l L. 461 (2011).

Petty, Ross D., *The "Amazing Adventures" of Super Hero*®, 100 Trademark Rep. 729 (2010).

CHAPTER 9

Sale of Securities and Investor Protection

Chapter Objectives

1. To know the role and purpose of the Securities and Exchange Commission in regulating securities transactions in the United States
2. To know the purpose of the Securities Act of 1933 and understand how it helps protect investors
3. To know the purpose of the Securities Exchange Act of 1934 and understand its impact on publicly held companies
4. To understand the law, ethical issues, and consequences of insider trading
5. To understand the ethical obligations of corporate boards, executives, and traders in protecting investors and the public
6. To know the major provisions of the Sarbanes-Oxley Act of 2002.

Practical Example: Forest Corporation*

Bike Courier Services Corporation (Bike) provides courier services for businesses located in Boston. It guarantees that all deliveries will be completed in a nonstop format, from pickup to delivery point. Normal deliveries are guaranteed to be completed within four hours. Rush deliveries are guaranteed to be made within two hours. All deliveries are handled by trained personnel who use bicycles for all deliveries.

Charles works for Bike during the summers while attending college at a local university. He is majoring in business and has taken several accounting and finance courses. He recently completed a course in the legal and ethical environment of business.

From these courses, Charles has learned quite a lot about the stock market and investment strategies. For example, during the most recent semester, he learned that a company's stock can appreciate significantly in value after a takeover bid by another company has been announced.

Recently, Charles was delivering documents for a major law firm in Boston. A law associate at the firm instructed Charles to deliver the documents to Forest Corporation. She informed Charles that the documents were highly confidential and under no circumstances was he to review or read the documents. The law associate placed the documents in a large envelope marked "confidential." However, the associate forgot to seal the envelope.

As Charles was peddling from the law firm to Forest Corporation, he swerved his bicycle to avoid hitting a pedestrian. This unexpected movement caused Charles to lose control of the bicycle and he hit the ground with a jolt. When he recovered from the fall, Charles noticed that the envelope had opened and the documents were spread over the sidewalk. As Charles gathered the documents, he noticed some familiar terminology on several documents, including the word "takeover." Even though Charles knew he should not read the documents based on the instructions from the law associate, his curiosity compelled him to read the first three pages of the document. Charles thought there was little harm in simply reading the first couple of pages. After all, he needed to take a few minutes to recover from his fall.

Much to his amazement, Charles discovered that Forest Corporation was the target of a takeover. He also learned from the document that the management of Forest Corporation expected the value of the company's stock to increase about 25 percent after the takeover announcement.

Charles received a significant inheritance from his grandmother's estate about six months ago. He has been exploring different options for investing his $3 million inheritance. It suddenly struck him that he had just found the perfect investment opportunity: invest the $3 million in Forest Corporation before the takeover bid is announced. He began thinking about the possibility of a 25 percent return on his investment by simply holding on to the Forest Corporation stock for just a couple of days.

Charles assembled the documents, placed them back into the envelope, sealed the envelope, and delivered the envelope to officials at Forest Corporation. He told no one of his accident or his viewing of the documents related to the takeover bid of Forest Corporation.

About an hour after he delivered the envelope, Charles called his broker and purchased 5,000 shares of Forest Corporation.

---

*Forest Corporation is a fictitious company developed by the authors to demonstrate and illustrate key legal and ethical concepts, theories, practices, and strategies.

To help understand the laws and regulations enacted to safeguard the U.S. economy and to protect institutional and private investors, the preceding practical example illustrates some of the issues involved in regulating the U.S. securities market. As you read the chapter, consider Charles's decision to purchase 5,000 shares of Forest Corporation.

State Securities Laws

This chapter focuses mostly on federal securities laws. These are common rules and regulations that apply to all companies offering securities to the public in the United States. However, each of the 50 states also has its own set of state-based securities laws and regulations, commonly referred to as *Blue Sky Laws*. For a company to be in compliance, it must adhere both to

The stock market crash of 1929 led the U.S. Congress to enact the Securities Act of 1933 and the Securities Exchange Act of 1934.

federal securities laws and relevant state securities laws. A company and its management team must remember that federal and state securities laws may be similar in some ways but very different in other ways. For example, a company may be required to file certain reports under state law but be exempt from filing them under federal law.

The Securities and Exchange Commission

In all likelihood, you know something about the stock market crash of 1929. You may have read about the crash in prior academic courses, or you may have heard it discussed by family members who knew someone who experienced the aftermath of the crash. Regardless of the source of your knowledge about the stock market crash of 1929, you know that it caused the United States to suffer through the Great Depression of the 1930s. While nearly every facet of the private sector in the United States was trying desperately to rebuild during those years, the U.S. Congress focused on developing new laws, regulations, and agencies to ensure this calamity would never happen again. This chapter explains and illustrates the important legislation that the U.S. Congress enacted during the years following the Great Depression.

Two major pieces of legislation emanated from the stock market crash of 1929. These legislative acts are referred to as the Securities Act of 1933 and the Securities Exchange Act of 1934. The Securities Exchange Act of 1934

Exhibit 9.1. Mission of the Securities and Exchange Commission

- Protect investors
- Maintain fair, orderly, and efficient markets
- Facilitate capital formation

Source: U.S. Securities and Exchange Commission www.sec.gov/about/whatwedo.shtml.

created the most significant federal agency dealing with the U.S. stock market, the Securities and Exchange Commission (SEC). The mission of the Securities and Exchange Commission is presented in Exhibit 9.1.

The **Securities and Exchange Commission** plays a critical role in protecting private and institutional investors. Investors expect a return on their investment in the form of dividends, interest, and capital gains. For the common investor, investments represent a means for financing current expenses as well as a strategy for planning for future needs. For example, many people invest in the stock market to help finance educational costs for children, to help purchase a first home, and to plan for retirement. While no investment is risk free, the SEC, as a regulatory agency, helps minimize the risk of investing in companies by reviewing and monitoring the information companies are required to generate and disseminate to the general public.

The SEC also plays a major role in helping to control the various stock markets in the United States. It helps to stimulate the economy by facilitating capital formation and growth. For example, creating new jobs, producing new products, starting new businesses, and maintaining a strong overall economy requires a vibrant, well-controlled stock market, which holds the confidence of investors.

The Securities Act of 1933

The **Securities Act of 1933** (Securities Act) covers the purchase and sale of securities in the United States. To help protect investors and assist companies in offering its securities for sale to the public, the Securities Act includes two main objectives:

- To help ensure that private and institutional investors receive accurate, complete, and valid information about publicly held companies
- To minimize the likelihood of a company engaging in fraud or deceit when offering securities for sale to the public

Registration with the Securities and Exchange Commission

The first step in making securities available to the general public is to make what is called a *public offering*. If this is a company's first time making its stock available to the public, the offering is referred to as an **Initial Public Offering (IPO)**. As part of making a public offering, the Securities Act of 1933 requires a company to provide information about itself, the type of securities being offered, and similar kinds of information.

**Exhibit 9.2. Summary of Information Provided to the SEC
as Part of the Registration Process**

Description of the company's business, property, and industry

Description of the major risks of investing in the company

Discussion and analysis of the company's financial results and financial condition as seen through the eyes of management

Presentation of the company's audited financial statements

Listing of the company's officers and directors and their compensation

Description of material transactions between the company and its officers, directors, and significant shareholders

Description of material legal proceedings involving the company and its officers and directors

Description of the company's material contracts

Description of the security being offered, e.g., common stock

Plans for distributing the securities

Description of the intended use of the proceeds from the sale of the securities

---

Providing information to the Securities and Exchange Commission requires companies to register with the SEC. The registration process is divided into two parts. The first part requires the completion of what is called a prospectus. Many people view a **prospectus** as a kind of "selling document." Like any selling document, a prospectus describes the mission and objectives of a business along with details about a company's business operations. Detailed financial information is also provided along with information about the management team of the company. A prospectus explains the major risks and opportunities associated with a business. The law requires that companies include audited financial statements in a prospectus. The SEC requires companies to distribute a prospectus to all parties interested in buying the company's stock and to those who presently own the company's stock.

The second part of the registration process requires companies to provide confidential information, including items such as recent sales of unregistered securities, copies of significant contracts, etc. Exhibit 9.2 provides a summary of the information provided to the SEC as part of the registration process.

Once a company has registered with the SEC, the SEC assigns professional staff members to review the information provided by the company. The information is included in a set of documents referred to as a **registration statement**. In general, the review ensures that the contents of the registration statement conform to applicable rules and regulations. It is a compliance review as opposed to a meritorious review (i.e., the SEC does not comment on the merits of the offering). Investment decisions about the merits of a particular offering are left to the investing public.

Exemptions from the Registration Process

Because of the high cost and onerous time requirement often associated with the registration process, several types of offerings may qualify for exemption status. Exemption allows a company to offer its securities without going

"Going public" allows a company's stock to be traded on a national exchange, such as the New York Stock Exchange.

through the formal registration process. An offering of securities can be exempt based on the following factors:

■ Private placement offerings — securities are offered only to people who understand the risks, appreciate the risks, and can bear the risks of the investment
■ Offerings limited in size
■ Offerings confined to a single state, often referred to as intrastate offerings (issuer and purchaser are from the same state)
■ Offerings of municipal and state governments, and the federal government

One of the most commonly used exemptions is the private placement exemption, which falls under section 4(a)(2) of the Securities Act. Essentially, this section exempts from registration "transactions by an issuer not involving any public offering." Companies must satisfy the following three criteria in order to fall under the private placement exemption:

■ The purchasers of the private securities must be sophisticated investors. A sophisticated investor generally is someone who has the educational background and professional experience sufficient to allow the investor to assess the risks and merits of the private offering.
■ The purchasers must have access to all the information normally provided in a prospectus for registered securities.
■ The purchasers must agree in advance of any purchase not to sell or otherwise distribute the purchased shares to members of the general public.

By its very nature, a private offering is private; therefore, the offering company may not advertise the offering or disseminate any information to the general public about the offering. As a practical matter, the SEC strictly enforces the rules of a private offering. For example, if a company were to offer securities to

---

Exhibit 9.3. Benefits of Going Public

Enhance the credibility of the company and its products/services

Increase a company's access to cash to finance present and future projects

Attract talented officers and managers by offering stock options

Expand brand awareness

---

an investor who does not meet the above criteria, the entire offering may be challenged by the SEC.

While an exemption minimizes the time, cost, and processing of bringing an offering to the public, a number of federal securities laws continue to apply to companies that are exempt from the registration process. For example, the antifraud provisions of the federal securities laws apply to all securities transactions, even those that are exempt from registration. Application of the antifraud provisions means that the corporation itself along with its officers and directors are responsible for any false, deceiving, or otherwise misleading information disseminated by the company to shareholders or members of the general public.

Benefits and Burdens of "Going Public"

When a company considers the additional costs, time, effort, and administrative burden associated with a public offering, it is important to understand the benefits of "going public." Exhibit 9.3 presents some of the common reasons associated with "taking a company public."

When considering these benefits, a company should also consider the consequences of taking a company public. Exhibit 9.4 summarizes some of the primary consequences or burdens of going public.

Jumpstart Our Business Startups Act

In 2012, President Obama signed into law the Jumpstart Our Business Startups Act, commonly referred to as the JOBS Act. This legislation focuses on streamlining the registration process. The JOBS Act aims to facilitate the process of capital formation and make the registration process much easier for small businesses. One aspect of the legislation requires the SEC to develop

---

Exhibit 9.4. Burdens of Going Public

The founders of the company may lose control of the company they started

A public offering takes time and money to accomplish

A company assumes significant new obligations, such as filing SEC reports and keeping shareholders and the market informed about its business operations, financial condition, and management practices, which consumes a significant amount of time and adds to the cost of operations

A company may lose flexibility in managing company affairs

Information such as financial statements and disclosures about material contracts, customers, and suppliers, becomes available to the general public (including competitors)

rules and amend existing rules to make it easier for companies to raise capital without going through the formal registration process.

Securities Exchange Act of 1934

The Securities Act of 1933 and the Securities Exchange Act of 1934 are different and distinct legislative acts. While there are some obvious crossovers, the two acts stand on their own. Therefore, even if a company was exempt from registering its offering under the Securities Act of 1933, a company may nonetheless have reporting and filing requirements under the Securities Exchange Act of 1934.

Reporting Requirements

The **Securities Exchange Act of 1934** (Exchange Act) requires registered companies to report information regularly to the SEC about their business operations, financial condition, and management practices. Although the reports are sent to the SEC, the information included in the reports is public and is meant to provide investors with as much relevant information as possible about a registered company. Investors use this information to assist them in making decisions about whether to invest in a company, buy additional securities, or sell existing securities. Implicit in the objective of providing relevant and timely information to the investing public is the notion of transparency and full disclosure. The rationale is that if publicly held companies provide a regular flow of pertinent information about themselves in a consistent and understandable format, investors will have equal access to the information they need to make informed decisions.

Registration under the Securities Exchange Act of 1934

Section 12(g) of the Exchange Act requires a company to register its securities with the SEC if the following conditions are met:

- The company has more than $10 million in total assets and a class of equity securities, such as common stock, held by either (1) 2,000 or more persons, or (2) 500 or more nonaccredited investors;[1] or
- The company lists its securities on a U.S. stock exchange.

The following In-Depth Ethical Case Analysis demonstrates the SEC's power under the Securities Exchange Act of 1934 to investigate illegal activities and questionable ethical practices.

---

[1]The SEC considers accredited investors financially sophisticated and not in need of the same level of protection as nonaccredited investors. Accredited investors include banks, insurance companies, employee benefit plans, and individuals with financial means such as income over $200,000 per year or a net worth exceeding $1 million.

In-Depth Ethical Case Analysis

AUSA Life Insurance Co. v. Ernst & Young, 206 F.3d 202 (2000).

Facts

The plaintiffs invested in notes (securities) of JWP, Inc. (JWP). Ernst & Young (E&Y) served as JWP's independent auditors during the years in question. The plaintiffs purchased approximately $150 million of JWP's notes. The plaintiffs relied on JWP's financial statements and E&Y's certification of the financial statements when purchasing the notes.

The U.S. District Court (trial court) found that JWP failed to prepare its financial statements in accordance with generally accepted accounting principles (GAAP), which caused the financial statements to include misrepresentations. During the course of its examination of JWP's books and records, E&Y identified specific instances of GAAP violations and informed the appropriate parties at JWP. However, E&Y did not require JWP to correct the violations before issuing its audit report. Consequently, the financial statements continued to include GAAP violations with the resulting misrepresentations. E&Y's audit report made no reference to the misrepresentations.

The trial court determined that E&Y failed to insist that JWP make the required GAAP adjustments because of the close personal relationship that existed between the CEO of JWP and the partner-in-charge (PIC) of the E&Y audit. This relationship resulted in E&Y's personnel adopting a relaxed attitude about the audit, as noted by the court:

> *E&Y's failure lay in the seeming spinelessness of the partner in charge of the JWP audit and the other E&Y accountants in their dealings with JWP, and particularly with its CEO, [who] almost invariably succeeded in either persuading or bullying them to agree that*
> *JWP's books required no adjustment. Part of the problem was undoubtedly the close personal relationship between [the CEO and the Partner-in-Charge]. They had been partners [at E&Y's predecessor firm] and they continued to be good friends, regularly jogging together in preparation for the New York City Marathon.*

After JWP began to experience significant cash flow problems, a new CEO was hired. The new CEO identified accounting irregularities in JWP's financial statements and hired a new auditing firm, Deloitte & Touche (D&T), to review its books and records. After a thorough examination, D&T concluded that JWP's financial statements were inaccurate and required correction and restatement. The restatements resulted in significant reductions of JWP's previously reported annual profits. Ultimately, JWP could no longer pay its creditors and the company was forced into involuntary bankruptcy. As a result of JWP's insolvency, the plaintiffs sustained losses of approximately $100 million on their investments in JWP's notes.

Issue

Must a plaintiff alleging fraud under section 10b-5 of the Securities and Exchange Act of 1934 prove both *transaction causation* (the alleged fraud caused the plaintiffs to engage in the transaction in question) and *loss causation* (the damage suffered was a foreseeable consequence of the alleged fraud)?

Discussion

Section 10b-5 of the Securities and Exchange Act of 1934 provides that:

It shall be unlawful for any person, directly or indirectly, by the use of any means or instrumentality of interstate commerce, or of the mails or of any facility of any national securities exchange

- *to employ any device, scheme, or artifice to defraud,*
- *to make any untrue statement of a material fact or to omit to state a material fact necessary in order to make the statements made, in the light of the circumstances under which they were made, not misleading, or*
- *to engage in any act, practice, or course of business which operates or would operate as a fraud or deceit upon any person in connection with the purchase or sale of any security.*

In connection with the purchase or sale of securities, the court stated that a plaintiff must prove under section 10b-5 that the defendant (acting with scienter) made a false material misrepresentation or omitted to disclose material information. Additionally, a plaintiff must show that its reliance on the defendant's misrepresentation caused its injuries. In expanding on this point, the court observed that causation includes two elements: *transaction causation* and *loss causation*.

Transaction causation establishes that the misrepresentation caused [in fact] the plaintiff to engage in the transaction(s) in question. This element requires a plaintiff to prove that the misrepresentation caused the plaintiff to suffer an *actual* loss. Loss causation, analogous to the tort concept of proximate causation, establishes that the damages suffered were a foreseeable consequence of the defendant's misrepresentation.

Conclusion

The U.S. Court of Appeals for the Second Circuit determined that transaction causation was established by the plaintiff's reliance on E&Y's certification that JWP's financial statements were prepared in accordance with generally accepted accounting principles (GAAP). However, because the District Court (trial court) did not make any factual findings about loss causation, the Appeals Court remanded the case (sent it back to the trial court) for more factual findings about the question of loss causation because both transaction causation and loss causation are required.

Ethical Question

From an ethical perspective, do you believe it is important for professionals (e.g., auditors and corporate executives) to establish and maintain a mindset of "independence" when engaging in business dealings?

Ethical Theory Analysis

Auditors have serious social, economic, legal, and ethical obligations owed to their clients, investors, and the financial markets. Since, in addition to their clients, investors and the financial markets in general rely on these certified financial statements, they are acting in a fiduciary capacity with ethical obligations that extend beyond the auditor/client relationship. The auditors' professional obligations owed to their clients, investors, and the financial markets must take priority over any personal friendships they may have in their business dealings with the audited company. Their judgments must be based on GAAP, the code of professional ethics for certified public accountants (CPAs), and their own personal ethics.

W.D. Ross's prima facie duties of fidelity and nonmalfeasance apply to the auditors' ethical duties owed to the company, its investors, the financial markets, and the accounting profession.

Ross's prima facie ethical duty of nonmalfeasance (do no harm) obligates the auditors to prepare certified financial statements in accordance with GAAP and thereby not financially harm investors who rely on their accuracy. Investors engage in a degree of risk taking based on the auditors' certified financial statements that, when prepared in violation of GAAP, cannot be accurately assessed. The auditors in this case violated the ethical principles of fidelity and nonmalfeasance. They had an ethical duty to maintain an "independent mindset" that was compromised due to the personal relationship between the CEO and the partner in charge of the audit.

Insider Trading

Insider trading occurs when material nonpublic information is used by a person inside the company, such as a corporate officer or director, in the trading of a company's stock (see Exhibit 9.5). An insider is also a person who owes a fiduciary duty to the company, including employees, and uses material nonpublic information when trading in the shares of stock of the company. Although no precise definition exists, an insider is generally a person who

---

Exhibit 9.5. SEC Statement About Insider Trading

Insider trading is a term that most investors have heard and usually associate with illegal conduct. But the term actually includes both legal and illegal conduct. The legal version is when corporate insiders — officers, directors, and employees — buy and sell stock in their own companies. When corporate insiders trade in their own securities, they must report their trades to the SEC.

Illegal insider trading refers generally to buying or selling a security, in breach of a fiduciary duty or other relationship of trust and confidence, while in possession of material, nonpublic information about the security. Insider trading violations may also include "tipping" such information, securities trading by the person "tipped," and securities trading by those who misappropriate such information.

Examples of insider trading cases that have been brought by the SEC are cases against:

1. Corporate officers, directors, and employees who traded the corporation's securities after learning of significant, confidential corporate developments;
2. Friends, business associates, family members, and other "tippees" of such officers, directors, and employees, who traded the securities after receiving such information;
3. Employees of law, banking, brokerage, and printing firms who were given such information to provide services to the corporation whose securities they traded;
4. Government employees who learned of such information because of their employment by the government; and
5. Other persons who misappropriated, and took advantage of, confidential information from their employers.

Because insider trading undermines investor confidence in the fairness and integrity of the securities markets, the SEC has treated the detection and prosecution of insider trading violations as one of its enforcement priorities.

The SEC adopted a new rule [Rule 10b5-1], which provides that a person trades on the basis of material nonpublic information if a trader is "aware" of the material nonpublic information when making the purchase or sale. The rule also sets forth several affirmative defenses or exceptions to liability. The rule permits persons to trade in certain specified circumstances where it is clear that the information they are aware of is not a factor in the decision to trade, such as pursuant to a preexisting plan, contract, or instruction that was made in good faith.

Source: U.S. Securities and Exchange Commission, Insider Trading, http://www.sec.gov/answers/insider.htm.

has knowledge or facts about a company that are not available to the general public.

An insider may also be a person who operates "outside" the company and receives "insider" information through the normal course of providing professional services for the company, such as members of the company's accounting firm. An insider could also be a stock broker or financial advisor who receives information, often in the form of a tip, from someone who has access to inside information because of a fiduciary relationship with the company. Consider, for example, Forest Corporation, the company presented in the Practice Example at the beginning of the chapter. Based on the statement provided by the SEC in Exhibit 9.5, is it likely that Charles engaged in insider trading when he used information contained in the confidential envelope to purchase 5,000 shares of Forest Corporation's common stock?

What Is Inside Information?

Inside information is any information about a company's strategic and financial plans or current operations, such as planned mergers and acquisitions, research and development, and new product launches obtained from "inside" the company. Information obtained from inside the company means any information that is not otherwise available to the general public.

What Are the Penalties for Insider Trading?

There are two kinds of penalties: civil penalties and criminal penalties. In general, the **civil penalties for insider trading** consist of a violator being disgorged of any profit made or loss avoided as a result of using insider information. Under Section 21A of the **Securities Exchange Act of 1934**, a violator may be fined up to three times the amount of the profit earned or the loss avoided. Sanctions may also include restrictions on the types of activities the violator may engage in, such as not serving in certain types of positions in the future (e.g., a chief financial officer or a director of a public corporation).

Insider trading continues to be a high-priority area for the SEC's enforcement program. The SEC brought 58 insider trading actions in FY 2012 against 131 individuals and entities. Over the last three years, the SEC has filed more insider trading actions (168 in total) than in any three-year period in the agency's history. These insider trading actions were filed against nearly 400 individuals and entities with illicit profits or losses avoided totaling $600 million. Many of these actions involved financial professionals, hedge fund managers, corporate insiders, and attorneys who unlawfully traded on material nonpublic information, undermining the level playing field that is fundamental to the integrity and fair functioning of capital markets. SEC Enforcement Actions, Insider Trading Cases, http://www.sec.gov/spotlight/insidertrading/cases.shtml.

Examples of recent actions taken by the Securities and Exchange Commission regarding insider trading include:

■ A businessperson who obtained confidential information from the CEO of an oil and gas company that was about to secure a huge investment;

Insider trading is illegal and leads to the arrest and prosecution of major financial figures in the United States.

- A partner in a major accounting firm who obtained nonpublic information while serving as the partner in charge of a regional audit practice; and
- A portfolio manager who traded on the basis of inside information ahead of the quarterly earnings announcement of a major public company.[2]

In general, the **criminal penalties for insider trading** involve the Department of Justice through the local U.S. attorney's office, and not the Securities and Exchange Commission. The SEC imposes civil fines and sanctions on violators. On the other hand, the Department of Justice pursues a criminal prosecution of a violator under Section 32(a) of the Securities Exchange Act of 1934, as amended by the Sarbanes-Oxley Act of 2002. Generally, violators may face up to 20 years in prison for criminal securities fraud and a fine of up to $5 million for each "willful" violation of the act. Only fines, not imprisonment, apply if the defendant can demonstrate "no

> ### An Ethical Insight: Insider Trading and Ross's Prima Facie Duty of Fidelity
>
> W.D. Ross's duty of fidelity relates to keeping expressed or implied promises. Corporate insiders (e.g., board members and top-level executives) often have access to advanced strategic information that could be used to their financial advantage. Ross stated ". . . *To make a promise* [expressed or implied] . . . *is to put oneself in a new relationship . . . which creates a specifically new prima facie duty* [of fidelity]" . . .[*] [emphasis added]. SEC Rule 10b-5 that prohibits insider trading has its ethical foundation in a duty of fidelity.
>
> ---
>
> [*]Ross, W.D., *The Right and the Good*, Oxford at the Clarendon Press (1955), p. 38.

---

[2]SEC Enforcement Actions, Insider Trading Cases, http://www.sec.gov/spotlight/insidertrading/cases.shtml.

knowledge" of the rule or regulation that was violated. Corporations face penalties of up to $25 million.

For example, the Southern District of New York successfully prosecuted Raj Rajaratnam for insider trading. Rajaratnam was the managing member of Galleon Management LLC, the general partner of Galleon Management LP, and a portfolio manager for Galleon Technology Offshore Ltd. and certain accounts of Galleon Diversified Fund Ltd. He was convicted in May 2011 of 14 counts of conspiracy and securities fraud, following an eight-week jury trial. Rajaratnam was sentenced to 11 years in prison, one the longest sentences imposed for an insider trading offense.[3]

Legislative Initiatives of the Twenty-First Century

Sarbanes-Oxley Act of 2002

The financial collapse of Enron Corporation captured the attention of the world in late 2001. Enron was a major international energy-trading company located in Texas and the seventh-largest company in the United States. The aftermath of the collapse resulted in the prosecution of the scandal's major players. Congress passed the **Sarbanes-Oxley Act of 2002** which represents one of the most significant pieces of securities legislation since the Securities Act of 1933 and the Securities Exchange Act of 1934. Sarbanes-Oxley increases corporate responsibility and mandates higher levels of financial disclosures. Sarbanes-Oxley also created a new public oversight board. The Public Company Accounting Oversight Board (PCAOB) oversees the activities of the public accounting profession relative to the audits of publicly held companies.

Unlike the Securities Acts of 1933 and 1934, Sarbanes-Oxley focuses on a company's financial and corporate management practices. The emphasis on "management practices" aims to hold corporate officers and directors accountable for the accuracy, completeness, and validity of a company's financial reports. Before examining the key provisions of the Sarbanes-Oxley Act, consider the Manager's Compliance and Ethics Meeting scenario on page 275.

Presented below is a summary of the major provisions of the Sarbanes-Oxley Act of 2002.

Section 302: Corporate Responsibility for Financial Reports

Section 302 requires management to make assertions about the overall accuracy, completeness, and validity of the financial reports signed by the company's chief executive officer (CEO) and chief financial officer (CFO). This section of the act assures that the key members of a company's management team assume personal responsibility for the company's financial reports. For example, the CEO and the CFO must review the financial reports and state

---

[3]Bharara, P., Offices of the U.S. Attorneys, Securities Fraud, http://www.justice.gov/usao/briefing_room/fin/securities_fraud.html.

Manager's Compliance and Ethics Meeting

Whistleblower

Harrison Manufacturing Company (HMC), a multimillion-dollar (fictitious) international corporation, designs and manufactures medical devices and is listed on the New York Stock Exchange. In accordance with the Sarbanes-Oxley Act, it has a board of directors with an independent audit committee that established procedures to review the complaints of whistleblowers. The audit committee procedures require whistleblowers to bring all complaints to their department supervisor who makes the final decision about the merits of a complaint.

Sandra, a biotech engineer working for HMC, overheard her associate, a fellow engineer, speaking on her cell phone telling her friend to buy stock in HMC as it was about to file with the U.S. Patent Office a superior patent for an artificial knee replacement device that would substantially increase HMC's market value. All the engineers working on the device signed a nondisclosure agreement promising to keep progress on the new invention highly confidential.

Sandra reported this to her department supervisor who warned her not to start trouble since discussing the progress of a potential patent goes on all the time and would not in any way harm HMC. Sandra continued to insist that the situation be brought to the attention of upper management. When her complaint was ignored, she complained to HMC's compliance and ethics officer.

To assure company compliance with the Sarbanes-Oxley Act, HMC's compliance and ethics officer called a meeting of the audit committee to review its procedures on whistleblowers and the consequences of vesting complete authority to determine the merits of a complaint with the whistleblower's department supervisor.

Questions

1. Was the audit committee acting ethically in adopting its current set of whistleblower procedures?
2. Was Sandra's direct supervisor acting ethically in dismissing her complaint claiming that disclosure of the invention would not harm the company?

Be sure to use classical ethical principles in answering the questions and think about the following ethical considerations:

- W.D. Ross's Prima Facie Duty of Fidelity. Disclosing trade secrets can jeopardize a company's competitive position and ultimately its market value. Ross's prima facie duty of fidelity would be violated because the engineers all signed an agreement to keep their work on the proposed patent confidential.
- Utilitarianism — Rule utilitarianism. The greater happiness would be served by taking Sandra's complaint seriously and investigating the details of her complaint. Competition drives the free enterprise system, and keeping trade secrets confidential is an essential element of that process.
- Most ethical principles would find the audit committee's procedure unethical because allowing one person to rule on a complaint would defeat the purpose of carefully reviewing the merits of a whistleblower's complaint.

affirmatively that they have reviewed and assessed the overall content and quality of the reports. They must also state that the reports contain no misleading information, including no material untrue statements or omissions. By signing the report, the CEO and the CFO assert that the company's financial statements present fairly the results of operations and the financial condition of the company.

Another important aspect of Section 302 is that unlike the Securities Acts of 1933 and 1934, Section 302 places a company's system of internal control in the forefront of management's reporting requirements. For example, Section 302 places primary responsibility for the quality of a company's internal controls with the CEO and the CFO. Section 302 accomplishes this task by requiring the CEO and the CFO to include a statement in the company's annual report that they have reviewed and evaluated the internal controls of the company within the 90-day period preceding the issuance of the report. Section 302 requires them to report on the results of their review and evaluation of the internal control system, including statements about system deficiencies and fraudulent activities.

Section 401: Disclosures in Periodic Reports

Section 401 increases the disclosure requirements of a company's financial reports. One of the major problems in the Enron case related to the fraudulent use of off-balance sheet special purpose entities (SPEs). The SPEs were used to shift many liabilities from Enron's balance sheet to the balance sheets of the SPEs. This fraudulent process (approved by Enron's external auditors) allowed Enron's management to artificially and deceptively reduce the amount of debt reported on Enron's balance sheet. As a result, Enron's management team deceived shareholders and others, resulting in losses in the billions of dollars. To address this problem, Section 401 requires publicly traded companies to make complete disclosure of the use of any device, such as SPEs.

Section 404: Management Assessment of Internal Controls

At the conclusion of the Enron investigation, one of the major findings was the discovery of a significant breakdown in Enron's system of internal controls. Material transactions adversely affecting the company's financial condition were not included in the company's accounting system, and liabilities were fraudulently moved from Enron's accounting records to those of the special purpose entities. To address problems like those in Enron's financial records and reports, Section 404 requires management to include a statement in the annual report about the quality and integrity of the company's system of internal control. The statement must assert that management has assessed the quality and the effectiveness of the company's internal controls system. The statement must also disclose material breaches found in the control system. Finally, the statement must make it clear that management assumes responsibility for designing, implementing, and maintaining an adequate system of internal control. As a final check, Section 404 requires the accounting firm that audits a company's financial statements to corroborate management's assertion about the effectiveness of the company's internal control system.

Section 409: Real-Time Issuer Disclosures

While the Securities Acts of 1933 and 1934 require companies to report periodically to the SEC, Section 409, for the first time, requires companies to report information on a "real-time" basis. The real-time reporting requirement provides shareholders, regulators, investors, and others with current information about events that may have a material impact on a company's financial condition. Section 409 amends the Securities Exchange Act of 1934 by requiring that "each [company] reporting under [the Securities Exchange Act of 1934] shall disclose to the public on a rapid and current basis such additional information concerning material changes in the financial condition or operations of the issuer, in plain English, which may include trend and qualitative information and graphic presentations, as the Commission determines, by rule, is necessary or useful for the protection of investors and in the public interest."

Section 802: Criminal Penalties for Altering Documents

Section 802 imposes significant criminal sanctions on offenders who violate provisions of the Sarbanes-Oxley Act. The sanctions include the possibility of both imprisonment and the imposition of significant fines. Also, for the first time, external auditors may be criminally charged for knowingly and willfully violating the requirement of maintaining audit work papers for the required period of five years.

Dodd-Frank Wall Street Reform and Consumer Protection Act

Congress enacted the **Dodd-Frank Wall Street Reform and Consumer Protection Act** (Dodd-Frank) on July 21, 2010.[4] The legislation focuses on consumer protection, trading restrictions, credit ratings, regulation of financial products, corporate governance, disclosure, and transparency.

Dodd-Frank requires the Securities and Exchange Commission to create an **Office of the Whistleblower**. Whistleblower protection laws encourage employees to report inappropriate corporate activities to government officials, and they prevent companies from discharging or disciplining employees who report improper corporate activities.

---

[4]The Dodd-Frank Wall Street Reform and Consumer Protection Act of 2010 includes more than 2,300 pages of text and graphs. Many of its provisions have not yet been implemented.

Global Perspective: International Securities Law

Exhibit 9.6 presents excerpts from a speech delivered by Mary Jo White, Chairman of the Securities and Exchange Commission, on the topic of "Regulation in a Global Financial System."[5]

Exhibit 9.6. Regulation in a Global Financial System

As is our standard disclaimer, my remarks today are my own and do not necessarily represent the views of the Commission or other Commissioners.

* * *

Effective regulation of the U.S. financial system requires us to be a part of the fabric of a global financial and regulatory system that transcends political boundaries. And it demands that we match our regulatory and enforcement priorities with those of scores of jurisdictions around the world.

A defining fact of life at the SEC today is that we are not alone in the global regulatory space. And our duty to the investors, entrepreneurs, and other market participants who rely on us means that we must find common ground with our counterparts abroad, collaborate on everyday matters like enforcement and accounting, and knit together a regulatory network that offers protection, consistency, and stability to market participants — especially in the United States but abroad as well. This global reality was quickly and forcefully driven home to me almost from the moment I was sworn in. . . .

Over the last three weeks I have, for example:

- Attended meetings with the Secretary of the Treasury and central bank heads and regulatory chiefs from Canada, China, Europe, Japan, Mexico, Singapore and Switzerland.
- Been briefed for a meeting of the Financial Stability Board and a London meeting of the International Financial Reporting Standards Foundation Monitoring Board.
- Reviewed, shaped, and voted on a thousand-page proposal for regulating cross-border derivatives transactions, which I'll talk more about in just a few minutes.
- Held personal meetings with the Vice Chair of the Japan Financial Services Agency and the Australian Securities and Investments Commission Chairman, who also is Chairman of the International Organization of Securities Commissions.

---

[5]"Regulation in a Global Financial System," a speech by Chairman Mary Jo White, *U.S. Securities and Exchange Commission*, Investment Company Institute (ICI) General Membership Meeting, Washington, DC (May 1, 2013).

And this is only a partial list of my international activities. This has all occurred because — while I believe that the U.S. has the safest, most resilient and robust markets in the world — we are not the only game in town.

So throughout the SEC, we are cooperating with our foreign counterparts in ways that unleash the fullest potential of our capital markets to drive economic growth and create jobs — and to do so in a way that does not lower the bar or relax the regulatory and oversight standards that protect investors and stabilize markets.

What happens overseas matters here at home, and matters more every day. The fund industry knows this almost better than anyone. American investors and fund managers make decisions based on financial reporting standards developed and financial statements audited overseas. A bad derivatives trade executed by the Asian subsidiary of a Wall Street bank or a threat to an EU-based financial institution could mean layoffs, investor losses, and tighter credit here at home. And the fraudsters seeking to lure clients and tarnish the image of the industry you represent now cross international borders with the tap of a finger or the click of a mouse.

I remember a time when the only stock market reports you heard on the radio driving to work were yesterday's New York Stock Exchange and NASDAQ performances. Now you hear about the FTSE, the Nikkei, the DAX, and the Hang Seng all before breakfast, and it's simply assumed that a retail investor with, say, a reasonable retirement fund is interested in and affected by all of this.

U.S. investors rely on the SEC to be just as conscious of international financial market development as the business reporter on the local station.

And so the SEC is continuing to build on and strengthen its relationships with overseas regulators on a number of levels. It's a demanding and time-consuming task for the SEC staff and for me personally, but a critically important one.

One-on-one negotiations, membership in global organizations, participation in bilateral and multilateral discussions, domestic regulatory recognition of foreign reporting and accounting practices — these are a few of the ways the SEC is integrating itself into the global financial system.

Over the years, the SEC has played an active role in such international bodies as IOSCO and the Financial Stability Board — which themselves have helped to ensure coordination among financial regulators who share common regulatory objectives. Such coordination not only allows agencies to better achieve their own domestic agendas, but by encouraging the adoption of high-quality regulation around the globe it also helps to prevent regulatory arbitrage.

The SEC has long been at the forefront on multilateral efforts to ensure that broad standard setting is coupled with robust regulator-to-regulator assistance in oversight and enforcement matters. We have negotiated dozens of bilateral and multilateral cooperation arrangements that fill the gaps and facilitate sharing of critical enforcement and supervisory information with our overseas counterparts.

Regulatory globalization is now a continuous and ongoing process, and one that has gotten much more intensive and complex. We often find ourselves sailing in previously uncharted waters.

Until recently, for example, the multi-trillion dollar derivatives market was largely unregulated. In the United States, the SEC was essentially prohibited from regulating derivatives.

Now, in the wake of a financial crisis to which the opaque and potentially destabilizing nature of the derivatives market contributed, the SEC is charged with enhancing U.S. financial stability by working with other regulators to make multiple sets of rules from multiple regulators work in a global market.

* * *

International Oversight

Let me sum up my whirlwind international tour by saying that enhancing our profile as a globally-focused regulator is an ongoing priority at the SEC. From accounting standards to Ponzi schemes, from annual reports to OTC derivatives, the SEC is determined to maintain a regulatory structure that accommodates jurisdictional differences without lowering standards.

This isn't an effort aimed at the elite. Our collaborations with international regulators and considerations of international standards are also meant to protect America's mom-and-pop investors: workers, families, and future retirees who recognize that we live in a global marketplace and seek to maximize their options and returns by looking abroad — or to funds that invest abroad — for opportunities. They seek exposure to international markets through mutual funds, ETFs, and closed-end funds. And they rely both on our vigilance and your expertise as they invest their hard-earned dollars in the international market.

It's a challenge. Accommodating jurisdictional differences while promoting high standards is a delicate task. Understanding that, despite the size and dynamism of our markets, other jurisdictions have different priorities and solutions takes a conscious effort and a more expansive mindset. And weaving international concerns into even the most seemingly domestic rulemaking or policy takes time. But we understand an exclusively, or even largely, domestically-focused regulatory approach is no longer acceptable or effective. American investors are focused on international investing in a global marketplace. American regulators must be as well. That's what I'm committed to doing.

Source: "Regulation in a Global Financial System," a speech by Chairman Mary Jo White, *U.S. Securities and Exchange Commission*, Investment Company Institute (ICI) General Membership Meeting, Washington, DC (May 1, 2013), http:// www.sec.gov/news/speech/2013/spch050313mjw.htm.

The above speech reflects a growing recognition that securities laws and regulations are no longer the exclusive domain of one country. Indeed, as we move increasingly into a global economy, the markets and securities laws of the various countries must reflect this global transformation.

Summary

The Securities and Exchange Commission (SEC) plays a vitally important role in regulating the securities market in the United States. In fulfilling its mission, the SEC protects investors, helps maintain a fair, orderly and efficient market, and facilitates capital formation. The Securities Acts of 1933 and 1934 continue to serve as the foundation for securities laws and regulations in the United States. Insider trading and other corporate scandals have resulted in new legislation aimed at protecting the public and punishing offenders, such as the Sarbanes-Oxley Act of 2002 and the Dodd-Frank Wall Street Reform and Consumer Protection Act of 2010. Increasingly, securities transactions and transgressions have expanded beyond the borders of the United States, resulting in the need for closer cooperation among global regulators.

Questions for Review

1. Securities Act of 1933, the Securities Exchange Act of 1934, and the Sarbanes-Oxley Act of 2002

Jonathan owns Bright Sky Financial Services, Inc. (Bright Sky). He holds a controlling interest in the company. Jonathan manages seven mutual funds for approximately 150 high-wealth clients. Jonathan is a registered broker and Bright Sky is registered with the Securities and Exchange Commission. In total, the funds have a market value of just over $500 million. Jonathan's clients are very pleased with his handling of the funds, for the average investor receives a return of about 20 percent per year. Jonathan is highly regarded in his local community; he is known as a person who donates large sums of money to charitable organizations. Jonathan is also president of the local chapter of a financial planning organization. Recently, he published a popular book about successful investment strategies, and he is a regular speaker at regional and national conferences.

About three months ago, the Internal Revenue Service began an audit of Jonathan's personal tax return and the tax return of Bright Sky. During the course of the audit, the revenue agent discovered a discrepancy between the actual fund balance in one of Bright Sky's mutual funds and the reported balance on Bright Sky's tax return. The actual fund balance was $140,000 less than the amount reported on Bright Sky's tax return. Upon further inquiry, the revenue agent discovered that Jonathan had made seven wire transfers of $20,000 each from the fund in question to his personal bank account. The agent found that Jonathan had reported the $140,000 as dividend income on his personal tax return. However, the minutes of Bright Sky's board of directors' meetings did not indicate that any dividends had been declared. Furthermore, the reports filed with the Securities and Exchange Commission reported a fund balance that was $140,000 higher than the actual fund balance.

Discussion Questions

a. Based on the above facts, has Jonathan violated any of the provisions of the Securities Act of 1933, the Securities Exchange Act of 1934, or the Sarbanes-Oxley Act of 2002? Explain.

b. Based on the above facts, do you believe Jonathan has acted ethically in his dealings with his clients or the SEC? Explain.

2. Role of the Securities and Exchange Commission

Describe the SEC's role in regulating securities transactions in the United States. Discuss the mission and purpose of the SEC.

3. Ethics considerations

Madison Corporation (Madison) along with Sarah, Madison's chief executive officer (CEO), and James, Madison's chief financial officer (CFO), engaged in a practice known as using "dummy assets" to inflate credit ratings associated with an upcoming offering. Madison arranged to offer a collateralized debt obligation (CDO) to investors. The CDO promised to pay investors cash returns based on the amount of cash generated by the pool of investment assets included in the CDO. The price of the offering was based on the CDO receiving a certain rating from a national credit rating agency.

Shortly before the agency was due to rate the CDO, employees at Madison realized that the CDO would not satisfy two of the criteria used by the agency, which would result in the CDO receiving a lower than expected credit rating. To address this problem, Sarah and James inflated the assets of the CDO by including in the statements they sent to the rating agency $10 million of fictitious assets, so-called "dummy assets."

With the dummy assets included in the portfolio of the CDO, the agency provided the credit rating expected by Madison and the company proceeded to sell the notes associated with the CDO to shareholders. At the time of the sale, Sarah and James knew the investors were buying the notes based on false and misleading information, which led to the artificially higher credit rating. About six months after the sale of the notes, the economy took an unexpected downturn and the assets included in the CDO failed to produce the cash flow necessary to pay the investors. Ultimately, the notes became worthless.

Discussion Questions

a. Based on the actions of Sarah, James, and Madison Corporation to deceive investors by artificially inflating the value of the CDO's pooled assets, what federal securities laws may have been breached? Explain.

b. Madison Corporation along with its CEO (Sarah) and CFO (James) undermined the integrity of the financial markets in the United States and damaged the financial interests of the investors in the CDO notes. Discuss the ethical issues raised by the facts in this question. Do you believe Sarah and James acted ethically or unethically? Why? Is it possible for an artificial entity, such as Madison Corporation, to act ethically or unethically? Explain.

4. Insider trading

In a complaint filed by the Securities and Exchange Commission (SEC) against Thomas P. Flanagan and Patrick T. Flanagan in the U.S. District Court Northern District of Illinois Eastern Division, the SEC made the following allegations:[6]

a. That Thomas P. Flanagan ("Flanagan"), a former partner and a Vice Chairman at the Big Four accounting firm Deloitte and Touche LLP ("Deloitte") engaged in repeated insider trading. Flanagan traded in the securities of multiple Deloitte clients on the basis of inside information that he learned through his duties as a Deloitte partner. The inside information concerned market moving events such as earnings results, revisions to earnings guidance, sales figures and cost cutting, and an acquisition. Flanagan's illegal trading resulted in profits of more than $430,000.

---

[6]*U.S. Securities and Exchange Commission v. Thomas P. Flanagan and Patrick T. Flanagan*, civil complaint filed in the U.S. District Court Northern District of Illinois Eastern Division, Case 1:10-cv-04885, filed Aug. 4, 2010.

b. That Flanagan shared the information with his son Patrick. Patrick then traded based on the information. Patrick's illegal trading resulted in profits of more than $57,000.

What is the likely outcome of each allegation and why? Explain.

5. Securities Act of 1933 and Securities Exchange Act of 1934

Describe the major provisions of the Securities Act of 1933 and the Securities Exchange Act of 1934.

6. Insider trading

Joseph is a senior partner in a law firm representing a client interested in acquiring an interest in Liberty Software (a fictitious company). Liberty Software is a prominent social-networking company. His client is a member of the board of directors of Liberty Software. As a board member, Joseph's client received confidential information about a new patent in progress that would transform the way data could be stored and substantially increase the market value of Liberty Software's stock. Using the information acquired from his client, Joseph purchased a large amount of Liberty Software's stock at a low price and made millions of dollars on its sale. Section 10(b) and Rule 10b-5 prohibits insider trading. Joseph is convinced that his trading of Liberty Software stock based on the tip from his client is legal and ethical. He believes it is legal because he is not in a "fiduciary relationship or other relationship of trust" with the stockholders of Liberty Software. Joseph believes his actions are ethical because his trading in the stock may increase its market value and will not cause harm to the stockholders. Do you agree? Explain.

7. Sarbanes-Oxley Act of 2002

Describe the major provisions of the Sarbanes-Oxley Act of 2002.

8. International considerations

Based on the speech delivered by Mary Jo White, Chairman of the Securities and Exchange Commission, on the topic of "Regulation in a Global Financial System (see Exhibit 9.6), do you believe it is possible to regulate securities transactions on a global basis? Explain.

Further Reading

Garrison, M. J., and Knoepfle, T. W., *Limited Liability Company Interests as Securities: A Proposed Framework for Analysis*, 33 American Business Law Journal 577–644 (1996).

Mark, G., *Private FCPA Enforcement*, 49 American Business Law Journal 419–506 (2012).

Prentice, R. A., *Stoneridge, Securities Fraud Litigation, and the Supreme Court*, 45 American Business Law Journal 611–683 (2008).

Prentice, R. A., and Donelson, D. C., *Insider Trading as a Signaling Device*, 47 American Business Law Journal 1–73 (2010).

Prentice, R., Richardson, V. J., and Scholz, S., *Corporate Web Site Disclosure and Rule 10b-5: An Empirical Evaluation*, 36 American Business Law Journal 531–578 (1999).

Veliotis, S., *Rule 10b5-1 Trading Plans and Insiders' Incentive to Misrepresent*, 47 American Business Law Journal 313–359 (2010).

CHAPTER 10

Business Crimes

Chapter Objectives

1. To understand the basic concepts of criminal law and their direct application to business crimes
2. To know and understand the difference between civil law and criminal law
3. To know and understand the primary types of business crimes committed in the United States
4. To know and understand the common defenses to business crimes
5. To know and understand the criminal process and constitutional protections available to defendants

Practical Example: The Case of Iris*

Last year, the Boston office of the FBI launched an undercover operation to identify and arrest corrupt public officials. To assist in the operation, the FBI enlisted the services of Ken, a former certified public accountant (CPA) based in the San Francisco area. Ken had recently been indicted on charges of assisting ten of his clients in the preparation and filing of fraudulent tax returns. Ken was recommended by the FBI office in San Francisco as someone who possessed strong persuasive powers, as he was able to convince ten otherwise respectable and decent individuals (his clients) to conspire with

him to commit tax fraud. The FBI office in Boston interviewed Ken and then interceded on Ken's behalf to convince the prosecutor assigned to the case to reduce the charges against Ken. In exchange for the reduction in charges, Ken agreed to cooperate with the FBI.

During the FBI undercover operation in Boston, Ken played the role of a "well-connected" financial advisor and political strategist. Ken received a weekly stipend of $250 from the FBI to cover expenses related to his undercover operation. The FBI assigned an experienced special agent to work with Ken. The special agent assumed the name of Emily and played the role of a local business owner interested in constructing a building on federally owned property.

In his "hunt" for corrupt public officials, Ken attended conventions in the Boston area known for attracting local business owners and politicians. During coffee breaks at the conventions, Ken informed local business owners and politicians of his abilities to "get things done" in ways that others could not. During one of the breaks, Ken started a conversation with Iris. Ken learned that Iris served as a federal inspector responsible for approving building projects on federal property. Iris commented about how much she enjoyed her position, but acknowledged that her salary was insufficient to "make ends meet." Consequently, Iris held a second job with a construction company, working in the evenings and on weekends. Ken and Iris exchanged business cards.

About a week later, Ken called Iris and invited her to coffee. During their telephone conversation, Ken mentioned he had a proposal in mind that might be of interest to Iris. They met for coffee the next day. Eager to hear about Ken's proposal, Iris asked what he had in mind. Ken mentioned that an associate of his was interested in constructing a building on federally owned property. Ken mentioned that his associate was concerned that she might not be able to secure the permits necessary to construct the building. In response, Ken told Iris he had informed his associate about Iris, describing the position she held with the federal government. Ken then removed an envelope from his briefcase and told Iris it contained $10,000 in cash. He placed the envelope on the table. Ken said no more, and Iris changed the subject. Shortly thereafter, Ken and Iris left the restaurant without saying anything more about Ken's associate or the envelope containing $10,000. Iris did not touch the envelope, and Ken placed it back in his briefcase.

Over the next four weeks, Ken continued to see Iris at local conventions. He also joined the health club where Iris exercised on a regular basis. Ken started to call Iris a couple of times a week and invited her to attend a Red Sox game with him. Iris did not initiate any contact with Ken during

this period. Ken always approached Iris at the conventions, and he initiated all of the telephone calls. While many of their conversations covered general topics, inevitably Ken would mention to Iris how his associate wanted to start work on the building project and how his associate would do "whatever it takes" to secure the necessary federal permits. Ken explained to Iris how easy it would be for her to "earn" a quick $10,000. All she needed to do was issue the necessary permits to his associate. Iris commented that she found this type of business arrangement to be repugnant and that she had never participated in this type of financial transaction in the past. However, after six more telephone calls, all initiated by Ken, Iris finally agreed to meet with Ken's associate to explore some "options."

The next week, Ken arranged for Iris to meet with Emily and him. During the meeting, Emily spent two hours explaining the details of her plans. At the conclusion of Emily's presentation, Iris remarked about how impressed she was with Emily's plans and said the new building would benefit the community. Emily thanked Iris for her words of encouragement and enthusiasm. Emily then said she needed to leave for another meeting. As she was about to leave, Emily took an envelope from her briefcase and placed it on the table without saying a word. Iris looked inside the envelope and remarked about how much cash appeared to be enclosed. Iris hesitated, but then placed the envelope in her briefcase. At that point, Emily identified herself as an FBI special agent and arrested Iris, charging her with bribery in violation of 18 U.S.C. § 201 (Bribery of Public Officials and Witnesses).

Questions for Your Consideration

As you read the chapter, consider your responses to the following questions:

1. Is Iris legally responsible for her conduct in placing the envelope (filled with cash) in her briefcase?
2. To make your analysis as concrete as possible, assume you are a member of the jury charged with deciding Iris's fate: guilty based on the bribery charge, or not guilty based on an entrapment

defense. As you think about Iris's fate, ask yourself the following questions:

■ Did the idea for committing the crime of bribery originate with Emily, Ken, or Iris?

■ Has Iris participated in similar bribery schemes in the past?

■ Did Iris exhibit any reluctance to commit the crime of bribery? If there is evidence of reluctance, was Iris overcome by Ken's strong powers of persuasion?

■ If there is evidence of persuasion on Ken's part, what kind of persuasion and how much persuasion did he employ?

■ Should evidence about Ken's character and his past criminal behavior be considered by you (and the other members of the jury) as you consider Iris's fate?

■ Are there other questions you believe should be considered as part of your analysis?

---

* The Case of Iris is a fictitious case developed by the authors to demonstrate and illustrate key legal and ethical concepts, theories, practices, and strategies.

Basic Concepts of Criminal Law

Ethical Corporate Culture and Business Crimes

Corporate executives in orange jumpsuits with chains on their wrists and feet being led off to federal prisons and companies being fined in the millions of dollars are no longer scenes reserved exclusively for TV shows. When business crimes are committed, not only do the stakeholders of a company suffer from corporate criminal behavior, but also the image of corporate America is tarnished nationally and abroad.

The U.S. Congress has passed legislation and the U.S. Sentencing Commission has implemented rules aimed at reducing business crimes in the United States. Both groups have proposed compliance and ethics programs with vigorous "due diligence" and "risk assessment" requirements to encourage companies to strive for the elimination of business crimes and to create an ethical corporate culture. The first step in moving toward this objective is for companies to take aggressive measures to prevent business crimes. This chapter provides an introduction to the criminal justice system, business crimes, and ethical theories and standards that support sound business practices and ethical judgments. However, before jumping into a detailed discussion of business crimes, it will be useful to develop a broader understanding of the purpose and nature of criminal law in the United States.

Origin of Criminal Law in the United States

During the early years of colonization in the United States, the colonies adopted the various English common law crimes, such as battery, robbery, and murder. As the U.S. legislative and judicial systems matured, their understanding of these common law crimes began to change in ways that specifically reflected American society and culture. During the twentieth century, the various state legislatures and the U.S. Congress began to replace the concept of common law crimes with that of statutory crimes. Today, statutes enacted by legislative bodies define nearly all crimes prosecuted in the United States.

What Is a Crime?

In its simplest form, a **crime** represents the breach of a legal duty that is punishable by imprisonment and fines. A crime constitutes an offense against society as a whole. While most crimes involve a victim, the state brings the case forward against the perpetrator on behalf of the public it serves. The state does not prosecute a crime for the benefit of the victim; rather, the state prosecutes a crime as a means of preserving peace and pursuing justice for the benefit of society as a whole. This is not to say that the victim of a crime does not have legal rights. As will be discussed in Chapter 19, "Business Torts," a victim may be able to bring a civil lawsuit against the perpetrator of a crime. The desired outcome of a civil case is not to imprison the perpetrator, but for the victim to seek redress in the form of monetary damages.

For example, assume you are at a social gathering to celebrate the birthday of a college friend. During the course of the party, a fellow student confronts you. The student claims you took "his" parking spot near the dormitory where you both reside. You respond by saying that all parking is open and available to students on a "first-come" basis. As you turn to walk away from the student, the student slaps the side of your head. The slap does not cause you to fall, but it leaves a lasting "ringing" in your ear. A visit with your physician reveals that the ringing sound may last six months or more. Concerned about the possibility of a serious injury, you decide to seek the advice of a local attorney and decide to bring a private lawsuit against the student asserting battery as your legal claim. A *battery* is an intentional and offensive touching of a person without lawful justification. If you are successful in your private lawsuit against the student, the court will likely award you monetary damages,[1] which the student will be required to pay. Additionally, the state could decide to prosecute the student for the crime of battery. If convicted, the student could be incarcerated or fined.

Civil Law and Criminal Law

As demonstrated by the preceding example, the law encompasses two broad and distinct forms of rights and duties. In general, **civil law** covers the rights and duties individuals owe to one another, while **criminal law** involves the rights and duties that individuals owe to society. Consequently, important differences exist between civil law and criminal law, as shown in Exhibit 10.1.

---

[1]In general, the term *damages* is used to refer to monetary compensation for loss or injury to a person or property. Damages are covered in detail in Chapter 19, "Business Torts."

Exhibit 10.1. Characteristics of Civil Law and Criminal Law

Characteristics	Civil Law	Criminal Law
Goal	To resolve disputes between individuals or entities (such as corporations).	To punish offenders (individuals or entities) who violate the law.
Moving party	A private citizen (individual or entity) initiates a *civil* judicial proceeding.	A public employee (prosecutor) initiates a *criminal* judicial proceeding on behalf of the government.
Reason for the legal action	One party (individual or entity) injures another or their property.	An individual or entity commits a crime (violates the law).
Judicial process	A civil process where one party (wrongdoer/defendant) is compelled to answer to a complaint filed by an injured party/plaintiff.	A criminal process where one party (offender/defendant) is compelled to answer to the state (prosecutor) for the commission of an alleged crime.
Burden of proof	Preponderance of the evidence.	Beyond a reasonable doubt.
Outcome sought	Receipt of monetary damages for harm inflicted by the wrongdoer, or injunctive relief to prohibit the wrongdoer from continuing the harmful activity.	Punishment of the offender for harm inflicted on society. Fines and incarceration represent common forms of punishment.
Appeal	Either party may appeal a decision in a civil suit.	Only the defendant may appeal a court ruling in a criminal case. The prosecution cannot appeal if the defendant is found not guilty.

The goal of civil law is to resolve disputes between parties (individuals or entities).[2] For example, in the preceding illustration, you had a dispute with a fellow student. The civil law system allows you, the injured party, to resolve your dispute in a civilized, orderly fashion. Without this option, you might be tempted to "take matters into your own hands." The defendant in a civil case does not have to worry about the possibility of incarceration. On the other hand, incarceration and fines represent the goals of criminal law. The court in a civil case may require the defendant to compensate the injured party for damages suffered at the hands of the defendant.

The party who initiates a legal action in a civil suit is either a private citizen or a business entity, such as a corporation or a partnership. Conversely, a public employee (usually a prosecutor) initiates a criminal proceeding on

[2]The term *civil law* is also used to describe one of the two established legal systems in the Western world. The two systems are the common law legal system and the civil legal system. The common law system is a system of laws based on judicial decisions, rather than on statutes or constitutions. The United States adopted the English version of the common law system during the colonial years. The civil law system, which continues to influence some of the legal systems in continental Europe, originated in the Roman Empire.

behalf of the state. In a civil case, the injured party initiates a lawsuit by filing a complaint with the court. The term **plaintiff** describes an injured party who petitions the court for relief; whereas, the term **defendant** describes the party who caused the injury or damage.

In response to the plaintiff's complaint, the defendant prepares an answer to the various points made in the plaintiff's complaint. Like a complaint, an answer is a formal court document that addresses the merits of the plaintiff's case, typically by refuting some or all of the allegations made by the plaintiff. Additionally, the defendant uses the answer to establish relevant defenses and to state possible counterclaims. For example, a lender (plaintiff) might file a complaint against a borrower (defendant) for damages related to an unpaid loan. In answering the plaintiff's complaint, the borrower might include a counterclaim for damages based on fraudulent lending practices allegedly used by the lender.

Burden of Proof

The term **burden of proof** relates to a party's responsibility when attempting to prove an assertion. In a civil case, both the plaintiff and the defendant present evidence to prove their assertions. For example, in the earlier battery illustration, you could introduce the testimony of eyewitnesses to prove your assertion that the student hit the side of your head without provocation. You could also introduce the testimony of an expert witness to prove the nature and extent of the injury to your ear. On the other hand, the defendant would likely introduce evidence to challenge the veracity of your witnesses. After hearing all the evidence presented by you and the defendant's lawyer, assuming the defendant elects not to testify in keeping with his fifth amendment right to remain silent, the judge will charge (instruct) the jury on the applicable law and the jury will weigh the credibility of the evidence as part of deciding the outcome of the case.

Preponderance of the Evidence Standard

The burden of proof in a civil case is known as the **preponderance of the evidence standard**, which represents the standard of proof used by a fact-finder (a judge or a jury) in weighing the credibility of the evidence presented by the plaintiff and the defendant.[3] When delivering the case to a jury, the judge instructs the jury to find in favor of the party (plaintiff or defendant) who has presented the strongest and most credible evidence in support of their respective assertions. Under the preponderance of the evidence standard, the difference in the credibility of the evidence presented by the parties may be slight. Thus, the jury may find in favor of one party over the other when that party's evidence is

---

[3]Although used less frequently, another legal standard (*clear and convincing evidence*) is employed in some civil cases, particularly when the case involves fraud.

"more likely than not" true and correct. In practical terms, it often comes down to the jury deciding which eyewitness to believe when each is telling a different story about the same set of facts. Who is more believable or credible? Under the preponderance of the evidence standard, a jury can retain doubt about the credibility of both witnesses but still conclude that one witness is more credible than the other. Although many courts are reluctant to quantify the preponderance of the evidence standard, some legal commentators have suggested that a fact-finder must be only "51 percent" convinced to find in favor of one party over the other.

Beyond a Reasonable Doubt

The burden of proof used in a criminal case is called **beyond a reasonable doubt**. This standard differs significantly from the preponderance of the evidence standard. For example, in deciding whether the prosecution has proven its case, the jury begins its deliberations with a presumption that the defendant is innocent; whereas in a civil trial, the jury does not begin its deliberations with any presumptions. Additionally, unlike the preponderance of the evidence standard where the jury may have some doubt about its conclusions, the jury in a criminal case must be convinced "beyond a reasonable doubt" that the prosecution is correct in its assertions about the defendant's guilt.

Appeal

An **appeal** is the final step in a civil or criminal case. It represents a challenge to the decision of a court (judge or jury). As a challenge, an appeal asks a higher court to review and reconsider the decision of a lower court. In a civil case,

In a criminal trial, the jury determines if the prosecution has met its burden of proving guilt beyond a reasonable doubt.

either party (plaintiff or defendant) may appeal the decision of a court. While the defendant may appeal the verdict (the decision of the jury) in a criminal case, the prosecution may not appeal the verdict if the jury finds the defendant not guilty.

Felonies and Misdemeanors

Crimes are classified according to severity and the type of punishment incurred. For example, **felonies** are serious crimes. They are usually punishable by imprisonment for more than one year and often impose significant penalties. Examples of felonies include burglary, arson, rape, and murder. On the other hand, **misdemeanors** are less serious crimes and are usually punishable by minor fines and imprisonment for one year or less.

Criminal Intent and Criminal Act

The law recognizes two aspects of a crime: criminal intent and criminal act. **Criminal intent** deals with a defendant's state of mind when committing a crime. **Criminal act** refers to the specific acts performed by a defendant in carrying out a crime. Criminal intent is often referred to as the **mens rea**, which is the Latin term for "guilty mind." For most crimes, the prosecution must prove "beyond a reasonable doubt" that the defendant *intended* to commit the crime for which the defendant has been charged. In practical terms, a person's "intent" relates to that person's state of mind while performing an accompanying act.

The term **actus reus** relates to a defendant's criminal act, which is the Latin phrase for "guilty act." A defendant's criminal acts represent those deeds that comprise the physical components of a crime. Generally, the prosecution must prove beyond a reasonable doubt that a criminal act has occurred (actus reus) and that the defendant possessed the necessary mental intent (mens rea) to commit the crime. If the prosecution proves one of the elements of a crime (for example, the mens rea) but fails to prove the other (the actus reus), there is no crime, unless it is a strict liability crime.

Strict Liability Crimes

Strict liability crimes hold a defendant responsible based on a criminal act alone. No accompanying mental state (mens rea) is necessary. Strict liability crimes fall into a category of crimes known as "nonintentional" crimes: persons can be convicted of a strict liability crime even if the *mens rea* cannot be proven. Common examples of strict liability crimes include traffic violations and statutory rape.

Model Penal Code

The U.S. Constitution serves as the basis of all laws in the United States, including state laws, the law of the District of Columbia, and federal law. The U.S. Constitution reserves for the states the primary authority to define, enforce, and prosecute crimes. The United States does not have a single "national" criminal code. Rather, 52 criminal codes exist: one for each of the 50 states, one for the District of Columbia, and one for the federal government. Not surprisingly, each of the 50 states has a distinct criminal code. Even though the various criminal codes differ because of the history, culture, and heritage of each state, a high degree of commonality exists among the codes because of the influence of the **Model Penal Code**. The American Law Institute first published the Model Penal Code in 1962. It is not an official code (it serves as a model only), but it nonetheless has exercised significant influence in the shaping of state criminal codes over the past 50 years.

Business Crimes

Business crimes arise in a variety of national and international settings. They typically involve illicit activities characterized by deceit and a breach of trust.

Unlike the types of crimes popularized in the movies or depicted in television shows where armed intruders steal money through the use of physical force, business crimes occur in normal organizational settings without violence. We do not typically think of an educated individual with a degree from a business school as a person who commits a crime. Yet, these "white collar" professionals commit thousands of business crimes each year.

According to figures supplied by the Federal Bureau of Investigation (FBI), business crimes cost U.S. citizens billions of dollars each year.[4] Examples of business crimes include embezzlement, theft, money laundering, investor fraud, tax fraud, and similar kinds of nonviolent crimes. While individuals and organizations commit crimes for a variety of reasons, personal gain or business advantage often serve as motivation for the commission of business crimes. Before we

> ### An Ethical Insight: Aristotle and Virtue of Justice
>
> #### Why Corporations Need Ethics Policies and Training Programs
>
> As we think about the types of crimes committed by corporations along with the penalties imposed by the courts, including the frequently imposed requirement that corporations develop and implement ethics programs, consider the following observation by Aristotle, an observation made well over 2,000 years ago:
>
> "At his best, man is the noblest of all animals; separated from law and justice, he is the worst."
>
> Aristotle's "Virtue Ethics" helps us understand how some of today's corporate leaders fail to achieve the goal of being a "virtuous person." Rather than making the best decision for others, they too often make decisions that feed the avaricious appetites of a few greedy executives. Aristotle recognized that violations of just laws would lead to disastrous results. Violations of business criminal laws are especially unjust because they affect all stakeholders, not just business executives and managers.

---

[4]See the FBI, http://www.fbi.gov/.

begin our examination of business crimes, consider the following questions based on "An Ethical Insight: Aristotle and Virtue of Justice" on page 293: What is the consequence of being "separated from law and justice"? What does it mean for a corporation (including its board members, executives, and the professionals who serve it, e.g., attorneys and certified public accountants) to be at its "worst"? How can a corporation become a "noble" entity?

The consequences of being separated from law and justice and operating at one's worst are staggering. In addition to corporations paying fines in the hundreds of millions of dollars, people like you (honest, hard-working individuals) sometimes get caught up in a web of deceit and destruction. For such individuals, the U.S. Sentencing Commission reports that the majority of offenders serve prison terms and pay significant fines. And, if you have a professional license, such as an attorney or CPA license, you will likely have it revoked by a licensing board. In other words, your professional career may be over.

Case Illustration

As an illustration of investor fraud, consider the case of Bernard (Bernie) Madoff. This investor fraud case represents one of the largest and most publicized business crimes ever committed in the United States. The crime occurred over a 25-year period without detection until the arrest of its chief architect Bernie Madoff on December 11, 2008. For more than two decades, Madoff stole billions of dollars from his clients using a fraudulent investment system known as a Ponzi scheme.* Madoff's Ponzi scheme attracted billions of dollars from clients under the false pretense of investing their funds in high-return assets. However, instead of investing the funds as promised, Madoff enjoyed the lifestyle of a billionaire, not on the success of his investment abilities, but on funds stolen from trusted friends, charities, and others. Madoff's life of luxury and excess ended abruptly when a jury convicted him of numerous financial crimes and the judge imposed a 150-year prison term.

*A Ponzi scheme is a fraudulent investment scheme in which money contributed by later investors is used to cover the theft of funds from original investors. This type of business crime is named after Charles Ponzi, a Boston-based investor who was convicted of investment fraud in the 1920s.

Investor Fraud

In general, the term **fraud** represents a knowing misrepresentation of the truth or concealment of material facts that causes others to act in a way that is detrimental to their self-interest. For example, prosecutors often rely on wire fraud statutes or mail fraud statutes to prosecute fraudulent investment advisors who steal money from their clients. **Wire fraud** is a type of fraud perpetrated by using electronic communications. The federal Wire Fraud Act provides that any artifice to defraud by means of wire or other electronic communications (such as radio and television) in foreign and interstate commerce is a crime.[5] **Mail fraud** occurs when the offender perpetrates the fraud by using the U.S. Postal Service to make false representations and collect money illicitly.[6]

Business crimes affect not only the victims of the crimes, but all members of society. Business crimes, like the one committed by Bernie Madoff, erode

[5] 18 U.S.C. § 1343.
[6] 18 U.S.C. §§ 1341–1347.

Investor fraud harms individual investors and shakes the confidence of the financial community. A chilling example was provided by former stockbroker, investment advisor, and financier Bernard Madoff, shown here being escorted from federal court in New York City on January 5, 2009.

the trust we place in business professionals and place a significant financial burden on society.

Economic Crimes

An **economic crime** is a nonphysical crime aimed at obtaining a financial gain or a professional advantage. Economic crimes come in two forms. The first category consists of crimes committed by employees (or others who stand in a position of fiduciary responsibility) for personal gain without enhancing the profits of the company for which they work. Embezzlement is an example. The second type of economic crime arises when employees (or other individuals) commit crimes for profit on behalf of the company for which they work. Filing false financial statements showing artificially inflated profits with the Securities and Exchange Commission represents an example of this type of economic crime.

Corporate Crimes

Corporate crimes are crimes committed by a corporation's representatives acting on behalf of the corporation. Although a corporation, as an artificial entity, cannot commit a crime other than through its representatives, state and federal statutes provide for corporations themselves to be named as criminal defendants. (See *United States v. Park*, page 300.) To help mitigate the likelihood of corporate crimes occurring within business organizations,

Case Illustration

With several business associates, Brian Stevens, a certified public accountant (CPA), created a corporation called Summit Accomodators, Inc. (Summit). Through the use of lawful income tax planning techniques, Summit helped clients minimize their federal income tax obligations. Summit specialized in assisting clients who were planning to sell income-producing properties. Federal income tax laws allows taxpayers to defer paying taxes on the profits earned from the sale of such property as long as they purchase another income-producing property within a stated period of time after the sale. After clients sold their income-producing properties, Stevens told his clients that he would hold their funds in safekeeping until new properties could be purchased. Stevens reported to his clients that all funds would be deposited in the bank until used for the purchase of another income-producing property.

To the average observer, Brian Stevens and his business associates at Summit provided high-quality professional services to their clients. However, as revealed by an investigation conducted by the Federal Bureau of Investigation (FBI) and other law enforcement agencies, the individuals who benefitted from Summit's professional services were not clients, but the owners of Summit, including Stevens. Contrary to Summit's representations to clients about depositing their funds (ranging from $50 million to $100 million over a five-year period) in the bank, Stevens and his business associates at Summit used the funds to invest in personal real estate projects. They also used the funds to loan money to friends and businesses associates. To cover their tracks, Stevens and his associates sent false statements to clients misleadingly showing that the funds had been deposited in the bank.

As part of a plea agreement with the U.S. Attorney for Oregon, Stevens pleaded guilty to conspiracy to commit wire fraud and conspiracy to commit money laundering violations. Stevens admitted that he and his associates defrauded their clients, causing 91 clients to lose $13.7 million. Stevens was sentenced to 48 months in prison for defrauding his clients.* Brian Stevens, CPA, committed a serious business crime. As stated by the U.S. Attorney handling the case, "The sentencing of Mr. Stevens to four years in prison should tell every licensed professional there are serious consequences for misusing client funds."[†]

---

*This case was reported on the website of the Federal Bureau of Investigation (FBI) as "Breaking News" on May 8, 2012. See http://www.fbi.gov/.
[†] Id.

consider the Manager's Compliance and Ethics Meeting illustration on the following page.

Embezzlement

The crime of **embezzlement** involves the fraudulent taking of personal property with the intent to deprive the rightful owner of its usefulness and benefits. Typically, embezzlement occurs when a person has been entrusted with the care and management of another's property. Thus, the crime of embezzlement happens only after the offender assumes illegal possession of the property, for the offender otherwise has lawful possession of the property up to the point where the conversion occurs. Commonly, the embezzler has a fiduciary relationship with the rightful owner of the property. Most often, the relationship is an employer/employee relationship. Employees

Manager's Compliance and Ethics Meeting

Developing an Effective Ethics Training Program: U.S. Sentencing Commission Guidelines

Ethical corporate conduct begins with company employees not violating criminal laws. Alto, Inc., (a fictitious company) is a manufacturer of children's toys. It is in the process of developing a Corporate Compliance and Ethics Code of Conduct Program.

The U.S. Sentencing Commission defines the program as one that "exercises due diligence to prevent and detect criminal conduct and otherwise promote an organizational culture that encourages ethical conduct and a commitment to compliance with the law." Under the Federal Sentencing Guidelines, if one of its employees should commit a criminal act while on company business, Alto, Inc., could be exonerated or at least receive a mitigated fine and possible lesser sentence by showing it had implemented the adopted Program.

The company further seeks to develop an ethical corporate culture and often engages in "due diligence" to assure that employees are in compliance with the law. Since the 2001 Amendments to the Sentencing Guidelines require that the corporate board has ultimate responsibility to ensure the Compliance and Ethics Program is properly implemented, Alto's directors have insisted on a training program for all departments.

Beryl and her staff have been placed in charge of designing the training program. To complete this assignment, her first task would be to determine, with corporate counsel, possible criminal conduct that may apply to the employees in carrying out their job-related activities. Such conduct may include conflicts of interest, cheating on their expense reports, accepting improper gifts, violating trade secrets, or even failing to report a known offense engaged in by other employees. All possible illegal acts relevant to the nature of the business should be mentioned in the company's Code of Ethics.

Beryl and her staff should interview supervisors of each department and determine from them the nature of their subordinates' work and establish hypothetical cases that can be used in the training sessions. Each department should provide a typical "day in the life of an employee," including computer use on the company network anytime and place. Their activities should be reviewed for possible criminal and unethical conduct with a clear explanation of the consequential punishment. Beryl's report should be formally presented to the board of directors to assure compliance with the Amended Sentencing Guidelines. The training sessions should be compulsory and given throughout the year at designated dates and times.

With a Code of Ethics and a training program that implements the Code, Alto, Inc., is in a position to demonstrate that it engages in "due diligence" and thereby establish a defense to facilitating the potential criminal conduct of its employees and the potential criminal and civil liability of its directors and the corporation.

often have access to company property, creating the potential for embezzlement. The Case Illustration on page 298 is an example of employee embezzlement. This illustration and the ones that follow regarding money laundering and bribery were taken from the website of the Internal Revenue Service (IRS). They represent the commission of actual business crimes.

Case Illustration

On April 9, 2012, in Salt Lake City, Utah, Pamela Jane Madsen was sentenced to 46 months in prison, five years of supervised release, and ordered to pay $1,351,102 in restitution. She was also ordered to forfeit three snowmobiles and three four-wheelers. Madsen pleaded guilty in January 2012 to mail fraud and money laundering charges in connection with an embezzlement scheme to steal approximately $1.3 million from her employer. According to court documents, Madsen worked from May 2000 to October 2010 as a secretary at Professional Painting, Inc. (PPI), a commercial painting company. In 2007, her job duties expanded to include picking up the mail, filling out deposit slips for PPI's bank deposits, and preparing customer's checks for deposit into the company's bank account. In November 2007, Madsen opened a bank account in the name of Professional Painting, Incorp., a slight variation of PPI's name. Madsen was the only authorized signer on the account. Between November 2007 and February 2010, Madsen deposited checks representing payment from PPI's clients for services the company provided into her own account. To conceal the theft of the checks, she accessed PPI accounting records and made entries crediting the accounts of the customers whose checks she stole.

This case illustrates how a trusted employee can easily commit the crime of embezzlement. Although this crime was detected, many others go undetected for years costing companies billions of dollars.

Source: www.irs.gov/uac/Examples-of-General-Fraud-Investigations-Fiscal-Year-2012.

Money Laundering

In its simplest form, individuals use **money laundering** techniques to disguise the true source of money. The basic idea is to "launder" *dirty money* obtained from illegal activities and make it *clean money* by running it through legitimate business enterprises. The following statutory elements illustrate what prosecutors must prove to convict an offender of money laundering[7]:

- The defendant consummated a financial transaction;
- The defendant knew the transaction involved an unlawful activity;
- The funds generated by the transaction were, in fact, from illegal activities; and
- One (or more) of the following four situations was also present:
  - The defendant engaged in the transaction with the intent to further the illegal activity through the consummation of the transaction;
  - The defendant engaged in the transaction with the intent to commit tax fraud;
  - The defendant engaged in the transaction knowing that the transaction was designed to disguise the source of the money; or
  - The defendant engaged in the transaction knowing that the transaction was designed to avoid currency transaction reporting laws.

Bribery

The crime of **bribery** occurs when a public official provides a service beyond what is expected or required in the normal performance of the official's duties in exchange for money. Individuals (or entities such as corporations) who give a public official money or other valuable property in exchange for improper services (i.e., services beyond what is expected or required) may also be guilty

---

[7] 18 U.S.C. § 1956(a)(1).

of the crime of bribery. For example, consider the Case Illustration of Joseph Rivera involving an elaborate bribery scheme. Also, return to the Practical Example (The Case of Iris) at the beginning of the chapter. Do you think Iris committed the crime of bribery?

Foreign Corrupt Practices Act (FCPA)

In the United States, the main statute prohibiting overseas bribery payments is the **Foreign Corrupt Practices Act.** (Bribery in an international context is discussed in the Global Perspective section of the chapter, starting on page 314.) The FCPA was enacted in 1977 and amended in 1988 and again in 1998. For a violation of the FCPA to occur, three elements must be present. The FCPA prohibits payments (1) by certain individuals (2) to certain individuals (3) for an impermissible purpose. All three elements must be met to conclude that the FCPA has been violated.

The FCPA Prohibits Payments by Whom?

The FCPA applies to any U.S. resident or citizen or anyone acting on behalf of a U.S. individual or business (or non-U.S. company that is controlled by a U.S. company). It covers actions by any individual, company, officer, director, employee, or agent acting on behalf of a business. The act is not limited to corporations—it includes sole proprietorships, partnerships, and other types of businesses, too. Note that actions by an agent will render a U.S. principal liable under the FCPA, which is potentially a huge liability risk.

The FCPA Prohibits Payments to Whom?

Payments for prohibited purposes (see below) cannot be made to a foreign official. Foreign officials include government officers and government employees, as well as people who work for or are agents of public international organizations (such as the United Nations). It also prohibits payments to political candidates.

The FCPA Prohibits Payments for What Purpose?

The FCPA prohibits payments for the purpose of improperly influencing government decisions in order to obtain or keep business. The person making or authorizing the payments must be aware or substantially certain that the

Case Illustration

On March 28, 2012, in Camden, N.J., Joseph Rivera, a senior investigator with the N.J. Department of Labor and Workforce Development, Division of Wage and Hour Compliance, was sentenced to 60 months in prison with three years of supervised release and was ordered to pay $250,000 in restitution to the state Department of Labor and Workforce Development. The sentencing was in connection with a bribery scheme in which Rivera accepted $1.86 million from owners and operators of temporary labor firms in return for his official assistance. According to court documents and statements made in court, Rivera's responsibilities as a senior investigator included inspecting temporary labor firms working in southern New Jersey to verify compliance with state wage and hour laws and with regulations regarding taxes and workers' compensation insurance coverage. Between 2002 and 2008, Rivera solicited and accepted illicit cash payments from at least 20 owners or operators of temporary labor firms. In exchange for these illicit payments, Rivera used his position for the benefit of the temporary labor firms. He refrained from inspecting these firms and falsely certified that they were complying with state law. Rivera also attempted to evade paying taxes on the income derived from his bribery scheme.

This case shows that bribery occurs whenever a public official solicits or accepts money in exchange for providing "improper" services to individuals or entities.

Source: www.irs.gov/uac/Examples-of-Public-Corruption-Investigations-Fiscal-Year-2012.

United States v. Park, 421 U.S. 658; 95 S. Ct. 1903 (1975)

Facts: Mr. Park, the president of Acme Markets, Inc., was charged along with Acme Markets, Inc., with violating § 301(k) of the Federal Food, Drug, and Cosmetic Act* on the grounds that food in Acme's Baltimore warehouse had been exposed to rodent contamination. Acme Markets, Inc., entered a guilty plea. Mr. Park entered a not guilty plea.

Acme Markets, Inc., is a national retail food chain. Its headquarters, including the office of the president, Mr. Park, are located in Philadelphia. The government alleges that the defendants, Acme Markets, Inc., and Mr. Park, received food that had been shipped in interstate commerce and that, while the food was being held for sale in Acme's Baltimore warehouse, the defendants caused it to be held in a building accessible to rodents and to be exposed to contamination by rodents. The trial of Mr. Park took place in the U.S. District Court for the District of Maryland.

Evidence introduced at Mr. Park's trial demonstrated that the Food and Drug Administration (FDA) advised Mr. Park by letter of insanitary conditions in Acme's Philadelphia warehouse. Subsequently, the FDA found similar conditions present in Acme's Baltimore warehouse. During the trial, an FDA consumer safety officer provided evidence of rodent infestation and other insanitary conditions (discovered during a 12-day inspection) at the Baltimore warehouse. Furthermore, he testified that a second inspection of the Baltimore warehouse revealed that sanitary conditions had improved; however, there was still evidence of continuing rodent activity with many rodent-contaminated food items contained in the inventory.

The Chief of Compliance of the FDA's Baltimore office testified that he informed Mr. Park by letter of the conditions at the Baltimore warehouse after the first inspection. Following this testimony, Acme's divisional vice president in Baltimore stated that he responded in writing to the FDA's letter on behalf of Mr. Park and Acme Markets, Inc. His response described the steps taken by Acme Markets to remedy the insanitary conditions discovered by the inspections of the Baltimore warehouse. Acme's vice president for legal affairs and assistant secretary testified that Mr. Park functioned by delegating normal operating duties, including those involving sanitation. On the other hand, he stated that Mr. Park retained the responsibility of "seeing that all parts of the company worked together."

At the close of the government's case, Mr. Park's attorneys moved for a judgment of acquittal on the grounds that the evidence showed that Mr. Park was not personally connected with the Food and Drug violation. The trial judge denied the motion.

Mr. Park was the only defense witness. He testified that although all of Acme's employees were in a sense under his general direction, the company had an organizational structure for handling functional responsibilities, such as sanitation. Mr. Park identified the individuals responsible for sanitation, and stated that upon receipt of the January 1972 FDA letter, he had conferred with the vice president for legal affairs, who informed him that the Baltimore divisional vice president was investigating the situation. Mr. Park testified that he was told by the vice president for legal affairs that the Baltimore divisional vice president would be taking corrective actions regarding the rodent problem and would be preparing a summary of the corrective actions in his reply to the FDA letter. Mr. Park stated that he did not believe there was anything he could have done more constructively than what, he was told, was being done.

On cross-examination, Mr. Park conceded that providing sanitary conditions for food offered for sale to the public was something that he was responsible for in the entire operation of the company, and he stated that it was one of many phases of the company that he assigned to dependable subordinates. Mr. Park admitted that the Baltimore problem suggested that the company's system for handling sanitation wasn't working perfectly. Finally, Mr. Park acknowledged that as Acme's chief executive officer he was responsible for any result occurring within the company.

Issue: The question presented to the Court is whether managerial officers of a corporation, as well as the corporation itself, may be prosecuted under the Federal Food, Drug, and Cosmetic Act of 1938 for the introduction of misbranded or adulterated articles into interstate commerce where the managerial officer does not have a "consciousness of wrongdoing" and has not participated personally in the alleged criminal acts.

Holding: Mr. Park's motion for acquittal (based on the ground that the evidence showed that Mr. Park was not personally involved with the violations) was denied by the trial court judge following the close of the government's case. The jury then found Mr. Park guilty of violating § 301(k) of the Federal Food, Drug, and Cosmetic Act. On appeal, the U.S. Court of Appeals for the Fourth Circuit reversed the conviction of Mr. Park and remanded the case for a new trial. The Court of Appeals concluded that the trial judge's instructions to the jury might well have left the jury with the erroneous impression that Mr. Park could be found guilty in the absence of a "wrongful act" on his part. On appeal, the U.S. Supreme Court reversed the decision of the Appeals Court and upheld the guilty verdict of Mr. Park.

From the Court's Opinion: *The liability of managerial officers does not depend on their knowledge of, or personal participation in, the act made criminal by the statute. The Federal Food, Drug, and Cosmetic Act of 1938 dispensed with "consciousness of wrongdoing." Rather, the statute provides that an omission or failure to act is a sufficient basis for holding a managerial officer criminally liable. It is sufficient that, by virtue of the relationship the managerial officer bears to the corporation, the officer had the power to prevent the wrongdoing [the criminal act]. This Court has reaffirmed the proposition that the public interest in the purity of its food is so great as to warrant the imposition of the highest standard of care on distributors. The Food, Drug, and Cosmetic Act of 1938 punishes neglect where the law requires care, or inaction where the law imposes a duty. Thus, the Act does not make criminal liability turn on "awareness of some wrongdoing" or "conscious fraud." Accordingly, we reverse the decision of the Appeals Court and uphold the guilty verdict of Mr. Park.*

---

*21 U.S.C. § 331(k).

payment will be offered, given, or promised to the foreign official to induce the recipient to misuse his or her official position.

Bribery Prevention

Many companies from the United States and abroad are tempted to expand their markets into countries where bribery is commonplace because those countries often have fast-growing markets and lucrative business opportunities. When entering a market or engaging in business in a country known to have a high level of corruption, what can a company do to combat bribery? Companies can ensure a strong internal compliance and ethics program, including the practice of aggressive due diligence, risk assessment, a code of ethics that prohibits bribery, and Manager's Compliance and Ethics Meetings to explain the FCPA and why it is illegal and unethical to provide bribery payments of any kind. Managers should encourage employees to seek legal counsel in cases of doubt and take quick and thoughtful action if bribery is detected. Finally, a company should maintain a no-tolerance attitude regarding bribery throughout the company.

Common Defenses to Business Crimes

Exhibit 10.2 presents some of the defenses commonly used by defendants charged with committing a business crime.

Duress

As a defense, **duress** compels an individual to act contrary to his or her better judgment. A threat of harm to the individual underlies the compulsion to act opposite to one's beliefs. As shown in Exhibit 10.2, the defense of duress excuses a person's otherwise illegal acts. The theory underlying the defense holds that to convict and punish an individual who acts under duress is inappropriate and unfair. For example, assume that an employee embezzles funds from his employer because a known criminal has threatened to kill the employee's spouse and his children if the employee does not give the criminal $500,000. This significant threat may be sufficient to provide a basis for a duress defense. However, duress is often difficult to establish, and it may be equally difficult to convince a jury of its underlying merits.

Insanity

To assert the defense of **insanity**, a defendant states that he is not responsible for his actions during the time in question because he was suffering from a mental disorder. When the insanity defense is employed by a defendant, the outcome is usually not an outright acquittal. Rather, the defendant is often committed to a medical institution. In other words, if the jury believes the story

Exhibit 10.2. Common Defenses to Business Crimes	
Defense	**Characteristics**
Duress	Defendant asserts she was compelled to act contrary to her beliefs and judgment because of a threat of harm.
Insanity	Defendant states that a mental disorder caused him to commit the alleged crime.
Mistake of fact	Defendant claims she acted from an innocent misunderstanding of fact rather than with a criminal intent.
Mistake of law	Defendant asserts he failed to understand the criminal consequences of certain conduct.
Statute of limitations	Defendant assets that the case cannot be pursued by law enforcement because the time permitted by law to prosecute the case has expired.
Entrapment	Defendant alleges that a law enforcement officer induced her to commit the crime for which she has been charged.

told by the defendant about why he acted as he did the jury generally issues a special verdict holding that the defendant is not guilty "by reason of insanity." However, as the following case illustrates, a jury may decide to acquit the defendant.

Consider the well-known case of Daniel Sickles. During the battle of Gettysburg, General Sickles lost his leg and was later awarded a Congressional Medal of Honor. However, several years before the Civil War, Daniel Sickles served as a member of the U.S. Congress. After learning that his wife was having an affair with U.S. District Attorney Phillip Barton Key (son of the author of "The Star Spangled Banner," Francis Scott Key), Congressman Sickles shot and killed District Attorney Phillip Key. Sickles was arrested and charged with murder. His attorney asserted the defense of temporary insanity arguing that Sickles shot Phillip Keys because he became enraged upon learning of Key's affair with his wife and consequently experienced a period of "temporary insanity." The jury believed the defense and acquitted Sickles of the murder charge.

Mistake of Fact

In a **mistake of fact** defense, the defendant asserts that she acted from an innocent misunderstanding of fact rather than from a criminal intent to commit the crime in question. If the jury believes the defense, it accepts the notion that because of an honest and reasonable mistake of fact, the defendant did not possess the necessary mens rea (mental intent) to commit the crime. For example, assume that a person who buys stolen goods honestly and reasonably believes that the goods were the rightful property of the seller. This belief might serve to negate the criminal intent necessary to be convicted of the crime of receiving stolen property. However, this is a question of fact to be determined by the fact-finder.

Mistake of Law

In a **mistake of law** defense, the defendant states that he or she failed to understand the criminal consequences of his or her conduct. This defense is generally not as effective as a "mistake of fact" defense. Generally, a mistaken belief about a particular law is no defense to a violation of that law. All persons are presumed to know and understand the law. For example, assume you are accused of robbing your college roommate. However, in your defense, you state you were merely retrieving money that your roommate owed you. While you may believe that your action was appropriate, your mistaken belief that the law allows you to engage in so-called self-help practices may not convince the jury to find you not guilty of a robbery charge.

Statute of Limitations

The purpose of the **statute of limitations** defense is to protect defendants from having to defend themselves against charges associated with events that occurred many years ago. In practical terms, the problem relates to evidence that may have grown "stale" or may no longer exist. Thus, it may be difficult if not impossible for the defendant to identify and collect the evidence necessary to marshal an effective defense. While the statute of limitations is a complete defense, a defendant's failure to raise it prior to trial often results in a waiver of the defense.

Entrapment

In an **entrapment** defense, a defendant alleges that a law enforcement officer (or some other government official) induced her to commit the crime for which she has been charged. In a successful entrapment defense, the defendant convinces the jury that she would not have acted in a "criminal manner" *but for* the undue persuasion imposed on her by the law enforcement official. For example, if you were charged with the crime of insider trading, you would admit to committing the crime in question. However, using the defense of entrapment, you would argue that your illicit actions should be excused because you would not have engaged in the practice of insider-trading *but for* the inducement and encouragement of a law enforcement official who was operating "undercover." As another example, consider the Case of Iris introduced in the Practical Example on page 285. Do you think Ken's strong persuasive powers induced Iris to accept the bribe from Emily? Will Iris be able to use entrapment as a defense to the charge of bribery?

The Criminal Process and Constitutional Protections

The criminal investigative process and the constitutional protections provided by the Bill of Rights form an important part of the procedures used by law enforcement officials and prosecutors in performing their respective duties. Exhibit 10.3 depicts the overall process.

Law Enforcement Investigation

The criminal process begins with an investigation conducted by law enforcement officials. In the United States, law enforcement officials serve at different levels of government. For example, town and city police officers handle law enforcement at the local level. At the county level, the sheriff's office usually administers law enforcement, while state police troopers (sometimes called rangers) oversee law enforcement operations for each of the 50 states. At the federal level, highly specialized agents handle law enforcement for the nation. For example, FBI special agents, IRS special agents, and other federal law enforcement officials work individually or collaboratively to respond to a variety of federal crimes, including mail fraud, securities fraud, bribery, extortion, tax evasion, and environmental crimes. For purposes of this discussion, we will focus on law enforcement at the federal level. As part of the discussion, the terms *law-enforcement official*, *police*, and *federal agent* are used interchangeably.

Exhibit 10.3. The Criminal Investigative and Prosecutorial Process

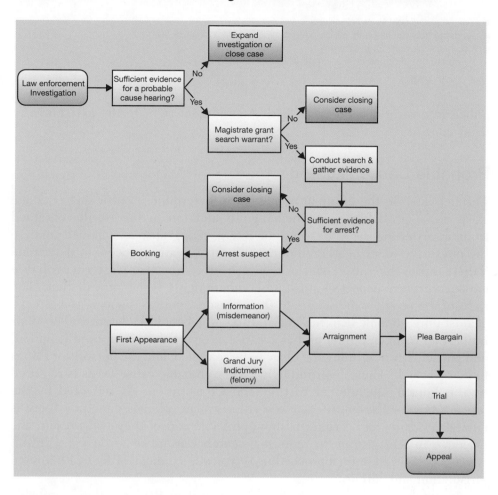

Police conduct **investigations** by inquiring systematically into a crime. Investigations typically include the process of interviewing individuals familiar with the crime and gathering physical evidence, such as computer files, paper documents, and so forth. An interview differs from an interrogation. An **interrogation** involves an intensive questioning by law enforcement officials of a person suspected of committing a crime. Once the investigation has moved from a general interview to a formal interrogation, an important constitutional protection comes into play. The law enforcement official conducting the interrogation is required to inform the suspect being interrogated of his or her constitutional right against self-incrimination. This task is usually accomplished by reading the suspect the Miranda warnings. The U.S. Supreme Court mandated the reading of the **Miranda warnings** (Exhibit 10.4 on page 306) to suspects as a means of protecting their Fifth Amendment right against self-incrimination during a

---

Exhibit 10.4. Miranda Warnings

- You have the right to remain silent.
- Anything you say can and will be used against you in a court of law.
- You have the right to an attorney.
- If you cannot afford an attorney, one will be appointed for you.

---

police interrogation and their Sixth Amendment right to the assistance of legal counsel.[8]

Probable Cause Hearing

The next step in the criminal process is to determine if sufficient evidence exists for a **probable cause hearing**. In addition to the results obtained from interviewing eyewitnesses and interrogating suspects, police analyze the physical evidence gathered during the investigative process to determine if there is probable cause that a crime has been committed. The term **probable cause** refers to a suspect's Fourth Amendment rights, which provide that: "The right of the people to be secure in their persons, houses, papers, and effects, against unreasonable searches and seizures, shall not be violated, and no Warrants shall issue, but upon probable cause, supported by Oath or affirmation, and particularly describing the place to be searched, and the persons or things to be searched." Thus, determining whether probable cause exists is required by the Fourth Amendment to the U.S. Constitution. As reflected by the process flow in Exhibit 10.3, if law enforcement officials conclude there is enough evidence of a crime to show probable cause, they will present the evidence to a magistrate to request a search warrant or an arrest warrant. A **magistrate** in a criminal proceeding is typically a judicial officer with limited jurisdiction and authority.

As emphasized by the U.S. Supreme Court in *Beck v. Ohio*,[9] probable cause does not exist merely because the police *subjectively* believe that a suspect committed the crime in question. The Supreme Court observed that if subjective good faith alone were the test, the protection of the Fourth Amendment would quickly vanish. Consequently, establishing probable cause requires the use of an *objective test*, not the mere subjective beliefs of the investigating officers. An objective test eliminates the subjective views of the police by requiring that a *reasonable person*, after viewing all of the evidence, would conclude that a crime had occurred. Once probable cause has been established, an **arrest warrant** authorizes law enforcement officials to arrest the suspect and present the suspect to the court. Similarly, once probable cause has been established, a **search warrant** authorizes the police

---

[8]*Miranda v. Arizona*, 384 U. S. 436 (1966).
[9]*Beck v. Ohio*, 379 U.S. 89, 85 S.Ct. 223 (1964).

to conduct a search of a specified place and to gather evidence relative to the crime in question.

Arrest

The term **arrest** refers to a forcible restraint of a suspect for the purpose of placing the suspect in police custody and bringing the suspect before a court of law. A **warrantless arrest** occurs without a warrant, based on probable cause of a felony or a misdemeanor committed in the presence of law enforcement officials. However, law enforcement officials may not arrest suspects in their homes without an arrest warrant.

Booking

After a suspect has been arrested, the next step is to "book" the suspect. The term **booking** refers to the process of capturing and recording relevant information about a suspect after the suspect has been arrested. The following information is normally captured during the booking process:

- Information about the suspect, including the suspect's name, birth date, social security number, driver's license number, address, telephone number, and emergency contact information.
- A photograph of the suspect. Police use photographs to identify the suspect and distinguish the suspect from other individuals with the same name.
- Collection and storage of the suspect's property. After the suspect's property has been collected, the police typically provide the suspect with a receipt of the property seized.

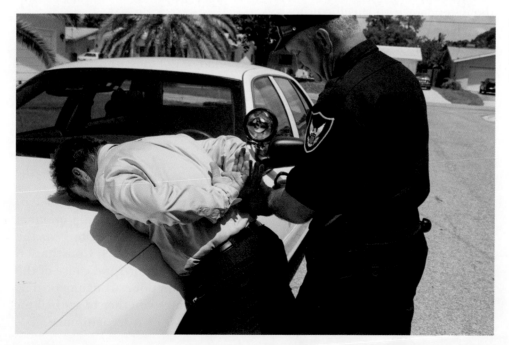

An arrest is often the culmination of a criminal investigation and the beginning of the prosecutorial process.

- Fingerprints of the suspect. Fingerprints of the suspect are matched against those identified at the crime scene. They are also entered into a national FBI database.
- Body search of the suspect. Body searches are conducted to discover the existence of possible contraband.
- Health screening of the suspect. A health screening protects law enforcement officials as well as other inmates from communicable diseases.

First Appearance

Following a booking, the next step in the prosecutorial process is referred to as a **first appearance**, also known as the initial appearance. A first appearance represents a defendant's first appearance in court. During the first appearance, court officers read the criminal charges to the defendant, advise the defendant of his legal rights, and inform the defendant of the court's bail determination. The first appearance is usually required by statute to occur without undue delay. In a misdemeanor case, the first appearance may be combined with the arraignment.

An Information and a Grand Jury Indictment

Following a suspect's first appearance, the process flow may take one of two paths: *an information* or a *grand jury indictment*. An **information** is a formal criminal charge made by the prosecutor without a grand jury indictment. An information is the legal device used to prosecute misdemeanors in most states. In a prosecution by an information, a formal document is issued that charges the defendant with specific crimes.

The second alternative following an initial appearance is the presentation of evidence to a grand jury. A **grand jury** is a body of citizens chosen to hear evidence of an alleged crime and decide whether or not to issue an indictment. An **indictment** is a formal written accusation of a crime, made by a grand jury and presented in court as part of the prosecution of the defendant. During a grand jury hearing, the defendant is not allowed to present evidence, provide witness testimonies, or appear in front of the grand jury.

Arraignment

Following either the issuance of an *information* or a *grand jury indictment*, the defendant is arraigned. An **arraignment** is the initial step in a criminal prosecution whereby the defendant is brought before the court to hear the charges and to enter a plea. The Sixth Amendment to the U.S. Constitution guarantees that defendants shall "be informed of the nature and cause of the accusation against them." Depending on the jurisdiction, arraignment may also be the proceeding at which the court determines whether to set bail for the defendant or release the defendant on his or her own recognizance.

Plea

Following the arraignment, the defendant next enters a plea. The term **plea** refers to the defendant's formal response to a criminal charge. Many criminal cases are resolved through a plea bargain, thus eliminating the need for a trial. The term **plea bargain** refers to a negotiated agreement between the prosecutor and the defendant whereby the defendant typically pleads guilty to a lesser offense in exchange for some concession by the prosecutor, usually a more lenient sentence or the dismissal of other charges.

Trial and Appeal

The term **trial** refers to a formal judicial examination of evidence and the determination of legal claims in an adversary proceeding. An **appeal** represents a proceeding undertaken to have the decision of a lower court reviewed and reconsidered by a higher court. In a civil case, either party may appeal the decision of the trail court. In a criminal case, the defendant may appeal a guilty verdict, but the prosecutor is precluded from appealing the decision of the jury if the jury finds the defendant not guilty.

Fifth Amendment Right Against Self-Incrimination

In *Rhode Island v. Innis*, the U.S. Supreme Court held that, for purposes of the Fifth Amendment right against self-incrimination, an interrogation

---

An Ethical Insight: Immanuel Kant and Thinking to Harm Another

"In law a man is guilty when he violates the rights of others. In ethics he is guilty if he only thinks of doing so."*

Kant insists that an ethical individual would not even contemplate an act that violates the rights of others. Kant's notion of unethical behavior is useful in understanding the concept of criminal intent. For example, someone may be civilly liable for negligence that caused great harm to another by acting carelessly without being held criminally liable for that injury.

Consider what you have learned about criminal intent (mens rea) and criminal acts (actus reus), the distinctions between civil law and criminal law, and the underpinnings of business crimes. What do you conclude about Kant's views on the difference between law and ethics?

To put this question in practical terms, have you ever deprived another of property by stealing it? According to Kant, if you answered this question affirmatively, you are *legally* guilty of violating the rights of others. Now, have you ever *thought* about stealing property, but did not follow through with the act? According to Kant, if you have thought about depriving another of property by stealing it, but did not follow through, you are *ethically* guilty. Does this make sense from your perspective? As you can see, the difference between illegal behavior and unethical behavior is not always clear, obvious, or discernible. Continue to consider the contrasts between ethical and legal behavior: An unethical act is not always illegal, and a person can unintentionally commit an unethical act. A successful compliance and ethics program, therefore, not only prevents criminal conduct, it ultimately maintains an ethical corporate culture.

---
*The Foundation of the Metaphysics Morals.

includes not only express questioning but also words or actions that the police should know are reasonably likely to elicit an incriminating response.[10]

The following In-Depth Ethical Analysis explores many of the issues associated with protecting a criminal suspect's Fifth Amendment right against self-incrimination.

In-Depth Ethical Case Analysis

Berghuis v. Thompkins, 130 S. Ct. 2250 (2010)

Facts

On January 10, 2000, two individuals (Samuel Morris and Frederick France) were shot in the parking lot of a strip mall in Southfield, Michigan. Morris died from multiple gunshot wounds, while France survived and recovered from his wounds. Shortly after the shooting, the police identified two suspects, Eric Purifoy and Van Chester Thompkins. Purifoy was arrested and charged with assault and the murder of Morris. Thompkins, however, fled before the police could arrest him. Thompkins eluded law enforcement officials for about a year before being arrested and charged with the murder of Morris. In the meantime, Purifoy was tried and acquitted of the assault and murder charges.

Shortly after his arrest, the police interrogated Thompkins about the shooting of Morris. Before the interrogation began, the police presented Thompkins with a written copy of his Miranda rights, which included the following language:

1. You have the right to remain silent.

2. Anything you say can and will be used against you in a court of law.

3. You have a right to talk to a lawyer before answering any questions, and you have the right to have a lawyer present with you while you are answering any questions.

4. If you cannot afford to hire a lawyer, one will be appointed to represent you before any questioning, if you wish one.

5. You have the right to decide at any time before or during questioning to use your right to remain silent and your right to talk with a lawyer while you are being questioned.

The police officers asked Thompkins if he understood these rights. Thompkins acknowledged his understanding verbally but refused to sign a written confirmation. The officers did not ask Thompkins if he wanted to waive his rights before starting the interrogation, and they made no further reference to the Miranda warning. The interrogation lasted approximately three hours. Thompkins remained silent throughout most of the interrogation, other than occasionally nodding his head or offering a very limited verbal response, such as "yeah," "no," or "I don't know." Toward the end of the interrogation, Thompkins was asked if he believed in and prayed to God. The police then asked Thompkins if he had asked God for forgiveness for shooting that boy [Morris]. Thompkins replied, "Yes."

---

[10]*Rhode Island v. Innis*, 446 U.S. 291, 100 S.Ct. 1082 (1980).

Issue

Can a defendant invoke his Fifth Amendment right during a three hour police interrogation against self-incrimination by remaining mostly silent?

Holding

At trial, the prosecution used Thompkins's "Yes" response as an admission to committing the murder of Morris. On appeal, defense counsel argued that Thompkins's constitutional right against self-incrimination had been violated. The Michigan Court of Appeals rejected Thompkins's argument, holding that the police had given Thompkins an effective Miranda warning. Thompkins next petitioned the U.S. District Court for the Eastern District of Michigan, which denied Thompkins's request for a new trial. Thompkins appealed the decision of the District Court to the Court of Appeals for the Sixth Circuit. The Sixth Circuit ruled in favor of Thompkins, as it found that Thompkins's so-called "waiver" of his Fifth Amendment right against self-incrimination was unreasonable because (1) Thompkins refused to sign an acknowledgement that he had been informed of his Miranda rights, and (2) Thompkins rarely made eye contact with the police officers throughout the three hour interrogation. Because of this error, the Sixth Circuit remanded the case to the trial court. However, the State of Michigan appealed the decision of the Sixth Circuit to the U.S. Supreme Court, which reversed the holding of the Sixth Circuit and ruled against Thompkins.

From the Court's Opinion

In a 5-to-4 decision, the Supreme Court determined that Thompkins failed to invoke his Miranda rights because he failed to invoke them in an "unambiguous" way. Moreover, the Court reasoned that Thompkins waived his Miranda right to remain silent when he "knowingly and voluntarily" made a statement to the police. In support of its decision, the Court noted that at no point did Thompkins say that (1) he wanted to remain silent, (2) he did not want to talk to the police, or (3) he wanted an attorney. Conversely, Thompkins argued that he implicitly invoked his right to remain silent by not saying anything to the police after nearly three hours of interrogation; therefore, the police should have stopped the interrogation before he made his inculpatory statements. In response to Thompkins's argument, the Court made the following observation:

> *[Thompkins] argument is unpersuasive. To invoke the Miranda right to remain silent an accused must do so unambiguously. A requirement of an unambiguous invocation of Miranda rights results in an objective inquiry that avoids difficulties of proof and provides guidance to officers on how to proceed in the face of ambiguity. Thompkins did not say that he wanted to remain silent or that he did not want to talk with the police. Had he made either of these simple statements, he would have invoked his right to cut off questioning.*

> * * *

> *The main purpose of Miranda is to ensure that the accused is advised of and understands the right to remain silent and the right to counsel. Thus the Miranda rule and its requirements are met if a suspect receives adequate Miranda warnings, understands them, and has an opportunity to invoke the rights before giving any answers. The record in this case shows that Thompkins waived his right to remain silent. There is no contention that Thompkins did not understand his rights. Thompkins was given a form that listed his rights and all of the rights were read aloud. Thompkins' answers to Detective Helgert's question about whether Thompkins prayed to God for forgiveness for shooting the victim is a course of conduct indicating waiver of the right to remain silent. There is no evidence that Thompkins' statement was coerced, nor were the police required*

to obtain a waiver of Thompkins' right to remain silent before interrogating him.

Dissenting Opinion

Justice Sonia Sotomayor, joined by Justices John Paul Stevens, Ruth Bader Ginsburg, and Stephen G. Breyer, dissented. Justice Sotomayor reprimanded the majority members of the Court for retreating from the broad protections afforded by *Miranda*, stating that now a criminal suspect waives his rights simply by uttering a "few one-word responses." Justice Sotomayor stated:

The Court concludes today that a criminal suspect waives his right to remain silent if, after sitting tacit and uncommunicative through nearly three hours of police interrogation, he utters a few one-word responses. The Court also concludes that a suspect who wishes to guard his right to remain silent against such a finding of "waiver" must, counterintuitively, speak — and must do so with sufficient precision to satisfy a clear-statement rule that construes ambiguity in favor of the police. Both propositions mark a substantial retreat from the protection against compelled self-incrimination that Miranda v. Arizona, 384 U. S. 436 (1966), has long provided during custodial interrogation.

Ethical Issues

The Supreme Court's analysis in *Berghuis v. Thompkins* focused on the meaning of one of the most often heard phrases in American movies and television shows, "You have the right to remain silent." This phrase emanates from the landmark 1966 Supreme Court ruling in *Miranda v. Arizona* that requires law enforcement officials to inform suspects of their constitutional rights before interrogating them. While the Supreme Court has heard many cases over the years involving different interpretations of its holding in *Miranda v. Arizona*, the

Court had not, before *Berghuis v. Thompkins*, dealt with the issue of an "implied" application of the *Miranda* right to remain silent. For example, after Thompkins was read his *Miranda* rights, he remained silent during nearly three hours of interrogation. He never said that he wanted to talk with a lawyer or that he wanted to exercise his right to remain silent. Essentially, Thompkins said nothing during three hours of interrogation, other than uttering the single word "Yes" at the end of the interrogation when asked if he prayed to God to forgive him for the shooting.

Did Thompkins make an implicit (unspoken) request to the police that he wanted to invoke his *Miranda* right to remain silent by sitting silently during three hours of tough interrogation? After one, or two, or three hours of watching Thompkins sit silently during the interrogation, should the police have "legally" if not "ethically" stopped the interrogation? A close examination of this case reveals that the Court addressed ethical as well as legal questions. For example, how does society balance the rights of the individual against the legitimate needs of a civilized society to enforce its laws? How does the Court decide a case? Are decisions based on a set of grounded ethical principles, or are decisions made on a more pragmatic need to protect society, even at the cost of individual rights and freedoms? Thus, if a suspect understands his Miranda right to remain silent but does not expressly assert that right when questioned by the police, is it appropriate, fair, or ethical for the police to continue the interrogation for nearly three hours as the suspect sits silently?

Ethical Theory Analysis

Ethical arguments supporting the majority decision: Thompkins waived his Fifth Amendment rights to remain silent during the interrogation.

Natural Law: Thompkins had a natural law right to a presumption of innocence until tried and convicted under a process that granted him "constitutional safeguards." That process begins very early in the interrogation by the police. His *Miranda* rights were read aloud to him and there was no evidence indicating he did not understand them. One could argue the police were acting ethically by continuing the interrogation under these circumstances.

Legal Positivism: John Austin, the founder of legal positivism, stated "A law . . . may be said to be a rule laid down for the guidance of an intelligent being by an intelligent being having power over him." One could argue the U.S. Supreme Court in the *Miranda* decision created rules for the guidance of the police before interrogating a suspect. In this case the *Miranda* rules were read to the defendant. After the suspect verbally states he understands them, there is no legal requirement to sign a written confirmation of that understanding. During the interrogation, Thompkins never asked to remain silent or talk to a lawyer. One could reasonably and ethically assume he waived his Fifth Amendment right to remain silent under these circumstances.

Ethical arguments supporting the dissenting opinion: Thompkins did not waive his Miranda rights by "uttering a few one-word responses."

Utilitarianism: English jurist William Blackstone stated, "Better that ten guilty persons escape than that one innocent suffer." If Thompkins's "single-word responses" after three hours of remaining silent had not been allowed into evidence because of a Miranda violation, he may not have been found guilty of murder. The utilitarian principle of "the greater good for the greater number" would support Blackstone's counsel and ensure that an innocent person does not go to jail unless he was aware of his constitutional rights under the Fifth Amendment to remain silent during a police interrogation. Under this theory, the police were acting unethically in continuing the interrogation for nearly three hours as the suspect remained mostly silent without reminding him of his right to remain silent and have any attorney present.

Rawls's Difference Principle states, "Social and economic inequalities are to be arranged so that they are . . . to be to the greatest benefit of the least-advantaged." A suspect being interrogated by the police, with a constitutional assumption of innocence, is surely among the "least advantaged." One could argue the police had an ethical obligation to clearly explain to Thompkins during the three hour interrogation that he could have remained silent and have a lawyer present and one would be provided free if he could not afford the cost. Individuals in Rawls's Original Position not knowing their place in society would ethically support the dissent.

Conclusion

The 5/4 split decision in this case indicates that reasonable people (justices) disagree on what constitutes a waiver of a defendant's *Miranda* rights. One could argue it would be highly unreasonable and unethical to require the police to do more than read the *Miranda* warning to a suspect once the suspect has been arrested. It would appear to be an unethical position to require more than a reading of the *Miranda* rules and a statement of understanding because an arrest often takes place in the street and in a dangerous situation that could put the police at risk of being harmed. If we were to confine the dissenting opinion to an interrogation room, one could construct an ethical argument that supports periodic informative statements by the police that the suspect could call a lawyer or not answer a question.

Global Perspective: International Business Crimes

Global Issues and Business Crimes

U.S. companies seeking international trade are subject to federal laws that, if violated, impose criminal liability on the corporation. Applicable laws should be carefully reviewed before contract negations with a foreign corporation. This review process is an essential part of a compliance and ethics program that provides for an aggressive "due diligence" and "risk assessment" overview of the planned international business by corporate legal counsel and high-ranking executives. The Case Illustration on the next page illustrates how companies doing business abroad can be criminally prosecuted for bribing foreign officials to obtain business. A convicted company can pay millions of dollars in fines with potential jail sentences for those who directly participated in committing the crimes. Although there are many business crimes discussed in this chapter, the crime of bribing foreign officials has been selected as it has significant legal, ethical, business, and social consequences.

Due Diligence

When a company is anticipating or engaging in foreign business transactions, corporate legal counsel should research the applicable laws and explain them to management to avoid potential criminal violations.

Risk Assessment

Top management should review all the details of the business risks involved in the planned foreign business arrangements, including any potential opportunities to bribe a foreign official to obtain contracts with the foreign company. The risks of violating the laws and unethical behavior should be explained to the sales personnel in detail. One method of transmitting that knowledge would be a Manager's Compliance and Ethics Meeting as illustrated throughout this textbook.

Manager's Compliance and Ethics Meetings

Managers should explain the company's code of ethics and what constitutes a bribe to the applicable employees and other agents who may be involved in the foreign business transactions. Corporate counsel should attend this meeting to demonstrate the seriousness of the company's position and the criminal consequence of breaking the law. The reasons why bribery is unethical as well as illegal should be explained to help employees better understand the Foreign Corrupt Practices Act, which was discussed earlier in the chapter.

Code of Ethics

Companies engaging in foreign business transactions should include a specific section in their code of ethics prohibiting the bribery of foreign officials with a reference to the Foreign Corrupt Practices Act. The code of ethics should be carefully explained to the employees to assure an understanding of the company's values. Management should be certain the employees understand the consequences of violating the code.

Ethical Corporate Culture

Since the objective of the company's compliance and ethics program is to maintain a sustainable ethical corporate culture, the entire corporate structure from the board of directors to rank-and-file employees should understand that the company's mission would be compromised by bribing foreign officials to obtain business, as that practice violates the law and ethical principles.

International Scope of the Problem of Bribery

Bribery, the payment of foreign officials to obtain business, is rampant on every civilized continent. The World Bank estimated in 2004 that globally about $1 trillion is transferred as bribes from the private to the public sector each year.[11] In addition, there are staggering economic costs to regions that support corruption and corresponding benefit for those effectively tackling the problem of bribery. Countries able to control the problem could expect a "governance dividend" of 400 percent — that is, "countries that improve on control of corruption and rule of law can expect (on average), in the long run, a fourfold increase in incomes per capita."[12] The Case Illustration involving Siemens AG illustrates the high cost of engaging in bribery schemes.

Efforts to Combat Bribery Worldwide. In recent years, there has been a surge of international interest, effort, and commitment to tackle and control the problem of bribery. As shown in Exhibit 10.5, this effort responds to the negative impact that bribery has on society. The United States significantly increased efforts to combat overseas bribery over the past few years. One U.S. government official said, "in 2004, [the Department of Justice] charged two individuals under the FCPA, the anti-bribery statute, and

Case Illustration

Siemens AG bribed officials and eventually paid $1.6 billion in fines and disgorgement. The bribery was committed by Siemens subsidiaries in Argentina, Bangladesh, and Venezuela and totaled $1.36 billion* over the course of about six years (2001–2007). In addition, Siemens subsidiaries in France and Turkey rigged kickbacks in connection with the UN Oil for Food program that totaled about $1.7 million. In its press release announcing the settlement of the case in 2008, the director of the Securities and Exchange Commission's Division of Enforcement, Linda Chatman Thomsen, said, "This pattern of bribery by Siemens was unprecedented in scale and geographic reach. The corruption involved more than $1.4 billion in bribes to government officials in Asia, Africa, Europe, the Middle East and the Americas." The Department of Justice also included this statement of gratitude for the way Siemens handled the bribery investigation: "Siemens AG and its subsidiaries disclosed these violations after initiating an internal FCPA investigation of unprecedented scope; shared the results of that investigation with the department efficiently and continuously; cooperated extensively and authentically with the department in its ongoing investigation; took appropriate disciplinary action against individual wrongdoers, including senior management with involvement in or knowledge of the violations; and took remedial action, including the complete restructuring of Siemens AG and the implementation of a sophisticated compliance program and organization."[†]

---

* Department of Justice Press Release, December 15, 2008. http://www.justice.gov/opa/pr/2008/December/08-crm-1105.html.
† Department of Justice Press Release, December 15, 2008. http://www.justice.gov/opa/pr/2008/December/08-crm-1105.html.

---

[11]"The Costs of Corruption," http://web.worldbank.org/WBSITE/EXTERNAL/NEWS/0,,contentMDK:20190187~menuPK:34457~pagePK:34370~piPK:34424~theSitePK:4607,00.html.
[12]"Six Questions on the Cost of Corruption with World Bank Institute Global Governance Director Daniel Kaufmann," http://web.worldbank.org/WBSITE/EXTERNAL/NEWS/0,,contentMDK:20190295~menuPK:34457~pagePK:34370~piPK:34424~theSitePK:4607,00.html.

Exhibit 10.5. Impact of Bribery on Society: Who Is Harmed by Bribery?	
Bribery from an economic and business perspective	• Discourages competition and creates barriers that prevent other companies from entering the market • Introduces inefficiencies in markets, slows industry growth, and retards economic expansion overall • Places legitimate, honest competitors and small companies at a disadvantage • Drives the proceeds of illegal transactions to foreign accounts, causing capital flight (since the proceeds of corrupt payments are often transferred abroad), thereby preventing money from being used in productive ways • Harms consumers because products and services are more likely to be substandard and more costly • Causes uncertainty and lack of confidence in markets because shareholders are unsure how their invested money is spent or believe it is spent unwisely
Bribery from a political and societal perspective	• Deflates morale among the citizenry and encourages people to think that the government and the judicial system are indifferent or incompetent • Weakens a government's credibility at home and abroad • Suggests to citizens that rule-breaking in other areas is permissible, fostering a culture of corruption • Can negatively affect a country or region's safety and security • Pits wealthier classes against poorer ones • Encourages and helps sustain poverty, hunger, disease, and crime
Bribery from an ethical perspective	• Corporate directors are fiduciaries who act on behalf of the stockholders and, in addition to making the company profitable and eventually issuing dividends, have an ethical obligation to "do no harm" to the business, including tolerating illegal and unethical business practices leading to adverse publicity and paying fines for criminal behavior. • Regardless of adverse publicity to the corporation, Kant's categorical imperatives demand a duty of ethical behavior irrespective of the consequences. Kant could argue if all companies paid bribes to get business, international trade would eventually be a disaster. • Aristotle's virtue ethics would find bribery a violation of justice and an unfair practice benefiting big business over small companies. • Rawls's Democratic Equality Principle states "Social and economic inequalities are to be arranged so that they are attached to offices and positions open to all under conditions of fair equality of opportunity." • Rawls's principle would be violated by bribing foreign officials because it provides for an "economic inequality" in the international marketplace.

collected around $11 million in criminal fines. . . . By contrast, in 2009 and 2010 combined, we charged over 50 individuals and collected nearly $2 billion."[13]

With the passage of the Sarbanes-Oxley Act in 2002, more companies have discovered and voluntarily disclosed bribery. As discussed in Chapter 9 "Sale of Securities and Investor Protection," the Sarbanes-Oxley Act significantly changed the reporting requirements of publicly traded companies, enhanced disclosure requirements, and improved transparency. Under Sarbanes-Oxley, CEOs and CFOs must personally verify company financial statements, and accounting records of publicly traded companies must "accurately and fairly" reflect financial activity. These rules have led to increased voluntary disclosure of bribery payments by publicly traded U.S. companies.

The movement to combat bribery has not been limited to the United States. The United Kingdom enacted the UK Bribery Act in 2010, dubbed "the toughest anticorruption legislation in the world."[14] Some countries, such as China and Russia, recently enacted antibribery laws that would prohibit illegal payments to foreign government officials. Other countries, such as Brazil and Indonesia, are reviewing newly proposed antibribery legislation.

A significant force behind much of the anticorruption activity globally is the Organisation for Economic Cooperation and Development (OECD). The OECD's central goal is stimulation of economic progress worldwide. It strives for economic progress through engaging in research, inviting countries to address policy questions and compare best practices, working with businesses and trade unions. The OECD itself does not have legislative or judicial powers, but to further its mission, it facilitated the Convention on Combating Bribery of Foreign Public Officials in International Business Transactions (also called the OECD Anti-Bribery Convention). Thirty-nine countries are signatories to the convention. The OECD provides support to signatory countries by monitoring corruption, making recommendations, and assessing the effectiveness of domestic anticorruption policies.

Summary

Criminal law differs from civil law. The goal of criminal law is punishment and deterrence; the goal of civil law is to resolve disputes and provide a remedy for injuries suffered. Business crimes arise in a variety of national and international settings, and they often involve illicit activities characterized by deceit and a breach of trust. A variety of defenses are available for defendants charged with perpetrating a business crime. Like other types of offenders, perpetrators of business crimes are afforded procedural guarantees under the Bill of Rights. Global trade is governed by international laws, and companies seeking business abroad must work closely with legal counsel to assure legal compliance. A well-designed compliance and ethics program must include ways to ensure the law is obeyed and ethical principles are upheld.

[13]"Assistant Attorney General Lanny A. Breuer of the Criminal Division Speaks at the 3rd Russia and Commonwealth of Independent States Summit on Anti-Corruption," http://www.justice.gov/criminal/pr/speeches/2011/crm-speech-110316.html.
[14]Russell, Jonathan, *Fears Bribery Act Will Harm UK plc*, The Telegraph (January 21, 2011).

Questions for Review

1. Mail fraud and computer crime

After quitting his job at Korn/Ferry, an executive search firm, David Nosal decided to start a competing business. To help get his new business off the ground, Mr. Nosal convinced some of his former coworkers at Korn/Ferry to use their employee credentials to log into the Korn/Ferry system and download confidential names and addresses from the Korn/Ferry files. The coworkers then sent this information to Mr. Nosal. In addition to being charged with various counts of trade secret theft and mail fraud, Mr. Nosal was charged with violating the Computer Fraud and Abuse Act (CFAA) by "aiding and abetting the Korn/Ferry employees in exceed[ing their] authorized access with intent to defraud." The CFAA defines "exceeds authorized access" as "to access a computer with authorization and to use such access to obtain or alter information in the computer that the accesser is not entitled to so obtain or alter." 18 U.S.C. § 1030(e)(6). This language can be read in two ways. Mr. Nosal believes that this should refer to someone who is authorized to access only certain data or files but who accesses unauthorized data or files. The government's position in the case is that this refers to someone who has unrestricted physical access to a computer but is limited in how he is allowed to use the information. Which interpretation do you find more convincing? Has Mr. Nosal aided and abetted in a violation of the CFAA? *United States v. David Nosal*, 642 F.3d 781 (9th Cir. 2011).

2. Civil law versus criminal law

Describe the differences between civil law and criminal law. What is the purpose of criminal law? What is the purpose of civil law?

3. Ethics

Immanuel Kant, a deontological philosopher, stated in "An Exposition of The Fundamental Principles of Jurisprudence as the Science of Right" that *"Judicial Punishment can never be administered merely as a means for promoting another Good either with regard to the <u>Criminal himself or to Civil Society</u>, but must in all cases be imposed only because the individual on whom it is inflicted has committed a crime. . . . The Penal Law is a Categorical Imperative and woe to him who creeps through the serpent-windings of Utilitarianism to discover some advantage that may discharge from the Justice of Punishment."* Kant would probably find it unethical for a defendant in a criminal case to be afforded the defense of mental incapacity (insanity). Do you believe it is ethical to convict a defendant who is mentally incapacitated? Use ethical principles to support your position.

4. Ponzi scheme, civil law and criminal law

In May 2010, Coquina Investments, a Corpus Christi, Texas–based investment firm brought a lawsuit against TD Bank alleging that through the fraudulent actions of its agents, TD Bank is responsible for Coquina's loss of millions of dollars. At issue in the case is an elaborate Ponzi scheme operated by disbarred attorney Scott Rothstein. As part of this scheme, Mr. Rothstein convinced investors to make cash payments to individuals expecting to receive settlement payments from pending legal disputes. According to Mr. Rothstein, in exchange for these cash payments, these individuals would assign to Mr. Rothstein (and the investors) the right to collect the future, larger settlement payments. Rothstein guaranteed the investors a 20 percent return on their investment. In reality, these settlements did not exist but rather were part of an elaborate Ponzi scheme that Rothstein ran through his law office and in which he channeled money through 38 TD Bank accounts. Rothstein pleaded guilty to racketeering, money laundering, and fraud conspiracy charges and is now serving a 50-year prison sentence. Investors, desirous of recouping millions of dollars of losses, have brought claims against TD Bank alleging that officers of TD Bank facilitated the continued existence of the scheme. The bank maintains that it was the bank for the Rothstein's law firm, Rothstein, Rosenfeldt, and Adler, and not for Scott Rothstein personally. Explain the differences between the government's prosecution of Scott Rothstein for criminal violations versus Coquina Investments' civil lawsuit against TD Bank for the alleged fraudulent actions of its agents. *Coquina Investments v. Rothstein*, 2012 U.S. Dist. LEXIS 108712 (S.D. Fla. 2012).

5. Defenses

List, describe, and provide examples of the various defenses available to a defendant charged with a business crime.

6. Federal crime and ethical issues

Erik recently accepted a position at Ocean Corporation as its chief operating officer (COO). As part of his responsibilities, Erik oversees the company's seafood processing operations. Ocean has been in business for 50 years and has been profitable for most of those years. Recently, however, Ocean has witnessed a steady decline in profits due in part to increased maintenance costs in the company's processing facility, which cleans, weighs, and packages seafood for distribution to restaurants in New England. In an effort to arrest the drop in profits, Ocean quietly introduced a program aimed at relaxing its previously high standards for cleanliness and sanitation procedures.

Ocean Corporation receives fresh seafood directly from fishing boats located in Maine, New Hampshire, Massachusetts, and Rhode Island. Because Ocean engages in the interstate transportation of goods and its primary business line involves the distribution of food,

Ocean falls under the statutory provisions of § 301(k) of the Federal Food, Drug, and Cosmetic Act.[15]

During his first month at Ocean, Erik took daily walks around the processing facility to introduce himself to employees. While talking with the employees, several offered suggestions about improving operational inefficiencies. Some of these same employees also complained about reductions in maintenance staff. They claimed the reductions have contributed to a serious decline in sanitation practices. Erik asked the employees if they could show him some examples of unsanitary conditions. To his surprise and astonishment, the employees led him to three storage rooms where wharf rats had eaten part of the packaged food. Erik asked why these packages had not been removed and discarded. The response Erik received caused great concern on his part. The employees informed Erik they had been instructed by "upper management" to repackage the damaged goods and ship the repackaged seafood to restaurants in the surrounding states.

After "sleeping on the situation" for three nights, Erik finally made his way to the office of Ocean's CEO. After reporting his discoveries about the unsanitary conditions in Ocean's processing facility and the repackaging of rat contaminated seafood, the CEO stared in silence for about three minutes. He then told Erik that "this conversation never occurred," and instructed Erik to stay away from those areas of the processing facility that may house contaminated seafood. Before Erik could respond, the CEO suggested to Erik that he take a long walk on the beach next to Ocean's processing facility and contemplate his future with the company.

Bella has worked at Ocean for the past five years. She serves as the company's chief financial officer (CFO). As a corporate officer, Bella is one of the employees responsible for

[15]21 U.S.C. § 331(k).

developing and implementing Ocean's corporate mission. Ocean's mission statement follows:

Ocean Corporation

Mission Statement

We strive to provide the freshest and healthiest seafood possible by purchasing our seafood directly from fishing boats each day and processing it with the most advanced and spotless technology available. We package and store our seafood using state-of-the-art techniques and facilities, ensuring that our customers receive the best seafood available in New England.

The mission statement is displayed prominently on the office wall of each corporate officer. It is also included in promotional brochures sent to current and prospective customers.

Shortly after Erik left the office of the CEO, he decided to talk with Bella about his conversation with the CEO (Jonathan). When Erik finished his account of the conversation, Bella shrugged her shoulders and said, "That's Jonathan. He wants to hear good news only. If it's bad news, he simply pretends he didn't hear it." Bella then told Erik that every company that processes seafood has rodent problems. She said it's impossible to eradicate them from the processing and storage facilities. Dismayed by Bella's comment, Erik pointed to the mission statement on her wall and asked Bella about the truthfulness of the assertions made in the statement. Bella laughed mildly and said "that's a joke."

Finding little comfort in his conversations with Jonathan and Bella, Erik decided to return to the employees who informed him initially about the rodent contamination problem. Erik invited two employees, Sarah and Andrew, to lunch, ostensibly to talk about their suggestions for improving operational efficiencies. However, after some perfunctory comments about efficiencies, Erik moved directly to the topic

of rodent contamination and the repackaging of contaminated seafood.

Sarah, who has been working at Ocean for the past seven years as a production manager, hesitated when Erik raised the topic of contamination. She stated immediately that she was not at fault for the eroding sanitary conditions. She mentioned that before "upper management" relaxed the high sanitary standards that had been in place for many years, she regularly hired part-time employees to conduct "spot checks" of key areas within the processing facility known for attracting rodents. However, when "upper management" instituted its cost-saving policies to improve short-term profits, Sarah was told she could no longer hire part-time employees to conduct spot checks. She was told that she would need to be more creative in developing ways of detecting rodent infestation. Sarah interpreted the comment about becoming more "creative" to mean that the days of "spot checking" had come to an end. When Erik asked Sarah if it was her decision to eliminate the spot checks, her exasperation with the situation manifested in her response to Erik: "No way! I'm tired of people pointing their fingers at me. I am a member of Ocean's middle management team. I don't make policy decisions. I simply follow them."

Andrew listened quietly as Sarah described the situation from her perspective. Andrew has been with Ocean for less than a year. He joined the company immediately upon graduation from college. Not wanting to "rock the boat," Andrew decided to focus on his job and not worry about what other employees may be doing or not doing. Andrew spends most of his time negotiating with fishing boat captains about the price of the daily catch and transporting seafood from the fishing docks to Ocean's processing facility. At the facility, Andrew helps other employees unload the refrigerated trucks and place the fresh seafood in storage containers housed in Ocean's processing facility.

Erik asked Andrew if he has seen any evidence of rodent contamination. Andrew's response was defensive: "My truck is clean, if that's what you're talking about." Erik explained calmly that he was more interested in any observations Andrew may have made regarding conditions within the processing facility. Andrew's response was curt: "I focus on getting my job done. I don't have time to see what others are doing. I've heard rumors about rodent infestation and contamination, but that doesn't affect my job. I buy seafood for Ocean and deliver it to the company's processing facility. Beyond that, I have no further duties, obligations, or responsibilities."

The day after Erik, Sarah, and Andrew had lunch, Sarah asked Erik if she could have a private conversation with him. Erik said "sure" and invited Sarah to his office. During the conversation, Sarah told Erik that during her seven years with Ocean Corporation she has witnessed a somewhat regular presence of rats in the processing facility.

Discussion Questions

a. Could Erik be found criminally liable for the unsanitary conditions in Ocean's seafood processing facility? What evidence could the government use to establish Erik's culpability? What defenses could Erik's attorneys use to exculpate him?

b. Could the government charge other employees at Ocean with criminal violations related to the company's unsanitary conditions? If yes, on what basis? Which employees?

c. What type of corporate culture exists at Ocean Corporation regarding ethical thinking and decision making?

d. Would you be surprised to learn that the board of directors of Ocean Corporation has not adopted a corporate code of ethics? Why? Why not?

e. If you were Erik, how would you respond to the situation at hand? Explain your rationale, motives, and decision-making process.

7. **Criminal process and constitutional protections**

Explain why a defendant in a criminal proceeding has significant constitutional protections afforded to her under the Bill of Rights. Use the Miranda warnings, as discussed in the chapter, to support your position.

8. **International**

This chapter discussed many of the problems associated with bribery. Do you think it is right or fair for some countries to have strong anti-bribery laws while other countries accept bribery "as a way of doing business"?

Further Reading

Dworkin, T. M., and Callahan, E. S. *Internal Whistleblowing: Protecting the Interests of the Employee, the Organization, and Society*, 29 American Business Law Journal 267–308 (1991).

Grafton, R., and Posey, C. *Tax Implications of Fraudulent Income Earning Schemes: Ponzi and Others*, 27 American Business Law Journal 599–610 (1990).

Hickox, S. A., and Roehling, M. V. *Negative Credentials: Fair and Effective Consideration of Criminal Records*, 50 American Business Law Journal 201–279 (2013).

Nichols, P. M. *The Business Case for Complying with Bribery Laws*, 49 American Business Law Journal 325–368 (2012).

Wen, S. *The Achilles Heel That Hobbles the Asian Giant: The Legal and Cultural Impediments to Antibribery Initiatives in China*, 50 American Business Law Journal 483–541 (2013).

CHAPTER 11

Antitrust

Chapter Objectives

1. To be able to define antitrust law and know what it is called outside the United States
2. To understand the principal types of antitrust violations
3. To understand the difference between a vertical and a horizontal restraint of trade
4. To be aware of the parties that can bring antitrust violations
5. To understand how antitrust law has developed at the international level

Practical Example: Cable TV — A Case of Illegal Bundling?

When students and recent graduates attempt to obtain cable television for the first time, they are often surprised and frustrated to learn that it is not possible to pay for only desired channels (say, TNT or ESPN). They must instead buy "packages" that include many channels they might prefer to forgo. Is the practice of bundling channels lawful? Antitrust law helps to answer this and other questions that involve business practices that allegedly harm competition to the detriment of consumers. In a recent lawsuit, Rob Brantley and other consumers sued NBC Universal,* Comcast, and other television programmers and distributors, seeking to compel them to sell each cable channel separately and thereby permit the plaintiffs to purchase only those channels that they desired. In a unanimous decision, the Ninth Circuit Court found no violation of the antitrust laws because, although consumer freedom of choice may be limited by bundling, there was no allegation of injury to competition. *Brantley v. NBC Universal, Inc.*, 675 F.3d 1192 (9th Cir. 2012). *Brantley* does not necessarily end the issue, however. As you read the chapter, think about what laws and arguments might be put forth in future litigation to more successfully challenge the practice of channel bundling.

---

* NBC Universal is a media and entertainment company, best known for its NBC television network, and since 2011 has been a subsidiary of Comcast, a cable company.

Overview of Antitrust Law

From the perspective of a business, there are a number of advantages to being large. Large businesses can exert significant leverage when negotiating with suppliers because those suppliers have more to gain from a large account. Large businesses may also be able to produce their products at a lower average cost per unit by spreading fixed costs over a greater number of units, a phenomenon economists refer to as "economies of scale." For example, a business must incur the fixed costs of creating a website whether it sells 1,000 units of output or 10 million units of output. These and other advantages of large size can sometimes result in benefits to consumers, such as lower prices.

At the extreme, however, a business could become so large that it is the only company selling a particular product or service. At this point the business would be known as a **monopolist**, and it would be able to set the price of its goods without worrying that a competitor might sell a similar product at a lower price. Even where two or more businesses compete in a given market, those competitors might agree to *act* like a monopolist, such as by agreeing to price products identically or to divide the market so that each competitor has a monopoly with respect to certain customers.

The Goals of Antitrust Law

Antitrust law attempts to draw a line between business growth and other business activity that is beneficial to society and that which is harmful. Although the boundary is often difficult to delineate precisely, there are a number of business practices that tend to be categorized as harmful and therefore condemned by the antitrust laws. These include price fixing, market division, boycotts, monopolization, predatory pricing, price discrimination, tying arrangements, interlocking directorates, and any other unfair method of competition. At the same time, it is sometimes beneficial for businesses to coordinate with each other. For example, joint ventures and collaborative research agreements can sometimes allow businesses to pool resources and thereby reduce duplicative spending. The challenge of separating permissible beneficial activities from prohibited harmful activities will be a recurring theme as each of these practices is examined throughout the chapter.

A Note on the Term *Antitrust*

Outside of the United States, antitrust law is known as *competition law*, a term that reflects the law's goal of promoting fair competition that ultimately

Exhibit 11.1. Structure of an Anticompetitive Trust: The Standard Oil Company

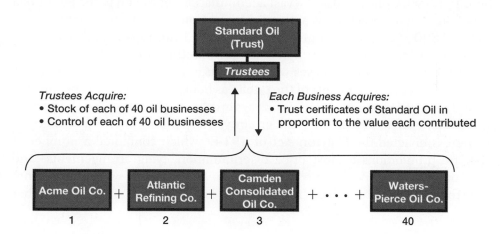

benefits consumers in the form of better products and lower prices. The term *antitrust*, more commonly used in the United States, derives from certain anti-competitive business practices of the late 1800s whereby two or more businesses would agree to restrain trade. For example, two or more parties might agree to fix prices or restrict output. In order to ensure that each party holds to the agreement, the rights to the aggregate profits of the parties could be placed under the control of a third party. In law, a third party that holds assets for the benefit of others is known as a "trustee," and the assets managed by the trustee are held "in trust" for benefit of those other parties. Laws seeking to limit this type of anticompetitive behavior thus became known as "antitrust" laws. The term is somewhat unfortunate because the antitrust laws do not prohibit all trusts, but only those that adversely affect competition. Indeed, the trust remains a common and lawful device for estate planning and other purposes.

Exhibit 11.1 illustrates the basic structure of an anticompetitive trust, using the example of the Standard Oil Company. Each conspiring business transfers its stock to a newly created company, Standard Oil, giving Standard Oil effective control over those businesses. In return, each business receives trust certificates in proportion to the value of stock transferred. Standard Oil then uses its dominant position to receive preferential rates from suppliers, to put out of business any competitors that refuse to join the trust, and to engage in other anticompetitive behavior. Finally, Standard Oil's profits are distributed among the conspiring businesses in proportion to the value that each contributed.

A Brief History of Federal Antitrust Law

In the years following the Civil War (1861-1865), a number of large firms came to dominate certain industries. Among them was the Standard Oil

Company, which, under the leadership of John D. Rockefeller, grew from its origins in 1870 to control as much as 95 percent of the U.S. oil industry. Other firms emerged to dominate the steel, tobacco, railroad, and sugar industries, among others. Concerned at the vast accumulations of wealth in the hands of a small number of corporations and individuals, Congress enacted the **Sherman Act of 1890**,[1] which sought to limit the ability of firms to monopolize markets or enter into trade-restraining agreements with other firms.

Although a number of cases were brought under the Sherman Act, it was criticized by certain segments of the public as being too weak, while businesses complained that its vague prohibitions against "monopolization" and "contracts in restraint of trade" created uncertainty. Responding to these concerns, Congress enacted the **Clayton Act of 1914**,[2] which contained a number of specific prohibitions against price discrimination, tying arrangements, and anticompetitive mergers, among others. The Clayton Act was intended not only to provide greater clarity, but to prevent mergers in their incipiency rather

At the turn of the twentieth century there was widespread popular condemnation of large business combinations called "trusts" that were perceived to be exerting unbridled control over both industry and government alike. This 1904 cartoon portrays the Standard Oil trust as an octopus that literally has within its grip the U.S. Congress, and the shipping, oil, and other industries, and is about to grab hold of the White House (lower left corner). Does this cartoon have relevance today? *Illustration entitled "Next!" by Udo J. Keppler*, Puck *magazine*, vol. 56, no. 1436 (Sept. 7, 1904), courtesy of the Library of Congress.

---

[1] 15 U.S.C. §§ 1–7.
[2] 15 U.S.C. §§ 12–27.

than waiting until they were consummated only to then break them up by enforcement under the Sherman Act. Earlier the same year, the **Federal Trade Commission Act** (FTC Act)[3] established the Federal Trade Commission (FTC) and broadly prohibited "unfair methods of competition."

State Antitrust Laws

Although the Sherman Act of 1890 was the first federal antitrust law, states had adopted their own antitrust legislation as early as 1867. By 1915, at least 35 states had adopted antitrust laws. Today every state and the District of Columbia have antitrust laws. Under the Supremacy Clause, state antitrust laws must not conflict with federal laws (see Chapter 3, "Constitutional Issues in Business"). Because state laws vary, the remainder of this chapter will focus on federal antitrust law except where noted.

The Sherman Act of 1890

The Sherman Act of 1890 contains two major provisions. The first, contained in § 1 of the statute, prohibits contracts or combinations that restrain trade. The second, in § 2, prohibits monopolization or attempted monopolization. The statute provides:

> **An Ethical Insight: Aristotle — Virtue of Justice and Antitrust Laws**
>
> "All virtue is summed up in dealing justly." This simple ethical principle is useful in the study of antitrust law, as competitors should be able to compete on a "level playing field," and a monopoly destroys that fairness.

§ 1: "Every contract, combination in the form of trust or otherwise, or conspiracy, in restraint of trade . . . is declared to be illegal."

§ 2: "Every person who shall monopolize, or attempt to monopolize any part of the trade or commerce . . . shall be deemed guilty of a felony."

The terms "restraint of trade" and "monopolization" are broad and may be viewed as providing little specific guidance as to what activities are prohibited. Fortunately, more than 120 years of interpretation by the judiciary have provided some degree of clarity as to what is prohibited under the statute. Each of the provisions, as interpreted by the courts, will be examined in turn.

Sherman Act § 1: Contracts in Restraint of Trade

Activities that violate § 1 of the Sherman Act fall within one of three principal categories: (1) price fixing, (2) market division, and (3) boycotting. Activities related to any of these three categories may be further classified as either horizontal or vertical. Furthermore, each type of activity may be condemned

---

[3]15 U.S.C. §§ 41–58.

Exhibit 11.2. Vertical Versus Horizontal Restraints

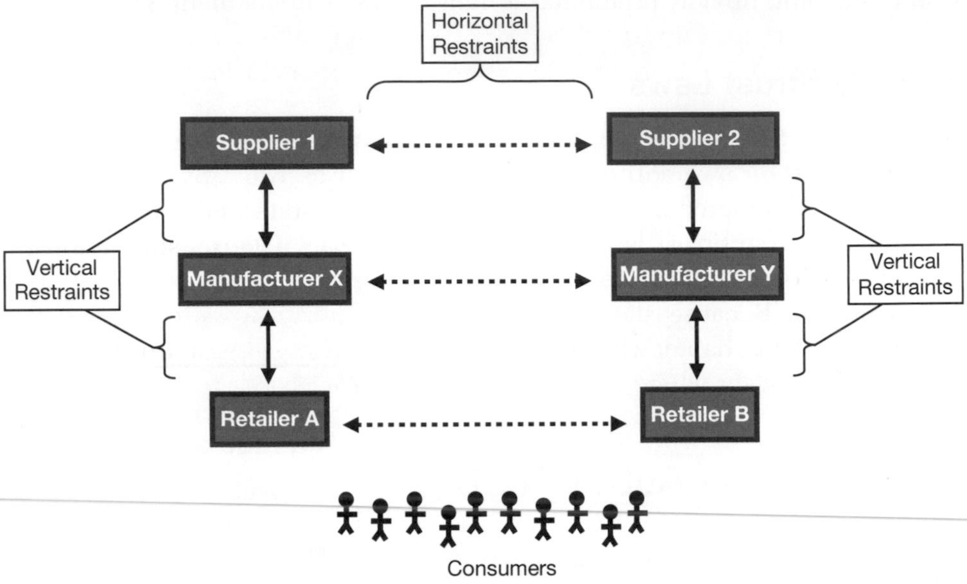

by the judiciary as illegal per se, or treated less harshly under the more flexible "rule of reason" standard.

Vertical Versus Horizontal Restraints

Horizontal restraints include those agreements or actions that involve businesses at the same level of the distribution chain. For example, an agreement between two or more suppliers to divide the market such that one sells only to manufacturers located east of the Mississippi River, and another sells only to manufacturers located west of the Mississippi River, would be classified as horizontal market allocation. **Vertical restraints** involve parties at different levels of the distribution chain. For example, an agreement between a manufacturer and a retailer by which the retailer agrees not to discount products below a certain price would be classified as vertical price fixing. Horizontal restraints are therefore often agreements among competitors, while vertical restraints are more commonly agreements between a party and its supplier or business customer (see Exhibit 11.2).

"Per Se" Versus "Rule of Reason"

Certain types of agreements are classified as **illegal per se** (illegal automatically, without further analysis). For example, horizontal price fixing is generally considered to be illegal per se. This means that once a court determines that horizontal price fixing has occurred, it will find the activity to be illegal auto-matically, irrespective of arguments by the defendants that the price-fixing arrangement served some beneficial purpose. Most business activities, however, are judged using the more lenient **rule of reason** standard, under which the court will consider the particular circumstances of the business environment and the likely effects of the restraint before determining whether or not it violates the antitrust laws. If the rule of reason standard is applied, the challenged activity is much more likely to be allowed.

Because the standard of analysis is not specified in the statute, it falls to the courts to determine whether a particular type of activity is to be judged under the per se or rule of reason standard. As a result, the standard used for a given type of activity may change over time as new evidence emerges or as judicial attitudes change. For example, until recently the Supreme Court had held that it was illegal per se for a manufacturer to agree with its distributor to set the minimum or maximum price the distributor could charge for the manufac-turer's goods. In two separate decisions in 1997 and 2007, however, the Court overruled its prior case law on this point. Therefore, vertical price restraints, whether minimum or maximum, are now judged under the rule of reason standard, meaning they are now more likely than before to be lawful.[4]

A Sliding Scale

Although the per se and rule of reason standards are often described as distinct categories, the Supreme Court has cautioned that "there is often no bright line separating *per se* from Rule of Reason analysis."[5] Instead, courts may flexibly analyze antitrust violations using a "sliding scale"[6] that allows for some intermediate amount of analysis. For example, where justice requires, a court may probe more deeply into the business context when analyzing alleged violations that might normally be judged under the per se standard. This flex-ible approach is illustrated by the case of *United States v. Brown University*, discussed in the In-Depth Ethical Case Analysis on page 330. The Third Circuit declined to rigidly apply the per se rule to a horizontal price-fixing agreement by a group of nonprofit universities.

Horizontal Price Fixing

Horizontal price fixing is the classic example of conduct that constitutes *a per se* violation of § 1 of the Sherman Act. In its most basic form, **horizontal price fixing** occurs where two or more parties at the same level of distribution agree to sell a product at a specified price. However, horizontal price fixing also

---

[4]*Leegan Creative Leather Prods. v. PSKS, Inc.*, 551 U.S. 877 (2007) (minimum price fixing); *State Oil Co. v. Khan*, 522 U.S. 3 (1997) (maximum price fixing).
[5]*Nat'l Collegiate Athletic Ass'n v. Bd. of Regents of Univ. of Okla.*, 468 U.S. 85 (1984).
[6]*Cal. Dental Ass'n v. FTC*, 526 U.S. 756 (1999).

includes less obvious means of "raising, depressing, fixing, pegging, or stabilizing" prices.[7] For example, an agreement between competitors to restrict the quantity of a product can have the effect of raising prices and would be classified as a horizontal price restraint. Horizontal price fixing often occurs in the context of a **cartel**, a group of producers or sellers that coordinate a product's price or volume.

A violation of § 1 of the Sherman Act cannot occur without **concerted action** (agreement) between two or more parties. For example, a retailer will generally not be held to violate the Sherman Act if it periodically monitors its competitors' prices and lowers its own prices to remain competitive. Indeed, the lowering of prices in response to competitive pressure is the essence of free competition.

The following case addresses alleged horizontal price fixing among Ivy League universities in setting their tuition, demonstrating that even nonprofit institutions are subject to the antitrust laws.

In-Depth Ethical Case Analysis

United States v. Brown University, 5 F.3d 658 (3d Cir. 1993)

Facts

In 1958, the eight Ivy League institutions (Brown, Columbia, Cornell, Dartmouth, Harvard, Princeton, the University of Pennsylvania, and Yale) and the Massachusetts Institute of Technology (MIT) began to coordinate financial aid offerings to students who were admitted by two or more of those institutions. The nine institutions agreed in writing "to share financial information concerning admitted candidates in an annual 'Ivy Overlap' meeting just prior to mid-April" of each year. The agreement further stated that "[t]he purpose of the overlap agreement is to neutralize the effect of financial aid so that a student may choose among Ivy Group institutions for non-financial reasons.... [Students and their families] will be asked to pay approximately the same amount regardless of the Ivy Group institution they choose to attend." Stanford refused an invitation to participate, believing that the agreement violated the antitrust laws.

The Antitrust Division of the U.S. Department of Justice (DOJ) brought a civil antitrust action against the universities, alleging horizontal price fixing in violation of § 1 of the Sherman Act. All eight Ivy League institutions immediately entered into a consent decree with the DOJ, leaving only MIT to defend the charges (the name of the case, *United States v. Brown University*, was nevertheless retained for the duration of the proceedings). MIT conceded that it had entered into an agreement with the other institutions but offered two principal justifications in defense. First, it argued that § 1 of the Sherman Act, which prohibits price fixing, did not apply to the agreement because the statute bars only "contracts ... in restraint of *trade or commerce*" (emphasis added), and that as a

---

[7]*United States v. Socony-Vacuum Oil Co.*, 310 U.S. 150 (1940).

nonprofit institution, MIT was not engaged in "trade or commerce." Second it argued that without the agreement, the universities would, "one by one, succumb to . . . pressures to attract the most desirable students and, eventually, engage in a bidding war for the 'best of the brightest' by offering merit scholarships and increased grant awards. As a consequence, the universities [would] find it necessary to shift 'limited' financial aid resources to highly qualified but non-needy students, which in turn [would] significantly decrease the availability of need-based aid."

Issue

May universities share financial aid data and thus "fix" the price of tuition?

Holding

Maybe. The universities' activities must be judged under the rule of reason.

From the Court's Opinion

The district court held that the agreement violated the antitrust laws, but the Third Circuit reversed and remanded. The Third Circuit first held that nonprofit organizations, including universities, were indeed subject to the antitrust laws. It reasoned that "[t]he exchange of money for services, even by a nonprofit organization, is a quintessential commercial transaction." The circuit court also implicitly concluded that the challenged agreement constituted a horizontal price restraint. However, the court allowed for the possibility that procompetitive and proconsumer implications of the agreement might outweigh the drawbacks. According to the circuit court:

> *A trade-off may need to be made between providing some financial aid to a large number of the most needy students or allowing the free market to bestow the limited financial aid on the very few most talented who may not need financial aid to attain their academic goals. Under such circumstances, if this trade-off is proven to be worthy in terms of obtaining a more diverse student body (or other legitimate institutional goals), the limitation on the choices of the most talented students might not be so egregious [as to require condemnation under the antitrust laws].*

Before the district court could issue another decision, however, MIT entered into a settlement agreement with the DOJ, under the terms of which neither party fully prevailed. MIT was prohibited from discussing individual student awards with other universities, as it had in the past, but could share aggregated financial aid data.

Note

Although horizontal price fixing is normally held to be illegal per se, the Third Circuit in this case indicated that a balancing of procompetitive and anticompetitive effects was required. Such balancing is normally reserved for the rule of reason standard and only rarely applies to horizontal price fixing or market allocation. The court held that this was one of those rare cases. It reasoned that the purpose of the challenged activity of fixing financial aid awards was to serve the public interest rather than to maximize profits, and noted that MIT "sets tuition considerably below its cost to begin with, and could fill its class each year with affluent students who do not need financial assistance." These factors made the activity sufficiently unlike ordinary horizontal price fixing to escape automatic condemnation under the per se rule.

Ethical Issue

Is it ethical for a group of universities to agree to offer the same financial aid package to admitted students rather than enter into a "bidding war for the best and brightest students," given that financial aid resources are limited and a bidding war would likely reduce the amount of available need-based financial aid?

Ethical Arguments Supporting the Overlap Agreement

Jeremy Bentham and John Stuart Mill — Utilitarianism

A utilitarian might argue that the overlap agreement is ethical. The most qualified students benefit by being able to choose the best academic institution without regard to financial aid, since all participating institutions agree to offer such students approximately the same financial aid package. Needy students benefit from the more generous financial aid offers made possible by the overlap agreement. A rule utilitarian would likely "subtract" from these benefits the loss of utility caused by highly qualified students receiving less financial aid than they would receive under a market-based system, but might conclude that the net gain nevertheless remains positive.

Oliver Wendell Holmes, Jr. — Legal Realism

A legal realist might argue that an overarching social goal is to provide broad access to high-quality education. Because highly qualified students are likely to attend a top university in any event, the overlap agreement promotes the social end of helping more people, particularly needy students, attend an Ivy Group institution of their choice. When possible, legal realism allows the facts to dictate the rules rather than imposing a formal rule of law, such as the per se illegality of horizontal price fixing, that must be rigidly followed.

John Rawls — The Original Position

Those in the original position would not know whether they would be one of the "large number of . . . most needy students" or "the very few most talented" students. Not knowing in which group they would belong, they might be willing to trade off the small possibility of additional merit-based financial aid for the greater certainty that, if admitted, they would receive sufficient aid to attend the institution of their choice.

Ethical Arguments Against the Overlap Agreement

Immanuel Kant — Categorical Imperatives

The overlap agreement reduces the aid that the most qualified students would otherwise be offered based upon their merit, for the purpose of achieving one or more social ends, such as the attainment of a more diverse student body. This could be viewed as violating Kant's categorical imperative to "act in such a way that you treat humanity, whether in your own person or in the person of another, always at the same time as an end and never simply as a means."

W.D. Ross — Prima Facie Duty of Nonmalfeasance

The *duty of nonmalfeasance* is a duty not to cause harm to others. In this case, the overlap agreement causes harm to some students by denying them the possibility of aid that they rightfully earned through hard work and achievement. In this view, universities are "consumers" of highly qualified students, financial aid is the price paid to attract those students, and the overlap agreement can be condemned as horizontal price fixing for the same reason it is condemned in other circumstances: it causes distortions and harm both to the market itself and to individual participants within that market.

Conclusion

This is a difficult case to analyze from an ethical perspective because it appears that qualified students not needing financial aid may be paying a financial price in the form of higher tuition costs in order to benefit needy students and the university environment. MIT's settlement agreement with the DOJ may be a reasonable and ethical compromise.

Vertical Price Fixing

Vertical price fixing (also known as resale price maintenance) occurs where a seller and a buyer agree to set the price at which the buyer may resell the product. The most common type of vertical price fixing is **minimum resale price maintenance**, where a supplier specifies the minimum price at which a retailer can resell a product. A resale price maintenance provision might be included in a contract for a number of reasons, such as to promote a product as a premium brand, or to ensure sufficient margins and thereby encourage retailers to provide customer service or to promote the product.

Vertical price fixing can also include the specifying of a *maximum* price at which a retailer can sell a product, also known as **maximum resale price maintenance**.

Case Illustration

In the landmark case of *State Oil Co. v. Khan*, a unanimous Supreme Court observed that a supplier of gasoline might wish to limit the price that one of its buyers (a retail gas station) could charge for gas. The supplier might wish to impose a price limit because "the higher the price at which gasoline is resold, the smaller the volume sold, and so the lower the profit to the supplier if the higher profit per gallon at the higher price is being snared by the [gas station]." The maximum price restraint was ultimately upheld as permissible under the rule of reason standard. *State Oil Co. v. Khan*, 522 U.S. 3 (1997).

Manager's Compliance and Ethics Meeting

Ethics of Collusive Bidding and Antitrust Law

Recall that a company's *compliance and ethics program* requires management to exercise *due diligence* to prevent and detect criminal conduct and encourage ethical behavior. Because antitrust violations can be serious crimes that can subject the corporation and its employees to criminal penalties, including fines and jail sentences, as well as civil liability, monitoring of employee conduct is the best legal and ethical practice.

A large construction company is bidding on a government contract, expected to total over $100 million, to build an extension to the building that houses the Environmental Protection Agency. The company wishes to stay clear of practices, often used in government contract procurement, that may violate the antitrust laws, such as bid rigging.

In accordance with the amendments to the *2001 Sentencing Guidelines* (see Chapter 2, "Ethics in the Business Environment"), Carol, the construction company's sales manager, has been asked by the CEO to prepare an effective training program for her sales force to review illegal practices in contract bidding. Carol has reviewed with corporate counsel the illegality of price fixing with other bidders. One of the sales employees has asked Carol if it is legal and ethical to agree with a small contractor that the latter not bid, or that it submit a high bid, in return for a promise to be given a lucrative subcontract. Carol has referred him to the *compliance and ethics program* that specifically references the Sherman Act and Federal Trade Commission Act that would subject the company and the employee engaging in that practice to criminal and civil liability with a corporate fine up to $100 million and an individual penalty for the employee of up to $1 million or imprisonment of up to 10 years, or both.* Civil suits allow an injunction against the contractor prohibiting the antitrust behavior and/or civil awards of up to three times actual damages plus attorney fees.

Carol has explained the ethics issue by examining a few ethical theories that are relevant to price-fixing and collusive bidding practices.

Kant — Categorical Imperative. Kant's categorical imperative that one "always act in such a manner that your actions could become a universal law" would prohibit the agreement with the smaller company. If all bidders engaged in such anticompetitive conduct, trust in the bidding system would erode, and government employees might turn to alternate means of selecting contractors, such as cronyism (favoring friends) or nepotism (favoring relatives). Honest bidders would be adversely affected.

John Rawls — The Original Position and Equal Basic Liberties. Those in Rawls's original position would not know whether they would be collusive bidders, honest bidders, the government entity seeking the bids, or taxpayers. If they are any of the latter three, they would favor a system that prohibits collusive bidding. He stated that "each person has the same indefeasible claim to a fully adequate scheme of equal basic liberties, which scheme is compatible with the same scheme of liberties for all." Collusive bidding would negate that principle.

Jeremy Bentham and John Stuart Mill — Utilitarianism. Any gain to collusive bidders in the form of higher prices will be offset by an equal loss to taxpayers, producing no net gain to society. In addition, harm to honest bidders and erosion of trust caused by collusion will create a net social loss.

W.D. Ross — Prima Facie Duty of Justice. The prima facie duty of justice would hold collusive bidding to be unethical because the assumption made by honest bidders and the government is that all bids are based on genuine estimates of cost and are not inflated by bid rigging.

Conclusion. Carol reported her extensive training session with the sales force to the CEO. If a salesperson later engaged in collusive bidding, the employee would be subject to criminal and civil liability, but since the construction company was in compliance with the 2001 amendments to the Sentencing Guidelines, it could present evidence of the training program to mitigate the resulting fine.

---

* Sherman Antitrust Act, 15 U.S.C. §§ 1–7; Federal Trade Commission Act, 15 U.S.C. § 45(a).

Horizontal Market Allocation

Horizontal market allocation occurs where two or more businesses at the same level of distribution agree that each will only sell to a defined portion of the market. Like horizontal price fixing, these agreements are illegal per se. For example, the Supreme Court has held that it is illegal for two providers of bar preparation courses (including market leader "BAR/BRI") to agree that one would market its course only to aspiring lawyers outside of the state of Georgia, while the other would market its competing course only to those within Georgia.[8] The BAR/BRI case is an example of geographic

---

[8]*Palmer v. BRG of Georgia, Inc.,* 498 U.S. 46 (1990).

market allocation. Other forms of illegal market allocation involve dividing markets by customer or by product (see Case Illustration at right).

Vertical Market Allocation

Manufacturers may wish to assign distributors or retailers exclusive territories in order to protect each distributor or retailer from competition, an arrangement known as **vertical market allocation**. One possible motivation for allocating exclusive territories is that it limits retailers from competing with each other on price, thereby preserving margins and allowing for higher levels of service or promotion. Without such exclusive territories, one retailer could "free-ride" on the promotional activities of another retailer and thereby sell at a lower price, which might cause the other retailer to eliminate its service offerings or reduce its promotion of the product. While vertical market allocation was formerly deemed to be illegal per se by the Supreme Court,[9] the rule of reason is now applied.[10]

Case Illustration

Blockbuster, Inc., offered thousands of movies for immediate viewing over the Internet, as well as more than 100,000 movies and games for rental via U.S. mail. Subscribers of the Blockbuster service brought suit against competitors Netflix and Wal-Mart, accusing them of dividing up the market for online DVD rentals such that Wal-Mart would only sell movies while Netflix would only rent them. The plaintiffs alleged that the price they paid for Blockbuster rentals was higher than it would have been had Wal-Mart stayed in the DVD rental market. In fact, Wal-Mart did exit the DVD rental market after the Netflix/Wal-Mart "promotional agreement" was announced, and two months after Wal-Mart's exit, Blockbuster announced a price increase for its rental service from $14.99 to $17.99 per month — the same price Netflix was charging. Despite the evidence that defendants Netflix and Wal-Mart had divided the market, the defendants nevertheless prevailed because, according to the court, the plaintiffs' injury was indirect (Blockbuster was not a party to the agreement, or to the suit) and the plaintiffs therefore lacked antitrust standing. *In re Online DVD Rental Antitrust Litigation*, No. M 09–2029 PJH, 2011 WL 1629663 (N.D. Cal. Apr. 29, 2011).

Group Boycott

A **group boycott** occurs when two or more parties refuse to buy from, sell to, or otherwise deal with a third party. Where the conspiring parties include entities at different levels of distribution, the boycott is a vertical boycott. Otherwise, it is a horizontal group boycott. It is important to note that the most common type of boycott — refusing to purchase from or otherwise deal with a seller for *political* reasons — is generally considered protected expression under the First Amendment and therefore unlikely to be condemned under the Sherman Act. Boycotts for *commercial* reasons, by contrast, are more vulnerable to antitrust scrutiny (see Case Illustration next page).

---

[9]*United States v. Arnold Schwinn & Co.*, 388 U.S. 365 (1967).
[10]*Continental TV Inc. v. GTE Sylvania Inc.*, 433 U.S. 36 (1977).

Case Illustration

Toys are sold in a number of different kinds of stores. At the high end are traditional toy stores and department stores, both of which typically sell toys for 40 to 50 percent above their cost. Next are the specialized discount stores such as Toys "R" Us that sell at an average 30 percent markup. General discounters like Wal-Mart and Target are next, with a 22 percent markup, and last are the warehouse clubs such as Costco, with a slender markup of only 9 percent or so. Warehouse clubs were a retail innovation of the late 1970s: the first one opened in 1976, and by 1992 there were some 600 individual club stores around the country. Faced with this competitive threat, Toys "R" Us orchestrated a horizontal agreement among its key suppliers (including Mattel, Hasbro, Fisher Price, and Tyco) to refuse to sell to the clubs. The FTC found that Toys "R" Us had engaged in an illegal boycott, a conclusion upheld on appeal to the Seventh Circuit. *Toys "R" Us, Inc. v. FTC,* 221 F.3d 928 (7th Cir. 2000).

Selling Versus Buying

Although Sherman Act § 1 is most commonly thought of as applying to agreements between *sellers* that restrain trade, agreements between commercial *buyers* may also be challenged under the antitrust laws (see Case Illustration next page). Buy-side agreements that potentially violate the Sherman Act may be more likely to arise in markets where a small number of powerful buyers are able to collude in order to depress the prices received by sellers, a situation known as an **oligopsony**.[11]

Sherman Act § 2: Monopolies

Section 1 of the Sherman Act prohibits agreements between *two or more* parties to fix prices, allocate markets, boycott third parties, or otherwise engage in unreasonable "restraints of trade" (Exhibit 11.3). Section 2 of the Sherman Act, in contrast, can be violated by a *single* party acting alone. It provides: "Every person who shall monopolize, or attempt to monopolize any part of the trade or commerce . . . shall be deemed guilty of a felony."

Exhibit 11.3. Sherman Act § 1, Summary Chart

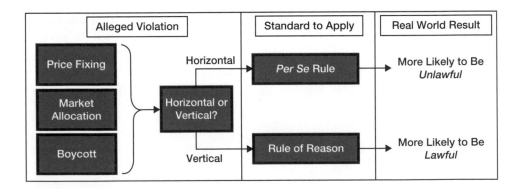

---

[11]In economic terminology, *oligopsony* (few buyers) and *monopsony* (single buyer) are the buy-side counterparts to *oligopoly* (few sellers) and *monopoly* (single seller).

What Is Monopolization?

In the context of antitrust, **monopolization** occurs whenever one firm has the ability to restrict output or raise prices above the competitive level *and* has attained this market power through anticompetitive (unfair) conduct. A business is more likely to be found to have market power where that business has a large market share in a given product and geographic market. Although there are no precise cut-offs, a market share of 67 percent (i.e., about two-thirds) or more is likely to suggest the presence of market power. Market share measures can be substantially influenced by both the geographic and product definition of the market.

A Sherman Act § 2 violation will not be found simply because a firm controls too much, or all, of a given market. In addition to the mere possession of monopoly power, the defendant must have engaged in unfair practices to achieve that power. The most commonly alleged unfair practice is **predatory pricing**, where the defendant sells a product below cost in order to drive competitors out of business. Once the competitor is forced out of the market, the party engaged in predatory pricing might then be able to raise prices above competitive levels, causing injury to consumers.

Case Illustration

In the state of Maine, wild blueberries are "farmed" by approximately 400 growers, who sell their berries to a small number of wild blueberry processors. In 2000, four of these growers brought suit under the Maine counterpart to Sherman Act § 1, alleging that the processors had conspired to fix at artificially low levels the prices they would pay to the growers. In addition, the seller-growers alleged that the buyer-processors had allocated the market by agreeing not to solicit each other's growers, and further that at least one defendant had threatened to boycott any grower that sold to a Canadian processor. A jury awarded the growers $18.68 million. *Pease v. Jasper Wyman & Son*, 845 A.2d 552 (Me. 2004).

Blueberry harvesting in Maine. Can antitrust law apply to agreements between buyers?

Case Illustration

Students irked at the high price of new textbooks may perceive a university bookstore to be "monopolizing" the market. In a Sherman Act § 2 monopolization action, the students would likely argue for a narrow definition of the geographic and product markets, while the bookstore could argue for a wider definition of the market. For example, the bookstore might argue that the relevant "market" should include Internet sales and sales from stores in neighboring towns (the geographic component) because the inclusion of these sources would make the bookstore's market share seem smaller. The bookstore might further argue that the "market" should be defined to include used textbooks in addition to new ones (the product component), for the same reason. The broader the market definition, the smaller percentage of the market the defendant will appear to control, and the less likely it will be found to have violated the antitrust laws.

An Ethical Insight: Jeremy Bentham — Utilitarianism and Antitrust Laws

Jeremy Bentham, the founder of utilitarianism, once stated: "It is the greatest good to the greatest number of people which is the measure of right and wrong." Bentham proposed that an act is ethical if a greater number of people benefits from its effect. A utilitarian could argue that antitrust laws are "right" because they encourage competition that benefits numerous consumers, even though competition may reduce the financial gain reaped by a much smaller number of sellers.

The Clayton Act of 1914

In contrast to the broad provisions of the Sherman Act, the Clayton Act provides more specific prohibitions against price discrimination (§ 2), tying (§ 3), anticompetitive mergers (§ 7), and interlocking boards of directors (§ 8). (These practices might also be challenged under the Sherman Act.) Each prohibition is examined in turn.

Clayton Act § 2: Price Discrimination

The Clayton Act § 2, as amended by the **Robinson-Patman Act of 1936**, prohibits certain types of **price discrimination**. Economists define price discrimination in general as the offering of identical or similar goods to different buyers at different prices, where the difference in price cannot be explained by differences in the cost of production. Price discrimination is a very common business practice, as reflected in the Case Illustration on page 339.

Although the movie theaters and universities are practicing price discrimination, this type of price discrimination is not prohibited by Section 2 of the Clayton Act (the section sometimes referred to as the Robinson-Patman Act), because the Clayton Act does not precisely follow the economic definition of price discrimination. Instead, § 2 makes it unlawful *to discriminate in price between different purchasers of commodities of like grade and quality . . . where the effect of such discrimination may be substantially to lessen competition or tend to create a monopoly in any line of commerce, or to injure, destroy, or prevent competition with any person who either grants or knowingly receives the benefit of such discrimination, or with customers of either of them . . . .*

The Clayton Act therefore does not prohibit all price discrimination, but only price discrimination "of commodities" that "substantially . . . lessen[s] competition or tend[s] to create a monopoly." Thus, the Clayton Act does not prohibit price discrimination in services, because services are not "commodities." (Price discrimination of services may, however, be subject to challenge under the Sherman Act, discussed above, and the FTC Act, discussed below.) Similarly, some forms of price discrimination do not run afoul of the antitrust laws because they do not substantially lessen competition or tend to create a monopoly. In the Case Illustration above, the movie theaters and universities escape Clayton Act condemnation both because their offerings are not "commodities" and also because price discrimination in these circumstances most likely cannot be shown to "lessen competition or tend to create a monopoly."

Case Illustration

Movie theaters practice price discrimination when they offer tickets for identical movies at different prices (e.g., regular price versus student price) to different buyers (e.g., general population versus students). Similarly, universities practice price discrimination when they offer different levels of financial aid to students, thus creating different tuition "prices" that different students must pay to attend the same university.

Price discrimination claims can be classified as primary line injury, secondary line injury, or tertiary line injury, depending on the identity of the injured party.

Primary Line Injury

A **primary line injury** involves price discrimination that injures *competitors* of the discriminating seller (see Exhibit 11.4 on page 340). It most frequently occurs where a defendant sells a product at different prices in different geographic locations, with the object of eliminating or stifling competition. For example, in the landmark predatory pricing case of *Utah Pie Co. v. Continental Baking Co.*,[12] Utah Pie alleged that it had suffered a primary line injury when the defendants priced their pies lower in the Utah market than they had elsewhere in the country, for the purpose of putting Utah Pie out of busi-

An Ethical Insight: Immanuel Kant and Antitrust Behavior

"So act that your principle of action might safely be made a law for the whole world." Imagine if no antitrust laws existed and powerful companies could put smaller ones out of business or keep them from entering the market. Viewed through this Kantian lens, anticompetitive behavior practiced without restraint throughout the world might be condemned because it would stifle fair competition, cause prices to rise, and potentially widen the gap between rich and poor.

ness. Following a landmark 1993 Supreme Court case[13] that reinterpreted and broadened the Sherman Act, § 2 of the Sherman Act (prohibiting monopolization) now overlaps with Clayton Act predatory pricing claims to such an extent that primary line cases under the Clayton Act are no longer frequent.

Secondary Line Injury

A **secondary line injury** involves price discrimination that injures competition among *customers* of the discriminating seller. This is the most common type of price discrimination claim under § 2. It also reflects the underlying motivation of Congress in implementing the Robinson-Patman amendments to § 2 of the

---

[12]386 U.S. 685 (1967).
[13]*Brooke Group Ltd. v. Brown & Williamson Tobacco Corp.*, 509 U.S. 209 (1993).

Clayton Act, namely, that Congress sought to prevent price discrimination that benefited large buyers while threatening small independent ones. Concern for small buyers can be understood by recalling that the Robinson-Patman Act was enacted in 1936, during the depths of the Great Depression, when chain stores proliferated in small towns and threatened the established business structure.

Tertiary Line Injury

A **tertiary line injury** involves price discrimination that injures the customers of the differently treated purchasers, even if the favored and disfavored purchasers do not compete with each other.

Defenses

Even if price differences that injure competition are found to exist, there will be no antitrust violation if the defendant can demonstrate that:

■ The differences in price were justified by differences in cost (e.g., volume discounts, higher transport cost).
■ Changing conditions necessitated a reduction in price (e.g., seasonal goods at end of season, going out of business sale, or discounts on perishable goods).
■ The lower price was made in good faith to meet an equally low price offered by a competitor.

Exhibit 11.4 illustrates one possible scenario involving primary, secondary, and tertiary line injury under § 2 of the Clayton Act. If Manufacturer X produces a gallon of milk at a cost of $1.50 and normally sells it to Wholesalers 1

Exhibit 11.4. Price Discrimination Under the Clayton Act: An Example

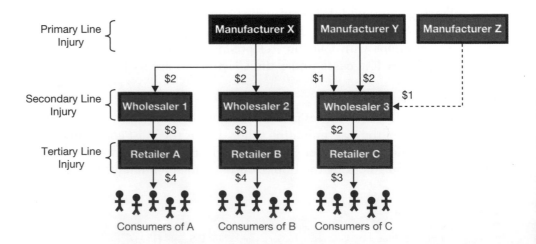

and 2 for $2.00, it cannot lawfully sell to Wholesaler 3 for $1 for the purpose of putting Manufacturer Y out of business. If X does sell at $1 to Wholesaler 3, Y could bring suit for primary line injury because Y is a competitor of the party engaged in price discrimination (X). However, if X reduced its price to $1 in order to meet a competing offer of Manufacturer Z, then X would have a valid defense to the claim of price discrimination.

Now suppose Z does not exist, and that a $1 markup is levied at each level of distribution. If X again sells at a lower price to Wholesaler 3, Wholesalers 1 and 2 (assuming they are in competition with Wholesaler 3) could bring a claim against X for secondary line injury, since they were customers of the discriminating seller and paid the higher price ($2 versus $1). Finally, Retailers A and B could bring a claim for tertiary line injury, since they might lose customers to Retailer C as a result of the price discrimination by X. The potential price-discriminating defendant is in dark red, while the potential plaintiffs are in green. As you might imagine from these examples, the details of complaints brought under the Clayton Act can be highly complex.

Recommendation to Repeal the Robinson-Patman Act

In 2002, Congress authorized an Antitrust Modernization Commission to evaluate and make recommendations to improve U.S. antitrust law. The resulting 2007 Commission Report described the antitrust laws as sound overall but recommended the repeal of the Robinson-Patman price discrimination provision (i.e., a repeal of Clayton Act § 2). The Commission explained that "[o]ver time, many businesses have found ways to comply with [§ 2] by, for example, differentiating products, so they can sell somewhat different products to different purchasers at different prices . . . [the effect of which is to] increase the seller's costs — and thus increase costs to consumers. . . ." In addition, the Commission found that the Robinson-Patman Act "makes it difficult for the United States to advocate against the adoption and use of similar laws against U.S. companies operating in other jurisdictions." In spite of the Commission's report (and similarly critical prior reports issued in 1955, 1969, and 1977), the price discrimination prohibition remains in force.

Case Illustration

The most infamous recent example of tying was Microsoft's decision to bundle its Internet Explorer (IE) Web browser (the tied product) with its Windows operating system (the tying product). Microsoft argued that IE and Windows were not separate products, and thus could not violate the tying prohibition. The district court disagreed, finding that consumers perceived them to be separate products. The court also rejected Microsoft's argument that the arrangement could not constitute tying because the Web browser was given away for free rather than sold, noting that consumers were forced to pay for IE as a part of the price paid for Windows. Later, however, the D.C. Circuit determined that the tying arrangement should be judged under the more lenient rule-of-reason standard due to the potential efficiencies of the bundling, and the plaintiffs eventually dropped the tying claim from the suit. *United States v. Microsoft Corp.*, 231 F.Supp.2d 144 (D.D.C. 2002), *aff'd sub nom. Massachusetts v. Microsoft Corp.*, 373 F.3d 1199 (D.C. Cir. 2004).

Clayton Act § 3: Tying Arrangements

Section 3 of the Clayton Act prohibits selling one item (the **tying product**) on the condition that the buyer also purchase a second item (the **tied product**).

Although tying is usually considered to be illegal per se, it is evident from the Case Illustration on page 341 that courts may apply the rule of reason standard if they feel it is warranted under the circumstances. Tying arrangements are prohibited as to both products (under § 3 of the Clayton Act) and services (under § 1 of the Sherman Act), and can also be challenged under § 5 of the FTC Act.

Tying and Price Discrimination

Businesses sometimes employ tying arrangements in order to generate additional revenue by forcing all consumers of the tying product to buy more than they desire. Sometimes, however, there may be a less obvious motivation at play, namely, the desire to charge high-volume users a higher total price than low-volume users by charging a relatively low price for the tying product and a relatively high price for the tied product. For example, businesses may charge a low price for video game systems, such as the Sony PlayStation, and a high price for games compatible with that system. Because gamers who play many hours per day can be expected to buy more games than those who play only infrequently, the high-volume users effectively pay more for their gaming activities. Other examples include printers (tying product) and ink cartridges (tied product), razors and razor blades, and smart phones and smart phone service contracts.

Although the sale of two complementary products is not unlawful in itself, businesses should exercise caution in conditioning the purchase of one product on the purchase of another if the effect would be to harm competition. In the landmark case *IBM Corp. v. United States*, the Supreme Court considered the legality of IBM's efforts to discriminate between high- and low-volume users by conditioning the lease of its computers on the purchase of its computer cards.

Clayton Act § 7: Mergers

Section 1 of the Sherman Act limits the ability of two or more firms to fix prices, allocate markets, or otherwise restrain trade. However, absent additional limits, businesses prohibited from *agreeing* with other firms to constrain trade could circumvent the Sherman Act prohibitions by simply *acquiring or merging with* competitors. Once merged, the now-enlarged company could do within a single firm what would have previously required an agreement between firms. Of course, should the merger result in monopolization, it could then be vulnerable to a claim under § 2 of the Sherman Act. After a merger is consummated, however, management teams may become intertwined and assets comingled, and at this point the merger would be costly and wasteful to

IBM Corp. v. United States, 298 U.S. 131 (1936)

Facts: In the 1930s, early computers called "business machines" could be used to sort, add, tabulate, and compare data entered and stored on punched cards that could be fed into the machines. International Business Machines (IBM) was the market leader, selling approximately 3 billion cards annually, constituting 81 percent of the market. Its success in the punched card market was linked to its success in the business machine market, in which it was a duopolist along with competitor Remington Rand. Rather than selling its business machines, however, IBM leased them on the condition that the lease would terminate if any cards not manufactured by IBM were used in the leased machines. Thus, customers needing to store and manipulate large amounts of data, including the newly created Social Security Administration, were forced under the terms of the lease agreements to purchase cards only from IBM.

Issue: May a company contractually prohibit those who lease one of its products (business machines) from purchasing a second product (punched cards) from any other company?

Holding: No. IBM's actions in attempting to control the market in punched cards violate § 3 of the Clayton Act, which prohibits tying arrangements.

From the Court's Opinion: *Despite the plain language of section 3 [of the Clayton Act],* *making unlawful the [contractual] tying clause when it tends to create a monopoly, [IBM] insists that [§ 3] does not forbid tying clauses whose purpose and effect are to protect the good will of the lessor in the leased machines, even though monopoly ensues. In support of this contention appellant places great emphasis on the admitted fact that it is essential to the successful performance of the leased machines that the cards used in them conform, with relatively minute tolerances, to specifications as to size, thickness, and freedom from defects. . . . The point is stressed that failure, even though occasional, to conform to these requirements, causes inaccuracies in the functioning of the machine, serious in their consequences and difficult to trace to their source, with consequent injury to the reputation of the machines and the good will of the lessors. [However, there] is no contention that [other punched card suppliers] cannot meet these requirements. It affirmatively appears, by stipulation, that others are capable of manufacturing cards suitable for use in [IBM's] machines. . . . Appellant is not prevented from proclaiming the virtues of its own cards or warning against the danger of using, in its machines, cards which do not conform to the necessary specifications, or even from making its leases conditional upon the use of cards which conform to them. . . . [S]uch measures would protect its good will, without the creation of monopoly or resort to the suppression of competition.*

undo. Section 7 of the Clayton Act therefore allows mergers to be challenged before they occur.

There are three main types of mergers: horizontal, vertical, and conglomerate. Each will be examined in turn.

Types of Mergers

The type of merger that creates the greatest concern from an antitrust perspective is the **horizontal merger**, a merger between competitors selling similar products in the same market. A **vertical merger** is a merger between businesses occupying different levels of operation for the same product, such as between a manufacturer and a retailer, or between a manufacturer and its supplier. A **conglomerate merger** is a merger between firms in unrelated lines of business or, according to the Supreme Court, "one in which there are no economic relationships between the acquiring and the acquired firm."[14]

Firms may seek to merge horizontally for legitimate reasons, such as to achieve economies of scale, acquire new technologies, or expand into new geographic regions. Vertical mergers may help to guarantee the supply of a required input or a means of distribution for a firm's product. For example, the Walt Disney Company acquired the American Broadcasting Company (ABC) in 1995, ensuring an important television outlet for Disney's feature films. The motivations for conglomerate mergers are less clear but may include the desire to reduce risk via diversification or the desire of firm management to build ever larger empires. Sometimes loosely considered to be subtypes of the conglomerate merger are the **market extension merger**, where a business seeks to expand into a new geographic or customer market via acquisition, and the **product extension merger**, where a business acquires another business in order to extend its product line. An example of the latter is provided in the following Case Illustration.

Case Illustration

Procter & Gamble (P&G) is a large, diversified manufacturer of low-price, high-turnover household products, including Crest toothpaste, Duracell batteries, and Folger's coffee. In 1957 P&G acquired the Clorox Chemical Company, thus adding Clorox bleach to its product line. The merger, however, was soon challenged by the FTC, and a decade of litigation ensued with the case ultimately finding its way to the Supreme Court. The Court first described the acquisition as a "product-extension merger," noting that the product of the acquired company (Clorox) was complementary to those of the acquiring company (P&G) in that it was "produced with similar facilities, marketed through the same channels and in the same manner, and advertised by the same media." Ultimately, the Court concluded that the acquisition was anticompetitive given that the liquid bleach market was already highly concentrated, that the acquisition meant P&G would not independently enter the market as a competitor of Clorox, and that the marketing power of P&G combined with Clorox's 48.8 percent market share might dissuade new entrants. The court ordered the divestiture of Clorox, which was completed in 1969. *FTC v. Procter & Gamble Co.*, 386 U.S. 568 (1967).

Premerger Notification

The **Hart-Scott-Rodino Antitrust Improvements Act of 1976** (HSR) requires large companies contemplating a merger to first notify the FTC and Antitrust Division of the Department of Justice (DOJ). This **premerger notification** provides a waiting period of 30 days, during which the FTC and DOJ can review the notification documents to determine whether the merger would, if consummated, violate the antitrust laws. A decision of the FTC and DOJ to allow a merger does not mean that the merger is necessarily immune from antitrust liability, however. States, individuals, and government regulators of foreign nations are not bound by the FTC-DOJ decision and may still file suit to oppose the merger (see Enforcement section on page 346).

In some cases, the FTC and DOJ will allow a merger to proceed only if one or both of the parties **divests** (sells off) a portion of its business so as to alleviate competitive concerns. For example, when pharmaceutical

---

[14]*FTC v. Procter & Gamble Co.*, 386 U.S. 568 (1967).

giants SmithKline Beecham and Glaxo Wellcome sought to merge to form GlaxoSmithKline, the FTC allowed the deal only on the condition (among others) that SmithKline divest certain antiemetic (anti-nausea) drugs used by cancer patients. Without this divestiture, the combined company would have controlled more than 90 percent of the market for this particular type of drug. Courts may also order divestiture as a remedy in an antitrust action.

FTC and DOJ Merger Guidelines

The FTC and DOJ jointly publish merger guidelines that are publicly available on the DOJ website, www.justice.gov. The guidelines are intended to assist businesses by increasing the transparency of the HSR premerger notification review process. For instance, the website explains that when determining whether a horizontal merger would result in an unacceptable increase in market concentration, the FTC and DOJ use the **Herfindahl-Hirschman Index**. This index is calculated by summing the squares of the market shares of individual firms and ranges from near zero (perfect competition) to 10,000 (monopoly). For example, a market with three firms with market shares of 40 percent, 40 percent, and 20 percent would have an index of 3,600 (i.e., $40^2 + 40^2 + 20^2 = 3,600$). A market with a single-firm monopoly would have an index of 10,000 (i.e., 100^2). Under the guidelines, if the market subsequent to the merger would have an index of less than 1,500, it is unlikely to be challenged as anticompetitive.

Celler-Kefauver Act of 1950

Section 7 of the Clayton Act originally applied only to mergers between competitors that took place via stock acquisition. This left a loophole, however, in that firms could still consummate an anticompetitive merger by simply purchasing the assets of another company rather than its stock. In addition, vertical and conglomerate mergers would not be limited because normally these types of mergers do not involve competitors. The **Celler-Kefauver Act of 1950** closed these loopholes, such that the Clayton Act now serves to limit all types of mergers, whether they take place via the acquisition of stock or of assets.

Clayton Act § 8: Interlocking Directorates and Officers

A **board of directors** is the governing body of a corporation, elected by the shareholders to oversee the corporation's major business decisions. An **interlocking directorate** exists when one or more individuals serve on the board of directors of more than one company. At the time the Clayton Act was enacted, there was concern that these interlocking directorates could present an easy opportunity for collusion, such as the coordination of production or marketing plans. As a result, Clayton Act § 8 prohibits individuals from serving at the same time as an officer or member of the board of directors of two or more corporations. The prohibition applies only if:

- each of the corporations exceeds certain financial thresholds, which are adjusted each year based on changes in U.S. gross national product (GNP); and
- the elimination of competition between the two corporations would constitute an antitrust violation.

The prohibition in § 8 extends to high-ranking officers who are chosen by the board, such as the chief executive officer (CEO), such that an individual could not avoid the reach of § 8 by serving as a member of the board of one large company and as the CEO of its competitor.

Federal Trade Commission Act of 1914

Enacted in the same year as the Clayton Act (1914), the **Federal Trade Commission Act** (**FTC Act**) created the Federal Trade Commission (FTC) and in § 5 of the act broadly empowered it to prevent "unfair methods of competition" and "unfair or deceptive acts or practices." The act reflected congressional discontent with early Supreme Court decisions in the 1890s that had interpreted the Sherman Act very narrowly. (The Sherman Act has since been reinterpreted much more expansively by the courts.)

If the Sherman Act prohibitions on "restraint[s] of trade" and "monopoliz-[ation]" seem broad or even vague, the FTC Act language is broader still. As with the Sherman Act, judicial interpretation has helped to bring clarity and definition to the broad language, a process that continues today as new court opinions are issued. Under the FTC Act, the phrase "unfair methods of competition" has been held to include not only violations of the Sherman and Clayton Acts, but virtually any trade practice declared unfair by the FTC (subject, of course, to judicial review). (See Exhibit 11.5.)

Antitrust Enforcement

Enforcement of antitrust laws is analytically complex, in part because the laws can be enforced by two principal federal agencies (FTC and DOJ), the attorneys general of all 50 states, and private parties.

Public Enforcement: FTC, DOJ, and Other Federal Agencies

Only the DOJ can enforce the criminal provisions of the antitrust laws, including Sherman Act § 1 (restraint of trade) and § 2 (monopolization). However, the Sherman Act also contains civil provisions, as does the Clayton Act, which can be enforced by either the DOJ, state attorneys general, or private parties.

Only the FTC is authorized to bring suit under the FTC Act provisions. Because the FTC Act's "unfair methods of competition" provision has been interpreted so broadly as to include Sherman and Clayton Act violations,

Act	Year	Principal Activities Prohibited	Comments
Sherman	1890	§ 1 — Contracts in restraint of trade	§ 1 includes price fixing, market allocation, and boycotts
		§ 2 — Monopolization	§ 2 monopolization only unlawful if attained through anticompetitive (unfair) conduct
Clayton	1914	§ 2 — Price discrimination	§ 2 applies only to *commodities*, and only where the effect is to *lessen competition*; amended by Robinson Patman Act of 1936
		§ 3 — Tying	
		§ 7 — Mergers	§ 7 amended by Celler-Kefauver Act of 1950
		§ 8 — Interlocking directorates	
FTC	1914	§ 5 — Unfair methods of competition	Includes violations of both Sherman Act and Clayton Act; FTC may also challenge any other method it deems to be unfair

Exhibit 11.5. U.S. Antitrust Laws, Summary Table

the FTC effectively has the ability to enforce all of the antitrust laws. However, the FTC cannot bring criminal actions. Other federal agencies exercise some antitrust enforcement powers over particular industry segments, including the FCC (communications) and the Board of Governors of the Federal Reserve System (banking).

Public Enforcement: State Attorneys General

State attorneys general may bring suits on behalf of **natural persons** (human beings) residing in the state. When an attorney general asserts this type of claim, the state is suing as **parens patriae** (the "parent of its people"), and the suit may be referred to as a *parens patriae* action. *Parens patriae* actions may not be brought on behalf of **artificial persons** (corporations or other business entities). State attorneys general may also bring suit under state antitrust laws. Through the National Association of Attorneys General (NAAG), state attorneys general may coordinate their antitrust strategies and can increase enforcement activities should they perceive federal enforcement to be lax.

Private Enforcement

Private parties that have sustained direct injuries, including both competitors and consumers, may also sue under the antitrust laws. Class actions suits may be brought to enforce the Sherman and Clayton Acts.

Exhibit 11.6 on page 348 summarizes the plaintiff or type of plaintiff that may sue under each antitrust law or type of law.

Exhibit 11.6. Enforcement Authority Summary Table					
	Sherman Act		**Clayton Act**	**State Antitrust Laws**	**FTC Act**
	Civil	**Criminal**			
FTC	Yes*	No	Yes	No	Yes
DOJ	Yes	Yes	Yes	No	No
State Attorneys General	Yes	No	Yes	Yes	No
Private Parties	Yes	No	Yes	Yes	No

* Via FTC Act.

Penalties and Remedies for Antitrust Violations

Both criminal and civil remedies are available under the antitrust laws. Civil remedies include both **legal remedies** (money judgments) as well as **equitable remedies**, such as injunctions or divestitures.

> ### An Ethical Insight: W.D. Ross — Antitrust and the Duty of Reparation
>
> **Damages and Fines Under Antitrust Laws**
> Ross's *duty of reparation* to compensate for injuries done to others supports the ability of both government and private parties to sue for injuries sustained in violation of the Sherman and Clayton Acts.

Criminal Penalties

The Sherman Act, as amended, provides for fines of up to $100 million and up to 10 years of imprisonment. This substantial penalty was increased from $10 million by a 2004 amendment, indicating Congress's view that the previous penalty was not a sufficient deterrent. In fact, a separate provision of law authorizes the imposition of fines *greater* than $100 million if the antitrust violation resulted in a wrongful gain (or loss) that was sufficiently large.[15] Some of the largest U.S. antitrust fines in history have been imposed by the DOJ on airlines for illegal price fixing: Air France, KLM, Cathay, and MartinAir in 2008 ($504 million, cargo only); and Korean Air Lines and British Airways in 2007 ($600 million, passenger and cargo).

Civil Damages and Equitable Remedies

In *parens patriae* actions under the Sherman Act, the state may recover **treble damages** (three times actual damages) plus attorney fees on behalf of its

---

[15]18 U.S.C. § 3571.

A potential customer examines an LCD panel made by Chi Mei. What effect do antitrust violations generally have on retail prices?

residents. Private parties may also sue to recover treble damages plus attorney fees. Because treble damages awards may motivate private parties to enforce the antitrust laws to the benefit of the general population, these plaintiffs are sometimes described as serving as "private attorneys general."

Divestiture, an equitable remedy, may be ordered to break up a company that would otherwise violate the antitrust laws. The FTC may issue administrative **cease-and-desist** orders (injunctions), discussed in greater detail in Chapter 4, "Adminstrative Law."

DOJ Leniency Program

The Department of Justice maintains a corporate leniency program designed to encourage voluntary disclosure of antitrust violations. Under the program, corporations and individuals can avoid criminal conviction and fines if they are the first to confess participation in a criminal antitrust violation. Violators may still be subject to private damages suits, but treble damages will be unavailable.

Case Illustration

A revolution in computer screen technology took place during the 1990s, as bulky displays based upon the cathode ray tube (CRT) began to yield to those using thin and lightweight liquid crystal display (LCD) technology. LCD screens are used in laptops, televisions, mobile phones, and other electronic devices, and confer the significant advantages of greater portability and lower energy consumption. In 1998, a Taiwanese company named Chi Mei began investing in a particular type of LCD technology known as "thin film transistor liquid crystal display" (TFT-LCD). According to the U.S. Department of Justice, between 2001 and 2006 Chi Mei participated in a conspiracy among major TFT-LCD producers, the primary purpose of which was to engage in price fixing in markets that included the United States, in violation of § 1 of the Sherman Act. Under a plea agreement reached in 2010, Chi Mei agreed to pay a $220 million fine to the United States. Across the Atlantic, the European Union imposed on Chi Mei a fine of almost €400 million. In all, fines totaling more than $1 billion were imposed on Chi Mei and its alleged co-conspirators, including LG and Chunghwa, and a number of executives were individually charged and jailed.

Case Illustration

In the LCD antitrust litigation described on page 349, Samsung escaped prosecution by both the DOJ and European Union Commission by being the first cartel member to report the conspiracy. Samsung's timeliness in confessing may have been motivated in part by its previous experience in defending antitrust actions brought by the DOJ. In 2005, Samsung had been sentenced to pay a $300 million fine over price fixing in the Dynamic Random Access Memory (DRAM) market, then the second-largest criminal antitrust fine in U.S. history (the largest at the time was a 1999 fine of $500 million against Hoffman La-Roche for antitrust violations in the vitamins market). Although Samsung did not have to pay fines to the U.S. government or the European Commission with respect to the LCD price-fixing conspiracy, it nevertheless faced a number of private lawsuits as well as prosecution by Korean antitrust authorities, with the latter imposing fines of 97 billion won ($89 million).

Exemptions and Limitations

A number of exemptions and carve-outs limit the reach of the antitrust laws. In order to ensure that the antitrust laws are not used to excessively constrain research collaboration between firms, Congress enacted the National Cooperative Research Act of 1984 (NCRA).[16] The NCRA stipulates that the rule of reason standard (rather than the per se standard) shall be applied when evaluating certain joint research and development ventures. In addition, if pre-notification of the joint venture is provided to the FTC and DOJ, only actual damages (and not treble damages) may be recovered. The NCRA was expanded in 1993 to include production activities,[17] and again in 2004 to include standard-setting activities.[18] Setting technical standards ensures compatibility and thereby has the potential to benefit consumers. Consider, for example, what would occur if there were no standardization or coordination with respect to railroad track gauge (width), electrical outlet voltage, or cell phone communication protocols.

Additional statutory or judicially created exemptions apply to insurance, labor union activities, cartels formed solely for export trade,[19] agricultural cooperatives, soft drinks,[20] and baseball.[21]

Global Perspective

Businesses must comply, at a minimum, with the antitrust laws of all countries in which they engage in business. As business increasingly occurs on a global basis, the jurisdiction with the strictest antitrust laws can in some cases determine the outcome of a proposed merger, intercompany agreement, or other competition-related business action.

---

[16]Pub. L. No. 98-462, 98 Stat. 1815 (Oct. 11, 1984) (codified at 15 U.S.C. § 4301(a)(6)).
[17]Pub. L. No. 103-42, 107 Stat. 117 (June 10, 1993) (codified at 15 U.S.C. § 4302).
[18]Pub. L. No. 108-237, 118 Stat. 663 (June 22, 2004) (codified at 15 U.S.C. § 4301).
[19]Webb-Pomerene Export Trade Act of 1918 (codified at 15 U.S.C. §§ 61–65).
[20]Soft Drink Interbrand Competition Act of 1980 (codified at 15 U.S.C. §§ 3501–03).
[21]*Federal Baseball Club v. Nat'l League of Professional Baseball Clubs*, 259 U.S. 200 (1922).

Multinational mergers and acquisitions, such as that of Owens-Corning and Saint-Gobain, (see Case Illustration, right), highlight the increasing need for antitrust coordination and harmonization at the international level. Not surprisingly, a number of efforts at coordination and convergence have taken place over the past several decades.

International Convergence of Antitrust Law

There is currently no multilateral treaty that coordinates antitrust law at the global level. Nevertheless, a number of factors have led to a dramatic convergence of antitrust law among the world's nations since 1980. In that year, the **UN Conference on Trade and Development** (**UNCTAD**), the branch of the United Nations that promotes the interests of developing countries, promulgated a set of model antitrust principles as a means of addressing the rising power of multinational firms. Around the same time, the **Organisation for Economic Cooperation and Development** (**OECD**), now a group of 34 mostly developed countries, began issuing a series of antitrust recommendations that, while nonbinding, have often served to influence government action and thereby harmonize the antitrust policies of different nations with one another. More recently, the International Competition Network, an organization whose membership includes the antitrust authorities from 92 countries, has actively promoted both the procedural and substantive convergence of antitrust laws. As a result of these and other factors, the number of countries with antitrust laws has increased dramatically from a few dozen before 1990 to around 130 today.

Despite the trend toward convergence, important differences remain. Only about 30 countries provide for criminal (as opposed to civil) penalties for cartel activity, although the number is growing. Furthermore, the antitrust laws of many countries do not allow for either treble damages or class-action suits, diminishing potential damages and thereby the likelihood that private plaintiffs will bring suit. In the United States more than 90 percent of antitrust actions are initiated by private parties. Considering that the antitrust agencies of many countries may lack resources, expertise, or a long tradition of antitrust law, enforcement in those countries has sometimes been criticized as lax, uncertain, and inconsistent.

U.S. Antitrust Law Applies to Overseas Conduct

Even in countries where antitrust laws have not been enacted or are inadequately enforced, businesses are not necessarily free to engage in anticompetitive activities. This is because the antitrust laws of one nation may apply **extraterritorially**, that is, to conduct occurring wholly outside that nation's borders. In the United States, antitrust law has been broadly defined by Congress to apply to conduct occurring outside the United States, provided that the conduct has a "direct,

Case Illustration

When Owens-Corning, an American fiberglass manufacturer with global operations, sought in 2006 to merge with Saint-Gobain, a French building materials company with global operations, the merger drew attention from antitrust authorities in the United States, the European Union, Mexico, Brazil, and South Korea, among others. Ultimately the transaction took place with significant modifications, including the divestiture of certain assets, as required by authorities in multiple jurisdictions. *In re Owens Corning*, Docket No. C-4210, FTC Decision and Order (Dec. 7, 2007).

substantial, and reasonably foreseeable effect" on U.S. commerce (see Case Illustration, below left).[22]

The application of U.S. law to conduct occurring elsewhere has the potential to undermine good relations and create conflict. In addition, there may be practical difficulties to enforcing judgments against foreign defendants, particularly where those defendants have no assets within the United States. A number of doctrines have therefore developed to temper the broad extraterritorial reach of U.S. law, including its antitrust law. Under the **political question doctrine**, courts may not decide issues, such as foreign policy matters, that are committed by the Constitution to the legislative or executive branches.[23] The doctrine rests on the principal of separation of powers and the recognition that the judiciary should not intrude where doing so might disrupt foreign policy.

The political question doctrine bars the judiciary from deciding issues that are committed to the discretion of other branches of its own government. In contrast, the **act of state doctrine** prevents courts from sitting in judgment of the acts of the government of another country, if those acts are done within that country's territory.[24] As with the political question doctrine, the act of state doctrine rests on the principal of separation of powers and seeks to prevent disruption to foreign relations. In the OPEC illustration on page 353, the act of state doctrine served to bar U.S. judicial scrutiny of the choices made by foreign governments with respect to the exploitation of natural resources found within their borders.

Case Illustration

Variable interest rates on student loans are often tied to a base interest rate known as the London Interbank Offered Rate (LIBOR) to yield a total applicable interest rate. Thus, a student loan might bear a variable interest rate of 4.5 percent, consisting of a 1 percent LIBOR rate plus a 3.5 percent rate based on an individual borrower's risk. Because student loans and other LIBOR-based financial instruments such as mortgages are traded in financial markets, market insiders can be tempted to influence the LIBOR rate and then profit by strategically buying or selling. In 2013, the U.S. Department of Justice (DOJ) fined the Royal Bank of Scotland (RBS) $150 million for its role in influencing LIBOR in conjunction with other banks, actions that were described by the DOJ as a "price fixing conspiracy in violation of the Sherman Act." Together with penalties imposed by the U.S. Commodity Futures Trading Commission, the total amount imposed on RBS and its subsidiary by U.S. regulators came to $475 million. Although RBS is a foreign corporation based in Scotland and LIBOR is set by a group based in London, the effects of RBS's actions were felt in the United States, thus allowing enforcement under U.S. antitrust law.

A third doctrine, that of **sovereign immunity**, developed under the common law to provide immunity to foreign governments from suit in U.S. courts as a matter of grace and comity (respect for another nation's laws and actions). The doctrine of sovereign immunity overlaps to some extent with the act of state doctrine. As codified in the Foreign Sovereign Immunities Act, sovereign immunity is broader than the act of state doctrine in that it applies to activities of the foreign sovereign regardless of whether they are done within that country's own territory. In another respect, however, sovereign immunity is narrower than the act of

[22]15 U.S.C. § 6a.
[23]*Japan Whaling Ass'n v. Am. Cetacean Soc.*, 478 U.S. 221 (1986).
[24]*Underhill v. Hernandez*, 168 U.S. 250 (1897) (emphasis added).

state doctrine, in that it does not provide immunity if the foreign government is engaging in a commercial activity, such as a state-run oil business.

Global Perspective: Competition Law in South Korea

The Korean Fair Trade Commission (KFTC) is the administrative agency that develops and enforces competition policy in accordance with Korea's 1980 Monopoly Regulation and Fair Trade Act. If a potential antitrust violation is reported, a KFTC examiner will begin an investigation. The examiner's findings, along with any comments or responses of the examinee, will be forwarded to the KFTC's nine commissioners who will deliberate and decide the issue following an administrative hearing in which the examinee may participate either directly or through counsel. Fines and cease and desist orders may result, and some cases may be referred for criminal prosecution. Decisions of the KFTC are subject to judicial review in the Seoul High Court, and ultimately in the Korean Supreme Court.

Korean antitrust law shares a number of characteristics with that of the United States. In addition to the availability of criminal penalties, the KFTC administers a Corporate Leniency Program that provides full amnesty to the first leniency applicant to provide evidence of cartel activity and fully cooperate with authorities, and a reduction in penalties of up to 50 percent to the second applicant to do so. Korean law also requires premerger notification for enterprises whose total assets or sales equal 200 billion won ($180 million) or more. To assist businesses in determining whether a contemplated merger would be anticompetitive, the KFTC has issued guidelines referencing the Herfindahl-Hirschman Index. If a proposed merger would result in an index below the thresholds specified in the guidelines, it will not be considered anticompetitive.

Case Illustration

The Organization of Petroleum Exporting Countries (OPEC) is an intergovernmental organization of 12 oil-rich countries, formed in the 1960s for the purpose of limiting the output of oil sold and thereby raising prices and profits. As noted above, a horizontal agreement to fix prices or restrict output constitutes the classic example of a per se violation of § 1 of the Sherman Act. Aware of the antitrust laws, two groups of gasoline retailers brought class action suits against a group of more than a dozen oil production companies affiliated with OPEC. Despite the clear prohibition contained in the Sherman Act, the extraterritorial reach of U.S. antitrust law, and the substantial and foreseeable effects felt within the United States, the OPEC defendants prevailed. The Fifth Circuit held that the suit was barred by the political question doctrine as well as the act of state doctrine. *Spectrum Stores, Inc. v. Citgo Petroleum Corp.*, 632 F.3d 938 (5th Cir. 2011).

Global Perspective: Competition Law in the European Union

Competition law in the European Union shares much in common with U.S. antitrust law. Articles 101 and 102 of the EU's Treaty on the Functioning of the European Union prohibit horizontal restraints and monopolization, respectively, in a similar manner to §§ 1 and 2 of the Sherman Act. A leniency policy is in place that provides either immunity or a reduction in fines for the first companies to disclose illegal cartel activities, end their own infringing acts, and cooperate with enforcement authorities. Contemplated mergers that exceed certain financial thresholds must be disclosed to the European Commission, which utilizes the Herfindahl-Hirschman Index as a measure of market concentration. This premerger notification applies extraterritorially to companies whose principal places of business, production facilities, or other activities are located outside the EU, if effects would be felt within the EU.

Case Illustration

The EU's strict view of mergers can best be seen in a famous 2001 decision in which the EU Commission declined to give approval to the merger of General Electric and Honeywell. The deal was blocked by the EU even though both companies were based in the United States, and even though the transaction had already been approved by the U.S. Department of Justice as well as the antitrust authorities of 11 other jurisdictions.

Source: Grant, Jeremy, and Damien J. Nevin, *The Attempted Merger Between General Electric and Honeywell: A Case Study of Transatlantic Conflict,* 1(3) J. Competition L. & Econ. 595 (2005).

Despite the similarities with U.S. law, there are several key differences. While the U.S. Supreme Court has taken a more permissive view toward vertical restraints since 1997, the EU continues to treat them skeptically. The situation is reversed with respect to price discrimination, where the EU as a whole takes a more permissive view toward price discrimination, barring it only where it is undertaken by a dominant firm in the context of Article 102 monopolization. A number of factors make private antitrust suits less likely in the EU, including the nonavailability or more limited availability of treble damages and class action suits, narrower rights of discovery, and the ability to shift attorney fees to plaintiffs who do not prevail. On the other hand, the less favorable environment for private antitrust suits in the EU is counterbalanced to some extent by more aggressive enforcement by the EU Commission.

Summary

Antitrust law (or, outside the United States, "competition law") seeks to draw a line between business conduct that is pro-competitive and that which is anticompetitive. The major antitrust laws include the Sherman Act of 1890, the Clayton Act of 1914, and the FTC Act of 1914. The Sherman Act § 1 prohibits contracts "in restraint of trade," including price fixing, market allocation agreements, and boycotting. Horizontal price fixing and horizontal market allocation agreements are illegal per se, while most vertical agreements and some horizontal agreements will be judged under the more lenient rule-of-reason standard. The Sherman Act § 2 prohibits market monopolization, the excessive control of a market by one firm that is achieved or maintained through anticompetitive conduct. The Clayton Act prohibits price discrimination, tying, exclusive dealing arrangements, interlocking directorates, and those mergers where the effect would be to substantially lessen competition. Under the Hart-Scott-Rodino Antitrust Improvements Act of 1976, companies exceeding certain financial thresholds must provide the DOJ and FTC with premerger notification, allowing time for these federal agencies to determine whether the merger would be anticompetitive if consummated. The DOJ and FTC, as well as the antitrust authorities of some foreign nations, use the Herfindahl-Hirshman Index to calculate market concentration and aid in the analysis of contemplated mergers. The FTC Act of 1914 created the Federal Trade Commission, an independent federal agency, and endowed it with broad power to define and prevent "unfair methods of competition." Antitrust enforcement is shared among the FTC, DOJ, state attorneys general, and private litigants. Severe criminal penalties may be incurred for antitrust violations, including fines of up to $100 million or more, and imprisonment for up to 10 years. Ethical theories support antitrust laws, which ultimately promote the common good of society.

Questions for Review

1. Merger/divestiture considerations

Anheuser-Busch, owner of the Budweiser and Bud Light brands, was once the largest brewer in the United States with a nearly 50 percent market share and annual revenues of $16 billion. In 2008, a group of Missouri beer consumers filed suit under the Clayton Act to enjoin the acquisition of Anheuser-Busch by InBev. InBev, itself the result of a merger of a large Belgian company with a large Brazilian company, was already the world's largest brewer at the time of the merger announcement. InBev primarily competed in the U.S. market by selling imported beers brewed in other countries, including the Stella Artois and Beck's brands,[25] but in most U.S. locations these beers account for less than 2 percent of the market. However, InBev also brewed and distributed in the United States the popular Labatt beer, which accounted for a significant portion of beer sales in some geographic locations, including Buffalo, Rochester, and Syracuse, New York. Ultimately, the merger was allowed to proceed. In general, what notification must large companies make to the DOJ and FTC prior to consummating a merger? For what purpose? As a condition of the merger, the DOJ required InBev to sell off one of its brands. Which brand do you think it was required to sell off? What is the term used to describe such a required sale of a part of a business? *Ginsberg v. InBev NV/SA*, 623 F.3d 1229 (8th Cir. 2010).

2. Coordinated licensing issues

Originally organized in 1920, the National Football League (NFL) is an unincorporated association that includes 32 separately owned professional football teams. In 1963, the teams formed the National Football League Properties (NFLP) to collectively license their intellectual property, such as by granting licenses to manufacturers of T-shirts, caps, and other memorabilia bearing NFL team insignias. In 2000, the NFLP switched from a system of nonexclusive licenses (where multiple manufacturers could each purchase rights to make memorabilia) and instead granted one company, Reebok International, an exclusive 10-year license to manufacture and sell trademarked headwear for all 32 teams. What law(s) might this concerted activity violate? What types of businesses or individuals might allege injury under this arrangement? What potential remedies might

---

[25]Javier Espinoza, *Merger Pays Off for AB Inbev*, Forbes, Mar. 5, 2009, http://www.forbes.com/2009/03/05/inbev-quarter-profits-markets-equity_drinks.html.

be available? *American Needle Inc. v. Nat'l Football League*, 130 S.Ct. 2201 (2010).

3. Ethics and the NFL (GF)

In 2011, quarterbacks Tom Brady, Drew Brees and Payton Manning, representing a class including current NFL players, claimed that the league-imposed lockout was a horizontal group boycott among competitors (the NFL teams) and a per se violation of Sherman Act § 1. The players argued that the NFL conspired to eliminate competition for professional football players through a series of anticompetitive restrictions, including a salary "cap" that fixed maximum amounts for player salaries, and the "franchise player" and "transition player" designations which limited players from receiving a contract from any NFL team other than the player's immediate prior team. Discuss the ethics, using principles from ethical theory, of the NFL practices that eliminate competition in the market for professional football players. *Brady v. Nat'l Football League*, 779 F. Supp. 2d 992 (D. Minn. 2011).

4. Predatory pricing

In 1990, Spirit Airlines began as a small, low-fare passenger airline. By 1996 it had experienced modest success and had grown to include 11 planes and about 455 employees. In 1995 and 1996, it expanded its routes to include the Detroit-Philadelphia market, which was also served by Northwest Airlines. Northwest was the fourth largest air passenger carrier in the United States, and held 72 percent of the Detroit-Philadelphia market. About six months after Spirit began the new route, Northwest dropped its lowest fares on that route from $189 to $49, the same price as Spirit, and three months later Spirit abandoned the route. Following Spirit's exit, Northwest raised the lowest fair to $271 and later to $461. Of what anticompetitive practice might Northwest be accused? Under which section(s) of which

act(s) do you think Spirit might have brought suit? *Spirit Airlines, Inc. v. Northwest Airlines, Inc.*, 431 F.3d 917 (6th Cir. 2006).

5. Predatory hiring

Selling at below-market prices is not the only means of putting a competitor out of business. A firm might also seek to hire individuals that have rare talents or skills, not for that firm's own business need, but to deprive competitors of those employees' skills and thereby drive the competitors from the market. Is such behavior a violation of the antitrust laws, or a creative but legal means to achieve or maintain market dominance? *Universal Analytics, Inc. v. MacNeal-Schwendler Corp.*, 707 F.Supp. 1170 (C.D. Cal. 1989).

6. Vertical and horizontal restraints

What is the difference between a vertical and a horizontal restraint? Which is more likely to be held to violate the antitrust laws?

7. Tying arrangements

Consumers rarely stop to pause at the many products and services are often sold together as "packages": Bicycle frames are usually sold with seats, wheels, and handlebars; vacation packages may bundle airfare with ground transportation and accommodations; universities provide courses on business law and poetry for a single tuition price. Are there any products or services that you have seen bundled together that you think should not have been so bundled? If so, what if anything differentiates these bundles from the bicycles, vacations, and university education mentioned above?

8. Global considerations

Yazaki Corporation and DENSO Corporation are both Japanese companies that supply electrical components to manufacturers of automobiles. Following an investigation by the U.S.

Department of Justice in 2012, the two companies agreed to plead guilty to price fixing and pay a total of $548 million in criminal fines. Four executives of the companies, all Japanese nationals, agreed to serve prison sentences ranging from 15 months to two years in U.S. prisons. Has Congress authorized the U.S. Department of Justice to investigate price-fixing violations where neither accused party is a U.S. business? If so, what is the legal standard? Once the companies have paid the $548 million in fines and the executives have served their prison terms, does this mean the companies and individuals have no further liability? What other authorities might impose further penalties or prison sentences, if any? What other plaintiffs might bring suit, if any? Press Release, *Yakazi Corp., DENSO Corp, and Four Yazaki Executives Agree to Plead Guilty to Automobile Parts Price-Fixing and Bid-Rigging Conspiracies*, Dep't of Justice, Jan. 30, 2012.

Further Reading

Antitrust Division, Department of Justice, http://www.justice.gov/atr/.

Antitrust Law Journal, American Bar Association, http://www.americanbar.org/groups/antitrust_law/publications.html.

Bureau of Competition, Federal Trade Commission, http://www.ftc.gov/bc/index.shtml.

Grow, Nathaniel, *In Defense of Baseball's Antitrust Exemption*, 49 Am. Bus. L.J. 211 (2012).

International Competition Network, http://www.internationalcompetitionnetwork.org/.

PART III

The Employee

CHAPTER 12

Agency Law

Chapter Objectives

1. To recognize how and when an agency relationship is formed
2. To understand the differences between agency and authority and what express, implied, and apparent authority mean
3. To understand the relationship between principals and agents, especially principals' legal duties to agents and agents' legal duties to principals
4. To identify when principals and when agents are liable to third parties for breaches of contract, torts, and crimes
5. To understand the importance of knowing when an agency has terminated
6. To understand how ethical principles support agency laws

Practical Example: Compare These Situations

What do the following situations have in common?

- Three brothers are in partnership together operating a pizza parlor. They have no written partnership agreement. One brother signs a contract to purchase supplies on credit for the business.
- A sales engineer is employed at a high-tech company. She negotiates a contract for the company to sell a large quantity of specially made optical lenses to a customer.
- The chief financial officer of a publicly traded corporation certifies the accuracy of the data in the financial statements that are filed with the Securities and Exchange Commission.

- A real estate broker agrees in writing to provide assistance marketing and selling a house, in exchange for compensation equal to a percentage of the home's selling price.
- A U.S. widget business interested in increasing its European sales hires a company in France to solicit and negotiate sales orders from Europe.
- A wife signs a power of attorney giving her husband the authority to make medical decisions on her behalf, such as authorization to sign forms for nursing home admission and for permission to perform surgery.

What Is an Agency?

Each of these examples presents a situation where one person is empowered to act on behalf of another. In each, a contract is made or facts are represented by one party (called the **agent**) on behalf of another party (called the **principal**). The principal can be a person (e.g., the wife who granted a power of attorney) or an entity (e.g., the corporation, as an entity, that employs the CFO). The agent can also be a person (e.g., the real estate broker) or an entity (the French company acting as trade representative). An agency relationship exists when the principal manifests consent to the agent to act (generally to contract) on the principal's behalf and subject to the principal's control, and the agent consents to do so. All the situations listed above exemplify such an arrangement: the brothers in the partnership are agents to the partnership and to each other; the sales engineer is an agent for her employer; the CFO is an agent for the corporation; the real estate broker is an agent for the seller; the French representative is an agent for the U.S. company; and the husband is an agent for his wife.

The concept of empowering a party to speak or act on behalf of another is a powerful one. The law of agency enables enormous expansion of business, facilitates many people working together toward common commercial goals, and allows for division of labor. In addition, the ability to speak on behalf of a principal or to bind the principal to an agreement can involve significant responsibility and trust. It is therefore not surprising that agents owe principals fiduciary duties.

A **fiduciary relationship** is a particular relationship in which one party (the fiduciary) acts on behalf of another and which the law recognizes as involving a high level of trust. This high level of trust warrants imposition of a higher standard of care on the fiduciary. Agency is consistent with the rationale underlying the imposition of fiduciary duties, a topic explored later in this chapter. Keep in mind as you read this chapter that business organizations, discussed in Chapter 7, "Business Organizations" are managed and operated by agent/employees. For a company to maintain an ethical corporate culture, the agents, including the board of directors acting on behalf of the stockholders, the CEO, CFO, other executives, managers, and supervisors all must act with a high standard of ethics and be accountable for their unethical conduct. For example, a manager, as an agent for the corporation, who overlooks the unethical behavior of a subordinate, is violating his ethical responsibility of integrity that an agent owes to a principal.

Forming the Agency Relationship

There are many ways in which a principal could manifest consent for an agent to speak or act on his behalf; therefore, there are many ways in which agency relationships can be formed.

Agency Formation in General

Agencies can be established **orally or in writing**. Examples of agencies established by writing include a written **power of attorney**, as where the wife authorizes her husband to sign nursing home admission documents, and the real estate broker's contract to help sell a home. The brothers operating a pizza parlor as a partnership without any written partnership agreement is an example of an agency created orally. Less commonly, agency status can also be implied from circumstances. For example, if a distributor regularly pays a business commission to an individual for selling its products, agency can be implied despite the lack of an oral or written agreement.

Sometimes agency arises not by agreement in advance, but by **ratification** after the fact. Ratification is a manifestation of assent to be bound to a past act. This can occur by written or oral communication or by action, as long as it is reasonably clear that the originally unauthorized act has been affirmed. A common example involves promoters entering into agreements during a business's start-up phase. For example, suppose Dan is starting a small business. Before incorporating, he negotiates commercial space with a landlord. On the lease, Dan signs his own name. Then, the business is incorporated. With the landlord's permission, the corporation could **ratify** the agreement by manifesting assent to be bound to the lease agreement, by vote of the newly formed board of directors. After ratification, the corporation will be liable on the lease.

Special Situation — Agency by Estoppel

Sometimes, a person or business makes it appear as if someone is an agent even though no agency exists. In such situations, it would be unfair for a court to deny relief to a plaintiff who reasonably believed that there was an agency relationship. Therefore, in such cases, the defendant is **estopped** (that is, prevented) from claiming that no agency exists. For example, suppose a company's receptionist is absent, and the company arranges for an administrative assistant, Vanessa, from a temp agency to fill the position. Vanessa answers the phone, and a customer, Adam, asks for a price quote. Administrative assistants

Case Illustration

Rostis Timoshchuk bought a Mercedes Benz car for $108,325.49 from Long Chattanooga Mercedes-Benz. Because Long did not have the exact car in stock, a car was transferred from a dealership in Atlanta called RBM. Long represented the car as new and told Timoshchuk there were 756 miles on the odometer. The certificate of origin, certificate of title, and CarFax report all stated that Timoshchuk was the car's first retail purchaser. The title history of the car revealed that Mercedes-Benz USA ("MBUSA") conveyed title to RBM; RBM sold the car to Long; and Long sold the car to Timoshchuk. MBUSA distributed vehicles to authorized dealers, such as Long and RBM. Long and RBM are legal entities separate from MBUSA. The Mercedes-Benz dealership agreement specified that dealers are neither agents nor representatives of MBUSA.

About four months after buying the car, Timoshchuk noticed the paint on the car looked slightly discolored in certain lighting. He discovered that the car's trunk had been repainted, and he notified Long. After various denials and further testing, RBM admitted that "the vehicle's trunk suffered minor damage while in transit from its port-of-entry to RBM." RBM had had the trunk repaired and repainted but had not informed Long of this. RBM offered to replace the trunk lid; Timoshchuk insisted on returning the vehicle. RBM refused, and Timoshchuk sued Long, RBM, and MBUSA.

Timoshchuk argued that Long's and RBM's acts should be imputed to MBUSA under an agency theory. The Court of Appeals of Tennessee upheld the lower court's decision in rejecting this claim. First, the language in the distributorship contract precluded a conclusion that express or implied authority exists. Second, there was no communication between MBUSA and Timoshchuk before the purchase of the vehicle so there could be no agency by estoppel. *Timoshchuk v. Long of Chattanooga Mercedes-Benz* Not Reported in S.W.3d, 2009 WL 3230961 Tenn.Ct.App., 2009.

at the company are not supposed to quote prices or take orders, but the company failed to tell Vanessa this so she quotes a price and takes an order from Adam. The price Vanessa quotes is too low for the company to make a profit. Must the company honor the sale? Yes. Adam can successfully claim agency by estoppel. Even though Vanessa was in fact not the company's agent, the company made it appear as if she was by arranging for her to answer the phone. Adam reasonably believed that Vanessa was the company's agent, and the company is prevented from arguing that she was not.

As in the case excerpted above, in situations where agency is contested, courts often examine all possibilities: whether an agency has been created expressly, implied, or through ratification or whether agency by estoppel applies.

Independent Contractors Versus Employees

A worker is classified as either an independent contractor or an employee. This distinction is made in several areas of law such as employment law, tax law, and agency law.

Why Is the Distinction Between Employees and Independent Contractors Important?

There are several reasons it is important to know whether a worker is classified as an employee or an independent contractor:

- *Benefits* Workers classified as employees receive numerous benefits mandated by federal and state law. For example, full-time employees may be legally entitled to vacation time and health insurance benefits. The law does not require that employers provide employment benefits to independent contractors.
- *Payroll implications* For workers classified as employees, employers must withhold a portion of earned wages and forward those funds, along with an accounting of them, to the federal and state governments as income tax payments on behalf of the worker.[1] Employers must also contribute a portion of social security for each employee. Employers hiring independent contractors need not withhold taxes.
- *Intellectual property rights* If a worker invents or creates something in connection with the work for which he is hired, who owns the intellectual property rights to the patent or copyright? The answer depends on the worker's status. For employees, the employer owns the intellectual property rights. In contrast, independent contractors own the intellectual property rights to their inventions and creations (unless the contract provides that the creation is a "work for hire").
- *Tort liability* If a worker commits a tort while acting within the scope of employment, could the injured third party receive compensation from the employer? Again the answer depends on the worker's status. For employees who commit torts within the scope of employment, the employer is liable to the injured third party. If the worker is an independent contractor, the employer is generally not liable (with some exceptions as noted on page 379–380).

From an ethical perspective, the employer should stand behind the wrongful acts of its employees causing an economic loss to others even if the company has training sessions that prohibited the act. The company's code of ethics should identify certain laws and regulations that apply to its transactions that could result in unintentional illegal behavior. This necessitates a strict code of accountability and supervision to identify careless employees and hold them responsible for their unethical and illegal conduct. The company should engage in "risk assessment' and explain to its employees possible examples of tortious conduct to be avoided. For example, a truck driver/agent/employee who carelessly drives into a pedestrian while making a delivery would cause the employer to be held liable for his careless driving. The company should require its

---

[1]Not all states have state income tax.

employees, by a written contract, to **reimburse the company for any losses** caused by their negligence. This practice would be supported by W.D. Ross's "prima facie" ethical *duty of reparation for injuries done to others.*

- **Status as agent** All employees are agents. (Note this does not mean employees have authority to bind the principal to *anything*, as explained below in the section on authority.) Some independent contractors are agents; some are not. Contrast two workers who both function as independent contractors: a plumber hired to fix a customer's sink and a real estate broker hired to help sell a home. The plumber is an independent contractor who is not an agent. This is because the customer *does not* manifest consent for the plumber to speak or enter into contracts on the customer's behalf. The real estate broker is an independent contractor who is an agent. This is because the customer *does* manifest consent for the broker to show the customer's home to prospective buyers, advertise the customer's home, communicate to others on the customer's behalf, and so forth.

The following Manager's Compliance and Ethics Meeting illustrates the legal and ethical obligations of salespeople bribing public officials to sell products.

Manager's Compliance and Ethics Meeting

Cash Paid to a Foreign Official by an Employee/Agent to Make a Sale Can Go a Long Way — to Jail!

You are the sales manager of Dishware Supreme, Inc., that employs sales personnel working in the United States and Mexico, all of whom are paid on a commission basis. You have noticed an unusually high volume of sales coming from Mexico. Some of the sales forces are complaining how difficult it is to sell in Mexico without offering and paying the custom officials cash payments. Legal counsel for the company has asked you to investigate the risk assessment of company sales personnel offering bribes to Mexican officials to acquire the sales transaction and to inform the employees of its illegality.

At the meeting you remind the sales force that engaging in bribing a public official in any manner will not be tolerated as it violates the Foreign Corrupt Practices Act (FCPA) and is prohibited in the company's Compliance and Ethics Program. In addition, the company code of ethics specifically prohibits paying "anything of value" to influence a foreign official, including any tangible and intangible property. The Code further states employees will be discharged if this provision is violated. A few sales personnel have informed you that offering bribes to foreign officials is a common practice with other companies and the most expedient way to ensure the sales contract is finalized. They further argue since there is no injury or fraud, cash payments to a foreign official to assure the contract is concluded will benefit Dishware Supreme and because it harms nobody is an ethical practice. They ask you to explain to them why this is considered an unethical practice by the company.

You respond that this is a violation of the FCPA and could implicate the company if it knew or should have known of this practice and remained passive in attempting to correct the potential crime. Since the employee/agent wanted to benefit not only himself by way of making a commission on the sale as well as the corporation/principal, the corporation could be held liable under an agency theory because the act of bribery by the employee/agent was motivated to benefit the company. A corporate fine for violating the FCPA would be a public relations disaster and a potential financial loss to the stockholders. Ethical theories that support the FCPA are:

W.D. Ross's duty to prevent harm. This unethical practice of bribing foreign officials to do business violates W.D. Ross's prima facie ethical duty to prevent harm to others, in this case the harm being the loss of the outstanding reputation of the company and the stockholders' potential market value loss. There is also the possibility of the company, Dishware Supreme, Inc., being held vicariously liable for the illegal bribe by its employees.

Kant's Categorical Imperative to always act in such a manner that your actions could become a universal law. This ethical principle would be compromised because bribing to obtain business as a "universal law" would favor those with the ability to pay the foreign officials over others who cannot and this would surely promote dishonesty in international trade. If all sales personnel bribed foreign officials to contract in a foreign country, global trade would be crippled; the prices of all goods would rise and corruption would be encouraged.

You document the discussion in the minutes of the meeting, referencing the proscribing of bribing foreign officials in the code of ethics and explain that the employee/agent engaging in such practice will be discharged. You send the written report to the board of directors, the ethics and compliance officer and corporate legal counsel. This would constitute appropriate "due diligence" by the company and could be used, along with other evidence, as a defense if Dishware Supreme, Inc., was sued for its agent/employees subsequently violating the FCPA.

Factors in Determining the Difference Between Independent Contractors and Employees

Because the distinction between employees and independent contractors impacts so many issues, it is important to understand the test for ascertaining the difference. Interestingly, a contract provision stating that the worker will be considered an independent contractor is only one of many relevant factors. Even where the parties agree by contract that the worker will be considered an independent contractor, a court could still decide that the worker is an employee. How, then, do courts determine the difference between employees and independent contractors?

The most important factor is the extent of control the principal exercises over the details of the work. The key here is not control over *what* the worker is being asked to do, but rather, over *how* the work is to be done. When the Internal Revenue Service examines whether a worker is an independent contractor or an employee, it uses evidence that falls into these three categories:

■ *Behavioral* Does the company control how the worker does the job? The type of instruction given, degree of instruction, evaluation systems, and training are examined.

Case Illustration

The Internal Revenue Service determined, in 1990, that Microsoft had misclassified workers as independent contractors instead of employees. In response to the IRS ruling, Microsoft offered some of the misclassified workers employee status, but most were offered the choice to "convert" to temporary status or cease working. Many workers stayed, were paid through one of several temp agencies, and signed an agreement with Microsoft stating that they were independent contractors and were responsible for their own benefits. In 1992, a class action lawsuit challenged the employment status of these temporary workers. After protracted litigation, Microsoft settled the case for $96.885 million. Microsoft also agreed to change its staffing and worker classification practices. *Vizcaino v. Microsoft*, 173 F.3d 713 (9th Cir 1999).

■ *Financial* Are the business aspects of the worker's job controlled by the payer? This involves whether the worker had to make a significant investment; whether expenses are reimbursed; the extent of opportunity for profit or loss; whether the worker works elsewhere; and the method of payment (periodic or a flat fee).

■ *Type of relationship* Is there a written contract stating the parties' understanding of the worker's status? Are employee benefits provided? Was the worker hired with the expectation of indefinite employment or hired for a specific project? Is the worker providing services that are a key aspect of the business?[2]

Types of Authority

Just because a person is an agent does not mean that he or she can bind the principal to any agreement. A critical concept in agency law is **authority**. After determining that an agency relationship exists, the next logical question is what is the agent authorized to do? And what happens when the agent exceeds the scope of authority? Large companies often have a vast array of agents performing different authorized functions on its behalf.

Actual Authority

Actual authority (also called "real" authority) is authority that the principal "actually" gives the agent. There are two kinds. A principal gives an agent *express authority* by telling the agent, either orally or in writing, what the agent is authorized to do or say. For example, a verbal conversation where Steve and Mary agree that Steve will sell Mary's car in exchange for 10 percent of the purchase price is a grant of express authority. Certain grants of authority must be in writing to be valid. If the agent is appointed to sign a contract that should be in writing pursuant to the Statute of Frauds,[3] then the grant of

---

[2]IRS, http://www.irs.gov/Businesses/Small-Businesses-&-Self-Employed/Independent-Contractor-Self-Employed-or-Employee.
[3]For an explanation of the Statute of Frauds, see Chapter 16, "Contract: Performance, Public Policy, and Global Contracts."

authority to the agent must also be in writing. For example, because a contract for the purchase of land must be in writing to be enforceable, the authorization of an agent for the buyer to sign documents at a real estate closing must also be in writing. The wife's power of attorney example at the beginning of this chapter is another example of express written authority. The appointment of an agent with authority to contract on behalf of the principal is always accompanied with ethical responsibilities by both parties. The principal/employer should inform its employee/agents about the company's compliance and ethics program and carefully review the terms of the code of ethics in the periodic training sessions as illustrated throughout this textbook.

Implied Authority

Often, it is difficult and laborious to articulate every situation in which an agent has authority. Most authority is not specifically described but is inferred. **Implied authority** is authority to do what is reasonably necessary, usual, and proper to perform the agent's work. This involves acting in a manner consistent with the principal's instructions and the agent's reasonable understanding of what is needed to effectuate those instructions. All implied authority is based on express authority, so it is important to examine express authority first.

Does handing keys to an agent imply authority?

Recall the example of the chief financial officer (CFO) of a publicly traded company. What might be sources of the CFO's express authority? The CFO's powers could be articulated in a job description, employment contract, or corporate bylaws section on officers' functions. Based on these writings and the job title, a CFO has the authority to sign documents related to financial reporting and recordkeeping. There is, however, no authority to sign an agreement to sell the business's primary plant because that would exceed what is reasonably necessary to perform the CFO job function.

Apparent Authority

Apparent authority exists when there *appears* to be authority despite the fact that there is not. Unlike actual authority, which is based on what the principal communicates or implies to the agent, apparent authority is based on what the principal communicates or implies to a third party. In this way, it is similar to agency by estoppel. Consider the example in the Case Illustration on page 370, where Hughes was LAI's agent but exceeded his actual authority. From the eyes of the third party (that is, Big Bear), does it appear as if Hughes had authority to negotiate an agreement for LAI?

Case Illustration

Chad Hughes was a newly hired sales representative for LAI Game Sales, Inc., which sold and manufactured gaming machines. At a trade show, Hughes met with the president of Big Bear, a seller of arcade-type games. After several conversations, they decided Big Bear would distribute a particular game produced by LAI. Hughes signed a purchase contract with Big Bear, and Big Bear proceeded to order a shipment of machines. After the first order was filled, LAI informed Big Bear that it would not sell any more machines because it was "inundated with minor service and setup issues on some of the games purchased by Big Bear's few existing customers." Soon afterward, LAI management learned that Hughes had signed a purchase contract with Big Bear, so LAI reaffirmed that it would send no more machines to Big Bear. Big Bear sued LAI. LAI filed a motion for summary judgment, arguing that Hughes did not have authority to bind LAI to this contract. The court ruled that Hughes did not have actual authority to enter into

the contract. (In fact, Hughes had even admitted "he had a feeling that he was not allowed to enter the purchase agreement.") However, the court denied summary judgment and held that whether there was apparent authority was a material question of fact. On one hand, Big Bear presented evidence that LAI hired Hughes as a regional sales manager to sell games and "sent [him] to the trade show where he met [Big Bear's President], and identified him with a booth decorated with LAI's logo, LAI clothing and a name-tag to market and promote LAI games." On the other hand, LAI argued that "it merely sent a newly hired sales representative to a trade show to stand at a booth that could have been staffed by a model or a child, that the representative was so excited to make a sale that he signed a contract he knew he had no authority to sign, and that LAI, upon learning of the agreement, quickly terminated it." *Big Bear Import Brokers, Inc. v. LAI Game Sales, Inc.* 2010 WL 729208 (D. Ariz.).

As you read the following In-Depth Ethical Case Analysis case, carefully note how ethical theories support the agency doctrine of apparent authority.

In-Depth Ethical Case Analysis

Motorsport Marketing, Inc. v. Wiedmaier, Inc., 195 S.W.3d 492 (Mo. App. 2006)

Facts

Wiedmaier, Inc. owned and operated a truck stop in Missouri. The company's sole owners and officers were Jerry and Marsha Wiedmaier. Their son, Michael, worked for Wiedmaier as a fuel

truck operator. Meanwhile, he also formed and was part-owner of Extreme Diecast, which marketed NASCAR merchandise. Michael met representatives of a supplier of racing collectibles, Motorsport Marketing, Inc., and expressed interest in selling Motorsport's products at the

Wiedmaier truck stop. He also discussed this possibility with Marsha. Pursuant to conversations with Michael, Motorsport faxed a credit application to Wiedmaier's place of business. Michael gave the account application to Marsha, and she signed it "in her capacity as 'Secretary-Owner' of Wiedmaier, Inc . . . . [and she] also signed as 'Individual Guarantor/Owner.'" When she signed it, the portion of the application that listed the names of all owners was blank. After she signed, Michael completed the owner identification portion of the application and listed his mother, his father, and himself. He then faxed the credit application to Motorsport and made several purchases on credit. Ultimately he stopped making payments, and Motorsport demanded payment from Wiedmaier, Inc. for the $93,388.58 owing on the account. At that point, Michael had moved to Columbus, Ohio.

Issue

Was Michael acting as an apparent agent for Wiedmaier, Inc.?

Holding

Yes. The Missouri Court of Appeals affirmed the judgment of the trial court, holding that Michael acted as apparent agent of Wiedmaier, Inc. in its dealings with Motorsport.

From the Court's Opinion

To establish the apparent authority of a purported agent, Motorsport must show that (1) the principal manifested his consent to the exercise of such authority or knowingly permitted the agent to assume the exercise of such authority; (2) the person relying on this exercise of authority . . . acting in good faith, had reason to believe, and actually believed, the agent possessed such authority; and (3) the person relying on the appearance of authority changed his position and will be injured or suffer loss if the transaction executed by the agent does not bind the principal . . . We find that Motorsport has

shown that each of the criteria for establishing Michael's apparent agency has been satisfied. First, Marsha manifested her consent to the exercise of Michael's authority or knowingly permitted Michael to assume the exercise of such authority by leaving the ownership section of the credit application blank . . . Second, Motorsport, relying on Michael's exercise of authority and acting in good faith, had reason to believe, and actually believed, that Michael possessed such authority. Motorsport received a credit application from Wiedmaier, Inc. signed by owner Marsha Wiedmaier, listing Michael as an owner . . . Third, Motorsport changed its position and will be injured or suffer loss if the transaction executed by Michael does not bind Wiedmaier . . . [because] Motorsport will suffer the loss of the balance due on the account. Motorsport Marketing, Inc. v. Wiedmaier, Inc., 195 S.W.3d 492 (Miss. 2006).

Ethical Issues

Are there ethical theories that support the agency doctrine of apparent authority? Yes.

Was Michael, the apparent agent, acting ethically, knowing he had no authority to contract on behalf of the principal/Wiedmaier, Inc., simply because the third party reasonably believed he had authority? No.

Ethical Theories Supporting Apparent Authority

1. **Mill's Utilitarianism**: The utilitarian ethical theory of *the greater good for the greater number* supports the legal doctrine of apparent authority. Mill wrote in *Utilitarianism*, Chapter IV, "*everyone who receives the protection of society owes a return for the benefits, and the fact of living in society renders it indispensable that each should be bound to observe a certain line of conduct towards the rest. This conduct consists, first, in not injuring the interests of one another; or rather certain interests, which, either by*

express legal provision, or by tacit understanding, ought to be considered as rights." In our business environment, a countless number of business representatives appear to have authority and others reasonably rely on that appearance and contract with them. The greater good to the business environment will require the principal who "knowingly permitted the agent to assume the exercise of authority" to ethically honor contracts made on its behalf. The doctrine of apparent authority is ethically supported on the theory that corporations receive the limited liability protection of society (Mill's "everyone who receives the protection of society owes a return for the benefits") and should observe ethical as well as legal conduct toward third parties who reasonably rely on the authority of agents acting on its behalf.

2. **Kant's Categorical imperative**: Kant stated, *Act so that you always use humanity, in your own person as well as in the person of every other, never merely as a means, but at the same time as an end in themselves.* Michael, the apparent agent, knowing he had no authority to contract on the behalf of the principal/Wiedmaier, Inc., acted unethically by taking advantage of the third party simply because the third party reasonably believed he had actual authority.

It violated Kant's categorical imperative because it treated the third party as a means to make money and not as an end to be respected.

3. **Rawls's Equal Liberty Principle**: Rawls's equal liberty principal states *Each person is to have an equal right to the most extensive basic liberty compatible with a similar liberty for others.* A person who reasonably relies on a contracting party who appears to have authority to represent the principal, should ethically have an equal right with the principal's right to sue the third party in the event of a breach of the contract. This is especially true in this case when the principal, Wiedmaier, Inc., "knowingly permitted the agent to assume the exercise of such authority" by the Treasurer, Martha Wiedmaier. We can assume that the apparent agent, Michael Wiedmaier, exceeded his authority in incurring the $93,388.58 debt and acted unethically in doing so since the corporation, Wiedmaier, Inc., was unaware of these transactions.

Conclusion

Ethical theories support the court's decision that found the principal liable under the doctrine of apparent authority. Note how classical ethical principles often support a court's legal reasoning and help in understanding the legal decision from a broader perspective.

Rights and Duties of Principals and Agents

When an agency relationship is established, the principal owes certain obligations to the agent, and vice versa. Depending on the situation, there can be many legal requirements in addition to those automatically imposed by virtue of the agency. For example, if the agent is an employee, federal and state employment regulations apply, as discussed in Chapter 13, "Employment Law". If the agent is a licensed real estate broker or insurance agent, then state licensing statutes apply. However, regardless of these rules, the following duties arise from the agency relationship.

Principal's Duties to Agent

Principals owe agents the following duties:

- *Compensation* The principal must compensate the agent when compensation is reasonably expected. Usually, there is an existing agreement between the parties regarding compensation. If there is no such agreement between the parties, the agent must be compensated a reasonable amount. If the agent is not an employee, the parties could agree that the principal will not compensate the agent; gratuitous agencies are legally permissible.

- *Reimbursement* The principal must reimburse the agent for expenses reasonably incurred while the agent executes authorized responsibilities. For example, if the manager of a high-tech company asks the sales engineer to attend a trade show, the company is obligated to reimburse the cost of any required entrance fee.

- *Indemnification* What if the agent sustains a loss in connection with work on behalf of the principal? Recall the practical examples at the beginning of this chapter. Suppose one of the brothers running the pizza parlor pays from his personal account for a delivery from a restaurant supplier, after which the supplier refuses to deliver and declares bankruptcy. Can the brother force the partnership to indemnify him for this loss? Yes. As Judge Learned Hand wrote, assuming the loss is not the result of the agent's mismanagement, "[t]he doctrine [of indemnification] stands upon the fact that the venture is the principal's, and that, as profits will be his, so should be the expenses."[4]

- *Cooperation* Having directed the agent to do certain work, a principal must cooperate with the agent's performance of that work. Suppose a homeowner hires a real estate broker to help sell his house in exchange for a percentage of the home's sale price. The broker tells the homeowner he is on his way to hand deliver a written offer from a prospective buyer. When the broker arrives, the homeowner refuses to open the door because the homeowner thinks he can locate a buyer on his own, thereby eliminating the need to pay a commission. This is a breach of the

> **An Ethical Insight: John Rawls and an Agent's Expectation to Receive What's Ethically Due from the Principal under the Agency Agreement**
>
> There are ethical as well as legal grounds for an agent to receive from the principal what is due under the agency agreement. Rawls stated the ethical principle that *". . . those who make and honor agreements have, by definition, a legitimate expectation of receiving the agreed amounts at the agreed times . . . , What individuals do depends on what the rules and agreements say they would be entitled to; what individuals are entitled to depends on what they do."*[*] The agent who performs the agreement has both legal and ethical reasons to legitimately expect that the principal will uphold its expressed and implied duties.
>
> ———————
>
> **Justice as Fairness*, p. 72, sec. 20.

———————

[4]*Admiral Oriental Line v. United States*, 86 F.2d 201 (2d Cir. 1936).

homeowner's obligation to cooperate with the broker and unethical behavior as illustrated in the Ethical Insight on page 373. Note how, under Rawls's ethical theory, an agent who performs an agency agreement has ethical as well as legal expectation to receive from the principal duties owed to him under the terms of the agency contract that may be expressed or implied.

The Fiduciary Duty

One of the most important concepts in business law is the fiduciary duty. As discussed in Chapter 7, "Business Organizations," the fiduciary relationship (from the word *fiducia*, meaning "trust" in Latin) is based on trust. The circumstances under which the law imposes a fiduciary duty are varied, but the common thread is this: party A entrusts party B with money or property or confidential information to use for party A's benefit. Party A owes a fiduciary duty to Party B. Common examples of fiduciary duties include:

- Doctor to patient (patient entrusts doctor with confidential medical information to use on patient's behalf)
- Board of directors to shareholders (shareholders contribute capital for corporation to use to generate wealth back to shareholders)
- Employee to employer (employer gives employee confidential information and authority to work on behalf of employer)

All agents, whether employees or independent contractors, owe a fiduciary duty to their principal.

Agent's Duty to Principal

Agents owe principals the following duties, many of which are based on fiduciary obligations:

Loyalty

The essence of the fiduciary duty is the duty of loyalty. Those entrusted with the property of another must be careful with that property. The law is clear that agents owe principals undivided loyalty. By corollary, the agent may not put her own interests ahead of the principal's and may not put a third party's interests ahead of the principal's. Doing so is a **conflict of interest**.

There are many ways in which an agent could breach the duty of loyalty. For example, the CFO diverts company assets to his own personal bank account. The real estate broker secretly agrees with a buyer to receive $5,000 for negotiating a price below the seller's asking price. At a trade show, a sales representative learns of a lucrative business opportunity, but instead of informing his employer of the opportunity, he forms a corporation and takes advantage of the opportunity himself. One of the brothers operating the pizza parlor partnership secretly invests in starting a competing restaurant across the street. The high-tech sales engineer gives her company's confidential information to a competitor. Many highly publicized scandals plaguing business in the United States have involved larger-scale breaches of the duty of loyalty — from the Enron scandal in 2001 to Bernard Madoff's dealings in 2008 to Raj Rajaratnam's insider trading conviction in 2011, to name a few. Upholding the fiduciary duty means that an agent cannot:

- Represent both the principal and another party to a transaction
- Use another person or entity as a "straw man" to circumvent conflict of interest rules
- Compete with the principal
- Disclose confidential information, even after the agency terminates
- Engage in self-dealing, where the agent takes personal advantage of a situation at the expense of the principal's interests
- Take a business opportunity that belongs to the principal

Case Illustration

The defendant, Citrin, had been the plaintiff's employee. While employed at International Airport Centers, Citrin decided to go into business for himself, in breach of his employment contract. When Citrin quit his job, he deleted all data before returning his computer. Because he had loaded a secure-erasure program onto the laptop, IAC was unable to undelete the data. Some of the deleted data would have revealed Citrin's improper conduct before he quit. His deletion of the data was a breach of the duty of loyalty and voided the agency relationship. *International Airport Centers, LLC v. Citrin*, 440 F.3d 418 (7th Cir. 2006)

Performance

Agents are obligated to perform their work with the "care, competence, and diligence normally exercised by agents in similar circumstances."[5]

Notification

In the course of acting and communicating for the principal, an agent often acquires information of interest to the principal. An agent must inform the principal, in a timely manner, of all facts the principal would reasonably want to know. For example, a real estate broker who receives an offer to purchase the seller's house must inform the seller, even if the offer is below the seller's asking price. This is because the seller would reasonably want to know the terms of any offer on the house. Because a principal is legally presumed to know what the agent knows, this rule is especially important. As a fiduciary, an agent has what W.D. Ross refers to as a prima facie ethical duty of fidelity to keep the principal informed. For example, an agent who represents a professional athlete attempts to obtain the highest salary possible on his or her behalf. As a fiduciary, an agent who finds the owner's salary offer unreasonably low is still obligated to keep the principal/professional athlete informed and allow him or her to accept or reject the salary offer made by the owner.

---

[5]Restatement 3d of Agency section 8.08.

Accounting

Agents have the duty to account to the principal both for money received and for money expended on the principal's behalf. In some sense, the duty to account is an extension of the duty to notify—a principal would reasonably want to know what revenue is received and what expenditures are made on its behalf.

Obedience

Since the purpose of agency is to structure a legal arrangement where the agent acts or speaks on behalf of the principal, it follows that the agent must obey the principal's directives. An agent has the duty to obey all reasonable instructions of the principal. Agents are under no obligation to obey instructions to act illegally or unethically.

Liability of Principals and Agents

The rules above govern the rights and responsibilities involved in the principal-agent relationship. Because the nature of agency involves agents negotiating contracts for principals and acting or speaking on behalf of principals, questions arise regarding liability to third parties. If the agent's acts lead to liability to a third party, who is responsible? Under what circumstances must a principal compensate a third party for something the agent has done? Is the agent also liable? The answers to these questions depend in part on the type of liability—contract, tort, or criminal. For each type of liability, both principal responsibility and agent responsibility should be examined separately.

Contractual Liability of Principal and Agent

Recall that if a principal makes it *appear* to a third party as though a person has authority, then the principal will be liable on a contract that person makes with the third party, as in the *Wiedmaier* case. But suppose that the person is an agent and is acting within the scope of authority. When a principal directs an authorized agent to negotiate a contract with a third party and the contract is ultimately breached, is the principal liable to the third party? Is the agent? Contractual liability of the principal and the agent turns on whether, in the agent's dealings with the third party, the principal is fully disclosed, partially disclosed, or undisclosed, as viewed from the vantage point of the third party.

A principal is **undisclosed** when the third party does not know that the agent is acting on behalf of a principal. When the principal is undisclosed, usually, the third party could bring any contract claims against the principal or against the agent.[6] Why would the law impose liability on the agent in this

---

[6]Courts are divided on the issue of an undisclosed principal's liability when the agent fails to make payment to the third party after receiving payment from the principal. The Restatement of Agency 3d favors the minority position that the principal should be liable in this circumstance.

situation? After all, the principal's business is the reason for the contract and the principal's purpose is being advanced. You will learn in Chapter 15, "Contracts: Contract Formation," the importance of evaluating and analyzing risk in contract negotiations. If the principal is undisclosed, the third party has no opportunity to investigate the principal's reputation or creditworthiness. Knowing nothing about the agent's connection to the principal forces the third party to assess doing business only with the agent, not the principal. If the third party chose to pursue a breach of contract claim against the agent, does the agent have any recourse? Yes. The agent could claim indemnification from the principal.

To illustrate, suppose the dishwasher in the pizza parlor breaks suddenly. The three partners/brothers quickly discuss the need to replace it, and one brother, Adam, is sent to a local appliance store to buy a new one. In his haste, he forgot the business's checkbook so he pays for the new dishwasher using his personal check. He takes the dishwasher to the restaurant and discovers it is the wrong size so he stops payment on the check. The store insists that the dishwasher was a final sale, refuses to allow its return, and files a breach of contract suit. In this case, the store could sue Adam, as agent, or the partnership, as principal. If the store received breach of contract damages from Adam, then Adam could receive indemnification from the pizza partnership.

A principal is **partially disclosed** when the third party knows that the agent is acting on behalf of a principal but does not know the identity of the principal. Generally, where an agent negotiates a contract with a third party and the principal is partially disclosed, both the principal and the agent are liable on the contract. For example, suppose a homeowner agrees with a real estate broker to cover the costs of advertising the home for sale. The broker arranges for a consulting firm to prepare an advertising layout but does not identify who the advertisement is for. The firm does the work, and then the homeowner refuses to pay. Is the broker responsible to pay the bill? Yes. The consulting firm knew that the broker was engaging services for a client but did not know the client's identity. Therefore, the homeowner is a partially disclosed principal. The consulting firm can choose to seek payment from the broker or from the homeowner. If the broker pays the consulting firm, the homeowner is obligated to indemnify the broker.

A principal is **fully disclosed** when the third party knows that the agent is acting on behalf of a principal and also knows the identity of the principal. Where an agent negotiates a contract with a third party and the principal is fully disclosed to the third party, the principal is liable on the contract and (absent an agreement to the contrary) the agent is not. From the perspective of contract law, this makes sense — the third party is fully aware that the deal is with the principal, not the agent. For example, suppose a sales engineer negotiates a purchase order for a customer to buy a large quantity of optical lenses from her employer. The lenses are delivered and the customer pays for them. Then the customer claims that the lenses fail to meet the contract's specifications and files suit. Because the customer knew that the sales

Exhibit 12.1. Contractual Liability for Agent's Authorized Actions		
	Principal's Liability for Contract	**Agent's Liability for Contract**
Principal is fully disclosed to third party	Yes	No, unless agent specifically agreed to be liable
Principal is partially disclosed to third party	Yes	Yes
Principal is undisclosed to third party	Yes	Yes

engineer was selling the lenses on behalf of her employer and knew exactly who the employer was, the company is liable but the agent is not.

Exhibit 12.1 summarizes the contractual liability for an agent's authorized actions. From the agent's perspective, these rules underscore the importance of communicating to the third party the existence of the agency and the identity of the principal. After all, only when this information is communicated will the agent be relieved of liability on the contract. What are some ways agents can ensure that third parties are aware of the agency and of the principal's identity?

- Names and titles on business cards
- Signature blocks on e-mails and letters
- Name tags with titles and identification badges
- Use of letterhead stationary
- Use of company charge card and company checks
- Signature on contract, followed by title and company (as in Philip Tanzani, sales agent for The Beatrice Company)

Tort Liability of Principal and Agent

What if the circumstances give rise not to contract liability, but to tort liability? Is the principal liable to compensate an injured third party for a tort, such as negligence? Is the agent liable?

The first steps in analyzing the legal liability of a situation involving agency and tortious conduct is to determine whether the wrongful action consisted of negligence, an intentional tort, or a crime and whether it has been committed by the principal, the agent, or both. General notions of personal responsibility in society dictate that agents and principals are each responsible for the torts and crimes they commit. An agent who commits a tort, whether or not in connection with agency business, is personally liable to injured third parties. A principal is also liable to third parties for tortious conduct the principal either commits or directs the agent to commit.

Especially when the principal is a business, sometimes the principal's negligent conduct, typically negligent hiring or negligent supervision, leads to the agent committing a tort or a crime. For example, suppose the pizza parlor needs to hire a driver to deliver pizza. Assume that at no time during the application or interview process do the managers ask the candidates about their driving records nor do they conduct any investigation into the candidates' driving records. The brothers who own the pizza parlor hire a person whose license was suspended for driving under the influence of alcohol, and they equip him with a car. He drinks excessively and as a result causes a car accident while delivering pizza. Although the driver was the direct cause of the accident (and is personally liable), the pizza parlor is also primarily liable for negligent hiring and negligent supervision. As with all negligence cases, foreseeability of risk is a key component. If the agent is being posted to a job that requires entry to customers' homes, supervising children, working with infirm people, and so forth, then the level of care required by the principal in hiring and supervising is correspondingly higher. Finally, suppose instead the pizza parlor hired an excellent candidate as driver but instructed her to exceed the speed limit regularly in order to deliver more pizzas and to deliver them faster. Again, although the driver was the direct cause of the accident (and is personally liable), the pizza parlor is also liable for directing the tortious conduct.

Could a principal be liable for an agent's tort even if the principal is entirely free of any wrongdoing? What would be the rationale for imputing liability on a blameless party? The principal has the opportunity to control the agent — to supervise him or her, to develop good business policies and practices, etc. Therefore in many instances, the principal can minimize risks to third parties. Also, recall that principals who must pay a third party might have insurance to cover the loss and/or can seek reimbursement from the agent for a breach of the agent's duty to the principal. Under what circumstances could the agent's tort liability be imputed to the principal?

Principal's Liability for an Independent Contractor's Negligence

Principals are usually immune from liability for the negligence of an independent contractor in the performance of contracted services. This is consistent with the rationale above; because principals usually do not have control over how independent contractors perform their work, they are not in a position to minimize third-party injury. However, principals could be liable for third-party injury in the following instances:

1. Recall that if a third party reasonably believes an agent has authority, then the principal will be bound under the theory of apparent authority. An independent contractor could have apparent authority. Several jurisdictions, for example, have found hospitals liable under apparent authority for the negligence of independent contractor personnel who are assigned by the hospital to perform support services.
2. Principals could also be found directly responsible for negligence in hiring or supervising an independent contractor.

Case Illustration

Domino's Pizza franchises its stores. A driver named Hoppock was delivering pizza for a Domino's franchise owned by J & B Enterprises when he allegedly caused a car accident that the plaintiffs, who were pedestrians, witnessed. While trying to assist the injury victims, they themselves were injured when another vehicle hit them. The plaintiffs claimed that Domino's Pizza exercised sufficient control over the activities of its franchisee that Domino's should be vicariously liable for the negligence of J & B Enterprises and Hoppock. On summary judgment, the District Court of Appeal of Florida reversed the trial court's conclusion that Domino's could not be held vicariously liable for J & B's negligence. In so holding, the court noted that the franchise agreement required the franchisee to "utilize the Company's business format, methods, specifications, standards, operating procedures, operating assistance, advertising services and the [trademarks]" and also required detailed specifics on "every conceivable facet of the business: from the elements of preparing the perfect pizza to maintaining accurate books; from advertising and promotional ideas to routing and delivery guidelines; from order-taking instructions to oventending rules; from organization to sanitation." This raised the material question of fact as to whether Domino's "retain[s] the right to control the franchisee to accomplish the required tasks." *Parker v. Domino's Pizza*, 629 So. 2d. 1026. Fla App. (1993).

3. Principals are vicariously liable for the tortious conduct of independent contractor agents if the independent contractor engages in inherently dangerous work (such as excavating). It would be unfair to allow principals to escape liability for inherently dangerous work simply by hiring an agent to do the work instead.
4. Sometimes principals do have sufficient control over the independent contractor to justify vicarious liability, as in the Case Illustration at left.

Principal's Vicarious Liability for an Employee's Negligence

As for agents who are employees, the doctrine of **respondeat superior** (Latin for "let the master answer") dictates that an employer is vicariously liable for the tortious act of an employee if the tort occurred in the **scope of employment**. According to the Restatement 3d of Agency, "[a]n employee acts within the scope of employment when performing work assigned by the employer or engaging in a course of conduct subject to the employer's control."[7] This involves consideration of

1. whether the agent's conduct was authorized by the employer,
2. whether the agent's conduct was controlled by the employer, and
3. the extent to which the employer's purpose and interests were advanced by the agent's conduct.

If the tort occurred when the employee was on a **frolic of his own**, then the employer is not vicariously liable. A **frolic of one's own** is defined as an "independent course of conduct not intended to further any purpose of the employer."[8] Sometimes employees engage in a minor deviation from the principal's business, referred to as a **detour**. Principals are responsible for the

---

[7]Restatement 3d of Agency, sec. 7.07(2).
[8]Restatement 3d of Agency, sec. 7.07(2)b.

When is an employer responsible for an employee's negligence?

negligent behavior committed while agents are on a detour. The distinction between detour and frolic is crucial because it marks the line for determining employer liability. Exhibits 12.2 and 12.3 on page 383 summarize liaibilty for third party harm caused by an employee/agent.

The following Ethical Insight illustrates the employee/agent's ethical duty not to cause vicarious harm to its principal/employer by misrepresenting the quality of the company's products to make a sale.

An Ethical Insight: W.D. Ross and the Ethical Obligations of an Agent at a Trade Show Not to Misrepresent the Quality of a Product

W.D. Ross's prima facie ethical duty of nonmalfeasance (not to cause harm to another) places an ethical duty on the employee/agent to carry out the agency function in a manner that does not cause vicarious liability to the employer/principal. For example, an agent/employee sent to a trade show who carelessly misrepresents the company's product to a customer, who in turn purchases it based on the agent's remarks, will cause the company to be vicariously liable to the customer for any losses he sustains in using the product. Employee/agents are often working on behalf of their principal/company on business trips, at home or abroad, for extended periods of time. A company's code of ethics should identify and prohibit an employee's potential illegal acts on business trips that may cause the principal/company to be vicariously liable for the agent's conduct.

Tort Liability of Principal and Agent — Intentional Torts and Crimes

There are several reasons why the imposition of liability on a principal for an agent's intentional torts and crimes would not be consistent with general legal principles. Recall from Chapter 10, "Business Crimes," that an essential element of most crimes is *mens rea*, that is, a culpable intent, and that, in general, the criminal system in the United States exists to and is designed to punish culpability. Imposing vicarious liability for crimes would contradict this; therefore, principals usually are not liable for the crimes of their agents unless the principal authorized or was complicit in the criminal activity. In addition, as explained above, a principal's liability for an agent's actions occurs when and because the agent is advancing the principal's interests. Ordinarily agents do not commit intentional torts and crimes in an effort to advance the principal's interests. Although courts are divided on this issue, the majority view is that a principal's vicarious liability for an agent's crime hinges on whether the criminal action involved an intent to serve the principal. Under an "intent to serve" theory, the injured third party must establish that the agent was motivated by the principal's interests when engaging in the intentional tort or crime.

Principals can also be vicariously liable for torts committed by agents who were "aided in accomplishing the tort by the existence of the agency relation."[9] This controversial concept opens principals to liability if, for example, an employee is entrusted by the employer with keys to rooms where the intentional tort or criminal activity takes place.[10]

---

[9]Restatement 2d Agency 219(2)(d).
[10]*Costos v. Coconut Island Corp.*, 137 F.3d 46 (1st Cir. 1998)

Exhibit 12.2 Summary of Principal's Vicarious Liability for Third-Party Injury Committed by an Employee/Agent

	Principal's Liability for Tort	Agent's Liability for Tort
Agent is acting within scope of employment	Yes	Yes
Agent is acting during a "detour"	Yes	Yes
Agent is acting on a frolic of his or her own	No	Yes

Terminating the Agency Relationship

Agency relationships can terminate in a number of different ways. The point at which a person is no longer an agent can be very important, especially from the principal's perspective. Suppose an agent has been given authority to enter

Exhibit 12.3. Analysis of Principal's Liability for Negligence

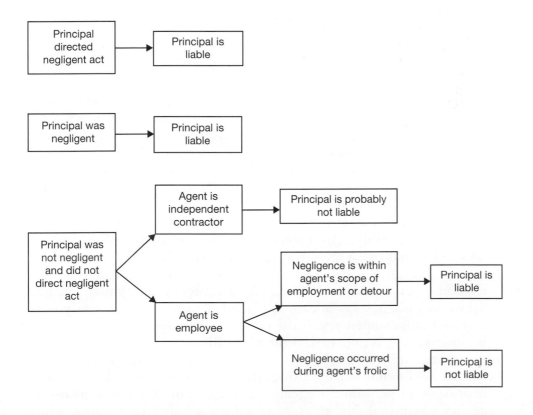

contracts on the principal's behalf and then the agency terminates. It is the principal's responsibility to notify third parties that the individual no longer represents the principal. Failure to notify others could lead to claims of apparent authority by a third party. For example, suppose a U.S. widget manufacturer appoints a company in France to solicit widget sales orders throughout Europe. The French company forwards sales orders and payment to the U.S. company, which fills the orders. The U.S. company terminates the agency but does not notify its European customers. The French company continues to receive payments but keeps the money. The European customers could claim apparent authority, leading to contractual liability for the U.S. company. Agencies can be terminated by the following:

- *Act of parties* Either the principal or the agent could terminate the agency relationship, typically through communication to the other party. Note that while such notice operates to halt ongoing principal/agent obligations and to terminate express authority, it does not necessarily follow that the parties are free of obligation to each other. A CFO with a two-year employment contract who chooses to resign after six months may terminate the agency but could be responsible for breach of the employment agreement.
- *Mutual agreement* The principal and the agent could mutually agree to terminate the agency relationship.
- *Purpose achieved* If the agency was created for a specific purpose and that purpose was achieved, then the agency is concluded. For example, assume a homeowner hires a real estate broker to help sell the home. Once the home is successfully sold, the broker is no longer the principal's agent.
- *Lapse of time* Sometimes principals and agents agree at the outset of the agency that the agency relationship will last for a certain period of time. Once that time has elapsed, the agency is over.
- *Occurrence of a specific event* Parties could agree at the outset of the agency that the agency will continue until a specific event occurs. The occurrence of the event triggers the termination of the agency.
- *By operation of law* Death and incapacity automatically terminate an agency relationship. An exception exists for a **durable** power of attorney — that is, a power of attorney specifically written to last beyond the principal's incompetency. For example, the wife who appoints her husband a power of attorney to authorize medical decisions and has specifically included a provision that the powers survive her incompetency. If the principal files bankruptcy, the agency is automatically terminated. If the agent files bankruptcy, the agency is terminated only if the agent's credit was important to the agency. Sometimes circumstances arising after the agency was created render it impossible to perform the agency's purpose. For example, suppose the agency was established to assist in selling a house or painting, which then is destroyed by fire.

Summary

Agency law enables businesses to expand beyond one individual. The law of agency enables enormous expansion of business, facilitates many people working together toward common commercial goals, and allows for division of labor. The ability to speak on behalf of a principal or to bind the principal to an agreement can involve significant responsibility and trust. Hence, agents legally owe principals fiduciary duties. In addition, the appointment of an agent with authority to contract on behalf of the principal is always accompanied by ethical responsibilities by both parties. The principal/employer should inform its employee/ agents about the company's compliance and ethics program and carefully review the terms of the code of ethics in periodic training sessions as illustrated throughout this textbook. Agency law is supported by ethical principles that should be explained at managers' meetings to employee/ agents to emphasize the ethical as well as the legal obligations employees owe to the company and its stakeholders. Employee/agents should be reminded that, as representatives of the company, they perform an essential role in the company maintaining an ethical corporate culture.

Questions for Review

1. Agency formation

The Church of God at Southaven entered into an agreement with a general contractor called National Church Services (NCS) for the construction of a sanctuary for about $1.1 million. NCS hired several subcontractors. Three of the subcontractors claimed that they had not been paid for construction work done on the sanctuary and that the church was responsible to pay them because NCS was acting as agent for the church when it hired the subcontractors. Was this argument valid? *Summerall Elec. Co., Inc. v. Church of God at Southaven* 25 So.3d 1090 (2010) Court of Appeals of Mississippi, 2010.

2. Agency formation and fiduciary duties

More than 600,000 residents of Pennsylvania participated in H&R Block's Rapid Refund program. The program was essentially a loan. Under the Rapid Refund program, qualified taxpayers who filed electronically and met certain eligibility requirements were automatically informed of the availability of a loan equal to their tax refund amount. For taxpayers selecting this option, Block would file the return simultaneously with the IRS and Mellon Bank. Within a few days, approved taxpayers receive a check for the amount of their refund less a transaction fee of either $29 or $35. When the taxpayer's refund from the government arrived, the government deposited the amount in a Mellon Bank account to repay the loan. Due to the short-term nature of these loans (about two weeks), the interest rates were as high as 151 percent. Block did not disclose to customers about the Mellon loan or that it shared profit on the rapid refund program. Was Block acting as agent for the taxpayers who chose the loan? If so, did Block breach its fiduciary duty to these taxpayers? *Basile v. H&R Block*, 563 Pa. 359 (2000).

3. Ethics of a company that benefited from an employee giving drugs and alcohol to procure sales

Alco, Inc., has a very progressive board of directors and CEO who are committed to creating and maintaining an ethical culture within its business environment. They have an extensive corporate compliance and ethics program, a code of ethics, and evaluate their supervisors on monitoring good ethical standards in their division. Alco, Inc., specifically prohibits the use of drugs and alcohol in the working environment. Harold, a top salesperson in the company, was discovered to be giving cocaine to buyers as an enticement to purchase Alco's merchandise. He was reprimanded by the company but not discharged. The Justice Department is prosecuting Alco under a theory of vicarious liability arguing the company has made thousands of dollars and benefited from Harold's illegal behavior. Alco argues its compliance and ethics program and code of ethics prohibit giving gifts to procure a sales contract for any reason, and its "due diligence" is a defense to vicarious liability. Alco introduces as evidence its company efforts to develop and maintain an ethical corporate culture. Was Alco, Inc., acting ethically, and were they correct in their argument? *United States v. Beusch*, 596 F. 2d 871 (9th Cir. 1979).

4. Apparent authority and an imposter

An imposter posed as a salesperson in a furniture store, took cash from a customer, promised delivery of the furniture, and then left. The customer sued the store based on apparent authority. What resulted and why? *Hoddeson v. Koos Bros.*, 135 A.2d 702 (N.J. Super. 1957).

5. Authority of attorneys

The plaintiff, Dennis Rubel, was permanently injured while working at Lowe's Home Center Inc., and hired Michael Dzienny to represent him in a personal injury lawsuit. When discussing a settlement with Lowe's, Rubel instructed Dzienny to "get the best he could get on this case." Dzienny then settled Rubel's case for $21,000 in exchange for Rubel's release of all claims against Lowe's. Rubel then stated that he never, expressly or impliedly, authorized Dzienny to accept a settlement on his behalf or to accept $21,000 as settlement of his claims against Lowes. Is Rubel bound by the settlement Dzienny negotiated? Why or why not? *Rubel v. Lowe's Home Centers, Inc.* 597 F. Supp. 2d 742 (2009).

6. Authority and service of process

A patient brought a medical malpractice lawsuit against a physician, Dr. Haynes, and Med-South, the healthcare group that employed Dr. Haynes. In connection with this lawsuit, a constable served Dr. Haynes with process (notifying him of the lawsuit) by giving the required papers to a customer service representative who greeted patients at the front desk reception area of MedSouth. The customer service representative was employed by MedSouth. She signed for medical records subpoenas and for certified mail but testified that she would not have signed had she known it was a lawsuit because she "did not know what to do about a lawsuit." When challenged in court, the Tennessee Supreme Court stated that "whether this constituted service of process upon Dr. Haynes hinges upon whether [the customer service representative] was "an agent authorized . . . to receive service on behalf of" Dr. Haynes. What resulted and why? *Hall v. Haynes*, 319 S.W.3d 564 (2010).

7. Authority in general

Laura Neilsen, a job specialist with Vocational and Educational Services for Individuals with Disabilities, responded to an advertisement in a New York newspaper for a position as a "shower," a job involving unlocking and locking apartments to assist real estate salespeople. The phone number listed in the ad corresponded to the Defendant, Manhattan Apartments, Inc., and a receptionist answered the call "Manhattan Apartments, Inc." Neilsen asked about the position and was transferred to another person who explained that the ad was for an entry-level position with Manhattan Apartments. Neilsen provided this information to the Plaintiff

Michael Halpert and suggested he apply. Upon arriving at the defendant's offices, the plaintiff was greeted by the defendant's receptionist who said she was expecting him and directed him to Robert Brook's desk. Brooks regularly hired assistants to work for him as showers, and he paid his assistants directly. In the interview, Brooks said that the plaintiff was too old for the position. When Neilsen called several days later to ask about the interview, defendant's receptionist told Neilsen that the plaintiff would not be hired because he was too old. Plaintiff sued for unlawful age discrimination. Did Brooks have actual or apparent authority to hire the plaintiff on the defendant's behalf? *Halpert v. Mahattan Apartments, Inc.* 2011 WL 5928782.

8. Principal's liability for agent's acts

In 2005, Sheila Newman decided to invest a large amount of her savings. Having little knowledge of investments, she researched companies online and decided to buy an annuity from National Western (NW). She called NW and was put in touch with Lynn Strickland, Jr., who told her that if she invested $200,000, she could live off the interest she received. Newman agreed, and Strickland instructed her to obtain two cashier's checks—one for $75,000 and one for $125,000—and that both checks should be made payable to Lone Star Financial "in order for him to be able to handle the money." Lone Star Financial is owned by Strickland.

Strickland went to Newman's house to give her a two-page application. She began completing it but did not finish because Strickland said he was in a hurry and she trusted he would take care of it. Part of the application stated, in capital letters, that "ALL CHECKS MUST BE PAYABLE TO NATIONAL WESTERN LIFE INSURANCE COMPANY." Newman's initials appeared next to the statement that the policy had been explained to her and that she had received and reviewed a copy of the consumer disclosures. She claimed her initials were forged and that she never received the disclosures.

Strickland deposited the $75,000 check in Lone Star's account and endorsed the $125,000 check over to NW. NW issued a policy to Newman for $125,000. Newman drew on the policy and received several checks from NW. Newman asked Strickland for a copy of the policy, but he gave her excuses or cancelled appointments with her. After about two years, she finally complained to NW that she never received a copy of her $200,000 policy. NW told her that the policy was for $125,000. Newman sued Strickland and NW. Is NW responsible for Strickland's acts? Why or why not? *National Western Life Insurance v. Newman* 2011 WL 4916434 (2011).

Further Reading

Bagley, Constance E., Lynn Sharp Paine, and Henry B. Reiling. *The Fiduciary Relationship: A Legal Perspective.* (Harvard Business School Publishing 2009).

Kistler, David S. *Independent Contractor v. Employee: The Never Ending Battle.* 43 Business Law Review 77-89 (2010).

Lazaro, Christine. *Fiduciary Duty—Now and in the Future.* 17 No. 2 PIABA Bar Journal (2010).

Musil, Thomas A., and John I. Halloran. *Arbitrating Real Estate Agency Disputes: The Complex Landscape of Real Estate Agency.* 67 Dipute Resolution Journal 85 (2013).

Sullivan, Charles A. *Mastering the Faithless Servant?: Reconciling Employment Law, Contract Law, and Fiduciary Duty.* 2011 Wisconsin Law Review 777 (2011).

CHAPTER 13

Employment Law

Chapter Objectives

1. To understand the concept of employment-at-will and the most common exceptions to this doctrine
2. To know the obligations of employers to employees, especially with regard to matters such as wages, medical leave, worker's compensation, and workplace safety
3. To understand that employees have a right to unionize and what unionization involves
4. To know the obligation of employees to an employer, especially with regard to loyalty, maintaining confidentiality, and refraining from competition with the employer
5. To understand the limits of privacy in the workplace

Practical Example: Starling Corporation*

While in her last of year of studies at Better Business University, Greta Graduate began to go through the interview process to secure full-time employment after graduation. She was thrilled to get an offer from Starling Corporation, a multinational corporation with corporate offices in many of the 50 states. When she arrived for her first day of work, she was greeted by a stack of papers in need of her signature. The human resources director explained to

Greta that signing the various agreements was a condition of her employment with Starling. Because Greta would never do anything to jeopardize her chance to work at Starling, she hastily signed the papers after only giving them a cursory glance. She did notice some key phrases such as, "you are considered an employee-at-will," "your Internet use will be monitored," "you have no privacy rights in e-mails sent and received through the Starling e-mail system," and "should your employment with Starling terminate for any reason, you shall not work for any competitor within a hundred mile radius for a period of three years." Some of these items certainly caused her to pause for a moment, but she quickly suppressed any hesitation and focused instead on how many skills she could develop at Starling and how impressive her work there would look on her résumé. Still, a part of Greta felt as if she were somehow going to be "checking her rights" at the door every time she entered the workplace, and she wondered just how extensive Starling's control over her everyday actions was going to be in the years to come. She also wondered what rights she had as an employee and how those rights would be protected and upheld.

Greta's experience is not unique. In fact, it is the norm for many employees in the workforce today to be presented with a variety of conditions of employment. As you read this chapter consider the following questions:

1. What does it mean to be an employee-at-will?
2. Are there any federal or state laws that will ensure that Greta has certain rights as an employee?
3. To what extent will Greta have any rights to privacy in the workplace? For example, is Starling permitted to monitor Greta's electronic communications? May they listen in on phone calls made on the office phone?
4. Can Starling dictate the type of employment opportunities Greta may engage in even after her employment with Starling has ended?

---

* Starling Corporation is a fictitious company developed by the authors to demonstrate and illustrate key legal and ethical concepts, theories, practices, and strategies.

The employer-employee relationship is central to a wide range of business transactions. It is a relationship in which each party has certain rights and duties. This chapter covers many of the laws that dictate an employer's obligations to its employees. It also explores the obligations of the employee to the employer as well as the employee's rights in the workplace. Ethical issues are discussed to assist you in understanding the moral obligations inherent in the employment relationship.

Employment-at-Will

Since the time of the Industrial Revolution the predominant approach taken toward employment relationships in the United States has been what is called **employment-at-will**. This means that employees have the option of quitting their employment at any time for any reason, and the employer has the option of firing those employees at any time, for any reason, or for no reason at all. Over time, a combination of state legislative and court decisions have chipped away at this broad latitude given to employers and have created exceptions to the employment-at-will doctrine. These exceptions include the public policy exception, the implied contract exception, and the implied covenant of good faith and fair dealing exception. In addition, if an employee has an employment contract with an employer or the employee has job security under terms of a union contract, that employee will automatically be exempt from employment-at-will status.

Public Policy Exception

When an at-will employee is terminated for reasons that offend a public policy, such termination will not sustain judicial scrutiny. What does this mean? Let us consider Greta from the opening example. Assume that sometime during the course of her employment at Starling, Greta's boss asks her to write a press release about the company that contains false information. Greta refuses, and she is fired immediately. While employment-at-will allows an employer to fire an employee for any reason, the public policy exception says "not so fast," there are some situations in which an employee should not be penalized. Whether Greta can be fired for refusing to write the false press release will depend on the law in her state. While the vast majority of the states recognize the public policy exception, there is wide variation in what activities are protected and how public policy is defined. The first issue to consider when deciding whether the public policy exception applies is how to define "public policy." In some states public policy only refers to state constitutional protections or state statutory law. Other states interpret public policy more broadly, including in the definition items such as a professional code of ethics and in some instances, general public sentiment.

The majority of public policy exception cases involve whistleblowers, employees who refuse to commit an illegal act, or employees who are terminated for exercising a right or privilege.[1] In some states public policy is defined very narrowly and may only include situations in which an employee gets fired because of their refusal to perform an illegal act, while in other states a public policy exception may be applied any time an employer acts in bad faith or with malice toward the employee.[2]

Whistleblower Protection

Blowing the whistle on an employer's wrongful actions often is accompanied by a risk of retaliation by the employer. Besides the potential for being ostracized within the workplace, the industry, and possibly even in their community, whistleblowing employees also run the risk of the termination of their employment. Is there any protection from termination for whistleblowers? The answer is, it depends. Wrongful acts reported externally, for example, to a government agency or law enforcement, often receive a greater level of

---

[1]Lichtenstein, Stephen and Darrow, Jonathan, *At-Will Employment: A Right to Blog or a Right to Terminate?* 11 Journal of Internet Law 9 (March 2008).
[2]Zachary, Mary-Kathryn, *Labor Law for Supervisors: Employment at Will and Public Policy,* 73 Supervision 11, p. 21 (Nov. 2012).

protection than acts reported internally to management within the workplace. Over time various Whistleblower Protection Programs have been developed and administered by the Occupational Safety and Health Administration (OSHA) to protect employees who report safety violations in certain industries such as airlines, food safety, maritime, and securities law. Recently OSHA announced that it would also be monitoring claims of retaliation against whistleblowers who come forward to report employer violations of the Patient Protection and Affordable Care Act. As described in Chapter 9, "Sale of Securities and Investor Protection," employees who come forward to report illegal corporate conduct may also find protection under Sarbanes-Oxley or Dodd-Frank.

Refusal to Perform an Illegal Act

An employer may not terminate an employee for that employee's refusal to comply with an employer's request to perform an illegal act. For example, Arthur Accountant, an at-will employee, keeps the accounting books and records for his employer, Shady Co. One day Arthur's supervisor informs him that the directors would like to keep the company's income tax liability as low as possible, and they would like Arthur to begin to keep a second set of books and records that understate income and overstate expenses. Arthur refuses to comply and his employment is immediately terminated. Ordinarily an employer may terminate the employment of an at-will employee for no reason at all. The public policy exception, however, ensures that employers cannot fire an employee for a "bad" reason. Arthur's termination is a clear violation of public policy and an exception to the rule of at-will employment.

Exercising a Right or Privilege

Employees cannot be terminated for exercising a lawful right or privilege. Consider, for example, the right of an employee to file a state workers' compensation claim for a work-related injury. There have been numerous cases of employees who have been terminated in retaliation for filing a state workers' compensation claim. In some cases, juries have awarded significant damages to the terminated employee. In 2010, an Illinois district court awarded Larry Holland $4.2 million in damages as a result of his termination by Schwan Home Services Inc. in retaliation for filing a workers' compensation claim. The jury award included $3.6 million in punitive damages intended to punish the employer for its actions.[3] In 2013 this judgment was affirmed by the appellate court.

The following case involves a whistleblower employee-at-will's claim for wrongful discharge. Notice the court's strict adherence to the facts of the case in denying the claim.

---

[3]*Holland v. Schwan's Home Service Inc.*, 2010 U.S. Dist. LEXIS 44624 (2010), affd. 2013 Ill. App. LEXIS 342 (May 30, 2013)

In-Depth Ethical Case Analysis

Sullivan v. Harnisch, **2012 WL1580602 New York Court of Appeals**

Facts

Joseph Sullivan was both an employee and minority owner (15 percent) of two related firms Peconic Partners, LLC and Peconic Asset Managers, LLC ("Peconic"). As an employee he fulfilled many roles simultaneously, including executive vice president, treasurer, chief operating officer, and chief compliance officer. Sullivan was fired by Peconic majority owner and president, William Harnisch. According to Harnisch, Sullivan's dismissal was based on performance reasons and misconduct. Sullivan challenged his firing on various grounds, but this particular case is only focused on one cause of action — Sullivan's claim that he was fired because he objected to certain deceptive stock transactions by Harnisch. These transactions allowed Harnisch to sell stock for his own personal account and for those of his family members but did not provide the same sale option for the firm's investment clients. According to Sullivan, these stock sales amounted to "manipulative and deceptive trading practices." Sullivan claimed that his firing was unlawful and qualified as an exception to the employment-at-will doctrine because he was a whistleblower and his dismissal was in violation of "a company policy to prohibit retaliation."

Issue

Was Sullivan's dismissal an unlawful termination under the public policy exception to employment-at-will?

Holding

The New York Court of Appeals denied Sullivan's wrongful discharge claim. This holding is consistent with the New York court's policy of only interfering with the employment-at-will relationship in narrowly tailored circumstances. "Absent violation of a constitutional requirement, statute, or contract," the employer could terminate Sullivan at will. The court did not find such a violation to exist. The court did not even find evidence of a company policy against retaliation as claimed by Sullivan, finding instead that Sullivan was relying on the general obligations under securities laws and the firm's code of ethics. According to the court, to prevail, Sullivan would have to be able to show that his regulatory duty as a compliance officer was intertwined with and central to his duties as an employee, a showing that the court did not find he could make, especially because he was only a part-time compliance officer and had many other roles at Peconic. The court went on to state that it should be left to Congress to create protection for employees such as Sullivan, pointing out as an example the Dodd-Frank Wall Street Reform and Consumer Protection Act (discussed in Chapter 9, "Sale of Securities and Investor Protection") that provides protection for employees fired by their employers for providing information of violations of securities laws to the Securities and Exchange Commission. The protection of the Dodd-Frank Act would not apply to Sullivan in this case because he did not provide information to the SEC but instead only confronted Harnisch about the stock trading. The dissenting judge in the case expressed concern that this opinion would potentially result in allowing further violations in the financial service industry to go unchecked.

Ethical Issue

Was it ethical, based on the facts of this case, for Harnisch to fire the plaintiff, Sullivan, for objecting to Harnisch's "manipulative and deceptive trade practice" that violated the company's code of ethics? Notice the majority decision's primary concern with Sullivan's regular duty as a compliance officer, which it found to be "intertwined and central to his duties as an employee." This is a contractual argument based on Sullivan's implied employment contract and ignores the unethical consequences of the decision. Judges are often restricted, as in this case, to a factual and legal resolution with a harsh result.

Ethical Theory Analysis

Utilitarianism is an ethical theory that follows rules that provide the greatest happiness to the greater number. Did the dismissal of Sullivan by Harnisch affect the public good? Assuming Sullivan's allegations are correct and the same sales option granted to Harnisch, the company president, and his family members was not given to the firm's investors to sell their stock amounted to a "manipulative and deceptive trade practice," could one argue Sullivan's dismissal was an ethical violation of utilitarianism because the greater number (the firm's investors) could not realize the same gain from the stock sale (as did the smaller number—Harnisch and his family)? Notice how utilitarianism is concerned with the *consequence of an action* and how it affects other company stakeholders, in this case the firm's investors. The immediate dismissal of Sullivan by Harnisch without a prompt review of Sullivan's allegations by an independent committee could be characterized as an unethical act

Kant's categorical imperative to "*act only on that maxim whereby thou canst at the same time will that it should become a universal law*" asks the ethical question did Harnisch's dismissal of Sullivan who accused him of engaging in a "manipulative and deceptive trade practice," violate that principle? Yes. If all CEOs and company presidents summarily dismissed the company chief compliance officers when they were accused of committing a wrongful act, the corporate culture of integrity would be nonexistent. Sullivan's allegations should have been investigated by an independent committee.

Effective Compliance and Ethics Program

It appears that Peconic, although it has a code of ethics, did not have an effective compliance and ethics program. In addition to the code of ethics, medium- and large-size corporations should have an auditing and monitoring committee that the compliance officer can report perceived wrongful acts to for their review. The company should have employee training programs that are also mandatory for the board of directors and corporate officers, periodic risk assessments that may have identified potential wrongful stocktrades, and in this case a specific mention in the code of ethics that those serving as compliance officers have authority to report all violations directly to the board of directors. The board should exercise oversight of the compliance and ethics program.

Compliance Officer's Duties Were Compromised

The dissenting opinion in this case by Chief Judge Lippman stated, "*The message that will be taken from the majority's decision is self-evident: if compliance officers (and others similarly situated) wish to keep their jobs, they should keep their heads down and ignore good-faith suspicions or evidence they may have that their employers have engaged in illegal and unethical behavior, even where such violations could cause or have caused staggering losses to their employers' clients.*" Of special note is Judge Lippman's reference to "unethical behavior" that this case seems to allow and legalize.

Conclusion

An ethical corporate culture has to hold all accountable for wrongful acts, including top management. Regardless of the many positions and part-time role of Sullivan as the chief compliance officer, he had an ethical duty to perceive and report wrongful conduct without fear of retaliation. An ethical analysis of this case does not support the majority decision. The ethical reasoning is more in line with Judge Lippman's dissenting opinion, which warns, ". . . *If compliance officers (and others similarly situated) wish to keep their jobs, they should keep their heads down.*" This position would hardly promote an ethical corporate culture.

Implied Contract Exception

Employees relying on the implied contract exception generally claim that continued employment was implied by the employer either through written or oral statements by the employer. You may be surprised to learn that even comments made by an employer during the interview process could be construed to create an implied contract. For example, let us assume that Joseph is an employee of Chesire Corporation. When Joseph first interviewed for the job at Chesire, the dialogue during the interview process included the following exchange:

JOSEPH: *What do you like best about working for this company?*

INTERVIEWER: *We are one, big, happy family at this company. Once you work for this company, your future is secure. We look out for each other and the company is loyal to us.*

It is likely that the supervisor who spoke these words to Joseph during the interview did not even realize the potential her comments had to create an implied contract of continued employment between the company and the employee. In addition to oral assurances, a written employee handbook or manual may also be evidence of an implied contract of continued employment. There is no uniform answer as to whether the language in an employee handbook creates an implied contract. In one case the Minnesota Supreme Court found that an employee handbook created an implied contract because the handbook outlined disciplinary procedures that would be followed in the event an employee violated company policy, and the company's termination of the employee without following the procedures outline in the handbook was a breach of that contract.[4] Other courts such as the Supreme Court of Pennsylvania rejected the notion that an employee handbook could create an implied contract because the terms of the handbook were not bargained for, and therefore, there was no "meeting of the minds" as required by contract law.[5]

Covenant of Good Faith and Fair Dealing Exception

The implied covenant of good faith and fair dealing requires that termination of employees be based on just cause, and not based on malice or ill will by the employer. This exception is only recognized in a handful of states. Examples of situations in which this exception has been utilized include an employer's discharge of a long-time employee in order to avoid payment of retirement benefits and discharge of an employee to avoid payment of sales commission. Other courts have rejected applying a covenant of good faith and fair dealing

---

[4]*Pine River State Bank v. Mettille*, 333 N.W. 2d 622 (1983).
[5]*Richardson v. Charles Cole Memorial Hospital*, 466 A.2d 1084 (1983).

standard to the employment relationship indicating that determining an employer's motivation in each termination case is too great a burden for the courts.[6]

Employers' Obligations to the Employee

Employers have a variety of obligations toward their employees under federal and state laws.

Minimum Wage and Hour Laws and Child Labor Restrictions

The **Fair Labor Standards Act**[7] (FLSA), passed in 1938, mandates federal standards for both hourly wages and overtime pay that apply to virtually all employers. This act covers employers engaged in interstate commerce and employers engaged in the production of goods for interstate commerce. Under this law, which is administered by the Wage and Hour Division of the Department of Labor, employers are required to pay their employees at least the federal minimum wage. The minimum wage amount is adjusted by Congress periodically for cost of living. Employers are also required to pay one and a half times the employee's hourly rate for any hours considered overtime (hours beyond 40 hours per week). Certain categories of employees, namely executives, administrative employees, professional employees, and outside salespersons, are exempt from this overtime requirement. The FLSA also imposes restrictions on child labor.

To ensure compliance with the requirements of the FLSA, the Department of Labor requires that employers maintain certain records. Exhibit 13.1 on page 397 summarizes these requirements.

Failure to comply with wage and hour laws may not only impact the business itself but may also result in personal liability for the business owners. Consider the following two examples. In one case, Phillip Franklin, the owner and president of Franklin Drywall, failed to pay employees the overtime rate of 1.5 times the regular rate and intentionally misstated the number of hours worked for purposes of reporting to the union and benefits fund. As a result, he was sentenced to two years in jail plus a potential fine of $3.3 million. In another instance, the owners and officers of International Detective & Protective Services were fined more than $200,000 for violating both the overtime and recordkeeping requirements of the FLSA.

In addition, states may have their own wage and hour laws in place that provide greater protections for employees than the FLSA. Employers must

---

[6]Muhi, Charles, *The Employment-at-Will Doctrine: Three Major Exceptions*, Monthly Labor Review (January 2001).
[7]29 U.S.C. ch. 8.

Exhibit 13.1. Recordkeeping Requirements Under the FLSA*

Records to Be Maintained

1. Employee's full name and social security number
2. Address, including zip code
3. Birth date, if younger than 19
4. Sex and occupation
5. Time and day of week when employee's workweek begins
6. Hours worked each day
7. Total hours worked each workweek
8. Basis on which employee's wages are paid (e.g., "$9 per hour," "$440 a week," "piecework")
9. Regular hourly pay rate
10. Total daily or weekly straight-time earnings
11. Total overtime earnings for the workweek
12. All additions to or deductions from the employee's wages
13. Total wages paid each pay period
14. Date of payment and the pay period covered by the payment

* U.S. Department of Labor, Fact Sheet #21, http://www.dol.gov/whd/regs/compliance/whdfs21.pdf.

---

comply with state laws or face financial consequence. Wal-Mart learned this expensive lesson when a jury in Alameda County, California, awarded plaintiffs $57 million in compensatory damage and $115 million in punitive damages for the company's failure to provide workers who worked more than a five-hour shift without the 30-minute meal breaks required by California wage and hour laws. It could be argued that the ethics of the FLSA, which provides for the less-advantaged employee, are supported by John Rawls, who stated in *A Theory of Justice* that "Justice is the first virtue of social institutions."

A more recent area of dispute under the wage and hour laws of the FLSA is the unpaid internship. An organization's ability to hire unpaid interns is premised on the fact that in return the organization will provide the intern with valuable training. However, when the organization fails to provide such training and simply uses the intern as an unpaid employee, the entity may be in violation of wage and hour laws. Consider the Case Illustration on page 398 regarding interns working on Fox Searchlight's movie *Black Swan*.

> **An Ethical Insight: John Rawls and the Fair Labor Standards Act**
>
> Rawls stated: "*Is it possible for the . . . less advantaged to be reconciled to a common principle? Should there be no such principle, the structure of the social worlds . . . . . . would be . . . hostile to the very idea of democratic equality.*"* A minimum wage, overtime pay, and other requirements of the Fair Labor Standards Act are ethically supported by Rawls's notion of a "common principle" (e.g., the FLSA statute) that provides a "structure of the social world" to protect the less advantaged low-ranked employees with little bargaining power with their employer and thereby helps promote democratic equality.
>
> ---
>
> *Rawls, John, *Justice as Fairness, A Restatement* 76 (Erin Kelley ed., Belknap Press of Harvard University Press).

Case Illustration

Two production interns working on the movie *Black Swan*, Eric Glatt and Alexander Footman, brought a suit against Fox Searchlight Pictures for back wages, claiming that instead of being given training in the field of production, they were required to perform tasks ordinarily performed by paid employees such as answering phones, taking lunch orders, tracking purchase orders, and taking out trash. The federal district court in the southern district of New York agreed that Fox Pictures violated federal and state minimum wage laws by failing to pay the interns. Relying on the criteria for unpaid internships adopted by the Department of Labor, Judge Pauley ruled that to qualify as an unpaid internship the work should be similar to vocational training given in an educational environment, the employer must not derive an immediate advantage from the relationship, the intern's work must not displace that of regular employees, and the experience should be for the benefit of the intern. *Glatt v. Fox Searchlight Pictures, Inc.*, S.D.N.Y. No. 11-06784 (June 11, 2013).

Family and Medical Leave Act

The **Family and Medical Leave Act** (FMLA) is a federal law enacted in 1993 that requires employers with 50 or more employees to provide employees with up to 12 weeks of unpaid leave for the birth or adoption of a child, or in the event of serious illness of the employee, or a spouse, child, or parent. To be eligible for leave under the FMLA, an employee must work for an employer for at least 12 months (nonconsecutive is fine) and have at least 1,250 hours of service for the employer during the 12-month period immediately preceding the leave. Employees are required to provide 30 days advance notice of the needed leave, when feasible. Since 2009, employers have been required to provide individual notices to each employee regarding their rights under the FMLA and an individual designation notice of whether the FMLA applies to their situation. During the period of leave, the FMLA requires that the employer continue to provide health benefits to the employee. In addition, upon returning from work, the employee must be given the same position or a position similar to the one he or she had before the leave with equivalent compensation, benefits, and responsibility. Employers who fail to comply with FMLA requirements face monetary liability for their actions. For example, employers who fail to continue the employee's health benefits will be liable for any damages the employee suffers in connection with this. The Case Illustration on the following page shows how important it is for employers to comply with *all* the requirements of the FMLA.

Maintaining Workplace Safety

The **Occupational Safety and Health Act** (OSHA) is the central piece of federal legislation designed to prevent workplace injury. OSHA, enacted in 1970, mandates safe working conditions for most workplaces to help ensure safe working conditions that are free from serious hazards. The secretary of labor is responsible for ensuring workplace safety standards are met by employers and has the right to authorize physical inspection of workplaces. Safety violations result in citations and corresponding civil penalties. Criminal penalties may also be imposed if an employer's willful violation of safety requirements results in the death of an employee.

OSHA health and safety compliance officers often conduct unannounced inspections. If an employer refuses to give the inspector access, the inspector could return with a warrant to inspect the premises. Employers who employ more than ten workers are required to keep detailed records of occupational injuries and illnesses and to make corresponding reports to the secretary of labor. Inspectors will also audit records to ensure compliance with these requirements. Records that indicate a higher-than-average rate of injury for that workplace often result in the inspector making a physical inspection of the entire facility. Workers injured on the job may be entitled to workers' compensation.

Workers' Compensation

Workers' compensation programs are governed by state law and ensure that compensation is provided to workers who are injured on the job. The workers' compensa-

Case Illustration

Wackenhut Corporation included in its employee handbook a general FMLA notice that outlined the rights of the employees under the act. The company also posted a FMLA poster provided by the Department of Labor. Wackenhut employee Jacqueline Young requested and took 12 weeks of FMLA leave for the birth of her child. When Young did not return to work when her leave expired, she was fired two weeks later. According to Wackenhut, Mrs. Young's leave expired on November 19, but they did not notify her of this until November 30. When she did not return to work on December 1, she was fired. In response Mrs. Young brought a claim against Wackenhut for interference with her rights under the FMLA for their failure to provide her with the required Notice of Eligibility and Rights & Responsibilities and the required Designation Notice. Mrs. Young prevailed. This case highlights the importance of employer compliance with all statutory law requirements. *Young v. Wackenhut Corporation*, 2013 U.S. Dist. LEXIS 14414 (D. NJ, 2013).

tion system helps to prevent disputes between the employer and the employee and helps to avoid the time and money that would be spent on litigation. The majority of state laws governing workers' compensation are similar. Workers' compensation amounts are set by state rules and paid from a state fund. Employers make contributions to the state fund, rather than compensating employees directly. The greater number of workers' compensation claims filed against an employer, the higher is the amount of required contribution for that employer, much like a premium increase in car insurance that results when a driver is at fault in an accident.

To recover damages, the employee does not have to show that the employer was at fault in causing the injury. All that is required is that the employee's injury occurred during the course of employment. In addition, the employee is not required to go to court to seek damages. The employee can file a form with the appropriate state agency seeking recovery. In most cases an employer will not contest the claim and damages will be paid. If, however, the employer objects to the claim, the next step would be an appeals hearing at the state agency. If the employee is unsuccessful on appeal, the employee retains the right to bring a case to the state court.

The amount of recovery an injured employee is entitled to receive is governed by state laws. In fact, in most states, workers' compensation is

OSHA officials inspect the scene of a 2012 collapse that took place during construction on the Horseshoe Casino in Cincinnati, Ohio.

considered to be the "exclusive remedy" available to employees for work-related injuries, meaning that they do not also have a right to bring a lawsuit against the employer for their injuries. The amounts recovered generally represent a portion of lost wages and do not include recovery for pain and suffering, unless the pain and suffering is at such a level as to be considered disabling. Because workers' compensation provides the primary relief, the employee is unable to bring a tort claim (for negligence) against the employer.

While the majority of employees come within the workers' compensation statutes, you should be aware that for a limited number of industries and employees, compensation for work-related injuries may be available instead under certain federal statutes. For example, federal employees are covered by the Federal Employees Compensation Act and certain industries have their own federal protection, e.g., Longshore and Harbor Workers' Compensation Act and the Federal Employers Liability Act (covering railroad workers and sailors).

Consolidated Omnibus Budget Reconciliation Act of 1985 (COBRA)

When an employee leaves his job or has a reduction in work hours so that he is no longer eligible for employer provided health benefits, **COBRA** ensures that the employee has the option to continue that coverage for an additional 18 months (29 months if the employee is disabled.) During the period of COBRA coverage, employees are required to pay for the health coverage themselves and may also have to pay a small administrative fee to the employer. COBRA does not cover situations in which the employee was fired for gross misconduct.

Employees' Right to Unionize

The **National Labor Relations Act** (NLRA), which became law in 1935, governs the relationship between management and employees. This law covers most industries and most categories of employees, although there are some exemptions for certain groups, such as temporary workers and agricultural workers. The purpose of the act is to secure the rights of employees and protect them from unfair labor practices by the employer. One of the employee's most basic rights under the act is the right to unionize and the right to take collective action. Workers who want to unionize must file a petition with the regional office of the National Labor Relations Board (NLRB) indicating that at least 30 percent of the employees have interest in a union. A committee from the NLRB oversees an election in which a majority of the votes cast must be in favor of the union. Should the union succeed, then both the union and the employer have an obligation to engage in collective bargaining in good faith. This does not mean that they have to come to a mutually acceptable decision, but they do have to try to reach an agreement in good faith.

Section 8 of the NLRA prohibits both employers and unions from engaging in unfair labor practices. Exhibit 13.2 on page 402 summarizes actions that constitute an unfair labor practice.

Exhibit 13.2. Unfair Labor Practices

Employer's Unfair Practices	Union Unfair Practices
Interfere, restrain, or coerce employees who seek to exercise their rights under the NLRA	Restrain or coerce an employee in the exercise of their rights under the NLRA
Dominate or interfere with the formation or administration of any labor organization or contribute financial or other support to it	Cause or attempt to cause an employer to discriminate against an employee whose membership in the union has been terminated
Discriminate in employment to discourage or encourage membership in any labor organization	Refuse to bargain collectively with an employer in good faith
Discharge or discriminate against an employee because the employee has filed charges or testified under the NLRA	Picketing or boycotting an employer for unlawful objectives (e.g., trying to compel an employer to recognize one union when another has been certified)
Refuse to bargain collectively with the employee representative	Charging excessive or discriminatory membership fees
	Causing an employer to pay for services that have not been performed

Workers at fast food restaurants, including Burger King, Wendy's, and Taco Bell, are shown with their supporters in front of the McDonald's in Times Square in New York City at a rally ending a one-day strike on November 29, 2012.

Employee Obligations to the Employer

As you learned in the preceding chapter on agency law, the employee has a duty of loyalty to the employer. This means that the employee must act in the best interest of the employer. There are other conditions of employment commonly imposed as well. As a condition of employment, many employees also sign both a confidentiality agreement and a covenant not to compete with their employer.

Nondisclosure Agreements

The confidentiality agreement ensures that the employee will not share the employer's trade secrets, business practices, marketing strategies, and so forth with others both during the course of their employment and after it ends. Recall from Chapter 8, "Intellectual Property," that it is essential for companies to monitor and protect trade secrets.

Covenant Not to Compete

Employers want to ensure that after termination, employees will not directly engage in competition with the employer.[8] To accomplish this, employers may prohibit employees from working in a competing activity within a certain distance and for a certain period of time after the employment relationship has ended. For reasons that will be further explained in Chapter 16, "Contracts: Performance, Public Policy, and Global Contracts," courts will uphold such covenants as long as they do not cover an unreasonable distance and are not for an excessively long period of time, in other words, as long as they do not unduly interfere with the employee's ability to make a living, and are reasonably tailored to protect trade secrets and other proprietary business information. In a recent Connecticut case[9] the court agreed that a fitness instructor was bound by the limitations of her noncompete agreement. In that case, Rebecca Hunt had signed a noncompete agreement with her employer, Bodyfit, which prohibited her from employment "in any business which engages in the same or similar business of the company or otherwise competes with the business of the company within a ten mile radius of any exercise studio owned and operated by the company." About a year after her employment with Bodyfit ended, Ms. Hunt secured employment with the Equinox gym, which was less than two miles from Bodyfit. The Superior Court of Connecticut agreed with Bodyfit that Ms. Hunt was in violation of her agreement. The court issued an injunction that prohibited Hunt from working at any exercise facility within ten

---

[8]State law governs noncompete agreements, and permissible restrictions vary between the states. In California, for example, noncompete agreements for employees and independent contractors are unenforceable. However, California does allow noncompete covenants signed in connection with the sale of a business.

[9]*Saylavee, LLC v. Hunt*, 2013 Conn. Super. LEXIS 1056 (May 7, 2013).

miles of Bodyfit, from revealing any of the company's proprietary business information, and from seeking the business of Bodyfit customers.

Privacy in the Workplace

To what extent does an employee have a reasonable expectation of privacy in the workplace? Keep in mind that in the private workplace there is no such thing as a constitutional right to privacy, although some constitutional provisions infer that a limited right to privacy may exist. As you learned in Chapter 3, "Constitutional Issues in Business," government employers are subject to heightened scrutiny and must act within the bounds of the Fourth and Fourteenth amendments. We will revisit this issue later in the chapter in the discussion of employer-provided cell phones. Claims for violations of workplace privacy in nongovernment settings are often based on the common law tort of intrusion on seclusion (invasion of privacy). In order to prevail on this tort claim, the employee must show that (1) the employee had a reasonable expectation of privacy and (2) the intrusion would be considered highly offensive to a reasonable person.

Before we consider the specifics of whether the employer can legally engage in various monitoring activities, let us first develop an understanding of why employers engage in monitoring activities, including monitoring electronic communications.[10] Employers do so, in part, to protect themselves from legal liability. Recall from Chapter 12, "Agency Law," the notion of *respondeat superior*. The employer is liable for all the actions of its agents/employees that the employer knew or should have known. For Chevron Oil Corporation, this was a very expensive lesson. Chevron settled a case for $2.2 million in response to a suit filed by four female employees alleging that they were the victims of sexual harassment based on receipt of sexually offensive e-mails sent via the employer's e-mail system. Employers also engage in monitoring activities to track employee job performance. Tracking performance ensures that employees are doing their job which increases efficiency. For example, tracking can include installing GPS systems on company-provided smartphones to allow employers to track the movements of delivery drivers during the workday. Employers monitor electronic communications to ensure that confidential documents, files, information, and trade secrets are not transmitted outside their organization. This concern is not unfounded, as an American Management Survey showed that 14 percent of employees have admitted to transmitting confidential employer information to third parties.[11]

---

[10]For a more in-depth discussion of this, see Jeffrey Mello, *Social Media, Employee Media, and Concerted Activity: Brave New World or Big Brother*, 165 Labor Law Journal (2012).
[11]*Id.*

Drug Testing

The high cost in terms of loss of productivity and increased accident rates resulting from substance abuse by employees has caused many employers to seek ways to reduce this problem. One way is through drug testing. Most states allow private employers to conduct both job screening drug tests as well as regular periodic screening of employees, but the states vary on the permissible limits of this testing. Government employers are limited by the Constitution, notably the Fourth Amendment limitation on unreasonable searches and seizures. A drug test will not run afoul of the Fourth Amendment if the employer has a reasonable basis for suspecting the employee of drug use. In addition, employees engaged in industries that involve public safety, such as transportation, can be subjected to random drug tests.

Polygraphs

The **Employee Polygraph Protection Act** (EPPA) was passed in 1988 to limit the ability of a private employer to use polygraph testing either as part of a preemployment screening process or during the course of employment. The EPPA covers a wide range of private employers — those affecting commerce or engaged in the production of goods for commerce. Certain employers are exempt from the act, including, for example, government employers and companies involved in the manufacture and sale of controlled substances. There are also some exceptions to the polygraph restrictions. If an employer is engaged in an ongoing investigation of a loss to the business (such as a theft of trade secrets), the company can ask an employee to take a polygraph test as long as the employer has a reasonable suspicion that the employee could be involved. If the police are conducting a criminal investigation of an incident occurring in the workplace, employers are allowed to cooperate in that investigation by allowing employee polygraph testing to be done by the police. The EPPA makes it unlawful for an employer to use the results of a polygraph test to discharge or discriminate against an employee.

Monitoring an Employee's Actions

Cameras in workspaces, listening to phone calls and voicemail, and reviews of employees' files are all traditional means used to keep tabs on employee performance. The ideal practice is for the employer to notify the employees that surveillance will take place, minimizing any expectation of employee privacy. There are, of course, limits to where in the workplace an employer can set up surveillance equipment. For example, installing such equipment in restrooms and locker rooms is not permitted. The Manager's Compliance and Ethics Meeting on page 406 requires you to think about the ethical and legal limits of permissible workplace surveillance and a reasonable expectation of privacy in your private office.

Manager's Compliance and Ethics Meeting

Changing Your Clothes in a Private Office — Is Someone Watching?

Holly, Mark, and Jacobs LLP (HMJ) is a fictitious law firm. It was recently ranked in a leading law journal as the best law office to work for in New York City, especially for women lawyers. One of its new renovations in the law firm was the establishment of a high-level gymnasium with private changing rooms and showers. Lydia, a New York Law School summer associate, was attracted to HMJ primarily because of its outstanding reputation in its fair treatment and promoting talented women to full partners. Lydia was told by other summer associates she could change into her gym clothing in her law office as the firm's gymnasium was only a few steps down the hall from all the summer associates' offices. At the end of the summer, during an exit interview, Lydia was informed by a partner that there was a hidden camera in her office to ensure the firm's awareness of any potential sexual harassment in the law offices. The partners installed the cameras in all offices to maintain their reputation as a firm especially sensitive to its reputation in protecting women from unwanted sexual conduct. Lydia was appalled and told the partners she had a "reasonable expectation of privacy" in her private office. The partners informed Lydia that the law office was the property of HMJ and it should not be used to change into gym clothing as the firm's gym had ample lockers and private changing rooms for women. When Lydia complained to her summer associate friends, they laughed at her and said that this goes on all the time in New York City offices and she was much too sensitive. Lydia was later informed the videos would be destroyed after six months and are viewed only by two senior partners and security. Lydia informed the senior partners she was considering bringing a lawsuit against the firm for invasion of privacy. A senior partner, who is also the ethics officer in the firm, is attempting to convince Lydia this was not only legal as she had no "reasonable expectation of privacy" in using her law office as a changing room but also ethical under any theory of ethics as the videos of her changing would be kept private by the firm and destroyed in six months.

The partner has decided to call a meeting of all the partners on the ethics committee to discuss the issues. A few partners have always had reservations on installing the cameras in the offices without notifying the summer associates and have raised a few ethical questions:

Is this practice ethical? Explain by using ethical principles as discussed in Chapter 2, "Ethics in the Business Environment."

Should they survey the next group of summer interns on exit interviews to discover what they think of this? In view of the facts in the case, are they ethically obligated to do so?

Does the firm have an ethical duty to respect privacy by immediately destroying the videos?

Would it be ethical for Lydia to "go public" with this incident and notify the *Wall Street Journal* and the *New York Times*, especially in view of the law firm's recognition as being the "best place to work in New York City, especially for women lawyers?"

Monitoring Electronic Activities

As technology has advanced, so has an employer's ability to monitor employees in the workplace. Technology brings with it many avenues of interaction and communication. E-mail and texts have all but replaced letter writing and phone calls. Websites such as Facebook and My Space offer incredible opportunities to share much information with others instantly. Technology has, without a doubt, revolutionized the workplace. According to the most recent survey on computer and Internet usage conducted by the Bureau of Labor Statistics,[12] approximately 77 million individuals (representing 55.5 percent of workers) use a computer at work, and about 40 percent of the workforce are connected to the Internet and have used e-mail on the job. The American Management Association conducted a study that showed that a majority of employers are engaged in some type of electronic monitoring, primarily Web usage and e-mail.[13]

The high-level monitoring that is now being conducted by employers begs the question of whether there is such a thing as privacy in the workplace. If there is, what are its limits? Consider, for example, that many individuals use an employer-provided computer in the workplace. May an employer track Internet usage on that computer? If the employer provides an e-mail account to the employee, may the employer monitor those e-mails? What happens when an employee uses the office computer to access his or her own personal e-mail account such as Gmail or Yahoo? Can employers monitor personal e-mail messages sent during work hours on the work computer? What if the employer provides the employee with a cell phone? May the employer monitor the tweets and texts sent by the employee via that cell phone?

For the courts, these questions represent a balancing act — how to balance an individual's right to privacy and the needs of the employer.

Protecting Privacy Rights in Electronic Communications

There are statutory laws in place to help protect privacy in electronic communications. The Electronic Communications Privacy Act of 1986 (ECPA) imposes civil and criminal liability on those who access data and electronic communications without authorization. Title I of this law, the Wiretap Act, prohibits the actual or attempted interception of any wire, oral, or electronic communication. Title II of this act, the Stored Communications Act (SCA), prohibits the access of electronic communications (such as e-mail) without authorization. It protects the files and records that are held by service providers.

---

[12]U.S. Department of Labor, Bureau of Labor Statistics, Computer and Internet Use at Work Summary, http://www.bls.gov/news.release/ciuaw.nr0.htm.
[13]2007 Electronic Monitoring and Surveillance Survey available at http://press.amanet.org/pres-releases/177/2007-electronic-monitoring-surveillance-survey./

Privacy in E-Mail Communications

At least 43 percent of employers engage in e-mail monitoring, and 28 percent of employers have terminated employees for improper use of the e-mail system.[14] It has been fairly well established through case law that an employee has little to no expectation of privacy in an employer-provided e-mail system. Consider the Case Illustration of *Smyth v. Pillsbury* involving an invasion of privacy claim brought by a Pillsbury employee.

Case Illustration

Michael Smyth, a Pillsbury employee, received e-mails from his supervisor over the employer's e-mail system. He engaged in an e-mail exchange with a supervisor via his home computer. Some time later, the company retrieved and read these messages and fired Mr. Smyth for what the employer considered to be "inappropriate and unprofessional comments" sent through the employer's e-mail system. The employee claimed that the firing was a violation of public policy because in reading his e-mails the employer invaded his privacy. The court disagreed and ruled for the employer despite the fact that the employer assured the employees that all communications would remain confidential and privileged. The court ruled that, "[T]he company's interest in preventing inappropriate and unprofessional comments or even illegal activity over its e-mail system outweighs any privacy interest the employee may have in those comments." *Smyth v. Pillsbury*, 914 F. Supp. 97 (E.D. Pa. 1996).

A federal district court in Texas relied on the holding in *Smyth* in finding that an employee suffered no invasion of privacy when Microsoft accessed his password-protected e-mail and files maintained on his employer-provided system.[15] In that case the employee was placed on suspension based on claims of sexual harassment and also due to concerns with whether he was responsible for inventory discrepancies. In conducting its investigation of the employee's conduct, Microsoft accessed and read through the employee's e-mails and files. In another case in Massachusetts, John Hancock Life Insurance Company[16] prevailed against its employee's invasion of privacy claim resulting from the company's review of the employee's e-mail. The employee at issue had been forwarding sexually explicit e-mails to fellow employees in violation of company policy. In the course of investigating a complaint by one of the recipients of such an e-mail, the company read through e-mail contained in password protected files on the company computer. When the company found evidence of the sexually explicit communication, the employee, Nancy Garrity, was fired. The court held that stated company policy, along with the fact that any e-mail transmitted had to pass through the company's system, defeated the employee's argument that she had a reasonable expectation of privacy.

We have already established that employees do not have a reasonable expectation of privacy in employer-provided e-mail accounts. Employees do, however, have an increased expectation of privacy in their own personal e-mail accounts that they access through the employer's system. Because the courts have made clear that e-mail comes within the scope of the ECPA, employers

---

[14]*Id.*
[15]*McLarren v. Microsoft*, 1999 Tex. App. LEXIS 4103 (1999).
[16]*Garrity v. John Hancock Mutual Life Ins. Co.*, 2002 U.S. Dist. LEXIS 8343 (D. Mass 2002).

who access an employee's personal e-mail accounts, which by definition are stored with service providers, may violate the SCA.

Cell Phone Privacy

As you consider an employee's reasonable expectation of privacy with regard to an employer-provided cell phone, keep in mind that the employer bears the cost of the cell phone, and it is often the employer that is a party to the cell phone contract. The purpose of the phone is for the employee to use it for work. Does this give the employer the right to access an employee's text messages? A recent Supreme Court case, *City of Ontario v. Quon*, discussed on page 410, will help you think about this issue.

Keep in mind that *Quon* involved a government employer and therefore raised Fourth Amendment concerns. In a separate action, Quon brought a claim against Arch Wireless, a private company, for a violation of the SCA. The Ninth Circuit agreed with Quon that by releasing the transcripts of the texts to the city, Arch Wireless, an electronic communications service (ECS), violated the terms of the SCA that prohibits an ECS from releasing information to a party that is not an addressee or intended recipient of the message. Because the city was neither, the release of the transcript violated the law.

Privacy in Social Media

Given the widespread use of social media sites such as Facebook and My Space, it is likely not surprising for you to learn that employers have increasingly been mindful of their employees' activities on such sites. Social media accounts that are not set to "private" or "friends only" are considered publicly available and therefore subject to review by an employer, or even a potential employer. In fact, 45 percent of employers have been shown to regularly use social media to screen job applicants.[17]

As a general rule, the courts have upheld adverse employment actions taken against an employee by an employer resulting from an employee's social media posting. As long as the employer has not accessed the information in a manner that violated the rules of the social media site, the employer's actions have been upheld. Consider, for example, the firing of a Florida deputy who posted inappropriate comments about women and other offensive remarks on his Facebook page along with a photo of himself in

Social media accounts that are not set to "private" or "friends only" are considered publicly available and may be viewed by employers and potential employers.

---

[17]See Damian LaPlaca and Noah Winkeller, *Legal Implications of the Use of Social Media: Minimizing the Legal Risks for Employers and Employees*, 5 J. Bus. Tech L. Proxy 1 (2010).

City of Ontario, California v. Quon, 495 U.S. 604 (2011)

Facts: Plaintiff Jeff Quon was a police sergeant and member of the SWAT team of the City of Ontario, California. Quon received from the city a pager that could send and receive text messages. Before the city purchased the pagers, the city distributed a document called "Computer Usage, Internet, and E-Mail Policy," which alerted employees that the city "reserves the right to monitor and log all network activity including e-mail and Internet use, with or without notice." Even though this policy did not include text messages when the city distributed the pagers, it alerted employees that it would treat text messages in the same manner as e-mails. When Quon went over on his monthly allotted usage of text messaging on the pager, he was given the option of reimbursing the city for the overage charge rather than having the city audit the messages to determine how many were for work and how many were personal. After several overages by Quon and another employee, the police chief decided to order a copy of all the text messages sent and received by Quon and the other employee to determine whether the text message plan was adequate or whether the city should contract for increased services. The wireless provider of the pager service, Arch Wireless, in response to the city's request, provided transcripts of the texts.

Most of the texts on Quon's pager were personal, and some sexually explicit. On a typical work day, Quon sent an average of 28 messages, and of these only three were work related. Some days Quon sent 80 messages. Quon sued the city for a violation of his Fourth Amendment right against unreasonable searches and seizures. The District Court found in favor of the city, and the Ninth Circuit Court of Appeals reversed.

Issue: Did the city violate Quon's Fourth Amendment rights by obtaining and reviewing the transcripts of the text messages?

Holding: No. The Supreme Court determined that even if Quon had a reasonable expectation of privacy in the texts, the city did not necessarily violate the Fourth Amendment in reviewing the texts. The court acknowledged that warrantless searches are generally per se unreasonable under the Fourth Amendment but decided that exceptions to this rule are available in certain circumstances. This search was found reasonable because it was motivated by a legitimate work-related purpose and was not excessive in scope.

From the Court's Opinion: *When conducted for a non-investigatory, work-related purpose[s] or for the investigatio[n] of work related misconduct a government employer's warrantless search is reasonable if the measures adopted are reasonably related to the objectives of the search and not excessively intrusive in light of the circumstances giving rise to the search. . . . Chief Sharf ordered the search to in order to determine whether the character limit on the City's contract with Arch Wireless was sufficient to meet the City's needs. . . . As for the scope of the search, reviewing the transcripts was reasonable because it was an efficient and expedient way to determine whether Quon's overages were the result of work-related messaging or personal use. . . . Under the circumstances a reasonable employee would be aware that sound management principles might require the audit of messages to determine whether the pager was being appropriately used.*

uniform. In another social media case, a waitress who criticized the tip left by a customer on her Facebook page in a post that identified the name of the restaurant was fired for violating a company policy that prohibited employees from publicly criticizing the employer or its customers. In both of these cases the employer was not liable.

Sometimes, however, the contents of social media postings can fall within the protection of the NLRA. Recall from the discussion earlier in this chapter that the NLRA protects the rights of employees to engage in "concerted activity." Employees have a right to work together to improve employment conditions. If a social media post falls within the protection of a concerted activity, the employee will be protected from termination as shown in this Case Illustration.

In response to employers' increased desire for access to social media accounts, some states (Arkansas, California, Colorado, Illinois, Maryland, Michigan, New Mexico, New Jersey, and Washington) have already passed laws restricting the ability of an employer to request access to social media accounts of both current and prospective employees. For example, Colorado legislation passed in May 2013 states that an employer may not "suggest, request, or require" access to an individual's social media account, and the employer cannot ask that the privacy settings be modified so that the employer has access. Employees cannot be forced to "friend" the employer or the employer's agents. Violations of the Colorado law result in a $1,000 fine for the first offense and $5,000 for subsequent offenses.

Case Illustration

Lydia Cruz-Moore, an employee of the nonprofit organization Hispanics United of Buffalo, expressed concerns to fellow employee Marianna Cole-Rivera that she and other employees were not doing enough to help the organization's clients. In response Marianna posted the following on her Facebook page: "Lydia Cruz, a coworker, feels that we don't help our clients enough at [Employer]. I about had it! My fellow coworkers how do u feel?" Four employees responded by posting Facebook comments in which they complained about their working conditions and the volume of work. Marianna and these four employees were fired for their postings on the grounds that the posts could be seen as harassing Lydia, the employee who made the initial comment, in violation of the company's anti-bullying policy. The NLRB ordered that the employees be reinstated. By firing the employees, the employer violated their right to engage in concerted activity regarding the conditions of their employment. *Hispanics United of Buffalo, Inc.*, 359 NLRB No. 37 (Dec. 14, 2012).

Global Perspective: International Aspects of Employment Law

U.S. corporations operating in foreign jurisdictions must comply with the laws of that jurisdiction. This necessarily requires that an employer be familiar with the legal requirements governing the employment relationship. This section briefly overviews concerns that arise in two key employment areas: employment-at-will and privacy in the workplace.

Employment-at-Will[18]

The ability of a U.S. employer to dismiss an employee employed in the foreign jurisdiction may be much more limited than that which the employer is accustomed

---

[18]Global HR Hot Topic: *Individual Employment Dismissal Obligations Outside the US, White & Case* (May 2013).

to under the U.S. employment-at-will framework. Many countries impose specific dismissal rules on employers. One aspect of these rules is a dismissal procedure that may include affirmative, procedural steps that should be taken before firing the employee. In some countries, this step is easier than others. Compare, for example, the requirements of the Czech Republic and France. The Czech Republic requires only that the dismissal be communicated to the employee in writing. France, on the other hand, first requires that the employee receive a letter in the French language notifying him or her of a meeting to discuss the issue. Following this meeting, additional notices, meetings, a waiting period, and an internal appeal are required.

In other countries the government itself is involved in the dismissal process. Some countries follow the notion of "lifetime employment," meaning that the employer cannot terminate the employee except for good cause or economic necessity. Such is the case, for example, in Japan where an employer can only fire an individual if it has good cause that a judge will ratify in court. If the court does not find good cause, the employer must reinstate the employee and also provide the employee with back pay.

Many countries require an employer to provide an employee with a pre-termination notice, although how much notice is required varies widely, from a week to a few months. For example, in South Africa the notice period is four weeks. In the United Kingdom one-week notice for every year of employment is required (to a maximum of 12 weeks).

Last, employers should keep in mind that many countries require that the terminated employee be paid either severance pay or liquidated damages.

Privacy in the Workplace

U.S. employers with workplaces abroad will encounter many of the same electronic communications privacy issues that are encountered in the United States. We will use examples from the European Union to illustrate this point.

As a general rule, privacy is a more fundamental right in the European Union than it is in the United States. Article 8 of the 1995 European Convention for the Protection of Human Rights and Fundamental Freedoms establishes that individuals have a right to secrecy in their correspondence which even extends to communications made while at work. Employer e-mail monitoring will only be justified if it is "necessary" and "legitimate." EU Directive 2002/58/EC is instructive. This directive prohibits the interception of private communications over networks, such as e-mails and phone calls. The directive, however, is designed to cover public employers and public employees. Private employers generally have internal policies that govern employee use of Internet and electronic equipment in the workplace. These policies become part of the contract between the employee and the employer and so are generally recognized by the European courts.[19]

The Case Illustration on the following page is representative of the current trend of case law in France regarding the protection of employee privacy rights.

---

[19]Internet Business Law Services (IBLS), Internet Law—European Approach to Privacy in the Workplace, http://www.ibls.com/internet_law_news_portal_view.aspx?id=2079&s=latestnews.

French courts are divided, however, on the employee's rights to maintain secrecy in social media.[20] The following two recent cases were decided in favor of the employer. In 2012 the Criminal Court of Paris fined an employee for posting an insulting message about the employer and the supervisor on company's union Facebook page, finding that the comments were beyond the level of acceptable criticism. The employer had terminated the employee for these actions. In 2011 the Court of Appeals in Besancon upheld an employer's termination of an employee resulting from the employee's inappropriate posting on the Facebook wall belonging to her friend because the friend's Facebook setting was not set to private and so the posting could be considered public. In a third case, the Court of Appeals in Rouen reached a decision in favor of the employee in a case involving a posting to a Facebook wall that was considered private. The court found that the employee's privacy settings on her account were adequate to consider the contents of her Facebook wall to be private and not accessible by the employer and the public.

Case Illustration

At issue in the case of *Jean Michael X v. Seit Hydr'Eau*, was the right of an employer to access and read information contained in an employee's computer folder that was marked with the employee's initials. The labor chamber of France's high court of appeal ruled that employee documents maintained on company-owned equipment can be presumed to be work related and, therefore, could be accessed by the employer without the employee's consent. Simply labeling files with the employee's initials was not sufficient to establish that the files were personal, protected data. Cass. soc. No. 07.43877 (November 2009).

Summary

The employer-employee relationship is central to a wide variety of business transactions. It is one marked by the flexibility of employment-at-will status and also by the federal and state regulation of the employment relationship and the workplace. Over time key pieces of federal legislation such as the FLSA, FMLA, and the NLRA have strengthened the rights of employees, providing both great flexibility and great regulation. It is a flexible relationship insofar as at-will employment allows employees to come and go from the workplace, with the corresponding ability of the employer to terminate an employee at any time for any reason, with exceptions made in those circumstances discussed in this chapter.

The employment relationship has many ethical attributes especially because of the economic hardships of losing a job. Promotions and pay raises may be perceived by the employees as being unethical if they are unsatisfied with the results. It is important for the company ethics and compliance officer, appropriate executives and the committees that review hiring, layoffs, promotions and raises to be ethically sensitive to their decisions in maintaining the good reputation of the company. The company's ethical respect for whistleblowers, employees' privacy, employees injured on the job, and those on medical leave is critical to establishing an ethical corporate culture.

---

[20]For more details on this issue see Proskauer, Cecil Martin, *French Employees Should Check Their Privacy Settings Before Posting on Social Media Platforms*, http://privacylaw.proskauer.com/2012/02/articles/online-privacy/french-employees-should-check-their-privacy-settings-before-posting-on-social-media-platforms/.

Questions for Review

1. FMLA

Nancy's mother has been diagnosed with a terminal illness. Nancy's mom lives with her in her home and, when not at work, Nancy is her mom's primary caregiver. A home-care nurse also comes to the home to help as needed. Nancy and her mother were granted a one-week trip to Las Vegas by the Fairygodmother Foundation, which grants wishes to individuals with a terminal illness. Nancy notified her employer, Enterprise, Inc., about the trip and requested leave under the FMLA for the one-week period. Does coverage under the FMLA include time spent accompanying someone on a trip as that person's primary caregiver? *Ballard v. Chicago Park District*, (NJ, 2012).

2. FLSA

A local theater company was seeking unpaid interns to be involved in their summer theater productions. The company hired several students from Better Business University to fill these slots. At the end of the summer, these student interns filed a claim against the theater seeking unpaid wages under the Fair Labor Standards Act for their work performed over the course of the summer. The theater company denied the claim stating that the students were aware that these were unpaid intern positions. What should the court take into account in deciding this case?

3. Ethics and Hollywood

Helen, a Hollywood actress, was required to do a dangerous stunt for an adventure movie. She insisted that a stunt actress perform the dangerous stunt, but the director wanted a close-up shot of Helen during her fall and demanded that she perform the stunt. Helen contacted the OSHA explaining that she refused to work in this high-risk stunt in which she could be seriously injured or even die. OSHA told Helen the movie studio was not within its authority. When Helen refused to perform the stunt, the movie director wanted her fired. Her attorney informed Helen there was not a provision in her contract that exempted her from doing dangerous stunts. The director asked the movie producers for permission to fire Helen. One of the co-producers stated that although it may be legal to fire Helen, it would be unethical and would bring unfavorable publicity to the movie. Do you agree? Explain the ethics of this case using ethical principles.

4. Public policy exception

An increasing number of states are opting to legalize marijuana for medicinal use, and some states have legalized this substance for recreational use as well. Paul Platt has a serious medical condition and as a result is a properly registered medical marijuana patient under state law. When a random drug test by his employer resulted in Paul testing positive for marijuana, he was fired. Paul is contesting the dismissal on the grounds that he was using this drug legally under state law. What resulted? *Casias v. Wal-Mart Stores, Inc.*, No. 11-1227 (6th Cir. 2012).

5. Covenant not to compete

You are considering accepting a job at Big Business Corporation. As a condition of employment, you must sign a covenant not to compete with Big Business in which you agree that when your employment at Big Business comes to an end you will not work for any competitor of Big Business within a 300-mile radius for a period of seven years. If you challenged the covenant in court, do you think the court is likely to rule in your favor? Why or why not?

6. **Polygraph testing**

   Discuss the situations in which an employee may be subject to a polygraph test.

7. **Privacy**

   What factors will a court find most important in deciding whether an employer may read the text messages on an employee's company-provided cell phone?

8. **International influence**

   Unlike the United States, many countries require that employees be given pre-termination notices. Discuss the impact such a requirement would have if it were adopted as U.S. law.

Further Reading

Bishara, Norman, and Michelle Westermann-Behaylo, *The Law and Ethics of Restrictions on an Employee's Post Employment Mobility*, 48 American Business Law Journal 1 (2012).

Gren, Ariana C., *Using Social Networking to Discuss Work: NLRB Protection for Derogatory Employee Speech and Concerted Activity*, 27 Berkeley Technology Law Journal 837 (2012).

Hodges, Ann C., *Bargaining Privacy in the Unionized Workplace*, 22 International Journal of Comparative Labour Law and Industrial Relations 147 (2006).

Kulow, Marianne Delpo., *Legislating a Family-Friendly Workplace: Should It Be Done in the United States?* 7 Northwestern Journal of Law & Social Policy 88 (2012).

Sadez Akril, Patricia, Arner Levin, and Alissa DelRiego, *Blurred Boundaries: Social Media Privacy and the Twenty-First Century Employee*, 49 American Business Law Journal 63 (2012).

CHAPTER 14

Discrimination in the Workplace

Chapter Objectives

1. To understand the protections guaranteed by Title VII of the Civil Rights Act of 1964 and be able to identify the distinction between discrimination which is intentional and that which is unintentional
2. To understand the protection against sexual harassment in the workplace and the situations in which employers will be held accountable for such conduct
3. To recognize that federal law guarantees protection from discrimination based on age or disability
4. To identify the defenses to a discrimination claim
5. To be familiar with the origin and purposes of affirmative action programs

Practical Example: Consider These Situations

Martha applies for a job at Auto Repair Shop. She has an automotive degree and several years of experience as a mechanic. Auto Repair Shop hires Ralph, who is less qualified for the job, but the owner feels he is a better fit for the workplace.

Katie is one of the most skilled accountants in an accounting firm of more than 300 employees. She has been with the firm for several years and has enjoyed her very spacious office. When Katie finds out that she is pregnant, she gives her employer notice that after the baby is born she will be taking a few months off for maternity leave. A few days after this conversation, Katie receives a memo from her manager indicating that there is to be a change in her office space. Katie is being moved from her spacious, three-window office into a much smaller interior office with no windows. The memo does not give any reason for the change.

Marco is a hard worker and is very good at his job as a systems analyst at Computer Corporation. He applies for a promotion when a staff manager slot becomes available. During the interview, Jill, the vice president of the company, promises Marco the promotion if he agrees to become romantically involved with her. Marco refuses and does not get the promotion.

Does Martha have a case against Auto Repair Shop? How about Katie? Can she bring a claim against the accounting firm for her disappointment? Does Marco have a claim against Jill? Against Computer Corporation?

This chapter begins with a discussion of the requirements an individual must meet to bring a claim under the antidiscrimination laws, followed by a review of the many dimensions of the statutes from a legal and ethical perspective.

An Ethical Insight: St. Thomas Aquinas: Unjust Laws and the Civil Rights Movement

St. Thomas Aquinas stated in the Summa Theologica, "An unjust law is no longer legal but rather a corruption of law." The Rev. Martin Luther King Jr. led the civil rights movement because racial discriminatory laws in the United States at that time were clearly unjust and violated natural law principles. Aquinas would argue an unjust law need not be obeyed. This ethical principle is the basis of "civil disobedience," and the violator must realize the consequence of breaking an unjust law could lead to his arrest and possible jail sentence.

Title VII of the Civil Rights Act of 1964

Since the close of the Civil War, various efforts, summarized in Exhibit 14.1, have been made by Congress to ensure racial equality. The most important piece of legislation designed to end discrimination in both public and private places of employment was the Civil Rights Act of 1964. This act prohibits discrimination in the workplace based on race, gender, religion, color, and national origin. These are referred to as "protected classes." To be covered by Title VII an employer must have 15 or more employees.[1] The law also covers most labor unions[2] and employment agencies.[3] State and local government agencies having at least 15 employees are also within

---

[1] A business is covered by the antidiscrimination laws if it has 15 or more employees who worked for the employer for at least 20 calendar weeks.

[2] All labor unions that either have at least 15 members or operate a hiring hall are covered by Title VII. Coverage under Title VII extends to any joint labor-management committee governing training or apprenticeship programs.

[3] Employment agencies are covered by the antidiscrimination laws if the agency regularly refers employees to employers, regardless of how many employees the agency has.

Exhibit 14.1. Legislative Efforts to Ensure Racial Equality	
Civil Rights Act of 1866 **14 Stat. 27–30**	Guaranteed the rights of all citizens to make and enforce contracts and to purchase, sell, or lease property
Fifteenth Amendment of the U.S. Constitution (1870) **16 Stat. 346; 16 Stat. 40–41**	Forbade any state to deprive a citizen of his vote because of race, color, or previous condition of servitude
Civil Rights Act of 1875 **18 Stat. 335–337**	Barred discrimination in public accommodations and on public conveyances on land and water; prohibited exclusion of African Americans from jury duty
Civil Rights Act of 1964 **P.L. 88–352**	Prohibited discrimination in public accommodations, facilities, and schools; outlawed discrimination in federally funded projects; created the Equal Employment Opportunity Commission to monitor employment discrimination in public and private sectors
Civil Rights Act of 1991 **P.L. 102–166**	Provided plaintiffs the right to receive monetary damages in cases of harassment or discrimination based on sex, religion, or disability; passed by the 102nd Congress (1991-1993) as S. 1745

Source: Black Americans in Congress: Historical Data. http://history.house.gov/Exhibitions-and-Publications/BAIC/Historical-Data/Historical-Data—Nav/.

President Lyndon Johnson meeting with Martin Luther King, Jr. and other civil rights leaders in 1966.

Title VII. Federal government agencies are automatically covered by this act regardless of the number of employees.

Procedure to File a Claim[4]

Persons wishing to file a claim against an employer for violations of Title VII must first file a claim with the **Equal Employment Opportunity Commission** (EEOC) to determine if that agency will bring a claim against the employer. The EEOC was created by the Civil Rights Act of 1964 to oversee and enforce the antidiscrimination laws. It is a bipartisan commission comprised of five members appointed by the president. Before investigating the claim, the EEOC may first attempt to get the individual and the employer to agree to mediation in the hopes of having the parties reach a voluntary settlement. If the claim does not go to mediation or the mediation fails, the claim will then be given to an EEOC investigator. Depending on the nature of the claim, the investigator may visit the workplace to gather evidence and interview witnesses, or alternatively, may simply gather information by phone and mail. On completion of the investigation, the EEOC will decide whether it will bring a claim against an employer. If it chooses not to bring a claim, the EEOC will give the individual a Notice-of-Right-to-Sue giving the individual the right to sue the employer. The lawsuit must be filed within 90 days after the individual receives this notice.

Discrimination under Title VII may be divided into two broad categories: intentional and unintentional.

Intentional Discrimination

Intentional discrimination, known as **disparate treatment**, is discrimination against an individual. To make a claim against an employer for disparate treatment an individual must initially prove that (1) he or she is a member of a protected class, (2) is qualified for and has applied for the job, (3) was rejected by the employer, and (4) the position has not yet been filled or, if filled, was filled by someone not in the protected class. If these four requirements are met, the individual has made what is called a prima facie case and has met the initial burden of proof. Consider for a moment Martha's situation in our opening example. It appears that she has enough evidence to make a prima

---

An Ethical Insight: John Finnis: Moral Absolutes and Workplace Discrimination

John Finnis, a prominent natural law scholar, would probably find discrimination to be a violation of a moral absolute. In his essay "Natural Law and Legal Reasoning," Finnis states: "The moral absolutes give legal reasoning its backbone: the exclusion of intentional killing, of intentional injury to the person and even the economic interests of the person . . . of enslavement which treats a human person as an object of a lower rank of being than the autonomous human subject." Title VII could be ethically viewed as a federal law codifying a moral absolute and "a backbone to legal reasoning." That ethical principle supports Title VII by excluding discrimination in the workplace because it "treats a human person as an object of lower rank of being."

---

[4]These procedures differ for federal employees seeking to bring a claim against the government.

facie case: (1) she is a woman (the protected class in this instance), (2) she is qualified as a mechanic as evidenced by her automotive degree and several years of experience before she applied for the job; (3) she was rejected by the employer; and (4) someone other than a woman, in this case Ralph, was hired for the job. Next the burden shifts to the employer to prove that there was a legitimate, nondiscriminatory reason for its actions. In Martha's case, the question is whether the employer had a legitimate reason for believing that Ralph would be better suited for the job that had nothing to do with his gender. If the employer makes this showing, the burden then reverts back to the Martha to prove that the reason provided by the employer is untrue (i.e., that the proffered reason is merely a pretext).

Unintentional Discrimination

Unlike intentional discrimination, unintentional discrimination, or **disparate impact**, results when an employer discriminates against an entire protected class. This discrimination may arise from the employer's interview practices, pre-employment testing, hiring procedures, or educational requirements. Often these methods appear neutral but statistically can be shown to have a discriminatory effect. Consider, for example, a supermarket that is seeking to hire someone to unload boxes from delivery trucks and stack them in a warehouse. The supermarket posts an ad that reads: "Help wanted to unload and stack food deliveries. Must be 6'1" and weigh at least 220 pounds." Since the average woman does not come within these height and weight restrictions, the supermarket has discriminated against women. Instead the supermarket should have kept the job description focused on the ability to do the job. For example, "Help wanted to unload and stack food deliveries. Must be able to lift boxes weighing up to 150 pounds."

There are a variety of methods for assessing disparate impact. One method looks to the pool of applicants in the labor market. If the employer's workforce does not reflect the labor market, this may be evidence of disparate impact as shown in the Case Illustration. Another method is the "four-fifths rule" explained in EEOC guidelines. This method identifies a disparate impact if members of a protected class are selected at a rate less than 80 percent of that of another group.[5] Consider

Case Illustration

Local 107 of the Steamship Workers Union accepted only new members who were sponsored by existing members. All of the existing members were white. During a six-year period, Local 107 admitted 30 new white members, all relatives of present members. The EEOC prevailed on its claim that this union practice constituted disparate impact discrimination. In reaching this result, the court found it compelling that during the years at issue the combined pool of potential African American and Hispanic applicants for union membership was between 8 and 27 percent of the overall pool of potential applicants, but during that time no African American or Hispanic was given Union membership. *EEOC v. Steamship Clerk's Union*, 48 F. 3d. 594 (1st Cir. 1995).

---

[5]EEOC's Uniform Guidelines on Employee Selection Procedures, 29 C.F.R. § 1607 *et seq.*

the case of a pre-employment test. If 70 percent of white applicants pass the test and only 40 percent of Hispanic applicants pass the test, this would be a pass ratio of 28 percent (40/70) for the applicants in the protected class indicating a disparate impact. In all of these cases, the initial burden is on the plaintiff to show a link between the challenged behaviors and the statistical disparity.

If the plaintiff makes a prima facie showing of disparate impact, the employer then has the burden of proving that its practice is "job-related for the position in question and consistent with business necessity."[6]

In-Depth Ethical Case Analysis

Ricci v. DeStefano, 129 S.Ct. 2658 (2009)

Facts

The city of New Haven, Connecticut, used a written firefighter exam to fill vacant lieutenant and captain positions. The results of the exam indicated that white candidates scored higher than minority candidates, raising some concern for the city that this exam might have a disparate impact on minority candidates. Threats of lawsuits from both sides emerged, and the city decided to disregard the results based on statistical racial disparity. Petitioners were the white and Hispanic firefighters who passed the exam and sued the city when it refused to certify the test results, alleging that ignoring the results intentionally discriminated against them based on their race in violation of Title VII of the Civil Rights Act of 1964. The city responded that had it certified the test results, it could be accused of adopting a practice having a disparate impact on minority firefighters.

The district court granted summary judgment for the defendants, and the Second Circuit affirmed. The U.S. Supreme Court disagreed with the lower courts and held that in

disregarding the test results the city intentionally discriminated against the plaintiffs in violation of Title VII.

Justice Kennedy delivered the opinion of the Court joined by Chief Justice Roberts and Justices Scalia, Thomas, and Alito. Justice Ginsberg filed a dissenting opinion joined by Justices Stevens, Souter, and Breyer.

From the Court's Decision

Title VII of the Civil Rights Act of 1964, as amended, prohibits employment discrimination on the basis of race, color, religion, sex, or national origin. Title VII prohibits both intentional discrimination (known as "disparate treatment") as well as, in some cases, practices that are not intended to discriminate but in fact have a disproportionately adverse effect on minorities (known as "disparate impact") ... Petitioners allege that when the [Civil Service Board] refused to certify the captain and lieutenant exam results based on the race of the successful candidates, it discriminated against them in violation of Title VII's disparate-treatment provision. The City counters that its decision was

---

[6]42 U.S.C. § 2000e-2(k)(1)(A)(i).

permissible because the tests "appear[ed] to violate Title VII's disparate-impact provisions."

Our analysis begins with this premise: The City's actions would violate the disparate-treatment prohibition of Title VII absent some valid defense. All the evidence demonstrates that the City chose not to certify the examination results because of the statistical disparity based on race — i.e., how minority candidates had performed when compared to white candidates. As the District Court put it, the City rejected the test results because "too many whites and not enough minorities would be promoted were the lists to be certified." . . . Without some other justification, this express, race-based decision making violates Title VII's command that employers cannot take adverse employment actions because of an individual's race. . . . Restricting an employer's ability to discard test results (and thereby discriminate against qualified candidates on the basis of their race) also is in keeping with Title VII's express protection of bona fide promotional examinations.

On the record before us, there is no genuine dispute that the City lacked a strong basis in evidence to believe it would face disparate-impact liability if it certified the examination results. In other words, there is no evidence . . . that the tests were flawed because they were not job-related or because other, equally valid and less discriminatory tests were available to the City. Fear of litigation alone cannot justify an employer's reliance on race to the detriment of individuals who passed the examinations and qualified for promotions. The City's discarding the test results was impermissible under Title VII, and summary judgment is appropriate for petitioners on their disparate-treatment claim.

Overview of the Ethical Dilemma

Standardized SAT tests are commonly used to evaluate a candidate's qualification for admission to a college or university. If a student paid for tutoring to do well on a SAT test and discovered her high score would be disregarded to better

racially integrate a university, would that be an unethical act by the administration of the university? In this case firefighters were promised that the standardized test scores for promotion to an officer's position would be used as part of their overall evaluation for promotion. Relying on that promise the applicants spent time and money preparing for the exam. Their test scores were not used to help in the evaluation of their promotion based on threats of the city of New Haven being sued by minority candidates who alleged that using the test results would be illegal because the testing would lead to unintentional racial discrimination.

Ethical Issue

Was it ethical to disregard the test scores of an exam to be used as part of an evaluation for promotion when that would intentionally racially discriminate against the test-takers in order to promote minority candidates?

One could ethically make different arguments to support or ignore the test results. The *ethical dilemma* is based on ignoring a candidate's higher test scores to bring about the greater good of an racially integrated fire department at the expense of candidates for promotion who relied on a promise that the test scores would be used as an important part of their evaluation.

Ethical Theory Analysis

Kant's Categorical Imperatives

One of Kant's categorical imperatives is *never to act unless your actions could become a universal law.* One could argue this means never to break a serious promise relied upon by another because if this became a universal practice serious promises would have no value in society. From this perspective, the city in ignoring the test results was acting unethically because if this became a common practice, people would lose trust in proposed procedures that were ignored at the whim of an administrator. Universalizing the practice of promising to use a test score for evaluating promotion and then disregarding it would violate Kant's categorical imperative and be morally and ethically impermissible. Kant would honor the duty to keep the promise regardless of the consequences.

John Rawls: "A Theory of Justice"

Rawls's equal liberty principle states that *"Each person has the same . . . equal basic liberties . . . with the same scheme of liberties for all."* Because minorities scored lower on the standard test, one could argue the objective of a racially integrated fire department is not achieved by this model, and it is therefore an unethical standard. Justice Ginsburg's dissent supports that principle when she states that "[t]he Court's recitation of the facts leaves out important parts of the story. Firefighting is a profession in which the legacy of racial discrimination casts an especially long shadow." Because the history of the firefighting profession is one of racial discrimination, minorities have not been granted "the same equal basic liberties . . . with the same scheme of liberties for all," and the rejection of the test scores could be ethically justified under that principle of justice. Rawls is concerned with the way society allocates power and opportunity. Under the equal liberty principle, one could argue it would be unethical to use the test scores in the promotion process if that would promote racial inequality in the fire department.

John Stuart Mill and Utilitarianism

"The greater good for the greater number" could find the use of the exam scores in evaluating a candidate to be ethically justified because the greater number would benefit under that process. The firefighter's exam for promotion to a captain's position is useful in determining who best understands the firefighter's role as an officer, and this will provide for the greater good of the department and ultimately for a safer society.

Justice Oliver Wendell Holmes, Jr. and Legal Realism

The founder of legal realism, Justice Oliver Wendell Holmes, Jr., stated *"the real justification of a rule of law, if there is one, is that it keeps bringing about a social end we desire."* The desired social end ought to be a racially integrated firefighter's department, and under this theory of legal realism a standardized test that frustrated that purpose could ethically be rescinded.

John Austin and Legal Positivism

Legal positivism takes the position that a law should generally be obeyed even though we happen to dislike it. Justice Alito's dicta that "sympathy is not what petitioners have a right to demand. What they have a right to demand is evenhanded enforcement of the law of Title VII's prohibition against discrimination based on race." A legal positivist would argue the test scores could be ethically used as they represent a racially neutral way of evaluating a promotion.

Thomas Aquinas and Natural Law

Natural law principles protect individuals from injustices, including racial discrimination, that violate human dignity and the common good. One could argue that disregarding the test scores to achieve a more racially balanced firefighter's officer corps would be ethically justified under a natural law theory of justice to provide equal protection of the law to racial minorities.

Conclusion

The important thing is to be aware of the relationship of the ethical theories to the legal arguments. From this ethical analysis you can see that reasonable arguments can be made to support the court's majority and minority opinions. You should decide what is in the best interests of society and construct ethical arguments to defend that position.

Protected Classes

Title VII prohibits workplace discrimination based on race, color, national origin, and gender.

Race/Color Discrimination

Race and color, although they may overlap, are two distinctly protected classes under Title VII. Discrimination based on race may result from characteristics associated with race such as skin color, hair texture, or certain facial features even though not all members of a race share those same features. Medical conditions that may be more prevalent among certain races can also not be used as a basis for discriminatory treatment. For example, the EEOC advises employers that a no-beard policy in the workplace may discriminate against African American men who have a predisposition to a medical condition making shaving difficult[7] if the policy is not job related and one of business necessity.

National Origin Discrimination

Title VII prohibits discrimination in employment based on an individual's national origin, which encompasses birthplace, ancestry, culture, or accent. Employers cannot make employment decisions based on an individual's accent or fluency in the English language unless such accent materially interferes with the ability of the individual to effectively perform his or her duties. For example, it is essential for a police or ambulance dispatcher to be able to speak English clearly and proficiently. Other types of positions, for example, an assembly line worker involved in the manufacture of clothing in a U.S. factory, would generally only be required to understand enough English to follow directions and safety rules. Some employers have sought to impose English-only rules in the workplace. They can generally do so only if this is necessary for the safe or efficient operation of the employer's business. For example, a hospital has the right to require the cleaning staff responsible for keeping the operating room sanitary to speak only English during job-related discussions while working in the operating room department.[8] Requiring employees, however, to speak English only on the company premises at all times, even during breaks, will be presumed to be discriminatory unless the employer can make a compelling case for the business necessity of this requirement. For example, an employer was unable to convince the court that its "English-only" rule that applied to the entire company premises (even the employee break room) and at all times (including during breaks, lunch, and when making personal phone calls) was necessary for maintaining "harmony"

---

[7]*Pseudofolliculitis barabae* results in a medical condition that primarily afflicts African American men and results in severe shaving bumps. See http://www1.eeoc.gov//eeoc/publications/fs-race.cfm?renderforprint=1.
[8]*Montes v. Vail Clinic, Inc.*, 497 F.3d 1160 (10th Cir. 2007).

EEOC v. Kelly Services, Inc., 598 F.3d 1022 (8th Cir. 2010)

Facts: Kelly Services Inc. is an employment agency that places individuals in temporary positions. Kelly makes placements in accordance with its business clients' needs and preferences. Asthma Suliman, a Muslim woman, filed a religious discrimination claim with the EEOC against Kelly Services when Kelly Services refused to refer her for a job at Nahan Printing, Inc., a commercial printing company, because of her refusal to remove her khimar* in the workplace. Nahan had a policy in place that prohibited employees from wearing loose clothing or headwear in the workplace. The EEOC brought this suit on Ms. Suliman's behalf.

Issue: Did the refusal of Kelly Services to refer Ms. Suliman for employment at Nahan Printing constitute religious discrimination?

Holding: The Court of Appeals affirmed the District Court's grant of summary judgment to Kelly Services finding that the agency provided a legitimate, nondiscriminatory reason for its failure to refer Ms. Suliman for employment at Nahan. Kelly based its decision on Nahan's neutral, safety-motivated dress policy. The court found no evidence that the reason offered by Kelly was merely a pretext for discriminatory behavior.

From the Court's Opinion: *Even if we assume that the EEOC established a prima facie case of religious discrimination by Kelly, Kelly would still be entitled to summary judgment, as it provided a legitimate, non-discriminatory reason for its failure to refer Suliman to Nahan for employment, and EEOC failed to show that this reason was pretextual. In a typical religious discrimination claim against an employer, once the plaintiff establishes a prima facie case, we require "the employer to offer a legitimate, nondiscriminatory reason for the adverse employment action." . . . We see no reason to vary from this burden-shifting scheme simply because the claim is against an employment agency instead of an employer. . . .*

Nevertheless, this inquiry is complicated by § 2000e(j)'s requirement that an "employer" accommodate a worker's religious beliefs unless doing so would create an undue hardship. 42 U.S.C. § 2000e(j) ("The term 'religious' includes all aspects of religious observance and practice, as well as belief, unless an employer demonstrates that he is unable to reasonably accommodate to an employee's or prospective employee's religious observance or practice without undue hardship on the conduct of the employer's business.") . . . But, in the present case, the EEOC sued Kelly in its capacity as an "employment agency," not an "employer," and nothing in § 2000e(j) suggests that an "employment agency," in defending itself against a claim of religious discrimination, must demonstrate that the employer to which it would be referring the temporary worker would suffer an undue hardship if it had to accommodate that worker. Therefore, the only question before us is whether Kelly has provided a legitimate, nondiscriminatory reason for declining to refer Suliman to Nahan for employment Here, Kelly's legitimate, nondiscriminatory reason for not referring Suliman to Nahan was Nahan's facially neutral, safety-driven dress policy prohibiting all employees — permanent and temporary — from wearing loose clothing or headwear of any kind. Kelly's understanding that Nahan would not permit temporary workers to wear any type of headwear, including khimars, was well established.

---

* A khimar is a headscarf that hangs to just below the waist.

in the workplace. Because the employer could not show that the policy was a business necessity or related to job performance, the employer was in violation of Title VII.[9]

Religious Discrimination

Title VII prohibits an employer from discriminating against employees because of their religion. In this context religion is defined broadly as any sincerely held religious beliefs, rather than membership in an established religion. Employers are also required to reasonably accommodate the religious practices of employees. Reasonable accommodations may include things such as leave for religious observances, time and/or place to pray, ability to wear religious garments, flexible scheduling, job swaps, and job reassignments. This requirement is not without limits, however, and an employer must only make an accommodation to the extent that it does not cause the employer undue hardship. Undue hardship may result, for example, when the accommodation requires more than ordinary administrative costs, infringes on the rights/benefits of other employees, diminishes workplace safety, or conflicts with another law or regulation. The case *EEOC v. Kelly Services* on page 426 considers whether an employment agency may lawfully refuse to refer a job applicant for a position because she wears a khimar (headscarf).

Case Illustration

Liberty Mutual Insurance Company had a policy that prohibited its insurance adjusters from attending law school. When Liberty Mutual discovered that both Ms. O'Connell and Ms. Chescheir were attending law school, these women were dismissed. It was determined that during this time three male employees were able to attend law school without consequence. In ruling on behalf of the plaintiffs, the court did not believe Liberty Mutual's assertion that it simply did not know that the men were attending law school. To the contrary, the court found that there were rumors that the men were attending law school, but Liberty Mutual chose to ignore and not investigate these rumors. However, when such rumors involved a female employee, the assertions were thoroughly investigated and action taken against the employee. Liberty Mutual was found liable under Title VII for a discriminatory application of company policy. *Chescheir v. Liberty Mutual Insurance Co.*, 713 F. 2d. 1142 (5th Cir. 1983).

Gender Discrimination

Employers are prohibited from making distinctions between male and female employees unless gender is an essential component of the job. Gender stereotyping is also prohibited by Title VII. An employer may not discriminate against an individual who does not conform to a traditional gender stereotype, and the EEOC has ruled that transgender status is within the protection of Title VII.[10] Sexual orientation is not protected under Title VII, but the EEOC's position is that sexual orientation discrimination may be prohibited gender stereotyping.[11] In addition, the EEOC advises

---

[9]*E.E.O.C. v. Premier Operator Services, Inc.*, 113 F. Supp. 2d 1066 (N.D. Tex. 2000).
[10]*Macy v. Bureau of Alcohol, Tobacco, Firearms, and Explosives*, EEOC Appeal No. 0120120821 (Apr. 20, 2012).
[11]*Veretto v. U.S. Postal Service*, EEOC, Appeal No. 0120110873 (July 1, 2011).

Discrimination based on pregnancy is considered gender discrimination.

employers that gender discrimination may also include treating someone differently because of that person's affiliation with an organization generally associated with people of a certain gender. To prevail in a gender discrimination claim, an individual must be able to prove that gender was a determining factor controlling the employer's actions. The Case Illustration *Chescheir v. Liberty Mutual Insurance Co.* on page 427 highlights an employer's disparate treatment of its employees based on gender.

Pregnancy Discrimination

Gender discrimination also includes discrimination based on pregnancy.[12] Pregnant employees must be permitted to work as long as they are able to do their job. They must also receive the same benefits as other employees. An employee unable to perform her job due to pregnancy must be given the same treatment as other employees who are temporarily disabled. Additional rights are sometimes granted to those with families. For example, as part of the Patient Protection and Affordable Health Care Act signed into law on March 23, 2010, employers are now required to provide a "reasonable break time for an employee to express breast milk for her nursing child for one year after the child's birth each time the employee has need to express the milk. The employer must also provide a "place, other than a bathroom, that is shielded from view and free from intrusion from co-workers and the public."[13]

---

[12]The Pregnancy Discrimination Act of 1978, 42 U.S.C. 2000e(k) expanded the scope of Title VII to include pregnancy.
[13]29 U.S.C. § 207(r)(1)(B) (2011).

Pay Differentials Based on Gender

Another concern with regard to gender distinctions arises in the context of equal pay. The **Equal Pay Act of 1963**[14] requires that men and women be paid equally for substantially similar work in the same establishment. Whether jobs are comparable is determined with reference to the level of skill, effort, and responsibility required for similar working conditions. If there is a pay differential between male and female employees, the Equal Pay Act places the burden on the employer to show that any differential was based on something other than gender. An employer's ability to invoke these distinctions has been limited somewhat by the Paycheck Fairness Act of 2009.[15] This act requires that employers be able to prove there is a "bona fide factor" other than gender, such as education, training, or experience, that necessitates the pay differential.

Sexual Harassment

Title VII prohibits unwelcome sexual conduct in the workplace. This harassment takes one of two forms: quid pro quo and hostile environment. **Quid pro quo harassment** results when an employer seeks sexual favors as a condition of employment, promotion, or receipt of other benefits. Quid pro quo harassment can also result if after a refusal to engage in a sexual favor, the individual is fired, demoted, or denied benefits. **Hostile environment harassment** results when the workplace is filled with discriminatory intim-

> ### An Ethical Insight: John Rawls and Title VII of the Civil Rights Act
>
> John Rawls stated in *Justice as Fairness*: "Social and economic inequalities are to satisfy two conditions: first, they are to be attached to offices and positions open to all under conditions of fair equality of opportunity; and second, they are to be to the greatest benefit of the least advantaged members of society." This principle supports opening the workplace to people of all races, genders, color, religions, and sexual orientations. It is an ethical principle that protects all classes, especially the "least advantaged."

idation, ridicule, or insult that interferes with the ability of an employee to do her work. Ultimately, whether the working environment is hostile is a decision made on a case-by-case basis taking into account all the facts and circumstances. The Ninth Circuit Court of Appeals has utilized a "reasonable woman" standard in deciding whether harassment has taken place.[16] This application has been broadened to the "reasonable worker" standard. Keep in mind that while women are the primary victims of sexual harassment in the workplace, men can be victims as well. Also, the harassment need not be by a member of the opposite sex; same-gender sexual harassment is also actionable.[17]

---

[14]29 U.S.C. § 206(d) (2011).
[15]P.L. No. 111-2 (January 20, 2009), Title II. Title I of this statute, entitled the Lilly Ledbetter Fair Pay Act of 2009, provides that the 180-day statute of limitations begins to run with each discriminatory paycheck received. This is a direct reversal of an earlier Supreme Court decision, *Lilly Ledbetter v. Goodyear Tire & Rubber Co.*, 550 US 618 (2007), in which the Court found that the statute of limitations began to run at the time the discriminatory pay was agreed upon by the parties.
[16]*Ellison v. Brady*, 924 F. 2d 872, (9th Cir. 1991) (court asks whether a "reasonable woman" consider the defendant's actions sexual harassment).
[17]*Oncale v. Sundown Offshore Services, Inc.*, 523 US 75 (1998).

Employer Liability for Harassment

Harassment by Supervisors

If a tangible employment action has been taken against an employee by a supervisor, the *employer* is liable for that action because the employer put the supervisor in the position of authority, and, therefore, the supervisor's actions are considered those of the employer. Tangible actions include hiring and firing, promotion and demotion, compensation decisions, and significant changes in work assignments. If the changes in the employee's status are insignificant, courts will often fail to find that a tangible employment action has taken place. For example, the court has found that a change that required an individual to report to a former subordinate, while possibly impacting the plaintiff's ego, was not a tangible employment action because there was no change to the individual's salary, benefits, and level of responsibility.[18] As shown in the Case Illustration *Vance v. Ball State University*, determining whether the individual committing the harassment qualifies as a supervisor is a significant component in a Title VII claim.

Even if the harassment by the supervisor does not result in a tangible employment action against the employee, the employer will be liable. However, the employer may avoid liability by raising an affirmative defense to show that the employer had taken actions to prevent such an occurrence. The employer must show that (1) reasonable care was taken to prevent and promptly correct such harassment, and (2) the employee unreasonably failed to take advantage of the preventative or corrective opportunities offered by the employer or failed to avoid harm otherwise.[19] Employers demonstrate reasonable care by providing training on sexual harassment in the workplace, establishing and distributing antiharassment policies, and outlining complaint procedures for employees alleging harassment. The employer must show that it has tried to prevent and correct harassment in the workplace. Exhibit 14.2[20] illustrates measures the EEOC recommends for employers to prevent and correct the effects of harassment.

Case Illustration

Maetta Vance, an African American woman, brought a claim against her employer, Ball State University (BSU), alleging racially hostile workplace harassment resulting from the actions of fellow employee, Saundra Davis. In this case the court considered the degree of authority that an employee must have to be considered a supervisor in order to determine whether Davis's actions could result in liability for BSU. The court concluded that a supervisor is an employee empowered "to take a tangible employment actions against the victim, i.e. to effect a significant change in employment status, such as hiring, firing, failing to promote, reassignment with significantly different responsibilities, or a decision causing a significant change in benefits." In ruling in favor of BSU, the Supreme Court rejected the broader definition of supervisor advocated by the EEOC which is "one with the ability to exercise significant direction over another's daily work." *Vance v. Ball State University*, 133 S. Ct. 2434 (2013).

---

[18]*Flaherty v. Gas Research Inst.*, 31 F. 3d 451 (7th Cir. 1994).
[19]*See Faragher v. City of Boca Raton*, 118 S. Ct. 2275 (1998).
[20]This information is derived from EEOC Publication: *Enforcement Guidance: Vicarious Employer Liability for Unlawful Harassment by Supervisors* (1999).

Exhibit 14.2. EEOC Recommendations

Measures to Stop Harassment and Ensure It Does Not Recur

1. Oral or written warning or reprimand
2. Transfer or reassignment
3. Demotion
4. Reduction of wages
5. Suspension
6. Discharge
7. Training or counseling of the harasser
8. Monitoring the harasser to ensure the harassment stops

Measures to Correct the Effects of Harassment

1. Restoration of leave taken because of the harassment
2. Expungement of negative evaluation(s) in the employee's personnel file that arose from the harassment
3. Reinstatement
4. Apology by the harasser
5. Monitoring the treatment of the employee to ensure that he or she is not subjected to retaliation by the harasser or others in the workplace because of the complaint
6. Correction of any other harm caused by the harassment (e.g., compensation for losses)

Harassment by Coworkers and Nonemployees

In the case of harassment by coworkers or nonemployees, an employer will generally only be liable if the employer knew or should have known about the harassment and did not take steps to prevent or end the harassment. The Case Illustration considers Pizza Hut's liability for harassment by its customers.

Discrimination Based on Age

Soon after the passage of Title VII, Congress set its sights on ending yet another form of discrimination — the discrimination of older workers in the workforce. The enactment of the Age Discrimination in Employment Act[21] (ADEA) of 1967 gave protection to employees age 40 and over. All employers having more than 20 employees are covered by this act. As with other types of discrimination, oversight authority of discrimination claims rests with the EEOC.

Case Illustration

A&M Industries, a Pizza Hut franchisee, was found liable for sexual harassment by its customers. The restaurant manager failed to prevent harm to the waitress Reba Lockard that resulted from sexually offensive behavior and contact by two male customers. Ms. Lockard had put the manager on notice that these two customers had made sexually inappropriate comments toward her in the past. Despite this, the manager insisted she wait on their table. *Lockard v. Pizza Hut, Inc.*, 162 F. 3d 1062 (10th Cir. 1998).

---

[21]Age Discrimination in Employment Act, Pub. L. No. 90-202, 81 Stat. 602 (1967).

Case Illustration

Richard Miller, age 53, was employed by Raytheon (and its predecessor company) for more than 30 years before being laid off by the company in 2008. According to Raytheon, the layoff was part of a reduction in workforce. Miller brought a claim against the company in Federal District Court alleging age discrimination under both ADEA and the Texas Commission on Human Rights. The jury found in favor of Miller. Evidence of age discrimination included the following: (1) two workers with similar skills, ages 34 and 46, were not included in the layoff; and (2) 77 percent of the employees who were laid off from Miller's division were over 48 years old. *Miller v. Raytheon Co.*, 716 F. 3d 138 (2013).

Making the Case

Even though the procedure for filing a claim under ADEA is the same as that for filing a Title VII claim, the employee in an ADEA action bears a higher burden of proof than the Title VII claimant. The employee must prove that he or she would not have suffered the adverse employment action *but for* the age discrimination. Age must be *the* motivating factor behind the discrimination.[22] Even a policy that applies equally to all workers can be a violation of this act if it has a negative impact on applicants and employees aged 40 and over. The Case Illustration considers an employee's age discrimination claim against Raytheon Co.

The Manager's Compliance and Ethics Meeting on page 433 deals with an age discrimination concern.

Discrimination Based on Disability

Congress enacted the Americans with Disabilities Act of 1990[23] to prevent discrimination against individuals with disabilities. Employers with 15 or more employees are covered by this law.

Understanding the Term *Disability*

An individual must meet one of three requirements to be covered by the ADA: the individual must (1) have a physical or mental impairment that substantially limits his ability to conduct one or more major life activities, (2) have a record of such impairment, or (3) be regarded as having such an impairment. The first inquiry is whether the individual has a condition that limits one or more major life activities. Until recently, the U.S. Supreme Court generally interpreted the term *disability* quite narrowly, but with the enactment of the ADA. Amendments Act (ADAAA)[24] in 2008 Congress expanded this definition and broadened the scope of protection available under the ADA. For example, major life activities were traditionally considered to include things such as breathing,

---

[22]In *Gross v. FBL Financial Services, Inc.*, 129 S. Ct. 2343 (2009), the Supreme Court clarified that the plaintiff in the case who alleged his age was a motivating factor in his employer's decision to demote him must be able to prove that "but for" his age he would not have been demoted.
[23]42 U.S.C. §§ 12101 *et seq.* (2011).
[24]Pub. L. No. 110-325, 122 Stat. 3553.

Manager's Compliance and Ethics Meeting

Company Layoffs and Age Discrimination

Due to budgetary constraints, as manager of the human resource department, you have been informed by the vice president of your company that each department must reduce its fixed overhead, including salaries, by 10 percent. The VP has asked you to design a strategy that will be used by each department in achieving this objective. You have called a meeting with your HR department to work on this proposal. At the meeting, the department profiles show that senior workers are making significantly more than others for doing the same work. The suggestion is to lay off as many senior workers as possible to reduce each department's fixed overhead.

A "due diligence search" to determine the "rule of law" shows that this is a violation of the Age Discrimination in Employment Act. *Aristotle's Virtue Ethics* would argue this is an unjust and unethical procedure as it deprives a group of competent and productive senior employees their right to equal treatment. This policy would also violate *Kant's categorical imperative* of respecting the human dignity of the senior employees as an end in itself and not to manipulate them to achieve the company's objective. *Rawls's equal liberty principle* would apply to older competent and productive employees to have the same rights as other employees. *W.D. Ross's prima facie duty of nonmalfeasance* would apply to this procedure as it would cause harm to qualified and productive senior workers. The suggestion to lay off senior employees is not only illegal but also unethical. The company should have a compliance and ethics program that prohibits this policy. A better ethical and legal strategy to accomplish the company's objective would be to lay off, if necessary, the unproductive members of a department that may include senior employees.

seeing, and hearing. Under the amendments, the law now recognizes other activities such as reading and bending as major life activities. The amendments also add major bodily functions to this list of activities. These include, for example, digestive, bladder, and endocrine function. In a departure from previous court interpretations, the act now states that corrective measures are not to be taken into account when deciding whether an individual has a disability. This means, for example, that if an individual has diabetes, that condition will be considered a disability even if the diabetes is well maintained and kept under control by insulin shots.

If an individual does not have a condition that substantially limits a major life activity, the individual may nonetheless come within the coverage of the act if the individual has a record of having such impairment or if an employer treats the individual as if he or she has a disability.

Employers are legally required to provide reasonable accommodations for employees with disabilities.

Genetic Testing

Congress passed the **Genetic Information Nondiscrimination Act of 2008**[25] (GINA) to prohibit employers from using genetic information in making employment-related decisions. For example, requiring potential employees to be genetically screened for possible inherited diseases that could lead to excessive insurance costs or time in treatment. Although the EEOC had previously determined that genetic discrimination would come within the provisions of the ADA, this result was not clear from language of the ADA, nor had the courts provided clear guidance on whether the protections of the ADA extended to genetic information. GINA provides employers and employees the needed clarity on this matter.

Making the Case

Procedurally, a plaintiff making an ADA claim must follow the same guidelines as a plaintiff bringing suit under Title VII. In this context, to make a prima facie case, the individual must show that he has a disability, is qualified for the job, and that the disability was the reason he did not get the job.

Reasonable Accommodation

If an employee with a disability requests an accommodation in the workplace, the law requires that the employer reasonably accommodate such a request.

---

[25]Genetic Information Nondiscrimination Act of 2008, Pub. L. No. 110-233, 122 Stat. 881 (codified in scattered sections of 26, 29, and 42 U.S.C.).

The nature of the accommodation will vary with individual circumstances but may include things such as modification of the physical facilities for their easy access (e.g., installing wheelchair ramp or widening doorways), modification of work schedules (e.g., an employee with diabetes may need regularly scheduled breaks to eat and check blood sugar), or providing braille typewriters and special computer note-taking devices for the blind and sign interpreters for deaf employees.

Undue Hardship

An employer will not be required to provide an accommodation if to do so would constitute an undue hardship for the employer. Whether something is an undue hardship is determined on a case-by-case basis and will take into account information such as the expense of the accommodation, the employer's size, and the employer's financial health. If more than one accommodation is possible, employers are permitted to choose the option with the least cost. The following case considers whether the PGA Tour must provide an accommodation for a professional golfer with a disability.

PGA Tour Inc. v. Martin, 532 U.S. 661 (2001)

Facts Casey Martin joined the PGA Tour in 2000. He was born with a condition called Klippel-Trenaunay-Weber Syndrome, which is a circulatory disorder. This disease, which is recognized as a disability under the ADA, makes it necessary for Mr. Martin to use a golf cart while participating in golf tournaments. When Casey requested use of a cart at PGA Tour events, his request was denied based on PGA Rules that required all players to walk the course.

Issue Did the refusal of PGA Tour Inc. to allow Casey Martin to use a golf cart violate the ADA?

Holding Yes, the Supreme Court, affirming the judgment of the appeals court, found the PGA in violation of the ADA because the golf cart is a "reasonable modification that is necessary."

From the Court's Opinion *Allowing Martin to use a golf cart, despite petitioner's walking requirement, is not a modification that would "fundamentally alter the nature" of petitioner's tours or the third stage of the Q-School [qualifying school for golf professionals]. In theory, a modification of the tournaments might constitute a fundamental alteration in these ways: (1) It might alter such an essential aspect of golf, e.g., the diameter of the hole, that it would be unacceptable even if it affected all competitors equally; or (2) a less significant change that has only a peripheral impact on the game itself might nevertheless give a disabled player, in addition to access to the competition as required by Title III, an advantage over others and therefore fundamentally alter the character of the competition. The Court is not persuaded that a waiver of the walking rule for Martin would work a fundamental alteration in either sense. The use of carts is not inconsistent with the fundamental character of golf, the essence of which has always been shot-making. The walking rule contained in petitioner's hard cards is neither an essential attribute of the game itself nor an indispensable feature of tournament golf.*

Defenses to Employment Discrimination

Once an employee has made a prima facie case against an employer for a violation of the antidiscrimination laws, the burden of proof then shifts to the employer to show that there is a legitimate, nondiscriminatory reason for its actions.

Bona Fide Occupational Qualification

Title VII allows employers to make certain employment distinctions based on religion, gender, or national origin in those instances where the employer can demonstrate that such qualification is "reasonably necessary to the normal operation of that particular business or enterprise."[26] For example, it is permissible for a department store to hire only female security guards to conduct spot checks of the female dressing rooms. Individual privacy concerns provide a reasonable justification for the gender distinction, as shown in the Case Illustration. Race and color may never be used as a bona fide occupational qualification.

Case Illustration

Frederick Fesel, a male nurse, applied for a nurse's aide position at the Masonic Home of Delaware, Inc., a nursing home facility, and was denied the position because of his gender. Masonic Home provides 24-hour care for its elderly residents, the vast majority of whom are female. In many instances, these residents require personal care such as dressing and bathing. Given the nature of the job and the fact that many of the female residents indicated they would not accept personal care from a male nurse, Masonic Home determined that being female was a bona fide occupational qualification for the position. Mr. Fesel brought suit against the Home for violations of Title VII. The court ruled that while Mr. Fesel had made a prima facie case against Masonic, the defendant successfully met its burden of proof and provided a legitimate, non discriminatory, reason for the discrimination. Not only did the defendant show that hiring a male would undermine the essence of its business operation, but also due to the relatively small size of its business enterprise, they could not arrange staff schedules so that at least one female nurse would always be on shift with a male nurse's aide. *Fesel v. Masonic Home of Delaware, Inc.*, 447 F. Supp 1346 (Del. 1978) *aff'd* 591 F. 2d. 1334 (1979).

Seniority or Merit Systems

Title VII allows employers to "apply different standards of compensation, or different terms, conditions, or privileges of employment pursuant to a bona fide seniority or merit system, or a system which measures earnings by quality or quantity of production"[27] as long as the purpose of this distinction is not to discriminate based on protected characteristics.

After-Acquired Evidence

After-acquired evidence refers to evidence of employee misconduct that an employer discovers after an employee has brought a suit against the employer under Title VII. This evidence does not serve as a complete defense for the employer,[28] but it will generally limit the plaintiff's remedies to recovery of back pay.

---

[26]42 U.S.C. 2000e § 703(e).
[27]42 U.S.C. 2000e § 703(h) (2011).
[28]*McKennon v. Nashville Banner Publ'g Co.*, 513 U.S. 352 (1995).

Retaliation

All of the antidiscrimination laws we have discussed in this chapter give an employee the right to bring a claim for retaliation against the employer. Employers are not permitted to take an adverse employment action against an employee because the employee complained about discriminatory conduct or sexual harassment, filed a claim against the employer, or otherwise participated in a discrimination investigation or lawsuit (e.g., serving as a witness for a fellow employee bringing a claim against the employer).

Remedies

A plaintiff who is successful in a claim for discrimination in the workplace may receive both compensatory and punitive damages. These remedies may include back pay, reinstatement, wage adjustments, retroactive promotions, and attorney fees.[29] If applicable, injunctive relief may also be awarded. In some instances of intentional discrimination, a plaintiff may also receive a punitive damage award if the plaintiff can show that the employer acted with malice or with reckless disregard for the employee's rights.

Affirmative Action

Affirmative action programs are programs implemented as a means of remedying past patterns of discrimination. These programs are applicable to government hiring and to private employers who seek to enter into government contracts. Affirmative action programs have generally been focused on the areas of jobs and education. Although the term *affirmative action* was first used by President Kennedy in 1961, the implementation of affirmative action initially began with President Franklin Roosevelt's Executive Order[30] outlawing discrimination against African Americans by defense contractors.[31] In a series of executive orders issued during the 1960s, affirmative action programs were mandated with the goal of eliminating racial bias in the employment practices of those engaged in government contracts and those projects receiving federal funding.[32] Affirmative action programs, despite the merits of their objectives, have been the subject of a significant amount of controversy

---

[29]The Civil Rights Act of 1991 imposed a liability cap on compensatory and punitive damages received for discrimination based on religion or gender. This cap ranges from $50,000 for employees with 100 or fewer employees to up to $300,000 for employers with more than 500 employees.
[30]Exec. Order No. 8802 (June 25, 1941).
[31]Times Topics, New York Times, Jan. 15, 2009.
[32]Exec. Order No. 10,925 (1941) (President Kennedy); Exec. Order No. 11,246 (1965) (President Johnson); Exec. Order No. 11,478 (1969) (President Nixon).

Exhibit 14.3. Employer Affirmative Action Programs

United Steelworkers v. Weber 443 U.S. 193 (1979)	A private, voluntary, race-conscious affirmative action plan that reserved 50 percent of the openings in a training program for African American employees was upheld by the court. The court found that the program was only a temporary measure to be used until there was an adequate representation of African American craftsmen in the workplace. The court also found that the plan did not interfere with the advancement of white employees.
Johnson v. Transportation Agency 480 U.S. 107 (1987)	The Supreme Court ruled that the employer appropriately took gender into account in making a promotion decision where the employer was seeking to promote balance in traditionally separated job categories.
Adarand Constructors, Inc. v. Pena 515 U.S. 200 (1995)	The Supreme Court applies a standard of "strict scrutiny" in judging affirmative action programs. This standard is met only if the program fulfills a "compelling government interest" and is "narrowly tailored" to fit a particular situation.

especially in those instances where the result has been reverse discrimination. Affirmative action policies have met with varied success in the courts. Exhibits 14.3 and 14.4 summarize some of the leading affirmative action cases. Exhibit 14.5 highlights state legislative action taken in response to affirmative action programs.

Exhibit 14.4. Educational Institution Affirmative Action Programs

Regents of the University of California v. Bakke 438 U.S. 265 (1978)	The Supreme Court ruled that the university's admissions practice of reserving a certain number of spots for minority applicants was a violation of Title VII resulting in reverse discrimination against a white applicant. The Court indicated that race could be used as a "plus factor."
Gratz v. Bollinger 539 U.S. 244 (2003)	The University of Michigan's undergraduate admission policy that used a point system for admission and awarded a set number of additional points to minorities was found by the Supreme Court to be unconstitutional.
Grutter v. Bollinger 539 U.S. 306 (2003)	The Supreme Court upheld the University of Michigan Law School policy of using race as one of the many components of their admission policy.
Parents Involved v. Seattle Schools* and companion case *Meredith v. Jefferson County Board of Ed. 551 U.S. 702 (2007)	The Supreme Court struck down as unconstitutional programs implemented in Louisville and Seattle that used race as a factor in assigning students to public schools.

Exhibit 14.5. Snapshot of State Legislative Responses	
California: Proposition 209 (1997)	Eliminates "preferential treatment to any individual or group on the basis of race, sex, color, ethnicity, or national origin in . . . public employment, public education, or public contracting."
Washington: Initiative 200 (1998)	Washington state abolishes state affirmative action measures by adopting an initiative similar to California's Proposition 209.
Florida: "One Florida" Initiative: Executive Order 99-201 (2000)	Florida legislature approves the governor's initiative aimed at ending affirmative action in college admission as well as in public employment and contracting.
Michigan: Proposal 2 (2006)	This proposal prohibits state and local agencies from granting preferential treatment based on race, color, gender, ethnicity, or national origin.
Nebraska: Initiative 424 (2008)	Eliminates affirmative action programs at state colleges and universities.
Colorado: Initiative 46 (2008)	This initiative, which would have ended affirmative action programs in public employment, education, and contracting, was defeated by voters at the ballot box.
Arizona: Proposition 107 (2010)	Arizona voters approve a ballot measure putting an end to the use of affirmative action measures in public employment, education, and contracting.

Although some states seem to be moving away from affirmative action programs, this does not signal the end of affirmative action measures. For example, in August 2013, two regulations were passed by the Department of Labor that require federal contractors and subcontractors to increase the number of employees who are veterans and also increase the number of disabled employees.

Global Perspective

A U.S. company doing business abroad is required to comply with the laws of foreign jurisdictions. This section will introduce you to a few of those laws that apply to employment discrimination.

The protections of the antidiscrimination laws that we have discussed in this chapter — Title VII, ADEA, and the ADA — extend to American citizens who have employee status when they are working abroad for a U.S. employer. Such protections do not extend, however,

Case Illustration

Armenian-born Shekoyan became a lawful permanent resident of the United States in 1996. He was hired by a U.S. consulting firm based in Washington, D.C., to be a training advisor for an accounting project in Tbilisi, Republic of Georgia. When the project the plaintiff was working on came to an end, he was not considered for a new position with the firm. The plaintiff brought a Title VII discrimination claim against the firm in U.S. district court on the basis of national origin discrimination. The plaintiff claimed that his supervisor discriminated against him and regularly ridiculed his accent and made negative comments about people from Armenia. The court ruled that Title VII does not extend beyond the U.S. boundaries for any person who is not a U.S. citizen. Because he was a permanent resident, and not a citizen, Mr. Shekoyan fell outside of the protection of the law. *Shekoyan v. Sibley Int'l. Corp.*, 217 F. Supp. 2d 59, affd. 409 F. 3d. 414 (D.C. Cir. 2005).

to non-U.S. citizens working abroad for the U.S. employer.[33] What, then, is the obligation of U.S. employers to foreign nationals working in locations outside the United States? To answer this question, consider the following example.

U.S. Employer ("Employer") operates a manufacturing operation in China. Two of its female employees, one a citizen of China and one a U.S. citizen temporarily working in Employer's factory in China, work side by side each day. Both women are sexually harassed by the plant manager. What recourse do they have? It is clear that the protections of Title VII will apply to the U.S. citizen. She may bring a claim against Employer for a violation of Title VII in a U.S. court. This is not the case for the Chinese employee. She is covered by the labor laws of China and must bring her claim through the Chinese legal system. It is important for the multinational employer to be mindful of the host country's employment laws. But what about a person who is not a citizen of the United States, but instead is a U.S. permanent resident, meaning that they have a green card?[34] Are they covered by Title VII when they go to work abroad for a U.S. employer? That was the subject of the Case Illustration *Shekoyan v. Sibley Int'l. Corp.*

As you read through the following descriptions of some of the nondiscrimination laws of the European Union, China, and India notice the similarities and dissimilarities with the antidiscrimination laws of the United States that you have learned about in this chapter.

Global Perspective: The European Union

The European Union (EU) is a union of sovereign nations that delegate some of their decision-making powers to shared institutions created by those nations, called *member states*. Within the European Union it is generally the European Commission that proposes new legislation that then may be considered for passage by the European Parliament and the Council of the European Union. The main forms of EU law are (1) regulations,[35] which have direct effect; and

---

[33]See, e.g., *Shekoyan v. Sibley International Corp.*, 217 F. Supp 2d. 59 (D.D.C. 2002).

[34]A holder of a green card is a foreign individual who has been authorized by the government to live and work in the United States.

[35]A regulation may be adopted by the Commission acting independently or by the Council working in conjunction with the European Parliament. Unlike a directive, a regulation is directly applicable to all member states and takes immediate effect.

(2) directives,[36] which must be implemented by the national legislatures of each member state.

In the year 2000, the European Union passed two significant directives aimed at putting an end to discrimination in the workplace. The Racial Equality Directive[37] provides protection from discrimination on the basis of racial or ethnic origin in employment and training, education, social protection, membership of organizations, and access to goods and services. The directive gives affected individuals the right to complain through a judicial or administrative procedure and provides penalties for those engaging in prohibited discriminatory actions. The burden of proof in such cases requires that the individual first provide evidence of the discrimination. The burden then shifts to the accused party to prove that no breach of the equal treatment principal has occurred.

The Employment Framework Directive[38] expanded the protected classes by adopting a principle of equal treatment in employment and training irrespective of religion or belief, disability, age, or sexual orientation. The directive requires employers to make reasonable accommodations to enable qualified, disabled individuals to participate in training or to join the employer's workforce. Limited exceptions to these rules are permitted. For example, a religious organization is permitted to hire someone with a shared belief to preserve the mission of the organization. Similarly, if an employer has a legitimate need for a person from a certain age group, a distinction based on age is permitted.

An illustration of how a member might implement an EU directive can be found in the United Kingdom's (UK) actions with regard to age discrimination. In response to the Employment Framework Directive, the UK enacted the Employment Equality Regulations in 2006. These regulations cover employees of all ages working in the UK, including foreign employees, so, unlike ADEA, the focus is not just on protecting older workers, but on protecting workers of all ages from discriminatory treatment based on age.

Global Perspective: China

As the most populated nation in the world, The People's Republic of China boasts a rapidly growing industrialized economy and benefits from substantial investment by multinational enterprises. China is a country with a long history of employment abuses, and multinational employers setting up businesses in the country should be aware that this is beginning to change as more and more workers seek to establish and protect their rights in the workplace.

---

[36] A directive may be adopted by either the Commission alone or by the Council working in conjunction with the European Parliament. A directive is addressed to member states, and its purpose is to align national legislation. While the directive is binding on member states as to the result that is to be achieved, the members may decide on the best means of adoption within their own legal system.
[37] Directive 2000/43/EU.
[38] Directive 2000/78/EU.

The 1994 Labor Law of China[39] provides protection from discrimination for various classes of people. Article 12 of this law protects all laborers from discrimination based on their ethnic group, race, gender, or religious beliefs. The law offers the following additional protection to women: "women shall enjoy the equal employment right with men. With exception of the special types of work or posts unsuitable to women as prescribed by the State . . . no unit may, in employing staff and workers, refuse to employ women by reason of sex or raise the employment standards for women."[40]

In addition to the Labor Law, the Law on the Protection of Rights and Interests of Women of the People's Republic of China, adopted in 1992 and significantly amended in 2005, provides further protection for women. Various provisions of this law work together to ensure that women receive compensation, benefits, and professional titles equal to those of men. Women may not be discriminated against due to pregnancy, maternity leave, or nursing.

In 2007 the Regulation on the Employment of the Disabled was adopted with the purpose of "promoting the employment of the disabled and safeguarding the labor rights of the disabled."[41] The regulation requires that employers enter into labor contracts with disabled employees and make accommodation to provide such individuals with a safe working environment, among other things.

Also in 2007, China enacted the Employment Promotion Law.[42] This law addresses discrimination based on ethnicity, race, gender, disability, and religious belief. Although its terms are similar to those of the Labor Law, one significant feature of the new law is that for the first time employees are given the right to bring a discrimination case against an employer in the People's Court of China. This is a significant change from the administrative remedies generally available under the earlier laws.

Global Perspective: India

In comparison to steps against discrimination taken by the European Union and China, the government of India has taken very little notice or action with regard to discrimination in the workplace. Instead, the bulk of efforts in the labor area have been to address basic rights for all employees. India has a myriad of such laws, 60 pieces of legislation in all, addressing things such as wages, hours, working conditions, benefits, and plant closing restrictions. Despite a lack of emphasis on discrimination, India has taken some steps to safeguard women in the workplace.

As early as 1946, with the passage of the Industrial Employment Act, India prohibited the sexual harassment of women in the workplace. This was followed

---

[39]Labor Law (promulgated by Standing Committee National Peoples Congress, effective January 1, 1995).
[40]*Id.* at Article 13.
[41]Adopted by the State Council Feb. 14, 2007; effective May 1, 2007, Article 1.
[42]This law became effective on January 1, 2008.

by the Maternity Benefit Act passed in 1961 allowing women a 12-week absence from the workplace following birth of a child or a miscarriage. In 1976 the Equal Remuneration Act was passed requiring the same or similar pay for men and women for the same or similar work. The act also prohibits employment recruitment practices that discriminate against women except in those cases where employment of women is restricted or prohibited by law.

In April 2013, India enacted the Sexual Harassment of Women at Workplace Act to prevent the sexual harassment of female employees. Sexual harassment was first acknowledged as a human rights violation by the Supreme Court of India in the *Vishaka v. State of Rajasthan* case. In that case the court provided guidelines that required employers to enforce the equal rights of women in the workplace and to provide a process by which women could report sexual harassment. The new law codifies the 1997 guidelines for vulnerable workers.

Other International Agreements

In addition to considering the laws of the foreign jurisdictions in which they operate, U.S. companies doing business abroad should also take into account the existence of any international or regional agreements that may impact employment rights. Exhibit 14.6 highlights some of these agreements.

Exhibit 14.6. Agreements Affecting Employment Rights

United Nations Universal Declaration of Human Rights (1948)	Article 7: "All are equal before the law and are entitled without any discrimination to equal protection of the law." Article 23(2): "Everyone, without any discrimination, has the right to equal pay for equal work."
Conference on Security and Cooperation in Europe: Final Act — Helsinki (1973)	"To ensure equality of rights between migrant workers and nationals of the host countries with regard to conditions of employment and work and to social security."
United Nations International Covenant on Economic, Social and Cultural Rights (1994)	Article 7(3): "Equal opportunity for everyone to be promoted in his employment to an appropriate higher level, subject to no considerations other than those of seniority and competence."
United Nations Convention on the Elimination of All Forms of Discrimination Against Women (1979, updated 1999)	Article 11: "Parties shall take all appropriate measures to eliminate discrimination against women in the field of employment in order to ensure, on a basis of equality of men and women, the same rights."
North American Free Trade Agreement (1994)	Cooperative activities with regard to: Article 11(1)(j): employment standards and their implementation Article 11(1)(m): the equality of women and men in the workplace

Summary

After reading and discussing this chapter, you should have an appreciation of the wide range of antidiscrimination laws in the U.S. workplace. Keep in mind that the statutory laws and judicial opinions that support our legal system have an ethical foundation. These laws are based on providing equal opportunity to all capable employees regardless of race, color, creed, national origin, gender, age, and disability. Notions of fairness and a just society that are found in the natural law theory of Thomas Aquinas and John Finnis remind us that anti-discrimination laws are "moral absolutes that give legal reasoning its backbone." John Rawls in his book *Justice as Fairness* defines in his difference principle a fair equality of opportunity for all. Aristotle in his famous book on *Ethics* remarks that laws should be a reflection of a just moral order. This chapter provides much more than a basic understanding of the antidiscrimination laws. The in-depth ethical analysis of the Supreme Court's decision in *Ricci v. DeStefano* offers a clear understanding of how ethical theory is related to judicial reasoning in interpretation of the antidiscrimination laws. Given the global nature of business enterprises today and the fact that U.S. companies doing business outside the United States must comply with the laws of the jurisdiction in which they operate, a global perspective is essential.

Questions for Review

1. Discrimination based on language

Robert Pierre and Jon LeFranc are assembly line workers employed by Manufacturing Inc,, a manufacturing company in Dayton, Ohio. Robert and Jon are good friends as they both grew up in the same town in France. Both are fluent in French and often converse in their native tongue during their mid-morning and lunch breaks. Manufacturing has an English-only rule for the workplace. One day the assembly line supervisor enters the lunchroom and hears Robert and Jon speaking to one another in French and immediately fires both of them for violating the employer's English-only rule. In response, Robert and Jon file a Title VII claim with the EEOC. Do they have a case? Why or why not? Explain the circumstance in which employers should be able to adopt and enforce an English-only requirement.

2. Americans with Disabilities Act accommodation

When the University of Maryland Medical System Corporation learned that one of its surgeons was HIV positive, the university offered him transfers to positions that did not involve surgery. The surgeon refused, and the university terminated him. The surgeon filed suit alleging in part a violation of the ADA. The surgeon claimed that he was "otherwise qualified" for his former position. What does he have to prove to win his case? Should he be reinstated? *Doe v. University of Maryland Medical System Corp.*, 50 F. 3d 1261 (5th Cir. 1995).

3. Ethics and employment discrimination

Bridget applied for a TV news commentator's job. She has adequate experience to satisfy the job description but was denied the job. Bridget has a substantial birthmark that covers one side of her face. The TV producer told her that viewers would find it distracting from her news commentary. He explained to Bridget that her interview would be discussed with upper management but she probably would not be hired. The TV ethics and compliance officer finds this grossly unfair to Bridget and is concerned about the company's legal liability if she brings a claim under the ADA. Explain the company's legal liability.

The ethics and compliance officer called a manager's meeting to discuss the ethics of not hiring Helen. Explain the ethical implications of the company's decision using ethical principles.

4. Sexual harassment

Estrella Medina-Rivera was employed by MVM, Inc., a company that provides security services for the Bureau of Immigration and Customs Enforcement (ICE). An ICE agent began disturbing Estrella by continually calling her at her personal phone number and harassing her sexually. Estrella notified her MVM supervisor that an ICE agent was "bothering" her with calls to her personal number. Sometime later, Estrella was sexually assaulted by this individual. The agent was fired within a few days of the incident. Estrella brought a claim against MVM, Inc., for failing to respond to her earlier sexual harassment complaint regarding this individual. What result? *Medina-Rivera v. MVM, Inc.*, 713 F. 3d. 132 (2013).

5. Sexual harassment

Beth has worked as a lifeguard for several summers while attending college. During the course of her employment, she and other female lifeguards were subject to "uninvited and offensive touching" by their supervisors. In addition, supervisors often made lewd comments and in general spoke about women in offensive terms. Does Beth have grounds for a sexual harassment claim? On what basis? What defenses, if any, may be available to Beth's employer? *Faragher v. Boca Raton*, 524 U.S. 775 (1998).

6. Title VII discrimination?

Cori McCreery was a store clerk at Don's Valley Market in South Dakota. Cori notified her employer that she is transgendered and would soon be starting the medical process of transitioning to a man. Shortly after this, Cori was fired. No reason was given by her employer for the firing. During the time of her employment, Cori had always received favorable performance evaluations. Cori has brought a discrimination claim against her employer. Explain the likely outcome of the dispute.

7. Affirmative action programs

Explain the pros and cons of affirmative action programs.

8. International consideration

Jillian Mitchell is a citizen and resident of Canada. She applies for a position as a film editor at the California offices of DreamWorks. Although she is highly qualified for the job, she is not hired. She later discovers that DreamWorks executives expressed preference to hire a male for the job believing that a man could better endure the often round-the-clock hours required during a movie editing job. Jillian believes that she has enough evidence to make a prima facie case under Title VII. As a Canadian citizen and resident, does Jillian have a right to bring a Title VII claim? Why or why not?

Further Reading

Equal Employment Opportunity Commission, http://www.eeoc.gov/.

Manning Magid, Julie, and Jamie Prenkert. *The Religious and Associational Freedoms of Business Owners*, 7 University of Pennsylvania Journal of Labor and Employment Law 191 (2005).

Notes, *The Title VII Tug-of-War: Application of U.S. Employment Discrimination Law Extraterritorially*, 40 Vanderbilt Journal of Transnational Law 833 (2007).

Selmi, Michael. *Why Are Discrimination Cases so Hard to Win?* 61 Louisiana Law Review 3 (Spring 2001).

Smith, Heather, Kevin Battle, and Jitendra Mishra. *Discrimination in the Workplace*, 6 Advances in Management 2 (Feb. 2013).

PART IV

The Business Sale

CHAPTER 15

Contracts: Contract Formation

Chapter Objectives

1. To understand the purposes for which contracts are used and the basic requirements of valid contracts
2. To become familiar with two significant bodies of contract law: the Uniform Commercial Code and the United Nations Convention on International Sales of Goods
3. To recognize when a valid offer and a valid acceptance has been made
4. To understand the concept of consideration and to know the minimum commitments each party must give and receive in order for an agreement to be binding
5. To understand the two types of required capacity for entering a valid contract: age capacity and mental capacity
6. To appreciate the ethical implications of committing to a contract

Practical Example: Mortgage Defaults

Approximately 70 percent of U.S. homeowners have a mortgage on their home.[*] A mortgage is a loan that is secured by real estate — that is, the mortgage lender has the right to foreclose on the real estate if the loan is not repaid. Foreclosure involves taking back the property, selling it, using the proceeds to pay the costs of the foreclosure process and the amount owed on the loan, and returning any remaining funds to the homeowner. If the proceeds from the sale of the property were inadequate to pay for the deficiency balance, the mortgage lender may proceed to sue the borrower for the balance due.

Housing prices climbed quickly and steadily in most regions of the United States during the late 1990s and early 2000s. Lenders loaned money freely, sometimes loaning large sums of money to people who had little prospects of repaying it. Then in 2007, housing prices plunged dramatically. Some homeowners found themselves owning homes that were worth less than the mortgage owed. This created an economic incentive to "walk away" from their homes and their mortgage obligations.

Some theorists believe that contractual obligations are purely economic propositions, so contracts should be breached if it makes economic sense to do so. In the context of the mortgage crisis, some homeowners assessed their options and risks and chose to default on their mortgages (called a *strategic default*). In some of these cases, the borrowers could not pay. In other cases, the borrowers had the means to pay and were current on their other debts but saw no prospect of their house ever regaining a value close to what they paid for it.

Other theorists assert that a contract creates an ethical obligation to complete the deal, even if circumstances change significantly for one of the parties.

As you read about contract formation in this chapter and contract performance and breaches in the next chapter, consider the following. What are the consequences of entering a contract like a mortgage? What specific provisions would help protect the borrower? The lender? Is it ethical for a lender to extend credit to a homeowner who is unlikely to be able to repay the debt in full? What are the consequences of breaching a mortgage? Is it ethical to strategically default on a mortgage when the borrower has the money to continue paying? Is it ever unethical for a lender to foreclose on a homeowner, even when it is legal to do so? When large numbers of borrowers choose strategic defaults, how is business impacted?

---

* Zillow Real Estate Research, Free and Clear American Homeowners, http://www.zillowblog.com/research/2013/01/09/free-and-clear-american-mortgages/.

What Is a Contract?

Contract Definition

A contract is a legally binding promise. In a contract, one party agrees to do or to refrain from doing something, in exchange for which the other party also agrees to do or refrain from doing something. The Restatement (Second) of Contracts, a well-respected, non-binding source of U.S. law, defines a contract as a "promise or a set of promises for the breach of which the law gives a remedy, or the performance of which the law in some way recognizes as a duty."[1] This chapter begins with an exploration of each aspect of this well-known definition by addressing these questions: (1) Which promises are legally binding? (2) What legal duties are recognized by the law? (3) What constitutes a breach? and (4) When a breach is established, how does a court provide a remedy?

---

[1]Restatement (Second) of Contracts section 1.

Contract Terms

The parties' specific responsibilities, obligations, and benefits in the contract are called the **terms** of the contract. Terms of a contract could include, for example, time of delivery of goods, how long a company could use an inventor's patent, when payment is due, and so forth. People who regularly enter into the same type of contract often begin with a form contract (or portions of a form contract), called a **boilerplate**, and then revise the language to reflect the individual aspects of the arrangement. For example, a company could use a contract for services that could include a boilerplate provision such as "The Contractor will furnish all personnel, equipment and materials necessary to perform the work described in Appendix A in an efficient and expeditious manner." The company could then change Appendix A to describe the specific services but keep the boilerplate language quoted above. Despite even careful attention to detail, it is often difficult or impossible for parties to anticipate and contemplate every possible future occurrence and the impact of future events on the contractual arrangement. Part of the role of contract law is to provide rules of convention that operate to fill in the gaps of the agreement.

The terms and conditions make up the essential framework of the contract.

Freedom of Contract

Parties have wide latitude to negotiate and commit to the terms they choose and to allocate business risks as they see fit, as long as their agreement meets certain tests and rules. This is sometimes referred to as **freedom of contract**. Despite a strong legal tradition of freedom of contract, some negotiated bargains fall outside the purview of legal enforceability.

There are two major reasons that a parties' agreement would not be legally enforceable. First, not all promises rise to the level of being considered a contract. Several requirements, explained later in this chapter, must be met in order to conclude that an exchange of promises is in fact a binding contract. Underlying these requirements is the theme of **voluntary assent**. That is, in general, courts will enforce only those promises that parties have voluntarily chosen to commit to. Many of the rules examined in this chapter exist as a way to test whether the agreement is in fact the product of the parties' free will. The rules surrounding offers and acceptances are designed to test for the manifestation of mutual assent. Once the law is satisfied that the agreement is the product of voluntary assent, then the parties are bound to adhere to the contractual terms[2] or will be liable for the consequences. Second, some types of contracts, such as employment

---

[2]Unless, for example, performance is excused. See Chapter 16 for more information on excuses from performing under a contract.

agreements and mortgages, are subject to extensive regulation by federal and/ or state authorities. In these situations, freedom of contract is restricted by the parties' obligation to comply with relevant statutory law, case law, and administrative law.

Role of Contracts in Business

The business world depends heavily on contracts. Bankers, suppliers, venture capitalists, retailers, entrepreneurs, consumers, and many others rely on the strength of a contract's legal validity. A party to a contract is able to rely on the other party's performance, knowing that if contractual obligations are not met, then there is a right to legal recourse. The confidence that contractual obligations will be met is what keeps the wheels of commerce moving. For example, assume Acme, Inc., needs to purchase sensors to use in its manufacture of televisions. Acme enters into a contract with Component Parts Inc. to supply the needed sensors by June 1. Acme and Component Parts both understand that the agreement is legally enforceable. Relying on receiving the sensors by June 1, Acme can estimate the length of time necessary to manufacture the finished product and can, with confidence, enter into a contract with the purchaser of the finished product. Similarly, Component Parts can rely on selling the sensors and receiving the money. Suppose Component Parts decides to apply for credit at a bank. In its request for credit, Component Parts could provide the bank with a copy of the contract with Acme as evidence of an anticipated payment amount and date. The bank's decision to extend credit relies in part on the Acme/Component Parts contract. Both the bank and the television purchaser could enter into other contracts, with similar ripple effect. In part, the wheels of commerce move because each business is relying on the strength of the contracts it has formed and on the strength of contracts others have formed.

Requirements for a Valid Contract

Not all promises rise to the level necessary for a binding contract. Which promises are legally binding? Only those promises that meet the tests for contract formation are legally binding. Contract formation requires (1) a valid offer, (2) a valid acceptance, (3) consideration, (4) capacity, and (5) legality. Each of these required elements must be present before drawing the conclusion that the exchange of promises is a legally binding contract. For each, the law has developed definitions, rules, and tests. Many of these legal rules help ascertain whether the exchange of promises[3] has been the product of mutual assent and whether the parties involved are acting voluntarily. Later sections of this

---

[3]Occasionally, assent to a contract is manifested through conduct rather than by an oral or written promise.

chapter examine the concepts and rules relating to each of the five required elements.

Sources of Contract Law

As addressed in Chapter 1, the legal system in the United States is a federalist one. Both the federal (national) government and individual states have the authority to legislate, within the framework and constraints of the U.S. Constitution. Early in the nation's history, one of the challenging effects of this system was that each of the many state legislatures passed laws applicable to business transactions. Many of these laws (and their interpretations through caselaw) differed from and conflicted with each other, creating confusion for businesspeople. The uncertainty resulting from differences in rules inhibited business, decreased confidence in the enforceability of contracts, and discouraged complex commercial transactions, especially interstate ones. In recognition of these obstacles, professional legal organizations drafted standardized sets of rules for business transactions. Similarly, the variation in rules across country borders caused confusion and legal uncertainty to those transacting business internationally. Three seminal works were developed in an effort to provide guidance and standardization of business rules across state and international borders: the Uniform Commercial Code (UCC), the Restatement (Second) of Contracts, and the United Nations Convention on Contracts for the International Sale of Goods (CISG). (The CISG is more fully explained in Chapter 17, "Sales Law, Consumer Protection, and E-Commerce.")

Uniform Commercial Code (UCC)

Originally completed in 1952, the Uniform Commercial Code was written to cover all aspects of routine business transactions. It covers contracts between merchants[4] and also between merchants and consumers. The drafters of the UCC had no power to enact the rules, but eventually, 49 of the 50 states adopted the UCC as law in their state, sometimes with modifications. Louisiana, whose legal system is derived from the French, adopted only part of the UCC.

The UCC is comprised of nine articles, or chapters. Each article is devoted to a different aspect of commercial transactions—contract formation and breaches, financing, collateral, checks and banking, and so forth. Article 2 of the UCC governs the sale of goods. By UCC definition, the term **goods**

---

[4]The UCC definition of a merchant is "a person who deals in goods of the kind or . . . holds himself out as having knowledge or skill peculiar to the practices or goods involved in the transaction." UCC section 2-104.

means all things that exist and are movable.[5] (For a more in-depth discussion of Article 2 coverage, see Chapter 17). If there is no UCC provision that addresses the question (or if the contract is not governed by the UCC), apply common law principles and look for applicable statutes from the relevant jurisdiction.

Restatement (Second) of Contracts

The Restatement of Contracts was first published in 1932, and a revision, known as the Restatement (Second) of Contracts, was released in 1980. Just as its name implies, the Restatement is not law itself but rather a compilation of contract-law principles, rules, definitions, commentary, and examples. Despite its nonbinding status, the Restatement (Second) of Contracts is well respected throughout the legal community in the United States and is sometimes used by judges and lawyers looking for guidance on matters of contract law.

Agreement in General

In most business deals, evidence of a manifestation of mutual assent takes the form of an offer by one party (the **offeror**), followed by an acceptance by the other party (the **offeree**).[6] This is sometimes referred to as a "meeting of the minds." A **meeting of the minds** occurs when, taking all communications between the parties and all circumstances into account, a reasonable person would conclude that an offer had been extended and accepted and that the parties agree on all material (that is, important) terms. This is taken from the objective vantage point of a third party. Neither internal communication within a company (such as internal company e-mails) nor a party's private thoughts, for example, are relevant. In reference to the reasonable person standard, Judge Easterbrook wrote, "The objective approach is an essential ingredient to allowing the parties jointly to control the effect of their [contract]. If unilateral or secret intents could bind, [then] parties would become wary and the written word would lose some of its power."[7] Natural law ethically supports the notion of the reasonable person standard. Often the collective judgment of a jury will determine if a reasonable person could conclude from the negotiations if and when an offer has been made. This objective standard rather than the subjective intent of one of the contracting parties is based on the natural law ethical principle that we have an inherent ability to judge what is reasonable after reviewing all the relevant facts and evidence.

---

[5]Uniform Commercial Code section 2-105.
[6]Restatement (Second) of Contracts section 22(1).
[7]*Skycom Corp. v. Telstar Corp.* (C.A.7, 1987), 813 F.2d 810, 815.

Point of Commitment

The difference between a general expression of interest in doing business with another party and the present intent to be bound to a business arrangement can be critically important. Again, to quote Judge Easterbrook: "parties should be able to choose with precision the point at which they can no longer back out . . . A rule of law that could bind the parties to a deal in the midst of resolving these uncertainties . . . would make transactions riskier."[8] So, when during the course of negotiations do parties become legally bound? Parties are bound when a valid offer has been extended and a valid acceptance has been made.[9] The next sections explain the rules of legally valid offers and acceptances.

Valid Offers

When does a communication — an e-mail, a phone conversation, or an in-person conversation — rise to the level of being a valid offer?

Definition and Requirements for a Valid Offer

An offer is a definite proposal by one person to another indicating a present intent to enter a contractual relationship. To determine present intent, the reasonable person standard is applied to these factors:

- There is language of present commitment.
- The terms are fairly definite.
- The offer must be communicated.

Each of these requirements is explored in more detail below.

Offers are within the sole control of the offeror. A well-known common law adage describes the offeror as "master of the offer." She may choose the exact terms of the offer, the method of delivery of the offer, and how any acceptance will be conveyed. By law, none of these must be reasonable. Recall that contract law permits parties significant freedom to contract — this freedom begins with the offeror choosing whatever proposal he thinks best under the circumstances, but the proposal need not pass a test for fairness or reasonableness. Of course, if the

> **An Ethical Insight: W. D. Ross's Prima Facie Duty of Fidelity and "Promise Keeping"**
>
> Ross's prime facie duty of fidelity to "promise keeping" enhances the well-being of society. Business and personal relationships are based on trustful assurance of what was offered and accepted in a contract. For example, life insurance contracts that promise to pay the beneficiaries of the policy owner in exchange for the paid premiums must be supported by a reliable ethical insurance company and a legal system to enforce the claim, if necessary. The insurance company and the policy owner rely on mutual promises for their security and well-being.

---

[8]*Skycom Corp. v Telstar Corp.*
[9]This presumes that the three other elements required for a valid contract are also in place: consideration, capacity, and legality.

offeree finds the offer undesirable, she need not accept. The Ethical Insight on page 455 explains ethical reasons for a promise to help ensure a secure society.

Language of Present Commitment

Most offers in the business world are communicated by the offeror to the offeree either orally or in writing. Careful evaluation of the offeror's words, in context, is necessary to determine whether, from a reasonable person's perspective, the offeror demonstrated present commitment. Words uttered in anger or jest do not qualify.

Sometimes even when there is no evidence of anger or jest, it can be difficult to determine when, during the course of business negotiations, words rise to the level of establishing the intent to commit. Despite the difficulty, this is an important issue to be mindful of when conducting business. Accidentally becoming bound to a deal that is disadvantageous or has been prematurely agreed to is problematic from many perspectives.

Definite Terms

Parties need not conclude every detail for a contract to be binding. In fact, "[w]here the parties have intended to conclude a bargain, uncertainty as to incidental or collateral matters is seldom fatal to the existence of a contract."[10] However, contract terms must be *reasonably* certain. Why? Why doesn't the freedom of contract allow parties to agree to a loose or ambiguous set of terms as long as both parties agree to it? There are two reasons. First, imagine you are a judge deciding a breach of contract case. The plaintiff successfully proves the existence of a contract with the defendant. If the contract terms are too vague or scant, how will you determine whether there has in fact been a breach? And if you do decide there was a breach, how will you calculate the amount of damages the plaintiff is entitled to because of the breach? These questions can be difficult or impossible to answer unless the contract terms are reasonably certain. Second, the more specificity a proposal includes, the more likely it implies commitment to the deal. There must be enough agreed-upon terms and enough specificity for courts to infer that the parties reached a point of commitment. For these reasons, the

Case Illustration

In a famous 1893 decision, an appeals court in Illinois reviewed a case involving these facts. The defendant owned an old harness, worth about $15. The harness was stolen, and the defendant, in an "explosion of wrath," involving "rough language and epithets concerning the thief" vowed to "give $100 to any man who will find out who the thief is." Subsequently, the plaintiff discovered who stole the harness and revealed the thief's identity. When the defendant refused to pay the reward, the plaintiff sued, claiming that a contract had been formed and breached. But the Illinois Appeals Court disagreed. Given the circumstances, the defendant's statement was not a valid offer — it was "indicative of a state of excitement so out of proportion of the supposed cause of it, that it should be regarded rather as the extravagant exclamation of an excited man than as manifesting an intention to contract." *Higgins v. Lessig*, 49 Ill. App. 459 (1893).

---

[10]Restatement (Second) of Contracts, Section 33 comment a.

offer must be "sufficiently definite to be specifically enforced,"[11] and the more definite the terms of the proposal, the more likely it is an offer.

When terms are definite enough to warrant that an offer was made and accepted but not fully comprehensive, how does the law settle disputes over the ambiguities or the missing terms? Part of the answer depends on whether the contract is governed by the UCC. If Article 2 of the UCC applies, then courts utilize legal conventions to fill in the gaps, as explained more fully in Chapter 17. In cases where the UCC does not apply (such as contracts for real estate, services, or licensing of intellectual property), courts try to ascertain what the parties intended based on the available evidence. To accomplish this, courts may use:

- Usage of trade — that is, what is customary in this trade or industry?
- Course of dealing between the parties — what patterns of conduct did parties use previously?
- Factual implication — what can be reasonably inferred based on what the parties actually said or did?

Case Illustration

Mr. Leonard claimed a television commercial he watched was an offer. In the commercial, Pepsi launched a promotional where customers could collect points by buying Pepsi products and redeeming the points for various prizes. The commercial featured a teenage boy getting ready for school. When he is shown wearing a T-shirt, the number of Pepsi points needed to redeem the T-Shirt flashes on the screen, followed by a jacket, sunglasses, etc. Then, an announcer states "Introducing the new Pepsi Stuff catalog," during a camera shot of the catalog. Finally, a Harrier Jet flies into view, accompanied by the subtitle "HARRIER FIGHTER 7,000,000 PEPSI POINTS." The Harrier jet was not listed in the catalog, but Mr. Leonard collected 7,000,000 Pepsi points and submitted them to Pepsi to redeem the jet. Pepsi declined, and the case went to court. How do you think the court decided? *Leonard v. Pepsico* 88 F. Supp. 2d 116; U.S. Dist. Ct. S.D.N.Y. 1999.

Communication to the Offeree

Communicating the offer to the offeree is an essential requirement of a valid offer. If a proposal is not communicated, perhaps the offeror is still contemplating the deal. Conversely, the communication of an offer implies that the offeror is serious in his intent. An offer becomes valid when it is sent, not when it is received.

As "master of the offer," the offeror alone has the power to choose the offeree(s). The ability to identify the offeree is critical in business. For example, a seller might permit one buyer to purchase goods on credit but would not extend the same offer, or might not extend an offer at all, to a less creditworthy buyer. Unless dictated otherwise by statute, the offeror also has the power to select how the offer is conveyed to the offeree — orally, by e-mail, by letter, and so forth.

---

[11]*Oglebay Norton Co. v. Armco* 52 Ohio St.3d 232, 556 N.E.2d 515 (1990).

An offeror can make an offer to one person, to a group of people, to one person who is yet to be identified (e.g., the "tenth caller"), or to the public at large. In cases where the validity of an offer is in doubt, though, a proposal communicated to a specific person is more likely to be an offer than a proposal communicated to the public. Again, this is further proof of a manifestation of intent to be bound — an offeror who singles out a particular offeree is exhibiting evidence of a deliberate effort to engage in a contract.

Case Illustration

A store advertised in the newspaper "1 Black Lapin Stole Beautiful, worth $139.50 . . . $1.00 First Come First Served [on Saturday]." Mr. Lefkowitz was the first to arrive on Saturday, but the store refused to sell him the stole for $1. He sued the store and won. In its opinion, the Supreme Court of Minnesota relied on the principle that where the advertisement is "clear, definite, and explicit, and leaves nothing open for negotiation, it constitutes an offer, acceptance of which will complete the contract." *Lefkowitz v. Great Minneapolis Surplus Store*, 86 N.W.2d 689 (Minn. 1957).

Special Situations — Advertisements, Online Auctions, and Bids

In some circumstances, invitations to discuss or to transact business do not rise to the level of being a valid offer without some further evidence of commitment. Advertisements, online auctions, and bids raise questions about the distinction between a valid offer and an invitation to negotiate.

In general, advertisements, catalogues, price lists, circulars, order forms,[12] and promotional materials are not offers; they are invitations to negotiate. Suppose We Are Gadgets sends its catalogue to Machine Maker, a potential customer. Machine Maker then sends to We Are Gadgets a purchase order for 10,000 Grade A Model Z42 widgets, which are listed in the catalogue. Has a contract been formed? No — not without further action by We Are Gadgets. Legally, the brochure operates as an invitation to negotiate and the purchase order is an offer. In the event We Are Gadgets replies with a confirmation (sometimes called an "order acknowledgement"), then Machine Maker's offer has been accepted and a contract has been formed.[13]

Occasionally, advertisements contain so much detail and specificity that they are an exception to the rule that advertisements are not offers. Compare the two Case Illustrations above and on page 457. What are the similarities between Mr. Lefkowitz's case and Mr. Leonard's? Both plaintiffs responded to advertisements. In Mr. Lefkowitz's case, the court ruled that the advertisement constituted an offer. Is the same true in Mr. Leonard's case? No, according to the U.S. District Court in New York. The commercial was not definite enough

---

[12]*Mesaros v. United States*, 845 F.2d 1576 (Fed.Cir.1988).
[13]Note that federal and state consumer protection laws regulate advertising and prohibit false advertising practices, such as "bait and switch." Bait and switch involves "baiting" customers by advertising a low price and then, when customers arrive to buy the goods, "switching" the advertised product with a higher-priced one. Therefore, even though an advertisement is not an offer, advertisers are sometimes held to deliver on their advertised promises.

because it specifically directs the viewer to the catalog for further terms. In contrast, the newspaper ad in Mr. Lefkowitz's case identified exactly who could accept. Also, the commercial lacked evidence of present commitment: "In light of the obvious absurdity of the commercial, the Court rejects plaintiff's argument that the commercial was not clearly in jest."[14]

A solicitation of bids through a live or online auction or through the construction bidding process, for example, is an invitation for offers. Those submitting bids are extending offers that the seller (in an auction) or builder (in a construction setting) must accept for a contract to be formed. An exception applies where the auctioneer specifically states that auction items are offered **without reserve** or where a builder specifically states that the lowest bid meeting the required specifications will be accepted. In such cases, the bid solicitation is an offer, and the submission of the bid is an acceptance.

Before committing to any contract, it is important for a company to do its **due diligence.** Due diligence is a common legal phrase referring to the diligence that is due in a particular situation. For example, before entering a contract, it is important to investigate the other contracting party's creditworthiness, reputation, solvency, etc. The Manager's Compliance and Ethics Meeting on page 460 illustrates how documenting its due diligence could be used as evidence of legal compliance in a criminal case.

Termination of Offers

A valid offer empowers the offeree to accept, but only as long as the offer remains in effect. For how long is an offer valid? Offers can terminate in one of four ways:

1. By the lapse of time
2. By operation of law
3. By revocation
4. By rejection

Once the offer is terminated in any of these ways, the offeree's power to accept is extinguished.

Termination of Offers by Lapse of Time

As master of the offer, the offeror may include in the offer a specific time for its expiration. The offer expires at the time specified by the offeror. This rule is valuable for businesspeople, who may wish to control the timing of the negotiation process and allow time for exploration of other business opportunities if

---

[14]*Leonard v. Pepsico, Inc.* 88 F. Supp. 2d 116; U.S. Dist. Ct. S.D.N.Y. 1999. *Leonard v. Pepsico, Inc.* was appealed to the U.S. Court of Appeals, Second Circuit and affirmed "for substantially the reasons stated" in the District Court's opinion.

Manager's Compliance and Ethics Meeting

Contract Criminal Liability

The remedy for breach of contract is a civil case in which the aggrieved party, who has sustained an economic loss as a result of the breach, is seeking damages. In some instances, there could be criminal liability as well. Companies have to engage in due diligence for many reasons, including ensuring that their contracts do not violate a criminal statute. A Compliance and Ethics Program should be implemented that "exercises due diligence to prevent and detect criminal conduct. . . ." Suppose you are the manager of a construction firm that regularly submits bids on large construction government projects. During negotiations there is a pre-award stage where your company submits to the government detailed information on the materials it will provide, including its cost. Section 1001 of 18 U.S. Code states, among other rules, *"whoever makes any materially false, fictitious, or fraudulent statements or misrepresentations shall be fined or imprisoned not more than 5 years."* The false statements at this pre-award stage may be oral as well as written. You, as the ethics and compliance officer, have called a manager's meeting to inform all employees submitting bids of the ethical care and legal compliance necessary not to violate the federal criminal statute and to be especially careful what they submit and say about the materials the company will provide for the construction costs. Minutes of the manager's meeting should be detailed and forwarded to the chair of the board and CEO for safekeeping. In the event the corporation is later criminally prosecuted by the federal government for the crime of making "false, fictitious, or fraudulent statements," for the construction of a government project, the Corporate and Ethics Program, the company's code of ethics, and the minutes documenting the Manager's Compliance and Ethics Meeting are relevant evidence that may be used at the criminal trial to prove "due diligence" and possibly exonerate the company or reduce its fine and/or the employees' sentence.

the offer is not accepted. For example, suppose Rita is a real estate developer who owns five condominiums for sale. She offers them at a specified price and on specified terms to Lance. It is likely that Rita would want to specify in the offer a time at which it will expire. Inclusion of an expiration date and time will free Rita to offer the units to another prospective buyer as soon as the offer expires.

In cases where the offeror does not specify a time for expiration of the offer, an offer expires after a reasonable time. What is reasonable depends on several factors: the subject matter of the offer, method by which the offer was communicated, industry practice, and prior dealing between the parties. For example, if Michael phones Sophia with an offer to buy 1,000 red roses that are available for delivery immediately, a reasonable time will be much shorter than if an offer for dry goods is sent to a prospective buyer by mail. In fact, many courts would hold that Sophia's power to accept Michael's offer ends when the phone call ends. Another important consideration is the volatility of price fluctuations. An offer to buy a commodity that is subject to sharp price increases and decreases will expire sooner than an offer to buy a commodity with historically stable pricing.

Termination of Offers by Operation of Law

Certain events automatically terminate an offer: the death or incapacity of the offeror or the offeree, or the death of a person or destruction of a thing that would have been essential to the deal. Keep in mind that these events will terminate an *offer*; the same events do not necessarily release parties from obligations under a *contract*. For example, Homeowner offers to sell her house to Buyer. After making the offer but before Buyer responds, Homeowner dies. The offer is terminated. However, suppose Homeowner offers to sell her house to Buyer, who accepts. After the contract is formed, Homeowner dies. Buyer is entitled to purchase the house from Homeowner's estate because the contract is not terminated by Homeowner's death.

Termination of Offers by Revocation

As master of the offer, in general, the offeror has the right to revoke at any time prior to acceptance. Even if the offeror promises to keep the offer open, it may still be revoked, although doing so would obviously give rise to ethical and reputational concerns. Any clear manifestation of unwillingness to enter into the proposed bargain operates as a revocation and, like an offer, a revocation is valid when received. However, there are certain instances in which an offeror may not revoke.

Option Contracts

In a strict sense, an option contract is not really an exception to the rule that offerors can revoke offers, because it is a contract itself. The offeror sells his power to revoke in exchange for the offeree giving something of value. For example, suppose Mary would like to sell the contents of her aunt's home, which contains numerous antiques, for $100,000. Stella, an antiques dealer, is considering buying the items but must obtain financing to do so. While she is applying for a loan, Stella does not want Mary to sell to someone else. Stella pays Mary $200 to hold the offer opened for Stella to consider for 30 days. During the 30 days, Stella may choose to accept the offer and Mary may not revoke the offer. At the end of the 30th day, the offer is terminated. At that point, Mary is free to sell to someone else and may keep the $200.

UCC Firm Offers

Recall that Article 2 of the Uniform Commercial Code applies to sales of goods only. Under UCC 2-205, if an offer is:

■ Signed
■ By a merchant

■ For the purchase or sale of goods
■ Stating that the offer will be held open for the offeree to consider

Then it is irrevocable:

■ For the time stated in the offer or
■ If no time is stated, it is irrevocable for a reasonable period of time; and
■ In no event can the period of irrevocability exceed three months.

What is the rationale for the UCC requiring merchants to adhere to their promises to hold offers opened, while nonmerchants may legally break such a promise? Offers involving merchants are more likely to involve complex arrangements. If a merchant makes an offer to sell $1 million worth of batteries, what is involved in the offeree's evaluation of the offer? Perhaps the offeree needs time to investigate alternative proposals, to determine whether the batteries are suitable for the offeree's purpose, to arrange for financing, to plan space to store the batteries in a warehouse, and so forth. While investing time in researching these issues, it would be unfair if the offeree were suddenly informed that the offer was no longer valid.

Offer for a Unilateral Contract

A unilateral contract involves an offer that can only be accepted through an act of performance. Suppose Wenda says to Hongling, "If you get an A in your business law class, I will pay you $500." How can Hongling accept? She can accept only by getting an A. If instead she replies, "Sure, I'll get an A," she has not accepted because Wenda's offer invites only performance as a method of acceptance. Now suppose that after Wenda extends his offer, Hongling has an A average and Wenda stops her on the way to the final exam. Can Wenda revoke the offer? No, because an offeree's beginning substantial performance of a unilateral contract terminates the offeror's power to revoke.

Promissory Estoppel

A theme of law in the United States is recognition that businesses, consumers, and others rely on assertions and promises and should be able to do so, within reason. One example is the doctrine of promissory estoppel. **Promissory estoppel** is a legal theory that plaintiffs can sometimes invoke when there is no consideration (discussed below) to support a contract, but an injustice has occurred. To establish a claim under promissory estoppel, the plaintiff must show:

1. The promisor should reasonably expect to induce action or forbearance on the part of the promisee;
2. Such action or forbearance is in fact induced; and
3. Injustice can only be avoided by enforcing the promise.

If an offeror knows that extension of his offer will induce some substantial action or restraint by the offeree, and the offer does in fact induce substantial

Is a handshake a "manifestation of mutual assent"?

action or restraint, then the offer is binding "to the extent necessary to avoid injustice." For example, suppose a general contractor solicits bids to prepare a proposal to a real estate developer. An electrician submits a bid for the necessary electrical work. (Recall that a bid is an offer.) The general contractor then tells the electrician that his bid will be used in submitting the final proposal to the developer. While the developer is considering the general contractor's proposal, can the electrician revoke his bid? No. The electrician knew the general contractor was relying on the bid, and the general contractor has a reasonable time to notify the electrician whether the developer accepted the proposal. To allow the electrician to withdraw his bid or to demand more money while the developer is considering the proposal is unfair to the general contractor.

Termination of Offers by Rejection and Counteroffers

When an offeree rejects an offer, he loses the power to accept. A **rejection** occurs when, viewed objectively, the offeree manifests an intention not to accept the offer. Careful examination of the offeree's words and surrounding circumstances is sometimes necessary. Complications can arise when a counteroffer is made, as is often the case when parties negotiate. This is a critical aspect of law to consider when negotiating a business deal, because except for offers involving sales of goods, a counteroffer operates as a rejection of the original offer. Responses to offers should be phrased carefully to avoid inadvertently extinguishing an offer that the offeree would still like to consider. For example, is there a difference between an offeree stating, "The price you quoted seems high to me — I wonder if you could do any better than that?" compared to "Would you take $5,000 instead?" The first example is not a rejection or a counteroffer. According to the Restatement (Second) of Contracts, "A mere inquiry

Richard Davis, originator of *Flip That House*.

regarding the possibility of different terms, a request for a better offer, or a comment upon the terms of the offer, is ordinarily not a counteroffer."[15] However, the second example is a **counteroffer** because it proposes a bargain different than the original offer. As such, it extinguishes the original offer.

Valid Acceptances

Once a valid offer has been made (and has not been terminated), the offeree is empowered to accept. One way to view an offer is that it enables an offeree to accept, thereby concluding the bargain.

Requirements for a Valid Acceptance

An **acceptance** is an offeree's "manifestation of assent to the terms . . . in a manner invited or required by the offer."[16] The **mirror image rule**, which is applied to negotiations for all bilateral contracts except sales of goods,[17] requires that the offeree assent to the exact terms proposed by the offeror. An acceptance is valid only if it mirrors the offer. Proposed variations or additions constitute a counteroffer.

The rules for determining whether the offeree's response is an acceptance are similar to the rules for determining whether the offeror's statement was an offer. Offers and acceptances require indicia of voluntary assent; the same level of commitment, proof of present intent, and requirement of communication are necessary. However, recall that the offeror may choose the means by which an offeree may accept. If the offeror specifies the means and timing of acceptance, the offeree must abide; any deviation does not operate as an acceptance.

Exhibit 15.1. Summary of Rules for Validity of Offers, Acceptances, Rejections, and Revocations	
	Valid when
Offer	Received by offeree
Acceptance	Dispatched by offeree
Rejection	Received by offeree
Revocation	Received by offeree

---

[15]Restatement (Second) of Contracts, section 39 comment b.
[16]Restatement (Second) of Contracts, section 50.
[17]For the rules relating to acceptance of offers of sales of goods, see Chapter 17.

One difference between rules of acceptances and rules of offers relates to timing. The **mailbox rule** states that an acceptance is valid when dispatched, as long as the communication (e-mail, letter, etc.) is correctly addressed. Contrast this rule with the timing of offers, revocations, and rejections, which become valid when received. An offer, revocation, or rejection is "received" even if the e-mail, text message, or letter has not been opened but could be opened (Exhibit 15.1).

In the following In-Depth Ethical Case Analysis case, note the ethical basis that supports the court's holding that, based on all the relevant facts, a reasonable jury could find that the offer was accepted.

In-Depth Ethical Case Analysis

Trademark Properties Inc. v. A&E Television Networks, 422 Fed.Appx. 199, 2011 WL 1350758 (C.A. 4 S.C.)

Facts

Richard Davis was a South Carolina real estate broker who owned and operated a business called Trademark Properties Inc., which bought, sold, and renovated underpriced homes. He approached A&E Television Networks with an idea for a reality television show based on "flipping" homes. Charles Norlander, an A&E employee, viewed a pilot episode Davis had created, and Norlander and Davis spoke by phone for about an hour. During the conversation, Davis proposed that he would bear all financial risks of selling and reselling the homes featured on the show and that they would divide profits from the show evenly. At the end of the conversation, Norlander said, "Okay, okay, I get it."

Shortly thereafter, Norlander arranged for Davis to speak with three other employees at A&E about the terms of the agreement. Norlander arranged for Davis to meet with a production company, and a senior vice president at A&E e-mailed Davis, "[t]he board approved the money for our series." There was no formal written contract.

The parties filmed 13 episodes of *Flip This House*, and the show was successful. A&E never paid Davis anything.[*]

Davis sued for breach of contract. A&E claimed there was no contract. The case was sent to a jury that returned a verdict awarding Davis about $4 million (half the profit from the first season). The defendant then filed a motion for judgment as a matter of law and requested a new trial. The District Court denied the motion, and the defendant appealed.

The Court's Decision

A reasonable jury could conclude a reasonable person in Plaintiff's position after such extensive bargaining could plausibly interpret "Okay, okay, I get it," in conjunction with the statement that the only condition is board approval, as acceptance. In addition, there is sufficient, though not unequivocal, evidence from which a reasonable jury could conclude that Plaintiff objectively treated Nordlander's statement as an acceptance of his offer to make a television series and split the revenues equally. Plaintiff allowed himself and his company to be the subject of thirteen television shows made by Defendant.

Overview of Ethical Dilemma

Keep in mind that the law is often, but not always, supported by ethical principles. Carefully review the fact pattern in this case. From an ethical perspective, one could ask: (1) Was it reasonable to assume, based on this phone conversation with an employee, without proof that Norlander had the authority to bind the corporation, that there was an ethical obligation for Norlander to stand behind his promise or were they merely negotiating without any moral or ethical commitments at this stage? (2) Was the conversation with the three other employees enough to ethically create a moral obligation to fulfill the exchanged promises made earlier between Davis and Norlander? Can one continue to speak in general terms about a commitment without creating an ethical obligation to fulfill its terms? (3) A conversation with a senior vice president about a company venture takes on a serious tone beyond a discussion with mere employees. The ethical issue is when the vice president e-mailed Davis, "The board approved the money for our series," was there an ethical obligation on the company to do so even if there was no formal contract?

Ethical Theory Analysis

W.D. Ross's Duty of Fidelity

Ross's prima facie duty of fidelity would find an ethical obligation based on a promise made by the senior vice president's e-mail. The corporate board acts in a **fiduciary relationship** on behalf of the stockholders and is accountable to them for its executive decisions. A senior vice president generally has authority to relate board decisions to others on behalf of the board. An ethical and moral obligation exists at this point to honor the promise unless, Ross says, "the consequences of fulfilling a promise . . . would be so disastrous to others that we judge it right not to do so." If the decision to participate in the show would be "disastrous" to the company and ultimately to the stockholders, there could be ethical grounds to break the promise.

John Rawls's Equal Liberty Principle

Those in Rawls's Original Position functioning behind a "veil of ignorance" would discuss the ethics of this case not knowing if they were Davis or A&E Television Networks. Their guiding ethical standard would be the equal liberty principle that "Each person has the same . . . claim to . . . equal basic liberties . . . compatible with the same . . . liberties for all." The freedom to contract is supported by this ethical principle granted to both parties. Relying on the promise of a senior vice president would be reasonable and an ethical commitment.

John Stuart Mill's Utilitarianism

The ethical theory of **utilitarianism** often abbreviated as "the greater good for the greater number" could be used by A&E to ethically renege on its promise if the stockholders could lose money based on this venture. One could argue this is a significant undertaking, and the parties were in an early stage of precontract negotiations without any moral or ethical obligation. The "greater good" would ethically require both parties to now decide if they want to formalize the new business venture with a written contract. At that point there would be ethical and moral obligations to fulfill the contract terms or be subject to a claim for damages.

Conclusion

There are sufficient ethical arguments to support the court's decision that a reasonable jury could conclude there was an acceptance.

---

*At one point, A&E offered Davis a per-episode fee plus 5 percent of revenue attributed to the show, which Davis rejected.

Silence as Acceptance

Save for the exceptions below, an offeree's silence is not an acceptance. Imagine the burden on society if the reverse were true. Anyone could send offers by mail or voicemail or e-mail or text and simply state, "If I don't hear from you in the next 30 minutes, I will assume you accept." A recipient might not even be aware of the offer. To hold that a contract would be formed after 30 minutes of silence would wreak havoc to businesses.

Instead, the offeree's silence is an acceptance only in these limited situations:

1. *The offeree signals in advance that her silence will constitute an acceptance.* For example, Lucinda extends an offer to Luis. Luis replies, "If you don't hear from me in three days, assume I accept." If three days pass and Lucinda does not hear from Luis, a contract has been formed.
2. *The offeree takes the benefit of the offered services, knowing the offeror expects compensation.* John phones a cleaning company, Spotless, Inc. Spotless tells him that the first housecleaning is $50 and each subsequent cleaning is $100. Spotless cleans John's house and John pays $50. A week later, Spotless employees arrive to clean John's house again, although this had not been pre-arranged. He lets them in and observes that they clean his house. When they are finished, he must pay them. He took the benefit of the offered services, knowing compensation was expected.
3. *Previous course of dealings between offeror and offeree establish a pattern of contract formation through offeree's silence.* Homeowner signs a contract to have home heating oil delivered to her house regularly for one year at a specified price. When the year is over, the contract has expired but the oil delivery company continues to deliver oil and homeowner continues to pay when invoiced. This continues for five months. In the sixth month, when oil is delivered, the homeowner is bound to pay.
4. *The offeree acts in a manner inconsistent with the offeror's ownership of the offered property.* Michael walks into a convenience store, grabs a bottle of soda, opens it, and begins drinking it in the store before paying. His acts of opening and drinking the soda are inconsistent with the store's ownership of the soda, and he is obligated to pay for it.

Other Expressions of Agreement

Negotiations can take a variety of forms. Sometimes, parties choose to memorialize some of their agreement in writing.

Term Sheets, Letters of Intent, and Memorandum of Understanding

In more complex situations, **term sheets, letters of intent** and **memorandum of understanding** are sometimes used as vehicles to express some measure of agreement or intent and to advance contractual negotiations, with minimal or no level of legal commitment. In general, a **term sheet** is a list of the major terms one party proposes to another. Parties draft, revise, and submit term sheets to each other as a way to identify the terms they agree upon and those that require further proposals and negotiation. **Letters of intent** express the nonbinding intent to come to an agreement. As discussed in the Ethical Insight, a letter of intent consists of a serious promise with ethical consequences.

Both term sheets and letters of intent usually anticipate that a more formal document will be forthcoming, articulating more comprehensively the parties' specific obligations. **Memoranda of understanding** memorialize principles that parties agree on in a cooperative venture, business or otherwise. For example, the ground rules for debates between candidates for the U.S. presidency are memorialized in memoranda of understanding. Exhibit 15.2 compares these three types of documents.

An Ethical Insight: Kant's Ethics on a Letter of Intent

Although not legally binding, a *letter of intent* should always be taken seriously. For the company to maintain an ethical reputation there should be sound reasons for not following through with its intent to contract. Treating a letter of intent frivolously would violate Kant's categorical imperative of universalizing one's conduct. Kant could argue that although the letter is not legally enforceable, if everyone did not try to fulfill a letter of intent, society and businesses would suffer. This ethical principle does not preclude the option to ethically renege on the letter of intent if there are strong legitimate reasons for doing so.

Exhibit 15.2. Comparison of Term Sheets, Letters of Intent, and Memoranda of Understanding

	Form of Document	Binding?	Use
Term sheet	Bullet point or list of material terms, typically proposed by one party	Not usually binding but used to facilitate negotiations leading to a binding contract	Valuable tool in helping parties identify points of agreement and disagreement during negotiation
Letter of intent	Letter outlining basic obligations of both parties and expressing intent to continue negotiation to bring the deal to fruition	Not usually binding but can contain binding terms, such as a promise not to negotiate with other parties	Expression of intent to enter a binding contract in future
Memorandum of understanding	Typically a formally written document signed by all parties	Not binding and usually not intended to lead to a binding agreement	Can be used in business but more commonly used in nonbinding arrangements where parties work cooperatively; for example, multiparty community projects

Agreements to Agree

Recall that sometimes parties negotiate a contract by exchanging term sheets or expressing intent to enter a contract through a letter of intent. Term sheets, letters of intent, agreements to agree, and similar documents present thorny issues for businesspeople. Despite the complications, it can be crucial for parties to identify whether they are bound and if so, the exact point at which they became legally obligated.

An **agreement to agree**, in which one or more material terms are left open for further negotiations or which is subject to future negotiation, is unenforceable. Similarly, a letter of intent that states that it is subject to final agreement is also not binding. Regardless of the name of the document, "if it appears to be no more than a statement of some of the essential features of a proposed contract and not a complete statement of all the essential terms,"[18] then it is not a binding agreement. Whether an agreement is binding depends on two questions: "(1) whether the parties intended to be bound by the document; and (2) whether the document contains all the essential terms of an agreement."[19]

The Consideration Requirement

What Is Consideration?

Assuming a valid offer has been accepted, the next requirement for establishing a contract is consideration. Adequate **consideration** exists when parties bargain to give each other something or refrain from doing something that confers benefit on the other party and for which there was no previous obligation to do or refrain from doing. With this definition in mind, determine whether the offer in each example below is a valid consideration.

Example A

Randy says to Kerry, "I'll sell you this book for $50."

Kerry replies, "Sure," and hands Randy $50.

Consideration? Yes. The parties have bargained for the purchase and sale of the book for $50. Randy's promise to transfer the book to Kerry induced Kerry's payment to Randy.

Example B

Randy says to Kerry: "I'll sell you this book for $50."

Kerry replies, "Sure."

Randy has not yet given Kerry the book, and Kerry has not yet paid Randy.

---

[18]*Glazer v. Dress Barn*, 274 Conn. 33, 873 A.2d 929 (2005).
[19]*Pharmathene, Inc. v. Siga Technologies, Inc.* Not Reported in A.3d, 2011 WL 4390726 (Del. Ch. Sept.22, 2011).

Consideration? Yes. Randy's *promise* to give Kerry the book and Kerry's *promise* to pay Randy is valid consideration. Randy had not previously been legally obligated to transfer the book to Kerry, and Kerry had not previously been legally obligated to pay Randy. In fact, most business contracts are more like this example than example A. In business, ordinarily parties are attempting to secure performance of some kind—payment, services, goods, and so forth—at a point in the future.

Example C

Randy says to Kerry: "I'll sell you this book for $50."

Kerry replies, "Sure."

Kerry then discovers that the book is worth $2.

Consideration? Yes. An old legal maxim is that courts do not inquire into the fairness of consideration. Parties are free to negotiate terms largely unrestricted by judicial second-guessing or legislative interference. As a result, for an exchange of promises to be considered a valid contract, consideration must *exist*, but courts will not examine whether what parties receive in a given deal is fair or approximates fair market value. Gross overpayment could, however, be symptomatic of some other legal problem, such as fraud or duress.

Example D

Dinesh causes a car accident that injures Lyle. Dinesh offers to pay Lyle $50,000 if Lyle agrees to release Dinesh from all claims that relate to the accident. Lyle agrees.

One example of consideration is exchanging or promising to exchange something of value.

Consideration? Yes. There is bargained-for exchange of something of value. Recall that consideration can be based on the promise to give something of value or to *refrain from* doing something one is legally permitted to do. Lyle has a valid legal claim against Dinesh, and his promise not to pursue the claim constitutes valid consideration.

Example E

Dinesh and Lyle were never involved in a car accident. Lyle says to Dinesh, "If you don't pay me $50,000, I will file a lawsuit against you claiming that you injured me in a car accident."

Consideration? No. Forbearance of a claim only constitutes consideration if the claim involves an honest dispute. In essence, Lyle is not really giving anything (nor is Dinesh actually receiving a benefit), so the definition of consideration is not met.

The Ethical Insight on page 472 illustrates how Aquinas argues, from an ethical and moral perspective, that an ethical selling price should be based on it being "necessary or virtuous." A markup on goods or services sold is often necessary and moral to maintain a profitable business. Generally contract law allows competent parties to agree on any price unless there are extenuating circumstances that would make the contract "grossly unfair" or unconscionable.

Case Illustration

Recall the Case Illustration from Chapter 12, "Agency Law." LAI was a manufacturer, promoter, and seller of gaming machines. Big Bear was a manufacturer and seller of arcade-type games. A sales representative of LAI met the president of Big Bear at a trade show. They had several meetings about the possibility of Big Bear becoming a distributor of one of LAI's popular gaming machines, the "Stacker." After negotiations, they entered into an agreement that stated, among other things, that Big Bear could terminate the contract at any time by providing written notice of termination, but LAI could terminate only for insolvency, fraud, assignment, or bankruptcy. LAI filled Big Bear's first order for 20 machines but refused to ship any more, citing numerous small service and setup issues with the few customers Big Bear had sold to. Big Bear sued. Did the parties have a contract?

The court decided that there was no consideration. Big Bear did not have to purchase anything and could get out of the agreement at any time and because Big Bear could terminate at any time, the promise was illusory. The court stated, "The Purchase Contract did not obligate Big Bear to render any performance. Instead, Big Bear could withdraw from the contract at any time, for any reason, and never purchase Stacker machines at all." Therefore, the agreement was void.[*]

---

[*]*Big Bear Import Brokers, Inc. v. LAI Games Sales, Inc.*, 2010 WL 729208 (D. Ariz. Mar. 2, 2010).

What Is Not Consideration?

What kinds of situations fall outside the scope and definition of consideration? Some of the most common situations involve (1) past consideration and (2) preexisting duties.

Past Consideration

Generally, a promise made in recognition of a benefit that the promisor has already received is not valid consideration. If the promisor received the benefit first and then chose to make a promise, the inducement component of the consideration definition is lacking. In fact, the phrase "past consideration" is a misnomer; to quote another old legal adage, "Past consideration is no consideration."

An Ethical Insight: Aquinas, an Excessive Selling Price, and Contract Consideration

In his *Summa Theologica*, Question 77, Article 4, Aquinas states: "For if he sells at a higher price something that has changed for the better, he would seem to receive the reward of his labor. Nevertheless the gain itself may be lawfully intended, not as a last end, but for the sake of some other end which is necessary or virtuous."

According to Aquinas, the sale of a product that has appreciated in value has "changed for the better" and may be sold at a higher price than its acquisition cost. However, Aquinas would argue that in order for the motive of the gain (the increased resale price) to be ethical, it must be "necessary or virtuous." Aquinas is seemingly uncomfortable with an extravagant gain in the selling price, and he would find an excessive or greedy profit motive in the sales price to be unethical.

Aquinas appears to be hinting toward the contemporary doctrine of an "unconscionable contract" (discussed in Chapter 16, "Contracts: Performance, Public Policy, and Global Contracts") where the court may examine the adequacy of consideration if the sales price would "shock the court's conscience" to enforce it, allowing the judge to adjust the contract accordingly. This is a highly unusual procedure, and in the absence of fraud, duress or misrepresentation, a competent adult/buyer generally has to honor an agreed upon excessive contract price.

Preexisting Duty Rule

Consideration involves the giving and receiving of something of value. But a promise has no value if the promisor is already legally obligated to do or not to do that thing, whether as a result of a contractual provision, a statute, etc. This idea is formalized in the **Preexisting Duty Rule**, which states that a promise to do something the promisor is already legally bound to do (or to refrain from doing something the promisor is already not permitted to do) does not constitute valid consideration.

At first, it might appear as if few business contracts involve bargaining with someone to do what that person is already obligated to do. When might a party wish to make the same promise twice and claim that the second promise is valid consideration? Consider the debt settlement arrangements described below. Is there valid consideration when a creditor and debtor agree that the creditor will extinguish the claim in exchange for payment of less than the full amount owed? The answer turns on whether the debt is uncertain or disputed in some way.

Suppose Daniel borrowed $10,000 from Lucy, which he promised to repay on December 31, along with $500 of interest. On December 31, Daniel asks Lucy, "If I pay you $9,000 on December 31, will you discharge the debt?" Lucy says yes, takes the $9,000 on December 31, and then sues for the $1,500 balance. Will she win?

Yes. Applying the preexisting duty rule, the agreement to pay $9,000 on December 31 to discharge the debt was not supported by consideration. In agreeing to take the $9,000 on December 31, Lucy was not receiving any type of benefit. In promising to pay $9,000 on December 31, Daniel was doing something he was already legally obligated to do.

Suppose instead that Daniel contacts Lucy and offers to make a $9,000 payment on July 1 (six months before payment is due) in order to satisfy the debt. Lucy agrees, takes the $9,000 on July 1, and then sues for the $1,500 balance. Will she win?

No. Here, the agreement to pay $9,000 on July 1 did provide Lucy with a benefit — she gains use of the money earlier than originally planned. Moreover, Daniel has agreed to do something he was not previously obligated to do — he agreed to make payment earlier than he had to. There is valid consideration, and the agreement to discharge the debt is valid.

Gifts and Donations

In general, the promise to give a gift in the future is not legally enforceable. If a donor is not receiving something in return, the promise to give a gift does not meet the definition of consideration. A donor is receiving no benefit; the recipient is not obligated to do or refrain from doing anything; and there is no bargained-for exchange. Suppose a donor promises to give a gift to a charity and then has a change of heart. Can the charity sue for breach of contract? Some states have statutes addressing this question. In the absence of a statute, the charity cannot sue for breach of contract because there is no consideration and therefore no contract.

Capacity to Contract

Recall that contract formation is based on the concept of voluntary assent. In essence, the law requires evidence of voluntary assent of both parties before an exchange of promises is considered legally binding. In furtherance of this, the law also requires that the parties to an agreement possess capacity. Broadly, capacity means the ability to give voluntary assent; if a party lacks capacity, any assent is not truly voluntary. There are two ways in which a person could lack legal capacity:[20] (1) the person has not reached the age of majority, and (2) the person lacks the requisite mental capacity.[21]

Minors

The age of majority is set by each individual state's statute. For purposes of entering a contract, 18 is the age of majority in all states except Alabama and Nebraska (where the majority age is 19). A person who enters into a contract before reaching the age of majority may avoid the contract, at his or her election, at any time before reaching the age of majority or for a reasonable time thereafter.[22] This is a bright-line rule. It does not matter whether the person was particularly mature or particularly inexperienced for his or her age. The rationale behind the long-standing rules regarding minors lacking

---

[20]Previously in U.S. history, other segments of society were deemed incapable of entering a contract, such as spendthrifts, the elderly, prison convicts, Native Americans, and married women. See Restatement (Second) of Contracts, section 12 comment b.

[21]Note that there are several different tests for both age capacity and mental capacity in the law. Requisite capacity to execute a will, to get married, to enter a valid contract, and to enlist in the military, for example, each mandate application of a different legal test.

[22]Some states limit the time for avoiding the contract to one year after reaching the age of majority.

capacity to contract is protection of young people. Presumably, due to their youth, minors lack the judgment, experience, and wisdom necessary to negotiate and become legally bound to contracts.

There are three possible outcomes when a minor does enter into a contract. First, the minor could choose not to disaffirm or could choose to ratify the contract after attaining the age of majority, in which case the parties would proceed with performance of the contract. Second, the minor could choose to disaffirm the contract at any time before reaching the age of majority and for a reasonable period of time thereafter. This would usually involve notifying the other party and returning to the adult whatever the minor originally received under the contract (when and to the extent this is possible). Assume a 16-year-old purchases a car for $5,000. While driving the car negligently, he is involved in a car accident that renders the car worth $200 as scrap metal. In some states, the minor could disaffirm the contract and receive back the full contract value of $5,000. In other states, the minor disaffirms the contract and receives back only $200, the value of whatever is returned to the adult.

Third, the minor might not have a choice to disaffirm and must honor the contract. This is based on an exception to the rule allowing minors to disaffirm contracts. Where the subject matter of the contract involves necessary goods or services, a minor cannot disaffirm. Agreements for medical services, health insurance, educational loans, and groceries, for example, cannot be disaffirmed. What is the rationale underpinning this exception? After all, if minors lack sufficient life experience to buy a car, don't they also lack sufficient life experience to purchase health insurance? View these transactions from the perspective of an adult seller. Knowing that minors can disaffirm, adult sellers are and should be reluctant to sell to minors (especially goods of significant value). The exception for necessities protects minors by removing sellers' concerns that the contract could be subsequently disaffirmed. This exception enhances minors' ability to procure goods and services that are necessary and basic for living.

Mental Capacity

A person could lack required mental capacity for a variety of reasons, such as mental illness, intoxication, or substance abuse.[23] Regardless of the underlying cause, a person lacks mental capacity to enter a valid contract if, because of mental illness, intoxication, or substance abuse, the person:

1. Is unable to understand the nature and consequences of the transaction; and
2. Is unable to act in a reasonable manner with respect to the transaction.

As with minors, a person lacking mental capacity can choose to avoid the contract or can choose to ratify it.

---

[23]There are many tests for mental capacity in law. There are different rules for testing a person's mental capacity to execute a will or to get married, for example. The test described here can be used only for contract formation.

Case Illustration

In 1954, the Supreme Court of Virginia faced the questions of mental incapacity and mutual assent in the famous case *Lucy v. Zehmer.* Mr. Lucy and Mr. Zehmer had known each other about 20 years, and Lucy had tried several times to buy from Zehmer several acres known as the Ferguson Farm. On the Saturday afternoon before Christmas 1952, several friends and neighbors had visited Zehmer at the restaurant he and his wife ran, and he had "a good many drinks." Lucy stopped by the restaurant at about 8:30 P.M., taking a partial bottle of whiskey with him to offer Zehmer a drink. Zehmer subsequently testified: "I was already high as a Georgia pine, and didn't have any more better sense than to pour another great big slug out and gulp it down, and he took one too." After the men started drinking Lucy said, "I bet you wouldn't take $50,000" for the Ferguson Farm. Zehmer replied, "Yes, I would too; you wouldn't give fifty" and said he doubted Lucy had that much money in cash. For about 40 minutes, the men continued to drink, joke, and intermittently discuss the Ferguson Farm. Lucy again said he would pay $50,000 and told Zehmer that if he didn't believe it, he should write up an agreement to that effect. Zehmer wrote on the back of a restaurant check, "I do hereby agree to sell to W. O. Lucy the Ferguson Farm for $50,000 complete." Lucy told him he should change "I" to "We." Upon viewing the writing at trial, Zehmer exclaimed, "Great balls of fire, I got 'Firgerson' for Ferguson. I have got satisfactory spelled wrong. I don't recognize that writing if I would see it, wouldn't know it was mine."

According to Zehmer's testimony, Lucy said, "Get your wife to sign it." Zehmer then tore up what he had written and rewrote it to include Mrs. Zehmer and also to include a provision for title examination, at Lucy's suggestion. After the rewrite, Zehmer asked his wife, who was busy working in the restaurant, to sign it. Zehmer testified that at first his wife did not want to sign, but then he told her it was just a joke and she signed. (Mrs. Zehmer testified that she read before signing and thought it was a cash sale that night, subject to clear title.)

After Zehmer's wife signed, Zehmer brought it back and gave it to Lucy, who offered him $5 which Zehmer refused. Lucy testified that Zehmer said, "You don't need to give me any money, you got the agreement there signed by both of us." Zehmer testified that he refused the $5 Lucy offered and said, "Hell no, . . . that is beer and liquor talking. I am not going to sell you the farm. I have told you that too many times before." All witnesses confirmed a significant amount of alcohol was or appeared to be consumed by both men. Zehmer characterized the situation as "just a bunch of two doggoned drunks bluffing to see who could talk the biggest and say the most."

The next day, Lucy began preparations to buy the farm, and shortly thereafter, he retained legal counsel to examine the title. When a clean report of title returned, he wrote to Zehmer to arrange a closing and to confirm that he was ready to pay in cash. Zehmer replied that he never agreed to sell Ferguson Farm.

Lucy sued for specific performance of the contract. The Zehmers claimed that the writing "was prepared as a bluff or dare to force Lucy to admit that he did not have $50,000; that the whole matter was a joke; that the writing was not delivered to Lucy and no binding contract was ever made between the parties."

The Supreme Court of Virginia held that Lucy was entitled to specific performance and ordered the transfer of the farm to Lucy in exchange for $50,000. There was agreement to sell Ferguson Farm, and "Zehmer was not intoxicated to the extent of being unable to comprehend the nature and consequences of the instrument he executed, and hence that instrument is not to be invalidated on that ground." *Lucy v. Zehmer*, 196 Va. 493; 84 S.E.2d 516 (1954).

Summary

As legally binding promises, contracts provide the lifeblood of a business. They are a vehicle for helping to ensure stability and predictability in all aspects of business—they can cover buying supplies, taking out a loan, providing services to customers, purchasing real estate, and much more. But not all promises are legally enforceable.

The laws relating to contract formation are based on the idea that there has been a manifestation of mutual assent between the parties. In general, parties have broad freedom to contract, and if there has been a valid offer, valid acceptance, consideration, legal capacity (age and mental), and a lawful purpose, then parties will be legally bound to the promises they made.

It is good practice for corporate legal counsel to review major contracts before they are signed to ensure their terms and conditions are enforceable and represent what is in the company's best interests. In addition, companies should use due diligence and should be confident that promises undertaken can be performed in the future. A company cannot claim it is committed to maintaining an ethical corporate culture and then renege on its published promises, such as promises made to consumers in its code of ethics, online privacy policies with promises to the subscribers not to disclose personal information, or promises contained in online terms of use, unless there are serious business reasons for doing so. The company's ethics and compliance officer should work with corporate legal counsel in reviewing the code of ethics and any published online promises.

Questions for Review

1. Freedom to contract

The introduction to this chapter referred to ways in which parties have considerable freedom to contract but that the freedom to contract is restrained by certain legal parameters. What are some examples of how expansive the law is in allowing freedom to contract? What are some examples of the restraint on this freedom?

2. Valid offer

For each of the following, decide whether there has been a valid offer:

a. "Would you like to buy my family's cabin in Maine? It's a beautiful piece of lakefront property and could sell for more than $500,000 if I used a real estate broker to sell it."

b. "I'm looking to make some extra money over summer vacation. I'll paint the exterior of your house, two coats, nice job, if you'll pay me $20 an hour."

c. "I know it's only June, but I'm expecting a crop of McIntosh apples in October and can sell you 10 bushels at $15 per bushel."

d. "I will be able to mow your lawn for $50 as soon as possible."

e. A contractor and a homeowner agree that the contractor will build a house according to certain specifications and plans drawn and approved by an architect, for a stated price. The homeowner will be given a range of choices for appliances, interior and exterior paint colors, and carpet, but the homeowner has not yet selected these.

f. "Some of the coins in my collection are pretty rare. Maybe you'd be interested in the older ones?"

3. Ethics and job offers

Liz, a graduate MBA student at a prestigious business school, received three job offers late in April just before her May graduation. On

April 30 she accepted the job at ABC Corp, which she considered to be the best offer of the three. Liz started working on May 5 and was very pleased with her new position. On May 15 Liz notified the other two companies that she had accepted another offer and thanked them for considering her request for employment. On May 27 she was notified by ABC Corp that the department where she was to work was going to be reorganized and the company could employ her no longer. Liz was extremely upset and informed the other two companies that made her an offer that she was available for immediate work. They both informed her that the positions were now filled. Her lawyer explained to Liz she was a mere employee-at-will,[24] and the company was under no legal obligation to retain her. Aside from any legal theory of recovery, did the company have any ethical obligation to retain Liz, perhaps in another department? Was Liz acting ethically in not notifying the other two companies that made her job offers late in April that she accepted another offer on April 30? Be sure to use classical ethical principles in your answer.

4. Contract formation

DJ Slick was a radio show host on WLTO-FM, based in Lexington, Kentucky. As a promotional, he announced that he would reward "loyal listeners with a chance to win one hundred grand" by calling the station at a specified time. Norreasha Gill listened to the radio for several hours and was the tenth caller at the specified time. When she called, Slick put her on air and asked whether she planned to go on a shopping spree. She replied that she would like to put a down payment on a house, buy a minivan, and treat her three children. She went to the radio station the day after she won to collect the money but was told to return later. When she arrived home, an answering machine message from the station manager informed her that it was actually all a joke, and that her prize was a candy bar called $100,000, not $100,000 in cash. Subsequently, the station manager offered her $5,000 to settle, but she refused and sued the company that owned WLTO, Cumulus Media, for the $100,000. Was there a valid offer? Was there a valid acceptance? Was there valid consideration? Explain.

5. Rejection of an offer

An offeror extends an offer to settle a claim for $15,000. The offeree responds, "Could your $15,000 offer be increased to $17,500?" Is this a rejection? *Jackson v. Federal Reserve Employee Ben. System*, Slip Copy, 2009 WL 2982924 D.Minn., 2009.

6. Contract formation

Senior Settlements (SS) sent an offer to Growth Trust Fund (GTF) and stated that the offer would expire on July 23, 2004. GTF sent an acceptance on August 10, 2004. SS took steps to perform the contract, but these steps were not communicated to GTF until November 2004. However, on October 28, 2004, GTF sent a letter stating that GTF did not want to enter into a contract. When, if ever, is a contract formed? *Senior Settlements LLC v. Growth Trust Fund* Not Reported in F. Supp. 2d, 2008 WL 2036777 D.N.J., 2008.

7. Consideration

In a landmark case, William E. Story told his nephew in March 1869 that if the nephew "would refrain from drinking liquor, using tobacco, swearing, and playing cards or billiards for money" until he turned 21 years old, then he

---

[24]Recall from Chapter 13, "Employment Law," that an employee-at-will, in general, can be discharged for any reason or no reason.

would give him $5,000. The nephew agreed and did not partake in any of the listed activities. In the days following his 21st birthday, the nephew and uncle corresponded by letter. The uncle acknowledged that he owed the $5,000 but the two agreed that the uncle would keep the money, with interest, until the nephew was older. The uncle died. His estate claimed that there was no contract because there was no consideration. Who won and why? *Hamer v. Sidway* 124 N.Y. 538 (1869).

8. Contract formation

Fiona lost her pet dog and told Mary, "If you find my dog and return him to me, I'll pay you $200." Mary said nothing in response but found the dog and returned him. Fiona refused to pay because when she'd originally made the offer, Mary did not make any kind of promise to return the dog. Is Fiona correct? Why?

What if, instead, Fiona lost her pet dog and said nothing to Mary. Mary found the dog and returned him. Fiona was so grateful that, on being reunited with the dog, she exclaimed, "Mary, in appreciation for finding my dog, I'll give you a $200 reward!" A week later, Fiona refused to pay Mary and claimed that there was no valid contract between them. Is Fiona correct? Why?

Further Reading

Alces, Peter A. *Guerilla Terms.* 56 Emory Law Review Journal 1511–1562 (2007).

DiMatteo, Larry A. *Strategic Contracting: Contract Law as a Source of Competitive Advantage.* 47 American Business Law Journal 727–794 (Winter 2010).

Jacobson, M.H. Sam. *A Checklist for Drafting Good Contracts.* 5 Journal of the Association of Legal Writing Directors 79 (Fall 2008).

Jeffries, Browing. *Preliminary Negotiations or Binding Obligations? A Framework for Determining the Intent of the Parties.* 48 Gonzaga Law Review 1 (2012).

Mootz, III, Fancis J. *After the Battle of the Forms: Commercial Contracting in the Electronic Age.* 41 Journal of Law and Policy for the Information Society 271–343 (2008).

CHAPTER 16

Contracts: Performance, Public Policy, and Global Contracts

Chapter Objectives:

1. To recognize when an agreement is illegal due to statutory violations, public policy violations, or unconscionability
2. To understand which contracts must be in writing, to appreciate the reasons that written contracts are preferable, and to be familiar with conventions for interpreting contract language
3. To recognize valid defenses to the enforcement of a contract on the grounds of misrepresentation, fraud, duress, and undue influence
4. To know the circumstances under which a party may transfer rights or obligations under a contract or claim benefits under a contract
5. To identify how a party can be relieved from contractual obligations — either through performance of the contract obligations or through a legal excuse from performance
6. To determine whether a contract has been breached and understand the implications of different types of breaches
7. To determine the measure of damages a party has sustained as a result of a breach of contract and the theories underlying a court's role in providing just compensation for a breach

Practical Example: Unannounced Inspections at the Health Club

Muscles 4U is a national health club franchise. Elana signs a franchise contract allowing her to manage and profit from one of the Muscles 4U locations located in New Jersey. Among other things, the franchise contract provided for unannounced inspections by the franchisor to ensure high standards of cleanliness. If the club location Elana is running falls below the specified standards, it would be closed for a weekend and cleaned at the franchisee's expense. Assume after a few months, Elana's club was inspected just after a busy weekend and found to be in violation of the cleanliness standards. The franchisor insisted on closing the club for a weekend and sending in its clean-up crew at the franchisee's expense. Elana pleaded for another chance because paying outside help to clean would be an expense she could not afford at that time. The franchisor had a choice of demanding that the club be closed for cleaning or putting the franchisee on notice that if it happened again, the club would be closed and cleaned at the franchisee's expense. Note that this is a legal and an ethical choice. Although the contract permits weekend closure to clean the club at Elana's expense, there may be ethical reasons to give her another chance. In many instances throughout the chapter, performance of a contract is based on rules of law where the parties to the contract are confronted with a choice of performance or nonperformance with legal and ethical consequences.

"The best laid schemes of mice and men go often awry."[1] Even when parties have laid the groundwork for an agreement, unforeseen events can arise. A party might have had every intention of fulfilling contract obligations, but circumstances prevent contract performance. A disaster may have occurred since the contract was formed, or the party might simply wish to transfer rights or obligations to another party because the business environment changed. When unexpected circumstances arise, when should a party be excused from contractual promises? How do we determine when the contract has been breached? And how does the court "remedy" (or fix) a breach of contract? This chapter will address these questions as well as the ethical issues relevant to the performance or nonperformance of the contract and the remedies for a breach.

---

[1]"To a Mouse, on Turning Her Up in Her Nest with the Plough," poem by Robert Burns, 1785.

Legality and Public Policy Considerations

Even with a valid offer, acceptance, consideration, and capacity, there could still be a reason to prevent the recognition or enforcement of a contract. Take an intuitive example. A beautifully written and enthusiastically endorsed agreement for the purchase and sale of heroin will not be enforced by any court.

The nature of the underlying agreement can give rise to three reasons courts refuse to enforce part or all of the parties' obligations on the grounds of illegality.

Statutory Violations

Numerous federal and state statutes and regulations and local ordinances invalidate or even criminalize certain types of agreements. The heroin purchase is one such example. There are many other examples in the business world: consider agreements to lend money at an interest rate exceeding the maximum statutory amount; to distribute pharmaceuticals that have not been approved for use by the U.S. Food and Drug Administration; or to buy timber harvested from a wildlife protected area.

Public Policy Versus Enforcement of Agreements

Occasionally, public policy prevents the enforcement of a contract. A court will declare part or all of an agreement unenforceable on the grounds of public policy only after weighing the factors on both sides. How do courts ascertain what public policy is? From existing legislation and judicial decisions, courts can extrapolate the intent of the legislature and further those policies. If it will help further a public policy, a court could invalidate all or part of the agreement. For example, assume ABC Gadget Corp. tells Steve, a well-known blogger who writes about the gadget industry, that ABC will pay him $100,000 if he writes something in his blog that both parties know is false and harmful about a competitor of ABC. Steve agrees and publishes the false and harmful statement in his blog. If ABC refuses to pay and Steve sues, a court will not honor the agreement. Paying someone to commit a tort (disparagement of business) is a violation of public policy. Public policy is ethically concerned with recognizing there is often a greater good served than the private contract between the parties. Contracts do not exist in a vacuum, and their performance may negatively impact the general public who are not parties to the agreement.

Unconscionable Agreements

Recall that neither general unfairness nor gross disparity of consideration in an agreement is enough to release parties from contractual obligations. However, in extreme cases, courts can invalidate all or part of an agreement based on **unconscionability**. The UCC does not define unconscionability, but case-law precedent often describes unconscionability as the "absence of meaningful choice together with terms unreasonably advantageous to one of the parties." The strongest cases for unconscionability involve both procedural and substantive unconscionability.[2] *Procedural unconscionability* refers to unconscionability during negotiations and contract formation. *Substantive unconscionability* refers to unconscionability of the contract's terms or the contract as a whole. If a court determines that the contact is unconscionable, it may annul it completely or reform it.

Competent contracting parties can agree to an arrangement that is considerably more advantageous to one party, resulting in an unfair contract. What are the legal implications of such a deal? Suppose a recent college graduate, Ben, required his clients sign a retainer contract granting him a payment of $400 per hour. The client signed the contract, and later, when he discovered the consultant was a recent college graduate, refused to pay the bill, alleging the contract was unconscionable. The judge would declare the contract unconscionable if, for example, it appeared unreasonably advantageous and the client had no choice but to enter the contract. It is unlikely the client could show there was no choice.

Adhesion Contracts

Contracts of adhesion are contracts formed by parties with unequal bargaining power, resulting in the stronger party offering boilerplate contract terms on a take-it-or-leave-it basis. Adhesion contracts are not automatically unconscionable and in fact are commonplace. However, the adhesive nature of a contract can be considered in determining whether the contract is unconscionable.

Are the terms of use on websites adhesion contracts? They are unilateral and nonnegotiable and the consumer lacks "meaningful choice." Many are "unreasonably advantageous" to the website company. This fits the legal definition of an adhesion contract, but most courts uphold the terms of use because they have become a trade practice and should be expected as a condition of doing business online. That rationale is a utilitarian argument supporting the greater good for the greater number.

Usury Law

State law dictates the maximum rate of interest that can be charged when loaning money or property. Interest charged in excess of the maximum rate is **usury**. The effect of a contract providing for a usurious interest rate varies from state to state. Some states, such as Texas,[3] treat such an agreement as void and refuse to allow the lender to recover unpaid interest or principal. Other states, such as Georgia,

---

[2]Some states, like New York and Texas, do not require a showing of both substantive and procedural unconscionability. Other states, like Florida, do require both substantive and procedural unconscionability.
[3]*Kinerd v. Colonial Leasing Co.*, 800 S.W.2d 187 (1990).

treat only the usurious interest provision as void and allow for the recovery of principal. In addition, some statutes criminalize the receipt of usurious interest.

Noncompetition Clauses

The United States has a long tradition of disfavoring, rendering illegal, and even criminalizing agreements between parties who promise not to compete with each other. (Chapter 11, "Antitrust," addresses the many prohibitions on agreements to restrain trade.) Yet in some circumstances, noncompetition provisions are valid. They are most commonly included in an employment agreement where the employee promises that, upon leaving the job, he or she will not work for a competing firm. They are also found in agreements for the purchase and sale of business, where the seller agrees not to open a competing business. Most states[4] will not strike down a noncompetition clause as illegal due to public policy or due to antitrust laws if it meets these tests:

1. The noncompetition clause must be part of an agreement for some other purpose — for example, part of an employment contract or an agreement to buy and sell a small business.
2. The clause must be reasonable in time, scope, and geographic area. When is the time too long, the scope too broad, and the geographic area too large? What is reasonable in this context depends on what interests are being protected and in what business the company is engaging. Limitations on competition should be narrowly tailored to protect the confidential information and trade secrets. Limitations that exceed this are invalid. For example, in the purchase and sale of a recycling business that had one production location in Northern California, the court decided that a prohibition on the business's seller from opening a competing operation within a 1,000 mile radius was overbroad. The company being sold had never done business in much of the 1,000-mile radius area, and the court based its conclusion on the fact that noncompetition agreements are limited to the area where the sold business had conducted business.[5] Similarly, the scope of responsibilities a former employee is restricted from may be extensive only if the employee's job responsibilities were extensive. An employee with significant responsibilities would have access to extensive important proprietary information, and less so with a lower-ranking employee.
3. The clause must not impose an undue hardship. This is a high bar for those seeking to invalidate a noncompete on this basis. Having to move to a different region of the country, for example, is not an undue hardship.
4. The clause must serve a legitimate business interest. What serves as a legitimate business interest? Protection of trade secrets and confidential

---

[4]California is a notable exception. California does not recognize the validity of noncompetition clauses in employment contracts.
[5]T.J.T., Inc. v. Mori; 266 P.3d 476 (2011); 2011 WL 5966870; Idaho, 2011.

information are legitimate business interests for these purposes. Simply wanting to be free from having to compete with an employee after he or she departs or with the seller of a business after the transaction is consummated not only is not a legitimate business interest, it is potentially a serious violation of antitrust law.

When Do Contracts Have to Be in Writing?

Origins of the Statute of Frauds

In 1677, the English Parliament enacted the Statute of Frauds to combat a particular kind of fraud. For centuries, the rule in England had been that oral contracts were valid if witnesses testified to the existence of the agreement. However, unscrupulous bands of thieves designed scams to take advantage of this rule. One conspirator would claim in court that he made a contract with a defendant which was then breached. His co-conspirators would perjure themselves, claiming they witnessed the making of this fictitious agreement. Unable to prove otherwise, the defendant would be forced to pay damages, and the thieves would divide the proceeds. In response, Parliament passed the Statute of Frauds, which requires reliable evidence of the existence and terms of certain types of contracts. With some changes, the Statute of Frauds remains in effect in the United States. In approaching a Statute of Frauds problem, ask (1) Is this contract within (that is, covered by) the Statute of Frauds; (2) If yes, is there written evidence of the contract sufficient to satisfy the statute? (3) If there is no such written evidence, is there an applicable exception?

Agreements Subject to the Statute of Frauds

The Statute of Frauds does not change the general rule that oral contracts are valid. Rather, it requires that, unless an exception applies, particular types of contracts must be in writing to be enforceable. At first, the list of contracts that must be in writing appears random. But the common theme is that these types of agreements are most likely to be subject to the type of fraud described above. The following types of contracts are subject to Statute of Frauds rules:

Some contracts can be oral and some must be in writing to be enforceable.

- *Marriage.* If the consideration to support a contract is the promise to marry, the contract is subject to the Statute of Frauds.
- *Suretyship.* **Suretyship** involves the assurance by one party to pay the debt of another. The main purpose of the agreement must be to benefit *another* person. To illustrate, suppose Ron's business is in financial trouble. His brother, Harry, tells Ron's creditor that he (Harry) will pay Ron's debt if Ron does not. Harry's main purpose is not to benefit himself; it is to benefit Ron. Therefore, his promise to pay Ron's debt falls under the Statute of Frauds. Suppose instead that Harry is Ron's business partner. Ron owes a personal debt to Lulu, and Harry is concerned that Lulu could attach Ron's business interest or otherwise interfere with Ron's ownership and management of the business. For this reason, Harry tells Lulu that he (Harry) will pay Ron's debt if Ron does not. Harry's main purpose is to benefit himself, not Ron. Therefore, his promise to pay Ron's debt does *not* fall under the Statute of Frauds.[6]
- *Executor's and administrator's agreement to pay personally for the decedent's debt.* Among other duties, the executor (or administrator in the absence of a will) of an estate is responsible to use the decedent's assets to pay for the decedent's debts. In the course of handling the decedent's financial affairs, if the executor promises to pay the decedent's debts from the executor's personal funds, the promise must be in writing.
- *Interest in land.* Contracts to transfer an interest in land are covered by the Statute of Frauds. This includes not only contracts for the purchase and sale of real estate, but also mortgages and easements.[7] Conceptually, leases fall into the category of interests in land because a lease is the conveyance of exclusive possession of real or personal property. However, the law often treats residential leases differently from other business transactions or real estate interests because they involve a tenant's home. In some states, tenants cannot be evicted for failure to execute a written lease.
- *Contracts that cannot be performed within one year.* If, at the time parties enter a contract, there is no possibility that one or both parties will be able to completely perform the contractual obligations within one year, then it is subject to the Statute of Frauds. Consider the implications of proving the terms of an agreement long after the agreement was made. The quality of evidence declines because witnesses die, move away, or forget. Relying solely on the memories and testimony of witnesses to prove a contract's existence and its terms is difficult and could result in unfairness.
- *Contracts for the sale of goods costing $500 or more.* Under the Uniform Commercial Code section 2-201, the sale of goods that cost $500 or more is subject to the Statute of Frauds.

---

[6]Note that the requirement of a writing could still be imposed by some other law — for example, the Federal Truth In Lending Act, which applies to transactions involving consumer credit.
[7]Again, terms of a mortgage could be required to be in writing under the Federal Truth in Lending Act or another law.

Writing Sufficient to Satisfy the Statute of Frauds and Electronic Signatures

Assume a contract falls under one of the Statute of Frauds categories described above. What type of writing suffices to prove the existence and terms of the contract? Must both parties sign the contract? Can parts of the agreement be written in different documents?

All terms need not be memorialized in a single document. The essential terms can be understood by reference to one or more documents. Recall that especially in complex transactions, parties may choose to negotiate by agreeing on one or a few terms at a time. Evidence of the essential terms of the contract can be proven through writing(s) that are signed by or for[8] the party to be charged — that is, the party against whom enforcement is sought. In furtherance of the Statute of Frauds' purpose to prevent scams involving fabrication of an agreement, a plaintiff alleging a breach by a defendant must produce a document with the defendant's authenticated signature.

Exceptions to the Statute of Frauds

Even when an agreement falls under the Statute of Frauds and insufficient written evidence exists to establish agreement, there could be an exception that permits enforcement of the contract:

- *Promissory estoppel.* As with agreements that lack consideration, courts will enforce an unwritten contract if the promisor should reasonably expect to induce action or forbearance; such action or forbearance is in fact induced, and injustice can only be avoided by enforcing the contract.
- *Part performance.* Suppose an agreement falls under the Statute of Frauds but there is nothing in writing. One party performs part of the contract. Does the performing party have any rights? For example, Roger and Michael enter an oral agreement for Roger to sell land to Michael. Michael pays Roger $20,000 as deposit for the land. Two questions arise:
    - Can Michael obtain restitution for the value of what was given — that is, can he force the refund of $20,000? Yes.
    - Can Michael force Roger to convey the land in exchange for the balance of the purchase price? No, because the Statute of Frauds renders this agreement prospectively unenforceable.
    - What if instead, after entering an oral agreement for Roger to sell land to Michael, Roger invites Michael to begin developing architectural plans to build a commercial office complex. Michael does so, and with Roger's knowledge, consent, and encouragement, Michael begins construction. Roger then repudiates. Can Michael force Roger to convey the land in exchange for the purchase price? Yes. The Part Performance Doctrine states that even when there is failure to comply

---

[8]For rules relating to when a person can legally sign on behalf of another, see Chapter 12, "Agency Law."

with the Statute of Frauds, the contract will be enforced if the party seeking enforcement reasonably relied on the deal and injustice can only be avoided by enforcement of the contract.

■ *Merchant's memo for sales of goods.* As explained in more detail in Chapter 17, "Sales Law, Consumer Protection, and E-Commerce," in some instances, the Uniform Commercial Code holds merchants[9] to a higher standard than nonmerchants. One example involves an exception to the rule that a party asking for enforcement of an agreement which is subject to the Statute of Frauds must produce a writing with the *other* party's signature. When certain conditions are met, a merchant can enforce an agreement against another merchant even if the writing is signed only by the party seeking enforcement.

  ■ Suppose Rosa and Martin agree that Rosa will buy coconuts from Martin for $10,000. Close to the time for delivery, Martin tells Rosa he refuses to sell because the cost of coconuts has risen, yielding less profit than he had expected. Rosa has nothing signed by Martin evidencing their agreement. Nevertheless, she is still able to enforce the agreement if she can show each element of this rule:

  ■ The agreement is between merchants;

  ■ Rosa sent a confirmation of the contract within a reasonable time after they made the agreement;

  ■ Martin received Rosa's confirmation and had reason to know of its contents; and

  ■ Martin did not send written evidence of his objection to Rosa within 10 days of receiving her confirmation.

■ *Specially manufactured goods.* If an unwritten contract is made for a seller to manufacture for a buyer goods that cannot be sold to another customer, and the seller begins manufacture or buys materials needed for manufacturing, then the contract is enforceable even without a writing. The rationale for this exception is that the costs involved in producing goods under these conditions exhibit a high likelihood that there was a genuine agreement and the seller is not fabricating its existence.

■ *Admission in court proceedings.* A contract is enforceable if the party to be charged admits the existence of the agreement in a court document or by stipulation or testimony.

Results of Noncompliance

If an agreement falls under the Statute of Frauds, insufficient written evidence exists to establish an agreement, and there are no applicable exceptions, the contract is *unenforceable*. Courts will not order performance or compensation for performance that was promised but not yet delivered. Recall that under the Part Performance Doctrine, courts will compensate one party who has performed without compensation.

---

[9]A merchant, according to UCC 2-104, is "a person who deals in goods of the kind [in the contract] or . . . holds himself out as having knowledge or skill [regarding] goods involved in the transaction."

Writing, Interpreting, and Proving the Terms of a Contract

Whether or not a contract must be in writing, there are practical business reasons to document the agreement. The exercise of writing the agreement itself can underscore differences between the parties which can be decided before the contract becomes binding, thus helping to prevent later disputes. Writing contracts has other advantages, too. In *Trademark Properties v. A&E Television Networks* on page 465, would litigation have ensued had there been a written contract? Probably not. Reducing an agreement to writing provides reliable evidence of both the existence of the deal and of its terms. It is also wise to draft contract language carefully and completely. Recall that sometimes, memorandum of understanding, letters of intent, and term sheets are employed to assist parties in advancing business negotiations. Several rounds of correspondence and documents often volley between the parties before they agree on terms.

Sometimes there is sufficient evidence to show mutual assent and that a contract between parties exists but disputes arise in connection with interpretation of the terms. The Restatement (Second) of Contracts provides several rules of convention to help settle disputes and to encourage clear contract writing.

Rules of Contract Interpretation

Over time, rules of convention have developed to assist in interpreting contractual language. The most common of these rules appears in Exhibit 16.1.

Parol Evidence Rule

Once there is an agreement, can the parties' pre-agreement communication be used in a dispute regarding interpretation of the contract? The **parol evidence rule** establishes a framework for the permissible use of documents, correspondence, and conversations that took place before a final agreement. The parol

---

Exhibit 16.1. Rules for Interpreting Contract Language

Courts strive to effectuate the intent of the parties at the time of contracting.

If the parties omit a term that is essential in determining rights and responsibilities, then the court will supply a term that is reasonable given the circumstances.

If a term in the contract is ambiguous, the ambiguity will be construed against the party that drafted the contract.

Specific terms and technical language are given greater weight than general language.

Terms that were added (for example, by hand) to a standardized contract form are given greater weight than boilerplate language.

The course of prior dealings between the parties and how terminology is used in the parties' trade can be used to interpret a contract term.

evidence rule is actually not a rule of contract law—it is a rule of evidence. The law of evidence establishes the circumstances under which a court can consider particular testimony, documents, and other forms of evidence in determining the facts of a case. The parol evidence rule states, "A binding integrated agreement discharges prior agreements to the extent that it is inconsistent with them."[10] An *integrated* agreement is a written document that is the final expression of one or more terms of an agreement. Once a contract (or a finalized portion of it) has been memorialized in writing, neither party can use written or oral statements made during negotiations to alter the meaning of a document that was intended to be the parties' final expression of their agreement. This helps eliminate the potential for maneuvering and encourages fair, clear, and careful drafting. The rule also encourages parties to be complete and accurate in writing their final agreement. There are a few limited reasons a party can introduce parol evidence where there has been a binding integrated agreement: to prove additional, consistent terms; to clarify or explain ambiguity; to prove that the agreement was void, voidable, or unenforceable; or to prove that the parties agreed to cancel the contract and make a new deal.

Types of Contracts

Contracts can be categorized in different ways, and these categorizations can be important when applying particular principles of law.

Bilateral Contracts

A bilateral contract is a contract in which parties exchange promises. For example, Vidur promises to paint Sarah's house for $500 on June 1. Each party is promising performance. Most business contracts are bilateral contracts.

Unilateral Contracts

In contrast to bilateral contracts, a unilateral contract is one in which a promise is exchanged for an act of performance—by its terms, the offer can only be accepted through an act of performance, not by responding with a promise. Consider, for example, the *Leonard v. PepsiCo* case in Chapter 15, "Contracts: Contract Formation." Pepsi's offer to provide Pepsi merchandise required customers to accept by purchasing Pepsi and sending in the required number of "Pepsi points." If instead a customer wrote to Pepsi stating "I promise to send to you 1,000 Pepsi points before the promotional expires" then no contract would be formed. Unilateral contracts are used most

---

[10]Restatement to (Second) of Contracts, section 213.

frequently in contests, competitions, and promotionals, such as the Pepsi example.

It can take time for an offeree to prepare for the requested act of performance. Recall that unless an exception applies, an offeror can revoke an offer at any time. What if the offeree is busy getting ready to perform when at the last minute, the offeror revokes the offer? To prevent unfairness, an offer to enter a unilateral contract becomes irrevocable once the offeree begins substantial performance. Suppose a magazine distributor offers $500 to the person who can sell the most magazine subscriptions prior to October 1. By September 25, Rachel has sold the most subscriptions but the distributor revokes the offer on September 27. Would Rachel's breach of contract suit be successful? Yes. Rachel's performance rendered the offer irrevocable.

Valid, Voidable, and Void Agreements

There are other ways to classify agreements. Agreements can be *valid*, *voidable*, or *void*. A *valid contract* is an agreement that meets the required elements for legal recognition (offer, acceptance, consideration, capacity, and legality). A *voidable contract* is one that one or both parties may choose to void (i.e., invalidate); if no election is made to void the contract, it remains valid. A *void agreement* is one for which the law does not recognize a legal obligation to perform. Void agreements are sometimes called "void contracts;" however, because the term "contract" means a legally binding agreement, in truth, there is no such thing as a "void contract."

Enforceable and Unenforceable Contracts

Not all valid contracts are enforceable. Recall that even where all legal requirements are met, a contract could be unenforceable due to Statute of Frauds rules. Also, certain statutes or rules could render a valid contract unenforceable.

Executed and Executory Contracts

Another way to classify contracts relates to whether performance under a valid contract has been completed. An **executed contract** is a contract under which both parties have fully performed their obligations — that is, performance has been executed by both parties. An **executory** contract is a contract under which one or both parties must still perform an obligation.

Assent and Contract Defenses

Recall that the law of offer and acceptance helps ensure that an agreement is the product of mutual assent. In addition, a variety of contract defenses evolved over the centuries for the same reason — to ensure that courts only enforce agreements that are truly the product of mutual, voluntary assent of the parties. Even where there is a valid offer, acceptance, consideration, capacity, and lawful purpose, courts will release parties from their promises based on theories that assure voluntary assent to the deal, such as misrepresentation, duress, or undue influence. The integrity of the free bargaining process is undermined where one party's assent has been compromised, and therefore, such agreements are voidable at the option of the injured party. Note that either the plaintiff or the defendant could be raising these theories. A plaintiff could invoke them to seek rescission and restitution in a complaint. A defendant in a breach of contract action could assert them to show the agreement is not legally binding.

Misrepresentation and Fraud

The required elements for establishing misrepresentation are

1. The party claiming misrepresentation has been induced by justifiable reliance
2. On the other party's misrepresentation
3. Of a material fact.

Based on this definition, can misrepresentation be shown every time a party is lied to? No. First, the party claiming misrepresentation must have relied on the misrepresented fact. Even if the person did rely, reliance must be *justifiable*. Also, the misrepresentation must be of a fact, not an opinion. And, the misrepresented fact must be a *material* one.

A potential source of confusion arises in connection with the requirement that the misrepresentation be factual. Statements regarding the past and present can be factual; statements regarding future events are not facts. Also, opinions ("that dress looks gorgeous on you!") are not generally facts. This includes opinions of quality or value. However, society generally relies on certain types of opinions more heavily. These are considered a "fact" for purposes of a misrepresentation claim:

1. Opinions made by a fiduciary in the context of a fiduciary relationship (such as a doctor saying to a patient, "I think you need your gallbladder removed.").
2. Opinions made to a relying party who is unusually vulnerable (for example, infirm or elderly).
3. Opinions made by a party who has superior skill or judgment (for example, a mechanic says, "I think you need a new muffler.").

Can silence ever qualify as a misrepresentation? A party's concealment of a fact does not give rise to a successful misrepresentation claim, unless

1. Failure to disclose the fact would lead to serious harm;
2. The party failing to disclose is a fiduciary; or
3. The nondisclosed fact is a material one.

The sale of children's goods floods the marketplace each year, especially during the holidays. The case discussed in the Manager's Compliance and Ethics Meeting involves the sale of play tents for children under 12 that could collapse and cause a child to suffocate. Potentially injurious products pose special ethical issues.

Manager's Compliance and Ethics Meeting

Ethics of Selling Potentially Unsafe Play Tents

Your company is a manufacturer of play tents for children under 12 years of age. This product is subject to regulation by the Consumer Product Safety Commission (CPSC), an independent federal regulatory agency. One of its many mandates is to protect the public "against unreasonable risks of injury associated with consumer products." The company lawyers informed the vice president that penalties for violations of CPSC regulations are severe, including civil fines of up to $15 million for a series of violations. She is especially concerned to have discovered that corporate directors and officers of the company are subject to criminal penalties of up to five years imprisonment for willful violations. She has asked you to meet with your department's engineers to determine if there are any risks associated with children under 12 using the play tents. The play tents are already being sold and are very successful items on the market. A few engineers raised the remote possibility of the tent collapsing and a child suffocating. Others at the meeting found this to be highly unlikely but possible. You remind them that the CPSC only prohibits an "unreasonable risk of injury" and since this is a highly improbable occurrence perhaps it should be overlooked. The company's compliance and ethics program states in its code of ethics that it is "primarily concerned with child safety."

What are the ethical issues in continuing to sell the play tents? Is there an inherent fraud or misrepresentation in selling a child's product that may cause death although that's highly unlikely? Do you think the continuous manufacturing of the play tents is ethical even though there may be no "unreasonable risk of injury?"

The required elements for establishing *fraud* are the same as misrepresentation, with the additional element of *scienter*. Coming from the Latin *scientia*, meaning knowledge, *scienter* means that the party knew its misrepresentation was false. In other words, the falsehood was not made carelessly or negligently; it was deliberate.

Usually, a finding of misrepresentation or fraud will render a contract voidable, and a court will release parties from contractual obligations (through rescission) and order each party to return benefits received from each other (through restitution).

Duress

A party whose agreement to enter a contract was the product of duress did not assent voluntarily. Physical harm or the threat of physical harm deprives a person of free will to enter a contract. A contract is voidable (by the victim) on grounds of duress if

1. The contract was induced by an improper threat (such as a crime or tort); and
2. The victim had no reasonable alternative but to enter into the contract.[11]

If duress is economic, the economic need must be coupled with the fact that the economic conditions were created by the party against whom duress is claimed. This is rare. Most cases of financial difficulty result from economic downturns, inflation, fluctuations in supply prices, tight credit, changes in customer preferences, or other business factors. None of these qualify for excuse from contract performance.[12]

Undue Influence

A party who is operating under undue influence when assenting to a contract is not assenting voluntarily. A contract is voidable (again, only by the victim) on the grounds of undue influence if

1. The contract is the product of unfair persuasion; and
2. The victim is under the domination of the person exercising the persuasion (usually because of a special position, such as a guardian or relative in a position of trust).

Assignment and Delegation

Recall that an important role of contracts in business is to secure a set of promises so that contracting parties can arrange their affairs in reliance on the expected performance. If the parties' exchange of promises meets the tests for a valid contract, the law ensures that each party will receive *what*

---

[11]Restatement (Second) of Contracts, section 175.
[12]Those contract defense theories that are similar to duress but which apply only to sales of goods (such as commercial impracticability) will be discussed in Chapter 17.

was promised (or the value of what was promised). But in some circumstances, the law allows flexibility as to *who will perform the obligations* and *who will reap the benefits* under a contract.

This flexibility can prove useful in a variety of business situations. For example, a supplier who contracts to sell component parts to several buyers might be taken over by another company in an acquisition. A business in need of cash might wish to transfer its accounts receivable[13] to a bank in exchange for cash. Or a company with three years remaining on its lease might wish to relocate. Each of these situations raises questions about the permissibility of transferring one party's rights or obligations under a contract. When negotiating a contract, sometimes a party wants the flexibility of transferring its rights under a contract to another party, as in the example of a business wishing to transfer its accounts receivable. However, in other circumstances, a party might not want the other party to transfer duties. For example, a commercial landlord who selected a tenant based on the tenant's creditworthiness might not want the tenant to be able to transfer lease obligations to another party. Under what circumstances can a party legally transfer to another party the duties it promised to perform? The rights it contracted to receive?

Contracts involve both rights and duties. A party has the right to seek enforcement of the other party's promise and also has the duty to perform what she has promised. Both rights and duties can be transferred under the circumstances described below.

Assignment

The transfer of a right is called an **assignment**. A party transferring a right is called the *obligee* (because someone is obliged to do something for his or her benefit) or the *assignor* (because the party is assigning the right to a third party). The party to whom the right is transferred is called the *assignee*.

In general, contractual rights can be assigned without permission of the other party. Assignments of contractual rights are not permitted if (1) the assignment would materially (that is, significantly) change the obligor's responsibilities, (2) it is prohibited by statute, or (3) the original contract precludes assignments.

The business in need of cash can permissibly assign its right to receive payment from its customers to a company (called a *factor*) at a discount in exchange for cash. Ordinarily, this may be done without permission of the customers. Once an assignment is completed, the assignor no longer has the legal right to collect from the customers.

---

[13]Accounts receivable refers to the right to collect money from others.

Delegation

The transfer of a duty is called a **delegation**. Most contractual duties can be delegated without permission of the other party, just as assignment of rights. An exception is the obligation to perform personal duties, which may not be delegated. For example, promises to teach, to perform at a concert, or to design a building may not be delegated to a third party.

Suppose Mary and Steve enter a contract for Mary to buy 1,000 of Steve's smartphones for $100 each to be delivered on June 1 to Mary's place of business. Steve's obligation is to deliver the phones to Mary, and unless the contract prevents delegation, he is permitted to delegate this duty to a third party without her consent. Steve also has the right to receive $100,000 from Mary, and, again, unless the contract prevents assignment, he is permitted to assign this right without her consent.

What if Steve chooses to delegate his duty to deliver the phones to Dan, but Dan does not perform. Is Steve still obligated under the contract? Yes. What if Mary chooses to delegate her duty to pay for the phones to Frayda, but Frayda does not perform. Is Mary still obligated under the contract? Yes. A party's responsibility to fulfill an obligation under a contract is not discharged by virtue of delegating the duty to someone else. Until performance is completed, the original obligor is still responsible for performance. These rules are summarized in Exhibit 16.2.

These rules are consistent with themes in contract law discussed in the introduction of this chapter. Contract law aims to provide parties with significant freedom and flexibility to manage, adjust, and account for changing circumstances, new situations, and unforeseen opportunities and challenges. Therefore, the law provides for the ability to transfer both contractual benefits and responsibilities. However, freedom of contract also involves respect for parties' ability to choose exactly who to do business

Exhibit 16.2 Delegation Example

Steve's duty to deliver phones	Mary's duty to pay $1,000
May be delegated to Dan unless contract specifies otherwise. However, delegation to Dan does not extinguish Steve's duty to perform.	May be delegated to Frayda unless contract specifies otherwise. However, delegation to Frayda does not extinguish Mary's duty to perform.
Steve's right to receive $1,000	**Mary's right to receive phones**
May be assigned unless contract specifies otherwise. If assigned, Steve's right to receive the $1,000 is extinguished.	May be assigned unless contract specifies otherwise or delivery to third party would materially increase Steve's burden under the contract. If assigned, Mary's right to receive the phones is extinguished.

with. The unfettered ability to substitute one obligated party for another, without permission, would mean that a trusted business whose credentials were examined and which was carefully selected could simply be substituted for an unknown obligor. Therefore, the law maintains that the original party remains obligated to perform assigned duties.

Discharge

Completion of the Contract or Discharge by Agreement

When both parties fully perform all duties under a contract, the contract has been completed. Recall that this is called a fully **executed** contract. Sometimes the parties determine that the contract is no longer viable or desirable and they discharge the contract by agreement. In both of these situations — full performance and discharge by agreement — the contract is at an end.

While full completion of contractual obligations is the goal, there are other circumstances under which a party's duty to perform arises, but the law recognizes a valid excuse from performance. These excuses are limited to a few specific legal theories, the most common of which are listed below.

An Ethical Insight: W. D. Ross and the "Impossibility of Performance"

W. D. Ross wrote, "Unless stronger moral obligations override, one ought to keep a promise" (*The Right and the Good*). Ross would consider it ethical to break a contract when "stronger moral obligations override" the situation. Contract law reflects that ethical position with the doctrine of "impossibility of performance" due to conditions beyond the control of the breaching party.

Excuses from Performance: Impossibility

Impossibility refers to performance that becomes impossible after the contract is made. In such circumstances, the parties' performance is excused. To justify relief, the party must show that performance of his or her duties is genuinely impossible — not that it is more difficult or more expensive. The Ethical Insight illustrates the justification for breaking a promise when there are extenuating circumstances.

The In-Depth Ethical Case Analysis illustrates the legal and ethical reasons a court may discharge a non-cancellable contract.

Excuses from Performance: Commercial Frustration

When entering a contract, parties can take all kinds of risks. But most risks that become reality are not valid reasons to be released from contractual obligations. A party is not entitled to be relieved from contractual responsibilities merely because he will not be able to achieve his anticipated profit margin or that performance becomes financially burdensome. But what if a disruptive

In-Depth Ethical Case Analysis

Parker v. Arthur Murray, 295 N.E.2d 487 (Ill. App. 1973)

Facts

In November 1959, the plaintiff, a 37-year-old college-educated bachelor who lived alone in a one-room attic apartment in suburban Chicago, went to a dance studio to redeem a certificate for three free dancing lessons. During the lessons, the instructor said that plaintiff had "exceptional potential to be a fine and accomplished dancer." Upon hearing this, plaintiff signed a contract for 75 hours of dance instruction at a cost of $1,000. He continued taking lessons regularly, and despite a lack of progress, he continued receiving praise and encouragement and continued signing contracts for further dance instructions. Eventually, he contracted for a total of 2,734 hours of lessons for which he paid $24,812.80.[*] Each contract he signed included, in bold typeface: "NON-CANCELLABLE CONTRACT."

In September 1961, the plaintiff was severely injured in a car collision and was unable to continue taking dance lessons. He requested a refund but was refused. He filed suit on the grounds of impossibility of performance and fraud. The court agreed and discharged the contract.

Ethical Issue

This case illustrates a clear written exchange of promises in the contract stating it could not be cancelled. In view of Parker's physical disability was it ethical for the court to ignore the agreement and cancel the contract?

Ethical Theory Analysis

Virtue Ethics
Aristotle. Aristotle's book, *Nichomachean Ethics* stated the principle that no one should be enriched at another's expense. The Murray studio had a promise for 2,734 hours of dance instruction, and Parker paid $24,812.80 in advance. For the Murray studio to keep this money in view of Parker's impossibility of continuing to take dancing lessons would unethically enrich the studio at his expense.

Legal Realism
Justice Oliver Wendell Holmes Jr. In his classic essay *The Path of the Law*, 10 Harvard Law Review, 457, Justice Holmes wrote, "For the rational study of the [rule of law] man may be the man of the present, but the man of the future is the man of statistics and the master of economics." Legal realism will look beyond the rule of law (such as, in this contract, a non-cancellable clause) to the economic consequences of a breach of contract to determine an ethical and fair result. In this case, for the Murray studio to keep the deposit it has not earned is unfair enrichment and would be an unfair and unethical economic result.

Prima Facie Duties
W.D. Ross. In his book *The Right and the Good*, Ross, who insisted on "promise keeping," made an exception when "the consequences of fulfilling a promise would be so disastrous to others that we judge it right not to do so." Assuming Parker has limited financial means, this ethical principle obligates the Murray studio to return the deposit to Parker, as his loss of $24,812.24 for services not rendered would be an "economic disaster."

Conclusion

Classical ethical principles support the court's decision in discharging the "non-cancellable" contract.

---

[*] This equals approximately $150,000 today.

event is so severe or dramatic that it could not reasonably have been foreseen by even careful and experienced businesspeople? The doctrine of **commercial frustration** excuses a party from performance if the principal purpose of the contract is substantially frustrated due to no fault of the party.

The landmark case in this area of law, *Krell v. Henry*, is an English case from 1903. In anticipation of the expected coronation of Edward VII, a party rented a room along the planned coronation parade route for the day of the coronation. He gave the lessor a deposit of one-third the rent. Subsequently, the coronation was postponed due to Edward VII's poor health. The lessor demanded the remainder of the rent and the lessee demanded the return of his deposit. The court applied the doctrine of commercial frustration to release the parties from their contractual obligations. The essential purpose of the contract was for the lessee to rent the room in order to view the coronation. (This was evidenced by the fact that the rent was much higher than would normally be the case.) Could the doctrine of impossibility have applied instead? No. It was still possible to rent the room, but the main purpose of the contract was frustrated.

When is a cancelled event a valid reason to excuse contractual obligations? This photograph shows the royal carriages proceeding down St. James Street for the coronation of King Edward VII of England in August 1902. The delay of the ceremony, originally scheduled for June, gave rise to the famous 1903 case *Krell v. Henry*.

Excuses from Performance: Terrorism and Other Force Majeure Conditions

Commercial frustration is difficult to prove. Sometimes parties want to expand the scope of available contract excuses to cover situations that are unusual but do not fit the limited circumstances necessary for commercial frustration. Inclusion of a force majeure clause in a contract allows parties to be released from responsibility under broader circumstances. From the French for "superior force," a **force majeure** clause excuses a party from performance if performance is prevented due to any one of a list of extraordinary events. Common examples include fire, flood, earthquake, hurricanes, outbreaks of war, terrorist attacks, blockades, quarantine restrictions, and acts of God.

Excuses from Performance: Waiver

Sometimes, one party may choose to release the other from its obligation to perform or may waive its right to demand performance by the other party.

Statute of Limitations

For claims involving written contracts, the length of time within which a claim must be brought varies from three years in Alaska, Delaware, District of Columbia, Maryland, New Hampshire, North Carolina, and South Carolina, to 15 years in Ohio and Kentucky. A plaintiff who fails to file a breach of contract complaint within the specified time frame loses the right to pursue the claim.

Third Parties and Contracts

Many people could benefit from a contract — benefit could inure to the parties and to those around them. If a contract is breached, who could successfully assert a claim?

1. The original parties to the contract;[14]
2. Assignees; and
3. Third parties who the contracting parties intended to benefit.

Intended Beneficiaries

An **intended beneficiary** is a third party (that is, not one of the original contracting parties) who one or both contracting parties intended to benefit. The *promisee* is the person to whom a promise is addressed, and the *beneficiary* is a person other than the promisee who will benefit by performance of the promise.

---

[14]Except, as noted above, that an assignor's right is extinguished on assignment.

Assume Varoom Corp. owns several cars and is interested in selling one. To make the sale more attractive to a prospective buyer, Varoom contracts with ABC Insurance Company that ABC will cover fire and theft insurance for the car for a year after its sale. Varoom then sells the car to Margaret and tells her about the insurance policy. In this case, ABC is the promisor because ABC promised to keep coverage on the car for a year. Varoom is the promisee because Varoom is the party to whom ABC promised to keep coverage for a year, and Margaret is the intended beneficiary.

In this example, what are the rights of each party? Suppose Margaret's car is stolen within a year after she buys it, and ABC failed to pay her claim. Can she successfully sue ABC even though she was not an original party to the contract? Yes. According to the Restatement (Second) of Contracts,[15] "[a] promise in a contract creates a duty in the promisor to any intended beneficiary to perform the promise, and the intended beneficiary may enforce the duty." Therefore, ABC, as promisor, owes a duty to Margaret, and she has the right to enforce that duty.

Intended beneficiaries are either *creditor beneficiaries*, where the intent of conferring the benefit is to satisfy a debt owed by the promisee, or *donee beneficiaries*, in which case the promisor is agreeing to give a gift to the third party. The difference between creditor beneficiaries and donee beneficiaries is important because a creditor beneficiary has a legal action against both the promisor and the promisee, whereas a donee beneficiary has a legal action against the promisor only.

To illustrate, suppose a juice-making company, Just Squeezed Fruit, Inc. (JSF), purchases a bottling machine from Machines Are Us, Inc. (MAU) on credit. It uses the machine for a while, and three years later, there is a balance owing to the seller of $200,000. JSF agrees to sell the machine to U.S. Bottling Co. (USB). Under the terms of their contract, USB will pay JSF $500,000 and will also continue to pay the remaining $200,000 balance. Shortly thereafter, USB ceases payments to MAU. Who can MAU successfully sue for the remaining balance? JSF? USB? The answer is: both. An intended beneficiary who is a creditor beneficiary has rights against the promisee under the original contract (in this case, JSF) and against the promisor (in this case, USB).

Situations involving donee beneficiaries present a different outcome because a third party receiving a gift from the promisee has rights only against the promisor. A common example involves a life insurance company (promisor) promising to pay a sum of money to a person's spouse (intended donee beneficiary) upon the death of that person (promisee). In this situation, the original contract between the insurance company and the insured was made for the benefit of the spouse. The spouse is therefore an intended, donee third party beneficiary. Upon the insured's death, if the insurance company fails to pay, the spouse can successfully sue.

---

[15]Restatement (Second) of Contracts, section 304.

Case Illustration

NASCAR and Sprint Nextel agreed in 2003 that, beginning with the 2004 race car season, Sprint Nextel would become an official sponsor of NASCAR Nextel Cup Series. The agreement provided that Sprint Nextel would be the only telecommunications company to sponsor the NASCAR Cup Series races and that competitors of Sprint Nextel were not able to advertise or sponsor the Cup series. At the time, Cingular Wireless LLC was already sponsoring car #31, which was owned by RCR, and the parties agreed that Cingular's sponsorship of car #31 could continue and would be an exception to Sprint Nextel's exclusivity rights. In exchange, Sprint Nextel would pay $700 million over 10 years. NASCAR's agreement with RCR allowed RCR to renew its sponsorship "so long as the sponsor's brand position is not increased on the # 31 car."

Due to a corporate merger in late 2006, Cingular changed its name to AT&T Mobility LLC and transitioned its trademarks, including trade name and logos, to reflect this change. As part of the transition, RCR requested NASCAR's permission to repaint car #31 so that Cingular's logo would remain on the hood of the car, but the AT&T logo would appear on the rear quarter panel. NASCAR, believing that such a change would violate its agreement with Sprint Nextel denied the request to repaint. AT&T sued NASCAR for breach of contract and breach of implied covenant of good faith and requested a court order to place its trademarks on car #31.

The trial court decided that AT&T Mobility was a third-party beneficiary of the RCR Agreement and issued the order.

The U.S. Court of Appeals disagreed and held that under Georgia law, *"in order for a third party to have standing to enforce a contract . . . it must clearly appear from the contract that it was intended for his benefit. . . . [a] third party beneficiary need not be specifically named in the contract, but the parties' intention to benefit the third party must be evident from the face of the contract."* In this case, the RCR agreement did not require RCR to renew its sponsorship with Cingular. If RCR chose not to renew, it could seek sponsorship of any company that was not a competitor of Sprint Nextel. The fact that NASCAR permitted RCR to renew its sponsorship agreement was intended to benefit RCR because it protected RCR from a sudden loss of sponsorship. Any benefit to Cingular was incidental to the main purpose of preserving RCR's sponsorship. *"The promisor NASCAR made a promise only to the promisee RCR to preserve and protect RCR's sponsorship agreement with Cingular notwithstanding the exclusivity granted to Sprint Nextel. RCR was the intended beneficiary of that promise, not Cingular. Nothing in the RCR Agreement required NASCAR to ensure that RCR continued with Cingular as its sponsor."* AT&T Mobility, LLC v. National Association for Stock Car Auto Racing, Inc. 494 F.3d 1356 (2007).

Incidental Beneficiaries

Often, a third party benefits as a result of a contract between two parties, but the benefit was not an intended, purposeful one. The intended/incidental distinction is an important one. Intended beneficiaries have legal standing to enforce the promises made for their benefit; incidental beneficiaries do not. The outcome of the case on page 501, *AT&T Mobility LLC v. National Association for Stock Car Auto Racing, Inc.*, turned on the distinction between intended and incidental beneficiaries.

Conditions and Breaches of Contract

Conditions

All contracts require the performance of duties. Depending on the contract language, some duties can be **conditions**. A *condition* is an act or event that, unless excused, must occur before a duty under a contract arises. In keeping with freedom of contract, parties can agree to condition one party's performance on the performance of the other party or on some other event. (If you do X, I'll do Y.) Conditioning obligations on the occurrence of the other party's performance or on some other event allows businesses to negotiate according to the specifics of their situation, their bargaining power, and their chosen allocation of risk. In more sophisticated business contracts, parties often do not exchange performance simultaneously, and they often choose to qualify their duties by stating that performance is not required unless and until a particular event occurs.

For example, assume Philip wishes to buy a large number of widgets to use in his fabrication of time machines. He contracts with a widget supplier, Oliver. Their agreement states, first, Philip will pay Oliver $100,000 to make modifications to his factory. By January 1, Oliver will produce and send to Philip 50 prototype widgets for Philip to test in the machines. Philip will then notify Oliver of any necessary adjustments in widget specifications by June 1. On June 1, Oliver will begin mass production and will deliver 100,000 widgets on the first of each month. Depending on how the contract is written, the parties' duties could be conditional. For example, Oliver could condition his manufacture and delivery of the widgets on the receipt of Philip's $100,000. By doing so, Oliver shifts some of the risk of modifying his factory to accommodate manufacture of the widgets Philip needs. Philip's $100,000 payment to Oliver triggers Oliver's duty to modify his factory. If Philip never pays the $100,000, then Oliver is never obligated to modify his factory.

Breaches in General

Full performance of a contractual duty discharges that duty; anything less than full performance is a breach. Minor breaches of contract are common in business: a supplier delivers two days later than scheduled; a box contains 998 pencils instead of 1,000; a large quantity of bananas contains a few that are overripe or bruised. Which breaches are so significant that the nonbreaching party can suspend his own performance?

Material Breach

A material breach occurs in one of two situations. Either (1) a party fails to give substantial performance or (2) a party fails to comply strictly with an **express condition**. *Express conditions* are conditions that, according to the contract's language, must be strictly performed before the other party's performance under a contract is due. These conditions are designated through use of phrases such as "if and only if," "provided only that," or "this is an express condition." With respect to time, "time is of the essence" will turn a specified time deadline into an express condition. Suppose a contract for the purchase and sale of a condominium includes a time of 10:00 A.M. on May 1 for closing along with the phrase "time is of the essence." The buyer does not perform, and tells the seller he won't receive the necessary financing until May 2. Will a one-day delay in buyer's performance constitute a material breach? Yes, because the date and time were express conditions. Suppose instead that a shipment of shoes is to be delivered on May 1 and arrives one day late. If there is no clause stating time is of the essence, then the breach is not a material one.

Minor Breach

Minor breaches arise when a party has not performed exactly as promised in the contract, but has given substantial performance. (Note that a minor breach is never a breach of an express condition.)

The difference between material and minor breaches is important. A material breach of contract discharges the nonbreaching party's remaining obligations under a contract. The fairness underlying this rule is intuitive.

Case Illustration

The plaintiff, a builder, contracted to build a house for the defendant. The contract provided: "all wrought iron pipe must be well-galvanized, lap-welded pipe of the grade known as 'standard pipe' of 'Reading' manufacture." Plaintiff completed all requirements in the contract except that some of the pipe he installed was standard, well-galvanized pipe of the same grade as Reading, but a different manufacturer. The rest of the pipe in the house was the type required in the contract. The building was completed. The owner moved in and lived there several months before realizing that some of the pipe was not Reading brand. The homeowner refused to make the last payment of $3,483.46, and the plaintiff sued for this balance. In ruling for the plaintiff, the court stated, *"where by inadvertence or mistake a minor deviation has been made, which involves no damage to the defendant, and defendant takes possession of and continues to use the building, without seeking to disturb in any respect the work done by the contractor, the contractor is entitled to prove that he had substantially performed, that the defendant suffered no damage through such innocent mistake, and that what the owner received is what he had the right to expect to get under his contract." Jacobs & Young v. Kent*, 230 N.Y.239, 129 N.E. 889 (1921).

A party that has not received substantial performance should not have to continue to perform itself. On the other hand, if a breach is only minor, the nonbreaching party cannot withhold performance, as the landmark case *Jacobs & Young v. Kent*, left, illustrates.

Do you think this decision is unfair? After all, the defendant specifically included the need for all pipe to be Reading manufactured, yet he did not receive Reading pipe nor is any real remedy provided to him. What could you do if you were the homeowner and you wanted perfect performance? What are the disadvantages of making contractual requirements stricter?

Duty of Good Faith

The theories described in the previous section (duress, fraud, etc.) help establish parameters of fairness in making and negotiating contracts. Once a contract has been formed, parties are obligated to exercise a duty of good faith in the performance and enforcement of contracts. The UCC defines good faith as "honesty in fact in the conduct or transaction concerned" and, as applies to merchants, "honesty in fact and the observance of reasonable commercial standards of fair dealing in the trade." Under the Restatement (Second) of Contracts, "[e]very contract imposes upon each party a duty of good faith and fair dealing in its performance and its enforcement." What would a breach of the duty of good faith look like? Some examples of lack of good faith include lack of diligence in performing contractual obligations, willfully underperforming, and interfering with or failing to cooperate in the other party's performance. The terms "good faith" and "fair dealings" have ethical underpinnings and could be classified as part of natural law. Natural law holds that there is an inherent ability, common to all people of good will, to judge rightful conduct, including "good faith" and "fair dealings."

Anticipatory Repudiation

Suppose Luis and Linda enter into a contract for Luis to deliver 1,000 cameras to Linda on June 15, at which time Linda will pay Luis $1,000. On February 1, Luis e-mails Linda: "I will be unable to deliver cameras to you on June 15. My factory is being refurbished and we are shutting the facility for eight months."

What can Linda do? Must she wait until June 16 before she has sufficient cause to file suit? No. If one party has reasonable grounds to believe that the other party will materially breach, she may demand adequate assurance that performance is forthcoming and, if reasonable, may suspend her own performance. If no assurance of performance is given in a reasonable time, she may sue for breach of contract without waiting for the date of performance to pass.

Remedies

A breaching party is liable for damages even if the breach is unintentional or faultless — even if it could not have been prevented. This is because parties are entitled to rely on the performance (or its monetary substitute) of those with whom they enter into contracts. How does a court go about providing a remedy for what has gone wrong? When contractual promises are broken, how do courts fairly determine exactly what a plaintiff[16] is entitled to?

The rules relating to remedies aim to ensure fairness to both parties. Plaintiffs who successfully prove a breach of contract will be compensated for losses but will not receive a financial windfall. In general, defendants are protected by being ordered to pay the minimum amount necessary to compensate the plaintiff for losses suffered as a result of the defendant's breach.

Before awarding monetary damages, the following three requirements must be met:

■ *The plaintiff has the burden of proving financial losses with reasonable certainty.* Compensation for speculative losses is not permitted. The plaintiff can introduce evidence (sometimes through use of an expert witness) to substantiate the amount of loss sustained. Where a plaintiff seeks compensation for lost profit or good will, for example, exact mathematical

Case Illustration

In a famous nineteenth century British case, the plaintiff operated a flour mill in Gloucester, England. At that time, flour mills customarily owned two crankshafts — one used while the mill was in operation and a spare to be used when the main crankshaft broke. The plaintiff, however, did not own a spare crankshaft. When the sole crankshaft broke, the plaintiff entered into a contract for the defendant to transport the crankshaft to and from a foundry in Greenwich to be fixed. Although the defendant promised to get it back by a certain date, it took considerably longer. During this time, the mill was closed. In its suit for breach of contract, the plaintiff claimed entitlement to damages equaling the profit lost as a result of defendant's delayed delivery.

The court refused to award damages to compensate for plaintiff's lost profits. The defendant had no way of knowing that the crankshaft they were transporting was the plaintiff's only one and that their delay would cause the plaintiff lost profits. Had the defendant known the delay would cause the plaintiff lost profits, the defendant would have had the opportunity to act differently. The loss of profits cannot reasonably be considered as something that was in contemplation of both parties when they made the contract. As such, it is unfair to require defendants to compensate the plaintiffs for lost profits. *Hadley v. Baxendale*, 9 Ex Ch 341 (1854).

---

[16]The party seeking damages could be a defendant who is also a plaintiff-in-counterclaim, but for the sake of clarity, assume the party bringing a breach of contract action and seeking damages is the plaintiff.

precision is impossible. Damages need not be calculable with mathematical accuracy; reasonably certain approximations are acceptable.

■ *The plaintiff is only permitted to recover losses that were foreseeable to the defendant at the time the parties entered the contract*. The landmark case in this area of law, *Hadley v. Baxendale* (page 505), illustrates how this rule helps protect the defendant and ensure fairness.

Often, businesspeople intuitively reveal the least amount of information possible when negotiating a contract, especially information that exposes any weaknesses or vulnerability. Does the principle in *Hadley v. Baxendale* illustrate that a business can sometimes gain legal advantages and even legal rights by revealing information to the other party?

■ *The plaintiff has the duty to mitigate damages*. Suing for breach of contract is not an opportunity to claim a windfall. Where reasonably possible, it is incumbent on the plaintiff to mitigate damages. For example, if a roofing contractor breached a contract by failing to install a water-tight roof, a plaintiff may not idly observe furniture, rugs, and household objects being ruined and then claim their value in the lawsuit. If it is reasonably possible to move objects out of the way to protect them, then a court will not order compensation if they are ruined. Many cases relating to the issue of the duty to mitigate involve wrongfully terminated employees. To fulfill the obligation to mitigate damages, plaintiffs who show that their employment agreement has been wrongfully terminated are obliged to make reasonable efforts to obtain alternative employment.

Notice how, in the Ethical Insight, ethical theory supports the contract doctrine of mitigation of damages.

An Ethical Insight: W.D. Ross and the Ethical Duty to Mitigate Damages

W.D. Ross' prima facie duties include the duty of reparation. This ethical duty requires the defendant to compensate the plaintiff for injuries sustained as a result of reneging on an agreement. The plaintiff has an ethical duty to take reasonable steps to mitigate that loss.

Assume the plaintiff has successfully proven the existence of a valid contract with the defendant; the defendant's breach of that contract; and the three threshold requirements listed above. How does a court go about measuring damages? In general, there are three possible interests the law could protect in considering what damages to award: expectation interest, reliance interest, and restitution interest.

Damages for Expectation Interest

Protecting the plaintiff's expectation interest means damages should be awarded to put the plaintiff in the same position as if the contract had been performed. That is, the plaintiff is compensated for what he expected to get out of the contract.

Damages for Reliance Interest

Protecting the plaintiff's reliance interest means the plaintiff should be reimbursed for losses sustained by relying on the contract. That is, the plaintiff is compensated for those expenditures made because he relied on the defendant's promises.

Damages for Restitution Interest

Protecting the plaintiff's restitution interest means the defendant should return any benefit that the plaintiff conferred. That is, the plaintiff is entitled to receive the return or replacement of whatever he had given the defendant pursuant to the contract.

To illustrate, assume Roger enters into a contract engaging Paul's services to build a house. Roger gives Paul a deposit of $50,000 and applies for a building permit that costs $3,000 and expires in six months. Under the contract, Paul will begin building within two weeks and will complete the work within four months. Paul does not perform any work at all. Meanwhile, the permit expired. Roger seeks a replacement contractor and by the time he secures one, costs have risen. For doing the exact same work as Paul had promised, the replacement contractor will charge $10,000 more than Paul did. Roger sues Paul for breach of contract.

Does Roger have an expectation interest? Yes. It will now cost him an additional $10,000 to have the house built. To put him back in the same position he would have been in had the contract been performed, he is entitled to $10,000.

Does Roger have a reliance interest? Yes. In reliance on Paul's contractual promise to build the house, Roger spent $3,000 for a permit which is now expired.

Does Roger have a restitution interest? Yes. He gave Paul a deposit of $50,000 but received no value in exchange. He is entitled to the return of the $50,000.

The Ethical Insight illustrates the ethical duty to keep a promise to avoid harming those who reasonably relied on the promise and thereby sustained a loss.

> ### An Ethical Insight: Immanuel Kant and W.D. Ross on the Ethical Duty to Keep a Promise
>
> Society and business depend upon "promise keeping" to function in a competent, efficient manner. Imagine the chaos that would result if people could make serious promises and break them with impunity. Ethics has been defined as "doing the right thing" or "avoid harming another." Immanuel Kant's Categorical Imperative to "Act only on that maxim whereby thou canst at the same time will that it should become a universal law" would support the principle of promise keeping. W.D. Ross would find breaking a serious promise ethically justified only when "the consequences of fulfilling a promise . . . would be so disastrous to others that we judge it right not to do so." The business and social structure of society would deteriorate if a universal law allowed the breaking of serious promises.

Compensatory and Consequential Damages

Most damages awarded to plaintiffs in breach of contract cases are **compensatory damages**—that is, damages to compensate the plaintiff for the loss of bargain. Damages that arise as a consequence of the defendant's breach can also be awarded. To illustrate the difference between compensatory and consequential damages, suppose Billy agrees to sell Miriam a vintage bottle of wine for $500. Miriam enters a contract to resell the wine for $570. The price of the wine rises to $600, and Billy breaches the contract. Miriam's *compensatory* damages total $100 because this is the amount that compensates her for the loss of the bargain. Her **consequential** damages

BMW of North America, Inc. v. Gore, 517 US 559 (1996)

Facts Ira Gore, Jr. bought a new black BMW sports car from an authorized dealer in Alabama in January 1990 for $40,750.88. Nine months later, he took the car to an independent detailer (without noticing any flaws in the car's appearance) named Mr. Slick. Mr. Slick informed him that the car had been repainted. The plaintiff then brought suit against BMW for, among other things, fraud. He claimed that the fact that the car had been repainted was a material fact, and therefore failing to disclose that fact constituted fraud.

At trial, BMW admitted that it had a nationwide policy that if a car was damaged during the course of manufacture or transportation and the cost of repair was less than 3% of the suggested retail price, the car was sold as new without telling the dealer that any repair had been made. In the plaintiff's case, the cost of repainting the car was about 1.5% of its suggested retail price. The plaintiff claimed that the car was worth $4,000 less as a result of the paint job. He claimed punitive damages of $4 million because BMW had sold approximately 1,000 cars nationwide under the pretext of being new when they had actually been retouched. The jury found BMW responsible for $4,000 in compensatory damages and $4 million in punitive damages. BMW challenged the punitive damages and noted its policy meets the disclosure requirements for car sales in about 25 states. The Alabama Supreme Court reduced the amount of punitive damages to $2 million, and BMW appealed to the U.S. Supreme Court.

Issue Were the punitive damages awarded in this case excessive in light of the due process clause?

Holding Yes. The harm inflicted on the plaintiff was economic only, and BMW's conduct was not particularly reprehensible. An excessive award of punitive damages amounts to an arbitrary deprivation of property in violation of the due process clause.

From the Court's Opinion States may legitimately authorize punitive damages that are reasonably necessary to further states' interests in punishment and deterrence. *"Perhaps the most important indicium of reasonableness of a punitive damages award is the degree of reprehensibility of the defendant's conduct . . . In this case, none of the aggravating factors associated with particularly reprehensible conduct is present. . . . The harm BMW inflicted on Dr. Gore was purely economic in nature . . . The second and perhaps most commonly cited indicium of an unreasonable or excessive punitive damages award is its ratio to the actual harm inflicted on the plaintiff . . . The $2 million in punitive damages awarded to Dr. Gore by the Alabama Supreme Court is 500 times the amount of his actual harm as determined by the jury . . . we are not prepared to draw a bright line marking the limits of a constitutionally acceptable punitive damages award . . . we are fully convinced that the grossly excessive award imposed in this case transcends the constitutional limit."* Reversed and remanded.

total $70 because this is the amount she sustained as a consequence of the breach.

Punitive Damages

Punitive damages are relatively rare[17] in civil actions. This is particularly true in contracts cases — the purpose of awarding damages in contracts cases is to compensate, not to punish. However, punitive damages are allowed in breach of contract cases that also involve a tort for which punitive damages are recoverable. Often, such cases involve contracts and fraud, as in the well-known U.S. Supreme Court decision, *BMW of North America, Inc. v. Gore* on page 508.

Liquidated Damages and Limitation of Liability

The freedom to contract extends to the parties' ability to agree on a predetermined amount of (or formula for calculating) damages. Subject to the limitations below, parties are free to include a provision in the contract itself establishing what the damages will be if the contract is breached. This type of provision, called a *liquidated damages clause*, is enforced by courts as long as

1. The amount is reasonable in light of the loss caused by the breach;
2. Actual losses would be difficult to prove; and
3. The amount is not so large that it appears to be a penalty.

For most breaches of contract, monetary damages suffice to meet the plaintiff's expectation, reliance, and restitution interests. However, there are situations where monetary damages do not provide an adequate remedy for the plaintiff. When (and only when) monetary damages are inadequate, equitable remedies may be granted by a court. Broadly, an equitable remedy includes any type of court order to do something (other than pay money) or to refrain from doing something. The most common types of equitable remedies found in contract law are listed below.

Equitable Remedies — Rescission

Rescission of a contract means the contract has been terminated and parties are neither obligated to perform duties nor entitled to demand performance. A court order for rescission is often combined with an order for restitution. For example, in cases where a plaintiff proves that she entered a contract as

---

[17]According to Department of Justice statistics, punitive damages were awarded in about 5% of civil cases in state courts in 2005 where plaintiffs prevailed (http://bjs.ojp.usdoj.gov/content/pub/pdf/pdasc05.pdf). No doubt the number is much lower in cases involving solely breach of contract claims.

a result of fraudulent representations made by the defendant, a court would both rescind the contract and provide restitution to the parties. In such a case, both parties are returned to the position held before the contract was formed.

Equitable Remedies — Specific Performance and Injunction

An *injunction* is a court order requiring someone to do something or to refrain from doing something. *Specific performance* is a type of injunction where the court orders a party to carry out contractual duties. Specific performance is only available where monetary damages are an inadequate remedy for the non-breaching party. Interestingly, sometimes specific performance is only available to one of the parties in a contract. For example, suppose Ruth enters into a contract to sell Bill her house. If Bill breaches the contract, can Ruth get specific performance to force him to buy the house? No. Monetary damages would be adequate. A court would take into consideration any decline in market value between the time of Bill's breach and the time a replacement buyer is located. Additional advertising and marketing expenses could also be compensable. What if, instead, Ruth breached the contract? Could Bill get specific performance? Yes. Each parcel of land is presumptively considered unique due to its unique location. A monetary award will not enable Bill to be placed in the same position he would have been in if the contract had been performed.

Case Illustration

Brown University solicited bids to construct a state-of-the-art sports complex on its campus. The plaintiff submitted a proposal that Brown accepted. Although the parties planned to execute a written contract, disputes arose during negotiations and they were unable to agree on the scope of the work. Plaintiff nearly completed construction for which Brown paid $7,157,051. Plaintiff claimed that more was owed for "extras" not included in the original proposal, and Brown disagreed. Ultimately, the Supreme Court of Rhode Island decided that there was no express or implied agreement between the parties as to the scope of the project and the cost. A jury awarded more than $1.2 million on plaintiff's claim of unjust enrichment. The court affirmed the award, stating that the proper measure of damages in cases of unjust enrichment was the fair and reasonable value of the work done. *ADP Marshall, Inc. v. Brown Univ.*, 784 A.2d 309 (R.I.2001).

Unjust Enrichment

Sometimes, no valid contract exists, but one party would be unjustly enriched if a court did not take action. A **quasi-contract** is not a contract at all. It is an equitable remedy designed to prevent unjust enrichment. It applies when

1. The plaintiff conferred a benefit on the defendant;
2. The defendant knew of the benefit; and
3. The defendant accepted and retained the benefit under circumstances making it inequitable for the defendant to retain it without payment.

In addition to illustrating quasi-contract, the Case Illustration, left, shows the importance of preparing a written contract.

Global Perspective: Contracts

The execution of a contract between a U.S. company and a foreign corporation raises legal and ethical obligations for both parties. The performance of the contract may take place in the United States, in the foreign country, or in both.

Similarities and Differences between International and Domestic Contracts

Functionally, contracts between parties of different nationalities operate similarly to contracts between parties of the same nationality. Parties agree to exchange goods, services, money, permission to use intellectual property, or something else of value. Because a contract is a legally binding agreement, if one party fails to perform some or all its duties, a breach has occurred and redress is in order.

But there are some important differences. Recall from Chapter 5, "Legal Aspects of the Global Business Environment," that doing business internationally is often riskier than doing business within the United States. International contracts are written to shield against some of these risks and to help increase the predictability businesspeople want. For example, recall that *force majeure* clauses, described earlier in this chapter, excuse a party from performance if a particular event occurs. Controlling for the risks brought by severe weather, revolution, war, embargoes, etc., becomes even more essential when contracting with parties overseas, especially those parties operating in environments that are politically unstable or prone to weather-related or other disasters. The company's compliance and ethics program should require periodic "risk assessments" of international contracts and include appropriate *force majeure* clauses.

Forum Selection Clauses

A *forum selection clause* is a contractual provision specifying which judicial or arbitral forum would have jurisdiction over a dispute arising from the contract. While forum selection clauses are commonly used in agreements between U.S. parties, they are even more essential in international transactions. Distances between parties can be great; court systems can vary tremendously from one country to another; language barriers can hinder a party's ability to present its case; litigation overseas can be expensive. A forum selection clause can help overcome these difficulties. Courts in the United States recognize the validity of forum selection clauses unless "enforcement would be unreasonable and unjust, or . . . the clause was invalid for such reasons as fraud or overreaching."[18]

---

[18]*M/S Bremen v. Zapata Off-Shore Co.* 407 U.S. 1 (1972).

Choice of Law

Courts and arbiters usually, but do not necessarily, apply the law of the jurisdiction in which they are located. **Choice-of-law provisions** allow parties to identify which state's or which country's law will govern the interpretation of their contract in the event of a dispute or question. Like forum selection clauses, choice-of-law provisions are also often used in U.S. contracts because U.S. law varies from one state to another. In the international setting, the risks and uncertainties are magnified — imagine how much variation there is between, for example, the law of Illinois and the law of Brazil or Russia or China. Critical contractual obligations valid under the laws of one country might be illegal in another. Rather than leave uncertain which country's law would apply, choice-of-law provisions allow parties better control and predictability of the interpretation and effect of their agreement.

Choice-of-law provisions are valid in U.S. courts unless (1) the chosen state (or country) has no substantial relationship to the parties to the transaction and there is no other reasonable basis for the parties' choice; or (2) applying the law of the chosen state (or country) would contradict a fundamental public policy of the forum state or country. Under the UCC, choice-of-law provisions are permissible as long as the transaction "bears a reasonable relation to" the selected state or country. For example, an international contract between a Massachusetts company and a Chinese business which included a provision that, "In the event of a breach of this contract the parties agree that Nebraska law will apply" would not be enforceable because there is no reasonable relation with the selected state of Nebraska.

Summary

Entering a contractual relationship only begins the obligation to ethically and legally perform the contract under its terms and conditions. In certain circumstances, as explained in this chapter, performance is sometime excused. When not excused, nonperformance is a breach, and the injured party will seek a settlement of the case or its resolution through arbitration or litigation. Judges, juries, and arbitrators have ethical and legal obligations in performing their function in resolving the disputed performance. Businesses should view a contract's performance as a legal and ethical obligation unless there are serious grounds for excusing performance. Maintaining an ethical corporate culture demands that a contract's performance be ethical as well as legal.

Questions for Review

1. **Statute of Frauds**

   As explained in this chapter, the Statute of Frauds was enacted and continues in force today to help prevent people from fraudulently claiming that there is a contractual agreement when none exists. Do you think this is still a problem today? If so, is the Statute of Frauds effective in combatting the problem?

2. **Statute of Frauds**

   Recall the facts in *Leonard v. Pepsico* in Chapter 15. Had this been a contract, would it have been subject to the Statute of Frauds?

3. Ethical considerations

When a new health club opens, the owners offer a discount to the first 100 members who enter into a five-year contract. The fee is $2,400 annually for the first five years, prepaid, regardless of any fee increases throughout that period. Later, the health club alleges it faces an economic crisis due to the recession and notifies the 100 members who prepaid that the membership fee will increase, based on a provision in the contract that stated, "the health club reserves the right to review the fixed membership fee if it sustains an economic hardship during the five year period." The members have brought suit against the club for breach of contract and fraud. The subpoenaed financial records continue to show a small profit. What are the ethical issues and how would you resolve this case using classical ethical principles?

4. Noncompete clause

John J. William began working at Delaware Elevator as a branch sales manager in late 2004. The company manufactures components for elevators and installs and repairs elevators. It employs 175 people in Maryland, Virginia, Delaware, New Jersey, and Pennsylvania. Williams was based in Wilmington, Delaware. Before he began work, Williams signed a noncompete that stated that for three years after the termination of his employment, he "shall not, within a radius of one hundred (100) miles of any Delaware Elevator, Inc.'s office, directly or indirectly, enter into or carry on as owner, employee or otherwise a business or businesses that compete with the [Employer] or in any manner engage in competition with Employer." After working at Delaware Elevator for about five years, he resigned and formed his own competing elevator maintenance and repair business. Is the noncompete enforceable? If not, how should it be revised to ensure enforceability? *Delaware Elevator, Inc. v. Williams*, 2011 WL 1135080.

5. Anticipatory repudiation

Creusot-Loire, a French company, was the project engineer for the construction of ammonia plants in former Yugoslavia and Syria. Creusot-Loire contracted with Coppus Engineering for the purchase of burners that were capable of continuous operation using heavy fuel oil with combustion air preheated to 260°C. Coppus warranted the burners for one year from the start-up of the plants but not exceeding three years from the date of shipment. The burners for the Yugoslavia plant were shipped immediately, but due to construction delays the plant was not to become operational until four years later. Two years after receiving the Yugoslav burners, Creusot-Loire discovered that similar burners at the Syria plant (and also at a plant in Sri Lanka) were experiencing serious operational difficulties. Creusot-Loire wrote to Coppus asking for proof that the burners for the Yugoslavia plant would meet contract specifications. Is Creusot-Loire's request for assurances reasonable? Explain. *Creusot-Loire International v. Coppus Engineering Corp.*, 535 F. Supp. 45 (S.D. N.Y. 1983).

6. Public policy

Kimberly Ramirez joined a club called 24 Hour Fitness USA in December 2007. When she joined, she signed a membership agreement that had a release of liability that stated: "*24 Hour . . . will not be liable for any injury*, including, without limitation, personal, bodily, or mental injury, economic loss or any damage to you . . . resulting from the negligence of 24 Hour or anyone on 24 Hour's behalf or anyone using the facilities *whether related to exercise or not.*" Ms. Ramirez read, understood, and signed the agreement. About two and a half years later, Ms. Ramirez went to the club to attend a yoga class. While there, she slipped in a puddle of water and/or sweat and was injured. Ms. Ramirez sued, claiming that the release of liability clause was unconscionable because the contract pitted Ramirez, an uneducated person who was not a high school graduate, against a corporation and because the agreement was nonnegotiable. She also argued she had "limited workout options" and that "there surely is a public policy in favor of seeing to it that folks have reasonable access to a safe and clean facility and to retain the right to hold the facility accountable for failing to provide . . . a safe and clean workout facility." What resulted and why? *Ramirez v. 24 Hour Fitness USA, Inc.* 2013 WL 2152113 (S.D. Texas).

7. Statute of Frauds

A and B orally promise C a share in a partnership of which A and B are partners. C orally promises to contribute his services to the firm business. A and B own land as part of the partnership assets. Is this agreement covered by the Statute of Frauds?

8. Choice of forum clause

Zapata, a Texas company, entered into a contract for Unterweser, a German company, to tow an oil-drilling rig from Louisiana to Italy. The contract stated, "Any dispute arising must be treated before the London Court of Justice." While Unterweser was towing the rig in the middle of the Gulf of Mexico, a severe storm arose and damaged the rig. Zapata told Unterweser to tow the damaged rig to the nearest port, Tampa, Florida. Three days later, Zapata sued Unterweser in federal court in Tampa for damage to the rig. Unterweser moved to dismiss the suit, claiming that the suit should be heard in London. The case was ultimately appealed to the U.S. Supreme Court. What do you think resulted and why? *M/S Bremen v. Zapata*, 407 US 1; 92 S.Ct 1907 (2007).

Further Reading

Baird, Douglas G., ed. *Contract Stories* (Foundation Press 2007).

Bishara, Norman D., and Michelle Westermann-Behaylo. *The Law and Ethics of Restrictions on an Employee's Post-Employment Mobility.* 49 American Business Law Journal 1–61 (2012).

Garrison, Michael J., and John T. Wendt. *The Evolving Law of Employee Noncompete Agreements: Recent Trends and an Alternative Policy Approach.* 45 American Business Law Journal 107–186 (2008).

Miller, Geoffrey P. *Bargains Bicoastal: New Light on Contract Theory.* 31 Cardozo Law Review 1475–1522 (April 2010).

Petty, Ross. "Contracts." *Wiley Encyclopedia of Management, 3rd Ed.* Managerial Economics volume (Robert McAulliffe ed., Wiley 2014).

CHAPTER 17

Sales Law, Consumer Protection, and E-Commerce

Chapter Objectives

1. To recognize when the Uniform Commercial Code (UCC) Article 2 applies to a transaction
2. To understand the law of offers and acceptances as applied to sales of goods
3. To understand the Statute of Frauds rules as applied to sales of goods
4. To understand buyers' and sellers' obligations under sale of goods contracts and remedies for breaches of such contracts
5. To know when title of goods and risk of loss passes from seller to buyer
6. To know about the Convention on Contracts for the International Sale of Goods (CISG) and to recognize the important differences between the CISG and the UCC

Practical Example: Health Club Owner's Nightmare

Mary and Kathy execute plans to open a new health club. They sign a commercial lease and renovate suitable space, attract several new members in a pre-opening promotional deal, and launch a successful advertising campaign to announce the

515

grand opening for June 1. By contract, the seller of the exercise equipment, George, will deliver the equipment on May 25, giving Mary and Kathy time to set up the equipment before opening day. During phone conversations in early May, George indicates he might have difficulty delivering on time. By May 20, George admits delivery before the grand opening will not be possible. As soon as they hear this, Mary and Kathy begin researching their options. They learn they can order the equipment from a different supplier, pay extra for rush delivery, and have the equipment delivered, set up, and ready for opening day. But will doing this expose them to liability for breach of contract to George? What if George *does* deliver on May 25 and they end up with two sets of equipment? What should they do?

Sales Law

Contracts can involve the exchange of an enormous variety of promises. Some promises relate to real estate, cars, or the rights to a piece of music. Others involve employment services, architectural work, or the sale of a business. Still others involve loaning or investing money or the purchase of a cup of coffee. The two previous chapters examined contract law generally. Yet the history of commerce is largely devoted to *trade in goods*; today, domestic and international sales of goods remain a fundamental component of the U.S. and world economies. This chapter is devoted to an understanding of rules of law and ethics governing the sales of goods—initial contract formation, obligations of the parties, and remedies in the event the contract is breached.

For centuries, most business transactions involved the purchase and sale of goods. Trade in goods was conducted between tribes in Africa, on market days in medieval Europe, and between sailors and merchants in port cities all over the world. Expanding trade was a primary motivation for European colonization, ranging from the establishment of the British East India Company to the British settlement of the Western Cape in South Africa. Europeans began developing and relying on *Lex Mercatoria* (Latin for "merchant law") based on the customs and practices used on trade routes. Recall from Chapter 15, "Contracts: Contract Formation," that predictability of outcomes enables businesspeople to transact business with increased confidence; the development of *Lex Mercatoria* is another example of how law can support business by enhancing predictability.

Another effort to harmonize rules relating to business transactions is, as described in Chapter 15, the Uniform Commercial Code. Each of the American colonies, and later each state, had very different laws governing business transactions. The composition of the UCC was an effort to standardize these rules, thereby facilitating and encouraging commerce across state lines. The UCC covers a variety of types of business transactions, involving banking, Letters of Credit, secured transactions, and more. Although the United States is increasingly a service-based economy, there is still much reliance on the sale of goods, whether produced in the United States or abroad. Today, as in centuries

Current trade law is based on centuries of international commerce.

past, the purchase and sale of goods both at retail and between businesses continues to be a mainstay of the economy. Consequently, it is important to examine and understand UCC rules relating to the sale of goods and the ethical implications of these transactions.

Since manufacturing companies are engaged in selling products, their employees/sales personnel have an ethical obligation to assure their representations about the product are truthful. Sales law is replete with ethical consequences. For example, when the seller makes a valid offer to sell, a power of acceptance is available to the buyer and both sides have legal and ethical obligations in negotiating and concluding the sales transaction. Because sales law allows the seller to express a robust opinion about the product (called "puffing"), sellers must know when the **opinion** becomes a **false statement** and an unethical and illegal representation. For example, compare "this smartphone is the clearly the best on the market" (which is the seller's opinion and considered "puffing") with "this smartphone has the fastest connection time on the market" (which, if untrue, is a false representation that is illegal and unethical). This differentiation between a **seller's opinion** and **false representations** should be part of management's ongoing "due diligence" and "risk assessment" process. The **Manager's Compliance and Ethics Meeting** could be used by the ethics officer to explain the ethics of selling the company's product. As a practical matter, a well-designed **code of ethics** should reference the sales personnel's ethical duty in making honest and truthful contract representations about the products being sold. For example, Raytheon's Code of Conduct states "*Truthful and accurate communications of information about our* *products and services is essential to meeting our commitments to our customers."* The ethics officer should, at periodic meetings, explain the value of integrity in truthfully representing the product being sold to enhance the company's long-term ethical reputation to its customers.

Article 2 of the Uniform Commercial Code

Recall from Chapter 15 that the Uniform Commercial Code was written to cover all aspects of routine business transactions and that, with minor variations, it has been adopted by statute in nearly every state. As such, it carries the weight of a state statute and is read against the backdrop of common law. Several state opinions address questions of interpreting UCC provisions (including some excerpted in this chapter), and these decisions help interpret and explain ambiguities and gaps.

What Is a Contract for the Sale of Goods?

Each article of the UCC is devoted to a different legal topic. Article 2 is devoted to the sale of goods,[1] and Article 2A is devoted to the lease of goods. Ascertaining when a contract is for the sale or lease of goods is not always straightforward. Further, sometimes determining whether Article 2 applies to a contract is a critical issue in a dispute between buyer and seller. For example, a buyer who purchases from a merchant will automatically receive the benefit of certain warranties if Article 2 applies but might not receive the same warranties if Article 2 does not apply.

Consider a contract where Homeowner agrees to pay a masonry contractor to lay a brick walkway in front of Homeowner's house. The contractor will supply the bricks, mortar, and other materials and will also provide the labor. One price covers all labor and materials. Is this a contract for the sale of goods, in which case it is covered by Article 2? Or is this contract for the sale of services, in which case it falls outside the scope of Article 2 and is governed by the common law of contracts?

In hybrid cases where a contract involves a combination of goods and services, if the contract is predominantly for the sale of goods, with services incidental, the contract is governed by Article 2. Conversely, if the contract is predominantly for services, with the sale of goods incidental, the contract falls outside Article 2's scope. A comparison of the value of goods with the value of services is relevant and important but is not the only factor to consider. What is the thrust, the purpose of the contract? What is the nature of the supplier's business? Reconsider the brick walkway contract in light of these factors. The cost of masonry exceeds the cost of the bricks. No doubt the mason is hired for his skill in working with bricks. Probably, what is important

---

[1] UCC 2-102.

to both parties is the workmanlike care with which the bricks are laid, rather than the purchase and sale of the bricks and the mortar. This contract is not covered by Article 2 because it is predominantly for services, with goods incidental.

Hybrid situations also occur when intellectual property is digitized into something tangible. One federal court provided the following guidance on this issue: "Computer programs are the product of an intellectual process, but once implanted in a medium are widely distributed to computer owners. An analogy can be drawn to a compact disc recording of an orchestral rendition. The music is produced by the artistry of musicians and in itself is not a 'good,' but when transferred to a laser-readable disc becomes a readily merchantable commodity. Similarly, when a professor delivers a lecture, it is not a good, but, when transcribed as a book, it becomes a good."[2]

When faced with a contracts question involving the sale of goods, consult UCC Article 2 first to see if a relevant provision addresses the issue and solves the problem. If so, the UCC provision, and any legal cases serving as precedent for the interpretation of that provision, will govern the legal issue. If there is no relevant provision, then common law applies.

Merchants and Consumers

Who Is a Merchant?

UCC Article 2 applies to sales of goods transactions, whether between merchants or between a merchant and a consumer. However, certain Article 2 provisions apply only to merchants.[3] It is therefore important to distinguish between a merchant and a nonmerchant. In this context, a **merchant** is a person who

1. Deals in the type of goods that are the subject of the contract; or
2. Holds herself out as having knowledge or skill peculiar to the type of goods that are the subject of the contract; or
3. Hires or appoints an employee or agent who holds herself out as having knowledge or skill peculiar to the type of goods that are the subject of the contract.

Why Is a Merchant Treated Differently Than a Consumer?

Many of the Article 2 provisions that relate specifically to merchants hold merchants to a higher standard of care than consumers. Others impose the possibility of slightly higher risk to merchants than to consumers. Why these

---

[2]*Advent Systems Limited v. Unisys Corp.*, 925 F.2d 670 (1991).
[3]UCC provisions that apply only to merchants specifically state so.

differences? Wouldn't this distinction operate to discourage commerce? The rationale behind the difference in treatment is that, by definition, merchants are more experienced, more skillful, and more knowledgeable. It is therefore fair to hold them to a higher standard of care or to impose a bit more risk on them than on consumers, who lack similar experience. As you read the provisions that relate only to merchants, keep in mind the ethical underpinnings of this difference in treatment. For instance, suppose a seller/merchant of smart TVs is aware of many customer complaints of an Internet feature on a particular TV brand that he is selling. If the salesperson continued to sell that brand without advising the customers of the problem, is he acting ethically? Is the merchant acting as a "commercially reasonable" seller in not disclosing the material defects of the TV?

An Ethical Insight: Karl Llewellyn and Reasonable Commercial Transactions

Karl Llewellyn was a law professor at Columbia Law School and the University of Chicago Law School, a world renowned legal scholar, and the principal drafter of the Uniform Commercial Code. As a legal realist his primary concern was to make the Uniform Commercial Code reflect "commercial reasonableness" to facilitate the sale of goods in the marketplace. Although the word "ethics" is not used in the Uniform Commercial Code, sales transactions are required to be "commercially reasonable." Llewellyn placed more emphasis on the practical trade practice of a sales transaction than a strict rule of law. The facts of a specific case and what is "commercially reasonable" under the circumstances often will govern the sales transaction.

UCC Article 2A — Lease of Goods

In the context of the UCC, a lease is a contractual agreement where one party is given the right to use personal property in exchange for payment.[4] Leases of goods are common for vehicles, machinery, and equipment. There is a separate UCC article, Article 2A, governing leases, but many of the principles are similar to those for the sale of goods.

Firm Offer by a Merchant

Recall from Chapter 15 that, barring an exception, the offeror may revoke an offer at any time before acceptance. One of the exceptions to this rule is UCC 2-205, sometimes called a **merchant's firm offer**.

Under this provision, if an offer is

■ Signed
■ By a merchant
■ For the purchase or sale of goods
■ Stating that the offer will be held open for the offeree to consider,

---

[4]The term "lease" can also be used in reference to real property, as in an apartment lease, however UCC Article 2 covers only leases of goods.

then it is irrevocable

- For the time stated in the offer or
- If no time is stated, it is irrevocable for a reasonable period of time; and
- In no event can the period of irrevocability exceed three months.

There are strong reasons behind the rule that merchants' written offers are irrevocable. In merchant-to-merchant negotiations, offers are more likely to be complicated and, presumably, offerees will need to expend time, effort, and perhaps financial resources in deciding whether to accept, reject, or counter-offer. It would be unfair to the offeree if the offeror could revoke before the offeree has had a chance to evaluate the offer. But what about the offeror? Does it seem unfair to you that a merchant is not legally permitted to revoke a signed, written offer made to another merchant? In fact, there is also protection for the offeror. As master of the offer, the offeror can choose when the offer expires (even if the length of time is short). And if the offeror does not choose an expiration date for the offer, it will only last for a reasonable period of time (and not more than three months).

Suppose a seller makes a written promise to the buyer to discount cell phones for a 30-day period. Does the seller have an ethical duty to keep that offer open during the 30-day period? If so, which ethical theory supports that obligation? W.D. Ross's prima facie ethical **duty of fidelity** relates to "promise keeping." According to Ross, a person who makes a serious promise is ethically obligated to stand behind it unless "extraordinary circumstances excuse its performance." If the merchant/seller's written contract to the buyer stated a time period during which the offer is to remain open, for instance, "the cell phones are discounted 10 percent for the next thirty days," he has an *ethical duty* to keep that promise open during the time period as the consumer may rely on it and use that time to decide whether he wants to purchase that brand of cell phone or another. Even without consideration, there is an ethical and legal duty to keep the offer open during the stated time.

Acceptance of an Offer to Buy, Sell, or Lease Goods

Recall that the Mirror Image Rule states that an offeree's response is not a valid acceptance unless it is an exact mirror image of the offer. In an effort to provide flexibility in the sales of goods (and thereby encourage commerce), the UCC takes a different, much broader, approach to acceptances. Unless the offeror specifies otherwise, an acceptance can be made "in any manner and by any medium reasonable in the circumstances."[5] Not only is there latitude in allowing the *manner* of acceptance; there is also flexibility in the *content* of the

---

[5]UCC 2-206.

response. The UCC defines a valid acceptance as a "definite and seasonable expression of acceptance or written confirmation which is sent within a reasonable time . . . even though it states terms additional to or different from those offered."[6] This rule increases the likelihood that an agreement will be a legally binding contract and provide options for how the offeree accepts.

Acceptance by Shipping

Suppose Nikita e-mails Ajay and asks to buy 1,000 widgets for $1,000. Ajay does not respond to her e-mail, but he ships the widgets. Has a contract been formed? If it has, Nikita may not refuse the widgets. She is obligated to take them and pay for them. If it has not, then she need not accept or pay for them. Under the UCC, unless the offeror specifies otherwise, an offeree/seller can accept an offer by shipping the goods. Therefore, Nikita *is* legally bound to accept and pay for them. What if Ajay responded to Nikita's e-mail request by shipping defective widgets? Would this put him in the curious position of both accepting and breaching at the same time? The UCC provides a potential escape for the seller in this case. If, after shipping, Ajay realizes the goods are nonconforming and notifies Nikita that the goods are offered as an accommodation, not as intended acceptance, then there is no contract or breach.

Acceptance by Responding

Naturally, instead of answering Nikita's request by shipping the goods, Ajay could have submitted an acceptance in writing. As described above, a definite and seasonable expression of acceptance of Nikita's order would have operated as an acceptance.

Special Situation: Shrink-wrap Acceptance

Software has presented many thorny issues for courts since its arrival on the commercial market. One such issue has been whether shrink-wrapped software is a service or a good. Another complex issue has been whether acceptance occurs when the product is purchased or when it is opened and installed. The case illustration *ProCD, Inc. v. Zeidenberg* provides a landmark example of how one court decided this issue.

Determining the Contract Terms

Even though the UCC's broader definition of acceptance makes the formation of contracts easier, it also raises new questions. If the parties do not need to have perfect agreement on every term in order to form a contract, then what guidance do courts use in the event of a dispute? What happens when the

---

[6]UCC 2-207(1).

Case Illustration

The plaintiff compiled information from more than 3,000 telephone directories into a computer database. The database cost more than $10 million to compile and could be used by individual consumers for personal use as well as by businesses that used it as a marketing tool. The software package was shrink-wrapped with the license terms inside the package. The defendant bought the software and, ignoring the licensing terms, formed a company to resell the information in the database. The defendant's company sold the data, via a website, for less than the cost charged by the plaintiff for the same information. When the plaintiff sued, the 7th Circuit Court of Appeals held that (1) the defendant's purchase of the software was a sale of goods contract governed by Article 2 of the UCC and that (2) the license terms inside the box were the terms of the contract between the parties.

Regarding contract formation, the court noted that many transactions involve the exchange of money first, followed by the communication of detailed terms of the contract. The plaintiff extended an offer that a buyer can accept by using the software, after having the opportunity to read the licensing terms. The defendant was required to click to indicate acceptance or he would be prohibited from proceeding further. In addition, if the defendant read the terms and found them unsatisfactory, UCC 2-606 would have permitted him to reject the goods. Defendant could have either rejected the plaintiff's offer to enter into a contract or could have rejected the goods after inspecting them, but he did neither. There was a contract. *ProCD, Inc. v. Zeidenberg*, 86 F.3d 1447 (7th Cir. 1996).

offeree responds to the offeror with a definite expression of acceptance but with terms different than the offeror's original proposal? Or with additional terms—that is, terms that were not included in the original offer? When, if ever, do different and additional terms become part of the contract? What if neither the offer nor the acceptance addresses a particular term?

Open Terms

Whether the business situation is simple or complex, negotiations do not always lead to a contract in which every term has been negotiated and finalized. Consider the following examples:

- Sarah sends an offer to Juan proposing to sell him 1,000 widgets. The offer contains several terms written on a preprinted form, one of which is that payment is due on delivery. Juan sends back an acceptance on his company's preprinted form, which includes a provision that payment is due 30 days after delivery.
- Juan agrees to buy and Sarah agrees to sell 1,000 widgets. Other details are finalized, and part of their agreement is that they will agree to a price at a future time. Later, they are still unable to agree on a price.[7]

---

[7]Note that if they had not intended to be bound until there was an agreement on price, there would be no contract at all. UCC 2-305 (4).

Exhibit 17.1. UCC Terms Covering Contract Gaps

Open Price Term
Reasonable price at time of delivery

Open Delivery Term
Buyer will pick up at Seller's place of business

Open Time for Delivery
Reasonable time

Open Time for Payment
Payment is due at time and place at which buyer receives the goods

---

■ Juan agrees to buy and Sarah agrees to sell 1,000 widgets. Several terms are agreed upon, but Juan and Sarah completely forget to discuss whether the widgets will be picked up or delivered.

In each of these scenarios, there is a contract because the "definite and sea-sonable expression of acceptance" standard has been met. The agreements are definite enough by UCC standards. But what if a dispute arises over the contract's terms? In light of the law's recognition of and respect for parties' freedom to contract, how does a court settle a dispute involving a term that the parties did not agree on? In such cases, the UCC will fill in the "gaps" of the parties' contract using the rules of convention listed in Exhibit 17.1.

In reviewing the types of open terms that the UCC gap-fills, note which common term is missing: quantity. If parties to a sale of goods agreement do not agree on the quantity (by a fixed number or by a formula for determining the quantity), then there is no contract. The agreement fails to be definite enough meet the standards for an enforceable contract. Why is the quantity term treated differently? If the parties do not agree on quantity and the con-tract is breached, the courts will lack the basis upon which to calculate an appropriate remedy. In other words, without a definite quantity term, there is no way for a court to calculate how much a plaintiff should be compensated for a breach of contract.

Different Terms in a Valid Acceptance

Suppose Michael sends Adam an offer to purchase 100 official Red Sox sweat-shirts for a total price of $4,000, payable upon delivery on June 1. Adam sends back a response stating that he will definitely buy the sweatshirts for $40 each and that delivery should be on April 1 instead of June 1 so that he will be able to stock them in time for the opening of the baseball season. Assume the parties agree they have a contract. What is the delivery date?

Curiously, the UCC does not address how to resolve this question. Several states, such as Michigan, Pennsylvania, and Rhode Island, have adopted the **knock-out rule**, meaning that differing terms in the offer and acceptance are both treated as unenforceable and the court applies the UCC's gap-filling provisions to supply the term. Under the knock-out rule, in the example above, the delivery date is neither June 1 nor April 1. It is a reasonable time, as dictated by the UCC gap-filling provision.

Additional Terms in a Valid Acceptance

Suppose instead that Adam's response to Michael's offer states that he will definitely buy the sweatshirts for $40 each and that the sweatshirts should be packaged 10 to a box. The parties agree they have a contract. But must the sweatshirts be packaged 10 to a box? Under 2-207, the answer depends on several factors:

- *If the parties are not merchants.* Between nonmerchants, additions in an offeree's response serve as proposals for an addition to the contract, requiring assent by the offeror. In this case, Adam's response is a request that the sweatshirts be boxed 10 to a box. Michael can choose to agree to that term, in which case there is a contract and he is bound to box the sweatshirts 10 to a box; or he can choose not to agree, in which case there is a contract, and he is free to package them as he likes.
- *If the parties are merchants.* If the parties are both merchants, additional terms in the acceptance *automatically* become part of the contract unless
  - The offer expressly limits acceptance to the terms of the offer; or
  - The addition materially alters the contract; or
  - Notification of an objection to the additional term is given within a reasonable time.

In the example above, if Adam and Michael are both merchants, must the sweatshirts be packaged 10 to a box? Probably. There is no indication that Michael's original offer expressly limited acceptance to the terms of the offer. Packaging the sweatshirts 10 to a box is probably not a material change because it probably does not impose additional cost or risk on the seller, nor does it significantly alter the deal between the parties. What if Michael really did not want to comply, even if there were no additional cost or risk? Michael could always object to the term that the sweatshirts be packaged 10 to a box. If he does object, the parties still have a contract, but he can package them as he chooses.

Exhibit 17.2. Battle of the Forms: Lessons Learned

1. Read the terms you send to the other party.
Be familiar with your business's preprinted forms.

2. Read the terms the other party sends to you.

3. Be careful with your language.
If the other party offers a proposal with a term that is a "deal-breaker" for you, do not accept. Use language such as "I cannot accept until term X is removed" or "I will only accept if term X is changed to Y."

4. If the other party's acceptance contains additional terms that you find objectionable, notify the other party in a reasonable time, in writing.

Implied Duty of Good Faith

UCC Section 2-103 (b)

"Good faith" in the case of a merchant means honesty in fact and the observance of reasonable commercial standards of fair dealing in the trade.

Sometimes the law imposes an obligation or a right on a party to a contract by operation of law. One such automatic obligation is the **duty of good faith**, which the UCC imposes in every sales contract. Good faith is defined as "honesty in fact and the observance of reasonable commercial standards of fair dealing in the trade." A breach of the "duty of good faith" by a merchant is the basis of a claim for recovery in court in a sales contract case.

The Difference Between Good Faith and an Ethical Standard of Care

The legal definition of *good faith* is determined by trade practice in the industry. Other companies' actions in a similar situation help show whether a defendant merchant acted in good faith. Such evidence is relevant to prove a "reasonable commercial standard of fair dealing in the trade." For example, if a manufacturer of a children's toy discovered that the toy caused a small number of physical injuries, and competitor companies with similar toys have experienced approximately the same number of complaints, is the manufacturer acting with a "reasonable commercial standard of fair dealing in the trade" in continuing to sell the toys? One could argue that if the toy manufacturer has complied with all regulatory laws and warranties, it is acting in good faith. If so, is that ethical?

Assuming the toy manufacturer was acting in good faith under the UCC standard, a company committed to maintaining an ethical culture would seek a higher commercial standard than the existing trade practice. This ethical commitment would encourage the company to adopt a compliance and ethics program. A vigorous policy of due diligence would ascertain legal violations, assess risks to ensure that toys are safe, and instill an ethic of manufacturing safe toys appropriate for children at a certain age. This ethical standard, which exceeds the UCC definition of good faith, would ensure ethical corporate values in the safe design of children's toys.

The Statute of Frauds — UCC 2-201(1) and UCC 2A-201(1)

Recall from Chapter 15 that, as a general rule, oral contracts are enforceable, but if the subject of the contract falls under one of the Statute of Frauds categories, then the agreement must be in writing to be enforceable. Under the UCC, sales of goods costing $500 or more or lease contracts for total payments of $1,000 or more are subject to the Statute of Frauds. They therefore must be in writing (or subject to an exception) in order to be enforceable.

Special Rules for Merchants — UCC 2-201(2)

Suppose an agreement for the sale of goods exceeds $500. Recall from Chapter 16, "Contracts: Performance, Public Policy, and Global Contracts" that a writing or e-mail signed by the party to be charged (that is, the party against whom enforcement is sought) is sufficient to satisfy the Statute of Frauds. Under the UCC, between merchants, there is an exception to this rule, expanding the likelihood that a contract is enforceable. Between merchants, written evidence of the contract signed *by the charging party* (that is, the party claiming the existence and enforcement of a contract) is sufficient evidence of the contract if the recipient does not answer within ten days. Is this exception inconsistent with the underlying rationale of the Statute of Frauds? After all, the Statute of Frauds is designed to prevent people from fraudulently claiming the existence of a contract when there really is no such agreement. Under the exception, what prevents an unscrupulous merchant from sending out a fictitious sales order confirmation and then claiming in court that the order was legitimate?

There are several safeguards against this. First, a duty of good faith is implied in all UCC transactions. Claiming the existence of a contract when there isn't one violates the duty of good faith. Second, the rule only covers situations where a written confirmation by the charging party goes unanswered. Suppose Jessica and Sam are both merchants. Jessica is claiming in court that she had a contract with Sam to sell him $5,000 worth of widgets. The agreement falls under the Statute of Frauds because the subject of the contract is the sales of goods exceeding $500. Jessica produces a written confirmation she sent to Sam on April 1. If Sam received this confirmation but had never ordered the widgets, as a merchant, he should have contacted her to tell her there was no such order. Third, if the contract is contested in court, the charging party will also have to testify that he or she really did send the confirmation. This provides another safeguard against falsely claiming an agreement because many people will be hesitant to swear under oath to a falsehood.

Specially Manufactured Goods

If goods are manufactured specially for the buyer, and they are not suitable for sale to others in the seller's ordinary course of business, then no written evidence of the agreement is necessary, as long as the seller has made a substantial beginning in the manufacturing of the goods or procurement of necessary supplies to manufacture them. For example, suppose a towel manufacturing company receives an oral order to manufacture 1,000 plush bath towels for the Castles in the Sky hotel chain. The order's specifications require that the towels be monogrammed with "Castles in the Sky." After producing and monogramming 230 towels, the hotel cancels the order and claims that because there is no written evidence, there is no enforceable contract. The towel manufacturer need not produce written evidence of the agreement because the specially manufactured goods exception applies.

Admitting to a Contract

It is possible that the party against whom enforcement is sought could admit to the existence of a contract in court documents or in testimony. In such a case, the contract is enforceable, but not beyond the quantity of the goods admitted.

Part Performance

Even if a contract is covered by the Statute of Frauds, a party is obligated to perform under the contract to the extent the other party already has performed. For example, suppose Paul and Judy orally agree that Paul will sell Judy 5,000 widgets, to be delivered in shipments of 1,000 on the first day of each month. Judy will pay after all deliveries have been made. After two deliveries, Judy tells Paul she does not want any more widgets and that she will not pay for the two deliveries he made. Can Paul force Judy to pay for the two shipments he made? Yes. The doctrine of part performance allows Paul to recover payment for the widgets he already delivered, despite the lack of a written agreement. Under the doctrine of part performance, can he force her to accept the three remaining deliveries? No. The Statute of Frauds prevents enforcement of the balance of the contract. Similarly, if Judy had paid Paul a deposit for the widgets, she would be entitled to receive the portion of the widget shipment equal to her deposit, but she could not enforce Paul's obligation to deliver widgets beyond these shipments.

Exhibit 17.3. Statute of Frauds Decision Tree for Contracts for Sales or Leases of Goods

Question 1: Is the subject of the contract the sales of goods for more than $500 or the lease of goods for more than $1,000?

Question 2: If no, then an oral contract is enforceable.
   If yes, is there written evidence to substantiate the agreement?

Question 3: If the contract is subject to the Statute of Frauds but there is no written evidence of the agreement, does one of the exceptions apply?

A. Between merchants
B. Specially manufactured goods
C. Admission in court
D. Part performance

Obligations of the Seller

Assume that a valid, enforceable contract for the sale of goods has been formed and that the terms of the contract have been determined, either through agreement by the parties or by gap-filling or other rules of convention described above. With contract enforceability and terms settled, what performance is required by the seller?

Conforming Goods

Goods that meet all contract specifications are called *conforming goods*.[8] The seller is obligated to provide conforming goods to the buyer under the contract.

Place of Delivery—UCC 2-308

Exercising their freedom to contract, the parties can agree upon a place for the seller to deliver the goods. This could be the seller's own place of business, the buyer's place of business, or some third location, such as a customer of the buyer. As noted above, where the parties omitted designation of a place for delivery, the UCC will fill the gap and require that the buyer pick up the goods.

Tender of Delivery—UCC 2-503(1)

Under the UCC, **tender of delivery** requires that the seller transfer conforming goods and place them at the agreed-upon location. Tender rules also require the seller to give whatever notice is reasonably necessary for the buyer to take possession of the goods. This involves offering the goods at a reasonable hour and making the goods available for a long enough period of

---

[8]UCC 2-106(2).

Tender of delivery requires that the seller transfer the goods to the agreed-upon location.

time for the buyer to take possession. The seller's delivery must be made at a reasonable hour and in a reasonable manner.

Perfect Tender Rule and Its Exceptions

Tender refers to the transfer of goods from seller to buyer. The UCC specifies the manner in which tender must be made, but there are many exceptions to the rule.

Perfect Tender Rule—UCC 2-601

The UCC requires that the seller's performance when tendering the goods complies perfectly with every contractual provision. Variations in how the goods were manufactured, whether the goods meet the contract specification and description, how they were packaged, or whether the quantity is correct would violate the perfect tender rule. If tender is not perfect, the buyer has the option to

1. Reject all the goods;
2. Accept all the goods; or
3. Accept any commercial unit(s) and reject the rest.[9] (A **commercial unit** is a single whole for purposes of sale, such as a single machine, a crate of wine, a carton of packages of paper, a bushel of apples.)

Exception: Cure — UCC 2-508

It is commonplace and understandable that a seller might vary slightly from contractual specification, thereby violating the perfect tender rule. Does violating the perfect tender rule mean that the seller loses the right to all or part of the buyer's payment? No. The seller has a right to cure (that is, to fix) the improper tender. This right depends in part on when delivery has been made.

■ *Delivery before the time for performance.* If the seller delivers the goods before the contract time for performance and the buyer rejects the tender as nonconforming, then the seller can promptly notify the buyer of the intent to cure the defect(s) before the contracted delivery time. In such a case, the seller may then repair or fix the defects before the contracted delivery date.

■ *Delivery after the time for performance.* If the seller delivers the goods on the delivery date specified in the contract or afterwards, the seller is given reasonable time to substitute conforming goods if (1) the buyer rejected the nonconforming tender; (2) the seller had reasonable grounds to believe that the goods would be acceptable to the buyer; and (3) the seller notifies the buyer.

Do these rules seem fair to you? There is protection for both seller and buyer. On one hand, the buyer is protected because tender must be perfect; seller's substitution of conforming goods must occur before the contract delivery date or must be reasonable under the circumstances; and the buyer must receive notice of seller's intent to cure. On the other hand, the seller is protected because there can be opportunities to rectify any defect before the contracted delivery date and rectify minor defects after the contracted delivery date.

---

[9]UCC 2-601.

Exceptions: Substitution of Carriers — UCC 2-614(1)

Often, one of the terms parties agree to in a sale of goods contract is the means by which the goods will be transported from seller to buyer. If, due to no fault of the seller or buyer, the agreed-upon manner of delivery becomes impracticable, but a reasonable substitute method is available, then the substituted method not only may be chosen, but must be used. This is one of many examples of the UCC's underlying policy to keep the wheels of commerce moving when feasible.

Exceptions: Commercial Impracticability — UCC 2-615(a)

In general, freedom of contract allows parties to allocate risk as they see fit and in whatever manner they negotiate. Recall that *force majeure* clauses are sometimes used to allocate the risk of unusual events beyond the control of the parties. However, sometimes circumstances arise that parties did not and could not reasonably have foreseen. UCC 2-615 provides that a seller is not in breach for failing to deliver or delaying delivery if

1. The seller did not assume the risk of a particular unknown contingency;
2. The nonoccurrence of the contingency was a basic assumption on which the contract was made; and
3. Occurrence of the contingency made performance impracticable.

A common argument sellers advance in hopes of being released from contractual obligations is soaring supply costs. In reference to this problem, the UCC states, "Increased cost alone does not excuse performance unless the rise in cost is due to some unforeseen contingency which alters the essential nature of performance. Neither is a rise or a collapse in the market in itself a justification, for that is exactly the type of business risk which business contracts made at fixed prices are intended to cover."[10]

What situations, then, could be excused under the doctrine of commercial impracticability? Courts have excused a seller's nonperformance when a contract required the seller to use parts that were manufactured at a specific manufacturing plant and that plant ceased production. Sudden, unforeseen action by the government, such as a declaration of war, that significantly changes the parties' initial assumptions at the time of contract formation can also form the basis of excuse under commercial impracticability. Other examples include an embargo or a crop failure. Suppose the buyer informs the seller that delivery by a specified date is an essential term of the sales contract and the seller agrees. However due to a hurricane all air flights are grounded for prolonged periods of time, resulting in a late air delivery. The seller would be legally excused from that delivery date under the doctrine of

---

[10]UCC 2-615 comment 4.

commercial impracticability. This is also ethically supported by W.D. Ross's rule that exceptional cases excuse performance when "the consequences of fulfilling a promise . . . would be so disastrous to others (the seller's additional expenses due to the buyer for a late delivery) that we judge it right not to do so."

Exceptions: Destruction of Identified Goods — UCC 2-613

Goods are **identified to the contract** when, during contract formation, the parties designate exactly which goods are the subject of the contract. For example, a farmer contracts to sell the apples that will be ready for harvest in October from a particular orchard. This is not a sale of *any* apples; it is a contract for the sale of *those particular* apples.

If goods that have been identified to the contract suffer a casualty due to no fault of the parties, then the parties are excused from performance. If only part of the goods have suffered such a casualty, then the buyer has the choice of treating the contract as void or accepting the goods at an appropriately reduced price.

Exceptions: Noncooperation — UCC 2-311(3)(b)

Assume Bob enters into a contract to sell Amy 10,000 imported Chinese dressers on June 1. The contract specifies that by May 1, Amy will tell Bob which of five different dresser models she will select. On May 1, Amy refuses to identify which models she would like. Bob asks again a week later, by which point it is getting late for him to arrange for delivery from China. Amy still refuses to

---

Exhibit 17.4. Recap of Perfect Tender Rule and Exceptions

Perfect Tender Rule: Seller's performance when tendering goods must comply perfectly with the contract.

Buyer's Options: If tender is not perfect, buyer may (1) accept all the goods, (2) reject all the goods, or (3) accept any commercial units and reject the rest.

Exceptions to the Perfect Tender Rule:

Cure. Before the contracted delivery time, the seller can notify the buyer and cure. After the contracted delivery time, the seller has reasonable time to substitute conforming goods if (1) the buyer rejected the nonconforming tender, (2) the seller had reasonable grounds to believe that the goods would be acceptable to the buyer, and (3) the seller notifies the buyer.

Substitution of carriers. If, due to no fault of the seller or buyer, the agreed-upon manner of delivery becomes impracticable, then a reasonable substituted method must be chosen.

Commercial impracticability. A seller is not in breach for failing to deliver or delaying delivery if (1) the seller did not assume the risk of a particular unknown contingency, (2) the nonoccurrence of the contingency was a basic assumption on which the contract was made, and (3) the occurrence of the contingency made performance impracticable.

Destruction of identified goods. If goods that have been identified to the contract suffer a casualty due to no fault of the parties, then the parties are excused from performance.

Noncooperation. One party's failure to cooperate excuses the other party from failing to perform.

cooperate. Bob does not deliver on June 1. Is his breach excused? Yes. One party's failure to cooperate (when such cooperation is needed) excuses the other party from failing to perform. Failure to cooperate can be treated as a breach. So, Bob could choose to treat Amy's refusal to submit her model choices as noncooperation, and he is therefore excused from failing to deliver.

The perfect tender rule and its exceptions are summarized in Exhibit 17.4 on page 533.

Obligations of the Buyer

As before, presume that a valid, enforceable contract for the sale of goods has been formed and that the terms of the contract have been determined, either through agreement by the parties or by gap-filling or other rules of convention. With contract enforceability and terms settled, what performance is required by the buyer?

Payment at the Time and Place the Buyer Receives the Goods — UCC 2-310(a)

As part of the UCC's gap-filling provisions, if the parties do not address in the contract when the buyer must pay for the goods, then payment is due at the time and place the buyer receives the goods. How is this rule consistent with principles regarding risk allocation in basic contract law? By paying before receiving the goods, the buyer takes on risk in a deal. By extending credit to allow a buyer to pay after receiving the goods, the seller takes on risk in a deal. The gap-filling provision equalizes risk between the parties. By requiring payment at the time goods are delivered, risk is more evenly distributed.

Acceptance by the Buyer After a Reasonable Opportunity to Inspect the Goods — UCC 2-606(1)(a)[11]

The UCC carefully defines when a buyer has accepted goods. **Acceptance of goods** has important significance — once goods have been accepted, they cannot be rejected, and the buyer's obligation to pay is triggered. Under the UCC, **acceptance of goods** can occur in a number of different ways.

First, a buyer has legally accepted goods if the buyer acts in a manner inconsistent with the seller's ownership of the goods. For example, a buyer purchasing cola syrup for use in making soft drinks receives delivery of the syrup from the seller, opens the container, and begins using the syrup in manufacturing. This use, inconsistent with seller's ownership of the product, constitutes acceptance.

---

[11]Note that this section applies to acceptances *of goods*, not to be confused with acceptance *of an offer*.

In all other cases, the buyer has the right to inspect the goods. The time given for inspection is a reasonable time, depending on the circumstances. Some goods take longer to inspect than others. Perishable goods, by their nature, demand shorter time within which to inspect. Once the buyer has had a reasonable opportunity to inspect, there are three possibilities:

1. The buyer may signify to the seller that the goods are conforming;
2. The buyer may signify to the seller that the goods are nonconforming but that he or she will retain them despite the nonconformity; or
3. The buyer fails to make an effective rejection of the goods on reasonable grounds. (Recall the rules for rejection and the perfect tender rule, above. For an application of these rules, see the Case Illustration below.)

Anticipatory Repudiation

Recall from Chapter 15 that sometimes one party indicates in advance that performance under the contract will not be forthcoming. In an effort to provide businesspeople with flexibility, the UCC does not require a party to wait until the time of performance has arisen in order to take action. Where one party repudiates before time for performance is due, the other party may choose

Case Illustration

Brandeis Machinery & Supply Company rented to Capitol Crane Rental, Inc., a 35-ton crane, with an option to buy. Capitol leased the crane for several months. On June 16, 1999, the parties entered into a contract for Capitol to buy the crane "as is — where is" for $291,773.46, with payment to be made within 10 days, plus late charges. Brandeis sent an invoice for the crane to Capitol on June 29, 1999. At about this time, the crane's boom was damaged. Capitol bought parts from Brandeis and repaired it. Meanwhile, a national crane rental company expressed interest in buying Capitol. Capitol's owner, Steve Dotlich, returned the crane to Brandeis's lot. When a Brandeis employee phoned Dotlich to ask about the returned crane, Dotlich replied that he "did not want to buy [the crane] any more" and that he planned to sell the business. Brandeis managers told their staff not to sell the crane because it belonged to Capitol, not Brandeis, and they placed a sign on the crane to indicate it had been sold to Capitol. Eventually,

in order to sell it to someone else, Brandeis spent $9,794.86 to inspect the repairs Capitol had made to the crane. Brandeis sued for the full purchase price, plus late charges, claiming that Capitol had accepted the crane before returning it. Capitol claimed that it had not accepted the crane.

Referencing the UCC provision applicable to buyers' acceptances, the Indiana Court of Appeals held that the trial court did not err in finding that Capitol returned the crane in a reasonable time and that this return constituted a "wrongful, yet effective, rejection." The return was within a reasonable time, Brandeis had timely notice of the rejection, and Brandeis had a pattern of cancelling contracts in the past after customers signed but before money changed hands. Further, it was not clear from the evidence whether Capitol received the invoice before or after returning the crane. *Brandeis Machinery & Supply Co., LLC v. Capitol Crane Rental, Inc.* 765 N.E.2d 173 (2002).

(1) to wait for performance by the repudiating party or (2) to resort to a remedy for breach. Under either option, the nonrepudiating party may suspend its own performance. For example, in the case of the health club owners in the introduction to this chapter, once the original supplier indicated clearly that she could not deliver in time for opening day, Mary and Kathy could order the equipment from a new supplier without breaching the contract with their original supplier. In fact, by ordering immediately from a new supplier, they are potentially minimizing the damages that could be owed by the original supplier. The Manager's Compliance and Ethics Meeting on page 537 illustrates the ethics of anticipatory reputation in a sales transaction between the manufacturer of software and a commercial airlines buyer.

Remedies

Remedies of the Seller

When a buyer breaches a sale of goods contract, what options does the seller have? Recall from Chapter 16, that the purpose of remedies in contract law is to put the nonbreaching party in the same position he would have been in had the contract been performed. How does this apply to sale of goods cases — that is, contracts governed by UCC Article 2? Suppose that on June 1, Judy contracts to sell 500 bushels of fresh New England apples from a specific orchard to Paul. They agree that Paul will pay half the purchase price on September 1 and the balance on delivery on October 15. Then the price of apples drops. On September 1, Paul does not pay the deposit. Judy requests payment and Paul refuses, wanting to buy cheaper apples from a different supplier. Must Judy deliver the apples? What remedies and options does she have?

1. Judy has the **right to withhold delivery**. She need not deliver the apples on October 15.
2. Judy has the **right to resell** the apples and in fact, if she is able to, she *should* resell the apples because she is obligated to mitigate damages. Since the price has dropped, a new buyer will likely pay her less. If a good faith resale of the apples yields a lower price than what Paul was contractually obligated to pay, Judy can recover from Paul the contract price minus the resale price.
3. Judy has the **right to recover damages**. She can also recover incidental costs relating to the resale (for example, additional transportation costs) but must deduct the consequential damages she saved as a result of Paul's breach.
4. Judy has the **right to recover the purchase price** for the apples. This is available if, for example, she is unable to resell them because Paul breached too late for Judy to resell the apples and they spoiled or if she had delivered all the apples to Paul and then he failed to pay her.
5. Judy has the **right to cancel** the contract. If Paul had made a deposit and then refused delivery, Judy could have returned the deposit and treated the contract as cancelled.

Manager's Compliance and Ethics Meeting

The Ethics of Anticipatory Repudiation of a Sales Contract

Your company, Best Instruments, Inc., manufactures and sells software products used in commercial aviation aircraft. You have been informed by your company's marketing vice president that a software product sold to a commercial airline was to be used by its entire fleet. Under the sales contract, your company's engineers and technicians, who are experts in the installation and use of the software, were to provide the training and implementation of the product at the airline's expense. You were recently informed that the airline company wants to use its own experts because it claims there are government regulations that require, for safety purposes, the software meet certain standards. They have informed your company this repudiation is nonnegotiable. This would amount to a significant loss of profit to your company under the sales contract. The marketing vice president has asked you to meet with your department and provide him with your due diligence and risk assessment findings with a special emphasis on the ethical reasons for anticipatory repudiation of the contract. The marketing vice president's concern relates to the company's corporate compliance and ethics program, including the company's published code of ethics, which states, "We are especially committed to providing safe installation of our software products to prevent any potential loss to our customers."

At the meeting with your aeronautical engineers, you discuss the legal and ethical aspects of anticipatory repudiation.

You report to the marketing vice president that because the terms of the contract were changed by the airline company after its acceptance, your company is ethically justified in holding the airline company to its promise. However, the airline company may ethically argue that the government regulation makes the contract performance impossible because they could be held criminally liable for noncompliance if the software malfunctioned. They could argue that having your company install the software is too great a risk.

From an ethical perspective, **W.D. Ross's** prima facie duty of nonmalfeasance may justify the buyers' repudiation of the contract if "the consequence of fulfilling the promise would be disastrous." Because your company has certified safety engineers, the airline company's argument is rather weak.

Aristotle's *Virtue Ethics* (Nicomachean Ethics, Book V) states, "Justice alone of the virtues is 'the good of others' because it does what is for the advantage of another." This ethical principle would find that the best practice would be to determine if the government standards for safety could be maintained ("the good of others") by your company's engineers and technicians. If so, and the airline refused to allow your company's engineers to implement the software and provide training in accordance with the contract terms, your company would be ethically and legally justified to anticipate repudiation by the buyer airline company and immediately resort to a remedy for its breach.

Rule utilitarianism would ask the question: if your company's safety engineers were adequately qualified to ensure the equipment meets the safety standards established by the federal government, would their training and installation of the software bring about the greatest increase in happiness to all involved, especially the passengers on the aircraft? Once that question is answered with an unequivocal positive response, it would be ethical to insist your company's engineers perform as stated in the sales contract.

Ethical principles would support anticipatory repudiation of this sales contract if the airline company insisted on its own engineers installing the software in violation of the contract.

Remedies of the Buyer

Assume the same facts as above: Judy and Paul enter a contract for the purchase and sale of apples. This time, Paul makes the required deposit but the price of apples rises. Judy never delivers the apples, thinking that she can now obtain a buyer who will pay a higher price. What remedies and options does Paul have?

Case Illustration

Recall that in the *Brandeis Machinery* case, the seller sued for the full purchase price of the crane. Given the rules on remedies on page 536, what is the appropriate measure of damages Brandeis should receive for Capitol's breach? Capitol made a wrongful yet effective rejection. The court held that the appropriate measure of damages was the difference between the contract price and the fair market value of the crane, plus the cost of inspection of the repairs.

1. Paul has the **right to cover**. Presuming he still needs apples, he can purchase them in good faith from another supplier. Since the price has increased, a new seller will likely charge him more. If a good faith purchase of the apples yields a higher price than what Paul was contractually obligated to pay, he can recover from Judy the additional cost — that is, the new purchase price minus the contract price.

2. Paul has the **right to recover damages**. Paul can also recover incidental costs relating to the new purchase (for example, additional commission costs if a broker is involved).

3. Paul has the **right to reject the goods**. Suppose that instead of failing to deliver, Judy delivered nonconforming apples. Recall that under UCC 2-606, if the goods are nonconforming, Paul may reject them all, accept them all, or accept any commercial unit and reject the remainder.

4. Paul has the **right to acceptance**. Suppose that some of the bushels of apples were rotten. Paul can choose to accept nonconforming goods and recover damages for the nonconformity. As noted previously, the buyer must, within a reasonable time, notify the seller of the existence and nature of the nonconformity.

In "Health Club Owner's Nightmare" at the beginning of this chapter, the exercise equipment seller's failure to deliver was a breach of contract. What remedies do Mary and Kathy have? They have the right to cover — they can purchase from an alternative exercise equipment seller so they will be ready for the grand opening. They also have the right to incidental damages. They can recover the cost of rushed shipping from the breaching seller.

Title to Goods and Risk of Loss

What does it mean to own something? Ownership is sometimes defined as the exclusive right to possess property. It is comprised of several rights, classically referred to as a bundle of ownership rights. For example, a property owner has the right to sell the property, to give it as a gift, to pledge it as collateral, or to pass it by will.

Legal title is evidence of ownership. Sometimes, legal title takes the form of a document. A certificate of title is record evidence of car ownership. Real property ownership is transferred by a deed. For sales of goods, title and possession might not be vested in the same person. For example, suppose Luis plans to move from Boston to Chicago. He hires a moving company to transport his furniture. During transit, the moving company has possession of the furniture, but Luis still owns it. In a lease of goods, as in Brandeis's lease of the crane to Capitol discussed previously, the lessor retains title of the property while the lessee is granted to right to use the property in exchange for payment.

In a sale of goods transaction, at what point does title pass from seller to buyer? This can be an important question if, for example, the goods are lost, stolen, or damaged. Is the party who has title always the party to bear the risk of loss? Can one party insure the goods even before taking title or possession of them? The answers to these questions help parties allocate and manage their risks during the packaging, loading, transport, and transfer of the goods.

Passage of Title

When title to goods passes is dependent on several factors:

- Whether the parties have provided in the contract the time for title passage;
- Whether the goods are identified to the contract;
- Whether the seller must deliver a document of title along with the goods;
- Whether the seller is required to deliver the goods to a carrier for transportation to the buyer, or whether seller is required to deliver them to the buyer; and
- Whether the seller has delivered nonconforming goods.

To determine the time at which title passes, refer to the following rules, in order:

1. **Contractual provision addressing passage of title**. Freedom of contract allows parties to designate in the contract when title will pass. Any such agreement by the parties will govern. It is, however, often the case that parties do not make such a provision, and title passage is, by default, determined in accordance with UCC rules.
2. **Goods are identified to the contract and seller completed delivery obligations**. If a contract requires that goods be identified (recall that this means *specific* apples instead of *any* apples), then title cannot pass until goods are identified to the contract. This rule is based on the common-sense notion that a person cannot own something until it is clear exactly *what* is being owned. Once goods have been identified to the contract, title passes at the time and place where the seller completes his responsibilities for delivery of the goods. Some sellers use their own transportation service to deliver the goods to the buyer. However, most sellers are not in the delivery business, so it is more likely that the seller is required to deliver the goods to a third-party carrier for shipment to the buyer. A contract where the seller is required to deliver the goods to a carrier (for shipment to the buyer) is called a **shipment contract**. A contract requiring the seller to

deliver to the buyer's destination is called a **destination contract**. In both, title passes when the seller has completed performance with respect to the physical delivery of the goods.

3. **Documents of title**. Sometimes the title to goods is evidenced by a document, such as a **bill of lading**. A bill of lading is a receipt signed by the carrier when the seller delivers goods to the carrier. It serves as a seller's receipt for the goods. A **negotiable bill of lading** means that title to (and right to possess) the goods is evidenced by the paper itself. A buyer who produces a negotiable bill of lading with the buyer's name is entitled to receive the goods from the carrier. In such a case, title passes when and where the document is delivered.[12]

4. **Goods are identified to the contract and delivery is made without moving the goods**. If the sale will occur without moving the goods and if no document of title is involved, then title passes at the time and place of contracting (assuming goods are identified to the contract).

The In-Depth Ethical Case Analysis illustrates the legal and ethical obligations of a party seeking legal title to take timely positive steps to claim ownership or lose that claim under the equitable doctrine of laches.

In-Depth Ethical Case Analysis

Bakalar v. Vavra, 819 F. Supp. 293 (S.D.N.Y. 2011)

Facts

Egon Schiele: *Seated Woman with Bent Leg (Torso)*, 1917 (Kallir D. 1974). Photo courtesy Galerie St. Etienne, New York.

Prior to World War II, a Jewish art collector named Grunbaum purchased a 1917 drawing, "Seated Woman With Bent Leg" by an artist named Egon Schiele. When the war came, Grunbaum was sent in 1938 to Dachau concentration camp, where both he and his wife died. Years later, in 2002, an Austrian court declared that Milos Vavra ("Vavra") and Leon Fischer ("Fischer") were both the rightful heirs of the Grunbaum estate. In July 2008, the Court applied Swiss law to the issue of whether Bakalar acquired title to the Drawing and awarded judgment to the Grunbaums. On investigation, it was proven that Grunbaum's sister-in-law, Lukacs, sold the drawing after the war to a gallery that purchased it in good faith and sold it to another gallery, which sold it to Bakalar.

---

[12]UCC 2-401(3)(a).

Ultimately, Bakalar sued for declaratory judgment, seeking a court order stating that he was the rightful owner of the drawing. Was Bakalar the rightful owner? Instead of waiting, should Vavra and Fischer have pursued a claim to the drawing when they were declared the Grunbaum estate heirs?

The Court's Decision

The court analyzed several potential theories for determining who had valid title to the drawing. First, the court noted that under New York law, a thief cannot pass good title—but was the drawing looted by the Nazis and confiscated from Grunbaum? In fact, the court stated that "Lukacs' possession of the Drawing after World War II strongly indicates that such a seizure never occurred. Accordingly, what little evidence exists—that the Drawing belonged to Grunbaum and was sold by one of his heirs after World War II—suffices to establish by a preponderance of the evidence that the Drawing was not looted by the Nazis." Second, there was insufficient proof that the Grunbaums had given Lukacs the drawing as a gift. The mere possession by a family member of an object does not establish that it was given as a gift—for example, the custodian may have it for safekeeping. Third, Bakalar argued that Lukacs may have had voidable title. But the court held that voidable title refers only to those who buy goods for a price and is inapplicable to gifts. In an interesting conclusion to its opinion, the court decided that, even though Bakalar failed on all three grounds to substantiate the claim to clear title, Vavra and Fischer lost the case due to laches—that is, the defendants were aware of their claim, inexcusably delayed taking action, and Bakalar was prejudiced as a result.

Ethical Issue

Did Vavra and Fisher have an ethical duty to pursue in court, as soon as possible, their alleged ownership rights to the drawing? Was their "inexcusable delay in taking action" unethical? Is the doctrine of laches, that decided this case, supported by ethical theory?

Ethical Theory Analysis

Kant's Categorical Imperatives

Kant's categorical imperative "Act only on that maxim whereby thou canst at the same time will that it should become a universal law" would support an ethical duty to complain of a wrongful act as soon as possible. One could argue that Kant would find a moral duty to take immediate action when necessary to prevent a wrongful act, regardless of the consequences as something we all "ought" to do. If we do not complain of wrongful acts as soon as possible, our rights would deteriorate. A universal moral law to object to wrongful acts as soon as reasonably possible supports the court's judgment for the petitioner, Bakalar, as the rightful owner of the drawing. Vavra and Fischer violated their ethical obligations in their "inexcusable delay" in taking actions to assert their alleged claim of ownership in the Schiele Drawing as the alleged rightful heirs of the Grunbaum estate. Kant would hold the timely objection to a wrongful act is a moral duty regardless of the consequences or happiness of others.

John Stuart Mill and Utilitarianism

The ethical utilitarian maxim "the greater good for the greater number" would support a timely complaint. Vavra and Fischer waited until 2008 for the court to rule they were the rightful heirs of the Grunbaum estate violated their ethical duty to act in a timely fashion and constituted an "inexcusable delay." Vavra and Fisher should have pursued, if necessary in court, ownership rights to the drawing as soon as they discovered it was sold by Grunbaum's sister-in-law Lukacs. Following this moral rule would provide the greater good and happiness to all, as the rightful owner would be established, if necessary, by litigation. The consequences of claiming ownership rights in the drawing would create a moral rule that would bring the greater good to the litigants as the court would settle the dispute one way or another and bring closure to the controversy. Notice how this rule differs from Kant's categorical imperative that demands moral conduct (in this case an immediate claim to ownership of the drawing by Vera and Fisher) regardless of the consequences of the greater good or happiness to those involved.

Ethics Supports the Equity Doctrine of Laches that Decided this Case

The above ethical analysis supports the equity doctrine of laches that states "equity aids the vigilant and not those who procrastinate their rights." English philosopher Edmund Burke said, "The only thing necessary for the triumph of evil is for good men to do nothing." One could paraphrase Burke and state "evil will triumph if good men and women procrastinate in claiming a violation of a right."

Risk of Loss

Students are sometimes surprised to learn that risk of loss and passage of title might not occur at the same time. The reason for this is that "[t]he underlying theory of [the UCC] on risk of loss is the adoption of the contractual approach rather than an arbitrary shifting of the risk with the 'property' in the goods."

To determine the time at which risk of loss passes, refer to the following rules, in order:

1. **Contractual provision addressing risk of loss.** As with passage of title, freedom of contract allows parties to designate in the contract who will bear the risk of loss and at what point the risk will pass. Any such agreement by the parties will govern. And, as with passage of title, if parties do not specify, then risk of loss is determined by default, in accordance with UCC rules.
2. **Shipment and destination contracts.** The risk of loss in shipment and in destination contracts passes when the seller completes the responsibilities for delivery. Therefore, for shipment contracts, the risk passes when the seller delivers the goods into the hands of the carrier. For destination contracts, the risk passes when the seller delivers the goods into the hands of the buyer.
3. **Documents of title.** If the goods are transferred pursuant to a negotiable bill of lading, then the risk passes to the buyer upon receiving the negotiable bill of lading.
4. **If none of the above apply.** If none of the above rules are applicable to the situation, then if the seller is a merchant, the risk of loss passes to the buyer when he receives the goods; if the seller is a nonmerchant, the risk of loss passes upon tender of delivery.
5. **Breaches by buyer or seller.** If a seller's delivery fails to conform to the contract, then the risk of loss remains with the seller until the seller cures or the buyer accepts the goods. Similarly, if a buyer repudiates or is in breach

of contract and the goods have been identified to the contract, then the risk is on the buyer for a commercially reasonable time after the seller has learned of the breach and only to the extent of any deficiency in the seller's insurance coverage.

Suppose Carlos enters into a contract to ship to Nancy 5,000 pounds of steel bars from Pittsburgh to Los Angeles. The contract specifies that Carlos will deliver the steel to a freight carrier in Pittsburgh and Nancy will arrange for transportation to her warehouse in LA, but it contains no provision regarding when risk of loss would pass. The steel bars are damaged during transportation. Whose loss is this? The loss is Nancy's because this is a shipment contract. What if the steel that Carlos delivered to the carrier was defective? Carlos would be responsible for the loss because his delivery failed to conform to the contract.

Insurable Interests

In order to procure insurance coverage to protect against losses due to theft, destruction, damage, and the like, a party must have an insurable interest in the property. A person cannot, for example, procure an insurance policy on a neighbor's car. This is because such an arrangement would be more like gambling than selling risk to obtain protection. Once goods have been identified to the contract, they are insurable by the buyer, even if title and risk of loss have not passed.[13] As long as the seller has title, he, too has an insurable interest in the goods. Therefore, in a destination contract where the goods are identified to the contract, while the goods are being transported, both parties have an insurable interest. The seller has an insurable interest because title does not pass from seller to buyer in a destination contract until the goods have arrived at the buyer's destination. The buyer has an insurable interest because the goods were identified to the contract.

E-Signatures

A tremendous number of contracts, especially consumer contracts, are formed online. The terms and conditions of the agreement appear online. The parties can sign online, by, for example, pasting their scanned signatures or typing their names or clicking "I accept." To what extent are e-contracts and e-signatures valid? Most types of contracts and legal documents may be formed and signed online. Notable exceptions include foreclosure notices and eviction notices, wills, and notices of cancelation of utility services.

---

[13]UCC 2-501(1).

Further, as discussion of the following laws shows, e-signatures enjoy widespread validity.

Uniform Electronic Transactions Act (UETA)

Recall from Chapter 16 that federal law mandates that signatures and contracts in electronic form have the same legal effect, validity, and enforceability as paper signatures and contracts. The Uniform Electronic Transactions Act (UETA) states that any electronic signature (which includes signatures produced by many types of technology) satisfies any law requiring a signature. Because UETA is a uniform law designed to serve as a basis for individual states to model their state statutes, states choose whether to adopt UETA and whether to modify it before adopting it. All states have adopted UETA except Illinois, New York, and Washington,[14] which have nonetheless adopted statutes recognizing electronic signatures.

Electronic Signatures in Global and National Commerce Act of 2000 (E-SIGN)

In the year 2000, in an effort to standardize the effect and application of electronic signatures, the federal government passed the Electronic Signatures in Global and National Commerce Act (called "E-SIGN"). Like UETA, E-SIGN mandates that a record, signature, or contract may not be denied legal effect or enforceability solely because it is in electronic form. The importance of E-SIGN is that, as a federal law, it is applicable to all states. Although the preemption implications of E-SIGN are complicated, in essence, the federal government gave states some latitude to enact their own legislation regarding e-signatures and to make modifications as each state saw fit. However, all states must obey the basic requirement that e-signatures on most documents and contracts have the same legal effect as traditionally written ones.

Consumer Protection Law

History of Consumer Protection Law

For centuries, the legal principle governing common law consumer transactions was *caveat emptor*, Latin for "let the buyer beware." When buyers purchased defective goods, no recovery was available in U.S. or British courts. Then, in the mid-nineteenth century, a New York pharmacist was sued for mislabeling belladonna (a poisonous substance) as dandelion extract

---

[14]National Conference of State Legislatures, Uniform Electronic Transactions Act, http://www.ncsl.org/issues-research/telecom/uniform-electronic-transactions-acts.aspx (April 15, 2012).

(a harmless medicine).[15] Overturning precedent, the New York Court of Appeals held in 1852 that the pharmacist was liable to the injured plaintiff, even though he had not sold the product directly to the plaintiff. This decision, and others that followed, paved the way for the development of greater legal protection for consumers.

It is not coincidence that the advent of consumer protection occurred in the wake of the Industrial Revolution. The Industrial Revolution brought many more product choices into the marketplace. Advertising became more prevalent, more important, and sometimes more confusing, as consumers attempted to distinguish between products. Previously, a merchant's market was limited to sales to fellow villagers. Advancements in transportation facilitated the ability to sell and purchase goods from long distances. Yet it was difficult for buyers to evaluate the reputation of a distant seller and the public opinion of local buyers no longer helped prevent merchant indiscretions and dishonesty. Eventually, increased wealth among the average consumer, coupled with an ever-increasing choice of investments, meant more people were putting more money into more investments. By the twentieth century, consumers not only invested in companies and other ventures, but also obtained credit through credit cards, mortgages, car loans, and so forth. The complexity of these transactions created opportunities for enterprises to take advantage of consumers.

Over time, all these issues led Congress to pass several consumer protection statutes. Some of these statutes created federal agencies empowered to enforce Congressional mandates by promulgating regulations, investigating alleged violations, issuing reports, and so forth. States also created similar agencies with similar purposes and powers. And of course, the courts have been responsible for interpreting these laws and regulations and for deciding disputes involving them. The result is a complex, interwoven body of consumer law.

What Does Consumer Protection Law Cover?

Consumer protection law extends to goods, services, and investments. For example, the purchase and sale of stocks, bonds, and other investments are regulated, as are the use of credit cards and the maintenance of bank accounts.[16] The purchase of houses, condominiums, time shares, and hotel rentals are all subject to numerous laws. Airline tickets, mobile phone service, insurance, and utility usage are regulated, in part, to protect consumers.

Although consumer protection law covers a vast array of consumer transactions, our focus is federal laws governing the purchase of goods. All types of goods are regulated — sales of everything from cribs, cars, cigarettes, packaged

---

[15]*Thomas v. Winchester*, 6 NY 397 (1852).
[16]For more information on investor protection, see Chapter 9, "Sale of Securities and Investor Protection."

foods, shampoo, and bicycle helmets are regulated, to name just a few examples. In part, product liability theories discussed in Chapter 20, "Product Liability and Warranties," like express and implied warranties, negligence, and strict liability, help protect consumers who purchase goods. These theories allow consumers to initiate lawsuits against the offending merchant, manufacturer, wholesaler, or other business. In addition to these bases for recovery, there are many specific federal and state administrative agency regulations specifying, for example, exactly how a particular product can (or cannot) be made, the temperature at which it should be stored and transported, where component parts can be sourced, what to include in directions on how to use the product, what to include in warnings on how not to use the product, how it can be advertised, and more. Violations of these statutes and regulations may provide other bases for consumer lawsuits, give rise to investigations conducted by government agencies, trigger agency complaints and administrative agency hearings, and potentially, result in civil fines, criminal penalties, compensation to injured consumers, and even imprisonment.

Consumer Protection Federal Statutes

Described below are three of the most important and most comprehensive federal acts pertaining to product-related consumer protection: the Federal Trade Commission Act; the Federal Food, Drug, and Cosmetic Act; and the Consumer Product Safety Commission Act. Note that each state has legislation on consumer protection issues as well.

The Federal Trade Commission Unfair and Deceptive Acts and Practices

The Federal Trade Commission Act of 1914 (FTCA) established a federal agency, called the Federal Trade Commission (FTC), and empowered it to prevent people and businesses from "using unfair methods of competition in or affecting commerce."[17] Accomplishing these goals is critical to a healthy, free market economy. Preventing unfairness and deception in the marketplace helps increase consumer confidence, minimize economic waste, and establish sound, ethical commercial practices. All this lays the groundwork for a vibrant and healthy marketplace.

The FTC is the major federal consumer protection agency. Its primary function is to help prevent fraud, deception, and unfair business practices virtually anywhere in the marketplace. Its work involves data security, deceptive advertising, identity theft, financial services and mortgage scams, price disclosures, and a broad range of representations made to consumers.

---

[17]15 USCA 45.

It accomplishes its goals through efforts on several fronts. For example, it investigates complaints lodged by consumers, consumer groups, attorneys general, competing businesses, and other government agencies. Once a complaint is made, the FTC conducts an investigation and can ask an offender to sign a voluntary compliance affidavit promising to stop the prohibited activity. The FTC also has an important educational function — it provides information to consumers and businesses regarding their rights and responsibilities. It also has regulatory, compliance, and enforcement powers. It can bring lawsuits against alleged violators, establish industry guidelines, and promulgate rules. It can impose a variety of sanctions, such as ordering a company to counteradvertise (to correct a misimpression), imposing cease-and-desist orders (requiring the company to stop doing something and not to do it in future), imposing penalties, and ordering restitution (providing restoration to injured parties).

Many different actions could constitute unfair and deceptive acts. An act could be unfair without being deceptive, be deceptive without being unfair, or be both unfair and deceptive. Even where a business is in compliance with all other federal regulations, there can still be a violation of the FTCA.

A act or practice is *unfair* if it meets this test:

1. Causes or is likely to cause substantial injury to consumers,
2. Cannot be reasonably avoided by consumers, and
3. Is not outweighed by countervailing benefits to consumers or to competition.[18]

An act or practice is *deceptive* if it meets this test:

1. It is a representation, omission, or practice that misleads or is likely to mislead a reasonable consumer; and
2. The misleading representation, omission, or practice is material.[19]

As the definition above implies, a statement blatantly lying to consumers is only one form of illegal deception. A business could be liable by implying an untruth, telling a half-truth or omitting or failing to state something, as long as it is likely to mislead a reasonable consumer and is material to the consumer.

Deceptive Advertising

Deceptive acts or practices can occur in many different settings. One common situation is advertising. Deceptive advertising includes advertising that is in

---

[18]15 USCA 45.
[19]FTC policy statement, October 14, 1983.

print, online, faxed, telemarketed, on billboards, television, radio, or even claims printed on the product itself. Deceptive advertising includes:

1. Advertising that is facially incorrect. This includes statements about the product that are empirically false as well as phony product endorsements and photographs. It also includes misstating a competitor's prices; advertising that a product is on sale when its price is actually not reduced; and artificially raising the original retail price of a product so that it appears the discount is greater than it actually is.
2. Advertising that is actually correct but appears misleading (as in the *Kraft, Inc. v. FTC* case on page 549); and
3. Bait and switch where a seller advertises a low price for a product (the bait); the product is actually not available and the seller instead offers a more expensive (or less-discounted) product (the switch).

Federal Food, Drug, and Cosmetic Act and the Food and Drug Administration

Because the food we eat, the drugs we use, and the cosmetic products we apply impact our health and well-being so much, their regulation plays a vital role in public health. Federal regulation of food and drugs dates back to 1906, and the responsible federal agency, the Food and Drug Administration (FDA), is "the oldest comprehensive consumer protection agency in the U.S. federal government."[20] One of the FDA's major responsibilities is to administer the Federal Food, Drug, and Cosmetic Act (FFDCA), passed by Congress in 1938. The FFDCA prohibits "adulterated or misbranded food, drug, device, tobacco product or cosmetic" in interstate commerce.[21] To enforce this, the FDA regulates the testing, manufacturing, labeling, packaging, shipment, distribution, and sale of foods, drugs, cosmetics, medical devices, and medical products.

Just the regulation of food alone is a huge task for the FDA. One of the FDA's primary responsibilities is to remove "adulterated food" from the U.S. food supply. *Food* is defined as "(1) articles used for food or drink for man or other animals, (2) chewing gum, and (3) articles used for components of any such article."[22] (There are a few exceptions; for example, the Department of Agriculture has authority to regulate labeling of meat, poultry, and eggs.) Food is *adulterated* if it

■ Contains a poisonous substance that renders it harmful or unsafe;
■ Is in whole or in part a "filthy, putrid or decomposed substance or if it is otherwise unfit for food";

---

[20]U.S. Food and Drug Administration About FDA, http://www.fda.gov/AboutFDA/WhatWeDo/History/default.htm.
[21]21 U.S.C.A. 331 sections a and b.
[22]21 U.S.C.A. 321(f).

Case Illustration

One of the most well-known deceptive advertising cases involved Kraft processed cheese food slices.[*] In an effort to compete against manufacturers of imitation slices, which were less expensive and less nutritious, Kraft launched an advertising campaign designed to convince consumers that Kraft singles cost more than imitation slices because they are made from five ounces of milk (as opposed to less expensive ingredients). The advertisements focused on the nutritional importance of calcium and the milk content of Kraft cheese food slices. Kraft called it the "five ounces of milk" campaign. In fact, Kraft did use five ounces of milk per slice. However, approximately 30% of the calcium from the milk was lost during the manufacturing process. In addition, "the vast majority of imitation slices sold in the United States contain 15% of the U.S. Recommended Daily Allowance of calcium per ounce, roughly the same amount contained in Kraft Singles."[†]

The FTC argued that two of Kraft's advertisements in this campaign were deceptive. In one advertisement, a woman says, "I admit it. I thought of skimping. Could you look into those big blue eyes and skimp on her? So I buy Kraft Singles. Imitation slices use hardly any milk. But Kraft has five ounces per slice. Five ounces. So her little bones get calcium they need to grow. No, she doesn't know what that big Kraft means. Good thing I do." Among other visuals is an image of milk pouring into a measuring cup until it reaches the mark for five ounces. Originally, the advertisement stated "Kraft *has* five ounces per slice," which Kraft changed to "Kraft *is made from* five ounces per slice."

Another advertisement featured a group of children assembling for a school photograph. An announcer says, "Well, a government study says that half the school kids in America don't get all the calcium recommended for growing kids. That's why Kraft Singles are important. Kraft is made from five ounces of milk per slice. So they're concentrated with calcium. Calcium

the government recommends for strong bones and healthy teeth!"

The FTC argued that, taken from the vantage point of a reasonable consumer, Kraft's claim that Singles have the same amount of calcium as five ounces of milk is deceptive. The FTC concluded that these were material claims and issued a cease-and-desist order. On appeal, Kraft argued that the FTC should "rely on extrinsic evidence rather than its own subjective analysis in all cases involving allegedly *implied* claims" and that, had it used this standard, the FTC would have found that consumers would not have believed that each Single contained the calcium value of five ounces of milk.

The U.S. Court of Appeals disagreed and held that "when confronted with claims that are implied, yet conspicuous, extrinsic evidence is unnecessary because common sense and administrative experience provide the Commission with adequate tools to make its findings. The implied claims Kraft made are reasonably clear from the face of the advertisements, and hence the Commission was not required to utilize consumer surveys in reaching its decision."

The court also held that the conclusions the FTC drew were substantially supported by evidence: "the ads emphasize visually and verbally that five ounces of milk go into a slice of Kraft Singles; this image is linked to calcium content, strongly implying that the consumer gets the calcium found in five ounces of milk. Furthermore, the Class Picture ads contained one other element reinforcing the milk equivalency claim, the phrase '5 oz. milk slice' inside the image of a glass superimposed on the Singles package." Even though the claims are literally true (they are made with five ounces of milk), the claim is impliedly deceptive.

The court also held that the claims were material. In Kraft's own surveys, "71% of respondents rated calcium content an extremely or very important factor in their decision to buy

Kraft Singles." The court also found that the claim was material because Kraft chose to run the advertisement even after an advertising agency, a television network, and a consumer group raised concerns about it. In response to the concerns, a high-level Kraft executive recommended the ad run unaltered because "the Singles business is growing for the first time in four years in large part due to the [advertisement]." The Court upheld the FTC's cease-and-desist order prohibiting Kraft from running these two advertisements and from advertising any calcium or nutritional claims, on Kraft Singles and all Kraft cheeses and cheese-related products, which are not supported by reliable scientific evidence.

---

* *Kraft, Inc. v. Federal Trade Commission*, 970 F.2d 311 (7th Cir. 1992), cert. denied, 113 S. Ct. 1254 (1993).
† *Ibid.*

- Has been prepared, packed, or stored in unsanitary conditions;
- Is the product of a diseased animal; or
- Has a container that is poisonous or may render its contents harmful.[23]

A food additive (that is, anything that is not inherent to the food product) is adulterated if it is injurious to any group in the general population.

Recognizing that it is "economically impractical to grow, harvest, or process raw products that are totally free of non-hazardous, naturally occurring, unavoidable defects,"[24] the FDA tolerates small amounts of prohibited material. It publishes the "maximum levels of natural or unavoidable defects in foods for human use that present no health hazard."[25] For example, for 100 grams of chocolate, the FDA may tolerate up to 60 or more insect fragments and one or more rodent hairs. But it is incorrect to assume that a manufacturer is in regulatory compliance if foods are below the stated defect levels. Rather, "levels represent limits at which FDA will regard the food product 'adulterated' and subject to enforcement under . . . the Food, Drug, and Cosmetics Act."[26]

In addition to prohibiting adulterating food, the FFDCA also prohibits misbranding food. Most prepared foods are required to have a nutrition facts label detailing fats, cholesterol, sodium, etc., in a specified format. Labels must also list ingredients and additives. The FDA standardizes vocabulary so that consumers and manufacturers alike understand the meaning of terms such as *organic* and *natural*.

As noted, the FDA also regulates many nonfood items that impact public health. For example, it regulates prescription and nonprescription drugs,

---

[23]This is a partial list. For the complete list of adulterated foods, see 21 U.S.C.A. 342(a) (1-7).
[24]U.S. Food and Drug Administration, Defect Levels Handbook, The Food Defect Action Levels, Introduction, http://www.fda.gov/Food/GuidanceRegulation/GuidanceDocumentsRegulatoryInformation/SanitationTransportation/ucm056174.htm#intro.
[25]U.S. Food and Drug Administration, Introduction, http://www.fda.gov/Food/GuidanceRegulation/GuidanceDocumentsRegulatoryInformation/SanitationTransportation/ucm056174.htm#intro.
[26]U.S. Food and Drug Administration, Defect Levels Handbook, The Food Defect Action Levels, Introduction, http://www.fda.gov/Food/GuidanceRegulation/GuidanceDocumentsRegulatoryInformation/SanitationTransportation/ucm056174.htm#intro.

dietary supplements, vaccines, medical devices, and even electronic products that emit radiation, such as microwave ovens and x-ray machines. As with food, these items may not be adulterated or misbranded. The FDA regulates how they are prepared and packaged, what they may be used for, and whether a prescription is required. In the case of prescription and nonprescription medication and medical devices, the FDA must issue approval before sale.

What constitutes a "medical device" is not always straightforward. In one recent case, the FDA issued warning letters to companies that manufactured candles used to remove ear wax. The user places the candle, which is a hollow tube made of fabric soaked in wax or paraffin, in one ear and sets the other end on fire. Because ear candles are used to treat headaches, colds, congestion, and the like, the FDA claimed that ear candles were medical devices, and therefore required FDA approval.[27]

FDA approval includes approval of the product itself, permitted uses, directions for use, and warnings about potential side effects. Once the FDA approves a drug or device, advertising representations about the drug, dosages, strengths, ingredients, warnings, and labels are also regulated. And even when a company adheres to all FDA regulations, it is still possible that the product is adulterated or misbranded.

The FDA has extensive powers to enable it to accomplish its many responsibilities. It is authorized to promulgate regulations, issue safety alerts and advisories, recall contaminated products, obtain search warrants, conduct inspections, seize and sample condemned products, detain shipments of imported products, obtain injunctions, maintain a registry of dangerous foods, and even instigate criminal prosecution.

Consumer Product Safety Act and the Consumer Product Safety Commission

An important part of consumer protection law involves product safety. While the FFDCA aims to ensure the safety of food, drugs, and cosmetics, consumers purchase and use many other types of products that could be hazardous in many ways. Congress passed the Consumer Product Safety Act (CPSA) in 1972 for these purposes:

1. To protect the public against unreasonable risks of injuries and deaths associated with consumer products;
2. To assist consumers in evaluating the safety of consumer products;
3. To develop uniform safety standards for consumer products and to minimize conflicting state and local regulations; and
4. To promote research and investigation into the causes and prevention of product-related deaths, illnesses, and injuries.[28]

---

[27]Manufacturers of ear candles challenged the FDA warning letter, but their complaint was dismissed because the FDA warning letters were not a "final action" and therefore could not yet be appealed. *Holistic Candlers and Consumers Association v. FDA*, 664 F.3d 940 (2012).
[28]15 U.S.C.A.

The CPSA also established the Consumer Product Safety Commission (CPSC) to administer the act. As with the FTC, the FDA, and most other administrative agencies, the CPSC accomplishes its goals through a variety of efforts on multiple fronts. It promulgates detailed regulations and issues both mandatory and voluntary standards for product safety. It collects data from consumers and from industry and conducts research on consumer product safety issues and problems. It reports on the causes and injuries resulting from everything from toys to ATVs.

The CPSC can also ban hazardous products completely, issue mandatory product recalls, or suggest voluntary product recalls. The specifics of product recalls are posted on the CPSC website to notify the public. CPSC violations can result in civil penalties, criminal penalties, imprisonment, injunctions, and seizures of dangerous products.

The Federal Trade Commission, Federal Food and Drug Administration, and Consumer Product Safety Commission are not the only federal agencies involved in assuring consumer protection. Other federal statutes target specific areas of consumer protection, such as consumer lending (Truth-in-Lending Act and Fair Credit Reporting Act) or investing in securities (Securities and Exchange Acts). Also, state agencies that operate under state statutes add to the regulatory scheme and provide additional protection to consumers.

Global Perspective

Suppose Philip, a furniture distributor in the United States, enters into an agreement to sell $10,000 worth of furniture to Vanessa, a buyer in Australia. There is no written contract, as their agreement was negotiated by phone. Is this agreement legally enforceable? Does it matter whether Vanessa is a merchant or is buying the goods for her own use? The answer to these questions depends in part on whether the agreement is governed by the Convention on Contracts for the International Sale of Goods.

The Convention on Contracts for the International Sale of Goods

The U.N. Convention on Contracts for the International Sale of Goods (CISG)[29]
Recognizing the benefits of harmonizing contract rules, the U.N. Commission on

---

[29]Excellent resource on the CISG: http://www.uncitral.org/uncitral/en/uncitral_texts/sale_goods/1980CISG.html (official website).

International Trade Law (UNICTRAL) adopted a set of conventions and rules relating to international trade in 1980. The stated purpose of this body of law is "that the adoption of uniform rules which govern contracts for the international sale of goods and take into account the different social, economic and legal systems would contribute to the removal of legal barriers in international trade and promote the development of international trade."[30] The result, the CISG, is a treaty that currently more than 75 countries have adopted, including the United States.[31]

When does the CISG apply?

For the CISG to apply to an agreement, all the following requirements must be met:

Sale of goods. The subject matter of the contract must be the sale of goods (not, for example, services, securities, or licensing of intellectual property).

Excludes consumer contracts. Unlike the UCC, which applies when selling goods to the ultimate consumer, the CISG does not apply to sales of goods bought for personal family or household use. For example, the CISG would be inapplicable to an online book order for two books placed by a U.S. consumer to an Israeli bookseller.

Signatory countries for both parties. The parties must both have their principal places of business in different countries and each of those countries have agreed to be bound to the CISG.

Opt out. Parties have not agreed to opt out of CISG provisions in their contract. Why opt out? Due to familiarity with the UCC, many U.S. attorneys prefer counseling their clients to opt out of the CISG, and insisting that the contract be governed by the UCC.

If the parties choose to opt out and if U.S. law governs the agreement (either through conflict of laws or because the parties contractually agree to the application of U.S. law), then the UCC will apply to the contract. It is therefore common that a choice funnels down to the application of either the CISG or UCC. To determine the implications of both, consider some of the most important distinctions between the two.

Major Differences Between CISG and UCC. To evaluate the implications of the application of the CISG versus the UCC, consider the differences described in Exhibit 17.5 on page 554.

---

[30]Preamble, CISG (1980).
[31]Notably, Brazil, India, South Korea, and the United Kingdom are not signatories.

Exhibit 17.5. Major Differences Between the CISG and the UCC

	Convention on Contracts for the International Sale of Goods (CISG)	Uniform Commercial Code (UCC)
When is the law applicable?	The contract must be between merchants and for the sale of goods; parties' principal places of business must be in different countries; and those countries must be signatories.	The contract must be for the sale of goods and the law of any U.S. state governs the contract.
Can parties choose which law governs their contract?	Parties may opt out of the CISG and select a governing law to apply.	Parties may choose which law applies to their contract as long as the choice is reasonable.
Under what circumstances are offers irrevocable?	An oral promise that an offer is irrevocable is permissible.	Between merchants, offers stating they are irrevocable must be in writing.
When forming a contract, on what essential elements must parties agree?	Parties must agree on subject matter, quantity, and price.	Parties must agree on quantity.
What constitutes a valid acceptance?	Offeree's response must be an exact mirror image of the offer to qualify as acceptance.	A "definite and seasonable expression of acceptance" qualifies as an acceptance, even if it contains different and/or additional terms.
Must a contract be written?	A contract need not be in writing to be valid.	Sales of goods costing $500 or more must be in writing to be enforceable.
Does seller have the right to cure a defect after the contract delivery date?	Yes, the seller has the right to remedy a failure or defect in performance if doing so is possible without unreasonable delay and without causing the buyer unreasonable inconvenience.	Yes, if the buyer rejected the tender; the seller had reasonable grounds to believe the goods would be acceptable; and the seller notifies the buyer.
If seller breaches, what remedies are available to the buyer?	Buyer may require seller to perform contractual obligations.	Unless goods are unique or have been identified to the contract, monetary damages are awarded.

With these differences in mind, would it matter (and how would it matter) whether the CISG or the UCC applied to Philip's agreement to sell $10,000 worth of furniture to Vanessa in Australia? First, determine whether this transaction qualifies for coverage under the CISG and under the UCC. Because it is a sale of goods, the UCC can apply. If Philip and Vanessa are both merchants, then the CISG could also apply. However, if Vanessa is a consumer (that is, she is buying the furniture for her own use), then the CISG does not apply.

Assume that Philip and Vanessa are both merchants and therefore both the CISG and the UCC could apply. Is the oral agreement to sell $10,000 worth of furniture to Vanessa enforceable? Under the CISG, a contract need not be in writing to be valid, so this agreement *is* enforceable. Under the UCC, sales of goods costing $500 or more must be in writing to be enforceable, so this agreement *is not* enforceable.

This example helps illustrate the importance of knowing which body of law applies to a given transaction by showing that outcomes can vary. Problems and uncertainty can be avoided with advanced planning. Businesspeople should understand which law would apply to a given transaction and negotiate a choice of law provision that prevents uncertainty and confusion.

Summary

Sales transactions can be complex legal and ethical undertakings. Major contracts should be reviewed by legal counsel to assure compliance with the Uniform Commercial Code and other relevant regulations. Companies should insist on truthful and accurate representations of the product in its advertising campaign and the truth of remarks made by the sales force to potential buyers. Websites should reflect the truth about the product with appropriate disclaimers in the terms of use. The company Compliance and Ethics Program and the Code of Ethics should reference the obligation of truthful representations of the product enforced by diligent training sessions that assures the sales force clearly understands the importance of truthfully negotiating contracts. Due diligence and risk assessment should review all significant sales transactions to assure legal and ethical compliance. Although this is a burdensome process, it will contribute to the company's mission of creating and sustaining an ethical corporate culture.

Questions for Review

1. **Article 2 coverage**

   Which of the following is a sale of goods and therefore is covered by Article 2 of the Uniform Commercial Code?

   a. Buyer purchases a Hitachi computer system, including installation. (*OneBeacon Insurance Company v. Datalink Corp.* 2009 WL 1311787.)

   b. A health center provided services before, during, and after surgery to facilitate implementation of a sling. (*Brandt*, 204 Ill.2d at 652-53, 275 Ill.Dec. 65, 792 N.E.2d at 303.)

   c. A contract for the purchase of chicken feed and advice and support from the seller regarding formulation of the feed. (*Kietzer v. Land* *O'Lakes*, N.W.2d, 2002 WL 233746 Minn. App., 2002.)

2. **Terms included in the contract**

   Aangi sends Anil a purchase order stating that only her terms apply and that in the event of a dispute between the parties in connection with the transaction, the dispute will be submitted to arbitration. Anil replies with a confirmation form that indicates that only his terms will apply and that in the event of a dispute between the parties in connection to the transaction, there will be no arbitration. Anil ships the goods, Aangi accepts them, and a dispute develops. What results and why?

   What if, instead, the purchase order had mentioned nothing about arbitration, but Anil's confirmation included a provision for arbitration. What results and why?

3. Ethical considerations

Online purchases of personal property are commonly governed by a sales contract between the online merchant and the consumer in the "terms of use" that are usually found as a "hot link" at the bottom of the seller's home page. The first sentence in the terms often reads, *"Unless you agree to the following please do not order our merchandise. Use of this site and ordering merchandise constitutes acceptance of the terms and conditions of this contract."* Research has shown that the overwhelming number of users do not read the "terms of use" and order merchandise without any idea of their contract obligations. Is it ethical for online merchants to utilize this practice even when it may be legal to do so? Explain.

4. Knockout rule

The results of the knockout rule may seem unsatisfactory because potentially, *neither* party is getting what he wants. What could an offeror do to prevent the knockout rule from "knocking out" any of his terms? What could the offeree do to prevent the knockout rule from knocking out any of his terms?

5. CISG and international considerations

Describe all the types of contracts to which the CISG does not apply and why it does not apply.

6. Article 2 coverage

Plaintiffs operated a concession foods business called Festival Foods that provided food services at carnivals and festivals. The tangible assets of the business included a truck and servicing trailer, refrigerators, freezers, roasters, chairs and tables, fountain service, signs, and lighting equipment. The defendants had several conversations with plaintiffs about purchasing the business and entered into an oral agreement to do so for $150,000. The defendants paid $10,000 immediately, took possession of the truck and equipment and promised to pay the remaining $140,000 upon receiving the proceeds of a bank loan. The defendants operated the business for the next few months but returned the equipment and refused to pay the balance because the income was not as high as they had anticipated. Does UCC Article 2 apply to this dispute? *Jannusch v. Naffziger* 379 Ill.App.3d 381, 883 N.E.2d 711 (2008).

7. Consumer product regulation

When should consumer products be regulated? Is our society overregulated and if so, by what standards should we decide when and what to regulate? When should consumer products be regulated at the federal level and when at the state level? What are the advantages and disadvantages of regulating consumer products?

8. International considerations

Over the course of about six years, Hanwha Corp., a Korean company, entered into 20 separate contracts to purchase petrochemicals from Cedar Petrochemicals, Inc. While negotiating for the twenty-first contract, Hanwha sent a bid, Cedar accepted it and included a provision for NY law to govern. Hanwha crossed out the reference to NY law, stated that Singapore law would apply and also stated that no contract would "enter into force" unless Cedar countersigned Hanwha's proposed version of the contract documents. Cedar refused to accept Hanwha's terms and e-mailed Hanwha saying that the contract would be finalized only if Hanwha accepted Cedar's original terms and asking Hanwha to sign the original version of the contract documents. Hanwha started arranging for financing, but Cedar said there was no contract unless Hanwha signed the original terms. Hanwha sued for breach of contract. Which law applies—Korean, New York, Singaporean, or CISG? Do you think the parties did form a contract? From this scenario, what lessons can you learn about good business practices? *Hanwha Corporation v. Cedar Petrochemicals, Inc.* 760 F. Supp. 2d 4246 U.S.Dist Ct (S.D.N.Y. 2011).

Further Reading

Consumer Product Safety Commission, http://www.cpsc.gov/.

Federal Trade Commission, Bureau of Consumer Protection, http://www.ftc.gov/bcp/index.shtml.

Food and Drug Administration, http://www.fda.gov/.

Petty, Ross, "International Advertising Law and Regulation: A Research Review and Agenda—the Devil Is in the Details" *Handbook of International Advertising Research* (Hong Cheng ed., Wiley/Blackwell 2014).

United Nations Commission on International Trade Law, U.N. Convention on Contracts for the International Sale of Goods (Vienna, 1980) (CISG), http://www.uncitral.org/uncitral/en/uncitral_texts/sale_goods/1980CISG.html.

CHAPTER 18

The Debtor-Creditor Relationship

Chapter Objectives

1. To understand the purpose and use of liens in a debtor-creditor relationship
2. To know and understand the roles of a surety and guarantor
3. To understand the differences between a secured creditor and an unsecured creditor
4. To understand the purpose of bankruptcy laws
5. To know the basic elements of a Chapter 7 Bankruptcy and a Chapter 11 Bankruptcy

Practical Example: Creative College Painters, Inc.*

Maxwell owns an older home that requires many repairs. For example, the exterior of Maxwell's house needs immediate attention, as the house was last repainted about 20 years ago and now shows signs of excessive peeling. After interviewing several companies, Maxwell decided to sign a contract with Creative College Painters, Inc. (College Painters). Among other provisions, the contract calls for College Painters to use a shade of green known as "Southern Green Moss." When Krista, the owner of College Painters, purchased the paint she accidentally ordered "Southern Green Mist" rather than "Southern Green Moss." The shades are similar and the difference is not discernable to the average person.

When College Painters began painting the house, Maxwell noticed that the newly applied paint was the wrong shade of green. However, he said nothing about the error until the job was complete. When Krista presented the bill to Maxwell, he told Krista that she used the wrong shade of green. Therefore, Maxwell informed Krista that he would be willing to reimburse her for the cost of the paint, but he would not pay for the cost of the labor to paint the house. Krista dismissed Maxwell's statements as being ludicrous. She stated emphatically that Maxwell should have raised his concerns much earlier and that he was responsible for paying the full price called for in the contract. Maxwell responded with a simple laugh and told Krista he would not pay one dollar more than the cost of the paint. At that point, Krista informed Maxwell that she planned to place a lien on his house and would not remove the lien until Maxwell paid the full amount called for in the contract.

Consider the following legal and ethical questions as you read the chapter.

1. Does Krista have a legal right to place a lien on Maxwell's property?

2. Will Maxwell be required to pay the amount demanded by Krista in order to secure a discharge of the lien?

3. Do you believe it was ethical of Maxwell not to mention the different shade of paint to Krista until the job was complete?

4. Do you believe it would be unethical of Krista to refuse to repaint the entire house the shade of green called for in the contract?

---

* Creative College Painters, Inc., is a fictitious company developed by the authors to demonstrate and illustrate key legal and ethical concepts, theories, practices, and strategies.

When individuals or businesses are unable to collect monies owed to them, the law provides legal rights and remedies to assist them in their collection efforts. Conversely, if individuals or businesses are unable to pay their debts, the law also provides protection and relief for them. The relationship between the party trying to collect money (the creditor) and the party responsible for paying money (the debtor) is known as the **debtor-creditor relationship**. This chapter covers the laws that address the rights and responsibilities of both debtors and creditors, and it examines ethical issues involved in resolving debtor-creditor disputes. The concept of "fairness" plays an important role in understanding the laws and the ethics of the debtor-creditor relationship.

The Debtor-Creditor Relationship

The law involving the debtor-creditor relationship comes into play when one party (the debtor) is unable to pay the full amount of its financial obligations to another party (the creditor). A **debtor** is an individual or an entity, such as a corporation, that owes money to another individual or entity. A debtor is often referred to as the borrower. A debtor may owe money to a creditor because it received services, purchased goods, or borrowed money from a creditor.

A **creditor** is an individual or an entity that is owed money by another individual or entity. A creditor is often referred to as the lender.

Types of Creditors

Generally, three types of creditors operate within the business community: secured creditors, unsecured creditors, and preferred creditors.

Secured Creditors

A **secured creditor** is an individual or an entity that has protected its monetary interest by securing a lien, holding a mortgage, or requiring some other form of collateral from the debtor as part of the lending process. For example, assume John purchases an automobile on credit. The automobile costs $40,000. Concord Finance Company (CFC) agrees to finance John's loan. As part of the finance agreement, CFC requires John to sign a promissory note, which is a promise to repay the loan according to the terms agreed upon by the debtor and the creditor. The note stipulates that John must repay the principal amount of the loan ($40,000) and interest (8 percent per annum) over the next three years. To protect its monetary interest ($40,000 plus interest), CFC requires John to pledge the title to the automobile to CFC as collateral in support of the loan.

During the third year of the loan agreement, assume John defaults on the loan. The outstanding loan balance is $10,000 at the time of the default. Because title to the automobile has been pledged to CFC as collateral,

When purchasing a car on credit, the buyer pledges the title to the automobile to the finance company, often a bank, as collateral to support the loan.

CFC may repossess and sell the automobile to satisfy the remaining $10,000 loan balance plus any accrued interest. If CFC sells the automobile for less than $10,000, John continues to owe CFC the difference. On the other hand, if CFC sells the automobile for more than $10,000, CFC must return the difference to John, less the amount of any accrued interest, penalty fees, and reasonable expenses incurred in repossessing and selling the automobile.

Unsecured Creditors

An **unsecured creditor** is an individual or an entity that has extended credit to a debtor but has not protected its monetary interests through the use of a lien, a mortgage, or other form of collateral. Use of a credit card represents one of the most common types of unsecured credit transaction. Unlike a secured creditor, which requires some form of collateral to protect its interests, an unsecured creditor relies exclusively on the creditworthiness of the debtor. While most unsecured creditors collect the amounts owed to them, debtors sometimes become insolvent (that is, unable to satisfy their financial obligations). When this occurs, an unsecured creditor's option for collecting an unsatisfied debt is to sue the debtor for breach of contract. If the court decides in favor of the unsecured creditor, the creditor may use the judgment as a basis for seizing the debtor's nonexempt assets.[1] The assets may then be sold to satisfy the debtor's financial obligations.

As discussed later in the chapter, if a debtor files for relief under the bankruptcy laws of the United States, the collection process is suspended, and unsecured creditors must stop all actions to collect debts or seize property. As a general rule, unsecured creditors receive very little, if any, money from an insolvent debtor who has filed for bankruptcy protection. As a result, unsecured creditors generally assume a high level of risk when extending credit to a debtor. Consequently, unsecured credit transactions, such as credit card transactions, usually carry a higher rate of interest than secured credit transactions.

Preferred Creditors

A **preferred creditor** is an individual or an entity that has a statutory right over other creditors to receive payment from a debtor. For example, federal law grants to the Internal Revenue Service a preferential right over other creditors to collect an outstanding tax liability from an insolvent debtor. This statutory right is based on the U.S. Federal Priority Statute, which entitles the federal government to be paid first in certain circumstances when a debtor is unable to satisfy its financial obligations.[2]

---

[1]As discussed later in the chapter, some of the debtor's assets are exempt from the collection process, such as the debtor's primary residence.
[2]31 USC § 3713(a)(1)(A).

Secured Transactions — UCC Article 9

Article 9 of the Uniform Commercial Code (UCC) provides creditors with a statutory means of protecting their monetary interests by securing transactions with debtors. A creditor secures a transaction with a debtor by completing and signing a security agreement. A **security agreement** names the parties to the transaction, states the essential terms of the agreement, and specifies the property to be used as collateral in support of a corresponding credit arrangement. Article 9 restricts the collateralized property in a security agreement to a debtor's personal property, such as inventory, stocks, bonds, and other types of personal assets. A debtor's real property (often referred to as real estate), such as an office building or warehouse, may not be used as collateral in an Article 9 security agreement.

Perfecting a Security Interest

An important part of a secured transaction under Article 9 involves the requirement of "perfecting" a security interest. **Perfecting** a security interest establishes the right of a secured party to collect a debt before other non-perfected creditors. The process of perfecting a security interest requires that the secured creditor gives notice to other creditors. This notice indicates the creditor has a priority interest in the collateralized property. Article 9 provides three ways of perfecting a security interest:

- File a public notice (financing statement) with an appropriate governmental agency;
- Take possession of the secured property; or
- Establish legal control over the secured property.

Mortgages and Real Estate

Unless a business has enough cash to fund a real estate acquisition internally, it will need to seek financing from an external source, such as a bank. To protect its monetary interests, the bank will require the business to use the purchased real estate as collateral in support of its loan. A specialized type of security agreement, known as a mortgage, is used to collateralize real estate. Like other types of loans, the bank will require the business to sign a promissory note. The bank (creditor) will also require the business (debtor) to sign a mortgage agreement. A **mortgage agreement** is a document that describes the real estate used as collateral for a loan and allows the creditor to take title and possession of the property should the debtor default on its loan. In a real estate transaction, the creditor is referred to as the **mortgagee** and the debtor the **mortgagor**.

Foreclosure occurs when a homeowner (mortgagor) is unable to make the necessary mortgage payments to the bank (mortgagee).

The mortgagor is required to give notice to others that the mortgagee has a collateralized interest in the real estate covered by the mortgage agreement. This notice helps protect the mortgagee's interests, as any future potential lenders will be aware that the property is already pledged as collateral. Typically, the mortgagor accomplishes this requirement by recording the mortgage with an appropriate governmental agency, such as a local registry of deeds. Real estate and mortgages fall outside the purview of the UCC. Rather, real estate and mortgages are governed by the common law and relevant statutes of the various states. For example, state laws specify the requirements for transferring legal title to real estate from one party to another. State law also determines the methods for creating and recording mortgages, and the means by which a mortgagee may foreclose on collateralized real estate. **Foreclosure** allows a mortgagee to assume legal ownership and take possession of collateralized real estate should a mortgagor default on its loan obligations. Once foreclosure has occurred, the mortgagee may sell the collateralized real estate and use the proceeds to help satisfy the mortgagor's loan obligations.

Sureties and Guarantors

What alternatives exist for a high credit-risk individual or business that is unable or unwilling to pledge assets as collateral in support of a loan?

In general, an individual or a business in this situation will need to fund acquisitions using internally generated resources or rely on a third-party surety or guarantor. In general, sureties and guarantors provide security for the debt of another person or entity. However, the degree of responsibility each assumes may differ. Generally, a **surety** is a third party who cosigns a promissory note or other form of credit agreement with the debtor and the creditor and assumes responsibility for paying the creditor if the debtor defaults. A **guarantor** is like a surety except a guarantor usually becomes liable only after the debtor defaults and the creditor has pursued all available legal options against the principal debtor.

For example, assume Sarah wishes to purchase a tractor for her farming business. Sarah approaches a retailer about buying a new tractor on credit. After investigating Sarah's credit history, the retailer informs Sarah that her credit rating is poor, and will not support a loan in her name alone. In this situation, Sarah will need to find a willing surety or guarantor to cosign a promissory note with her.

Garnishment

As part of the collection process, creditors will sometimes ask a court to issue a garnishment order. A **garnishment order** is a judicial decree instructing a third party, such as a debtor's employer, to turn over a portion of the debtor's property to the creditor. In the case of a debtor-employee, the order instructs the employer to withhold a certain amount of the debtor's pay each period and transfer it to the designated creditor. Because of its possible adverse effect on a debtor's ability to pay living expenses, garnishment is not a common collection technique. However, garnishment can offer a creditor a highly effective means of collecting a debt. In addition to employers, third parties include banks and other type of institutions that hold funds on behalf of others.

Liens

A **lien** provides a creditor with a legal right or interest in a debtor's property. A lien encumbers a debtor's property and usually gives the lienholder a priority interest in the property over other creditors. Although a lien does not provide a creditor with an ownership interest in a debtor's property, it gives a creditor a legal claim to the property. A lien affects the title of property and restricts the owner's use of it. The title is no longer "free and clear." Different types of liens include an artisan's lien, a mechanic's lien, and a judgment lien.

Artisan's Liens — Personal Property

An **artisan's lien** provides a creditor with a security interest in a debtor's *personal* property when the creditor performs work on the property. Typically, the creditor has incurred labor and material costs associated with the work and has a legal right to retain the property until the creditor has paid for the work performed. For example, assume Kara leaves her car at Jason's Automobile Repair Shop to have work performed on the automobile's transmission. Jason repairs the transmission and informs Kara that her car is all set. Jason tells Kara that the repair costs total $1,550 (labor costs of $450; material costs of $1,100). When Kara arrives to pick up her car, she informs Jason she has only $1,000 and this amount "will have to do." Jason responds by telling Kara that he expects to be paid the full amount of the invoice ($1,550) and that he will retain possession of the car until the bill is paid.

Does Jason have a legal right to retain Kara's car? Yes. Because Kara requested that Jason repair the transmission of her car and Jason performed the work, Jason holds an artisan's lien on Kara's automobile. In most jurisdictions, the attachment of an artisan's lien occurs by operation of law. Thus, Jason's artisan's lien on Kara's car occurred automatically when Jason took possession of the car and performed work on it. An artisan's lien allows Jason to keep the automobile in his possession until Kara pays the full amount of the bill. If the bill remains unpaid for more than 90 days, Jason has the right in most jurisdictions to sell Kara's car and use the proceeds to satisfy the debt. Jason must return any excess monies to Kara less any costs associated with selling the car. In most jurisdictions, Jason must complete the following steps before selling Kara's car:

- Provide Kara with a "notice of intent" to sell her car. Jason could satisfy this requirement by sending a letter to Kara;
- Publish the "notice of intent" in a local medium. Jason could satisfy this requirement by publishing the notice in a community newspaper; and
- Post the "notice of intent" at his place of business. Jason could satisfy this requirement by posting the notice on a bulletin board in the customer waiting area of his repair shop.

Mechanic's Lien — Real Property

A **mechanic's lien** provides a creditor with a security interest in a debtor's *real* property when a creditor performs work on the property or supplies materials. The creditor may be a general contractor, a laborer, an architect, a supplier, or other party who has provided services for or delivered materials to the debtor's real property. A mechanic's lien differs from an artisan's lien because of the nature of the property to which the lien attaches. Because a mechanic's lien attaches to real property, it is impossible for a worker or supplier to retain possession of the property. Therefore, a creditor is required to file a mechanic's lien with an appropriate state agency, such as the registry of deeds. The filing of a mechanic's lien secures an interest for the worker or supplier in the debtor's real property and notifies potential buyers and subsequent potential creditors of the security interest. *Tremont Tower Condominium, LLC v. George B.H. Macomber Company* demonstrates the use of a mechanic's lien.

Tremont Tower Condominium, LLC v. George B.H. Macomber Company, 767 N.E.2d 20 (2002)

Facts: George B. H. Macomber Company (Macomber) signed a contract with Tremont Tower Condominium, LLC (Tremont) to serve as the general contractor for a construction project. The contract called for the building of a condominium tower. Shortly after signing the contract, Macomber established a mechanic's lien on the property by recording a "notice of contract" at the local registry of deeds. The purpose of the lien was to secure payment for Macomber's labor and materials. Several months later, Tremont requested that Macomber withdraw its mechanic's lien because the lenders providing the funds for the project refused to release any funds until Macomber withdrew the lien. To allow the project to continue, Macomber complied with Tremont's request and dissolved its lien by recording a "notice of dissolution" at the registry of deeds.

Construction commenced shortly thereafter. However, a dispute between Macomber and Tremont brought construction to a halt about a year later. Macomber claimed that Tremont had failed to satisfy its financial obligations; it owed Macomber approximately $3 million. At this time, Macomber reestablished its lien on the property by recording a second notice of contract at the registry of deeds. Tremont again informed Macomber that the lenders would not release any funds until Macomber dissolved its lien. This time, Macomber refused, and Tremont filed a lawsuit asking a trial judge to discharge Macomber's lien claiming that state law precluded Macomber from recording a second lien after having dissolved its initial lien. The trail court judge ruled in favor of Tremont holding that the previous dissolution barred Macomber from establishing a second lien. Macomber appealed the trial court's decision, and the Massachusetts Supreme Judicial Court heard the case on direct appeal.

Issue: Does a voluntary dissolution of a mechanic's lien prevent a lienholder from subsequently recording another timely lien on the same property?

Holding: A voluntary dissolution of a mechanic's lien does not prevent a lienholder from later recording another lien on the same property.

From the Court's Opinion: *Mechanic's liens are created and governed purely by statute. The primary purpose of the lien is to provide security to contractors, subcontractors, laborers, and suppliers for the value of their services and goods provided for improving the owner's real estate. At the same time, the statute contains filing and notice requirements to protect the owner and others with an interest in the property. We look then to the statutory provisions concerning the creation, perfection, and enforcement of a lien to determine whether Macomber has met the statutory prerequisites for a valid and enforceable lien.*

A person who has entered into a written contract with an owner of real property for improvements to that property, or for the furnishing of equipment, appliances, or tools for such improvements, shall have a lien upon such real property to secure the payment of all labor, including construction management and general contractor services, and material or rental equipment, appliances, or tools which shall be furnished by virtue of said contract. In order to claim such a lien, the contractor must record a notice of contract in the registry of deeds for the county in which the property is located. The statute sets a deadline for the recording of such a notice of contract, and calculates that deadline according to the way that the contract is either terminated or completed. If the parties to the contract have filed a notice of substantial completion (signifying the parties' agreement that the work under the written contract is sufficiently complete so that it can be occupied or utilized for its intended use, the contractor must file the notice of contract no later than sixty days after the filing of the notice of substantial completion. If the contract has been terminated and the owner has filed a notice of termination, the contractor must file the notice of contract no later than ninety days after the filing of the notice of termination. Or, in the absence of any such notice of substantial completion or notice of termination, the deadline for filing a notice of contract is ninety days after the contractor last performed or furnished labor or materials or both labor and materials. A notice of contract may be recorded at any time after execution of the written contract, as long as it is recorded before the applicable deadline.

The recording of the notice of contract establishes the priority of the mechanic's lien. As a general matter, the lien takes priority over all other later-recorded encumbrances on the property. Thus, once filed, the notice of contract sets the date for the lien's priority.

Here, there is no dispute that Macomber filed both its notices of contract within the time frame set. Macomber relies on the literal language of that section, which allows such a notice to be filed at any time, and contains no prohibition on the filing of subsequent or duplicate notices.

The issue, however, centers on Macomber's filing of a notice voluntarily dissolving its lien after its first notice of contract was recorded. Macomber contends that what was dissolved by that notice was the originally filed notice of contract, i.e., that Macomber forfeited the priority position it had acquired by that first filing, but did not extinguish the underlying right to a lien. The right to a mechanic's lien still existed, and could be perfected and enforced by later filings (as long as they were timely), but the priority of that lien would only be established as of the later date when the second notice of contract was recorded. According to Macomber, the lien itself is only created on the filing of the notice of contract, and therefore a notice dissolving that lien dissolves only the precise lien that was created by that filing. Dissolving that lien does not forfeit the right to another lien being established sometime in the future.

Tremont Tower argues, however, that a lien is created by the mere signing of the construction contract, and is thus in existence prior to any recording of the notice of contract. Recording the notice of contract only establishes the priority of an already existing lien. Thus, it argues, a notice dissolving the lien permanently dissolves the underlying lien itself, and not just its priority position. As such, Tremont Tower contends, there was no lien remaining after Macomber's notice of dissolution was filed, and thus no basis for filing the second notice of contract to prioritize a nonexistent lien. The judge in the Superior Court agreed with Tremont Tower that the lien came into being at the time the underlying construction contract was signed, not at the time the notice of contract was filed, and that a notice of dissolution of lien therefore dissolved the entirety of the lien rights that had been created by the construction contract.

We disagree. Although the wording of the statute is not perfectly clear on this point, it tends to support Macomber's position. It does not appear that any form of "lien" actually exists prior to recording a notice of contract. The contractor has a statutory right to such a lien, but the lien itself does not exist until the contractor does something to assert that right.

* * *

---

* Statutory references omitted.

Judgment Lien

A **judgment lien** attaches to the property of the party who loses a lawsuit. The losing party is often referred to as the judgment debtor and the winning party as the judgment creditor. A judgment lien gives the judgment creditor a legal interest in the judgment debtor's property, which helps the judgment creditor collect the money awarded by the court. In most states, the judgment creditor must record the judgment by filing it with the appropriate state agency in order to create a judgment lien against the judgment debtor's real or personal property.

To generate the cash necessary to pay the award given to the judgment creditor, the court usually orders the debtor's property to which the lien has been attached to be sold by a court official. The proceeds of the sale are then used to pay the award. If any cash remains, the debtor receive the difference after applicable court costs have been paid. For example, assume Allison sues Thomas for breach of contract and the court awards Allison $50,000 in damages. To secure her interest in Thomas's property, Allison will first record her judgment by filing it with the appropriate state agency, which allows her to attach a judgment lien against Thomas's nonexempt property. Next, the court will order that Thomas's non-exempt property be sold to satisfy Allison's judgment.

Exempt Property

In general, a debtor has a legal right to keep certain kinds of property from the grasps of creditors. For example, most states allow a debtor to protect the investment in his home and household items up to a certain value under what is known as a homestead exemption. Thus, while a creditor may attach a lien to a debtor's home, the debtor does not have a right to attach the entire value of the property. For example, assume Erik owes Jonathan $600,000. If Erik's home is worth $500,000 and the homestead law provides that homeowners may "exempt" $150,000 from creditors. Jonathan's

---

Exhibit 18.1. Illustration of Personal Property Exempt from Creditors

The following personal property items are exempt from creditors subject to the value limitations noted below:

An individual is entitled to an exemption in property not to exceed an aggregate value of $3,000 chosen by the individual from the following categories of property:

- Household goods and clothing reasonably necessary for one household;
- Books and musical instruments if held for personal use; and
- Family portraits and heirlooms of particular sentimental value.

Additionally, an individual is entitled to an exemption of jewelry, not exceeding $1,000 in aggregate value, if held for the personal use of the individual or a dependent. An individual is entitled to an exemption, not exceeding $2,800 in aggregate value, of implements, professional books, and tools of the trade.

Source: Alaska Statutes, Chapter 09.38, § 09.38.020: Exemptions of personal property subject to value limitations.

lien is not for $500,000, but $350,000. Exhibit 18.1 on page 569 provides an illustration of exempt personal property using the state of Alaska as an example.

Lien Discharge

Liens may be discharged in several ways. If a debtor satisfies an obligation by making payment in full, the lien is discharged. When this occurs, the debtor should receive written notice from the creditor stating that the amount has been paid in full. Depending on the type of lien involved, the debtor may need the creditor's assistance to discharge the lien. If a mechanic's lien is involved, the debtor should ask the creditor to arrange with the appropriate state agency, such as the registry of deeds, to remove the lien. Liens may also be discharged through the expiration of time based on state statutes. A court may also discharge a lien through a judicial process.

While the discharge of a lien may seem to be the final step in a debtor-creditor relationship, ethical issues involving the relationship should also be considered. The following Manager's Compliance and Ethics Meeting illustration demonstrates ethical decision making implicit in the debtor-creditor relationship.

Manager's Compliance and Ethics Meeting

Is It Ethical to Violate the Terms of a Debtor/Creditor Agreement If No One Is Financially Harmed?

Quick Rental, Inc., rents limousines to customers for graduations, weddings, anniversaries, and other celebratory events. Quick Rental leases its 800-vehicle fleet from Limo Financial Associates. The terms of the lease agreement between Quick Rental and Limo Financial Associates prohibit the limousines from being rented to Quick Rental's customers for periods exceeding one week or to commercial customers who intend to sub-lease the limousines. The lease between Quick Rental and Limo Financial Associates is secured by a promissory note that incorporates the terms of the lease and pledges Quick Rental's business assets as collateral in the event of a default on its monthly payments. Quick Rental operates in all six New England states and promotes itself as an "ethical and responsible rental company." It has an ethics and compliance officer, and its code of ethics is published on its website.

A Quick Rental salesperson was approached by a customer (Robert's Rentals) who wanted to lease 20 limousines for two months and sublease them to its customers. Robert's Rentals agreed to pay Quick Rental the rental fee for all 20 limousines in advance. When the salesperson approached his supervisor with the proposal, he was informed to go forward with the transaction and report it as separate one-week rentals to a noncommercial customer. Both the supervisor and the salesperson were aware of the prohibition against renting the limousines for more than one week or renting them to commercial customers. When the CEO of Quick Rental discovered this unusual arrangement, she was concerned about its ethics.

The CEO knows that the agreement creates a unique debtor-creditor relationship secured by a promissory note that pledges business assets as collateral. She is concerned about the consequences of Limo Financial Associates discovering the proposed lease agreement violation. She has asked the compliance and ethics officer to call a manager's meeting to discuss the ethics of the proposed deal. The CEO wants to know if Quick Rental should inform Limo Financial Associates about the proposed rental agreement before it is signed.

A few classical ethical principles follow:

W. D. Ross's prima facie duty of fidelity relates to "promise keeping" and calls for an ethical duty to adhere to contractual terms. The lease and promissory note provisions were the basis of the bargain between Quick Rental and Limo Financial Associates. Ross's duty of fidelity would argue that Quick Rental has a moral obligation to perform in accordance with the terms of the lease contract. However, Ross does not require an absolute moral obligation to perform a contract regardless of the consequence. Ross stated *"when the consequences of fulfilling a promise would be so disastrous to others . . . we judge it right not to do so."* That situation does not

apply in this case because receiving the full payment in advance from Robert's Rentals for renting the 20 limousines from Quick Rental, Inc. does not ethically justify breaching the terms of the contract that Quick Rental has with Limo Financial Associates. Although this is a lucrative transaction, the absence of it would not create a "disastrous" situation that would otherwise justify not fulfilling its promise to Limo Financial.

Kant's categorical imperative of "truth telling" states *"I ought never to act except in such a way that I can also will that my maxim should become a universal law."* In this case, the proposal to lease 20 limousines to a commercial company (Robert's Rentals) for two months would violate the terms of the lease Quick Rental has with Limo Financial Associates as well as Kant's duty to universalize our conduct as found in his categorical imperative. For instance, if everyone was allowed to break an agreement, our personal integrity would be seriously compromised with adverse consequences to the business environment. If this were to become a universal business practice, everyone would be looking for ways to breach a contract for his or her own advantage.

Conclusion. The compliance and ethics officer and the members of Quick Rental's management team are committed to maintaining an ethical corporate culture; therefore, the proposed transaction should not be pursued.

Federal Bankruptcy Laws

Article I, Section 8, of the U.S. Constitution authorizes Congress to enact uniform bankruptcy laws. Section 8 follows:

> The Congress shall have the power . . . to establish . . . uniform laws on the subject of bankruptcies throughout the United States.

Bankruptcy law is exclusively federal law. The current set of "uniform laws on the subject of bankruptcies" was enacted by Congress in 1978. This body of law is referred to as the **Bankruptcy Code of 1978**, which is codified as Title 11 of the United States Code.

The U.S. Constitution gives Congress exclusive jurisdiction over all bankruptcy cases in the United States.

Purpose of Bankruptcy Laws

By giving the federal government exclusive jurisdiction over all bankruptcy cases, the framers of the U.S. Constitution intended to give individuals (and businesses) a "second chance" in resolving their debts in a uniform manner. Also, in order to facilitate freedom of movement among the states and encourage commercial development throughout the United States, the framers believed that the handling of bankruptcy cases could not be left to the individual states.

Bankruptcy Court

Because of the goal to provide a uniform set of laws for all bankruptcy cases, the U.S. Congress established federal **bankruptcy courts**. And, to provide reasonable access to the federal bankruptcy court system, Congress enacted legislation to ensure that each judicial district in the United States has at least one bankruptcy court. Today, there are 90 bankruptcy districts in the United States.

Like any other federal court, the judge hearing a bankruptcy case has the power to apply the law to a given set of facts. However, unlike the proceedings in most federal courts, bankruptcy proceedings usually occur outside the courtroom and not in the presence of the sitting judge. This unusual arrangement results from the nature of a bankruptcy proceeding, which is mostly administrative in form and substance. If a judge does not handle the actual proceedings of a bankruptcy case, who does? Once again, this is where a bankruptcy case deviates from most other types of cases. A trustee is appointed by the court to conduct nearly all of the administrative processes associated with a bankruptcy case.

How do debtors and creditors work with bankruptcy judges and bankruptcy trustees? To the surprise of most people unfamiliar with the bankruptcy process, debtors rarely appear before a bankruptcy judge. In fact, debtors almost never walk into a federal bankruptcy courtroom. Most of the time debtors deal exclusively with a bankruptcy trustee. The same process holds true for creditors. In most cases, there is only one required meeting between the debtor and the creditor. This required meeting is often referred to as a Section 341 meeting. Not surprisingly, this meeting takes its name from the bankruptcy code section that requires debtors to attend at least one meeting with creditors, which affords creditors the opportunity to ask debtors questions about their income, assets, and other financial holdings. A Section 341 meeting usually lasts less than five minutes, and creditors rarely attend the meeting.

Bankruptcy Discharge

Giving people a second chance through the bankruptcy process is accomplished through the concept of a "discharge." A **bankruptcy discharge** brings finality to a person's debt-related problems. A discharge in federal bankruptcy court provides individuals or businesses with a "clean slate" and prevents creditors from harassing debtors. Think of a discharge as a process that not only relieves debtors of personal liability, it also serves to protect debtors from any future actions by creditors. For example, once a bankruptcy court has discharged a particular debt, creditors are prevented from trying to collect the debt in the future.

The discharge process is a remarkably simple process. Unless creditors object to a discharge and initiate litigation, a discharge occurs through an automatic process. Once the time period for an objection has lapsed, the court simply mails a copy of the discharge order to all creditors. At this point, the discharge process terminates. What this means for debtors and creditors is significant. For the debtor, it means financial freedom from previous debts. For the creditor, it usually means that the creditor will never collect the amount of the discharged debt. Creditors may not harass debtors in any way. If a creditor attempts to collect a discharged debt, serious legal consequences follow. For example, a bankruptcy court has the power to hold a misbehaving creditor in contempt of court. A **contempt order** could result in fines being paid by creditors who attempt to collect a debt after it has been discharged.

Types of Bankruptcy

The Bankruptcy Code provides six types of bankruptcies. Exhibit 18.2 on page 574 provides a summary of each type. The two most commonly used by individuals and businesses are Chapter 7 Liquidations and Chapter 11 Reorganizations. A detailed discussion of these two types of bankruptcies follows the summary provided in Exhibit 18.2.

Exhibit 18.2. Types of Bankruptcies	
Type of Bankruptcy	**Description**
Chapter 7 Liquidation	Applies to individuals, partnerships, corporations, and other forms of business entities. A court-appointed trustee assumes responsibility for the debtor's assets and obligations. The trustee liquidates the debtor's estate (subject to the rights of secured creditors and the rights of the debtor to retain exempt assets) and distributes the proceeds to creditors.
Chapter 9 Adjustment of Debts of a Municipality	Applies to municipalities, such as cities, towns, and counties. A court appointed trustee works with the debtor and the creditors to allow the debtor to continue operations under a court-approved plan. The plan usually calls for creditors to be repaid a reduced amount of the original obligation.
Chapter 11 Reorganization	Applies to commercial enterprises, such as corporations and limited liability companies. Like a Chapter 9 Adjustment, a court-appointed trustee works with the debtor and the creditors to allow the debtor to continue operations under a court-approved plan. The plan usually calls for creditors to be repaid a reduced amount of the original obligation.
Chapter 12 Adjustment of Debts of a Family Farmer or Fisherman with Regular Annual Income	Applies to family farmers and fishermen who have a regular income. A court-appointed trustee works with the debtor and the creditors to develop a plan to repay creditors over a period of time, usually 3 to 5 years.
Chapter 13 Adjustments of Debts of an Individual with Regular Income	Applies to individuals who have a regular income. Like a Chapter 12 Adjustment, a court-appointed trustee works with the debtor and the creditors to develop a plan to repay creditors over a period of time, usually 3 to 5 years.
Chapter 15 Ancillary and Other Cross-Border Cases	Applies to cross-border bankruptcy cases, usually involving international parties and a debtor who is subject to the laws of the United States.

Chapter 7 Liquidation

A Chapter 7 Liquidation requires a court-appointed trustee to identify and sell the assets of the debtor subject to the rights of secured creditors and the rights of the debtor to retain exempt assets. The bankruptcy code allows the debtor to retain certain assets, such as the debtor's home. These assets are referred to as **exempt assets.**

Eligibility
Who is eligible to file a Chapter 7 bankruptcy petition? The bankruptcy code provides that individuals, partnerships, corporations, and other types of business entities are eligible to file a Chapter 7 petition. Other than the "means test" described below, there are no limits imposed on candidates interested in filing for Chapter 7 relief. For example, Chapter 7 is available regardless of the amount of debt owed and whether the debtor is solvent or insolvent.

An Exception
An exception to eligibility for a Chapter 7 Liquidation was enacted by Congress in 2005. The exception represents an amendment to the bankruptcy code and

A Chapter 7 Liquidation requires the court-appointed trustee to sell the debtor's non-exempt assets.

is included in the **Bankruptcy Abuse Prevention and Consumer Protection Act**. This law requires all applicants to undergo a "means test" to determine if the debtor's income exceeds the threshold limits of the act. If the debtor's income exceeds the threshold limit, the debtor may not be eligible for a Chapter 7 Liquidation bankruptcy.

Property, Income, and Creditors

As part of the process of determining the debtor's financial condition, the trustee requires debtors to report the following types of information:

■ A detailed list of all creditors, including information about the nature of the debt, the amount owed, the property acquired by the debt, and whether collateral is associated with the debt;

■ A statement about the source and amounts of income earned by the debtor;

■ A detailed list of all of the debtor's property (real, tangible, and intangible); and

■ A detailed accounting of the debtor's monthly living expenses, such as food, clothing, shelter, transportation, and so forth.

Payment and Discharge

After the trustee has accounted for all exempt property and property subject to a security interest or lien, the trustee sells the remaining assets and distributes the cash among the unsecured creditors. In most cases, the unsecured creditors receive much less than the original amount of the debt. For example, credit card companies generally fall into the category of unsecured creditors and may receive much less than the outstanding balance due. In many Chapter 7 Liquidations, most of the assets of the debtor are either exempt or subject to a security interest or lien. The common term used for these kinds of bankruptcies is "no asset cases." As discussed earlier, after the trustee has distributed the property to the unsecured creditors, the debtor receives a discharge from the court relieving the debtor from personal liability for all discharged debts.

Chapter 11 Reorganization

A Chapter 11 Reorganization is typically used by business entities, including corporations, limited liability companies, and limited liability partnerships. Unlike a Chapter 7 Liquidation, which requires the sale of assets and provides the debtor with a fresh start, a Chapter 11 Reorganization allows the debtor to stay in business without the need to liquidate some or all of its assets. A Chapter 11 Reorganization calls for the preparation of a reorganization plan aimed at reducing the level of debt carried by the debtor while at the same time determining a fair and appropriate amount to pay creditors. The court must approve the plan. Creditors have a right to review the plan and offer comments. However, creditors do not have the right to approve or reject the plan. Only the court has the authority to approve or disapprove the reorganization plan.

Restructuring Business Operations

A court-approved plan allows debtors to discharge part of their debt and terminate existing contracts and leases. Allowing debtors to terminate existing contracts and leases affords debtors the opportunity to reshape and rescale existing business operations including executive salaries and workers' wages.

A Chapter 11 Reorganization allows a company to stay in business while working with creditors to restructure its debts.

Consequently, after a Chapter 11 Reorganization has occurred, a business typically is smaller, leaner, and more focused.

Disclosure Statement

Like a Chapter 7 Liquidation, the debtor in a Chapter 11 Reorganization must provide certain kinds of information to the trustee, including:

- A detailed listing of all assets and liabilities;
- A detailed listing of income and expenses;
- A detailed listing of all contracts and leases; and
- A statement of financial affairs.

The information collected from the debtor is included in a **disclosure statement**. The disclosure statement is presented to all creditors to allow them the opportunity to make an informed judgment about the plan of reorganization. After the creditors have responded to the disclosure statement, the court holds a confirmation hearing. Once the hearing has been held, the court decides whether to confirm or reject the plan of reorganization.

The Trustee

The court-appointed trustee assumes responsibility for monitoring the progress of the reorganization plan. The trustee supervises the administration of the plan. As part of the administrative process, the trustee receives regular information from the debtor and meets periodically with the creditors. During meetings with the debtor, creditors are allowed to ask the debtor questions under oath about the debtor's operations and other aspects associated with the debtor's business.

Creditors' Committee

The trustee appoints the membership of a creditors' committee. The committee is composed mostly of unsecured creditors. The committee plays a major role in the formulation of the plan, the administration of the plan, and the reporting associated with the plan. The committee has the right to investigate the conduct of the debtor. Importantly, the committee has the right to hire its own professionals, such as accountants, attorneys, and business analysts to ensure that the debtor is complying with the terms of the reorganization plan.

> **An Ethical Insight: Utilitarianism and Chapter 11 Bankruptcy Reorganization**
>
> Utilitarianism is a consequential ethical theory that justifies moral decisions that benefit the "greater good for the greater number". This ethical theory could be applied to justify a Chapter 11 bankruptcy reorganization that allows an insolvent company to remain in business under a court approved plan among the creditors, who agree to take a lesser amount than what they are due. The end result often benefits not only the creditors and the insolvent company but also the greater number of the company's stakeholders, including its employees, customers, and society. Classic examples are some of the major airline companies continuing in business under a Chapter 11 Reorganization plan.

Fraudulent Transfers

In general, a **fraudulent transfer** is a transfer of property made with the intent to defraud creditors by placing the transferred property beyond the reach of creditors. Establishing the *intent to defraud* on the part of a debtor is critical to ascertaining whether a particular transfer is fraudulent or not. Because it is often difficult to determine whether a debtor subjectively intended to defraud a creditor, courts often examine objective facts and circumstances surrounding a particular transfer. For example, a secretive transfer made by a debtor to a relative for nothing in exchange may be evidence of the intent to defraud a creditor. The transfer of real property without recording the transfer publicly at the registry of deeds may also serve as evidence of the intent to defraud creditors. Further, debtors who transfer all of their assets to another party in exchange for minimal consideration provide creditors with strong evidence of the intent to defraud.

Most state legislatures have adopted some version of the Uniform Fraudulent Transfer Act (UFTA), which creditors must follow when asking a court to set aside an alleged fraudulent transfer. Exhibit 18.3 presents the factors to be considered under the UFTA to determine if a transfer is fraudulent.

The In-Depth Ethical Case Analysis on page 579 explores some of the legal and ethical issues associated with fraudulent transfers. As you read the case, consider not only the legal aspects of the UFTA but also the ethical ramifications of a debtor purposefully placing property outside the reach of a creditor.

Exhibit 18.3. Fraudulent Transfer Factors

1. A transfer made by a debtor is fraudulent if the debtor made the transfer:
   - With *actual intent* to hinder, delay, or defraud a creditor, or
   - Without receiving a reasonably equivalent value in exchange for the transfer, and the debtor was engaged or was about to engage in a business or a transaction for which the remaining assets of the debtor were unreasonably small in relation to the business or transaction.
2. In determining the existence of *actual intent*, consideration may be given to whether:
   - The transfer was to an insider;
   - The debtor retained possession or control of the property transferred after the transfer;
   - The transfer was disclosed or concealed;
   - Before the transfer was made, the debtor had been sued or threatened with a lawsuit; or
   - The value of the consideration received by the debtor was reasonably equivalent to the value of the asset transferred.

Source: Uniform Fraudulent Transfer Act, Section 4 (Transfers Fraudulent as to Present and Future Creditors).

In-Depth Ethical Case Analysis

ACLI Government Securities, Inc. v. Daniel Rhoades and Nora Rhoades,
653 F. Supp 1388 (1987)

Facts

The plaintiff, ACLI Government Securities, Inc. (AGS) was awarded approximately $1.5 million by a jury verdict in an earlier lawsuit involving Daniel Rhoades (Daniel), a defendant in the case at hand. One day before the court entered the $1.5 million judgment against Daniel, he conveyed his interest in a parcel of real property to his sister Nora Rhoades (Nora) for $1.00 and unspecified "other good consideration." The property, owed by Daniel and Nora as tenants in common, was worth approximately $325,000 at the time of the conveyance. In addition to their commonly owned property, Daniel and Nora were partners in a law firm.

After Daniel failed to pay the $1.5 million judgment, AGS brought a lawsuit against Daniel and Nora Rhoades alleging that the property conveyance was a fraudulent transfer. By asking the court to declare the transfer fraudulent, AGS sought to have the property available to satisfy part of its $1.5 million judgment against Daniel.

AGS alleged that the property conveyance was fraudulent because it occurred between family members without Daniel receiving a reasonably equivalent value from his sister Nora in exchange for his transferred interest in the property. AGS also alleged that the conveyance rendered Daniel insolvent, thus providing further evidence of his intent to defraud AGS. In response, Daniel asserted that the conveyance was a valid (nonfraudulent) transfer because it was supported by "other good consideration" based on a debt owed by him to his sister Nora. Daniel also asserted that the conveyance did not render him insolvent.

Issue

Is the conveyance of real property between related parties for less than fair market value one day before a $1.5 million court ordered judgment a fraudulent transfer under New York law?

Discussion

In reviewing the evidence presented at trial, the court determined that the defendants (Daniel and Nora) failed to establish the existence of any debt owed by Daniel to Nora. Therefore, the court found that the transfer was not supported by "other good consideration." Furthermore, the court found the evidence presented at trial by Daniel allegedly showing his "solvency" at the time of the transfer to be unconvincing.

The court stated that a plaintiff, such as AGS, must present evidence of *actual intent* on the part of the defendant (Daniel) to defraud the plaintiff. The court acknowledged that by its very nature direct proof of fraudulent intent is rare. Consequently, actual intent is usually established by examining the facts and circumstances surrounding an alleged fraudulent transfer. The court enumerated the following factors from which actual intent to defraud another party may be inferred:

1. A close relationship among the parties to the transaction;

2. Secrecy and haste of the sale;

3. Inadequacy of consideration; and

4. The transferor's knowledge of the creditor's claim and his own inability to pay it.

In reviewing these factors, the court observed that the case at hand possessed all of the classic forms of evidence of actual intent to defraud another party. The court noted that the defendants were not only brother and sister, but they were also partners in a family law firm. Furthermore, the conveyance was made in secret, and it occurred just one day before the court entered a $1.5 million judgment against Daniel.

Conclusion

The court concluded that Daniel fraudulently transferred his interest in the conveyed property to his sister Nora.

Ethical Questions

1. Was it ethical for Daniel to transfer to his sister Nora (one day before the court entered a $1.5 million judgment against him) his share of the property interest for $1.00 and unspecified "other good consideration" when the court determined the so-called *other good consideration* to be nonexistent?

2. Was it ethical for Daniel and Nora to assert that a debt existed between them in support of the property transfer when in fact they were unable to provide any credible evidence of the debt?

Ethical Theory Analysis

In the case at hand, the judgment awarded by the court amounted to $1.5 million. The transfer of the real estate, valued at $325,000, one day before the judgment was rendered by the court could be construed as an unethical act because it was made to avoid paying the just debt owed to the plaintiff (AGS).

Anticipating insolvency, a debtor may seek to transfer his assets to family members and friends before falling into what is known as a "technical state" of insolvency. Once a debtor is technically insolvent (unable to pay his debts when they become due), it is considered a *fraud on creditors* and an illegal and unethical act to transfer any assets to avoid paying bona fide creditors. Indeed, some financial advisors recommend to their clients that they transfer their assets prior to the state of technical insolvency. This type of

advice remains ethically problematic and seems to depend upon the extent of avoiding the payment of a just debt.

W. D. Ross's *prima facie duty to prevent harm* would be violated when a debtor, who knows insolvency is imminent, takes steps to transfer assets beyond the reach of creditors. In this case, Ross's ***prima facie duty of fidelity*** would find a contractual obligation to pay the debt based on the jury's verdict. Daniel is now a debtor and legally and ethically obligated to liquidate his assets to pay this just debt. A fraudulent conveyance, as in this case, should be set aside by a court in order for the debtor's assets to be liquidated under court supervision to satisfy the judgment rendered.

Aristotle's virtue ethics found justice to be the most important virtue as it seeks to give to others what they are rightfully due. Transferring an asset worth $350,000 the day before a judgment is ordered violates the virtue of justice and is an unethical act.

"Credible evidence" of a debt is commonly found in a promissory note, a mortgage, a lease, or other formal document signed by the debtor and the creditor. These formal documents are dated and generally indicate, among other promises, a formal promise by the debtor to pay the debt according to a schedule of payments. Without the evidence of a written document, the claim of money due is suspicious because most people are aware of the need to document a debtor/creditor relationship, even if a sister and a brother are involved. Without documentation of a substantial debt, it becomes untenable to assume there was "fair consideration in exchange for the conveyance of an interest in property." One could argue that absent the presence of a formal written document, there is a strong suspicion of unethical conduct by both parties, which may be the situation in the case at hand.

Kant's categorical imperative to "*Act in such a way that you treat humanity, whether in your own person or in the person of another, always at the same time as an end and never simply* *as a means*" is germane to the case at hand. The act of transferring property should be moral or ethical in itself and not a means to accomplish an ulterior motive such as to avoid paying a just debt. Daniel's transfer of his share in the real property for $1.00 and other "unspecified good consideration" to his sister the day before the final verdict was clearly a means to avoid paying a just debt and violated Kant's categorical imperative.

Global Perspective

International Debtor-Creditor Issues

Optimally, in a sale of goods transaction, the seller wishes to be paid before releasing goods and the buyer wishes not to pay until receiving the goods. From the seller's perspective, stakes are high if the transaction is international; merchants selling goods overseas assume more risk than merchants selling goods domestically. Why? First, transportation costs are usually higher than for domestic sales. If the buyer refuses delivery due to a change of mind or insolvency, the seller has already incurred shipping costs, with perhaps more shipping and insurance expenditures needed to recover or redirect the goods to a substitute buyer. Second, it is more difficult for a seller to evaluate the creditworthiness of an overseas buyer.

Financial accounting conventions might not conform to U.S. rules; financial information could be in a foreign language; and/or the seller might have limited access to credit reports. Last, if the buyer refuses to pay, pursuing a legal claim can be more difficult. Jurisdictional questions are more complex in an international setting, and enforcing legal rights in a foreign court system can be slow and uncertain. Even when a judgment against a buyer can be obtained, it can be more difficult to enforce than a U.S. judgment. It can also be more expensive, involving travel costs and the need to retain overseas legal counsel.

Payment Options in International Sale of Goods Contracts

There are several payment options possible in international transactions, some of which help minimize the risks and expense associated with nonpayment. Payment in full in advance and payment after goods are delivered are, of course, options. To gain an advantage over competitors, a seller could offer an open account, meaning the buyer is extended credit for a certain period of time (typically 30, 60, or 90 days after delivery). A less risky option is the use of a correspondent bank. Commercial banks sometimes have correspondent banks in other countries. A **correspondent bank** is a bank that operates as an agent for another bank. For example, assume a U.S. buyer is a customer of ABC Bank in New York. If ABC has a correspondent bank in London, then ABC can draw money from the customer's account and transfer the money to the correspondent bank in London. Then the correspondent bank will forward the funds to the British seller.

Letters of Credit

A well-established vehicle for securing payment in international sales of goods transactions is the letter of credit. A **letter of credit** is a bank document that guarantees that the bank (called the *issuing bank*) will pay a stated amount if certain conditions are met within a set period of time. This enables the seller to look to the issuing bank, instead of the buyer, for payment. Letters of credit have been used for centuries to guarantee payment in international trade. Today, they are widely viewed as a secure, convenient, and flexible way to ensure prompt payment.

One reason the letter of credit system has endured so long and is so popular around the world is that it serves many different functions. First, it operates as a payment instrument, enabling the seller to collect funds from the buyer through the transfer of the documents. Second, it operates as a guarantee instrument because it guarantees the buyer will perform payment obligations. Third, it operates as a finance instrument because the letter of credit itself can be transferred from one holder to another or be pledged as collateral.

Letter of Credit Process

Although there is some variation, an international sales contract invoking use of a letter of credit fundamentally involves the following steps:

1. The buyer and seller execute a contract for the sale of goods. The contract provides that to finance the transaction, the buyer will obtain a letter of credit naming the seller as beneficiary. The buyer's receipt of the goods is conditional on this obligation. The contract also specifies the exact circumstances under which funds will be released to the seller. This could include, for example, timing of shipment, shipping method, insurance coverage, product description and quantity, and certificate of inspection.

2. The buyer obtains a letter of credit from the issuing bank, usually in the same country as the buyer. This arrangement is separate and independent of the sales contract between the buyer and the seller. The bank agrees to issue a letter of credit in favor of the seller for the amount of the cost of the goods. The bank also promises to release funds upon receipt of the documents required by the sales contract. In return, the buyer promises to reimburse the issuing bank. The issuing bank charges a fee, based on a percentage of the transaction, for the service of issuing a letter of credit.

3. The issuing bank forwards the letter of credit to a nominated bank that is located in the seller's country. This bank is called a nominated bank because it has been "nominated" by the issuing bank to honor the documents required by the sales contract.

4. The nominated bank forwards the letter of credit to the seller.

5. The seller ships goods. Having received the letter of credit, the seller can now ship the goods with confidence, knowing payment is assured. Although letters of credit can be revocable or irrevocable, when used in international trade, they are universally irrevocable — that is, they can only be canceled or modified with the consent of both the seller/beneficiary and the issuing bank. This provides critical security to the seller. If instead, the issuing bank or buyer could revoke the letter of credit, then the seller would not want to deliver the goods to the carrier because there would be no assurance of payment.

6. The seller assembles the documents required by the letter of credit and delivers them to the nominated bank. The letter of credit will require those documents that the buyer instructed the issuing bank to include. Typically, letters of credit require the following documents:

- **A clean, negotiable bill of lading.** When the seller delivers the goods to the carrier for shipment, the carrier gives the seller a bill of lading. A *bill of lading* acknowledges that goods were delivered to the carrier. It describes the goods, names the carrier, and is signed by the carrier (or agent). Sometimes sales contracts require that the bill of lading name the ship and note that the goods have been loaded on board. Sometimes sales contracts require that the seller is responsible for international shipping charges, in which case the bill of lading must note "freight prepaid." A bill of lading is *clean* if it has no notations indicating damage to the goods when they were received by the carrier for shipment. A *negotiable* bill of lading entitles the holder to receive the goods. The seller retains title to the goods until the bill of lading has been transferred to the buyer;
- **A commercial invoice**, detailing the parties, description of goods, quantity, and price;
- **An insurance policy**, detailing the amount of coverage and dates of coverage. Coverage should include loading of the goods to and from the ship;
- **A certificate of origin**, declaring the country in which the goods were manufactured, produced, or grown; and
- **A certificate of inspection**, showing the results of an inspection, typically by a third party. For example, a certificate of inspection could state that the goods comply with certain safety standards or are composed of a certain material.

7. The nominated bank examines the documents and pays the seller. If the documents comply with the letter of credit, the nominated bank sends them to the issuing bank and pays the seller. Essentially, the bank is purchasing the documents from the seller, on behalf of the buyer. But to receive payment, the seller must produce documents that strictly conform to the requirements of the letter of credit (not the requirements of the sales contract). If the bill of lading, commercial invoice, and other required documents vary, even in small ways, from the specifications set forth in the letter of credit, the bank will deny payment. This is known as the *strict compliance principle*. To avoid problems, parties should review the sales contract carefully to ensure that the letter of credit requirements correspond to the sales contract requirements. The more complexity in the letter of credit requirements, the greater the likelihood of disputes and problems. If it turns out that the seller is unable to comply with the letter of credit terms (for example, if more time is needed for shipping), the seller can request a modification that the buyer and the issuing bank must agree upon.

8. The nominated bank forwards the documents to the issuing bank.

9. The issuing bank examines the documents. If the documents comply with the letter of credit, the issuing bank will charge the buyer's account, send the documents to the buyer, reimburse the correspondent bank, and be reimbursed by the buyer.

10. The buyer takes the bill of lading to the port and is able to obtain the goods from the carrier when they arrive in port.

Standby Letters of Credit

One variation on the standard letter of credit is the standby letter of credit. In a **standby letter of credit**, the bank "stands by" and only pays the seller if the buyer fails to pay for the goods. A standby letter of credit operates as a guarantee of payment in the event a buyer defaults. It is often used in conjunction with an open account. If the buyer fails to remit payment in accordance with the open account terms, the bank will pay the seller according to the terms of the standby letter of credit.

Summary

The debtor-creditor relationship encompasses a wide array of protections for parties to a credit transaction. The creditor enjoys benefits afforded by liens, security agreements, and garnishment. Creditors are also protected when third parties (sureties and guarantors) assume the risk of default by a party to a credit transaction. On the other hand, debtors benefit from a uniform set of federal bankruptcy laws. Bankruptcy protection gives debtors a "fresh start" to their personal or business lives, or allows commercial debtors to continue running their businesses while operating under a court-supervised plan to repay creditors. The debtor-creditor relationship involves both legal and ethical issues, which require debtors and creditors to confront the concept of fairness in business dealings.

Questions for Review

1. Artisan's lien

A used car dealer sold an automobile to a customer (Robert) on an installment basis. The installment sales contract calls for Robert to make monthly payments of principal and interest. The contract also provides the dealer with a certificate of title, which gives the dealer a lien on the property. After Robert took possession of the car, he drove it to a local tire store to have all four tires replaced. Robert returned to pick up the car but refused to pay the bill. Consequently, the tire store owner retained possession of the car claiming his rights under an artisan's lien theory. The tire store owner asserts that his artisan's lien has priority over the dealer's lien. Do you agree? Explain. *Bond v. Dudley*, 426 S.W.2d 780 (1968).

2. Mechanic's lien

Morison Supply Company (Morison) sells building materials to contractors for high-end construction jobs, such as luxury condominiums. The average cost of materials for a given job ranges from $2 to $3 million. Morison works exclusively with three general contractors and ships materials to them on a credit basis. Morison does not record a mechanic's lien with the local registry of deeds each time it executes a written contract with one of the general contractors.

What is the nature of the risk that Morison assumes by failing to record a mechanic's lien with the local registry of deeds each time it executes a written contract with one of the general contractors? Explain.

3. Ethics and a loan application

Hi-Cloud, Inc., is a start-up tech company. It is seeking a substantial line of credit from a federally insured commercial bank. Among other questions, the loan application requires disclosure of the compensation paid to company executives. Barbara, Hi-Cloud's CEO, was drawing a salary of $800,000 at the time of the application. She intentionally omitted disclosing her salary in an effort to increase Hi-Cloud's net worth. The bank was satisfied with the application and granted Hi-Cloud a line of credit for $1.5 million.

Under Section 1014 of Title 18 of the U.S. Code, it is a crime "*to knowingly make a false statement or report or willfully overvalue . . . property in a credit application to a federally insured bank . . . [the applicant] shall be fined not more than $1,000,000 or imprisoned for not more than 30 years, or both.*" Hi-Cloud has made all payments under the line of credit for the last three years and continues to be in good standing with the bank. The compliance and ethics officer of Hi-Cloud discovered the omission and is counseling Barbara on the best ethical and legal approach to avoid criminal prosecution. Barbara is convinced the omission of her salary was not a "false statement," and because the bank was satisfied with the application and did not ask her to disclose her salary despite the fact it was left blank on the application, she asserts that she was acting ethically and legally.

As the compliance and ethics officer of Hi-Cloud, what advice would you give to Barbara? Explain.

4. Mechanic's lien

Conway Crafters, LLC, negotiated two promissory notes with Gotham Bank. Conway secured the loans to help finance the construction of a new commercial building. Separate mortgages secured each note. The mortgage language instructed Conway to take "any action reasonably requested" by Gotham Bank to preserve the bank's priority interest in the property. After Gotham Bank made the final cash disbursement according to the terms of the loan, Conway hired Sunset Paving Company to pave the lot of its new commercial building. After Sunset completed the job, Conway refused to pay the full amount of the invoice. Shortly thereafter, Sunset filed a mechanic's lien on the new commercial property. Gotham Bank believes its mortgage interest in the new commercial property takes priority over Sunset's mechanic's lien. Do you agree? Explain. *F.R. Carroll, Inc. v. TD Bank, N.A.*, 8 A.3d 646 (2010).

5. **Fraudulent transfers**

   List and describe the factors a creditor may use when asking a court to set aside an alleged fraudulent transfer of property under the Uniform Fraudulent Transfer Act (UFTA).

6. **Bankruptcy**

   Discuss the purpose of federal bankruptcy laws from a debtor's perspective, and from a creditor's perspective.

7. **Chapter 7 Bankruptcy and Chapter 11 Bankruptcy**

   Explain the similarities and dissimilarities of a Chapter 7 bankruptcy proceeding and a Chapter 11 bankruptcy proceeding.

8. **International considerations**

   Explain how letters of credit protect sellers in overseas sales of goods transactions. Explain how they protect buyers in overseas sales of goods transactions.

Further Reading

Han, S. and G., Li *Household Borrowing After Personal Bankruptcy* 43 Journal of Money, Credit and Banking 491–517 (2011).

Landry, R. J., *Ethical Considerations in Filing Personal Bankruptcy: A Hypothetical Case Study* 29 Journal of Legal Studies Education 59–93 (2012).

Rapheal, J. S., *The Status of the Unsecured Creditor in the Modern Law of Secured Transactions* 1 American Business Law Journal 26–38 (1963).

Rotem, Y., *Governmental Concessions in Corporate Bankruptcy Proceedings: A New Approach* 50 American Business Law Journal 337–411 (2013).

Solomon, D., *The Rise of a Giant: Securitization and the Global Financial Crisis* 49 American Business Law Journal 859–890 (2012).

PART V

Business Liability

CHAPTER 19

Business Torts

Chapter Objectives

1. To understand the concept and implications of tort liability
2. To know the types of intentional and unintentional torts that affect business entities
3. To understand the ethical implications of business torts
4. To know the types of damages that result from tort liability
5. To know the defenses that may be raised in response to a business tort claim
6. To understand the relationship between ethics and business torts

Practical Example: Skyview Corporation*

Skyview Corporation is a family-owned business located in San Diego, California. Skyview has operated a flight training center since 1970. The center is approved by the Federal Aviation Administration (FAA).[†] Skyview issues a private pilot certificate to students who complete its flight training program.[‡] As part of its instructional program, Skyview maintains a fleet of 15 aircraft, each of which has an airworthiness certificate issued by the FAA.[§] Skyview also maintains a staff of ten FAA certified flight instructors.[**]

With the exception of the current year, Skyview has enjoyed steady profits since its inception. Its revenues have increased on average about 10 percent per year. For most of these years, about 60 percent of Skyview's customers have come from referrals generated by the California Referral Corporation (CRC).[††] For each customer referred by CRC, Skyview paid CRC a $200 referral commission, which is a standard rate paid by schools included in the CRC Flight Training Program Network. The remaining 40 percent of Skyview's customers have been generated from ads placed in local media outlets and recommendations from satisfied customers.

About a year ago, CRC increased its commission rate from $200 to $250 per customer referral. After careful consideration of the price increase, Jennifer,

589

the president of Skyview, concluded it would not be economically feasible for Skyview to maintain its membership in the CRC network. Accordingly, Skyview terminated its relationship with CRC according to the terms of CRC's network contract.

Within six months of its severance from the CRC network, Skyview experienced a 20 percent decline in revenues. Concerned about this precipitous drop, Skyview hired Kate to pose as a prospective flight school student to determine if CRC was making derogatory comments about Skyview. Several days later, Kate spoke with Kevin, a CRC customer representative, about flight school programs in the San Diego area. During the course of their conversation, Kevin did not mention Skyview. However, as Kate was about to leave, she asked Kevin if he knew anything about the Skyview training program. Kevin hesitated at first, but then offered several pejorative comments about the low quality of Skyview's flight instructors and the poor conditioning of its instructional aircraft. When Kate asked Kevin if he was sure about his statements regarding Skyview, Kevin said that CRC's president told him that he had an ethical obligation to tell prospective students about the inadequate flight instructors and equipment at Skyview.

While attending professional conferences in the southern California area, Jennifer attempted to establish networking relationships with companies similar to the relationship Skyview had with CRC. However, she found it difficult to form new relationships because of the negative comments made by CRC's customer representatives. Additionally, the management of CRC made it known that it would view unfavorably companies doing business with Skyview.

Within a year of severing its relationship with CRC, Skyview's revenues dropped by 40 percent. The management of Skyview is convinced that the pejorative comments made by CRC representatives contributed directly to Skyview's decline in revenues. Skyview also believes it has been unable to establish a new networking relationship because of CRC's comments about viewing companies unfavorably if they did business with Skyview.

For the past two months, Jennifer has been talking with Stella, a client representative at Pilots Network. Pilots Network operates a referral business similar to the model used by CRC. Jennifer and Stella have been discussing the possibility of Skyview joining Pilots Network and paying a referral rate of $190 for each customer referral. Negotiations were nearing closure when Stella received a call from Brian, the director of customer relations at CRC. Brian told Stella he was aware of her discussions with Jennifer about the possibility of Skyview joining Pilots Network. He stated in unequivocal terms that Skyview would be an unworthy and unreliable client and that Pilots Network would be wise to sever all communications with Skyview. Brian emphasized the low quality of Skyview's flight instructors and its inadequately maintained fleet of aircraft. Shortly thereafter, Stella told Jennifer that Pilots Network was no longer interested in continuing negotiations with Skyview. With an eroding customer base, Skyview's revenues continued to plunge.

Jennifer believes that Skyview may have several legal claims against CRC. She also believes that CRC and some of its representatives may have acted unethically in their dealings with Skyview. As you read about the business torts covered in this chapter, consider what legal claims may be available to Skyview as well as some of the ethical issues raised by the behavior and actions of CRC and its representatives.

---

* Skyview Corporation is a fictitious company developed by the authors to demonstrate and illustrate key legal and ethical concepts, theories, practices, and strategies.

† Chapter 54, Part 142, Section 6 of the FAA regulations provides guidelines about flight training centers including the evaluation of training programs, curricula for training programs, flight training equipment, etc.

‡ Chapter 9 of the FAA regulations outlines the requirements for issuing and obtaining a private pilot certificate.

§ Chapter 14 of the FAA regulations provides guidelines regarding the airworthiness certificate processes and the requirements.

** Chapter 14 of the FAA regulations describes the requirements for obtaining and renewing a flight instructor certificate.

†† The California Referral Corporation is a fictitious corporation created solely for the purpose of educational instruction.

Torts and Business Torts

A **tort** is a civil wrong, as opposed to a crime, that occurs when one party (wrongdoer) breaches a legal duty, imposed by law, owed to another party (victim), and the victim seeks a remedy, usually in the form of damages. In general, **tort law** protects individuals and entities from three types of injuries: (1) injury to the person, (2) damage to property, and (3) impairment of economic interests. Even though different names are used to describe injuries to an individual's or an entity's economic interest, the term **business torts** is commonly used in business and in the legal profession. The business torts covered in this chapter include

- Fraudulent misrepresentation
- Negligent misrepresentation
- Intentional interference with contractual relations
- Intentional interference with prospective economic advantage
- Conversion
- Product disparagement

Unintentional Torts (Negligence)

Negligence occurs when one party (wrongdoer) fails to use the standard of care reasonably expected of others in like situations, and the wrongdoer's failure causes injury to another party (victim). For example, assume that a handrail in a department store became loose after years of use by thousands of customers. As you grip the handrail for support, the handrail detaches completely from the brackets holding it in place, causing you to fall and seriously injure your arm. When this type of injury occurs, the victim (you, in this case) should ask the following question: What standard of care does the department store owe to its customers? To prove a negligence case against a defendant such as the department store in the preceding example, the plaintiff must establish and prove the following five elements: duty, breach of duty, actual causation, proximate (legal) causation, and damages.

A **duty** is a legal obligation that one party (individual or entity) owes to another party (individual or entity). A duty owed by one party causes another party to have a corresponding right. For example, in the preceding scenario, the department store has a legal duty to provide its customers with a reasonably safe environment for browsing or shopping. Conversely, customers have a corresponding right to expect that the store will provide a reasonably safe environment. This set of obligations and rights establishes the legal relationship between the parties. A **standard of care** principle serves to protect individuals and entities against injuries that may result from situations involving *unreasonable risks of harm*. We measure "standard of care" based on how a reasonable person would act in a similar situation. A **reasonable person** is one who routinely exercises the degree of care called for in a given situation. For example, the reasonable person who manages a department store might routinely inspect safety devices, such as a handrail, to ensure their stability and functionality.

A **breach of duty** occurs when one party fails to satisfy the standard of care it owes to another party. For example, in the preceding illustration, if the department store fails to inspect safety devices, such as a handrail, on a routine basis, and the handrail detaches from its holding brackets, causing injury to a customer, arguably the department store has breached its duty to provide customers with a safe environment for browsing and shopping.

Actual causation relates to the conduct that caused an injury. In determining whether a party's conduct caused an injury, the following question is often asked: "but for" the defendant's conduct, would the injury have occurred? Alternatively, some jurisdictions have moved away from the "but for" analysis in favor of a "substantial factor" analysis. A substantial factor analysis requires the injured party to show a direct link between the defendant's conduct and the plaintiff's injuries. For example, under a substantial factor analysis, the injured party in the preceding illustration must show that a direct link exists between her injury and the department store's detached handrail.

Proximate causation places a limit on the extent to which an injured party may assert that her injuries were the direct result of the wrongdoer's conduct. The element of proximate causation narrows a negligence claim to those situations where a close relationship exists between the victim's injuries and the wrongdoer's conduct. For example, if a court determines that the relationship between the victim's injuries and the wrongdoer's conduct is too remote, the court may determine as a matter of law that the wrongdoer is not liable for the victim's injuries.

Damages relate to the harm caused by the wrongdoer. A successful negligence case requires the victim to prove **damages**. A comprehensive discussion of damages is presented toward the end of this chapter.

Defenses

Defenses to a negligence claim include comparative negligence, contributory negligence, and assumption of risk. **Comparative negligence** allows a defendant to argue that a victim's own conduct contributed to the injuries sustained by the victim. For example, in the preceding illustration, the department store might argue that the victim fell and injured her arm because she was texting and not paying attention to the stairway at the time of her fall. If successful in pursuing this argument, a court could reduce the amount of damages awarded to the injured party in proportion to the degree of fault attributed to the conduct of the injured party.

Contributory negligence works like comparative negligence in that it allows the defendant to show that the victim's conduct contributed to her injuries. However, unlike comparative negligence that apportions responsibility for an injury between the defendant and the injured party, contributory negligence is "all or nothing." Thus, if a court decides that the victim's own conduct contributed to the sustaining of her injuries, recovery of damages from the defendant is barred altogether.[1] All but four states (Alabama, Maryland, North Carolina, and Virginia) and the District of Columbia have eliminated contributory negligence as a defense and have adopted comparative negligence.

Assumption of risk comes into play when a victim has knowledge that the defendant's conduct may cause harm, but nonetheless voluntarily chooses to place herself within the sphere of the defendant's conduct. For example, in the department store scenario, if the store had detected a problem with its handrail and placed barriers and warning signs in front of the stairway but a customer nonetheless uses the handrail and falls, the department store could use "assumption of risk" as a defense.

To demonstrate the various elements of negligence, consider the Case Illustration of *Campbell v. Weathers.*

Intentional Torts

All intentional torts possess a common element: a party acts with the intent to cause a certain result. Intent comes in two forms: desired intent and substantial certainty intent. *Desired* intent occurs when the wrongdoer wants the result of her action to occur. For example, X wishes to harm Y's business reputation; therefore, X contacts Y's customers and tells them false information about Y's products. If the communication with Y's customers impairs Y's business reputation, then X has achieved the desired result of her intended action.

Substantial certainty intent, on the other hand, occurs when the wrongdoer knows with "substantial certainty" that the result of her action will occur, even if she does not desire the result. For example, assume that X does not desire to harm Y's reputation, but she

Case Illustration

The defendant (wrongdoer), Weathers, operated a convenience store that included a small restaurant. The plaintiff (victim), Campbell, entered the defendant's store, but did not purchase anything. Campbell remained in the store for about 15 to 20 minutes. During this time, he walked down the hallway of the defendant's store to use the restroom. As he approached the restroom, Campbell fell through an opened trapdoor in the floor of the hallway breaking his right arm and sustaining other injuries. A box had been left directly in front of the opened trapdoor, thus obstructing Campbell's view. Campbell sued Weathers for damages related to his injuries. In defense, Weathers argued that he owed no duty to Campbell because Campbell did not purchase any merchandise while in his store. However, the Kansas Supreme Court held for the victim Campbell. The Court reasoned that because Campbell was an invited guest of Weathers' store, Weathers owed Campbell a duty of care to protect him from foreseeable risks, such as leaving a box in front of an opened trapdoor. *Campbell v. Weathers*, 111 P.2d 72 (1941).

---

[1]An exception to this harsh standard may be made in situations in which the plaintiff can prove that a defendant acted with wanton (reckless) disregard of the rights or safety of others.

nonetheless spreads falsehoods about Y's products while attending a business conference, which is also attended by many of Y's customers. If X's dissemination of falsehoods about Y's products harms Y's business reputation, a court could find that X knew with "substantial certainty" that the result of her actions (spreading falsehoods) would result in an injury to Y's business reputation.

With the preceding discussion serving as an introduction to torts in general, we now move to the main topic of this chapter: business torts.

Business Torts

The following business torts are covered in this section of the chapter: fraudulent misrepresentation, negligent misrepresentation, intentional interference with contractual relations, intentional interference with prospective economic advantage, conversion, and product disparagement.

Fraudulent Misrepresentation

Assume you are interested in buying a used automobile. You identify a car that meets your criteria on a popular website. After contacting the owner, you arrange to meet for the purpose of inspecting the car and asking the owner some questions. During your discussion with the owner, you ask the owner if he is aware of any mechanical problems with the car. The owner states the car is in great shape and there are no mechanical problems. In fact, however, the owner was told by the mechanic at his automobile repair shop that the car's transmission was in need of a major overhaul. You purchase the car for $10,000, which approximates the fair market value of the car assuming it "is in great shape with no mechanical problems." Two days after you purchase the car, the transmission fails. Your mechanic estimates it will cost about $2,000 to repair the transmission.

Did the owner of the automobile make a misrepresentation when he said the car "is in great shape and there are no mechanical problems?" What is a misrepresentation? In its simplest form, a **misrepresentation** is nothing more than a statement that varies from the truth. For example, when the owner told you the car did not have any mechanical problems, when in fact he knew it did have mechanical problems (transmission issues), he misrepresented the truth. The owner's misrepresentation about the mechanical condition of the car resulted in an economic impairment (loss) for you. Instead of buying a car at a price equal to its fair market value ($10,000),

Parties to a contract are expected to provide accurate and truthful representations about services rendered and products sold. For example, the buyer (homeowner) of a newly constructed house expects the seller (contractor) to make truthful representations about the quality of the materials used in the construction of the house.

you will need to spend an additional $2,000 to make it operational. Therefore, the amount of the economic harm inflicted on you by the owner is $2,000. This economic harm, *intentionally* inflicted on you by the owner, resulted from the owner's fraudulent misrepresentation of the condition of the car. In this case, you could consider suing the seller in tort for fraudulent misrepresentation.

To be successful in advancing a legal claim based on the business tort of **fraudulent misrepresentation**, the victim must prove the following elements:

- The wrongdoer made a false representation of a past or present fact;
- The wrongdoer had knowledge of the representation's falsity, or made the representation without knowing whether it was true or false;
- The wrongdoer intended to induce the victim to act in reliance on the representation;
- The wrongdoer's representation caused the victim to rely on the representation; and
- The victim suffered pecuniary (money) damages as a result of the reliance.

Another issue that often surfaces in fraudulent misrepresentation cases is the *nondisclosure* of a material fact. As a general rule, nondisclosure becomes an issue only when one party has a legal duty to inform another party about a problem related to a prospective decision or action. Determining when a "nondisclosure duty" arises is often unclear. However, it is generally accepted that when one party has superior knowledge over another party (and the other party cannot reasonably gain access to similarly superior knowledge), the party with superior knowledge has a duty to inform the other party. For example, consider the Case Illustration of *Griffith v. Byers Construction Co. of Kansas, Inc.*

It is important to distinguish between puffery and a fraudulent representation. **Puffery** is a seller's opinion, often in the form of vague generalizations, where such generalizations lack a factual basis. For example, a sales representative who states his opinion that "this car is the best car for its price on the lot" is engaging in puffery. The sales representative's statement is not specific enough to approach that of a fraudulent

Case Illustration

Griffith brought a claim of fraudulent misrepresentation against Byers Construction Co. of Kansas, Inc. (Byers), a real estate developer. Byers developed and advertised the real estate in question as a choice residential area. Previously, the property had been used as an oil field that included a saltwater disposal area. Griffith argued that Byers knew or should have known that the soil would not support the growth of vegetation because of the property's previous use as a saltwater disposal area. Furthermore, Griffith argued that Byers graded and reworked the soil in such a way that made it impossible to detect the saline conditions of the soil. After new homes were constructed, Griffith discovered that it was impossible to grow grass, shrubs, and other kinds of vegetation because of the saline condition of the soil. At no time did Griffith inquire about the quality of the soil nor did Byers give any assurances about the fertility of the soil. Nonetheless, in holding for Griffith, the Court stated that "[w]here a vendor has knowledge of a defect in property which is not within the fair and reasonable reach of the vendee and which he could not discover by the exercise of reasonable diligence, the silence and failure of the vendor to disclose the defect in the property constitutes fraudulent [misrepresentation]." *Griffith v. Byers Construction Co. of Kansas, Inc.*, 510 P.2d 198 (1973).

misrepresentation. Thus, if a buyer is influenced by a sales representative's puffery about a particular vehicle, it is unlikely that the buyer will be successful in advancing a fraudulent misrepresentation claim when the buyer discovers that the vehicle is not as "great" as the sales representative said in his "puffery" statement.

Negligent Misrepresentation

Negligent misrepresentation is similar to fraudulent misrepresentation, except the victim is not required to establish that the wrongdoer had knowledge of the falsity of the representation. Rather, the legal standard for a negligent misrepresentation claim requires that the wrongdoer made a representation with reckless disregard of the truth. For example, a person may be viewed as having "acted recklessly" if she makes a representation without weighing or

Case Illustration

The plaintiff (International Products Company) was expecting a shipment of goods to be delivered to the defendant's (Erie Railroad Company) place of business. In advance of the arrival of the goods, the plaintiff requested that the defendant keep the goods in a safe place until the plaintiff was able to retrieve them. The defendant accepted the plaintiff's offer and stored the goods in one of its warehouses. The plaintiff wished to insure the goods while they remained in the defendant's warehouse; therefore, the plaintiff asked the defendant to identify the particular warehouse where the goods were stored. The defendant mistakenly gave the plaintiff incorrect information about the location of the goods. A fire broke out in the warehouse where the plaintiff's goods were stored, destroying all the plaintiff's goods. The insurance company refused to indemnify the plaintiff for its loss because the goods were stored in a warehouse different from the one listed on the insurance policy. The plaintiff brought a claim against the defendant for negligent misrepresentation. In finding in favor of the plaintiff, the court made the following statements about the tort of negligent misrepresentation:

Confining ourselves to the issues before us we eliminate any theory of fraud or deceit. Had they been present other questions would arise. We come to the vexed question of liability for negligent misrepresentation. . . . In some cases, a negligent statement may be the basis for a recovery of damages. . . . Liability in such cases arises only where there is a duty to give the correct information. And that involves many considerations. There must be knowledge or its equivalent that the information is desired for a serious purpose; that he to whom it is given intends to rely and act upon it; that if false or erroneous he will because of it be injured in person or property. Finally the relationship of the parties, arising out of contract or otherwise, must be such that in morals and good conscience the one has the right to rely upon the other for information, and the other giving the information owes a duty to give it with care. An inquiry made of a stranger is one thing; of a person with whom the inquirer has entered or is about to enter into a contract concerning the goods which are or are to be its subject is another. . . . Here, as we view the facts, the duty to speak with care rested on the defendant. . . . And, the defendant's breach of that duty caused the plaintiff's loss. *International Products Company v. Erie Railroad Company*, 155 N.E. 662 (1927).

considering the possible harm that such representation may cause, or foresees the possibility of harm but nevertheless continues to make the representation. For example, consider the Case Illustration of *International Products Company v. Erie Railroad Company* on the previous page.

Note the court's reference to "morals and good conscience." Although it is unusual for a judge to mention ethics or morals in a decision, there is a natural law right, assuming one acts in good conscience in contract dealings, to reasonably rely on the accuracy of the information received from another party.

Intentional Interference with Contractual Relations

Interference covers two types of business torts: (1) intentional interference with contractual relations, and (2) intentional interference with prospective economic advantage. The first type of interference, *intentional interference with contractual relations*, requires a plaintiff to prove the following five elements:

- The existence of a valid contract;
- The defendant had knowledge of the contract;
- The defendant intended to disrupt the contractual relationship between the plaintiff and another party;
- The defendant's actions *in fact* disrupted the contractual relationship; and
- The disruption injured the plaintiff, causing an economic impairment.

Interference with contractual relations is an intentional tort; therefore, the defendant's knowledge of the existence of a contractual relationship between the plaintiff and another party is essential. Without such knowledge, it would be impossible for the defendant to "intentionally" interfere with an existing contractual relationship. For example, assume Robert interferes with a contractual relationship between Alexa and Emily. If Robert can establish he was unaware of the contractual relationship, he has a strong defense against a claim of intentional interference with contractual relations, even if his interference disrupts Alexa and Emily's contractual relationship.

The In-Depth Ethical Case Analysis of *Mathis v. Liu* on the next page discusses the legal basis for establishing a claim of intentional interference with contractual relations.

In-Depth Ethical Case Analysis

Mathis v. Liu, 276 F.3d 1027 (2002)

Facts

In an effort to increase sales, Pacific Cornetta, Inc. executed a contract with Lawrence Mathis. The contract called for Mathis to solicit orders from Kmart and other department stores in return for a 5 percent sales commission. The terms allowed either party to terminate the contractual relationship at will. Approximately one year after Mathis signed the contract with Pacific Cornetta, he hired John Evans to work for him as a subagent. Evans agreed to solicit orders from Kmart for the products handled by Mathis in exchange for a 1 percent sales commission. The contract between Mathis and Evans stated that each party could terminate the contract only after providing the other party with a six-month written notice.

Several months after Evans began working for Mathis, Pacific Cornetta initiated discussions with Evans about joining its workforce. As part of these discussions, Pacific Cornetta persuaded Evans to terminate his contract with Mathis. Pacific Cornetta was aware of the contractual provision requiring Evans to provide Mathis with a six-month written notice before terminating the contract. Based on these discussions, Evans accepted the offer to work for Pacific Cornetta. The following day, Evans terminated his contract prematurely with Mathis. Two days later, Pacific Cornetta also terminated its contract with Mathis. Mathis then filed a lawsuit in Federal District Court against Pacific Cornetta and its officers (Ching and Alex Liu) for intentional interference with the contractual relationship between him and Evans.

Issue

Did the defendant, Pacific Cornetta, intentionally interfere with the contractual relationship between Mathis and Evans?

Holding

To be found liable for intentional interference with a contractual relationship, Arkansas law states that the "interference" must be "improper." Determining whether an interference is improper requires an analysis of the following elements:

1. The nature of the actor's conduct;

2. The actor's motive;

3. The interests of the other party with which the actor's conduct interferes;

4. The interests sought to be advanced by the actor;

5. The social interests in protecting the freedom of action of the actor and the contractual interests of the other party;

6. The proximity or remoteness of the actor's conduct to the interference; and

7. The relations between the parties.

The jury determined that the defendants were liable for intentionally interfering with the contractual relationship between Mathis and Evans, and awarded Mathis compensatory damages. For reasons unrelated to the issue at hand, the trial judge set aside (overturned) the verdict of the jury and Mathis appealed to the U.S. Court of Appeals for the Eighth Circuit.

From the Court's Opinion

The Appeals Court concluded that the jury was entitled to conclude as a *matter of fact* that the defendants acted "improperly" when they induced Evans to breach his contract with Mathis. However, the Appeals Court determined as a *matter of law* that Mathis was not entitled to receive compensatory damages. The Appeals Court found that Mathis had failed to introduce at trial, as required by state law, sufficient evidence to "fix damages in dollars and cents" and to "present a reasonably complete set of figures [about the loss of anticipatory profits] to the jury." Consequently, the Appeals Court concluded there was no legal basis for the awarding of compensatory damages to Mathis, even though the jury concluded as a matter of fact that the defendants had intentionally interfered with the contractual relationship between Mathis and Evans.

Ethical Issue

In the end, Lawrence Mathis was unsuccessful in his claim for damages as a result of Pacific Cornetta's intentional interference with his contractual relationship with John Evans.

Mathis lost his case because of a failure to demonstrate adequately to the jury his specific economic loss that "fixed damages in dollars and cents." Even though the interference may have been "improper" and therefore illegal, a plaintiff must prove damages in court. Mathis had to prove an actual loss of anticipated profits (economic impairment) due to the interference with the contract, and he failed to satisfy this requirement.

Separate from the legal analysis, was Pacific Cornetta's interference with the contract that Mathis had with Evans unethical? Keep in mind that the defendant (Pacific Cornetta) knew that the contract between Mathis and Evans required a six-month written notice prior to termination, yet the defendant purposefully and intentionally induced Evans to prematurely breach his contract with Mathis.

Ethical Theory Analysis

As potential business executives, you should be conscious of creating a corporate ethical culture and must be especially aware of respecting the diverse business relationships existing in the business environment. They are often, but not always, evidenced by a formal contract.

This case enumerates what constitutes an improper interference with an existing contractual relationship based on the interests and motives of the interfering party. An ethical analysis differs from a legal analysis and should be reviewed if a company sincerely wants to create and project an ethical culture and a value system reflective of its published code of ethics.

Kant's Categorical Imperatives

Kant in his Fundamental Principles of the Metaphysics of Morals (p. 179) stated, "The imperative duty may be expressed thus: Act as if the maxim of thy action were to become by thy will a Universal Law of Nature." This categorical imperative would find Pacific Cornetta's interference unethical and improper because a universal allowance of interfering with a contract that required a six-month notice for a legal termination would cause chaos in contract law. If everyone was allowed to interfere with a contract, the legal system would be substantially weakened.

W. D. Ross and Prima Facie Duties

Ross stated in *The Right and the Good,* "unless stronger moral obligations override, one ought to keep a promise." He insisted on "promise keeping" unless "fulfilling a promise . . . would be so disastrous that we judge it right not to do so." One of Ross's prima facie duties is the duty of nonmalfeasance that requires one not to harm others. Interfering with a contract to acquire an advantage at the contracting party's expense, which causes economic harm, represents an unethical practice.

Conclusion

Mathis lost his case because he failed to prove that Pacific Cornetta's interference with his contractual relationship with Evans resulted in a measureable economic loss. However, the ethical principles discussed above illustrate that this contractual interference was, nonetheless, an unethical act.

Case Illustration

The defendant, Toyota Motor Sales, U.S.A., Inc. (Toyota), introduced its new Lexus brand automobile to the U.S. market. Anticipating a high demand for the Lexus in Japan, Toyota barred U.S. dealers from reselling Lexus automobiles to customers in Japan. Toyota also barred U.S. dealers from transacting business with U.S. businesses that resold Lexus automobiles to customers in Japan. The plaintiff, Penna, owned an automobile wholesale business. Penna was not one of Toyota's dealers in the United States. However, Penna purchased Lexus vehicles from an official Toyota dealer and resold them to customers in Japan. When Toyota discovered that its U.S. dealer was selling Lexus automobiles to the plaintiff, it threatened to cut off future sales to the dealer if the dealer continued to transact business with Penna. Shortly thereafter, the dealer terminated its relationship with Penna, and Penna's business suffered. Penna brought an action for damages against Toyota asserting a claim of "intentional interference with prospective economic advantage."

In its opinion, the California Supreme Court noted that "the following elements of the cause of action [for intentional interference with prospective economic advantage] must be satisfied:

■ An economic relationship . . . containing the probability of future economic benefit to the plaintiff;
■ Knowledge by the defendant of the existence of the relationship;
■ Intentional acts on the part of the defendant designed to disrupt the relationship;
■ Actual disruption of the relationship; and
■ Damages to the plaintiff proximately caused by the acts of the defendant.
As to the third element, [we are of the opinion that the defendant's intentional acts must also be] wrongful . . . . Wrongfulness may lie in the method used or by virtue of an improper motive."

In its opinion, the California Supreme Court established the rule that a plaintiff seeking to recover for an alleged interference with prospective economic advantage must establish that the defendant engaged in *wrongful* interference. Because the trial court had not considered the question of "wrongfulness" on the part of Toyota's interference with Penna's economic relationship with the dealer, the California Supreme Court sent the case back to the trial court to determine if Toyota's interference was "wrongful." *Della Penna v. Toyota Motor Sales, U.S.A., Inc.*, 902 P.2d 740 (1995).

Intentional Interference with Prospective Economic Advantage

As demonstrated by the Toyota Motor Sales case, intentional interference with prospective economic advantage provides a basis for a victim to bring a legal action against a wrongdoer for intentionally interfering with a prospective business relationship. For the claim to be successful, the business relationship between the plaintiff and another party must have advanced to the stage of what is commonly referred to as preliminary contract negotiations.

A plaintiff must prove the following five elements to establish a successful intentional interference with prospective economic advantage claim:

- An economic relationship existed between the plaintiff and another party, with the probability of the relationship developing into a future economic benefit for the plaintiff;
- The defendant had knowledge of the relationship between the plaintiff and the other party;
- An intentional *wrongful* act by the defendant aimed at disrupting the relationship between the plaintiff and the other party;
- Actual disruption of the relationship between the plaintiff and the other party by the defendant; and
- An injury (economic impairment) to the plaintiff proximately caused by the defendant's wrongful act.

Generally, the plaintiff must prove that the defendant's intentional interference was *wrongful*. Some states have defined a wrongful interference as one that is unlawful pursuant to a constitutional, statutory, regulatory, common law, or other recognized legal standard.

Conversion

As an intentional tort, a **conversion** occurs when one party (wrongdoer) intentionally interferes with the personal property of another party (victim). To prove a conversion claim, the victim must satisfy the following four elements:

- The victim owns or has a legal right to possess the property in question;
- The wrongdoer intentionally interferes with the victim's property;
- The interference disrupts or deprives the victim of use or possession of the property; and
- The wrongdoer's interference causes injury to the victim.

For example, assume that a fellow student (John) intentionally took possession of your smartphone without your permission. John retained possession of the phone for a month. Because you use your smartphone on a daily basis, John's possession of the phone for a month "interfered" with your use and possession of it. Therefore, John may be liable to you for any damages he caused based on his "conversation" of your property.

Commercial Disparagement

The business tort of **commercial disparagement** provides a legal remedy for the publication of a false statement about a victim's products or services. Consider the Ethical

> **An Ethical Insight: John Rawls: The Equal Liberty Principle and the Ethics of Commercial Disparagement**
>
> Commercial disparagement is a false "published" statement that causes harm to a victim's commercial reputation and economic interests. Publishing harmful false remarks about another is unethical behavior that violates ethical principles. For example, John Rawls's equal liberty principle states "*Each person has the same indefeasible claim to a fully adequate scheme of equal basic liberties, which scheme is compatible with the same scheme of liberties for all.*" This ethical principle of equal liberty calls for the right to maintain a professional reputation compatible with that same right for others.

Case Illustration

Forbes magazine published an article about Granada Biosciences, Inc., and its parent company, Granada Corp. The article was entitled "The Incredible Shrinking Empire," and it dealt with the financial condition of Granada Corp. The article noted that the *Wall Street Journal* had described Granada Corp. as a "corporate star of the future" and that the organization had garnered much favorable publicity. However, the *Forbes* article stated: "There is less to Granada than meets the eye. Actually, its total revenues, $1 billion as recently as 1988, will scarcely be $200 million for 1991. Profits: zilch. Granada's work force has shrunk to below 900 from 2,200; and its cattle herd has dwindled to 25,000 from 1 million." Based on the article, Granada Corp. sued *Forbes* for commercial disparagement.

In its discussion, the court noted that a commercial disparagement claim is similar in many respects to a defamation claim. However, the two torts differ in the following way. A defamation action protects the personal reputation of an injured party; whereas, a commercial disparagement claim protects the economic interests of the plaintiff. The court also stated that the plaintiff must prove actual malice in a commercial disparagement claim. The court noted that actual malice is "a term of art; it is not ill will, spite, or evil motive." Instead, actual malice requires proof that the defendant made a statement with knowledge that it was false or with reckless disregard of whether it was true or not. In holding for *Forbes*, the court determined that Granada Corp. failed to establish the requirement of actual malice on the part of Forbes. *Forbes, Inc. v. Granada Biosciences, Inc.*, 124 S.W.3d 167 (2003).

Insight on page 601 as you think about the intentional tort of commercial disparagement. Commercial disparagement causes harm to a victim's economic interests. The harm usually takes place in a business setting where a wrongdoer makes some kind of false disparaging statement about the victim's products or services. See, for example, the above Case Illustration of *Forbes, Inc. v. Granada Biosciences, Inc.*

A victim must prove the following elements to establish a successful commercial disparagement claim:

- The wrongdoer published a false statement that was received by a party other than the victim;
- The false statement was aimed at the victim's products or services (economic interests);
- The wrongdoer published the statement with knowledge of the statement's falsity or with reckless disregard of its truth or falsity (actual malice);
- Economic impairment of the victim's interests was intended or foreseeable; and
- The publication of the false statement resulted in an impairment of the victim's economic interests.

The following Manager s Compliance and Ethics Meeting addresses the ethical considerations of posting a disparaging statement on a company's website.

Manager's Compliance and Ethics Meeting

The Business Tort of Commercial Disparagement

Arco, Inc., an automobile dealership, recently launched an interactive website for its online customers. Arco has published its code of ethics online, which recites its corporate values. Its customers and others are invited to post comments about the quality of Arco's customer service and compare it with Arco's competitors on Arco's website's bulletin board. One of the comments posted by an unknown party accused Harrison Motors (HM), Arco's largest competitor, of being "financed by organized crime and a place for buying drugs." The party who posted the defamatory statement informed Arco that "the statement is not true and is only a joke." Based on this disparaging comment, a large number of customers who search the web for automobiles are now going to the Arco dealership, and HM has lost substantial business. Arco's lawyer has informed the company that under the Communications Decency Act (CDA) Arco has no legal obligation to remove the disparaging statement and the only person liable is the defamer who posted it on Arco's bulletin board. Arco's vice president called a manager's compliance and ethics meeting to discuss the ethics of leaving the disparaging statement on Arco's website.

Some of Arco's sales representatives have said, "If it's legal, leave it alone and let's hope the alarmed customers continue to come to our company for business." Others have reservations. Following are several classical ethical principles that are helpful in analyzing Acro's ethical dilemma.

Virtue Ethics: Aristotle

Aristotle would argue that HM has a civil right not to be subjected to disparaging comments. Aristotle "recognized rights within the political community par excellence — the Greek city-state — and this was the historical seed out of which the more familiar theories of natural rights grew in the late medieval and early modern eras." (Aristotle's Theories of Political Rights, Fred D. Miller, Jr., Aristotle and Modern Law, Brooks and Murphy, p. 328). Aristotle would argue that the disparaging statements violate HM's natural right to a good business reputation and should be removed from Arco's website.

Natural Law: Aquinas

Aquinas states in his ***Summa Theologica***, Sixth Article, in response to "Whether He Who Is Under a Law May Act Beside the Letter of the Law?" answered "He who in a case of necessity acts beside the letter of the law, does not judge the law, but the particular case in which he sees the letter of the law is not to be observed." Although Arco is acting within the law (i.e., The Communications Decency Act), and "the letter of the law" allows Arco to keep the disparaging comment on its website, Aquinas would argue that natural law ethically dictates its removal because "*the letter of the law is not to be observed*" in this "*particular case*" because it would cause a grave injustice to Harrison Motors.

Prima Facie Duties: W. D. Ross

Ross would argue that two of his "prima facie duties" require removal of the disparaging statement: (1) the duty of nonmalfeasance not to harm another; and (2) the duty to prevent harm. Clearly, Harrison Motors is being harmed by the website posting.

Ethical Resolution

This case illustrates that what may be legal is not always ethical. Because Arco, Inc., is committed to developing a corporate ethical culture and its posted Code of Ethics on the company's website defines its core values, Arco should remove the disparaging comments even though the company is not legally required to do so.

As noted above, to prove that a wrongdoer made a disparaging statement, the victim must establish that the wrongdoer made the statement with *actual malice*. To establish actual malice, a victim must show that the wrongdoer made the disparaging statement with knowledge that the statement was false or made with reckless disregard of whether the statement was false or not.

Damages

Courts award damages to victims for injuries caused by wrongdoers. The theory underlying damages is to make an injured party "whole" through the awarding of monetary damages. Assume, for example, A drives recklessly and smashes into B's automobile causing damages in the amount of $10,000. In this case, A would be expected to pay B $10,000 in monetary damages to bring B's automobile back to its state prior to the accident.

In general, tort-based damages fall into three categories: nominal damages, compensatory damages, and punitive damages as shown in Exhibit 19.1.[2]

Nominal Damages

Nominal damages provide victims with a token monetary award. Typically, the award is used as a means to establish a legal right. For example, assume that A constructs a fence that encroaches on B's property. To clarify the boundary line, the court could order A to remove the fence from B's property and award B nominal damages (often one dollar) as a symbolic gesture of B's successful legal action. Because B did not suffer personal injuries, incur property damage, or suffer economic loss, B does not require the awarding of damages beyond the symbolic gesture of a nominal monetary award.

Compensatory Damages

Courts award **compensatory damages** to *compensate* individuals for personal injury, property damage, or economic loss. Compensatory damages require the party who caused the injury to "make whole" the injured party. Courts accomplished this goal by requiring the offending party (the wrongdoer) to pay a monetary amount to the victim that is equivalent to the amount of damage caused. For example, assume A is hiking along a commonly used trail and B is riding a bicycle on the same trail at an extremely fast speed. Because of B's negligence, B collides with A causing serious injury to one of A's legs. In this situation, the court could require B to

---

[2]In addition to torts, courts award damages for other types of civil wrongs, including breach of contract, employment discrimination, and other types of civil violations.

Exhibit 19.1. Categories of Tort Damages

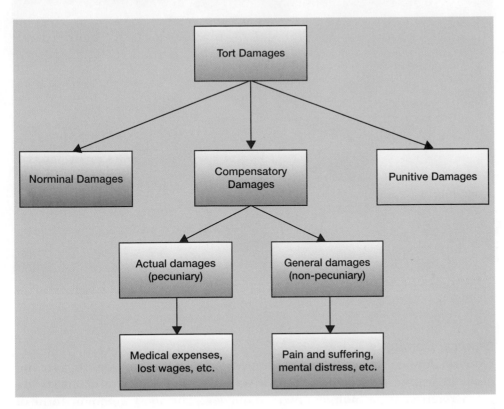

pay compensatory damages to A in an amount equal to A's medical bills and lost wages.

Actual Damages

Returning to Exhibit 19.1, we can see that compensatory damages come in two forms: actual damages and general damages. **Actual damages** relate to personal injuries, property damage, or impairment of economic interests, and they are susceptible to objective measurement in monetary terms. For example, in the above illustration, A would likely seek actual damages in the form of reimbursement for expenses related to his doctor and hospital bills. If A was required to miss work because of the injury, he could seek monetary payments equal to any lost wages and pursue reimbursement for the cost of household help and nursing assistance during his period of recuperation. As demonstrated by this illustration, actual damages are often referred to as **pecuniary damages** because of their financial components and characteristics.

When one party injures another party, the injured party (victim) expects to receive damages from the party (wrongdoer) who caused the harm.

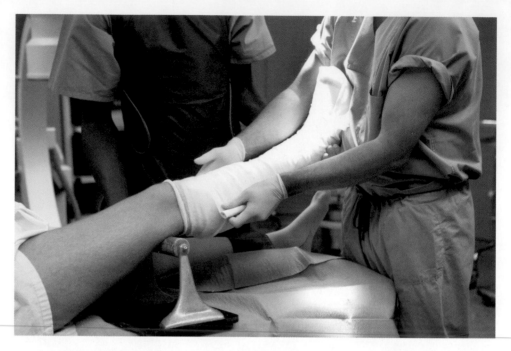

General Damages

General damages are designed to compensate parties for injuries that are not easily measured in pecuniary terms. Not surprisingly, general damages are often referred to as **nonpecuniary damages**. The most common form of harm associated with general damages is emotional or mental "pain and suffering" injuries. When allowed, pain and suffering encompass both physical pain and emotional pain. Physical pain could assume the form of chronic headaches related to the wrongdoer's actions. Emotional and mental pain may relate to the agony of losing a spouse, parent, or child. Other forms of emotional and mental pain and suffering include acute depression, loss of opportunity, public humiliation, anguish related to a bodily disfigurement, and loss of consortium (benefits of a relationship). Given the nature of these kinds of injuries, it is often difficult to measure them precisely and objectively. The plaintiff's attending physician will generally testify about the degree of physical pain or mental anguish the patient suffered from the injury.

Punitive Damages

As shown in Exhibit 19.1, punitive damages (often referred to as exemplary damages) represent the third and final category of tort-based damages. Courts award punitive damages in a civil case as a means of punishing and deterring the egregious conduct of a wrongdoer. **Punitive damages** are awarded on a discretionary basis, and they differ significantly from compensatory damages. Punitive damages focus on the repugnant and loathsome behavior of the wrongdoer and are awarded to make an example out of the defendant's wrongful conduct whereas compensatory damages focus on losses sustained by the victim.

The goal of compensatory damages is to make the victim whole by requiring the wrongdoer to pay damages in the form of monetary compensation; the goal of punitive damages is to punish the wrongdoer for what society views as willful and malicious conduct by the wrongdoer.[3] For example, a court might decide to award punitive damages in a situation where a company's negligent acts have the potential of harming many customers. Punitive damages are awarded as an addition to compensatory damages, not as a substitute for compensatory damages.

Damages: Reform Legislation

Because of the increasingly large sums of money awarded by juries to plaintiffs for general damages (pain and suffering) and punitive damages, members of the healthcare community and others have called upon members of the U.S. Congress and state legislators to enact tort reform legislation. The thrust of the debate centers on the impact that large jury awards have on the cost of healthcare, including medical insurance premiums, in the United States. The tort reform debate gained momentum in the mid-1970s with the passage of tort reform in California. As an illustration of tort reform, Exhibit 19.2 presents the main elements of the California Medical Injury Compensation Reform Act (MICRA) of 1975.

The California legislation is very clear and definite. The maximum amount that an injured plaintiff can receive for most forms of general damages is $250,000. For some observers and commentators, this amount is significantly too low to compensate individuals seriously injured as a result of negligence by healthcare providers, such as doctors. Many commentators also note that the $250,000 cap has not increased since the legislation was enacted in the 1970s. For others, the limit of $250,000 is too high because of the difficulty in measuring (quantifying) general (nonpecuniary) damages. As discussed previously, actual damages, such as reimbursement for medical cost and lost wages, are susceptible to objective measurement. Although the California statute has been the subject of numerous court challenges, it remains a primary example of a state's efforts to curb medical costs through tort reform.

---

[3]You will recall that punishment was discussed in detail in Chapter 10, "Business Crimes." The focus was on punishing offenders because of their criminal behavior. The punishment typically comes in the form of incarceration or the payment of a fine to the government. In the context of a civil action, punitive damages are like the payment of a fine to the government in a criminal case, only the payment of the "fine" goes to the injured party.

Exhibit 19.2. California Civil Code

California Civil Code Section 3333.2 provides that:

(a) In any action for injury against a health care provider based on professional negligence, the injured plaintiff shall be entitled to recover noneconomic losses to compensate for pain, suffering, inconvenience, physical impairment, disfigurement and other non-pecuniary damage.

(b) In no action shall the amount of damages for noneconomic losses exceed two hundred fifty thousand dollars ($250,000).

(c) For purposes of this section:

(2) "Professional negligence" means a negligent act or omission to act by a health care provider in the rendering of professional services, which act or omission is the proximate cause of a personal injury or wrongful death, provided that such services are within the scope of services for which the provider is licensed and which are not within any restriction imposed by the licensing agency or licensed hospital.

Global Perspective

Alien Tort Statute

Tort law often has international applications. For instance, the Alien Tort Statute (ATS) is a federal act permitting non-U.S. citizens to sue in U.S federal court for tort-based claims. May an individual or entity file a claim under the ATS based on conduct that occurs outside the United States? This was the question addressed by the U.S. Supreme Court in a case involving Nigerian nationals. Chief Justice Roberts delivered the opinion of the Court.

Large jury awards have caused some state legislatures to enact statutes aimed at limiting the amount injured parties may receive in tort-based cases.

Kiobel v. Royal Dutch Petroleum Co., 133 S. Ct. 1659 (2013)

In the words of Chief Justice Roberts (citations omitted) . . .

Petitioners, a group of Nigerian nationals residing in the United States, filed suit in federal court against certain Dutch, British, and Nigerian corporations. Petitioners sued under the Alien Tort Statute, 28 U.S.C. § 1350, alleging that the corporations aided and abetted the Nigerian Government in committing violations of the law of nations in Nigeria. The question presented is whether and under what circumstances courts may recognize a cause of action under the Alien Tort Statute, for violations of the law of nations occurring within the territory of a sovereign other than the United States.

* * *

Passed as part of the Judiciary Act of 1789, the [Alien Tort Statute] ATS was invoked twice

in the late 18th century, but then only once more over the next 167 years. The statute provides district courts with jurisdiction to hear certain claims, but does not expressly provide any causes of action. We held in Sosa v. Alvarez-Machain, however, that the First Congress did not intend the provision to be "stillborn." The grant of jurisdiction is instead "best read as having been enacted on the understanding that the common law would provide a cause of action for [a] modest number of international law violations." We thus held that federal courts may "recognize private claims [for such violations] under federal common law." The Court in Sosa rejected the plaintiff's claim in that case for "arbitrary arrest and detention," on the ground that it failed to state a violation of the law of nations with the requisite "definite content and acceptance among civilized nations."

The question here is not whether petitioners have stated a proper claim under the ATS, but whether a claim may reach conduct occurring in the territory of a foreign sovereign. Respondents contend that claims under the ATS do not, relying primarily on a canon of statutory interpretation known as the presumption against extraterritorial application. That canon provides that "[w]hen a statute gives no clear indication of an extraterritorial

application, it has none," Morrison v. National Australia Bank Ltd., and reflects the "presumption that United States law governs domestically but does not rule the world."

This presumption "serves to protect against unintended clashes between our laws and those of other nations which could result in international discord." As this Court has explained:

> *For us to run interference in . . . a delicate field of international relations there must be present the affirmative intention of the Congress clearly expressed. It alone has the facilities necessary to make fairly such an important policy decision where the possibilities of international discord are so evident and retaliative action so certain. Benz v. Compania Naviera Hidalgo, S. A. The presumption against extraterritorial application helps ensure that the Judiciary does not erroneously adopt an interpretation of U.S. law that carries foreign policy consequences not clearly intended by the political branches.*

* * *

We therefore conclude that the presumption against extraterritoriality applies to claims under the ATS, and that nothing in the statute rebuts that presumption. "[T]here is no clear indication of extraterritoriality here," and petitioners' case seeking relief for violations of the law of nations occurring outside the United States is barred.

On these facts, all the relevant conduct took place outside the United States. And even where the claims touch and concern the territory of the United States, they must do so with sufficient force to displace the presumption against extraterritorial application. Corporations are often present in many countries, and it would reach too far to say that mere corporate presence suffices. If Congress were to determine otherwise, a statute more specific than the ATS would be required.

In ruling for the defendant (Royal Dutch Petroleum Co.), the Court of Appeals for the Second Circuit dismissed the plaintiff's (Kiobel) complaint, reasoning that the ATS does not apply to tortious acts occurring outside the United States. The U.S. Supreme Court affirmed the decision of the Court of Appeals, ruling in favor of the defendant.

The global consequences of the Supreme Court's decision in *Kiobel v. Royal Dutch Petroleum* for future tort litigation involving claims arising under the Alien Tort Statute are far-reaching. The decision affects both multinational corporations and the victims of alleged wrongdoing by multinational corporations doing business outside the United States. The decision makes it clear that the United States will not serve as "world host" for litigating tortious acts occurring beyond the borders of the United States.

Summary

Although tort law in general protects individuals and entities against wrongdoing involving injuries to the person, damage to property, or impairment of economic interests, business torts focus on economic injuries. Knowing the common types of torts that affect businesses helps future business managers and leaders act ethically and plan for and protect against legal claims based on the types of business torts discussed in the chapter.

Questions for Review

1. **Intentional interference with prospective economic advantage**

   Richard Foust worked as a project manager at San Jose Construction, Inc. (SJC). During the first part of 2004, he was managing 18 different projects. Foust grew unhappy with his employment situation at SJC and spoke with Richard Furtado, the CEO of South Bay Construction Company (South Bay), about his discontentment. South Bay and SJC were competitors. Because of Foust's "proven track record," Furtado offered Foust a project manager position with South Bay. Foust believed that many of the 18 accounts that he was managing for SJC would come with him to his new employer, South Bay. An SJC employee assisted Foust in copying more than 200 documents related to Foust's projects onto a computer disk. The documents were later uploaded to the computer system at South Bay. Shortly after Foust left SJC and joined South Bay, some of SJC's clients terminated their arrangements with SJC and gave their work to South Bay requesting that Foust manage their projects. SJC sued Foust and South Bay alleging among other claims that they intentionally interfered with SJC's prospective economic advantage. Do you believe SJC will be successful in its case against Foust and South Bay? Explain. *San Jose Construction, Inc. v. S.B.C.C., Inc.,* 155 Cal. App. 4th 1528; 67 Cal. Rptr. 3d 54 (2007).

2. **Intentional interference with contractual relations**

   Jennifer completed her graduate studies three years ago. She holds a PhD in philosophy. Her area of expertise is business ethics. After finishing graduate school, she accepted a position with Waltham University (WU) as an assistant professor. Jennifer has a tenure-track appointment and knows she is expected to conduct rigorous research and publish papers in top academic journals. The university also expects tenure-track faculty, like Jennifer, to be effective classroom teachers and advise students as part of their contributions to the academic community. Jennifer experienced much success during her first three years at WU. She published ten articles, four of which are in "A" journals, three in "A–" journals, and three in "B+" journals. Remarkably, she also was presented with WU's highest teaching award at this year's commencement ceremonies.

Based on this high level of performance, Jennifer's contract for her fourth year at WU included a significant merit increase, an internal research grant that was twice the size of regular research grants, and a research expense account to support conference travel and similar kinds of research activities. Jennifer signed the contract in June of the current year and began using the internal research grant to support two ongoing research projects. She also used $2,450 of her research expense account to defray the cost of attending a conference.

One week before the start of the fall semester, Acton University (AU) approached Jennifer about joining its full-time faculty as an associate professor with tenure. The dean at AU told Jennifer that she considers Jennifer to be one of the new "stars" in the business ethics area. AU offered Jennifer a starting salary that was 30 percent higher than her current salary. AU also offered Jennifer a larger research grant than she was receiving at WU. The AU dean was aware of Jennifer's contract obligations with WU at the time she made the offer to Jennifer. Jennifer accepted AU's offer. She informed WU's dean of her decision just three days prior to the start of classes.

a. Does WU have a basis for a lawsuit (cause of action) against Jennifer and AU? If so, what legal arguments could WU advance? Explain.
b. What types of damages could WU seek in its lawsuit against Jennifer and AU? Explain.

3. Ethics and harmful remarks on e-mail

Veronica's expense report was reviewed by her company and she was accused of taking her best friend on a business conference to Paris and charging all expenses for both of them on a company credit card. The company fired Veronica for this dishonest and unethical behavior.

Veronica admitted it was her fault and reimbursed the company for the charged personal expenses. The company then sent a general distribution e-mail to its 300 employees stating that Veronica was fired because of her dishonesty in submitting a false expense report, making it clear that this kind of dishonest behavior would not be tolerated. The e-mail did not mention that Veronica reimbursed the company for the charged personal expenses. Do you believe the company acted ethically when it sent the e-mail about Veronica to its 300 employees? From an ethical perspective, should the company have mentioned in its e-mail that Veronica reimbursed the company? Explain.

4. Fraudulent misrepresentation

Jack L. Hargrove is president and majority shareholder of Jack L. Hargrove Builders, Inc. (Hargrove). Gerald A. Heinz is president and majority shareholder of Gerill Corporation. After engaging in a series of preliminary discussions, Heinz and Hargrove decided to form a joint venture for the purpose of developing a tract of 110 acres of undeveloped land. The land in question was owned by Gerill and was called "the Woodridge properties." As part of the joint venture, Gerill agreed to contribute the land. Hargrove agreed to assume primary management responsibilities. He oversaw the construction process and managed the financial affairs of the joint venture. Hargrove secured a $352,000 loan from the Concordia Federal Savings and Loan Association.

He used part of the proceeds to loan $290,000 to the joint venture, which in turn was used to pay off a mortgage held on a parcel of land in the Woodridge properties. Subsequently, Hargrove approached Heinz about having one partner purchase the interest of the other partner.

At Heinz's request, Hargrove prepared a 19-page list of the joint venture's outstanding debt, including all outstanding loans and unpaid invoices. Determining that he had insufficient resources to purchase Hargrove's interest, Heinz approached a third party (Rosch) about the possibility of Rosch purchasing the interest. Roach decided to purchase Hargrove's interest. The parties signed a contract specifying that Rosch would pay $200,000 for Hargrove's interest. The contract included the following assurance by Hargrove:

That to the best of Jack L. Hargrove Builders, Inc. and Jack L. Hargrove individual's knowledge, they have advised the Gerill Corporation, Gerald Heinz and John Rosch of any and all open invoices and any and all liabilities in the form of monies due and owing on the properties.

The contract also stated "that Rosch, Gerill, and Heinz would assume all liabilities and responsibilities for the Woodridge properties and hold Hargrove harmless and indemnify him from any and all debts, liabilities and claims of every kind and nature which may arise in reference to said Woodridge properties." After the parties signed the contract, it was discovered that the liabilities of the joint venture were significantly understated by Hargrove. Based on this discovery, Rosch, Gerill, and Heinz filed a legal complaint in court against Hargrove alleging among other complaints that Hargrove had purposely misrepresented the facts and intentionally defrauded them. Do you believe Rosch, Gerill, and Heinz will be successful in their case against Hargrove? Explain. *Gerill Corporation v. Jack L. Hargrove Builders, Inc.*, 538 N.E.2d 530 (1989).

5. Intentional interference

List and describe the legal elements that comprise the intentional torts of *intentional interference with contractual relations* and *intentional interference with prospective economic advantage*. Describe the key differences between the two types of torts. Provide two examples of each type of *interference* tort.

6. Commercial disparagement

E.I. Du Pont De Nemours & Company (Du Pont) manufactured and sold Teflon. The plaintiff (F&F) purchased Teflon from Du Pont and used it as the primary ingredient in a product (Tufoil) it manufactured and distributed as a motor oil additive. The label on Tufoil listed Teflon as a primary ingredient. After conducting various tests and analyzing data from external sources, Du Pont concluded that Teflon was not useful as an ingredient for products marketed and sold as oil additives. Therefore, Du Pont issued a press release saying that it would discontinue supplying Teflon for use as an ingredient in oil additives or oils for lubricating internal combustion engines. Shortly after Du Pont issued the press release, F&F filed a lawsuit against Du Pont claiming that Du Pont had severely injured its reputation and economic interests by impugning Tufoil through the press release and had therefore committed the tort of commercial disparagement. Do you believe F&F will be successful in its case against Du Pont? Explain. *Flotech, Inc., and Fluoramics, Inc., v. E.I. Du Pont De Nemours & Company*, 814 F.2d 775 (1st Cir. 1987).

7. Damages

Describe and illustrate the following four types of damages:

- Nominal
- Actual
- General
- Punitive

8. International considerations

Twenty-two Argentinians (hereinafter "the plaintiffs") initiated a lawsuit against Daimler-Chrysler Aktienge-sellschaft (DCAG). In its complaint, the plaintiffs stated that a subsidiary of DCAG, Mercedes-Benz Argentina (MBA), collaborated with Argentinian security forces to kidnap, detain, torture, and kill them and their relatives. Of the 22 plaintiffs, one is a citizen of Chile but a resident of Argentina. The remaining 21 are Argentinian citizens and residents. The plaintiffs either worked at MBA or had relatives who worked there. The plaintiffs alleged that MBA brutally punished them and their relatives because MBA saw them as union agitators. The complaint further alleged that MBA decided to collaborate with the Argentinian security forces as a means of brutalizing the workers. The plaintiffs filed their lawsuit against DCAG in the District Court for the Northern District of California under the Alien Tort Statute (ATS). The plaintiffs selected the United States as a forum for its lawsuit, in part, because DCAG maintained a physical presence (an operational headquarters) in Auburn Hills, California. Do you believe the plaintiffs will be successful in their case against DCAG? Explain. *Bauman v. DaimlerChrysler Corp.*, 644 F.3d 909 (9th Cir. 2011).

Further Reading

Anenson, T. L., *Beyond Chafee: A Process-Based Theory of Unclean Hands*, 47 American Business Law Journal 509–574 (2010).

Daller, Morton F., *Business Torts: A Fifty State Guide* (Wolters Kluwer 2013).

Langvardt, A. W., *A Principled Approach to Compensatory Damages in Corporate Defamation Cases*, 27 American Business Law Journal 491–534 (1990).

Mark, G., *Private FCPA Enforcement*, 49 American Business Law Journal 419–506 (2012).

Neyers, J., *Rights-Based Justifications for the Tort of Unlawful Interference with Economic Relations*, 28 Legal Studies 215–233 (2008).

Prentice, R. A., *Stoneridge, Securities Fraud Litigation, and the Supreme Court*, 45 American Business Law Journal 611–683 (2008).

Weber, C. M., *The Reasons Behind the Rules in the Law of Business Torts*, 2 American Business Law Journal 41–67 (1964).

CHAPTER 20

Product Liability and Warranties

Chapter Objectives

1. To understand the concepts of product liability and strict liability
2. To know the significance of design defects, manufacturing defects, and labeling defects from a legal and ethical perspective, and to be able to distinguish among them
3. To understand the importance of informing buyers about potential risks associated with products through proper warnings and labels
4. To know that warranties often attach to products by contract or by operation of law, and to know when they are required
5. To know the defenses available in product liability, strict liability, and breach of warranty cases

Practical Example: The Ultimate Energy Drink*

The Maximum Corporation designs, manufactures, and sells a trademarked beverage known as *The Ultimate Energy Drink* (Ultimate). This product has been on the market for about five years. During this period, the U.S. Food and Drug Administration (FDA) received reports of ten deaths allegedly connected with the consumption of Ultimate. The Maximum Corporation does not disclose the levels of caffeine or other ingredients contained in each bottle of Ultimate. The combination of high levels of caffeine and other stimulants is suspected by some members of the healthcare community to cause serious injury and, in some cases, death.

It is unclear how long the management team of Maximum Corporation has known about the potential adverse effects of Ultimate. Also unclear is whether the management team is aware of any dangers associated with the unique combination of Ultimate's ingredients. Public data regarding these questions are unavailable, and Maximum's management team has not disclosed any information about known hazards or dangers. However, media outlets are beginning to question whether the risks outweigh the benefits of drinking Ultimate.

Jenna enjoys drinking Ultimate. She believes it provides supplemental energy during workouts and rock-climbing excursions. During the past four years, Jenna estimates she has consumed around 900 bottles of Ultimate. Most often, Jenna purchased Ultimate from the Shop Here Convenience Store, located near Jenna's residence. Recently, Jenna was rushed to the emergency room of a local hospital. She was diagnosed with anxiety, abnormally high blood pressure, a dangerously high heart rate, vomiting, and convulsions — conditions associated with excessive consumption of energy drinks, including Ultimate. Jenna spent six days in the hospital recuperating from internal injuries. Jenna is concerned about her condition and wonders if there is any connection between her medical problems and the consumption of Ultimate.

One way to assess the health consequences of consuming energy drinks is to ask if a connection exists between the consumption of energy drinks and visits to the offices of healthcare providers or hospital emergency rooms. The FDA maintains a surveillance system that solicits, collects, and organizes data about problems related to consumer products such as energy drinks. For example, the FDA collected data about three popular energy drinks from 2004 to 2012 through its Center for Food Safety and Applied Nutrition.[†] During this period, the FDA received 145 reports[‡] regarding energy drinks. The reports cataloged symptoms related to the consumption of energy drinks, including anxiety, high blood pressure, abnormal heart rate, vomiting, diarrhea, chest pain, sleep disorders, dizziness, and depression. Of the 145 reports, 18 resulted in death, and 24 resulted in life-threatening conditions. In response to these alarming numbers, the FDA issued the report presented in Exhibit 20.1 on page 618.

The FDA report includes the following statement about energy drinks:

> The FDA cautions consumers that products marketed as "energy shots" or "energy drinks" are not alternatives to rest or sleep. It is important for consumers to realize that, while stimulants such as caffeine may make one feel more alert and awake, judgment and reaction time can still be impaired by insufficient rest or sleep. If you are thinking about taking one of these products, please consult your health care provider to ensure that you don't have an underlying or undiagnosed medical condition that could worsen as a result of using them.

As you read the chapter, consider the following questions:

1. Do you believe Maximum Corporation has an ethical obligation to disclose the FDA statement to consumers?

2. Even if it is legally acceptable to sell energy drinks to teenagers and young adults, is it ethical?

---

[*] This hypothetical example is completely fictional. It is not based on or associated with any past or present organization that produces energy drinks. The example draws on data reported on the website of the U.S. Food and Drug Administration (FDA).
[†] U.S. Department of Health and Human Services, Food and Drug Administration, Center for Food Safety and Applied Nutrition (CFSAN) Adverse Event Reporting System, Voluntary and Mandatory Reports on [High Energy Drinks] January 1, 2004, through October 23, 2012.
[‡] Each report captures data about patient visits to healthcare providers and hospital emergency rooms.

As consumers, we purchase, use, and enjoy a variety of products on a daily basis. Most of the time, we pay little attention to the technical design of a product, the materials used to make a product, or the warning labels attached to a product. Price, functionality, and appearance often dominate our thinking when deciding whether to buy a product. For example, when buying something as simple as a jacket, we might compare the price of one jacket to another, or we might consider the colors of two comparable jackets, or we might decide to buy one jacket over another because of its insulation capacity. On the other hand, we may not have considered a safety feature such as whether the jacket is made of flammable or nonflammable material. And, there is a good chance we may not have read any of the warning labels attached to the jacket.

This chapter focuses on the characteristics of products that are often overlooked by consumers. As we will see, these overlooked characteristics usually come into play only after a product has caused personal injury or property damage. Consumers might not be interested in knowing whether a jacket is made of flammable or nonflammable materials until after they have sustained a burn-related injury. For example, assume you are standing very close to an open flame at a campfire and your jacket suddenly ignites causing serious burns to your arm and hand. After you have been treated for your injuries, you will likely begin asking questions such as why did my jacket ignite? What type of material was used to make my jacket? If flammable materials were used, you might reasonably ask "why?" Could the manufacturer have reasonably and efficiently used a nonflammable material? These and similar questions form the basis of our study of product liability law and warranties.

To help illustrate the application of product liability law and warranties, the Practical Example introduced you to a product — energy drinks — that is very popular among young adults in the United States. Yet, little is known about the health consequences of consuming energy drinks. If you have ever consumed an energy drink, do you know what ingredients you ingested? Does it matter? Are there any immediate or long-term dangers associated with the consumption of energy drinks? As you think about these and other questions, consider the implications of the FDA report presented in Exhibit 20.1 on page 618.

What Is Product Liability Law?

Product liability law typically involves a lawsuit brought by a party who has suffered an injury or experienced property damage caused by a defective product. An injured party may base a product liability suit on a negligence theory, strict liability, or breach of warranty. For example, assume Robert is cooking on a gas grill designed and manufactured by Great Grill Company.

Consumers have the right to expect that the products they purchase are safe and contain appropriate warnings and labels.

Exhibit 20.1. FDA Report Regarding Energy Drinks

Energy "Drinks" and Supplements: Investigations of Adverse Event Reports*

The FDA is continuing to investigate reports of illness, injury, or death of people who took products marketed as "energy drinks" or "energy shots." The FDA takes every adverse event report seriously and investigates and evaluates other possible causes before deciding whether the product actually caused the medical problem. The existence of an adverse event report does not necessarily mean that the product identified in the report actually caused the adverse event. The FDA assesses the relationship, if any, between a product or ingredient and the reported adverse event.

"Energy" products are relatively new to the market, and manufacturers of these products have labeled some as dietary supplements and others as conventional foods. The FDA regulates both dietary supplements and conventional foods under the Federal Food, Drug, and Cosmetic Act (the FFDCA), but the requirements for them are different. A food additive cannot be used in a conventional food unless it has been approved for that use by the FDA. However, substances that are generally recognized as safe by qualified experts are not considered to be food additives and can therefore be added to conventional foods without preapproval from the FDA. Dietary ingredients (the "active ingredients" in dietary supplements) require no FDA preapproval to be used in a dietary supplement, and the FFDCA requires the FDA to prove that a product is unsafe under the conditions of use suggested in the labeling in order to take the product off the market.

Manufacturers, packers, and distributors of dietary supplements are required by law to report any serious adverse events to the FDA within 15 business days, and to provide (also within 15 business days) any additional medical information they obtain within a year of the adverse event report. However, the FFDCA does not require manufacturers, packers, or distributors of conventional foods to report serious adverse events to the FDA. Therefore, all adverse event reports that the FDA has received in connection with these products are voluntary.

It is important to note that while those who voluntarily report an illness or injury (such as medical professionals, family members, or the consumers themselves) typically identify the product that they believe may have caused the injury or illness, the FDA as a scientific public health agency must carefully investigate and evaluate other possible causes before deciding whether the product actually caused the medical problem.

* * *

The FDA cautions consumers that products marketed as "energy shots" or "energy drinks" are not alternatives to rest or sleep. It is important for consumers to realize that even though stimulants such as caffeine may make one feel more alert and awake, judgment and reaction time can still be impaired by insufficient rest or sleep. If you are thinking about taking one of these products, please consult your healthcare provider to ensure that you don't have an underlying or undiagnosed medical condition that could worsen as a result of using them.

* "Energy Drinks and Supplements: Investigations of Adverse Event Reports: How the FDA Investigates Adverse Event Reports Allegedly Related to Energy Drinks and Supplements," U.S. Food and Drug Administration, November 16, 2012.

As Robert flips a burger, one of the grill's gas jets suddenly and unexpectedly surges. The surge sends a flame high above the grill. The flame seriously burns Robert's arm. Robert could consider bringing a product liability suit against Great Grill Company arguing that his burn resulted from a defectively designed or manufactured gas grill.

Today, most product liability suits, such as the one Robert could bring against Great Grill Company, are based on the legal theories of negligence, strict liability, and breach of warranty. However, during the early years of product liability claims, strict liability and negligence were unavailable to support a product liability suit. As discussed below, contract law served as the legal basis for many of the early product liability cases.

Product Liability: Origin in Contract Law

During the first part of the nineteenth century, buyers typically purchased goods directly from the maker of the goods. After preliminary discussions had occurred, the maker and the buyer would negotiate the terms of the contract. Later on, if the goods were found to be defective, the buyer would sue the maker for breach of contract, arguing that the product failed to meet the buyer's expectations. As demonstrated by the Case Illustration, *Barnard v. Kellogg*, the courts were reluctant to find

Case Illustration

Barnard was a merchant who sold wool. Bond & Company served as Barnard's sales agent. Barnard instructed Bond to require all customers to inspect each and every bale of wool prior to purchase. A customer named Kellogg sent a representative to Barnard's warehouse to purchase some wool. Bond told the representative to inspect each and every bale of wool, but the representative decided to inspect only a sample. After the wool had been delivered, Kellogg discovered a significant amount of rotten wool due to a packing error. Barnard was unaware of the packing error. Kellogg demanded compensation for his losses, which Barnard refused to pay. Kellogg sued Barnard for damages arguing the contract promised that the wool would be packed correctly and that the wool in each bale would be similar to the samples inspected. The trial court held for Kellogg finding that an *implied warranty* existed in the contract whereby Barnard warranted that each bale would be properly packaged and would be similar to the samples inspected. The Court of Appeals affirmed the trial court's decision. However, the U.S. Supreme Court reversed, holding that the contract between Barnard and Kellogg called for each bale to be inspected prior to purchase. Therefore, the Court concluded that Kellogg must assume the responsibility of his decision not to inspect each and every bale of wool. The Court stated that it could not create a warranty where one did not exist in the original contract. *Barnard v. Kellogg*, 77 U.S. 383 (1871).

the maker liable for defective products unless the buyer could prove that the maker breached one or more of the terms of the contract.

As illustrated by the Kellogg case, courts exercised restraint in the early years of product liability suits. They were inclined to bind parties to the explicit terms of the contract and not search for alternatives beyond the four corners of the contract itself. However, as manufacturers began to use techniques and processes to "mass produce" goods, the earlier arrangement of the buyer purchasing goods directly from the maker largely disappeared. Consequently, injured parties and courts began to look for alternative legal theories to support product liability claims. During the first part of the twentieth century, the legal doctrine of negligence served as the most common alternative to be employed by the courts. And, by the middle part of the twentieth century, the legal doctrine of strict liability assumed prominence.

Case Illustration

The defendant, Buick Motor Co., designed and manufactured automobiles. The plaintiff, MacPherson, purchased a new Buick from a dealer. One of the automobile's wheels collapsed while MacPherson was driving. The collapse caused an accident that resulted in personal injury to MacPherson. MacPherson sued Buick Motor Co. based on a negligence theory. The evidence presented at trial indicated that Buick could have discovered the wheel's defect had it conducted a reasonable inspection. Buick purchased the wheels from an unrelated third party, and it did not inspect the wheels prior to placing them on the new Buicks. The jury held for MacPherson. The appeals court affirmed the decision of the trial court, finding Buick Motor Co. liable for failing to inspect the wheels prior to placing them on the new Buicks. The Court stated that if a manufacturer puts a finished product on the market without conducting a reasonable inspection, liability will follow whenever foreseeable danger is present. *MacPherson v. Buick Motor Co.*, 217 N.Y. 382, 111 N.E. 1050 (1916).

Product Liability Suits Based on a Negligence Theory

As mentioned above, the legal doctrine of negligence became the primary basis for advancing product liability claims during the first half of the twentieth century. *MacPherson v. Buick Motor Co.*, a 1916 seminal product liability case, introduced negligence as a basis for suing manufacturers and sellers of defective products.

The significance of *MacPherson* is that the Court allowed an injured party to sue the maker of a product (Buick Motor Co.) even though the injured party did not have a contractual relationship with the maker. MacPherson purchased his Buick from a dealer, not from the Buick Motor Co. As discussed earlier, a product liability suit based in contract would have denied MacPherson the opportunity to sue the Buick Motor Co. for lack of privity. However, the *MacPherson* Court based its decision not in contract law, but on a negligence theory.

The elements required to establish a successful negligence case were discussed in Chapter 19, "Business Torts." Let us remember that the

Companies that design, manufacture, or sell inherently dangerous products may be held strictly liable for injuries caused by their products.

elements apply to a particular set of facts and circumstances. For example, a negligence-based product liability case requires the injured party to establish that the manufacturer, the seller, or other parties in the chain of distribution breached their duty of care. The chain of distribution includes the designer of the product, the manufacturer, the retail seller, and other parties associated with the product. The duty is owed not just to the initial buyer, but to any reasonably foreseeable party who might have a connection with the product, such as second-hand users and innocent bystanders.

Although the "duty of care" will vary from one manufacturer to the next, it generally involves: (1) a duty to design a reasonably safe product to the extent economically feasible, (2) a duty to manufacture the product properly, and (3) a duty to label the product correctly.

Product Liability Suits Based on Strict Liability

The landmark 1963 case of *Greenman v. Yuba Power Products, Inc.* introduced the application of strict liability to product liability cases. In finding for the plaintiff in *Greenman*, the California Supreme Court held that a plaintiff need not prove negligence or breach of warranty to succeed in a product liability suit. Rather, the doctrine of strictly liability may be used as an alternative legal theory.

An Ethical Insight: John Locke — Actions Follow Thoughts: Why Do Some Executives "Cross the Line" and Place Profits Above Safety?

"I have always thought the actions of men the best interpreters of their thoughts."
John Locke (1632–1704)

Arguably, Locke's social contract theory, based on his conviction that human nature is characterized by reason and tolerance and that human nature allows individuals to be selfish, might help explain why some corporate executives feel entitled to "cross the line" in placing profits above safety. After all, Locke's belief that in a natural state all people are equal and independent and that all people have the natural right to defend their "Life, Health, Liberty, or Possessions" served as the basis for one of the opening phrases of the U.S. Declaration of Independence: *"We hold these truths to be self-evident, that all men are created equal, that they are endowed by their Creator with certain unalienable Rights, that among these are Life, Liberty and the Pursuit of Happiness."*

Unlike negligence, a product liability case based on strict liability does not require an injured party to prove that the manufacturer breached its duty of care in order to recover damages. **Strict liability** holds manufacturers responsible for their actions even when they acted with due diligence and reasonable care. As stated by the Court in *Greenman* (see the following Case Illustration), the concept underlying strict product liability is that the manufacturer is in a better position than the customer to know about the risks and dangers associated with its product. Manufacturers are also better able to absorb the costs associated with product-related injuries.

Even though an injured party need not prove *how* a product became defective in a strict liability case, the injured party must establish that the product was defective when it left the control of the manufacturer or seller. The injured party must also prove that it was the "defective condition" of the product that caused the injury.

Case Illustration

The plaintiff, Greenman, was seriously injured when he was operating a power tool manufactured by the defendant, Yuba Power Products, Inc. While using the power tool to trim a board, a piece of wood unexpectedly broke off from the board striking the plaintiff in the head. Thereafter, the plaintiff sued the defendant, seeking damages to compensate for the personal injuries he sustained. The trial court found no evidence of negligence or breach of warranty on the part of the defendant, Yuba Power Products. Therefore, the Court found in favor of the defendant. Greenman appealed his case to the California Supreme Court. In holding for Greenman, the California Supreme Court determined that a plaintiff need not prove negligence or breach of warranty in a product liability case. Rather, the Court held that "a manufacturer is strictly liable in tort when an article he places on the market, knowing that it is to be used without inspection for defects, proves to have a defect that causes injury to a human being." The Court stated that strict liability covers any defective product that creates unreasonable hazards. Furthermore, the Court noted that strict liability from a public policy perspective insures that "the costs of injuries resulting from defective products are borne by the manufacturers that put such products on the market rather than by the injured persons who are powerless to protect themselves." *Greenman v. Yuba Power Products, Inc.*, 59 Cal.2d 57, 337 P.2d 897 (1963).

Most states embrace strict liability as a theory for advancing a product liability suit; however, strict liability laws vary from state to state. For example, some states allow injured parties to seek damages for personal injury and property damage, while others allow damages for personal injury only. Some states support the awarding of compensatory and punitive damages, and others allow for compensatory damages only.

Restatement (Third) of Torts — Product Liability: Design Defects, Manufacturing Defects and Marketing Defects

The Restatement (Third) of Torts (Product Liability) takes a different approach to analyzing product liability law.[1] Rather than focusing on the legal doctrines of contract, negligence, and strict liability, it classifies product liability claims according to the type of defect: (1) design, (2) manufacturing, or (3) marketing (inadequate warnings and instructions). Although different in many respects, each category under the Restatement's classification scheme shares a common theme — examining the relationship between a product defect and an injury.

Need to Establish a "Defect" in the Product

Many products have the capacity to cause injury, but only those injuries associated with a defective product invoke the application of product liability law. Thus, if a person is injured while using a product that is not otherwise defective, a product liability suit would be inappropriate.

Design Defects

What is a design defect? A design defect is a defect resulting from something that the manufacturer planned or designed. At first glance, this may not make sense. Why would anyone purposely include a defect in the design of a product? Well, of course, they would not. Think of a design defect as an error in the planning process. If a product has a design defect, the defect will be present each time the product is used. Thus, if one person sustains injuries because of a defect in the design of a product, other users may expect to incur similar kinds of injuries.

---

[1]In 1997, the American Law Institute adopted the Restatement (Third) of Torts: Product Liability.

To prove a design defect, an injured party must examine the design plans. To accomplish this task, the injured party usually hires an expert to review the plans and express an opinion about risk and safety issues embedded in the plans. In weighing the opinion of an expert, courts recognize that manufacturers often have to balance product functionality with product safety. At times, this can be a difficult balancing act. Minimizing risk may sacrifice a product's functionality, efficiency, and effectiveness, and it may cost more to produce the product.

For example, assume that a company designs and manufactures a poison to eliminate household rodents. By its very nature, this is a highly dangerous and lethal product. If used inappropriately (placed near pets or young children), a risk exists that the poison could be consumed by someone other than the intended target—rodents. The manufacturer could reduce the risk of serious bodily harm or death by lowering the toxin levels in the product. However, by lowering the toxin levels, the product may no longer be suitable for its intended purpose—eliminating rodents. In this example, the need to balance risk and functionality is critical. No clear answer may seem obvious, but courts recognize that as a society we must be willing to assume some level of risk in order to have access to a broad range of products. Consider the Case Illustration of *Miller v. Dvornik*.

Voluntarily using an inherently dangerous product may preclude the awarding of damages for injuries sustained while using the product.

Case Illustration

The plaintiff, 19-year-old David Miller, sustained personal injuries when he was hit by an automobile and thrown from his Yamaha motorcycle. Miller sued the driver of the automobile, Dvornik, the manufacturer of the motorcycle, Yamaha Motor Corporation, U.S.A., and the retailer who sold him the motorcycle, Performance Center, Limited. The motorcycle did not have safety crash bars, an optional feature. Miller argued that the motorcycle was *unreasonably dangerous* because

- the design of the motorcycle failed to incorporate safety crash bars as a protective device for the user's legs;
- crash bars were not recommended to users as a safety option; and
- the motorcycle failed to provide a cautionary warning that motorcycles are inherently dangerous vehicles when operated without crash bars.

In its opinion, the court observed that motorcycles are a common mode of transportation for individuals of Miller's age. The court concluded that any competent 19-year-old person can be expected to know the dangers inherent in riding a motorcycle. Furthermore, the court stated, as a matter of common understanding, that crash bars attached to a motorcycle will not protect a rider who is thrown from a motorcycle. At best, crash bars protect riders only when the motorcycle falls over. The court stated that the risks associated with riding a motorcycle are obvious to the general public. Therefore, the court held for the defendants, stating that the law does not award damages to an injured party who voluntarily uses a product with *inherent risks* that are obvious to all who come in contact with the product, such as a motorcycle. *Miller v. Dvornik*, 501 N.E. 2d 160 (1986).

Manufacturing Defects

Manufacturing defects represent an error or mistake in the manufacturing process. Manufacturing defects are unintended flaws. They are mistakes that occur accidentally during the manufacturing process. A manufacturing error (defect) can be defined as a deviation from the intended design of the product. The error causes the finished product to be deficient in some way. Of significance to the user, the error may cause the product to malfunction and possibly cause injury to the user or damage to the user's property.

Under a negligence theory, the manufacturer might not be liable for a defectively manufactured product as long as the manufacturer exercised reasonable care in the production process. However, under a strict liability theory, the manufacturer may be liable, even in the face of exercising reasonable care, simply because the finished product ended up being defective and caused personal injury. This result may seem harsh and impose undue harshness on the manufacturer, but the alternative is to require that an innocent user or bystander absorb the cost of injuries caused by a manufacturer's error. As stated by the court in *Greenman v. Yuba Power Products, Inc.* (discussed earlier in the chapter), strict liability insures that "the costs of injuries resulting from defective products are borne by the manufacturers that put such products on the market rather than by the injured persons who are powerless to protect themselves."

The following example demonstrates the difference between a design defect and a manufacturing defect. If a boot is designed with a heel that is too thin to support a person's weight while walking at a normal pace and the person falls and suffers an injury, the injured person could argue that the injury resulted from a defectively designed heel. On the other hand, if the heel is properly designed but has not been properly glued to the rest of the boot and a person falls and sustains an injury, the injured person could argue that the injury resulted from an error (defect) in the manufacturing process.

In addition to the many legal issues associated with product liability, a variety of ethical issues surround a company's managerial decision-making when trying to balance a product's risk against its functionality. Consider the following scenario in the Manager's Compliance and Ethics Meeting.

Manager's Compliance and Ethics Meeting

The Fewer Yellow Teeth the Better

Your company, Whiter Teeth, Inc., manufactures an over-the-counter product that whitens teeth. After extensive testing and at great expense, the product has been approved by the U.S. Food and Drug Administration (FDA). Approximately 20 percent of the users have complained of extensive gum damage that includes, in many instances, loss of teeth. The company's research has revealed that the competition has experienced about the same rate of complaints (20 percent), and in some cases a higher percentage of problems with a similar product. Legal counsel has advised Whiter Teeth to continue production of the product in light of FDA approval and has argued that a percentage of users will probably always have an adverse reaction. A recent market survey demonstrated that the overwhelming majority of users are pleased with the product. Legal counsel has mandated that a now warning label be attached to the product. The warning states: "*Consult with your dentist before using this product as it may cause serious gum problems.*"

Whiter Teeth has a code of ethics that reads "*Our customer's health is our foremost concern and all our products are extensively reviewed for safety. If ever our products are found to cause harm, they are immediately removed from production.*" The ethics officer of Whiter Teeth, Inc., has called for a manager's meeting to review the ethical obligations of the company. The ethics officer recognizes that the product is legally approved by the FDA, and it appears to be no more dangerous than the competitions' products. Some of the managers are insisting that FDA approval and the new warning are sufficient legal protections; therefore, there should be no further discussion about this highly profitable product. However, the ethics officer is concerned about the promise made in the company's code of ethics and its commitment to maintain an ethical culture. The ethics officer argues that production should be stopped until the product has been further tested for safety in accordance with the company's code of ethics. What are the ethical issues presented in the facts? How would you resolve this ethical dilemma?

Utilitarianism. One approach to resolving the dilemma is to apply the utilitarian principle of *"the greatest happiness (good) for the greater number of people,"* an expression first used by Francis Hutcheon (1694-1746) and further explained in the utilitarian theories of Jeremy Bentham (1748-1832) and John Stuart Mill (1806-1873). Because the product is approved by the FDA and 80 percent of the users are pleased with it and have not suffered any adverse effects, one could argue that the principle of *"the greatest happiness (good) for the greater number of people,"* resolves the dilemma by holding that no intervention is necessary. Further, since almost all drugs have side effects, it could be considered unethical to deny public access to the product when a minority of users will experience physical problems. A **rule utilitarian** argument would balance between the benefit of 80 percent of the users being pleased with an effective (functional) product and the risk that a smaller percentage of users (20 percent) may suffer gum damage. This is "consequential ethics" based on the result that justifies bringing a useful product to the majority of consumers. With the new warning on the container advising customers to seek the approval of a dentist before using the product, it is safe to assume that some dentists may not recommend the product to their patients. This ethical utilitarian argument supports the managers who want to continue to produce the product. Do you agree?

Kant's Categorical Imperatives. One could argue that Kant would find an absolute moral obligation to stop production because the consumers should be treated as an end in themselves and not merely as a means for profit. Kant would argue that we have a duty to do the right thing (stop production and attempt to fix the problem) regardless of the consequences, including a possible decline in revenues. The company's code of ethics is a promise to the public that if a product causes harm, it will be immediately removed from production. Breaking that promise and exploiting 20 percent of the customers who are unhappy with the product and may sustain injuries is ethically wrong regardless of the consequences. Do you agree?

Your answer should address the many issues presented in the case: 20 percent of customers sustain serious gum disease and loss of teeth; FDA approval of the product; a new warning suggesting approval by a dentist and disclosing adverse effects; a promise to the public in the code of ethics; and a profitable product with an 80 percent approval rating. If you believe it is ethical for the company to continue production, suppose that 40 to 50 percent of consumers were injured from its use, would sustaining the product under these circumstances be unethical?

Marketing Defects

While design and manufacturing defects relate directly to a flaw in the product itself, **marketing defects** address what the manufacturer or seller says about the product. A product may be properly designed and manufactured yet still cause harm because of deficient (defective) warnings or instructions. Marketing defects deal with questions such as whether the manufacturer properly described and illustrated how to use the product safely (operating instructions), or whether the manufacturer provided adequate warnings about any dangers associated with the product (warning labels).

For example, consider the In-Depth Ethical Case Analysis of *Liriano v. Hobart Corporation*, in which the court found the manufacturer of a meat grinder liable for failure to warn the user of the danger of operating the product without a protective shield.

In-Depth Ethical Case Analysis

Liriano v. Hobart Corporation, 170 F.3d 264 (2d Cir. 1999)

Facts

The plaintiff, Luis Liriano, injured his arm while operating a meat grinder owned by his employer, Super Associated. The defendant, Hobart Corporation, sold the meat grinder to Super Associated. In its original design, the meat grinder included a safety guard. However, Super Associated removed the safety guard and allowed its employees, including the plaintiff, to use the meat grinder without the benefit of a safety guard.

At the time of his injury, Liriano was 17 years old, not familiar with customs and practices in the United States (he had recently immigrated to the United States), and inexperienced (he had been on the job for only one week). The plaintiff had not received any instructions from his employer about how to use the meat grinder, and the defendant, Hobart Corporation, did not provide any warnings about the dangers of using the machine without the safety guard attached to it.

Liriano sued Hobart Corporation for failure to warn consumers, users, and bystanders about the dangers of using its meat grinders without the safety guard attached to it. The trial court held in favor of Liriano, awarding him monetary damages for his injuries. Hobart appealed, arguing that as a matter of law it had no duty to warn the plaintiff (or any other party) about the dangers of using its meat grinders because the dangers of using an inherently dangerous machine, such as a meat grinder, are obvious.

Issue

Are some dangers so obvious, such as operating a meat grinder, that no warning is required as a matter of law?

Holding

The Court held that, as a matter of law, the dangers of using an inherently dangerous machine, such as a meat grinder, are not sufficiently obvious to excuse a manufacturer from providing a warning, particularly when the warning could inform users about safer ways of using the machine.

From the Court's Opinion

In addressing the question of whether some dangers are so obvious, such as operating a meat grinder, that no warning is required as a matter of law, the Court stated that warnings do more than simply caution people about known dangers. They also assist people in making informed decisions. The Court noted that warnings communicate two types of messages. First, warnings caution people that a particular place, object, or activity may be dangerous. Second, warnings inform people about ways of avoiding dangers. The Court offered the following example to illustrate this point: *If a highway sign says merely Danger—Steep Grade, it says less than a sign that says Steep Grade Ahead—Follow Suggested Detour to Avoid Dangerous Areas.*

In expounding on this illustration, the Court observed that *if the hills or mountains responsible for the steep grade are plainly visible, the first sign merely states what a reasonable person would know without having to be warned. The second sign tells drivers what they might not have otherwise known: there is another road that is flatter and less hazardous. Drivers who believe the road up the mountainous pass is the only way to reach their destination might well choose to drive on the mountainous road despite its steep grade. However, drivers who are aware of an alternative (safer) road might choose to take the safer road even if it takes longer.* Based on this analogy, the Court concluded that one who grinds meat, like one who drives on a steep road, can benefit not only from being told that the activity is dangerous but from being told of a safer way of grinding meat.

Ethical Questions

1. Do designers and manufactures of inherently and obviously dangerous products have an ethical duty not only to warn customers, users, and bystanders about known and potential dangers, but also a duty to inform them about alternative, safer ways of using a product?

2. If designers and manufacturers are unaware of alternative, safer ways of using a product, do they have an ethical duty to search for safer alternatives?

Ethical Theory Analysis

What constitutes an "inherently dangerous product"? A piece of machinery that the average, reasonable person would immediately recognize as potentially dangerous? A snow blower, a high-voltage generator, a handgun? Throughout this textbook we have been emphasizing "due diligence" and "risk assessment" that should, among other things, identify products that are inherently dangerous and the manufacturer's obligation to attach adequate warnings to the

product along with safety and operational instructions. Ethically, managers should insist on providing warnings for the use of dangerous products and suggest the safest use "to avoid danger."

This case addresses the legal issue of a "defect by reason of inadequate warnings or instructions (marketing defect)" [The Restatement (Third) of Torts: Product Liability]. Did the manufacturer of the meat grinder have, in addition to a legal obligation, an ethical responsibility to inform the operator that the meat grinder should not be used without a guard to protect the worker's hands and arms? If so, is there an ethical duty to warn and provide a safer way to use a product? The court noted, "Plaintiff was only seventeen years old at the time of his injury and had only recently immigrated to the United States. He had been on the job for only one week. He had never been given instructions about how to use the meat grinder."

Should a manufacturer anticipate a novice worker, who perhaps is not proficient in the use of the English language, using the meat grinder? If so, should the warning be in a language other than English, such as Spanish or some other commonly spoken language in the United States? The designers of the meat grinder surely knew of possible dangers, not immediately obvious to a user, and how the dangers could be avoided. Managers, engineers, and legal counsel should exercise due diligence and risk assessment when designing and manufacturing a dangerous product and carefully assess what constitutes an adequate warning and set of safety instructions.

W. D. Ross's prima facie duty to prevent harm would impose a serious ethical obligation on the manufacturer of a dangerous product to attach an adequate warning to the product informing the user of potential harm if used improperly. Because the designers of the product test it for safety, they would be aware of the safest way to use the product, and they have an ethical duty to prevent harm by disclosing all relevant information to the user. Under Ross's duty to prevent harm, there is an ethical obligation to search for possible misuse of a product and to search for alternative ways to use a product more safely. Once discovered, there is an ethical obligation to inform users of all relevant information about the product. If one additional paragraph in a set of operational and safety instructions could save an arm or a life, why not include it?

Defenses to Product Liability Claims

One of the most common defenses in a product liability case is that the injured party substantially altered the product after it left the manufacturer's control. In these cases, the manufacturer argues that the alteration made by the victim caused the victim's injury. Another defense is available when the manufacturer is able to show that the victim used the product in a manner unforeseeable by the manufacturer and unrelated to the product's intended use. To maintain a successful defense, the manufacturer must show that the unintended use of the product is what caused the victim's injury. An increasingly popular defense is the state-of-the-art defense. The strategy of this defense is to show that the manufacturer used the best available technology and production processes to design and manufacture the product.

As discussed in Chapter 19, the traditional defenses used in a negligence case are available with equal force when negligence serves as the underlying theory for a product liability case. These defenses include contributory negligence, comparative negligence, and assumption of risk.

Warranties

A case brought forward on a warranty theory asserts that a manufacturer or seller is liable to an injured party because the manufacturer or seller breached a promise (warranty) made about the product. Product liability cases rely mostly on tort law (negligence and strict liability), but contract law may play an important role in the litigation of a product liability case, particularly when expressed or implied warranties are asserted. Article 2 of the Uniform Commercial Code (UCC) addresses breach of warranty claims.

Express Warranties

As the title suggests, a manufacturer or seller of a product makes an **express warranty** when it makes an explicit factual claim about the quality, safety, or functionality of the product. Express warranties are governed by Section 2-313 of the UCC, which provides that an express warranty is created in one of three ways:

- Any affirmation of fact or promise made by the seller to the buyer that relates to the goods and becomes part of the basis of the bargain creates an express warranty that the goods shall conform to the affirmation or promise;
- Any description of the goods that is made part of the basis of the bargain creates an express warranty that the goods shall conform to the description; and
- Any sample or model that is made part of the basis of the bargain creates an express warranty that the whole of the goods shall conform to the sample or model.

Implied Warranties

Unlike an express warranty, an implied warranty is not one that is affirmatively made by the manufacturer or seller. The UCC creates two types of implied warranties. Section 2-314 establishes an implied warranty of merchantability. Section 2-315 provides for an implied warranty of fitness for a particular purpose.

Implied Warranty of Merchantability

Unless excluded or modified by Section 2-316 of the UCC, an **implied warranty** of merchantability warrants that goods shall be merchantable. This warranty is implied in the contract for the sale of goods if the seller is a merchant regarding the kind of goods sold. To be merchantable under Section 2-314:

- Goods must pass without objection in the trade under the contract description;
- In the case of fungible goods, goods are of average quality within the description;
- Goods are fit for the ordinary purposes for which such goods are used;
- Goods run, within the variations permitted by the agreement, of even kind, quality, and quantity within each unit and among all units involved;
- Goods are adequately contained, packaged, and labeled as the agreement may require; and
- Goods conform to the promise or affirmations of fact made on the container or label, if any.

Essentially, an implied warranty of merchantability provides that a product will function in the way the buyer expects it to perform. For example, if a buyer purchases a new lamp, the buyer expects the lamp to provide light in an efficient and safe manner. The buyer does not expect the lamp to explode and set fire to a room. Some sellers may attempt to circumvent the rules surrounding an implied warranty of merchantability by selling a product in an "as is" condition. However, many states provide that an implied warranty of merchantability may not be avoided by using the words "as is" in the sale of goods.

Implied Warranty of Fitness for a Particular Purpose

Section 2-315 of the UCC provides that "where the seller at the time of contracting has reason to know any particular purpose for which the goods are required and that the buyer is relying on the seller's skill or judgment to select or furnish suitable goods, there is . . . an implied warranty that the goods shall be fit for such purpose."

Facts play an important role in determining the existence of an implied warranty. It is important to distinguish the "particular purpose" for which goods are to be used from an "ordinary purpose." For example, if a mountain climber is planning a trip to the Himalayas and the seller is aware of this plan, the sale of a sleeping bag by the seller should be viewed as a sale for a "particular purpose." The seller knows the sleeping bag must be of a quality to accommodate very cold temperatures, rather than the "ordinary" temperatures found in the locality of the store. If the buyer relies on the seller's recommended product selection, and the sleeping bag is not suitable for use in the Himalayas, then the seller is liable for breach of implied warranty of fitness for a particular purpose.

Global Perspective: International Product Liability Law

Many countries have adopted some form of legislation regarding product liability law. Although the particular requirements may vary from one country to the next, the basic tenants of product liability law remain consistent.

The Product Liability Directive of the European Union

The Product Liability Directive[2] represents one of the European Union's most important directives. Most of the countries that form the European Union have passed the Product Liability Directive, thus offering a vehicle for injured parties in those countries to seek monetary damages for injuries sustained from defective products.

The directive calls for member states to impose strict liability on the manufacturers of defective products that cause personal injury or property damage. The directive covers any defective product manufactured or imported into the European Union that causes personal injury or property damage. The directive applies to the sale of products; the rendering of services is not covered by the directive.[3]

---

[2]A Guide to the EU Directive Concerning Liability for Defective Products (Product Liability Directive), prepared for the U.S. Department of Commerce, Global Standards Program, Office of Standards Services, National Institute of Standards and Technology, Gaithersburg, MD 20899, by Helen Delaney and Rene van de Zande.
[3]*Id.*

International law cuts across national boundaries and is debated in settings such as the Berlaymont Building, the European Commission headquarters in Brussels.

Article 1 of the directive states that a manufacturer shall be liable for damages caused by a defect in its product. The directive includes the following elements:[4]

- It introduces the concept of strict liability (without fault) on the part of the producer in favor of the victim;
- It places the burden of proof on the injured party insofar as the damage, the defect, and the causal relationship between the two are concerned;
- It establishes joint and several liability of all operators in the production chain in favor of the injured party, so as to provide a financial guarantee for compensation;
- It provides for exoneration of the producer when the producer proves the existence of certain facts explicitly set out in the directive;
- It establishes liability limitations in terms of time, by virtue of uniform deadlines;
- It establishes illegality of clauses limiting or excluding liability toward the injured party;
- It establishes a limit for financial liability; and
- It provides for a regular review of the directive's content.

The above discussion provides only a sampling of product liability law in other countries, but it serves as a reminder to consult the laws of other nations when engaging in global business.

---

[4]*Id.*

Summary

Product liability law and breach of warranty claims hold the designers, manufacturers, and sellers of goods responsible for the safety and functionality of the goods they place in the marketplace. Injuries due to design defects, manufacturing defects, or inadequate warnings and labels will support legal claims based on product liability suits (negligence or strict liability) or breach of express or implied warranty claims. A variety of defenses are available to companies involved in product liability or breach of warranty lawsuits. In some instances, although a company may have a legal defense, it may have an ethical obligation to maintain a higher standard of safety in producing and selling a product than required by the law in order to sustain an ethical corporate culture.

Questions for Review

1. Strict liability and breach of warranty

Krista was a passenger in a rented van. She sustained injuries when the driver of the van slammed into a tree after the van's brakes failed. The driver of the van was not an authorized driver pursuant to the rental agreement with the rental company. The driver's brother-in-law signed the rental contract; he was not in the van at the time of the crash. He gave the driver of the van, his sister-in-law, permission to drive the van; however, he failed to list his sister-in-law as an authorized driver on the rental contract. Krista wishes to file a lawsuit against the rental company under two legal theories: strict liability and breach of warranty. Do you think Krista will be successful in pursuing her legal claims? Explain. *Banks v. International Rental and Leasing Corporation*, 680 F.3d 296 (3d Cir. 2012).

2. Design defects and manufacturing defects

Over the course of two days, Carmella heard repeated "pecking" sounds coming from the north side of her three-story house. Toward the end of the second day, she examined the exterior of her house and noticed two large holes located near the roof. To inspect the holes more closely, Carmella used a new extension-style ladder that she purchased recently at a local hardware store. With the ladder extended fully, Carmella climbed to the roof of her house and inspected the holes. She concluded the holes were caused by a woodpecker and decided to conduct some research to identify ways of keeping woodpeckers from damaging her house. As Carmella began to climb down the ladder, it suddenly collapsed causing serious injury to Carmella's right arm and shoulder.

What legal advice would you give to Carmella? Explain.

3. Ethics and the sale of I buprofen

Many drug companies sell an over-the-counter pain reliever that contains ibuprofen. Recent medical reports have claimed that excessive usage of ibuprofen can cause serious liver damage. Some companies sell Ibuprofen in an extra-strength pill that has a double dosage resulting in faster pain relief. Ibuprofen has been approved by the FDA with an acknowledgment of, in some instances, harmful side effects. Rachel, a compliance and ethics officer for a hypothetical drug company, is concerned that in view of the latest reports from the FDA, the labels and the package information used by her company about ibuprofen should be more explicit. About 10 percent of the company's customers have sustained serious liver damage by using the drug. The company's board members are split on her recommendation. Some are arguing it is best to leave things as they are because their competition has about the same percentage of injured customers. Other board members agree with Rachel's recommendation on the theory that, although some consumers may not buy the product after reading a more detailed label on Ibuprofen's side effects, over the long term, the best ethical course is to be sensitive to the new report and "do the right thing." Rachel has consulted you for your ethical advice. Respond to Rachel using ethical principles in support of your advice.

4. **Design defect, manufacturing defect, inadequate labels, and breach of warranty**

Describe and illustrate the differences among design defects, manufacturing defects, inadequate warnings and labels (marketing defects), and breach of express and implied warranties.

5. **Design defect**

James was driving a vehicle manufactured by a major automobile manufacturer. Accompanying him were his wife and two children. James accidently drove over a curb and crashed into the concrete base of a light pole while traveling at a speed of 25 miles per hour. Prior to the crash, James did not apply the vehicle's brakes. James's two children sustained injuries as a result of the crash. James believes the vehicle's seatbelts were defectively designed for children. Therefore, when the vehicle crashed into the light pole, the seatbelts failed to safeguard his children. James plans to file a lawsuit against the automobile manufacturer that designed and manufactured the vehicle. Do you think James will be successful in pursuing his legal claims? Explain. *Stark v. Ford Motor Company*, 365 N.C. 468; 723 S.E.2d 753 (2012).

6. **Manufacturing defect and breach of warranty**

The Greenshore Shoe Company is located in New Jersey along Interstate 95. It sells shoes directly to customers, many of whom visit Greenshore while traveling along Interstate 95. Greenshore purchases shoes directly from the Redhouse Corporation located in North Carolina. Marina purchased shoes recently from Greenshore during a trip from her home in Maine to a vacation resort in Florida.

During her vacation in Florida, Marina tumbled down a staircase in Whitehall Department Store breaking her left ankle and sustaining a mild concussion. After the accident, Marina examined the shoes she purchased from Greenshore and noticed a defect in the left heel of the shoe. Marina is exploring the possibility of suing Greenshore, Redhouse, and Whitehall. She hopes to recover compensatory (actual) damages and punitive damages.

What legal advice would you give to Marina? Explain.

7. **Defective design**

Brian worked as a painter for a major U.S. corporation. Over a period of nearly a decade, he was responsible for painting different aspects of the corporation's plant, including the floors, walls, and ceilings. A number of years after leaving this job, Brian developed a life-threatening form of cancer that ultimately claimed his life. Brian's surviving spouse would like to sue the company that designed and manufactured the paint Brian used during his employment with the major U.S. corporation. Supported by the conclusions of a number of medical expert witnesses, Brian's surviving spouse believes that an ingredient in the paint, benzene, caused her husband to develop the cancer that ultimately took his life. Do you think Brian's surviving spouse will be successful in pursuing her legal claims? Explain. *Schultz v. Akzo Nobel Paints, LLC*, 2013 U.S. App. LEXIS 13059 (7th Cir. 2013).

8. **International considerations**

What are the essential elements of the Product Liability Directive of the European Union?

Further Reading

Hurd, S. N., and F. E. Zollers, *Desperately Seeking Harmony: The European Community's Search for Uniformity in Product Liability Law*, 30 American Business Law Journal 35–68 (1992).

Leibman, J. H., *The Manufacturer's Responsibility to Warn Product Users of Unknowable Dangers*, 21 American Business Law Journal 403–438 (1984).

Metzger, M. B., *Products Liability and the Seller of Used Goods*, 15 American Business Law Journal 159–186 (1978).

Razook, N. M., *Legal and Extralegal Barriers to Federal Product Liability Reform*, 32 American Business Law Journal 541–582 (1996).

Singh, R., *Risk, Informational Asymmetry and Product Liability: An Enquiry into Conflicting Objectives*, 14 Pacific Economic Review 89–112 (2009).

CHAPTER 21

Environmental Law and Sustainability

Chapter Objectives

1. To understand that environmental issues transcend national borders
2. To recognize the widespread concerns regarding air pollution and understand the regulatory efforts being made to address this in the United States and internationally
3. To appreciate that unclean water poses one of the world's greatest health risks and to understand the actions legal systems have taken and continue to take to address this problem
4. To understand the regulatory measures that have been taken to prevent harm from toxic substances and to ensure the safety of waste disposal
5. To understand the efforts being taken to develop alternative energy sources
6. To understand the importance of making business decisions for a sustainable future

Practical Example: Two Approaches to the Environment

The rain forest of the New Guinea region in the Pacific Ocean has been a rich source of oil. Consider the following example of two different ways of interacting with the environment to extract this vital resource.[*]

The oil field on the island of Salawati was run by the Indonesian oil company, Pertamina. The field was marked by flames shooting out of a high tower, and natural gas burning off as part of the extraction process. Access roads of more than 100 yards wide had been cleared to create a path to the field. A distance of 100 yards was too wide for many of the native rainforest species to cross. Scattered throughout the area were numerous oil spills. Numbers of certain species of animals were dwindling in the Salawati region.

The oil field at Kubutu in the Kikori River Watershed of Papua New Guinea was run by a subsidiary of the Chevron Corporation. Before embarking on its extraction project, the corporation had retained the services of the World Wildlife Fund to learn how to minimize environmental damages caused by its operations. Access roads to the oil field were only 10 yards wide; just enough to fit two vehicles side by side and at a distance that allowed rain forest species to travel across easily. Oil spills were rare due to strictly enforced regulations governing behavior on access roads. Several species of animals were actually more numerous inside the company area than outside of it.

Two different approaches, two dramatically different effects on the environment.

As you read this chapter, think about how environmental law could be used to prevent the problem experienced on Salawati and the role of environmental law generally in improving the quality of life globally.

---

* Adapted from facts described in Diamond, Jared, *Collapse: How Societies Choose to Fail or Succeed*, Chapter 15, "Big Businesses and the Environment: Different Conditions, Different Outcomes" (Penguin Group 2005).

Protection for the Environment

As you read the above scenarios, your initial reaction might be that the actions of a multinational corporation in a distant rain forest are so far removed from your everyday life that they are not relevant or of immediate concern. Think again. Behind the approach of a multinational corporation doing business in a foreign jurisdiction such as New Guinea is a corporate code of ethics and responsibility that dictates how the corporation will conduct itself, not only in the rainforest but also in other areas of the world. With the ever continuous expansion of industrialization and the interconnectedness of the global community through improved methods of communication and transportation, it is clear that respect for the environment, or lack thereof, affects us all, whether we live in America's heartland, in one of its coastal cities, or on a remote island in the South Pacific.

Environmental issues transcend national borders, and so this chapter will explore a range of environmental concerns and how the law, both in the United States and elsewhere, has addressed those issues. Addressing environmental concerns is an important part of securing a sustainable future, both at the local and global levels. While there is no one, precise definition of sustainability, at a minimum, sustainability involves acknowledging the interconnectedness of all facets of society, the economy, and the environment and a keen awareness of the fact that actions have long-term consequences. Planning economic, social, and environmental actions that will work together to help preserve "Earth's life support system in the next two generations" is sensible long-term sustainability.[1] Sustainability involves operating in a delicate balance that ensures that the needs of the present generation are met, while at the same time conserving the resources available to future generations.

Keep in mind as you read this chapter that the number of environmental laws and regulations are numerous and coverage of all these rules is beyond the scope of this text. The goal of this chapter is to highlight some of the pressing environmental issues and some of the legal and ethical responses to those issues. Given the highly regulatory nature of environmental law, business managers must work closely with legal counsel to assure legal compliance. The format of this chapter is intentionally different from the other chapters in this text. Rather than including a global perspective section toward the end of the chapter, global material is dispersed throughout the chapter.

Notice in the Ethical Insight that there is an ethical principle that supports necessary environmental laws and regulations to prevent harming the public health.

Protecting the Air

Poor air quality is a threat to both health and sustainability. Worldwide, air pollution ranks seventh in the list of health risk factors and contributed to 3.2 million deaths in 2010. A recent scientific study of the leading causes of death worldwide found that outdoor air pollution contributed to 1.2 million premature deaths in China in 2010. In India such pollution was responsible for 620,000 premature deaths. The Organization for Economic Cooperation and Development based in Paris has stated that "urban air pollution is set to become the top environmental cause of mortality worldwide by 2050, ahead of dirty water and lack of sanitation."

> **An Ethical Insight**
> **John Stuart Mill: Utilitarianism and Environmental Law**
>
> In his essay "Utilitarianism," John Stuart Mills wrote, "Everyone who receives the protection of society owes a return for the benefit, and the fact of living in society renders it indispensable that each should be bound to observe a certain line of conduct towards the rest. This consists, first, in not injuring the interests of one another . . . by express legal provision." One could argue that Mill's ethical principle "not to injure the interests of one another" supports the need for laws and regulations to protect public health from dangerous pollution.

---

[1]U.N. Division for Sustainable Development, Global Sustainable Development Report Executive Summary (2013), http://sustainabledevelopment.un.org/index.php?menu=1621.

Air pollution in China has
reached record highs.

Clean Air Act

In the United States federal legislation was passed in 1963 with the goal of studying and cleaning up air pollution. In 1970, Congress recognized that stringent control was required, and comprehensive federal legislation in the form of the Clean Air Act of 1970 became law. In that same year the Environmental Protection Agency (EPA) was formed to carry out this and many other environmental laws. The Clean Air Act is federal legislation administered and enforced by the EPA, but both state and local governments often bear the primary responsibility for ensuring the act's requirements are met. In response to increased pollutant threats to air quality, in 1990 Congress once again expanded the reach of the Clean Air Act and gave the EPA even greater regulatory authority to ensure the reduction of air pollution emissions.

As a result of the 1990 amendments to the Clean Air Act, the EPA was required to set what is referred to as National Ambient Air Quality Standards (NAAQS). These standards have two goals: (1) protect public health from harmful air pollutants and (2) minimize public harm due to reduced visibility and damages to items such as livestock, crops, and buildings. The Clean Air Act also requires the states to develop State Implementation Plans (SIPs) that dictate how each state intends to regulate air pollution under the dictates of the Clean Air Act and maintain air quality within the guidelines of the NAAQS. Development of state regulations, policies, and programs often results from the combined effort of government, industry, and the public as the development process includes public hearings and an opportunity for public comment. State SIPs must be submitted to the EPA for approval. In reality, many states

Exhibit 21.1. States Included the Cross-State Air Pollution Rule			
Alabama	Kansas	Missouri	Pennsylvania
Arkansas	Kentucky	Nebraska	South Carolina
Florida	Louisiana	New Jersey	Tennessee
Georgia	Maryland	New York	Texas
Illinois	Michigan	North Carolina	Virginia
Indiana	Minnesota	Ohio	West Virginia
Iowa	Mississippi	Oklahoma	Wisconsin

establish clean air standards that are more stringent than those of the federal government.[2]

Parties that have suffered environmental harm often seek to recover damages for harm to their health and/or property. Environmental harm suits are often based on either negligence or strict liability. As seen in the Case Illustration of *Stevenson v. DuPont*, DuPont Chemical Corporation was sued by a landowner for harmful emissions from one of its manufacturing plants.

Private parties are not the only ones who have expressed concern with the harm caused by airborne particulates. Controversies have also developed between the states with regard to pollution crossing state borders. In response, the **Cross-State Air Pollution Rule** was passed by the EPA in July 2011 to help states reduce air pollution. This rule requires states to improve air quality by reducing power plant emissions that contribute to ozone or fine particle pollution in other states. A total of 28 states are included in the Cross-State Air Pollution Rule as shown in Exhibit 21.1.

Emissions Standards

Emissions from all mobile sources (which includes automobiles, trucks, motorcycles, locomotives, boats, ships, gasoline and propane industrial equipment, and aircraft) are regulated by the EPA under the provisions of the Clean Air Act. The EPA sets standards for the pollutants being emitted such as carbon monoxide, hydrocarbons, nitrogen oxides, and particulate matter. These guidelines were imposed on on-road vehicles in the

Case Illustration

DuPont is a U.S. chemical manufacturing company founded in 1802. One of the DuPont chemical production facilities burned hazardous waste that resulted in the emission of air particulates. Although these air particulates were invisible to the naked eye, the harm that they caused was evidenced in the property of the facility's surrounding neighbors. The paint on the home of plaintiff Stevenson began to peel and the screens began to become corroded. Stevenson sued DuPont for trespass. A trespass is the intentional or unintentional entry onto another's property without consent. Interpreting the Texas law on trespass, the court found that the air particulates from the plant had "actual physical entry upon the possessor's land, without the possessor's consent"; therefore, DuPont was liable to Stevenson for harm caused to his property. *Stevenson v. E.I. DuPont de Nemours and Company*, 2005 U.S. App. LEXIS 12734 (5th Cir.)

[2]EPA.gov, http://www.epa.gov/air/caa/.

1970s and in the 1990s were expanded to include nonroad engines. In addition, the EPA has set fuel standards to limit the sulfur levels of gasoline and diesel fuel.[3]

Beginning in 2010, the EPA, working with the Department of Transportation, issued regulations regulating vehicle emissions. The EPA also began to phase in requirements that new or modified "major greenhouse gas emitting facilities use the best available control technology." It is the responsibility of vehicle and engine manufacturers to comply with the emissions standards set by the EPA within the timeframe set by that agency.

Environmental Spotlight on California

California has consistently been the state with the most stringent emissions standards. In 2012, it went another step further in pushing America toward reduced emissions and clean energy when it became the first state in the nation to pass stringent new standards to help increase the production and sale of electric, hydrogen, and hybrid automobiles. The new rule, passed by the California Air Resources Board, requires that 15 percent of all new cars sold in the state by 2025 must run with zero emissions or near zero emissions (of air pollutants released into the air). This law, if effective, will result in approximately 1.4 million electric, hybrid, and hydrogen cars in use in California by 2025. A similar measure passed in California in 1990 required that 10 percent of new cars sold in California by 2003 be zero emission, but technology and consumer purchases did not keep pace with the requirement and so California had to abandon that requirement. It remains to be seen whether the 2025 target can be met. The California legislation also requires that by 2025 smog-producing pollutants must be cut by 75 percent and greenhouse gas emissions by 50 percent compared with today's levels.

Source: Wood, Daniel, Can California Change US Cars Forever? New Zero-Emissions Rules Take Aim, Christian Science Monitor (2012).

Greenhouse Gases

Greenhouse gases, such as carbon dioxide, methane, nitrous oxide, and fluorinated gases, are those that trap heat in the atmosphere. Concern regarding the effects of these gases on the climate has caused governments and industries to initiate studies of the effects of greenhouse gases and also to develop initiatives to reduce emissions. The In-Depth Ethical Case Analysis on the following page illustrates a dispute over greenhouse gases that developed between the EPA and several states. In *Massachusetts v. EPA*, legal action was brought against the EPA for the EPA Administrator's failure to regulate carbon dioxide. We can assume the EPA Administrator's decision was made in good faith after reviewing scientific evidence. Contrary evidence must have also existed, but he was persuaded his decision was in keeping with the best scientific findings. The ethical analysis of this case considers whether there is such a thing as unintentional unethical behavior. Keep in mind as you read this case that unlike most cases in this text that involve corporate behavior, this case deals with a government entity. Corporate managers have a code of ethics to help guide their business decisions; therefore, the ethical analysis is slightly different than that for decisions made by government employees who are making policy decisions.

---

[3]EPA.gov, http://www.epa.gov/.

In-Depth Ethical Case Analysis

Massachusetts v. EPA, 127 S. Ct. 1438 (2007)

Facts

Section 202 of the Clean Air Act requires the Administrator of the Environmental Protection Agency (EPA) to set the standards "applicable to the emission of any air pollutant from any class . . . of new motor vehicles . . . which in his judgment cause, or contribute to air pollution which may reasonably be anticipated to endanger public health or welfare." The EPA was asked by the state of Massachusetts and other parties to regulate carbon dioxide emission standards for automobiles because of the potential impact of carbon dioxide on climate change. In particular, Massachusetts claimed damages to its coastline caused by global warming. The EPA refused to regulate carbon dioxide based, in part, on the belief that the agency could not regulate carbon dioxide, because it was not considered to be an air pollutant contributing to air pollution as required by the statute. Massachusetts, eleven other states, three cities, and various environmental groups brought this lawsuit against the EPA to compel the EPA to take regulatory action.

Issue

One of the issues before the court in this case was whether the EPA was required by Section 202(a)(1) of the Clean Air Act to regulate carbon dioxide levels on the basis of its potential harmful effects.

Holding

The U.S. Supreme Court held that the EPA has authority to regulate carbon dioxide, finding that greenhouse gases are within the Clean Air Act's broad definition of air pollution. By refusing to decide whether greenhouse gases contributed to climate change, the EPA violated this statute.

Ethical Issue

The EPA, as a federal administrative agency, has broad discretionary powers to regulate the environment. The ethical issue in this case is whether the EPA's Administrator abused his discretionary powers and acted unethically in refusing to regulate carbon dioxide when he believed the evidence was not clear whether carbon dioxide presented a public health issue.

Ethical Theory Analysis

Could it be argued that the EPA Administrator had an ethical obligation under the Clean Air Act to regulate carbon dioxide even if scientific evidence was not conclusive on its public health effects? Consider the following ethical principles.

Utilitarianism

The abbreviated concept of utilitarianism is "the greater good for the greater number." Although reasonable expert scientific evidence may differ on the health hazards of carbon dioxide, the EPA statute allows broad discretionary power for the EPA's Administrator to regulate in this area. Public health is an expression used to identify the long-term common health and consequent goodness of the citizens. Utilitarianism would require the EPA Administrator to consider whether the "greater number" would benefit from a decision to regulate carbon dioxide. Under a utilitarian argument, one could argue that by not regulating carbon dioxide and refusing to decide whether it impacted public health, the administrator was not acting on behalf of "the greater good for the greater number."

John Rawls

The Difference Principle — Rawls stated "*Social and economic inequalities . . . are to be to the greatest benefit of the least-advantaged members of society.*"[*] Citizens depend upon the EPA to monitor hazardous public health air pollutants. This requires scientific evaluation by professional scientists working for the EPA because their knowledge of air pollution is beyond the competency of the people. From this perspective, one could argue the citizens are subject to social inequality if unregulated carbon dioxide is a public health hazard.

Conclusion

Federal agencies are public extensions of congressional powers staffed by experts in a particular field to regulate public activities for the common good (see Chapter 4, "Administrative Law"). Within that construct it can be argued that they have a duty to act ethically, in the same sense as Congress. Unethical conduct can be unintentional. In this case one could argue there was a failure to act, even assuming "good faith," when it was ethically obligated to regulate because there was a reasonable possibility that carbon dioxide is a public health hazard.

---

[*] Rawls, John, *Justice As Fairness, A Restatement* 42 (Belknap Press of Harvard University Press 2001).

In response to the Supreme Court's decision in this case, the EPA began the process of regulating greenhouse gases. At the end of 2009, the EPA determined that emissions from motor vehicles "cause, or contribute to air pollution which may reasonably be anticipated to endanger public health or welfare" and as a result, began to enact the emissions standards for greenhouse gases described at the start of this section.

Global Perspectives: International Efforts to Combat Air Pollution

This section will highlight some of the responses of the international community to the problem of air pollution. Actions to address the problem of air pollution seek to remedy any unacceptable levels of pollutants that threaten social, physical, and environmental well-being. Pollutants that degrade the quality of life are unsustainable.

The Kyoto Protocol

The **Kyoto Protocol** is an international agreement committing its signatory countries to reaching binding targets for reducing emissions. As part of the Protocol, developed nations (referred to as Annex I nations) agreed to reduce greenhouse gas emissions by at least 5 percent between 2008 and 2012. This was an overall target of 5 percent, with amounts differing between countries. For example, the European Union was to have cuts equal to 8 percent while Canada, Hungary, Japan, and Poland were expected to have cuts of 6 percent. Less developed countries were allowed to set voluntary reduction targets. In 2012, amendments known as the Doha Amendment to the Kyoto Protocol, were adopted. These amendments require signatories to commit to average overall emission reductions of 18 percent compared to 1990 levels from the period January 1, 2013, through December, 2020. The signatories have yet to agree on a revised list of greenhouse gases.

The United States has never ratified the protocol and so is not bound by its terms. In 2012, Canada and Russia withdrew from the Protocol, and in 2013 Japan also withdrew. Three former Soviet nations, Belarus, Ukraine, and Kazakhstan, are dissatisfied with the Doha Amendment and may also leave the Protocol.

Canadian Cooperation on Air Control Issues

The United States and Canada have a long-standing environmental relationship requiring cooperation between the U.S. government, the Canadian government, the states, and the Canadian provinces. In 1991 the two countries signed the U.S.–Canada Air Quality Agreement with the initial goal of reducing air emissions that cause acid rain and in 2000 extended its provisions to include smog emissions.

Protecting the Water

Unclean water is currently the world's biggest health risk and threatens the life and quality of health around the world. Water pollution impacts oceans, rivers, and lakes. Water pollution not only negatively impacts human health but also has a harmful effect on fish, soil, crops, and wildlife.

Environmental Spotlight on China's Smog Problem

Beginning in 2012, Beijing's air pollution began to reach record highs, and by 2013 the amount of air pollutants exceeded 10 times the level that is considered safe. On one particular day, levels were 30 times higher than levels deemed safe by the World Health Organization. The smog was so bad that the air was gray, flights were canceled, and roads were closed. Bloomberg News Service reported that for most of January 2013, Beijing's air was worse than that of an airport smoking lounge.

Japan is concerned with harmful effects of the toxic smog from China spreading into Japan. In fact, in 2013 the Japanese issued new guidelines that urge residents to stay indoors if the toxic smog coming in from China exceeds twice the allowable limit set by the government. Traces of Beijing's smog have also been detected in California.

In response to rising pollution, China's policymakers have started to pass stricter regulations governing existing coal plants and also passed even stricter regulations that will apply to new coal-fired power plants in 47 cities.[*]

Source: Jonathan Kaiman, Chinese Struggle through Apocalypse Smog, The Observer (February, 2013) available at http://www.theguardian.com/world/2013/feb/16/chinese-struggle-through-airpocalypse-smog.

Clean Water Act

As early as 1948, Congress passed the first major U.S. law addressing water pollution — the Federal Water Pollution Control Act of 1948. In 1972 this law was broadened and became known as the **Clean Water Act**. This act is now the central legislation protecting the nation's waters. A detailed discussion of the many provisions of this act is beyond the scope of this chapter, but Exhibit 21.2 on page 646 highlights the key components of the law.

The Clean Water Act was amended by the Beaches Environmental Assessment and Coastal Health Act of 2000 that permits the EPA to provide grants that will allow states and territories to set up beach water quality programs for both coastal and Great Lakes beach waters.

Exhibit 21.2. The Clean Water Act

* Requires states to establish standards in order to maintain safe water quality. Requires states to review these standards every three years.

* Makes it unlawful to discharge a pollutant into navigable waters, unless a permit has been issued by the EPA or a state program approved by the EPA.

* Implements pollution control programs, such as setting wastewater standards for industry.

* Imposes strict liability for discharge of oil and hazardous substances.

* Prohibits the discharge of dredge or fill material into the waters without a permit issued by the U.S. Army Corps of Engineers. (Recall that this provision was at the center of the dispute over Mr. Rapanos's desire to build a shopping center discussed in Chapter 1, "United States Legal System.")

* Authorizes the planning and construction of public sewage treatment plants.

* Authorizes individuals who have been harmed by a polluter's acts to bring private suits against the polluter for violation of the CWA.

Source: Adapted from Simonsen, Craig, *Essentials of Environmental Law* (Pearson 1998).

Safe Drinking Water Act

The Safe Drinking Water Act is the main federal law that protects the quality of drinking water in the United States. The law was initially passed in 1974, but it was amended in 1986 and again in 1996 becoming progressively more protective. Under the Act the EPA is authorized to set national standards of safety. To ensure these standards are met, the EPA works jointly with states and with both public and private water systems.

Marine Protection, Research, and Sanctuaries Act, *aka* Ocean Dumping Act

The Marine Protection, Research, and Sanctuaries Act was passed by Congress in 1972 with two basic goals: (1) to regulate intentional ocean disposal of materials and (2) to authorize research to bring about further improvements. Prior to passage of this act, industrial waste and sewage were regularly dumped in the water. Even though the EPA has primary authority for carrying out the law, it does so with assistance from the U.S. Army Corps of Engineers, the National Oceanic and Atmospheric Administration

Environmental Spotlight on BP Gulf Oil Spill, April 20, 2010

- This was the largest accidental oil spill in history.
- This was the most extensive environmental disaster in U.S. history.
- It caused 200 million gallons of oil to spill into the Gulf of Mexico.
- It caused the deaths of 11 people.
- The flow of oil was continuous for 87 days.
- Over 8,000 birds, 1,000 sea turtles, and 600 dolphins and whales were killed or injured, and this is likely a low estimate.
- This spill is more than 18 times the size of Alaska's Exxon Valdez spill, which had been the largest oil spill in U.S. history.
- The total settlement amount to date is approximately $7.8 billion.
- Criminal charges were filed against BP executives in 2012 for obstruction of justice and destroying evidence (text messages).

Source: OCEANA, The Spill — By the Numbers. http://na.oceana.org/en/our-work/climate-energy/offshore-drilling/gulf-oil-spill-response-center/the-spill-by-the-numbers.

Case Illustration

The U.S. Navy trains for war, in part, by conducting integrated training exercises at sea in which ships, submarines, and aircrafts train together as a strike force. A strike group cannot be deployed until it has successfully completed these training exercises that are designed to simulate hostile conditions. As part of this training, extensive work is done in the waters off the coast of Southern California to instruct sailors in the detection, tracking, and neutralizing of enemy submarines. During these exercises mid-frequency active sonar is used. Citing the many harmful effects such sonar has on marine mammals, the Natural Resources Defense Council, Jean-Michael Cousteau (a well-known environmentalist), and other groups dedicated to protecting the ocean habitat brought a suit seeking to enjoin the Navy from conducting exercises. In response the Navy pointed out that such sonar exercises have been conducted for forty years without a single documented injury to a

marine mammal. According to the Navy, the most harm the sonar could possibly cause is a temporary hearing loss or brief disruption of behavior patterns. The plaintiffs claimed the injuries were more extensive than this and included permanent hearing loss and decompression sickness. The Ninth Circuit Court of Appeals sided with the plaintiffs and issued an injunction imposing restrictions on sonar training. The Navy appealed to the U.S. Supreme Court, which reversed the Ninth Circuit, stating: "While we do not question the seriousness of these interests, we conclude that the balance of equities and consideration of the overall public interest in this case tip strongly in favor of the Navy. For the plaintiffs, the most serious possible injury would be harm to an unknown number of the marine animals they study and observe. In contrast, forcing the Navy to deploy an inadequately trained anti-submarine force jeopardizes the safety of the fleet." *Winter v. NRDC* 555 U.S. 7 (2008).

Workers use pressure washers to wash oil from the beach at Smith Island on Alaska's Prince William Sound in May 1989, in the aftermath of the *Exxon Valdez* oil spill.

(NOAA), and the Coast Guard. Certain items may not be dumped in the ocean: high-level radioactive waste, chemical and biological warfare agents, medical waste, sewage sludge, and industrial waste. Other items may be dumped after receipt of a permit from the EPA that will be granted if the EPA finds that "such dumping will not unreasonably degrade or endanger human health, welfare, or amenities, the marine environment, ecological systems, or economic potentialities."[4] Potential harm to marine mammals was the subject of the *Winter v. NRDC* Case Illustration on page 647. The Dumping Act has been amended several times since its initial adoption to strengthen protection of the waters.

In the following Manager's Compliance and Ethics Meeting, the ethics committee of the board of directors is troubled by the company's manner of trying to obtain a favorable report on wetland property.

Manager's Compliance and Ethics Meeting

Wetland, Civil Engineers, and the Ethics of Their Second Opinion

Connelly Construction Company is a commercial developer presently involved in building one of the largest retail malls in the United States. It has an ethics and compliance program and a code of ethics that states, "we always act within the law and hold our managers to the highest ethical standards."

Their attorney has brought to the CEO's attention that part of the proposed mall is on protected wetland property that, under state EPA regulations, prevents building unless adequate landfill and water filtration is provided. In addition, the state must approve of its construction. The cost of using adequate landfill and appropriate filtration to safeguard the environment would be in the millions of dollars and substantially reduce the anticipated profits to the construction company. The CEO knows competent and reputable civil engineers whom he has hired at a substantial fee. They are willing to investigate the wetland and give their opinion to the state on its safe development. After the investigation, the CEO has been informed by the chief engineer that the wetland is probably safe with adequate landfill and water filtration, although he has some reservations. The CEO asks the chief engineer and the other engineers to make a second, more in-depth analysis. The engineers agree.

The ethics committee, at a manager's meeting, asks your opinion on the ethical ramifications of asking the engineers for a second analysis. If the second analysis is even more unfavorable than the first, would it be ethical for Connelly Construction to ignore the second analysis and focus only on the conclusions in the first analysis to obtain the state permit?

---

[4] 3 U.S.C. § 1412(a), http://uscodebeta.house.gov/view.xhtml?req=granuleid:USC-prelim-title33-section1412&num=0&edition=prelim.

Global Perspective: International Efforts with Regard to Water Pollution

In 1982 the United Nations (UN) promulgated its Convention on the Law of the Sea, also called the Constitution of the Oceans, which sets out a legal framework for activities conducted in the oceans and seas. The UN established three institutions to help regulate these activities: the International Tribunal for the Law of the Sea, the International Seabed Authority, and the Commission on the Limits of the Continental Shelf. More recently, global efforts to ensure the protection of oceans and marine resources have increased as the important role that oceans and marine life play in achieving sustainable development goals has become clear. Exhibit 21.3, prepared by the UN Conference on Sustainable Development Secretariat, illustrates a list of commitments made by UN members in connection with issues involving water protection, management, supply, and sustainable development.

Exhibit 21.3. UN Commitments

Agenda 21 (Outcome of 1992 UN Conference on Environment and Development)
Goals:

1. Protection of water resources, water quality, and aquatic ecosystems:
   - Reduce prevalence of water-associated diseases, starting with the eradication of guinea worm disease and river blindness by the year 2000.
2. Integrated water resource management
   - Design and initiate national action programs, and put in place appropriate institutional structures and legal instruments by the year 2000.
   - To achieve targets of all freshwater programme areas by the year 2025.
3. Water resources assessment
   - To have studied in detail the feasibility of installing water resources assessment services by the year 2000.

Johannesburg Plan of Implementation (2003 World Summit on Sustainable Development)
Goals:

1. Access to safe drinking water
   - Provision of clean drinking water and adequate sanitation is necessary to protect human health and the environment. In this respect, we agree to halve, by the year 2015, the proportion of people who are unable to reach or to afford safe drinking water and the proportion of people who do not have access to basic sanitation.
2. Integrated water resource management
   - Develop integrated water resources management and water efficiency plans by 2005, with support to developing countries.

Millennium Declaration (Outcome of 2000 UN Summit of World Leaders)
Goal:

1. Access to safe drinking water
   - Halve, by 2015, the proportion of the population without sustainable access to safe drinking water and basic sanitation.

Source: UNCSD Secretariat, RIO 2012 Issues Brief. http://sustainabledevelopment.un.org/content/documents/338brief11 .pdf.

Environmental Spotlight on Water Supplies

In addition to the international efforts described in Exhibit 21.3, country and regional efforts regarding water supply are prevalent as highlighted in these examples from the Mideast and Western Asia and from Valencia, Spain.

Mideast and Western Asia: Intergovernmental forums are helping Arab countries to cooperate on managing shared water resources. The Arab Ministerial Water Council has adopted the "Arab Strategy for Water Security in the Arab Region" to help countries understand the challenges and importance of cooperation to meet the needs of sustainable development.

In addition, the UN Economic and Social Commission for Western Asia is helping at the regional level to encourage cooperation and sharing of resources by focusing on a common vision of increased access to supply.

Valencia, Spain: The region of Valencia is known for its network of irrigation canals that were built by the Romans two thousand years ago. Property owners derive their water supply from common canals. There are over 11,000 members in the community impacted by the irrigation canals. To regulate irrigation activities, community members have formed their own statutes. For more than a thousand years, a water tribunal in Valencia, Spain, has settled irrigation disputes in that region.

The Water Tribunal, consisting of eight administrators elected by the community, meet once a week and resolve disputes over alleged violations of the irrigation statutes. The UN has called the Tribunal an "Outstanding Example of Intangible Cultural Heritage."

Source: UN Educational, Scientific, and Cultural Organization, Water Cooperation. www.unwater.org/water-cooperation-2013/water-cooperation/water-cooperation.

Preventing Harm from Toxic Substances

Toxic chemicals are those which may cause harm. Chemicals can be labeled with varying degrees of toxicity—when a very small amount of a chemical is harmful, this is considered highly toxic. If the chemical is only harmful in large amounts, it is considered to be practically nontoxic.[5] As businesses take action toward ensuring a sustainable future, an important component of this includes providing consumers with safe products. For example, demanding that components and supplies are sourced from sustainable and safe materials contributes to long-term sustainability.

Toxic Control Substances Act

The **Toxic Control Substances Act** (TCSA) is a federal law passed in 1976 that regulates chemical substances and provides guidelines for the EPA on which chemicals may safely be used in manufacturing. The goal of the

---

[5]Washington Department of Labor and Industries, http://www.lni.wa.gov/wisha/p-ts/pdfs/toxicsubstances.pdf.

Exhibit 21.4. Authorized EPA Response to Unreasonably Dangerous Chemicals

Possible EPA Responses
Prohibit manufacture
Prohibit or limit use
Set quantity limits
Set concentration limits
Set quality control measures
Establish tests for compliance
Control disposal
Require adequate labeling
Impose recordkeeping requirements

Source: U.S. EPA, TSCA Section 6 Actions. http://www.epa.gov/opptintr/existingchemicals/pubs/sect6.html.

TCSA is to identify harmful substances before they are used in manufacturing. As part of its duties under this act, the EPA has compiled an initial list of more than 60,000 chemicals and since that time has added over 20,000 more to the list. Most of the EPA's actions under this act have been focused on new chemicals and new uses of existing chemicals. The EPA must be given a 90-day notice when a company plans to import, manufacture, or process a new chemical. One of the hurdles in terms of enforcement is deciding what is considered a "new" chemical, which involves comparing the molecular structure and chemical structure of the new substance against chemicals already on an EPA list.[6] The act also authorizes the EPA to require a manufacturer to conduct testing even on chemicals that are already included in the inventory list. Keep in mind, however, that legally a manufacturer can challenge in court the EPA's decision that testing should be done. To prevail, the EPA has the burden of showing "substantial evidence" of the need for testing.[7] Exhibit 21.4 summarizes the actions the EPA might take once it determines that a chemical poses an unreasonable risk.

Global Perspective: International Efforts with Regard to Toxic Substances

The International Labour Organization (ILO) is a special agency of the UN. It was originally created in 1919 to address social justice concerns and today continues its mission by working to promote rights in the workplace. It currently has 185 member countries. Consistent with its mission, the ILO has expressed concern with the safety of the working environment. To that end it developed the International Programme for Improvement of Working Conditions and Environment (PIACT) to, in part, promote actions by member countries to improve the quality of working conditions. In 1993, the ILO adopted the initiative, "Chemicals Convention, 1900," which was the result of an

---

[6]Craig Simonsen, *Essentials of Environmental Law* (Pearson, 1998).
[7]*Id.*

international conference devoted to the safe use of chemicals in the workplace. In conjunction with this the ILO issued "Safety in the Use of Chemicals at Work," guidelines to help minimize the risks associated with the large number of chemicals used in workplaces worldwide, in order to prevent or reduce the number of chemically induced illnesses or injuries. The guidelines were not intended to replace existing laws and regulations, but rather to offer guidance to authorities engaged in designing protocols for use of chemicals in the workplace and also to provide information for suppliers, employers, and workers' organizations.

Safely Disposing of Waste

Hazardous waste is that which contains properties that make it potentially harmful to human health or to the environment. The goal of hazardous waste regulation is to ensure proper handling of waste from the time it is generated, to its disposal, and even after its disposal.

Resource Conservation and Recovery Act

The Resource Conservation and Recovery Act (RCRA), passed by Congress in 1976, is the central legislation regulating the disposal of both solid and hazardous waste. Through both a solid waste program and a hazardous waste program, the RCRA aims to achieve the following goals:

- Protect human health and the environment from the potential hazards of waste disposal
- Conserve energy and natural resources
- Reduce the amount of waste generated
- Ensure that wastes are managed in an environmentally sound manner

In 1984 the Hazardous and Solid Waste Amendments were enacted to strengthen the efforts of the RCRA. As part of these amendments, land disposal of hazardous waste will be phased out. Also under these amendments the EPA was given greater enforcement authority, and an underground storage program was implemented to strengthen regulations governing underground tanks that store both petroleum and hazardous waste. Leaks in these systems have the potential to contaminate groundwater which could affect drinking water quality.

Comprehensive Environmental Response, Compensation, and Liability Act

The **Comprehensive Environmental Response, Compensation, and Liability Act** (CERCLA), also called Superfund, was passed by Congress in 1980 to allow the government to respond to releases or threatened releases of hazardous substances that could be harmful to public health and well-being or harmful to the environment. The law allows the EPA to force parties responsible for the contamination to clean it up. Alternatively, the EPA can authorize the clean-up and force the responsible parties to reimburse those costs.

There are four categories of parties that may be liable for environmental contamination under CERCLA:

- The current owner or the current operator of the contamination site.
- The owner or operator of a site at the time that disposal of a hazardous substance occurred.
- Anyone who arranged for the disposal of a hazardous substance or contaminant on the site.
- Anyone who transports a hazardous substance or contaminant to a site.[8]

As you read through the above list of possible parties, keep in mind that CERCLA issues have been the subject of much litigation. One question has been whether a party could be liable under CERCLA where its harmful activities occurred prior to the enactment of CERCLA. The court has made clear that this is permissible.

Electronic Waste

Cell phone manufacturers entice consumers with new gadgets on a regular basis. When Apple releases a new version of the iPhone or iPad, customers line up for hours to be among the first to purchase the new product. Corporations routinely upgrade computer systems and purchase new monitors for the workplace. But what happens to that outdated cell phone or computer monitor? They become part of the growing problem of how to safely dispose of electronic waste. Exhibit 21.5 on page 654 provides summary data from the EPA on whether this waste gets thrown into the trash (and winds up in landfills) or recycled. This chart should provide you with a clear sense of the magnitude of the problem of electronic waste management. As you consider the staggering numbers, think about the problem through the lens of ensuring sustainability, conserving resources, and being environmentally conscious. Even if safe waste disposal methods for dealing with this waste are put in place, can the environment sustain the current level of electronic waste production?

In 2010 the Interagency Task Force on Electronics Stewardship was created by the federal government to develop a national strategy for dealing with electronic waste. This task force released four recommendations:

- Create incentives for the design of greener electronics and enhance science, research, and technology development in the United States.
- Ensure that the federal government leads by example.
- Increase safe handling of used electronics in the United States.
- Reduce harm from U.S. exports of electronic waste and improve safe handling of used electronics in developing countries.[9]

---

[8]CERCLA, 42 U.S.C. § 107 (a)(1)-(4).
[9]Full Report available at http://www.epa.gov/wastes/conserve/materials/ecycling/taskforce/docs/strategy.pdf.

Exhibit 21.5. Trashed or Recycled: What Happened to Electronic Waste in 2010?

By the Ton

Products	Total Disposed**	Trashed	Recycled	Recycling Rate (percent)
Computers	423,000	255,000	168,000	40
Monitors	595,000	401,000	194,000	33
Hard copy devices	290,000	193,000	97,000	33
Keyboards and mice	67,800	61,400	6,460	10
Televisions	1,040	864,000	181,000	17
Mobile devices	19,500	17,200	2,240	11
TV peripherals*	Not included	Not included	Not included	Not included
Total (in tons)	2,440,000	1,790,000	649,000	27

By the Unit

Products	Total Disposed**	Trashed	Recycled	Recycling Rate (percent)
Computers	51,900,000	31,300,000	20,600,000	40
Monitors	35,800,000	24,100,000	11,700,000	33
Hard copy devices	33,600,000	22,400,000	11,200,000	33
Keyboards and mice	82,200,000	74,400,000	7,830,000	10
Televisions	28,500,000	23,600,000	4,940,000	17
Mobile devices	152,000,000	135,000,000	17,400,000	11
TV peripherals*	Not included	Not included	Not included	Not included
Total (in units)	384,000,000	310,000,000	73,700,000	19

What's included here? Computer products include CPUs, desktops, and portables. Hard copy devices are printers, digital copiers, scanners, multifunctions, and faxes. Mobile devices are cell phones, personal digital assistants (PDAs), smartphones, and pagers.
* Study did not include a large category of e-waste: TV peripherals, such as VCRs, DVD players, DVRs, cable/satellite receivers, converter boxes, or game consoles.
** *Disposed* means going into trash or recycling. These totals do not include products that are no longer used, but which are still stored in homes and offices.

Source: "Electronics Waste Management in the United States Through 2009," U.S. EPA, May 2011, EPA 530-R-11-002. http://www.epa.gov/wastes/conserve/materials/ecycling/docs/fullbaselinereport2011.pdf

In addition to federal efforts, many states, and even some cities, have passed laws to help ensure proper disposal/recycling of electronic waste. One of the major concerns with electronic waste is that some of this waste, such as circuit boards, contains precious metals that can be extracted. A growing problem involves this waste being exported to poor villages (many times illegally) around the world (primarily in China, India, Pakistan, and Nigeria) where workers are paid to remove these metals through fire and acid baths. Both processes expose these workers to toxins. These toxins are also released into the air potentially resulting in the degradation of the entire village.

The Coopermiti warehouse in São Paulo, Brazil, in March 2013. According to the United Nations Environment Programme (UNEP), Brazil generates the greatest amount of electronic waste (e-waste) per capita among emerging countries.

Global Perspective: International Efforts to Combat Hazardous Waste

As early as the 1970s, governments and industry began to recognize the growing problem of hazardous waste disposal. In 1992 a multinational treaty went into effect to combat this problem. This treaty, the Basel Convention on the Control of Transboundary Movement of Hazardous Wastes and Their Disposal, was signed with the stated objective of protecting "human health and the environment from the adverse effects of hazardous waste." Over 160 counties are signatories of this agreement and work along with industry to (1) minimize the generation of hazardous waste, (2) treat hazardous waste as close as possible to its source of origin to minimize the international movement of waste, and (3) develop guidelines to educate countries on safe handling techniques.

Alternative Energy

When alternative energy sources are considered in the United States, the objective is generally twofold: (1) reduce dependence on foreign sources (e.g., oil) and (2) conserve natural resources such as coal, oil, and natural gas that are nonrenewable sources of energy, which once depleted, cannot be replenished.

As a result, great efforts are being taken to develop renewable sources of fuel such as solar power, hydropower, wind power, geothermal power, and biomass power. Along with these efforts come considerable costs as industry develops ways to not only harness the power of the water, wind, sun, etc., but also develops ways to deliver this power to consumers. The Office of Energy Efficiency & Renewable Energy (EERE) within the U.S. Department of Energy develops opportunities for clean energy manufacturing. The EERE recently enacted the Clean Energy Manufacturing Initiative that focuses on increasing the competitiveness of the United States in producing clean energy products and increasing the competitiveness of U.S. manufacturers through increases in energy efficiency.[10]

Environmental Spotlight on California

In 2011 California Governor Jerry Brown signed into law the most ambitious clean energy plan in the United States. The plan requires that California obtain 33 percent of its energy needs from renewable sources by the year 2020.

The Energy Independence and Security Act

The **Energy Independence and Security Act** was passed in 2007 with the following goals:

To move the United States toward greater energy independence and security, to increase production of clean, renewable fuels, to protect consumers, to increase the efficiency of products, buildings, and vehicles, to promote research on and deploy greenhouse gas capture and

Windmill farms, such as this one on a California hilltop, can extend over several hundred square miles, often interspersed with other land uses, providing alternative energy for many hundreds of thousands of homes and businesses.

---

[10]Energy Efficiency & Renewable Energy, Clean Energy Manfacturing Initiative, http://www1.eere.energy.gov/energymanufacturing/.

storage options, and to improve the energy performance of the federal government.[11]

This legislation created energy management goals that included energy reduction for federal buildings, comprehensive evaluations of energy and water use at certain identified facilities every four years, the establishment of a Federal High-Performance Building Office and Advisory Committee to establish green standards for the federal sector, and requirements for federal agency use of vehicles that will ensure a reduction of petroleum dependence and an increase in alternative fuel sources.[12]

The federal government has committed significant resources to alternative energy initiatives including the funding of state alternative energy projects and a variety of tax incentives for both individuals and business adopting certain green practices. For example, tax credits (some as high as $7,500) are available for purchases of certain plug-in hybrid electric vehicles such as the Chevrolet Volt and the Ford Fusion Energi.

Environmental Spotlight on Cape Wind

Massachusetts has set a goal of deriving 20 percent of its energy from renewable sources by the year 2020. The Cape Wind Project could certainly help meet this objective. Initiated in 2001, the Cape Wind Project was one of the first offshore wind farms in the United States. The plan includes building 130 turbines in the Nantucket Sound which would then be able to supply three-quarters of the power needed by Cape Cod and the Islands. While the Project has passed nearly all of the required regulatory hurdles for construction to begin, the Project had also spent approximately $65 million complying with these requirements to obtain 17 state and federal approvals and also to defend legal challenges filed by those protesting these grants of approval. As the first-of-its-kind project in the United States, the Project was certain to come under intense scrutiny, but the extended battle period has now raised concerns about whether the Project can move ahead.

Source: Matthew Pawa, The Very Definition of Folly: Saving the Earth From Environmentalists, 38 Environmental Affairs 77 (2011).

Global Perspective: International Commitment to Alternative Energy

The United Nations dedicated the year 2012 as the International Year of Sustainable Energy for All. This helped to focus attention on renewable resources and generate even greater dialogue in the international community. The UN Secretary-General, in support of the year's theme, released an initiative entitled, "Sustainable Energy For All" to encourage countries, international organizations, the private sector, and civil society to work together toward ensuring access to energy for all, while at the same time committing to doubling the level of renewable energy by 2030. In June 2012, the UN Conference of Sustainable

---

[11]Summary of the Energy Independence and Security Act, http://www2.epa.gov/laws-regulations/summary-energy-independence-and-security-act.
[12]Energy Efficiency & Renewable Energy, Federal Energy Management Program, Energy Independence & Security Act, http://www1.eere.energy.gov/femp/regulations/eisa.html.

Development (The Rio+20) recognized that increased use of renewable energy is a vital part of the solution to the problem of sustainable energy and sustainable development.

Another international organization dedicated to promoting sustainability is the International Renewable Energy Agency (IRENA), an intergovernmental organization with 118 member countries. Since its first meeting was convened in Bonn, Germany, in 2008, IRENA has served as a platform for international cooperation and knowledge-sharing as countries transition to a more sustainable energy future. IRENA facilitates sharing of knowledge and technology with the goal of ensuring clean, sustainable energy for the world's population. It is the first intergovernmental organization to be headquartered in the Middle East, with its principal office in Abu Dhabi, United Arab Emirates. The organization has an Innovation and Technology Center in Bonn, Germany, and is planning a New York City location as well. IRENA encourages governments to adopt renewable energy policies and provides practical tools and advice to accelerate renewable energy deployment. IRENA promotes the widespread adoption and sustainable use of all forms of renewable energy, including bioenergy, geothermal, hydropower, ocean, solar, and wind energy in the pursuit of sustainable development, energy access, energy security, and low-carbon economic growth and prosperity.

Summary

Environmental issues transcend national borders. Regulatory measures have been adopted in the United States to address the problems caused by air pollution, water pollution, and toxic substances, as well as to address the ongoing problem of waste disposal. International measures concerning these issues have also been put in place, often within the frameworks provided by various agencies and committees of the United Nations. Increasingly, governments, businesses, and individuals are recognizing the interconnectedness of all facets of society, the economy, and the environment. Developing an understanding that individual actions and business decisions have far-reaching and long-term social, legal, and ethical consequences is vital to working toward a more sustainable future.

Questions for Review

1. **Sustainability in business**

   Edward Entrepreneur has an idea for a new business venture. He has designed an electronic gizmo, the Wonder Cleaner, to assist with routine household chores. Edward wants to set up a corporation to manufacture and sell this product in the United States and abroad. He is concerned about environmental issues and sustainability. He is wondering what actions he can take to factor sustainability into his corporate decisions.

   a. How can Edward Entrepreneur minimize the environmental impact of his company during the design phase?
   b. How does sustainability factor into the contracts Edward enters into with suppliers?
   c. What role, if any, can sustainability have in how Edward advertises his product?

d. What should Edward take into account when making decisions about the global distribution of the Wonder Cleaner to wholesalers and retailers if he is concerned about sustainability?

2. Psychological harm from environmental actions

In March 1979 one of the worst nuclear accidents in the United States occurred at the Three Mile Island nuclear plant in Pennsylvania. One of the nuclear reactors (Unit 2) at the plant had a partial meltdown and released small amounts of radioactive iodine and radioactive gases into the environment. After the accident, the operator of the plant, Metropolitan Edison Company, was ordered by the National Regulatory Commission (NRC) to keep the functioning reactor, Unit 1, shut down until it was determined that the plant could continue to operate safely. Initially, the NRC announced a notice of public hearing about the plant and encouraged comments on whether psychological harm should be considered in making a decision about the future operations of the plant. PANE (People Against Nuclear Energy) stated that restarting the reactor would cause serious psychological damage to people living in the vicinity of the plant. When the NRC decided not to take into account the potential for psychological harm in its decision making, PANE filed a petition in court claiming that the NRC was required to take this information into account. Government regulations under the National Environmental Policy Act (NEPA) require an agency to evaluate the "environmental impact" and unavoidable "adverse environmental effects" of a proposed action. What do you think the court will take into account to reach a result in this dispute? As a policy matter do you think psychological issues should factor into environmental decision making? *Metropolitan Edison Co. v. PANE*, 460 U.S. 766 (1983).

3. Ethics

Arco, Inc. is a small company that installs and repairs home and commercial heating and air-conditioning units. It has 75 employees and has recently started selling its stock to extended family, its employees, and friends. The company has never issued dividends to the stockholders. From its outset Arco has prided itself on being an ethical company and has a code of ethics that states "we are committed to setting the example of providing the best solutions to energy preservation." Arco has been very successful and is considering installing solar panels on its home office building at a substantial cost. The directors are concerned that the stockholders would rather receive a dividend than have company earnings spent on solar panels. The CEO has explained to the directors that Arco's accountant has informed him that over a period of five years the cost of the installation will be recouped in Arco's reduction of energy cost. He is convinced the company should start selling solar panels, and this new line of business would be helped by showing its customers how the solar panels work at Arco. At a stockholders' meeting, you have been asked to comment on the project from business and ethical perspectives. Should the stockholders receive a dividend distribution before the panels are installed? It is ethical to use corporate earnings for environmental purposes before issuing dividends?

4. University involvement

Research sustainability efforts that have been taken by colleges and universities. List three measures your school (or any school in your state) has enacted to address this concern.

5. Alternative energy

The amount of wind power produced through wind turbines steadily increases year after year, at a growth rate of about 25 percent. These wind turbines can be as tall as a twenty story building and have long, sharp blades. Wind farms have been found to kill thousands of birds annually, including golden eagles and hawks. In November, 2013, for example,

Duke Energy, operator of several wind farms in Wyoming, was fined $1 million for violation of the Migratory Bird Treaty Act for the harm caused to numerous migratory birds, including golden eagles. As a matter of public policy, discuss how to best balance the need for development of this important alternative source of energy with the potential harm caused by its operations.

6. Electronic waste

Hi Tech Corporation provides customers with access to the latest advancements in technology and software. Hi Tech replaces employee workstation computers every three years. Printers are replaced every five years. The High Tech board of directors believes such actions are essential to ensuring the Hi Tech environment maintains its reputation as a leading technology company. Assess these actions in light of sustainability concerns.

7. Next Generation Compliance

The EPA has been advocating its Next Generation Compliance initiative. Research and discuss the purpose of the initiative, its key components, and how it is designed to change the EPA's approach to enforcement of environmental regulations.

8. The Kyoto Protocol

As part of the Kyoto Protocol, member nations agreed to keep their emissions levels to certain allowable limits. Article 17 of the Kyoto Protocol allows countries that will not use all of their allowable emission amounts and, therefore, have emissions units to spare to sell their excess capacity to other nations who have exceeded their allowable amount of emissions. This is referred to as trading in carbon credits. Discuss the pros and cons of such an approach.

Further Reading

Bodansky, D., *The Art and Craft of International Environmental Law* (Harvard University Press 2010).

Environmental Protection Agency, http://www.epa.gov/.

Simonsen, C., *Essentials of Environmental Law* (Pearson 1998).

Stenzel, P., *Teaching Environmental Law and Sustainability for Business: From Local to Global*, 30 Journal of Legal Studies Education 249–293 (2013).

UN Sustainable Development Knowledge Platform, http://sustainabledevelopment.un.org/.

accede, accede to To join as a party to an international treaty.

accept by shipping Under the UCC, unless the offeror specifies otherwise, an offeree or seller can accept an offer by shipping the goods.

acceptance of an offer (common law) An offeree's manifestation of assent to the terms of a valid offer in a manner invited or required by the offeror.

acceptance of an offer (UCC) Under the UCC, a definite and seasonable expression of acceptance by the offeree.

act of state doctrine A doctrine that prevents courts from sitting in judgment of the acts of the government of a foreign country if those acts are done within that foreign country's territory.

act utilitarianism A teleological theory in which the acting agent calculates the greater good for the greater number at the time of its performance.

actual authority The authority that the principal "actually" gives the agent either through direct communication or by implication. Actual authority includes express authority, which is oral or written authority and implied authority, which is authority to do what is reasonably necessary, usual, and proper to perform the agent's work in light of the principal's instructions.

actual causation Relates to the conduct that caused an injury.

actual damages Personal injuries or property losses that are susceptible to objective measurements in monetary terms.

actus reus Latin for "guilty act." Relates to a defendant's criminal act.

adhesion (contracts of) Contracts formed by parties who have unequal bargaining power, resulting in the stronger party offering boilerplate contract terms on a take-it-or-leave-it basis. Adhesion contracts are not automatically unconscionable, but the adhesive nature of a contract can be considered in determining whether the contract is unconscionable.

administrative law judge A federal employee who presides over administrative agency adjudications.

affirmative action programs Programs implemented as a means of remedying past patterns of discrimination, especially in the areas of jobs and education.

Age Discrimination in Employment Act (ADEA) Federal law enacted in 1967 to protect employees age 40 and over from discrimination in the workplace. This Act covers all employers with more than 20 employees.

agency by estoppel Arises when a defendant (person or business) makes it appear as if someone is an agent, even though no agency exists, and a third party relies on this appearance. In such situations, the defendant is estopped (that is, prevented) from claiming that no agency exists.

agent A person or entity who is authorized to act on behalf of another party.

agreement to agree An arrangement in which one or more material terms are left open for further negotiations. Without further agreement, it is unenforceable.

alternative dispute resolution The means by which parties resolve a dispute without the involvement of the court, often through negotiation, mediation, or arbitration.

Americans with Disabilities Act (ADA) Federal legislation that prevents discrimination against individuals with disabilities in the workplace. Employers with 15 or more employees are covered by this Act.

anticipatory repudiation Occurs when one party to a contract has reasonable grounds to believe that the other party will materially breach. In such situations, he or she may (1) demand adequate assurance that performance is forthcoming; (2) if reasonable suspend his or her own performance; (3) if no assurance of performance is given in a reasonable time, he or she may sue for breach of contract without having to wait for the date of performance to pass; or (4) he or she may wait for performance by the repudiating party.

Anticybersquatting Consumer Protection Act (ACPA) A federal law that prohibits registering in bad faith a domain name that is identical or confusingly similar to the trademark of another.

apparent authority Situation when, based on what a principal communicates or implies to a third party, an agent *appears* to have authority, although in fact there is no authority.

appeal A proceeding undertaken to have the decision of a lower court reviewed and reconsidered by a higher court. It is the final step in a civil or criminal case. It represents a challenge to the decision of a court.

arbitrary Arbitrary marks are inherently distinctive and can be used as trademarks; they have no particular relation to the product or service.

arbitration A proceeding where a neutral third party hears a dispute between parties and issues a binding award. Typically the parties agree in advance to have their disputes resolved through arbitration rather than through the courts.

arraignment The initial step in a criminal prosecution whereby the defendant is brought before the court to hear the charges and to enter a plea.

arrest A forcible restraint of a suspect for the purpose of placing the suspect in police custody and bringing the suspect before a court of law.

arrest warrant Authorizes law enforcement officials to arrest the suspect and present the suspect to the court.

articles of organization Document prepared and filed by promoters, the individuals who want to start a business, in order the create a limited liability company or a corporation.

artificial persons Corporations or other nonhuman legal entities.

artisan's lien Provides a creditor with a security interest in a debtor's *personal* property when a creditor performs work on the property.

assign To effect a legal transfer of ownership.

assignment Transfer of a right under a contract. A party transferring a contractual right is called the assignor, and the party to whom the right is transferred is called the assignee.

assumption of risk When a victim has knowledge that the defendant's conduct may cause harm, but nonetheless voluntarily chooses to place herself within the sphere of the defendant's conduct.

authority The power given to an agent to act on the principal's behalf.

B-Lab An organization offering certification as "B Corporations" to those corporations that create a general public benefit as measured by an independent third-party standard and also meet other performance benchmarks to ensure that the company is meeting specific social and environmental performance standards.

Bankruptcy Abuse Prevention and Consumer Protection Act Among other provisions, requires bankruptcy applicants to undergo a "means test" to determine if the debtor's income exceeds the threshold limits of the Act.

Bankruptcy Code of 1978 The current set of uniform laws on the subject of bankruptcy in the United States.

bankruptcy court A federal trial court that hears only bankruptcy cases.

bankruptcy discharge Dismisses a debtor's financial obligations to creditors, bringing finality to a person's debt problems.

bankruptcy judge A federal trial judge who hears bankruptcy cases only.

bankruptcy trustee An individual appointed by the court to conduct and oversee most of the administrative processes associated with a bankruptcy case.

benefit corporations Hybrid corporate entities serving the dual goals of making a profit and having a positive social impact on society.

Berne Convention An 1886 treaty that protects copyrights internationally.

beyond a reasonable doubt The burden of proof used in a criminal case.

bilateral contract A contract wherein a promise is exchanged for a promise.

bill of lading A receipt signed by the carrier when the seller delivers goods to the carrier. It serves as a seller's receipt for the goods.

board of directors The governing body of a corporation whose members are elected by the shareholders.

boilerplate Part or all of a form contract that is used over and over again.

bona fide occupational qualification (BFOQ) A quality that is reasonably necessary to the normal operation of a particular business. It is used as a defense in an employment discrimination lawsuit. For example, it is permissible for a department store to hire only female security guards to conduct spot checks of the female dressing rooms.

booking The process of capturing and recording relevant information about a suspect after the suspect has been arrested.

breach of duty Occurs when one party fails to satisfy the standard of care it owes to another party.

bribery A crime that occurs when a public official provides a service beyond what is expected or required in the normal performance of the official's duties in exchange for money or something of value.

burden of proof A party's responsibility to prove an assertion.

business crimes Crimes which arise in a variety of national and international business settings and typically involve illicit activities characterized by deceit and a breach of trust.

business ethics Branch of philosophy that applies to ethical decision making in the business environment.

business torts Basis for lawsuits which involve impairment of some facet of a person's or an entity's economic interest. Business torts generally cause economic loss rather than bodily harm or property damage.

capacity to contract The ability of a party to give voluntary assent to a contract. There are two ways in which a person could lack legal capacity to form a contract: either the person has not reached the age of majority or the person lacks the requisite mental capacity.

cartel A group of producers or sellers that coordinate a product's price or volume.

categorical imperatives Immanuel Kant's deontological principles that create a duty to act in a manner that our conduct could be universalized and to treat others as an end in themselves.

cease-and-desist An order to refrain from some action.

Celler-Kefauver Act A federal law that amended the Clayton Act to limit all types of mergers, whether they take place via the acquisition of stock or of assets.

certification mark A distinctive word, name, symbol, or device that identifies an organization that certifies the quality or characteristics of another's products or services.

choice of law provisions Contractual provisions allowing parties to identify which state's or which country's law will govern the interpretation of their contract in the event of a dispute or question.

Clayton Act A landmark antitrust law that prohibits price discrimination, tying arrangements, and anticompetitive mergers, among other things.

Clean Air Act U.S. federal legislation, administered and enforced by the Environmental Protection Agency, that is designed to reduce air pollution and ensure regulations are developed at the federal and state levels to protect air quality.

Clean Water Act The central U.S. federal legislation protecting the nation's waters.

closely held corporations Corporations in which the investors (owners) often serve as corporate officers and help manage the business. A non-publicly held corporation (that is, stock is not traded on a public stock exchange).

COBRA Federal legislation that provides an employee with the option of continuing health coverage through the employer's health plan for a certain limited period of time after employment has ended.

code of ethics A document that clearly enumerates the legal compliance requirements of a company including its ethical values.

Code of Federal Regulations A comprehensive collection of administrative agency regulations, compiled and ordered by topic into a set of printed volumes.

collective mark A distinctive word, name, symbol, or device that identifies a group or organization, such as the Boy Scouts of America.

comity Doctrine holding that, in some circumstances, nations will recognize and defer to the legislative, executive, or judicial acts of other countries.

commerce clause A Constitutional power that allows Congress to regulate, among other things, commerce among the 50 states and prohibits the states from enacting laws that would interfere with interstate commerce.

commercial activity An exception to the Foreign Sovereign Immunities Act, applicable when a foreign government's activities are commercial, that is, of the type of commercial or trade actions in which a private party engages. In such instances, immunity from suit is not granted to the foreign government.

commercial disparagement A tort involving the publication of a false statement about a business's products or services.

commercial frustration Doctrine that excuses a party from contract performance if, after forming the contract, the principal purpose of the contract is substantially frustrated due to no fault of the parties.

commerical impracticability Under UCC Article 2, the doctrine that excuses a seller for failing to deliver or delaying delivery if (1) the seller did not assume the risk of a particular unknown contingency; (2) the nonoccurrence of the contingency was a basic assumption on which the contract was made; and (3) occurrence of the contingency made performance impracticable.

commercial speech Speech that has a commercial transaction as its goal, such as the sale of a product or service.

commercial unit A single whole for purposes of sale, such as a single machine, a crate of wine, a carton of packages of paper, or a bushel of apples.

comparative negligence Defendant's argument that a plaintiff/victim's own conduct contributed to the injuries he or she sustained, with the result that plaintiff's damages are reduced by the percentage a plaintiff was at fault.

compensatory damages Damages awarded by a court to compensate individuals for personal injury, property damage, economic loss, or loss of bargain in a breach of contract case.

compliance and ethics program An ongoing process that engages in vigorous due diligence, risk assessment, a corporate code of ethics, and periodic training programs to ensure the laws, regulations, and company values are understood and obeyed. They collectively maintain an ethical corporate culture that encourages ethical conduct and a commitment to compliance with the law.

Comprehensive Environmental Response Compensation Liabilities Act (CERCLA) Also called Superfund, this federal Act allows the government to respond to releases or threatened releases of hazardous substances that could be harmful to public health and well-being or harmful to the environment.

compulsory license Official permission granted by a government to a third party to produce a patented product without authorization from the patent holder.

concerted action Agreement between two or more parties that violates the antitrust laws.

condition An act or event that, unless excused, must occur before a duty under a contract arises.

confiscation Government seizure of private property in exchange for fair compensation to the owner of the property.

conflict of interest Arises when an agent puts his or her own interests in conflict with the principal's best interests or places the interests of a third party in conflict with the principal's best interest.

conforming goods Goods that meet all contract specifications.

conglomerate merger A merger between firms in unrelated lines of business.

conscious capitalism Theory that acknowledges corporations have a greater interconnectedness to society than ever before and, therefore, have a corresponding obligation to be more conscious in their decision making.

consideration A requirement for a binding contract. Consideration exists when parties bargain to give each other something (or refrain from doing something) that confers benefit on the other party and which they were not previously obligated to do (or to refrain from doing).

constituency statutes Statutes allowing corporate managers the option of considering more than just the interests of the shareholders when making business decisions.

constitutional safeguards Constitutional protections available to a person accused of committing a crime. Found in the Fourth, Fifth, and Sixth Amendments.

contempt order A court order declaring that a person (usually a party or a witness) has failed to obey a court order or request or has disrespected the court in some other way.

contract A legally binding agreement.

contributory negligence Allows the defendant to show that the victim's conduct contributed to his or her injuries. Unlike comparative negligence that apportions responsibility for an injury between the defendant and the injured party, contributory negligence is a complete bar to recovery.

convention A type of treaty where representatives of many countries meet, collaborate, discuss, and, if successful, achieve consensus on international or global issues of mutual concern.

Convention on Contracts for the International Sale of Goods (CISG) A UN-sponsored set of conventions and rules relating to international trade. It is designed to help standardize and harmonize the rules that govern contracts for the international sales of goods.

conversion An intentional tort which occurs when one party intentionally interferes with the personal property of another person.

copyright A temporary, government-granted right to prevent others from copying an original work of authorship.

Copyright Act of 1976 The principal federal copyright law.

corporate crimes Crimes committed by a corporation's representatives acting on behalf of the corporation.

corporate officers High-level employees who take direction from the board of directors and run the corporation on a day-to-day basis. Officers have the authority to commit the corporation to perform services, sell goods, and assume financial obligations.

corporate veil A legal shield that insulates shareholders (owners) from corporate creditors.

corporation A type of business organization that has a legal existence separate and distinct from its owners.

counteroffer A proposal by an offeree to an offeror of a bargain different than the original offer.

countervailing duties Duties designed to offset the effects of subsidies.

covenant not to compete An agreement signed by an employee by which the employee agrees to refrain from working in a competing activity within a certain distance and/or for a certain period of time after the employment relationship has ended. Covenants not to compete can also be included in contracts for the purchase and sale of a business.

creditor An individual or an entity that is owed money by another individual or entity.

crime The breach of a legal duty that is punishable by imprisonment, fines, probation, death penalty, or community service.

criminal act The specific acts performed by a defendant in carrying out a crime.

criminal intent A defendant's state of mind when committing a crime.

criminal law The laws governing activity prohibited by the government because it is deemed to threaten public safety and security.

Cross-State Air Pollution Rule Passed by the Environmental Protection Agency to help states reduce air pollution. This rule requires states to improve air quality by reducing power plant emissions that contribute to ozone or fine particle pollution in other states.

customary international law Widely recognized legal principles that have developed over centuries.

cybersquatting The bad-faith registration of an Internet domain name that contains the trademark of another.

damages Monetary awards ordered by courts to victims for injuries caused by wrongdoers or for losses caused by breach of contract.

de novo A standard of review by which a reviewing court will not give any deference to the judgment of a lower court or agency and instead will decide the matter anew.

debtor An individual or an entity, such as a corporation, that owes money to another individual or entity.

debtor-creditor relationship The relationship between the party owed money (the creditor) and the party responsible for paying money (the debtor).

defendant The party who allegedly causes an injury or damage in a civil case, or who is charged with a crime.

defenses Responses by a defendant to legal claims made by a plaintiff in a civil case or charges made by the prosecution in a criminal case.

deference The weight and respect given by a reviewing court to the determinations and decisions made by a lower court or agency.

delegation Transfer of a duty under a contract.

deontology An ethical theory based on a duty to act ethically under the circumstances, regardless of the consequences.

derivative works Works such as a translation, musical arrangement, or motion picture version based upon a preexisting work.

descriptive marks Marks that describe some aspect of the product or service they are associated with. They can be used as trademarks if they have acquired secondary meaning.

design defects A defect resulting from something inherent in the manufacturer's plan or design, as opposed to a defect in the manufacturing process.

design patent A patent that protects any new, original, and ornamental design for an article of manufacture.

destination contract A contract requiring the seller to deliver goods to the buyer's destination.

detour An agent's minor deviation from the principal's business. If a tort occurs during a detour, then the employer is vicariously liable.

difference principle A theory of John Rawls that states: "Social and economic inequalities are to satisfy two conditions; first they are to be attached to office and positions open to all under conditions of fair equality of opportunity; and second, they are to be to the greatest benefit of the least advantaged members of society."

directors The governing body of a corporation, elected by the shareholders and constituted as the board of directors.

disclosure statement A document that presents information (mostly financial) about a person or a company. It is used in many situations, such as in bankruptcy cases.

discovery The process that allows the parties in litigation to obtain relevant information from each other and also from third parties about the facts and circumstances of the case.

disparate impact Unintentional discrimination against an entire protected class. This discrimination may arise from the employer's interview practices, pre-employment testing, hiring procedures, or educational requirements.

disparate treatment Intentional discrimination toward an individual.

divestiture The selling of a portion of a business.

doctrine of impossibility Contract performance that becomes impossible after the parties form the contract is excused.

domain name The address for a website, such as www.google.com.

dormant commerce clause Defined by the courts as "the power to regulate commerce in its dormant state" and to "prohibit economic protectionism — that is, [to prevent] regulatory measures designed to benefit in-state economic interests by burdening out-of-state competitors." Even though Congress has not regulated a state's probation of interstate commerce, it has the power to do so under the dormant commerce clause.

double jeopardy A rule that precludes the government from prosecuting a defendant for the same offense after the defendant has been acquitted or convicted for that offense. It does not shield a defendant from being involved in a civil (private) lawsuit based on the same set of facts as those presented at the criminal trial.

due diligence An extensive method of legal review to ensure legal compliance.

dumping Occurs when products of one country are introduced into the commerce of another country at less than the normal value of the product.

duress Grounds for voiding a contract that was induced by a threat and that left the victim no reasonable alternative but to enter into it.

duty A legal obligation that one party (individual or entity) owes to another party (individual or entity).

duty of compensation Duty requiring principal to compensate the agent when compensation is reasonably expected.

duty of cooperation Requirement that the principal, having directed the agent to do certain work, must cooperate with the agent's performance of that work.

duty of good faith Required by every UCC contract, this is defined as "honesty in fact and the observance of reasonable commercial standards of fair dealing in the trade."

duty of indemnification Duty under which the principal must indemnify the agent for losses sustained in connection with work done on the principal's behalf, as long as the loss is not the result of the agent's mismanagement.

duty of loyalty Forms the essence of the fiduciary duty. It is a mandate that agents owe clear and undivided loyalty to the principal and must be careful with the principal's money, property, and confidential information.

duty of obedience Duty under which an agent must obey all reasonable instructions of the principal.

duty of performance Duty under which agents are obligated to perform their work with the care and diligence normally exercised by agents in similar circumstances.

duty of reimbursement Duty under which a principal must reimburse the agent for expenses reasonably incurred while the agent executes authorized responsibilities.

duty to account Requirement that an agent account to the principal both for money received and for money expended on the principal's behalf.

duty to notify Requirement that an agent must inform the principal, in a timely manner, of all facts the principal would reasonably want to know.

economic crime A nonphysical crime aimed at obtaining a financial gain or a professional advantage.

Economic Espionage Act A federal law that prohibits misappropriation of trade secrets.

embargo A government ban on trade with a particular country.

embezzlement The fraudulent taking of personal property that has been entrusted to the defendant, with the intent to deprive the rightful owner of its usefulness and benefits.

eminent domain The power of government to take private property for public use upon the payment of just compensation.

emissions Pollutants from all mobile sources (which include automobiles, trucks, motorcycles, locomotives, boats, ships, gasoline and propane industrial equipment, and aircraft) that are regulated by the Environmental Protection Agency under the provisions of the Clean Air Act.

Employee Polygraph Protection Act Federal legislation passed in 1988 to limit the ability of a private employer to use polygraph testing either as part of a pre-employment screening process or during the course of employment.

employment-at-will The option that allows an employee to quit a job and an employer to fire an employee at any time, for any reason, or for no reason at all.

enabling act Legislation that creates and empowers an administrative agency.

Energy Independence and Security Act Passed in 2007, in part, to help move the United States toward greater energy independence and security through the promotion of clean, renewable fuels.

enjoin To prohibit by court order.

entrapment A criminal defense based on a showing that a law enforcement officer (or some other government official) induced the defendant to commit the crime for which he or she has been charged.

Equal Employment Opportunity Commission (EEOC) A bipartisan commission comprised of five members created by the Civil Rights Act of 1964 to oversee and enforce anti-discrimination laws.

equal liberty principle John Rawls's principle of justice that states: "Each person has the same indefeasible claim to a fully adequate scheme of equal basic liberties, which scheme is compatible with the same scheme of liberties for all."

Equal Pay Act of 1963 Act requiring that men and women be paid equally for substantially similar work in the same establishment.

equal protection of the laws The Fourteenth Amendment states that no state shall "deny to any person within its jurisdiction the equal protection of the laws." This means that similarly situated individuals must be treated by the government in a similar manner under the law.

equitable remedies Damages other than money, such as injunction or divestiture.

estoppel *See* agency by estoppel.

ethics and compliance officer Performs the "risk assessment" function of constantly reviewing any risks associated with a business venture including potential civil or criminal liability for wrongful company conduct along with ongoing "due diligence" to ensure legal compliance and other roles including managing investigations into compliance issues, designing internal controls to ensure legal compliance, reviewing ethical complaints, working with a board of director's ethics committee, and generally overviewing the ethics and compliance program.

ethical corporate culture An ongoing development of the company's values and moral attributes for the ultimate benefit of its stakeholders.

exclusionary rule A rule of evidence that under the Fourth Amendment prevents the prosecutor in a criminal case from admitting into evidence unlawfully seized material.

executed contract A contract under which both parties have fully performed their obligations.

executory contract A contract under which one or both parties have yet to perform an obligation.

exempt assets Those assets that are generally unavailable to creditors to satisfy a debt, such as a debtor's primary residence.

exhaustion A doctrine requiring that plaintiffs must first pursue internal agency appeals prior to asking a court for judicial review of a decision.

expectation interest Damages that should be awarded to put the plaintiff in the same position as if the contract had been performed.

express conditions Conditions that, according to the contract's language, must be strictly performed before the other party's performance under a contract is due.

express warranty A warranty of a product by a manufacturer or seller making an explicit claim about the quality, safety, or functionality of the product.

expropriation Government seizure of private property without fair compensation to the owner of the property.

extraterritorial Outside a nation's borders.

Fair Labor Standards Act Federal legislation passed in 1938 that mandates federal standards for both hourly wage and overtime pay, applying to virtually all employers.

fair use A statutory right that permits use of a copyrighted work without authorization based on several nonexclusive factors.

Family and Medical Leave Act Federal law enacted in 1993 that requires certain employers to provide employees with up to 12 weeks of unpaid leave for the birth or adoption of a child, or in the event of serious illness of the employee, or a spouse, child, or parent.

fanciful Inherently distinctive marks that can be used as trademarks. They are invented terms that have no particular relation to the product or service.

Federal Trade Commission Act A 1914 federal law that created the Federal Trade Commission and broadly prohibited "unfair methods of competition."

federalist system Two systems of government operating side by side (one national and one regional).

felonies Serious crimes that are usually punishable by imprisonment for more than one year and the imposition of significant fines.

fiduciary relationship Particular relationships that the law recognizes as involving a high level of trust; therefore, the law automatically imposes higher standards. Typically, one party entrusts money, property, or confidential information to another to use for the first party's benefit. Examples include doctor/patient; lawyer/client; director/corporation; and partner/partner.

firm offer Under the UCC, a written offer for the purchase or sale of goods, signed by a merchant, which states that the offer will be held open for the offeree to consider. Such an offer is irrevocable for the stated time or, if no time is stated, for a reasonable period of time not to exceed three months.

first appearance In a criminal case, refers to a defendant's first appearance in court. A court officer reads the criminal charges to the defendant, advises the defendant of his or her legal rights, and informs the defendant of the court's bail determination.

first-sale doctrine Doctrine of copyright law that holds that once a copyrighted work is first sold with the permission of the copyright holder, it may then be freely resold.

first-to-file A principle of patent law that awards patent rights to the first inventor to file, in cases where inventorship is claimed by more than one party.

force majeure From the French for "superior force," a clause that excuses a party from performance if performance is prevented due to any one of a list of extraordinary events.

foreclosure Allows a mortgagee to assume legal ownership and take possession of collateralized real estate should a mortgagor default on its loan obligations.

Foreign Corrupt Practices Act A U.S. statute prohibiting overseas bribery payments.

Foreign Sovereign Immunities Act (FSIA) A U.S. statute that prevents a sovereign government's public-sector act from being subject to review and scrutiny by U.S. courts.

forum selection clause A provision in a contract designating which judicial or arbitral court would hear any dispute arising between the parties in connection with the contract.

fraudulent misrepresentation A knowing misrepresentation of the truth or concealment of material facts that cause others to act in a way that is detrimental to their self-interest. A party asserting fraud must prove that he or she was induced by justifiable reliance on the other party's misrepresentation of a material fact and that the misrepresentation was made with knowledge of its falsity.

fraudulent transfer A transfer of property made with the intent to defraud creditors by placing the transferred property beyond the reach of creditors.

freedom of contract Freedom to negotiate and commit to the terms parties choose and to allocate business risks as they see fit, as long as their agreement meets certain tests and rules.

Freeman, R. Edward Considered by many to be the father of contemporary stakeholder thinking.

Friedman, Milton Nobel-prize-winning economist often cited for his declaration that the purpose of a corporation is to make profit for its shareholders.

frolic of one's own An agent's independent conduct that is not intended to further any purpose of the employer. If a tort occurs during a frolic, then the employer is not vicariously liable.

fully disclosed principal In agency law, occurs when a third party knows that an agent is acting on behalf of a principal and also knows the identity of the principal. In this case, the principal is liable on the contract and (absent an agreement to the contrary) and the agent is not.

garnishment order A judicial decree instructing a third party, such as a debtor's employer, to turn over a portion of the debtor's property to a creditor.

General Assembly of the United Nations The United Nations' main deliberative and legislative body in which all members are participants.

general damages Damages designed to compensate parties for injuries that are not easily measured in pecuniary terms, such as pain and suffering or loss of consortium.

general partners All partners in a general partnership and those in a limited partnership who have unlimited liability and responsibility for managing the business.

general partnership A structure for running a business when two or more individuals decide to associate for the purpose of owning and operating a business. Different from a corporation, a limited liability company, or other type of artificial business entity.

generic Generic words describe the usual name of a product or service and cannot be used as trademarks.

genericide When a trademark becomes so well known that it becomes the generic term for a product, and trademark rights are lost.

Genetic Information Nondiscrimination Act of 2008 (GINA) Act prohibiting employers from using genetic information in making employment-related decisions.

geographical indications Trademark-like rights given to producers located within a given geographic region.

good faith Defined by the UCC as "honesty in fact in the conduct or transaction concerned" and, as applies to merchants, "honesty in fact and the observance of reasonable commercial standards of fair dealing in the trade."

grand jury A body of citizens chosen to hear evidence of an alleged crime and decide whether or not to issue an indictment.

group boycott Refusal by two or more parties to buy from, sell to, or otherwise deal with a third party, causing injury to competition.

guarantor One who becomes liable for paying a creditor only after the principal debtor defaults.

guidance Documents issued by agencies that help businesses understand how statutes or regulations will be interpreted by the agencies.

harmonize To make laws more similar and consistent with one another.

Hart-Scott-Rodino Antitrust Improvements Act A law that requires large companies contemplating a merger to first notify and receive approval from the Federal Trade Commission and Department of Justice.

Herfindahl-Hirschman Index A calculation used to determine whether a horizontal merger would result in an unacceptable increase in market concentration.

hold-up When a patented invention is a small component of a product and the patent holder uses the threat of an injunction for undue leverage in negotiations.

horizontal market allocation Where two or more businesses at the same level of distribution agree that each will sell only to a defined portion of the market.

horizontal merger A merger between competitors selling similar products in the same market.

horizontal price fixing An agreement between businesses at the same level of the distribution chain to sell a product at a specified price.

horizontal restraint An agreement or action that involves businesses at the same level of the distribution chain and that aims to restrict competition.

hostile environment harassment Occurs when the workplace is filled with discriminatory intimidation, ridicule, or insult that interferes with the ability of an employee to do his or her work.

identified to the contract Goods designated during contract formation; the parties designate which particular goods are the subject of the contract.

illegal per se Illegal automatically, without further analysis.

implied authority Authority to do what is reasonably necessary, usual and proper to perform the agent's work. This involves acting in a manner consistent with the principal's instructions and the agent's reasonable understanding of what is needed to effectuate those instructions. All implied authority is based on express authority.

implied warranty A warranty implied by law. The UCC creates two types of implied warranties: Section 2-314 establishes an implied warranty of merchantability. Section 2-315 provides for an implied warranty of fitness for a particular purpose.

import quotas Government-imposed restrictions on the number or value of goods that can be imported.

in personam jurisdiction The authority of the court over the parties in a dispute. This authority is generally based on the presence of the person or a business in the geographic region of the court but can also cover those with sufficient minimum contacts with a state.

in rem jurisdiction The authority of the court over property at issue in a dispute. This is determined by the physical location of the property.

incorporate by reference To make one document legally a part of another document by referring to it in the latter document.

independent contractor A self-employed individual who provides services and receives minimal supervision from a principal over how the work is to be completed.

indictment A formal written accusation of a crime, made by a grand jury and presented in court as part of the prosecution of the defendant.

information A formal criminal charge made by the prosecutor without a grand jury indictment. An information is the legal device used to prosecute misdemeanors in most states.

initial public offering (IPO) A company's first time making its stock available to the public.

injunction A court order requiring someone to do something or to refrain from doing something.

insanity A defense in which a defendant states that he is not responsible for his actions during the time in question because he was suffering from a mental disorder.

inside information Any material information about a company's strategic and financial plans or current operations, such as planned mergers and acquisitions, obtained from "inside" the company.

insider Generally, a person who has knowledge or facts about a company that are not available to the general public.

insider trading Trading in a company's stock based on material nonpublic information.

insurable interest The legally recognized right to procure insurance coverage to protect against losses due to theft, destruction, damage, and the like, on the property.

intellectual property (IP) A type of intangible property consisting of four principal categories: patents, copyrights, trademarks, and trade secrets.

intellectual property rights (IPRs) A term that collectively refers to patent copyright, trademark, and trade secret rights.

intended beneficiary A third party (that is, not one of the original contracting parties) whom one or both contracting parties intended to benefit.

intentional torts Torts in which the defendant acts with the intent to cause a certain result.

interference Principle covering two types of business torts: (1) intentional interference with contractual relations, and (2) intentional interference with prospective economic advantage.

interlocking directorate When one or more individuals serve on the boards of directors of multiple companies that compete with each other.

interrogation Intensive questioning by law enforcement officials of a person suspected of committing a crime.

investigation Law enforcement's systemic inquiry into a crime, typically including interviews with individuals familiar with the crime and the gathering of physical evidence, such as computer files, paper documents, and so forth.

judgment lien An order by a court to attach the nonexempt property of the party who loses a lawsuit.

knock-out rule Applicable in some states, this specifies that terms that differ between the offer and acceptance are both treated as unenforceable, and the court will apply the UCC's gap-filling provisions to supply the term.

Kyoto Protocol An international agreement committing its signatory countries to reaching binding targets for reducing emissions.

landmine Inadvertently violating the intellectual property rights of others.

Lanham Act of 1946 The principal federal trademark act in the United States.

legal remedies Compensation ordered to be paid by the defendant to the plaintiff to cover the loss, injury, or financial harm the defendant caused to the plaintiff.

letter of credit A bank document that guarantees that the bank (called the issuing bank) will pay a stated amount if certain conditions are met within a set period of time. A letter of credit enables the seller to look to the issuing bank, instead of the buyer, for payment.

letters of intent Expresses a nonbinding intent to come to an agreement.

Lex Mercatoria Latin for "merchant law." An ancient system of law developed mainly by European traders and based on the customs and practices used on trade routes.

lien A creditor's legal right or interest in a debtor's property.

likelihood of confusion The legal standard used to determine whether trademark infringement has occurred.

limited liability company (LLC) An unincorporated entity with a legal identity separate and distinct from its members.

limited liability partnership A partnership operating like a general partnership except that the partners' personal assets are protected against creditors for certain types of partnership liabilities.

limited partners Partners having limited liability and no responsibility for managing the partnership.

mail fraud Perpetrating a fraud by using the U.S. Postal Service to make false representations and collect money illicitly.

mailbox rule An acceptance is valid when dispatched, as long as the communication is correctly addressed.

maintenance fees Periodic fees that must be paid to the government to prevent a patent from falling into the public domain.

manufacturing defects Defects that occur in the manufacturing process; they represent a deviation from the design of the product.

mark A term that refers collectively to trademarks, service marks, collective marks, and certification marks.

market allocation Where two or more businesses agree that each will sell to only a defined portion of the market.

market extension merger A merger that allows a business to expand into a new geographic or customer market.

marketing defects Defects that emerge from what the manufacturer or seller says about the product. A product may be properly designed and manufactured, yet still cause harm because of deficient (defective) warnings or instructions.

mask work An integrated circuit layout design.

material breach Occurs when either (1) a party fails to give substantial performance or (2) there has not been strict compliance with an express condition.

maximum resale price maintenance A supplier's specification of the maximum price at which a retailer can resell a product.

mechanic's lien Provides a creditor with a security interest in a debtor's real property when a creditor performs work on the property or supplies materials.

mediation A voluntary, nonbinding, private process in which a neutral third party facilitates a negotiated settlement between the parties.

meeting of the minds Occurs when, taking all communications between the parties and all circumstances into account, a reasonable person would conclude that an offer had been extended and accepted.

memorandum of understanding Memorializes principles that parties agree on in a business or cooperative venture.

mens rea Criminal intent. Latin for "guilty mind."

merchant A person who (1) deals in the type of goods that are the subject of the contract; or (2) holds himself or herself out as having knowledge or skill peculiar to the type of goods that are the subject of the contract; or (3) hires or appoints an employee or agent who holds himself or herself out as having knowledge or skill particular to the type of goods that are the subject of the contract.

merchant's memo for sales of goods Written evidence of an agreement which is signed by the party seeking enforcement. When certain conditions are met, a merchant's memo is sufficient to satisfy the Statute of Frauds.

minimum resale price maintenance A supplier's specification of the minimum price at which a retailer can resell a product.

minor breach Occurs when a party has not performed exactly as promised in the contract but has given substantial performance.

Miranda warning A list of legal rights that is read to a suspect upon arrest, as mandated by the U.S. Supreme Court. The protections include the Fifth Amendment right against self-incrimination and the Sixth Amendment right to legal counsel.

mirror image rule Applied to negotiations for all agreements except sales of goods, this rule requires that the offeree assent to the exact terms proposed by the offeror. Any variation or additions by the offeree constitute a counteroffer.

misdemeanors Less serious crimes that are usually punishable by minor fines and imprisonment for one year or less.

misrepresentation A statement that varies from the truth.

mistake of fact With this defense, a criminal defendant asserts that he or she acted from an innocent misunderstanding of fact rather than from a criminal intent to commit the crime in question.

mistake of law With this defense, a criminal defendant states that he or she failed to understand the criminal consequences of his or her conduct.

Model Penal Code While not an official code (it serves as a model only), it nonetheless has exercised significant influence in the shaping of state criminal codes over the past 50 years.

money laundering Disguising the true source of money. The basic idea is to "launder" *dirty money* obtained from illegal activities and make it *clean money* by running it through legitimate business enterprises.

monopolist A seller that has no competitors.

monopolization When one firm has the ability to restrict output and raise prices above a competitive level *and* has attained this market power through anticompetitive (unfair) conduct.

mortgage agreement A document describing the real estate used as collateral for a loan and allowing the creditor to take title and possession of the property should the debtor default on its loan.

mortgagee In a financed real estate transaction, the creditor is referred to as the mortgagee.

mortgagor In a financed real estate transaction, the debtor is referred to as the mortgagor.

most favored nation (MFN) principle Required of all World Trade Organization members, MFN obliges each member to give equal trade privileges and benefits to all member nations in relation to the same imports. All member countries must be treated the same for trading purposes. This is sometimes referred to as the principle of **nondiscrimination**.

National Labor Relations Act Federal legislation passed in 1935 that governs the relationship between management and employees.

national treatment An antidiscrimination principle required of all World Trade Organization members that obliges each member to treat imports no less favorably than domestic goods.

natural law A teleological ethical theory that holds, regardless of cultural differences, all people with a good conscience have an innate ability and duty to make rational and ethical decisions.

natural persons Human beings.

negligence Occurs when one party (wrongdoer) fails to use the standard of care reasonably expected of others in like situations, and the wrongdoer's failure causes injury to another party (victim).

negligent misrepresentation Similar to fraudulent misrepresentation, except the victim is not required to establish that the wrongdoer had knowledge of the false representation.

negotiable bill of lading A bill of lading where the paper itself establishes title to (and the right to possess) the goods.

nominal damages Damages providing plaintiffs with a token monetary award.

nonrivalrous Capable of being used or enjoyed by one person without diminishing the ability of another to use or enjoy the same item.

nontariff barrier Any type of restriction on imports other than tariffs, such as import quotas, embargoes, and certain technical regulations.

normal value The price charged for a product in the exporter's home market.

obscene speech Speech that (1) appeals to the prurient interest, (2) depicts sexual conduct in a patently offensive way, and (3) lacks serious literary, artistic, political, or scientific value.

Occupational Safety and Health Act Federal law enacted in 1970 to prevent workplace injury by mandating safe working conditions for most workplaces.

Ocean Dumping Act Passed by Congress in 1972 with two basic goals: to regulate intentional ocean disposal of materials and to authorize research to bring about further improvements.

offer A definite proposal by one person (or entity) to another indicating a present intent to enter a contract.

offeree A person (or entity) who receives a valid offer.

offeror A person (or entity) who extends a valid offer.

Office of the Whistleblower A program of the Securities and Exchange Commission required by the Dodd-Frank Act in which employees are rewarded and protected for reporting inappropriate corporate activities to government officials.

oligopsony A market in which there are few buyers.

one-year on-sale bar A provision within U.S. patent law that requires an inventor to file a patent, if at all, within one year of selling or otherwise disclosing an invention.

open delivery term If the parties agree to a contract but leave an open delivery term, then the UCC will fill the gap by requiring that the buyer will pick up at the seller's place of business.

open price term If the parties agree to a contract but leave an open price term, then the UCC will fill the gap by requiring a reasonable price at time of delivery.

open time for delivery If the parties agree to a contract but leave an open time for delivery, then the UCC will fill the gap by requiring a reasonable time for delivery.

open time for payment If the parties agree to a contract but leave an open time for payment, then the UCC will fill the gap by requiring that payment is due at the time and place at which the buyer receives the goods.

operating agreement A written document regarding the management of a limited liability company and the conduct of its business, including guidelines about operational policies, practices, and procedures.

option contract A contract that allows a party, within a specified period of time, to buy or sell something at a stated price.

Organization for Economic Cooperation and Development (OECD) A group of 34 mostly developed countries coordinating efforts on a variety of economic initiatives.

orphan works Copyrightable works for which it is difficult or impossible to identify the copyright holder.

palm off To sell an imitation item intending that the buyer believe it is genuine.

parens patriae A Latin phrase meaning the "parent of its people."

Paris Convention An 1883 treaty that protects patents and trademarks.

Parol Evidence Rule A rule of evidence that establishes a framework for the permissible use of documents, correspondence, and conversations that took place before a final agreement.

part performance A UCC exception to the Statute of Frauds whereby a party is obligated to perform under the contract to the extent the other party already has performed.

partially disclosed In agency law, occurs when a third party knows that an agent is acting on behalf of a principal but does not know the identity of the principal. In this case, both the principal and the agent are liable on the contract.

pass-through entity A nontaxable business entity, whereby the profits and losses of the entity, such as a partnership, are reported on the owners' individual tax returns, rather than on the entity's tax return.

past consideration A promise made in recognition of a benefit that the promisor has already received. Since the promisor received the benefit first, and then chose to make a promise, the inducement component of the consideration definition is lacking; therefore, it is not a valid consideration.

patent A temporary, government-granted right to prevent others from making, using, or selling an invention.

patent troll An informal and pejorative term for a business that does not itself manufacture products but instead owns patents and asserts them against alleged infringers.

perfecting A process that establishes the right of a secured creditor to collect a debt before other creditors.

petition for writ of certiorari Request that a higher appellate court agree to review the decision of a lower court.

piracy The intentional copying of entire works without any lawful pretext, often on a large scale and for commercial gain.

plaintiff An injured party who petitions the court for relief.

plant patent A patent that protects any distinct and new variety of plant that may be asexually reproduced.

plea The defendant's formal response to a criminal charge.

plea bargain A negotiated agreement between the prosecutor and the defendant whereby the defendant typically pleads guilty to a lesser offense in exchange for some concession by the prosecutor, usually a more lenient sentence or the dismissal of other charges.

pleadings Written allegations provided to the court by both parties to the dispute.

political question doctrine A doctrine by which courts may not decide issues such as foreign policy matters, that, under the Constitution, are the purview of the legislative or executive branches.

power of attorney The authority to act for another person in legal or financial matters. Despite the word *attorney* in the term, the recipient of the power need not be a lawyer. A power of attorney is durable if it is specifically written to last beyond the principal's death or incompetency.

predatory pricing Selling a product below cost in order to drive competitors out of business.

pre-existing duty rule A promise to do something that the promisor is already legally bound to do (or to refrain from doing something that the promisor is already not permitted to do). In such cases, there is no valid consideration.

preferred creditor An individual or an entity that has a statutory right over other creditors to receive payment from a debtor.

premerger notification Notification given by large companies that are contemplating a merger to the Federal Trade Commission and the Antitrust Division of the Department of Justice.

preponderance of the evidence standard The burden of proof in a civil case; represents the standard of proof used by a fact-finder (a judge or a jury) in weighing the credibility of the evidence presented by the plaintiff and the defendant.

price discrimination Charging different prices for the same good to different buyers where the effect is to substantially lessen competition.

price fixing The agreement of two or more parties to sell a product at a specified price.

prima facie duties Deontological ethical duties used in resolving ethical dilemmas that establish a hierarchy where, considering all the circumstances, some duties prevail over others. They are especially useful as a reminder of the ethical duties to keep promises and not to harm others.

primary line injury Price discrimination that injures competitors of the discriminating seller.

principal A person or entity who authorizes another person or entity (called an agent) to act on his behalf.

private international law The law that applies to the resolution of disputes between private individuals and business entities, such as when parties are engaging in international commercial transactions.

probable cause hearing A hearing that focuses on a suspect's Fourth Amendment rights in a criminal case.

product extension merger Acquisition by a business of another business in order to extend its product line.

product liability The law involving a lawsuit brought by a party who has suffered an injury or experienced property damage caused by a defective product.

promisee The person to whom a promise is addressed.

promissory estoppel A legal theory used to enforce a promise, even where there is no consideration to support a contract. To establish a claim under promissory estoppel: (1) the promisor should reasonably expect to induce action or forbearance on the part of the promisee; (2) such action or forbearance is in fact induced; and (3) injustice can only be avoided by enforcing the promise.

promulgate To enact into law.

proprietor Someone who owns property, typically business property.

Prospectus Description of the mission and objectives of the business and details of the company's business operations, including financial information and information about the management team of the company. It is commonly viewed as a selling document.

proximate causation A principle placing a limit on the extent to which an injured party may assert that his or her injuries were the direct result of the wrongdoer's conduct.

public domain Information or works that are not covered by intellectual property protection.

publicly held corporations Corporations in which the management team operates separately and distinctly from the shareholders, and the company's stock is held by professional investors and the public at large.

puffery Vague generalizations, where such generalizations are so indefinite that a reasonable person would not view them as factual.

punitive damages Damages awarded on a discretionary basis and designed to punish the defendant in a civil case.

quasi-contract An equitable remedy designed to prevent unjust enrichment. It applies when (1) the plaintiff conferred a benefit on the defendant; (2) the defendant knew of the benefit; and (3) the defendant accepted and retained the benefit under circumstances making it inequitable for the defendant to retain it without payment.

quid pro quo harassment When an employer seeks sexual favors as a condition of employment, promotion, or receipt of other benefits.

ratification A manifestation of assent to be bound to a past act.

reasonable person One who routinely exercises the degree of care called for in a given situation.

registration statement A document containing information from a company about itself, as required by the Securities Act of 1933, concerning the type of security that is being offered and other kinds of information, mostly financial.

regulations Legally binding rules that are promulgated by administrative agencies.

rejection of an offer Occurs when, viewed objectively, the offeree manifests an intention not to accept the offer.

reliance interest Protecting the plaintiff's reliance interest means the plaintiff should be reimbursed for losses sustained by relying on the contract.

rescission A court order meaning the contract has been terminated and parties are neither obligated to perform duties nor entitled to demand performance.

respondeat superior Latin for "let the master answer." A doctrine imposing vicarious liability on an employer for the tortious act of an employee if the tort occurred in the scope of employment.

Restatement (Second) of Contract Although not binding law, this is a well-respected compilation of contract law principles, rules, definitions, commentary, and examples and is sometimes used by judges and lawyers seeking guidance on matters.

restitution A court order requiring the defendant to return any benefit the plaintiff had conferred.

right to acceptance Under the UCC, a buyer has the right to accept nonconforming goods and recover damages for the nonconformity.

right to cancel the contract Under the UCC, a seller has the right to cancel the contract if the buyer breached the contract.

right to cover Under the UCC, if a seller breaches a contract, the buyer has the right to procure substituted goods and recover from the seller the difference between the cost of the substituted goods and the contract price of the goods.

right to cure A seller has the right to cure (that is, to correct or fix) nonconforming tender any time before the contracted delivery date. Seller also has the right to cure a nonconforming tender for a reasonable time after the contract delivery date if (a) the buyer rejected the nonconforming tender; (b) the seller had reasonable grounds to believe that the goods would be acceptable to the buyer; and (c) the seller notifies the buyer.

right to recover the purchase price Under the UCC, a seller has the right to recover the purchase price if the buyer breaches and if the seller is unable to resell the goods to another buyer.

right to reject the goods Under the UCC, a buyer has the right to reject nonconforming goods.

right to resell Under the UCC, a seller has the right to resell goods if the buyer materially breaches.

right to withhold delivery Under the UCC, a seller has the right to withhold delivery if the buyer materially breaches.

risk assessment An extensive review of a wide range of potential business losses to the company, including possible corporate liability for carelessly enabling its employees to perform civil wrongs or criminal acts.

rivalrous Property is rivalrous if one person's use or enjoyment of the property diminishes the ability of another to use or enjoy the same property.

Robinson-Patman Act A federal law that prohibits price discrimination.

rule of reason A standard by which a court considers the particular circumstances of the business environment and the likely effects of the restraint before determining whether it violates antitrust laws.

rule utilitarianism The principle by which someone confronted with the ethical dilemma calculates the greater good for the greater number to benefit the common good.

scienter Having knowledge of the falsity of one's misrepresentation.

scope of employment The range of an employee's work assigned by or authorized by the employer; whether the agent's conduct was controlled by the employer; and the extent to which the employer's interests were advanced by the agent's conduct.

search warrant Authorizes the police to conduct a search of a specified place and to gather evidence relative to the crime in question.

secondary line injury Price discrimination that injures competition among customers of the discriminating seller.

secondary meaning A trademark possesses secondary meaning if consumers recognize the term as denoting a particular company or source rather than being merely descriptive.

secured creditor An individual or an entity that has protected its monetary interest by securing a lien, holding a mortgage, or requiring some other form of collateral from the debtor as part of the lending process.

Securities Act of 1933 Legislative act that covers the purchase and sale of securities in the United States.

Securities and Exchange Commission Federal government agency that plays a critical role in protecting private and institutional investors. It also plays a major role in helping to control the various stock markets in the United States and to stimulate the economy by facilitating capital formation and growth.

Securities Exchange Act of 1934 Legislative act that requires companies that meet certain thresholds to report information regularly about their business operations, financial condition, and management. These companies must file periodic reports or other information with the SEC.

security agreement Names the parties to the transaction, states the essential terms of the agreement, and specifies the property to be used as collateral in support of a corresponding credit arrangement.

service mark A distinctive word, name, symbol, or device that identifies a service.

service of process Complaint served on a defendant in order to give the defendant notice of the lawsuit.

shareholders The owners of a corporation.

Sherman Act of 1890 A landmark antitrust law that seeks to limit the ability of firms to monopolize markets or to enter into agreements with other firms to restrain trade.

shipment contract A contract where the seller is required to deliver the goods to a carrier, for shipment to the buyer.

social enterprise movement The notion of using private corporate enterprise to remedy social ills. Based, in part, on the belief that, acting alone, the government cannot solve social problems without help from private enterprise.

sole proprietorship A business structure where one person owns and operates a business enterprise.

sovereign immunity The principle by which courts in one country refrain from hearing lawsuits against foreign governments, resulting in immunity of a foreign government from suit in U.S. courts.

sovereign state A self-governing and independent country. Common characteristics of sovereignty include international recognition; control over a specified geographic region; a government that commands control over the population; identifiable symbols like flags and a national anthem; some uniform law; common currency; a postal system; and a defined population.

specific performance A court order requiring a party to perform contractual obligations.

stakeholder theory Requires that a corporation consider the effect of its action not only on its shareholders, but also on its customers, employees, vendors, suppliers, the community, and the environment.

standard of care The level of care required by law in a particular situation. This concept helps protect individuals and entities from injuries that result from situations involving unreasonable risk of harm.

standing to sue Requirement that the party seeking the aid of the court has an actual interest in the dispute.

stare decisis Principle by which judges place great weight on following the precedent of previous court decisions.

state sales tax A tax on consumer goods and services collected by the merchant and submitted to the state on a periodic basis.

Statute of Frauds Although in general, oral contracts are enforceable, the Statute of Frauds requires that, unless an exception applies, certain categories of contracts must be in writing.

statute of limitations The defined period within which a claimant must file a lawsuit or lose the right to sue. Its purpose is to protect defendants from having to defend themselves against charges associated with events that occurred many years ago.

statutory damages In copyright law, the amount a copyright owner can recover according to statute, irrespective of actual damages.

statutory laws Those laws adopted through the legislative process.

strict liability The principle holding manufacturers responsible for their actions even when they acted with due diligence and reasonable care.

strict liability crimes Crimes that hold a defendant responsible based on a criminal act alone. No accompanying mental state (mens rea) is necessary.

subject matter jurisdiction Refers to the authority of a court to hear the subject matter of a particular case. For example, the tax court has subject matter jurisdiction over tax cases.

subsidy A financial contribution by a government or any public body within the territory of a World Trade Organization member that confers a benefit. Under WTO rules, prohibited subsidies are automatically illegal, and actionable subsidies are illegal if the subsidy has an adverse effect on the complaining country.

suggestive Terms that are inherently distinctive and can be used as trademarks; they suggest a characteristic or quality of the product or service.

supremacy clause If a state or local law conflicts with a federal statute, regulation, or treaty, the federal law takes precedence.

surety A third party who cosigns a promissory note or other form of credit agreement with the debtor and the creditor and assumes responsibility for paying the creditor if the debtor defaults.

suretyship The assurance to pay the debt of another party.

sustainability Involves operating in a delicate balance that ensures that the needs of the present generation are met, while at the same time conserving the resources available to future generations.

tariff A tax levied on imported goods. Tariffs can be calculated as a percentage of the value of the imported good, on the basis of the number or weight of the imported goods, by the unit, or some combination of these.

teleology (consequential ethics) An ethical theory, often called consequentialism, in which the primary concern of the behavior is the consequence of the act.

tender of delivery Under the UCC, this requires that the seller transfer conforming goods and arrange for them to be brought to the agreed-upon location. Tender rules also require the seller to give whatever notice is reasonably necessary for the buyer to take possession of the goods.

term sheet A list of the major terms one party proposes to another. Parties draft, revise, and submit term sheets to each other as a way to identify which terms they agree upon and which require further proposals and negotiation.

terms and conditions In a contract, these are the parties' specific responsibilities, obligations, and benefits specified by the contract.

terms of reference A list of claims, unresolved issues, and applicable procedural rules that parties must submit to the arbiter and to the opposing party under International Chamber of Commerce International Court of Arbitration rules.

tertiary line injury Price discrimination that injures the customers of the customers of the discriminating seller.

tied product A product that a seller insists a buyer must purchase as a condition of obtaining another product.

Title VII Part of the Civil Rights Act of 1964 that prohibits discrimination in the workplace based on race, gender, religion, color, or national origin. The Act covers employers with 15 or more employees.

tort A civil wrong, as opposed to a crime, that occurs when one party (wrongdoer) breaches a legal duty owed to another party (victim), and the victim seeks a remedy, usually in the form of damages.

tort law Law that protects individuals and entities from three types of injuries: (1) injury to the person, (2) damage to property, and (3) impairment of economic interests.

Toxic Control Substances Act A federal law that regulates chemical substances and provides guidelines for the EPA on which chemicals may safely be used in manufacturing.

trade secret Any secret and valuable business information, such as a product formula, customer list, or undisclosed software code.

trademark A renewable, government-granted right to prevent others from using a confusingly similar symbol to identify competing products or services.

trademark dilution The blurring or tarnishing of a famous trademark's reputation by use of the mark on an unrelated product, even in the absence of confusion.

Trade-Related Aspects of Intellectual Property Rights (TRIPS) The most important intellectual property treaty today, providing minimum levels of protection and offers a meaningful enforcement mechanism.

treaty A written, international agreement that is signed by two or more states and is governed by international law. Bilateral treaties have two party signatories; multilateral treaties have three or more party signatories.

treble damages Three times actual damages.

trial A formal judicial examination of evidence and the determination of legal claims in an adversary proceeding.

tying product A product that a seller refuses to sell unless the buyer also buys another product.

typosquatting The registration of domain names that contain intentional misspellings of others' distinctive trademarks in order to divert Internet traffic to the typosquatter's site.

unconscionability The UCC defines this as the "absence of meaningful choice together with terms unreasonably advantageous to one of the parties." Contracts that contain unconscionable terms or were formed under unconscionable circumstances are illegal.

undisclosed principal Situation where a third party does not know that an agent is acting on behalf of a principal. Usually, in this case the third party could bring any contract claims against the principal or against the agent.

undue influence A contract is voidable (by the victim) on the grounds of undue influence if the contract is the product of unfair persuasion by a party who is under the domination of the person exercising the persuasion.

Uniform Commercial Code (UCC) An extensive set of rules written to cover all aspects of routine business transactions, including contracts between merchants and consumers, adopted in 49 of the 50 states.

Uniform Electronic Transactions Act (UETA) A federal act, the main provision of which states that any electronic signature satisfies any law requiring a signature.

Uniform Trade Secrets Act A model law that 46 states have adopted to protect trade secrets.

unilateral contract A contract where a promise is exchanged for an act of performance (not a promise to act).

unintentional torts Commonly referred to as negligence, occurs when a wrongdoer falls below the standard of care expected in everyday dealings and in conducting business, and such failure results in an injury to a victim.

United Nations A large, international organization whose purpose is to prevent and remove threats to peace, suppress aggression, and foster economic, social, cultural, humanitarian, and environmental cooperation among nations.

UN Commission on International Trade (UNCITRAL) A United Nations agency that helps modernize and harmonize international trade law and standardize commercial practices and agreements.

UN Conference on Trade and Development (UNCTAD) The branch of the United Nations that promotes the interests of developing countries.

UN Convention on the Recognition and Enforcement of Foreign Arbitral Awards (also called the New York Convention) A convention governing arbitration of private international disputes, ratified by 144 countries, including the United States.

UN Economic and Social Council A United Nations council responsible for preparing studies and arranging conferences relating to economic, social, cultural, educational, health, or human rights issues and problems and makes related recommendations to the General Assembly or to a specialized UN agency.

UN International Court of Justice The judicial branch of the United Nations.

UN Secretariat The administrative arm of the United Nations. It supports the UN's activities by providing day-to-day administrative services.

UN Security Council The United Nations body with primary responsibility for the maintenance of international peace and security. It has 15 members in total, five of whom (China, France, Russian Federation, United Kingdom, and United States) are permanent members.

U.S. Code A comprehensive collection of federal laws, compiled and ordered by topic into a set of printed volumes.

U.S. Patent and Trademark Office A federal administrative agency to which businesses can apply to obtain patent or trademark rights.

U.S. Sentencing Commission A federal independent agency that sets sentencing policies and practices for the federal courts, including appropriate form and severity of punishment for offenders convicted of federal crimes.

U.S. Sentencing Guidelines Requires compliance and ethics training for upper levels of management, all employees and agents of the organization.

unlimited personal liability One of the major disadvantages of organizing a business in the form of a sole proprietorship or a general partnership because business creditors can look for satisfaction of a debt by taking the personal assets of the sole proprietor or the partners.

unsecured creditor An individual or an entity that has extended credit to a debtor but has not protected its monetary interests through the use of a lien, a mortgage, or other form of collateral.

usury Interest charged in excess of the maximum rate. The effect of these agreements varies, depending on state law.

utilitarianism A teleological ethical theory that is summarized as seeking the "greater good for the greater number." It is useful in considering a management strategy that concerns the well-being of the stakeholders.

utility patent The most common type of patent.

valid contract An agreement that meets the required elements for legal recognition (offer, acceptance, consideration, capacity, and legality).

venue The most appropriate physical location for a trial.

vertical market allocation Where a manufacturer assigns distributors or retailers exclusive territories in order to protect each distributor or retailer from competition.

vertical merger A merger between businesses occupying different levels of operation for the same product.

vertical price fixing An agreement between businesses at different levels of the distribution chain to sell a product at a specified price.

vertical restraint An agreement or action that involves businesses at different levels of the distribution chain and that aims to restrict competition.

virtue ethics A teleological theory that, for business ethics purposes, relates to the character traits and virtues of a business executive.

void agreement An agreement for which the law does not recognize a legal obligation to perform.

voidable contract A contract that one or both parties may choose to void (i.e., invalidate). If no election is made to void the contract, it remains valid.

voluntary assent Parties freely and voluntarily agree. In general, courts will enforce only those promises that parties have voluntarily chosen to commit to.

waiver A party's choice to release the other from its obligation to perform under a contract or to waive its right to demand performance by the other party.

whistleblower In the context of employment law, an employee who brings an employer's wrongful acts to light.

wire fraud A type of fraud perpetrated by using electronic communications.

work made for hire A work that is prepared by an employee within the scope of employment, the copyright of which belongs to the employer.

workers' compensation System of remuneration provided to workers who are injured on the job.

World Intellectual Property Organization (WIPO) A specialized agency of the United Nations that is headquartered in Geneva, Switzerland, and promotes respect for intellectual property, administers 24 intellectual property treaties, and arbitrates intellectual property disputes.

World Trade Organization (WTO) Headquartered in Geneva, Switzerland, its goals are to open trade worldwide by establishing the rules of trade between nations and providing a forum for settling trade disputes The WTO began as the General Agreement on Tariffs and Trade.

TABLE OF CASES

Case illustrations and principal cases are denoted by italics.